Project Management by ICB4

Project Management by ICB4

First edition, first impression

IPMA®

Van Haren
PUBLISHING

COLOPHON

Title:	Project Management by ICB4
Authors:	Bert Hedeman (The Netherlands) Roel Riepma (The Netherlands)
Reviewers:	Peter Pürckhauer (Germany) Rebeka Vlahov (Croatia) Kristijan Robert Prebanić (Croatia)
Print:	First edition, first impression, September 2023
Ownership:	IPMA, Zurich - Switzerland
Publisher:	Van Haren Publishing, 's-Hertogenbosch - NL
ISBN hardcopy:	978 94 018 1092 0
ISBN e-book pdf:	978 94 018 1093 7
ISBN e-book ePub:	978 94 018 1094 4
Website:	www.shop.IPMA.world, www.vanharen.net
Final editor:	Bert Hedeman (The Netherlands)
Text editor:	Michelle Schuurman-Voorma (The Netherlands)
Editor in chief:	Reinhard Wagner (Germany)
Lay-out and DTP:	S&B IT Services, Amersfoort - NL

PREFACE

This book is intended for project professionals, students, and graduates of project management, and is arranged to reflect tools and methods behind the competences (People, Practice and Perspective) prescribed by the standard IPMA Individual Competence Baseline 4.0 (ICB4). It should be embraced as a guide for practicing project management on different levels of career development and project complexity. It is also intended as a book of knowledge for supporting the IPMA ICB4 when preparing for certification of competence in project management. For project managers, these are: IPMA Level A: Certified Projects Director, IPMA Level B: Certified Senior Project Manager, IPMA Level C: Certified Project Manager and IPMA Level D: Certified Project Management Associate. (more at www.ipma.world)

The book begins by emphasising the importance of the role of project manager, project management, and project setting and promotes project culture in everyday work. Thus it introduces the theoretical and practical components that constitute the field of project management.

Being both academic and practitioner in project management, I often witness project managers becoming so consumed in delivery and technical details that they forget the need to generate value for both clients and the people involved. The authors, Bert Hedeman and Roel Riepma so eloquently remind us of this need that beside technical aspects managers need to focus on their leadership and people skills and deliver value within a contemporary context. This is even more relevant considering the rapidly changing environment we are facing. With fewer resources, uncertain supply chains, less water, more carbon, labour shortage and a rapidly changing climate – project management can only get tougher, and more important.

Formal education and academia can grasp the opportunities to stimulate and inform future generations of project professionals... However, it is the current generation, who frequently have had little formal or systematic training in project management and who will immediately face the challenges and seize the opportunities. Therefore, this book is important for so called self-educated project professionals and ad hoc managers for improving their skills in everyday work.

Whether you are a serious project professional or a student in project management, you will find 'Project Management by ICB4' thought-provoking and will keep you willing to test the tools in real life. Reading this book will be enjoyable for anyone interested in the broad field of managing work through projects and is a required reading for those interested in contributing to project management discipline and continuously developing competences in project management.

This book is the product of two partnerships, IPMA and Van Haren Publishing. Many people have helped us to develop the ideas put forward in the book. Of course, the main authors: Bert Hedeman and Roel Riepma, but also the wide team of reviewers: Peter Pürckhauer, Rebeka Danijela Vlahov Golomejić and Kristijan Robert Prebenić and IPMA Publications Review and Editing team led by Reinhard Wagner have made this book a success.

Prof. Dr. Mladen Vukomanović,
Vice President Professional Development
IPMA

International Project Management Association (IPMA) is the oldest non-profit professional organisation dedicated to promoting excellence and professionalism in project, program, and portfolio management. It was founded in 1965. in Switzerland and nowadays operates in more than 70 countries worldwide through its Member Associations, thus providing a global platform for connecting practitioners and organisations, enabling collaboration and cooperation, sharing ideas and benchmarking, as well as advancing practices and competences in the field. Join the IPMA community at: www.ipma.world.

TABLE OF CONTENTS

GENERAL INTRODUCTION

IPMA observes an increasing number and importance of projects in business, public and people's lives, also known as 'projectification', which is why we need to engage more and more in projects. IPMA stands for *International Project Management Association* and is a federation of about 70 Member Associations for project management.

This book provides a knowledge base for developing individual competences for managing projects as described in the IPMA Individual Competence Baseline version 4.

IPMA defines a project as a unique, temporary, multidisciplinary and organised endeavour to realise agreed deliverables within predefined requirements and constraints. Projects drive the development of new products and services, expansions, new capabilities, implementation of new strategies and new generations of infrastructure, but also major maintenance and upgrade of existing facilities and infrastructure.

We recognise that projects begin and end with people and that their competent performance is at the heart of every successful project. This textbook describes the processes and steps applied in project management and the relevant knowledge basis for the people and perspective competences.

Please observe that some of this book's elements may be the subject of patent rights. IPMA shall not be held responsible for identifying such patent rights. Any trade name in this document is information given for users' convenience and does not constitute an endorsement.

PURPOSE

IPMA realises that no single book can contain the complete knowledge needed to develop project management skills and abilities. No two projects are the same, nor are the people who work on them, nor the stakeholders, nor the context within the project to be implemented. However, this book offers a knowledge base that can be built on further in developing individual competences in project management to make projects succeed.

Theories and practices for all ICB4 competences are described. They are logically sequenced, explained and enriched with practical theories, which can be learned and applied in the daily practice of project management. As such, it is entirely in line with IPMA's vision: to strengthen competence across society to enable a world in which all projects succeed. This book also supports obtaining an IPMA certificate as proof of your competence in projects.

AUDIENCES AND USES

Like the IPMA ICB4, this book is intended for a wide range of audiences across many uses. It was written with these audiences in mind. The audiences mentioned below are by no means exhaustive.

Project professionals – The primary audience is the project professionals, providing a basis for their professional development, as a reference guide, also as a basis to prepare for their certification. In the context of this book, project professionals are anyone who plays a role in managing the project and those who support them; these are the (sub-)project manager, work package leader, and project support staff. From convenience, we usually address the reader from their role as project manager.

IPMA Member Associations – This book is also intended for the various IPMA Member Associations (MAs), their certification boards, and assessors if they wish to strengthen their knowledge base for certifying project professionals and attract new members. This book may provide a solid foundation for that. Member Associations can add theories for certification on a chapter-by-chapter basis. Future versions of this book may include these theories.

Trainers and educators – Furthermore, this book may be used by trainers and educators as a basis for their curriculum and as a guide for delivering project management training. This applies, in particular, to those certified under the IPMA Education & Training Registration System (REG Partners).

Companies, governments, and not-for-profit organisations – Finally, this book is practical for decision-makers in companies, governments, and not-for-profit organisations to decide how to shape the competence development of project professionals within their organisations with the IPMA ICB4.

CERTIFICATION SCHEME

IPMA has developed a 4-level certification schema for project professionals based on the Individual Competence Baseline. The four levels of individual certification and their titles are described on the website of IPMA World (https://ipma.world).

Level D: Project Management Associate – An IPMA Level D certification requires that the candidate is knowledgeable in all Competence Elements (CEs) related to project management. As such, they possess broad project management knowledge and can work in a project team. No previous experience is required.

Level C: Project Manager – An IPMA Level C certification requires the candidate should have a minimum of three years of experience in the last six years as a project manager within projects of moderate complexity or in a responsible project management role assisting the project manager in complex projects.

Level B: Senior Project Manager – An IPMA Level B certification for project management requires that, in the last eight years, the candidate should have a minimum of five years of experience as a project manager, of which at least three years were in a responsible leadership function managing complex projects.

Level A: Projects Director – An IPMA Level A certification for project management requires that, in the last twelve years, the candidate should have a minimum of five year experience as a project manager in a responsible leadership function managing complex projects, of which a minimum of three years at a strategic level.

For Levels B, C and D, candidates should complete a self-assessment and pass an examination. The self-assessment is designed to provide a clear picture of an individual's experience in project-related environments. The exam aims to test your level of knowledge as a project professional. The knowledge tested is based on the competences described in the IPMA *Individual Competence Baseline*. The Certification Bodies of the IPMA Member Associations are responsible for the individual assessments and certification.

1. STRUCTURE OF THE BOOK

For project management, the Individual *Competence Baseline* version 4 (ICB4) describes 28 competences, subdivided into (see Table 1.01):

- 05 Perspective competences
- 10 People competences
- 13 Practice competences

Perspective competences		People competences		Practice competences	
4.3.1	Strategy	4.4.1	Self-reflection and self-management	4.5.1	Design
4.3.2	Governance, Structures and processes	4.4.2	Personal integrity and reliability	4.5.2	Requirements, objectives and benefits
4.3.3	Compliance, standards and regulations	4.4.3	Personal communication	4.5.3	Scope
4.3.4	Power and Interest	4.4.4	Relationships and engagement	4.5.4	Time
4.3.5	Culture and values	4.4.5	Leadership	4.5.5	Organisation and information management
		4.4.6	Teamwork	4.5.6	Quality
		4.4.7	Conflict and crisis	4.5.7	Finance
		4.4.8	Resourcefulness	4.5.8	Resources
		4.4.9	Negotiation	4.5.9	Contracts and procurement
		4.4.10	Result orientation	4.5.10	Plan and control
				4.5.11	Risk and opportunities
				4.5.12	Stakeholders
				4.5.13	Change and transformation

Table 1.01 ICB4 competence overview

The perspective competences define the contextual competences to navigate projects within and across the broader environment. The people competences define the personal and interpersonal competences required to succeed in projects. The practice competences define the technical aspects of managing projects.

ORDER OF SUBJECTS

To meet the readers' needs, this book starts with an introduction to projects and project management. Next, the practice competences are described, then the people competences, and finally, the perspective competences.

The practice competences are described in the sequence of the project lifecycle. Starting with the project preparation (Part 4), then project definition (Part 5) and finally, project delivery (Part 6). To do this logically, the ICB4 sequence has been changed, and competences have also been split up, as sections of certain ICB4 competences are particularly relevant for one particular project stage.

The people competences are described in Parts 7 and 8. The chapters in Part 7 focus mainly on managing yourself, and in Part 8, more on the interpersonal competences that connect with others.

The perspective competences are described in Parts 9, 10 and 11. The chapters in Part 9 focus on implementing change, Part 10 on the internal context of the permanent organisation, and Part 11 on the external context of the broader environment. Table 1.02 shows the book's structure with references to the chapters in the ICB4.

No.	ICB4	Title	No.	ICB4	Title
0		General Introduction	**8 Connecting with Others**		
1		Structure of the Book	8.01	4.4.4	Relationship and Engagement
2		Competence Development	8.02	4.4.5	Leadership
			8.03	4.4.6	Teamwork
Practice Competences			8.04	4.4.8	Resourcefulness
3	**4.3.2**	**Project Orientation**	8.05	4.4.10	Result Orientation
4 Project Preparation			8.06	4.4.9	Negotiation
4.01	4.5.10	Project Preparation Stage	8.07	4.4.7	Conflict and Crises
4.02	4.5.12	Stakeholders			
4.03	4.5.5	Project Organisation	**Perspective Competences**		
4.04	4.5.2	Requirements and Objectives	**9 Implementing Changes**		
4.05	4.5.11	Risk and Opportunity	9.01	4.3.1	Strategy
			9.02	4.3.2	Programme Management
5 Project Definition			9.03	4.3.2	Portfolio Management
5.01	4.5.10	Project Definition Stage	9.04	4.3.2	Support Functions and Implementing Project, Programme, and Portfolio Management
5.02	4.5.1	Project Design			
5.03	4.5.3	Scope			
5.04	4.5.6	Quality	9.05	4.3.2	Development Frameworks
5.05	4.5.4	Time			
5.06	4.5.8	Resources	**10 Internal Context**		
5.07	4.5.7	Finance	10.01	4.3.2	Organisation Theories
5.08	4.3.1	Business Justification	10.02	4.3.2	Personnel Management
			10.03	4.3.2	Financial Administration
6 Project Delivery and Close-out					
6.01	4.5.9	Procurement	**11 External Context**		
6.02	4.5.10	Change Control	11.01	4.3.3	Health, Safety, Security, and Environment
6.03	4.5.5	Information and Documentation	11.02	4.3.3	Sustainability
6.04	4.5.10	Control and Reporting	11.03	4.3.3	Laws and legislation
6.05	4.5.13	Organistational Change and Transformation	11.04	4.4.4	Power and Interests
6.06	4.5.10	Project Closure	11.05	4.4.5	Culture and Values
People Competences			**Annex**		
7 Managing Yourself			**A**		Glossary
7.01	4.4.1	Self-reflection and Self-management	**B**		Acronyms
7.02	4.4.2	Personal Integrity and Reliability	**C**		Literature
7.03	4.4.3	Personal Communication	**D**		Index

Table 1.02 Structure of the book with reference to the ICB4

VISION AND ROADMAP

In Figure 1.01, the book's structure has been translated into a roadmap to guide the reader. Central to the roadmap are the Practice chapters (Parts 3, 4, 5, and 6). This central block is carried by Part 7: Managing Yourself and Part 8: Connecting with Others (purple). Project results simply cannot be realised without insight into professional personal action, careful communication, and professional teamwork. This total is once again embedded in its environment (blue). The environment determines which project results are desired, which goals the project should contribute to and within which frameworks the project should be carried out (Parts 9, 10 and 11).

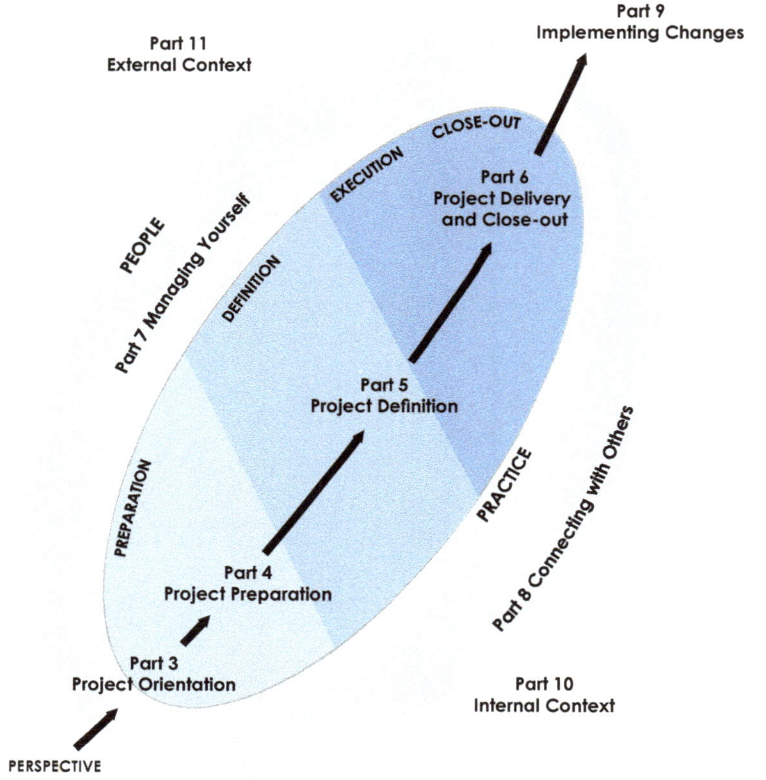

Figure 1.01 Vision and structure scheme of the book (© P. Pürckhauer)

STRUCTURE OF THE CHAPTERS

For each competence element, the book provides an overview of the knowledge, theories and beliefs the project professional can use to do the right things correctly. The chapters in this book, from chapter 3 onwards, have a consistent structure (see Table 1.03).

Chapter layout	Description
Purpose	The purpose of this chapter
Learning objectives	Subjects dealt within this chapter
Definitions	Most important definitions applicable in this chapter
Introduction	Description of the competence covered in this chapter
Positioning	Positioning subjects (except for People chapters)
Basic subjects	Basic knowledge areas
Sustainability	How to apply this competence from a sustainability approach (for Practice chapters)
Tailoring	How to apply this competence within an Agile environment (for Practice chapters)
Responsibilities	Responsibilities of those involved in this subject (for Practice and Perspective chapters)
Advanced subjects	Additional knowledge areas, if applicable

Table 1.03 Chapter layout

Advanced subjects

The basic subjects cover the primary knowledge areas needed for project success. They are also generally required for certification for IPMA D. The advanced subjects cover additional knowledge areas needed for more complex situations and are usually required for certification for IPMA C and or IPMA B.

2. COMPETENCE DEVELOPMENT

This book provides a sound basis for developing the competences of project professional. IPMA defines competence as 'the application of knowledge, skills and abilities in order to achieve the desired results'.

Following this, this book can be applied by the readers for:
- Knowledge development for passing the IPMA exams;
- Preparation of the self-assessment and project report to prove their skills and ability;
- Preparation for the IPMA assessment to substantiate chosen behaviour in certain circumstances.

Exams are mandatory at IPMA D, C and B levels. By completing them successfully, the candidate demonstrates sufficient knowledge and understanding of these competences at that level.

For the IPMA C certification, after passing the exam, the candidate has to prepare an experience document, an executive management summary and a self-assessment, after which an assessment interview can take place.

For the IPMA B certification, the candidate first has to prepare the experience document, executive management summary and self-assessment. After approval, they need to prepare a project report. After this is approved, they can proceed for the exam and then finally for the assessment interview.

For IPMA A certification, the candidate needs to follow the same procedure as for IPMA B, except an exam is no longer required.

In the self-assessment, the candidate reflects on their performance in all IPMA competences. The candidate can use the STAR technique to give form and content to the reflection for each competence element. STAR stands for:
- *Situation* – A description of the situation or problem that has occurred;
- *Tasks* – The tasks for which the candidate was responsible;
- *Activities* – The initiatives taken by the candidate in the described situation;
- *Results* – The result of the initiatives taken and their effect on the project.

Example STAR:
Situation – *Product-based planning is a prescribed approach for preparing plans within my organisation.*
Tasks – *Within the project, as the supplier's project manager, I am responsible for preparing the project plan and having it approved.*
Activities – *In a workshop with core team members and users, I defined the project and intermediate deliverables and prepared a first draft of the overall project schedule. Based on this, I had individual team members prepare their own timelines, which I then discussed with them. Following this, I prepared the final project plan and approved it by the project board.*
Results – *By jointly preparing the product-based planning, a high-quality plan was created, which was approved without much discussion, whereby the team members*

were motivated to deliver the work on schedule. We were able to complete the project without delay.

During the interview, the candidate can expect in-depth questions about their self-assessment. By answering adequately, the candidate demonstrates sufficient knowledge, skills, experience, and personality to lead projects. To prepare thoroughly for this, the candidate may use the content of this book.

PURPOSE OF COMPETENCE DEVELOPMENT

Competent action is expressed in the project professional's consciously chosen and actual behaviour. This book cannot enforce this behaviour. But by including examples in the text (provided with a blue marking on the left), the project professional can read about and reflect on the actual behaviour of others. Lessons can be learned from this.

Competence development is based on deepening and enriching successive areas of attention. These focus areas form the content of the circle that is visible in Figure 2.01.

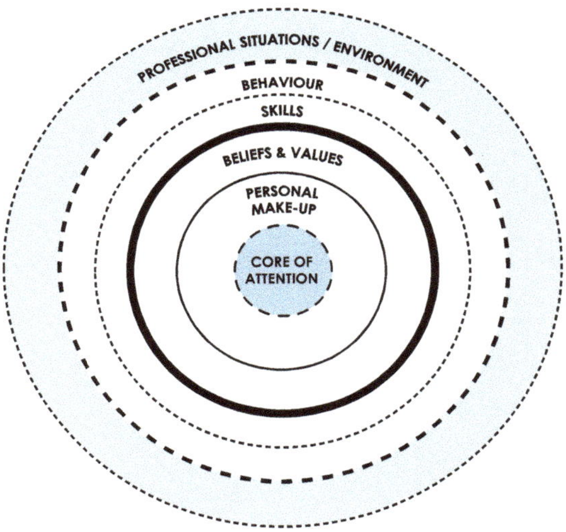

Figure 2.01 Focus areas of competence development

This circle can be regarded as the goal aspect of this book. Ultimately, it is about the reader having clear beliefs and values and using a self-conscious personal makeup, skills and behaviour appropriate to their professional environment.

All parts can be read against this background. Each part is ultimately intended:

- To better observe and understand the complex environments in which projects take place;
- To discover constructive beliefs and clear values that positively guide project work;
- To deepen and enrich personal behavioural skills related to project work;
- To gain insight into your personal makeup towards projects;
- To achieve a pure and concise form of attention that supports effective project management behaviour in complex environments.

Because this book is about projects, we begin with a broad introduction to projects.

PRACTICE COMPETENCES

3. PROJECT ORIENTATION

PURPOSE

The purpose of this chapter is to enable the individual to determine whether an initiative can best be carried out as a project and apply the principles of project management.

LEARNING OBJECTIVES

- What is a project and what is project management;
- Reasons to initiate a project;
- Prerequisites for and characteristics of a project;
- The different work forms;
- Project lifecycle;
- Staging, controlling and decision-making within projects;
- Control aspects in a project;
- Triple constraint and the iron square;
- Projects within the product lifecycle;
- Project at different levels;
- Project output, outcome, benefits, and goals;
- People and Perspective context of projects;
- Agile versus Waterfall;
- IPMA Project Excellence Baseline (advanced).

DEFINITIONS

Project: A unique, temporary, multidisciplinary, and organised endeavour to realise agreed deliverables within predefined requirements and constraints.
Project deliverable: A tangible or intangible element to be realised by the project.
Project output: The total of the project deliverables that forms the project result.
Project outcome: The result of a change enabled by the project output.
Project goal: The effect the sponsoring organisation or customer wants to achieve with the project output.
Sponsoring organisation: The organisation that commissioned and funds the work and makes the final go/no-go decisions. This can be corporate, programme management or an external client.
Customer: An individual, group or organisation receiving the deliverables.
Project sponsor: The individual accountable for the project's success to the sponsoring organisation or customer, and owner of the project's business case.
Project management: All managerial tasks necessary to deliver the project deliverables successfully, This involves planning, organising, monitoring, and controlling all aspects of the project, leading the team, and motivating all people involved.
Project manager: The individual responsible for the daily management of the project to achieve the project deliverables and enable project success.
Project stage: A period within a project, separated from other periods, with a predetermined output, and concluded with a go/no-go decision. Project stages cannot overlap.
Project phase: A period within a project with its own characteristics and with a predetermined output. Project phases can overlap.

Project decision: A decision by the sponsoring organisation or customer to go ahead with the project or not (go/no-go decision).
Decision point: A control point where the project is reviewed to decide whether or not it can proceed and whereby, if so, the budget for the next stage is released (gate).
Milestone: An important event that provides visible evidence of progress.

INTRODUCTION

The chapter lays the foundation for all other chapters, which is why it is so important. The chapter explains what a project is, why it is sometimes better to work on a project basis and sometimes not, what the characteristics and the necessary conditions are, and why working on a project is so different from business as usual. This chapter aims to provide a sound basis to enable you to understand and position the other competences.

POSITIONING

Understanding project management is, of course, essential when managing projects, but it is also vital before starting a project. We need to determine whether an endeavour is best carried out on a project basis or in a different manner. It is not self-evident to manage every endeavour as a project. Each approach has its pros and cons. And, if we opt for a project-based approach, we should be aware that certain conditions should be met before we can start the project. If these conditions are not met, we may encounter problems rapidly.

WHAT IS A PROJECT?

A project is a unique, temporary, multidisciplinary, and organised endeavour to realise agreed deliverables within predefined requirements and constraints. Deliverables are the tangible or intangible elements to be achieved. Projects can be stand-alone, part of a programme or part of a portfolio. However, a project is always a separate challenge for realising deliverables.

> *A project is a unique, temporary, multidisciplinary, and organised endeavour to realise agreed deliverables within predefined requirements and constraints.*

This definition sounds very obvious, but it isn't. To a great extent, it limits the scope of a project. A project is a temporary organisation to deliver a predefined product or service within predefined requirements and constraints. With these deliverables, the customer can implement the changes and realise the benefits they envision. That is the reason to start a project in the first place. However, it is not up to the project and the project manager to implement these changes and realise these benefits. It is the responsibility of the customer. Clearly, you need to know what they want to use the project output for to deliver one that is fit for purpose, but that's where the project ends. This should be clear to all stakeholders from the outset to avoid false expectations and prevent others from not taking responsibility for making the project a success.

A requirement is a criterion that a solution should meet to be acceptable. A constraint is a limitation within which the project should be implemented. For example, a requirement may be that the new engine is fully electrically powered. A constraint may be that the primary process should not be interrupted during the project.

WHAT IS PROJECT MANAGEMENT?

Project management is the whole of managerial tasks necessary to deliver the project deliverables successfully, involving planning, organising, monitoring, and controlling all aspects of the project, leading the team, and motivating all individuals involved.

> *Project management encompasses all managerial tasks necessary to successfully deliver the project deliverables, involving planning, organising, monitoring, and controlling all aspects of the project, leading the team, and motivating all individuals involved.*

In short, project management is the management of a project. This includes the management of the project itself, leading the team, and engaging the stakeholders. Project management is not an isolated task for the project manager but also a responsibility for the project sponsor and others, such as the work package leaders. The project sponsor is responsible for directing the project. The project manager is responsible for the daily management of the project to achieve the project deliverables and enable project success. The work package leaders should lead their teams and ensure that the agreed products are developed.

REASONS TO INITIATE A PROJECT

The permanent organisation is more efficient in routine work. A project organisation is often more effective in one-off activities. In the temporary setting of a project, different disciplines from different departments and even other companies can work together more easily to deliver the project output. Communication lines within the business organisation can also be relieved of the intensive coordination required to achieve such a one-off result. Especially since the work often cannot be specified in detail in advance.

Often a project is initiated because:

- The result is a one-off within a given context;
- Multidisciplinary teams need to be involved;
- The result cannot be specified in detail in advance;
- Many stakeholders need to be involved in the decision-making;
- The realisation transcends the individual domains;
- Much management attention is required;
- The work does not fit within 'business as usual'.

As a result, projects are usually more complex and risky than ordinary activities. But not everything is a project. The development of a new product is preferably carried out as a project. Replacing a plug is ideally done as part of regular maintenance. Transforming the organisation to a new way of working is best done as a programme (see Chapter 9.02 Programme Management).

POSITION PROJECTS

Projects can stand alone and be part of a programme or a portfolio (see Figure 3.01). A programme is a temporary organisation of interrelated projects, and business activities managed in a coordinated way to enable the implementation of change and the realisation of benefits. A portfolio is a set of projects and programmes brought together to provide optimum use of the organisation's resources to achieve its strategic goals. Both programmes and portfolios consist of projects and contain policies and frameworks within which a project should be implemented. However, the primary conditions and characteristics of a project remain the same.

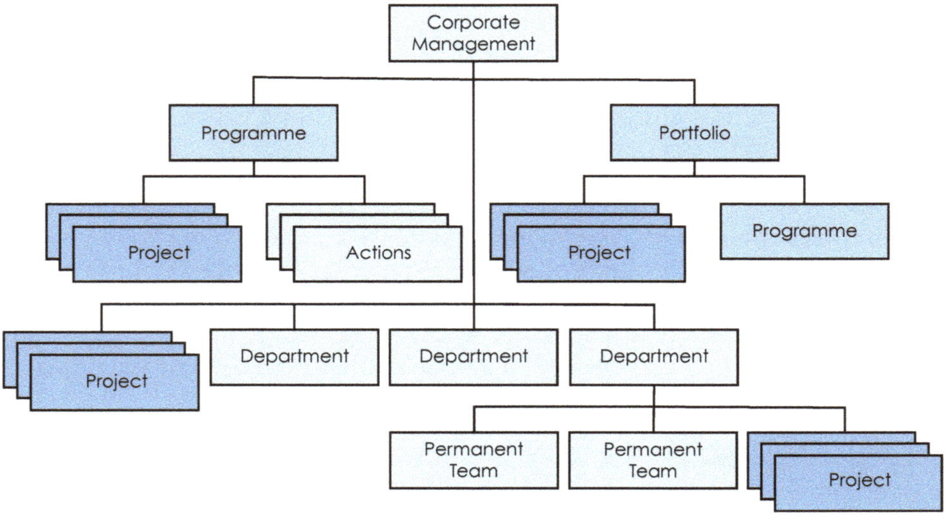

Figure 3.01 Position projects in the organisation

NECESSARY CONDITIONS FOR A PROJECT TO EXIST

Starting a project requires a conscious decision by the management. Projects cannot be created unilaterally. There should always be an agreement between the project sponsor and the project manager to start a project.

The necessary conditions for a project to exist are:

- A decision to carry out the endeavour as a project;
- A purpose and intended output;
- An agreement between the project sponsor and project manager;
- A defined start and end;
- A temporary organisation;
- A predefined scope and conditions.

The project sponsor and the project manager should first agree on the project outline before there is a project. The project output should be defined at least at key points. There should be an agreement on the scope, approach, and conditions under which the project needs to be implemented. Furthermore, it should be clear why the project should be carried out. Finally, the work should be authorised.

A decision is made to carry out the work on a project basis

It should not only be decided to develop a product or service but this also will be done through a project. Products and services can also be developed within the business as usual. Developing a product or service within 'business as usual' provides an entirely different set of tasks, responsibilities, and authorities than developing a product or service via a project. Given the differences in tasks, responsibilities, and authorities between these two approaches, agreeing that the product or service will be realised through a project beforehand is necessary.

There is a purpose and an intended output (product or service)

A project realises deliverables. This can be a product or a service. The purpose is the goal the sponsoring organisation or customer wants to achieve with the project output. We need to know the intended output in order to conclude an agreement to deliver this output. We need to know the purpose in order to design and specify the output during the implementation of the project since we usually do not know all the details of the project output at the start of the project and to adapt the work to changing circumstances.

There is an agreement between the project sponsor and the project manager

A project cannot be started unilaterally. A project does not start until there is an agreement between the project sponsor and the project manager on the project outline. The project manager is responsible for the output and how it will be achieved. If necessary, challenge the project sponsor and others to opt for a different result and or a different approach. Is the approach inclusive, is the project and the output sustainable, et cetera?

There is a defined start and end

A project has a defined start and finish. A project starts when there is an agreement between the project sponsor and the project manager about the assignment, and the sponsor authorises the project manager to start the work. The project ends when the acceptance of the project output is confirmed, or the project has nothing more to contribute, and the sponsor closes the project and officially discharges the project manager.

There is a temporary organisation

In projects, there is always a sponsoring organisation or customer and a supplier. The sponsoring organisation or customer defines the deliverables, requirements, and constraints. The supplier provides the resources and delivers the project output.

In projects, the project sponsor represents the sponsoring organisation or customer. The project manager is responsible for the daily management of the project to enable project success. The project teams will deliver the agreed deliverables. These roles, tasks and responsibilities should be defined and agreed upon before starting the project.

There is a predefined scope and conditions

In order to start a project, the scope and conditions of the project should also be known, as they determine the work to be carried out. Without a predefined scope and conditions, there can be no valid agreement about the project assignment. However, this does not mean that the scope and conditions should be defined in full detail at the start of a project; these just need to be specified in sufficient detail to form a valid basis for this project assignment.

WORK FORMS

There are three primary work forms: improvisation, plan-based work, and routine work (see Figure 3.02), besides all kinds of intermediate forms such as Agile. There is also no strict division between these work forms; they overlap in practice. We can also carry out parts of the work within one work form and other parts of the work on another work form. Within plan-based work, individual activities can be carried out ad hoc and routinely and vice versa. However, all these three forms of work have their own characteristics.

Improvisation – The work is performed ad hoc. This occurs when the work is highly demand-driven. Dependencies are unclear, and people do not work according to fixed procedures or based on a plan. The advantage herein is that there is a high degree of flexibility and that issues are often dealt with creatively. The disadvantage is that there is much uncertainty about whether the result is achieved. The consequences concerning time, money and capacity are also unclear in advance. Improvisation is quite effective as the work to be carried out is, to a large extent, unpredictable.

Routine work – Work is routine if the work is carried out over and over again according to set procedures and instructions. The process is work-orientated rather than change-orientated. A characteristic of routine work is that the same work is repeated over and over again according to a predetermined method. The result is clear in advance, as are the costs, time and resources to be spent. An important advantage is that the work can be performed very efficiently.

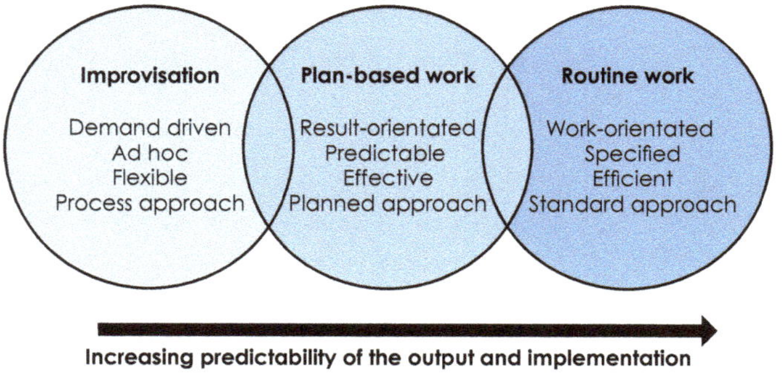

Figure 3.02 The three basic work forms (Groote, et al, 2011)

Plan-based work – Plan-based work is based on 'think first, then act'. Plan-based work is result-orientated. Plan-based work lies somewhere in between improvisation and routine work. The result to be delivered is relatively clear in advance but is not yet fully specified. The result gradually becomes more apparent during the realisation of the work. Risks can be estimated in advance.

Project work is a particular form of plan-based work. Project work is plan-based work for someone else and includes two additional steps. The first extra step is first agreeing on what the assignment is. The second extra step is to hand over the output to the other party upon completion. With that, project work includes the following steps (see Figure 3.03):

- Agree to the assignment > project preparation stage;
- Plan the assignment > project definition stage;
- Deliver the assignment > project delivery stage(s);
- Handing over the output > project closure at the end of the last delivery stage.

The project preparation stage is not an official part of the project itself, as there is yet no consent between the project sponsor and the project manager. The consent is the result of this stage. A project starts after the completion of the project preparation stage, the project assignment has been agreed upon, and the project sponsor authorises the start of the definition stage. Furthermore, project closure is not a separate stage in a project but only a part of the final delivery stage.

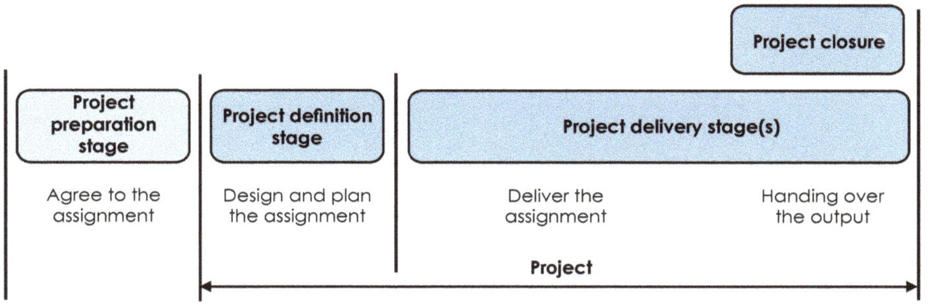

Figure 3.03 Steps in project-based work

> *Marian is a freelancer. She has been asked to manage a project to set up an online shop. She met with the Sales Director of Xantia to get a clear picture of what they want (agree to the assignment). On assignment, she should first draw up a plan of what needs to be done with an estimate of time and cost (plan the assignment). Marian hopes she gets the assignment and can start the project soon.*

STAGING, CONTROLLING, DECISION MAKING

Working according to plan does not mean that the plan is cast in stone. The characteristic of project-based work is that the project output becomes clearer as the project progresses. A project should therefore be designed in such a way that it is manageable but that sufficient room remains to respond to the ever-changing environment and the insights of the parties involved. Staging, controlling, and decision-making are, therefore, essential aspects of a project.

Staging

A project stage is a period within a project, separated from other periods, with a predetermined output, and concluded with a go/no-go decision. Based on the principle 'think first, act later', every project consists of at least two stages: the project definition stage and the project delivery stage. In the definition stage, the foundation is laid for the delivery. In the delivery stage, the actual development of the project output takes place. The project delivery stage may be split into successive sub-stages, depending on the control the sponsoring organisation wants to exert.

Each stage concludes with a project decision (go/no-go decision). The project can only continue after the sponsoring organisation has issued explicit authorisation. A decision point (gate) is a (usually) predetermined control point where the project is reviewed to decide whether or not a project can proceed and, if so, the budget for the next stage is released.

Project stages should be distinguished from the technical phases of a project. A project phase is a period within a project with its own characteristics and a predetermined output, such as engineering, tender, and construction. A project phase concludes with a milestone. A milestone is an important event that provides visible evidence of progress.

Project phases can overlap, but project stages do not. Project phases can coincide with project stages, but they don't have to (see Figure 3.04). The same applies to milestones. A milestone can coincide with a decision point, but it does not have to. Decision points and milestones should be included in the project plan.

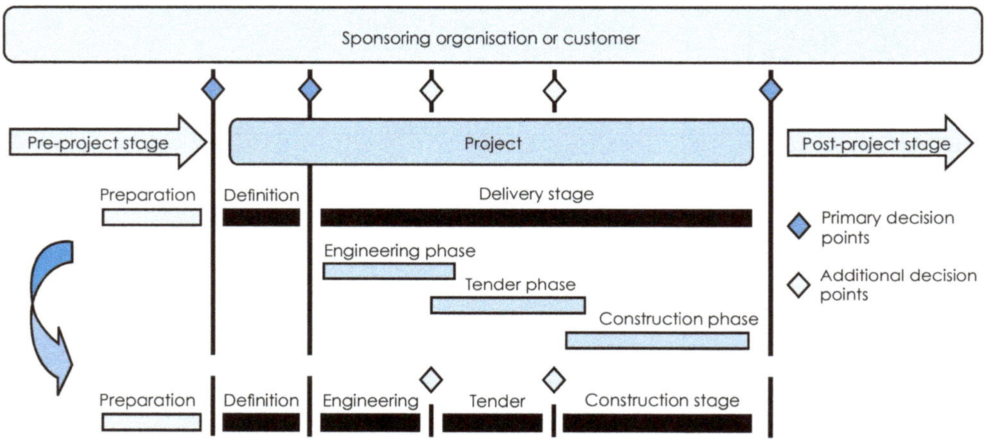

Figure 3.04 Project with additional stages and intermediate decision points

Control

Control in a project is necessary to ensure that objectives are met. Controlling involves drawing up a plan (Plan), putting the work into operation (Do), checking that everything is going according to plan (Check) and, if necessary, taking corrective actions (Act), after which the control cycle can be repeated. Part of the Check step is that the next management level is also informed so that they can exercise their own control responsibility. The control cycle should be carried out at each successive management level in the project.

This control cycle should be completed regularly to ensure that work is carried out according to plan, necessary changes are made in a timely manner, and maximum added value is realised. Primary control aspects are time, cost, scope, quality, risk and benefit. Nowadays, many projects include additional control aspects such as health, safety, security and sustainability. These aspects are becoming increasingly important.

Decision-making

Decisions should be made at every management level in the project. At the highest management level in the project (project sponsor/project board), stage transitions (decision points) are the ideal moments to evaluate the project's status and reconsider the project's further course. What is the status of the work? What still needs to be done? What is the best option forward? And does the project still provide sufficient added value, or is it better to close it prematurely?

Making choices is an important part of decision-making. Which alternatives are discarded, and with which should we continue? It is wise not to rush when choosing a particular design or approach and to retain freedom of action, but you cannot keep all alternatives open until the end. The latter costs too much time and money, and the team loses focus on the end result. That is why it is good to determine in advance which choices should be made and when to avoid acting in the spur of the moment.

Magic triangle and iron square.

Control aspects are interrelated. A change in one control aspect will affect one or more other control aspects, assuming the work is well planned. Reducing the budget will automatically affect time and or scope and vice versa to deliver a quality product. These are called the *triple constraints* and are visualised by the *magic triangle* (see Figure 3.05a). Today, the magic triangle is often replaced by the *iron square*, in which time, budget, quality, and scope are linked, as the quality to be delivered may also vary (see Figure 3.05b). If you change one aspect, at least one of the other aspects will also change to keep everything in balance. Nowadays we have to assess all control aspects, including health, safety, security and sustainability.

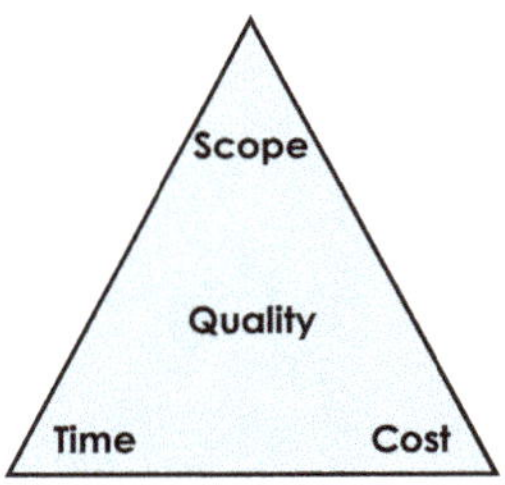

Figure 3.05a Magic triangle

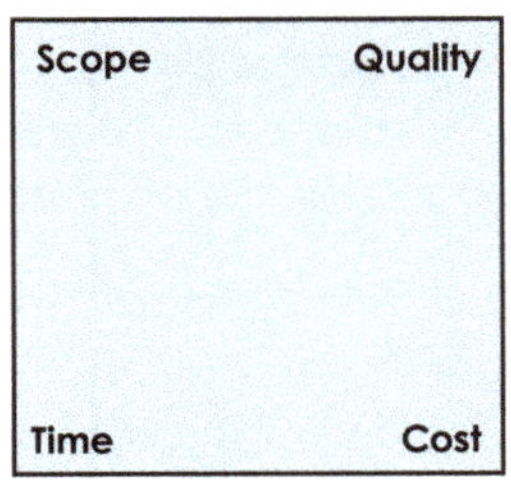

Figure 3.05b Iron square

PROJECTS WITHIN THE PRODUCT LIFECYCLE

Each product also has its own lifecycle. It starts with an initial idea, perhaps followed by a feasibility study to investigate whether the realisation and exploitation of the product are viable. If approved, the product is realised and put into use. Whilst in use, further major maintenance or product updates may be required. Finally, the product is disposed of, destroyed, or reused in another form or application. Every transformation during the product lifecycle can be carried out as a project, such as the feasibility study, the realisation, major maintenance, upgrades and repairs of the product, and the product's final de-commissioning and or demolition (see Figure 3.06).

Figure 3.06 Projects within the product lifecycle

PROJECTS AT DIFFERENT LEVELS

Projects can be defined at different levels (see Figure 3.07). They are comparable to Matryoshka dolls, whereby one Matryoshka doll fits snugly into another. The same applies to projects. A project at one level could be just a sub-project or a work package at another level.

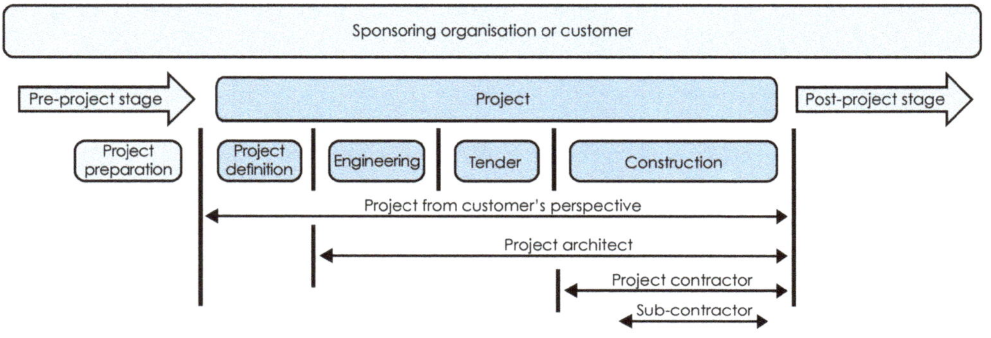

Figure 3.07 Projects at different levels

For the sponsoring organisation, the project includes the project definition and the project delivery stage. For a supplier, the project is the period from signing the contract to handing over the product to be delivered. This period may include several stages, up to just one work package in one of the stages.

In the context of this textbook, the project is viewed from the perspective of the sponsoring organisation or customer. In doing so, the project starts with authorising the project definition stage and ends with delivering the project output.

PROJECT OUTPUT, OUTCOME, BENEFITS AND GOALS

The project output is the total of the project deliverables that comprise the project result. This is the total of the project deliverables handed over to the customer.

The project output allows the sponsoring organisation or customer to implement the changes and realise the benefits for which the project was initiated in the first place. The project outcome is the result of the change enabled by the project output. Project benefits are the advances that result from the project outcome. The project goals are the effects the sponsoring organisation or customer wants to achieve with the project outcome and, thus, with the project output. The project goals should align with the strategic objectives and vision of the sponsoring organisation or customer.

PEOPLE AND PERSPECTIVE CONTEXT OF PROJECTS

The goal does not justify all means. The project should be legally sound and socially appropriate. In addition, the organisation can consciously opt for *Corporate Social Responsibility* (CSR) to voluntarily, but not without obligation, take on a social role that goes further than prescribed by law or what is socially appropriate.

Since projects usually are carried out to support changes in organisations, they should be directly aligned with the sustainability vision of the organisations involved. The project may even be initiated to contribute directly to this vision. Corporate social responsibility also draws attention to the beliefs and behaviour of the project manager and the project team regarding respect, transparency, sincerity, fairness, empathy, inclusivity, integrity, et cetera.

AGILE VERSUS WATERFALL

Agile is a conceptual approach to implementing changes iteratively and incrementally (see Chapter 9.05 Development Frameworks). in this context, iterative means that the products are developed cyclically and incremental means the output is delivered in a series of small steps. This contradicts the traditional Waterfall approach in which the output is developed linearly and entirely put into use at the end of the project (see Figure 3.08).

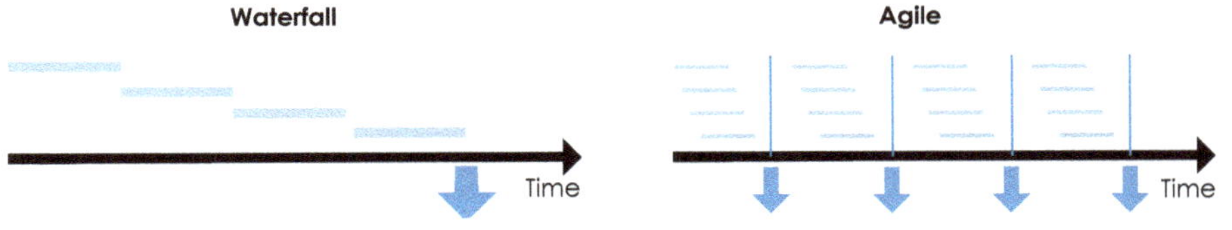

Figure 3.08 Agile versus Waterfall

Agile can be applied in any project where strong collaboration with users is required and incremental delivery is an option. The advantage of Agile projects is that developers and users work closely together from the start. Wherever this is important, an Agile approach delivers benefits. In Agile projects, the change authority is usually delegated to a product owner. The product owner is ultimately responsible for maximising the value of the envisaged product and maintaining the product backlog.

SUSTAINABILITY

Sustainability is one of the most significant challenges of our time. How can prosperity be developed without endangering the lives of future generations? Henceforth, the long-term social and environmental impacts of the project should be considered. The sustainability of the project and the project output to be delivered should be taken into account.

Focus on sustainability starts with recognising the context of the project. It also requires a greater emphasis on the outcome and value of the project than on its outputs and objectives. In other words, a more lifecycle-orientated and outcome-orientated approach rather than an output-orientated one. This affects all aspects of the project and of project management.

TAILORING

In organisations making substantial use of Agile development techniques, a conscious decision should be made whether new deliverables will be realised as part of continuous development or whether a temporary endeavour (project) should be initiated to realise these deliverables. In the latter case, special development teams should be created to realise those deliverables.

Before starting the actual development, we should first define the product vision (project preparation stage), the initial product backlog, and the additional capacity we need to realise the product vision (project definition stage). The project should be terminated when development is complete, has nothing more to contribute, or the regular development teams can do the remaining part (project closure). Within an Agile environment, these steps will often be performed less administratively but still need to be taken. Additional decision points can be scheduled during the delivery/ development stage to prevent this special endeavour from going unnoticed. These toll gates may coincide with planned releases.

RESPONSIBILITIES

The project sponsor is ultimately responsible for the project and should ensure the sponsoring organisation and customer that the intended output is delivered with which they can achieve their intended goals. The project manager is responsible for the daily management of the project to achieve the project deliverables and enable project success.

ADVANCED
PROJECT EXCELLENCE BASELINE (ADVANCED)

The *IPMA Project Excellence Baseline* (IPMA PEB, 2018) promotes project and programme management excellence. The IPMA PEB provides guidelines for assessing a project or programme. The IPMA PEB can be applied in any industry, within any profession and using any project management method.

Basic principles for excellent projects are:
- Excellent is a quality that surpasses ordinary standards;
- Excellent is a continuously moving target that should constantly be pursued;
- Excellent performance can best be achieved through continuous development.
- Achieving excellence is a long-term effort.

Leaders of excellent projects:
- Behave in a socially responsible manner with care for the weak;
- Understand the core elements of the project environment (People, Planet, Profit);
- Recognise the institutions pursuing sustainability as stakeholders of the project.

Sustainability is a core element of the IPMA PEB based on the UN Global Compact's *Ten Principles of Sustainability* (see Chapter 11.02 Sustainability).

The IPMA PEB can be used to assess a project or a programme. When assessing a programme, you can choose only to assess the programme management, one or more projects in the programme or a combination of both. The IPMA PEB cannot be used to assess a portfolio as a whole. The three key areas of the model are People & Purpose, Processes & Resources and Project Results (see Figure 3.09).

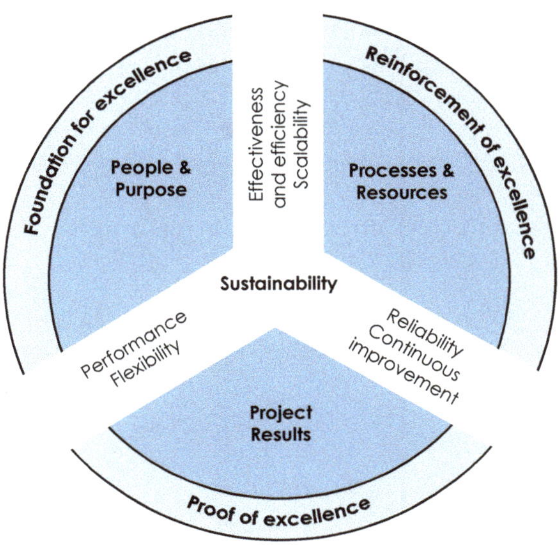

Figure 3.09 IPMA Project Excellence Baseline (IPMA, 2018)

- *People & Purpose* – This area includes Leadership & Values (A.1), Objectives & Strategy (A.2), and Project Team, Partners & Suppliers (A.3). It is considered to be the foundation of project excellence. The right people, led and supported by excellent leaders, all sharing a common vision of success, are crucial for driving improvements in a project and helping it achieve more than the set standards.
- *Processes & Resources* – This area includes Project Management Processes & Resources (B.1) and Management of Other Key Processes & Resources (B.2). It represents practices necessary to enhance excellence through sound processes and adequate resources used efficiently and sustainably.
- *Project Results* – This area includes Customer Satisfaction (C.1), Project Team Satisfaction (C.2), Other Stakeholder's Satisfaction (C.3), and Project Results and Impact on Environment (C.4). The project management approach can only be excellent if it leads to outstanding, sustainable results for all key stakeholders.

These areas are closely related to the result areas of the *European Foundation for Quality Management* model® (EFQM, 2021) often used for assessing organisational excellence (see Chapter 9.01 Strategy). This conscious linkage helps organisations use the EFQM excellence model to extend their excellence efforts into projects while remaining consistent with their organisation-wide initiatives.

Through good interaction between the three core areas of the IPMA PEB, the following elements of a project are secured:

- *Performance* – People driven by purpose are motivated and strive to achieve results.
- *Flexibility* – Regular observation of the results influences people's perception and leads to a better understanding of the project objectives and continuous refinement of its strategy.
- *Effectiveness and efficiency* – The right processes and resources used by people driven by purpose increase their effectiveness and efficiency.
- *Scalability* – People driven by purpose seek opportunities to increase their abilities by developing and using the appropriate processes and resources.
- *Reliability* – Proven processes and adequately managed resources help to secure short- and long-term results.
- *Continuous improvement* – Conclusions from the analysis of the results drive the development of processes and resources.

The assessment of project excellence enables the project team to understand how to achieve success and identify and use its strengths and improvement potential.

4. PROJECT PREPARATION

The project preparation is intended to arrive at a project assignment supported by the organisation.

Chapter 4.01 – Project Preparation Stage – Describes the different actions that need to be performed to prepare a project outline and obtain authorisation from the project sponsor to carry out the project definition stage.

Chapter 4.02 – Stakeholders – Maps out the different interest groups surrounding the project and discusses how these groups can be effectively involved in the project.

Chapter 4.03 – Project Organisation – Describes how the different interest groups are included in the project organisation, which roles can be distinguished, and the tasks and responsibilities of those different roles.

Chapter 4.04 – Requirements and Objectives – Describes the project goals, results and requirements and how they are related.

Chapter 4.05 – Risk and Opportunity – Describes managing risks and opportunities. Various risk and opportunity techniques are also discussed.

Together, these chapters contain the key elements a project manager has to deal with in preparing for the project.

4.01 PROJECT PREPARATION STAGE

PURPOSE

This purpose of this chapter is to enable the individual to develop and get agreement on the project outline.

LEARNING OBJECTIVES

- The activities to be undertaken in the project preparation stage;
- The project outline and the stage plan for the project definition stage;
- Preparing the initial project decision (decision to justify).

DEFINITIONS

Project preparation stage: The period prior to the start of the project in which the project outline is formulated and agreed upon.
Project mandate: The authorisation of the sponsoring organisation or customer to initiate the project.
Project outline: The description of the project assignment, which serves as the basis for the project definition stage.
Initial project decision: The decision to authorise the project definition stage (decision to justify).

INTRODUCTION

The purpose of the project preparation stage is to ensure that the conditions for the project definition stage are met. Do we have sufficient information? Is the project outline defined? Have the people for the key roles in the project been appointed? Has the work for the project definition stage been planned? Have the people needed for the definition stage been assigned?

In this stage, it is vital to ensure that the project assignment is aligned with the mission, vision and core values of the organisations involved and with regard to the project output to be realised. Without a proper project preparation stage, the chances of starting the project on the wrong track are high, and its chances of success are limited.

POSITIONING

The project preparation starts with the project mandate from the sponsoring organisation to the project sponsor to initiate the project. This is followed by the project request from the project sponsor to the project manager to prepare a project outline and a plan for the project definition stage. The project preparation ends when the project outline and the plan for the project definition stage are approved, and the project sponsor authorises the project manager to start the project definition stage.

Before the mandate is issued, one or more feasibility studies may already have been done to investigate whether an idea is feasible and the best option. These are projects in their own right and are not part of the project preparation stage itself (see Figure 4.01).

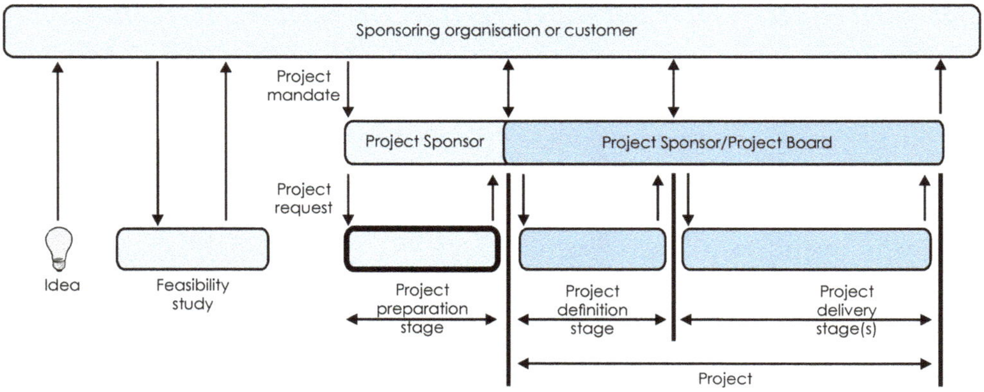

Figure 4.01.01 Positioning project preparation stage

PROJECT PREPARATION STAGE

As indicated, the project preparation stage starts with the mandate from the sponsoring organisation to initiate the project (see Figure 4.01.02). This can be a verbal notification or a formal document that almost describes the project assignment.

Next, the project sponsor selects and appoints you as project manager and assigns you to prepare the project outline and a plan for the project definition stage. Sometimes the sponsoring organisation has already determined who the project manager will be, but this should never be done without consulting the project sponsor.

It is then your task to develop the project mandate into a project outline. You will do this by studying it and the underlying documentation and entering into a dialogue with the project sponsor. After all, it is their mandate, and it is crucial to know how the project sponsor views it. What is necessary according to them? How do they want the project to be realised, and how do they want the stakeholders to be involved?

No two project sponsors are the same; therefore, no two assignments are the same. It is also essential to establish a bond of trust with the sponsor. The project sponsor should know that the project is in good hands with the project manager. In such a dialogue, you can also demonstrate that you know the business, understand what the sponsor wants, intend to carry out the project according to the sponsor's ideas, and can realise the desired project output. By this, the project sponsor can entrust the daily management of the project to you. It is also an excellent opportunity to bring in lessons learned from previous projects.

Furthermore, the project manager should initially assess whether the project has a business justification. You need to understand why the project should be implemented now, how the project output aligns with the organisation's strategic objectives, what alternatives have been considered, and why they have been dropped. What are the main risks associated with the project, and what effect does the organisation want to achieve with the project output? It won't be the first time that an initial assessment shows that it is doubtful whether the initiated project is or is not viable in the form the project sponsor has in mind.

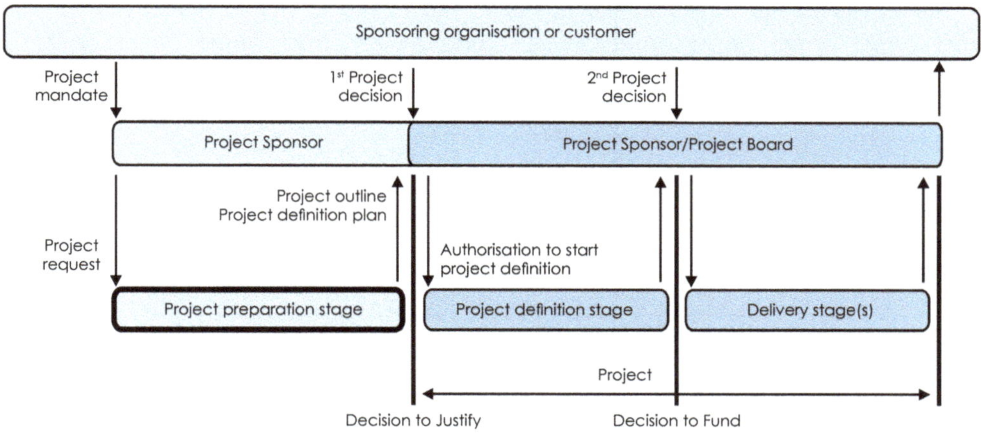

Figure 4.01.02 Project preparation stage

PROJECT MANDATE AND PROJECT OUTLINE

The project mandate authorises the project sponsor to initiate the project. In many organisations, the project mandate has a prescribed format. This is to ensure that no essential information is missed and to check afterwards whether the mandate was correctly provided. The latter is to improve the mandating process continuously. The content of the project mandate is often based on the results of a feasibility study conducted earlier.

> *The original idea for an online shop is two years old. Last year, Finance commissioned a feasibility study. A fortnight ago, Ben van Buren, the Sales Director, got the mandate from the management to start the project. Last week, he had an intake with Marian, a freelance project manager. She was recommended to him by a colleague. Marian made a good impression. Monday, as discussed, he received the project outline from her and a plan and quotation for preparing the project management plan. He discussed these today with management. They gave their authorisation. He has just sent her confirmation that she can start the project.*

Project outline

The project outline is prepared by the project manager, approved by the project sponsor and is, in principle, a tightening and deepening of the project mandate. In many organisations, the project outline also has a prescribed format. New topics in addition to the project mandate are usually the context, the demarcation of the scope, the conditions, the acceptance criteria associated with the individual quality expectations and the project approach. From the project manager's point of view, these topics are essential to developing a solid foundation for the project implementation in the project definition stage.

The project outline describes the project assignment that serves as a basis for developing the project management plan during the project definition stage. The project outline consists of the project definition, the outline business case, the outline quality expectations and acceptance criteria, the project organisation, the project approach, key risks, and the most important milestones (see Figure 4.01.03):

- *Context* – Describes the current situation; what is the actual situation?
- *Reasons* – The reasons why this project should be carried out now.
- *Project output* – The main products and services to be delivered by the project.
- *Project objectives* – The requirements for the implementation of the project, such as time and money.
- *Scope* – The total of products and services to be delivered and key activities to be performed in the project.
- *Demarcation* – The scope boundary, so the scope is more accurately determined.
- *Project goals* – The desired changes to be realised by the sponsoring organisation.

- Project definition
  - Context and reasons
  - Project output
  - Project objectives
  - Scope and demarcation
  - Project goals
  - Users and other stakeholders
  - Interfaces and prerequisites
  - Constraints and assumptions
- Outline business case
  - Business options declined
  - Alignment strategic goals
- Outline quality expectations and acceptance criteria
- Project organisation
- Project approach
- Key risks
- Most important milestones
- Reference documents

Figure 4.01.03 Composition project outline

- *Key stakeholders* – Users and other stakeholders to be involved in the implementation of the project and or affected by the desired changes.
- *Interfaces* – The dependencies on other initiatives that we need to consider.
- *Prerequisites* – Conditions that should be fulfilled before the project can start, for example, a permit that should have been issued.
- *Constraints* – Limitations within which the project should be carried out. For example, under no circumstances may the current operations be disrupted by the project.
- *Assumptions* – The assumptions made, for example, that sufficient qualified personnel is available.
- *Outline business case* – Why this project was chosen over other solutions and how this project aligns with the strategic objectives of the sponsoring organisation.
- *Quality expectations* – The customer's expectations regarding the project output.
- *Acceptance criteria* – The required values on a defined scale the project output should meet to be acceptable, each with a clear pass/fail result.
- *Project organisation* – The roles and responsibilities of those involved in directing and managing the project.
- *Project approach* – How the project output will be realised; are we going to outsource the work; are we going to work Agile or Waterfall, et cetera.
- *Key risks* – The main risks that may affect the delivery of the project output and the organisational goals to be achieved with it.
- *Project milestones* – The key events in a project at which the project's progress will be measured.
- *Reference documents* – The documents on which the project outline has been based.

The project mandate is also called the project charter. The project outline is also called the project brief or the draft project management plan. To avoid losing overview, work out the project outline as concisely as possible. Preferably, limit the project outline to one or two pages.

PLAN FOR THE PROJECT DEFINITION STAGE

Authorising the project definition stage also requires a plan for carrying out this stage. Who will be involved in developing the project management plan? What documents need to be prepared, how detailed should they be, and who should review and approve them? But also, how long will the definition stage take, and what are the total costs of this stage?

> *In the plan for the project definition stage, Marian indicated that she would first conduct several interviews with Xantia staff and then work with a small team from Xantia to draft the project management plan. She expects to complete it within four weeks.*

PROJECT DECISION

There are two project decisions at the start of a project. The first is at the end of the project preparation stage, in which the start of the project definition stage is authorised. This project decision is referred to as a 'decision to justify'. This decision is based on the project outline and the plan for the project definition stage. Along with this project decision, the project sponsor also appoints the project board and the key members of the project management team.

The second project decision is taken at the end of the project definition stage. With this decision, the actual delivery of the project is authorised. This project decision is referred to as a 'decision to fund'. This decision is made by the sponsoring organisation or customer based on (a summary of) the project management plan (see Chapter 5.01 Project Definition Stage).

Besides these first two project decisions, there is a project decision at each stage transition, when stage tolerances are threatened to be exceeded (see Chapter 6.04 Plan and Control) and at project closure (see Chapter 6.06 Project Closure).

SUSTAINABILITY

Two important aspects of the project outline are the desired changes the sponsoring organisation wants to realise with the project output (project goals) and how the project aligns with the sponsor organisation's strategic objectives (outline business case). The latter places the project in the broader context of the organisation's Corporate Social Responsibility. The former challenges the project sponsor and other key stakeholders to pursue a project output in the broader context of People, Planet and Profit. These two aspects directly affect all other parts of the project, such as scope, stakeholders, approach, quality criteria, constraints, and so on. Therefore, they should be taken into account from the start and also determine the (social) contract between the project sponsor and project manager on achieving the intended project results.

TAILORING

Another particular aspect of the project outline is the project approach; how will the project deliverables be achieved; traditional, through iterative and incremental delivery, or a hybrid combination? This will directly impact the project organisation, how stakeholders, particularly business users, will be involved, and the project's risks, resources, and business justification. Applying an initial assessment in the project preparation stage is recommended on whether to work Agile. What is the potential for iterative and incremental delivery? What is the flexibility on what needs to be delivered? What are the environmental conditions like? What is the level of collaboration? Can we assign a stable project team? What is the acceptance to work Agile, and so on? The project outline should capture the initial understanding of how to implement the project. In the case of an Agile approach, the project outline can be an elaborated product vision.

RESPONSIBILITIES

The sponsoring organisation appoints the project sponsor and issues the project mandate. The project sponsor appoints the project manager. The project manager and the sponsor are jointly responsible for the project preparation stage. The project manager should prepare the project outline and the plan for the project definition stage. You should also advise the project sponsor about the composition of the project board.

In consultation with the sponsoring organisation, the project sponsor approves the project outline and the plan for the project definition stage. Furthermore, they should make the necessary resources available for the project definition stage and appoint the project board. Finally, they need to authorise the project manager to start the project definition stage or end the project initiative.

4.02 STAKEHOLDERS

PURPOSE

The purpose of this chapter is to enable the individual to manage stakeholder interests and influence, engage stakeholders in the project, and effectively manage their expectations.

LEARNING OBJECTIVES

- Conduct a stakeholder analysis;
- Define a stakeholder strategy and prepare a communications plan;
- Effectively involve stakeholders in the project;
- Manage the expectations effectively of the various stakeholders.

DEFINITIONS

Stakeholder: Any individual, group, or organisation who has, or believes to have, interest or influence in an initiative.
Stakeholder interest-influence grid: A grid used to categorise and analyse stakeholders based on their level of interest and influence on an initiative.
Stakeholder management strategy: A high-level description of how stakeholders will be engaged in the project, including the intended outcome, processes, procedures, roles, responsibilities, and techniques to be applied.
Communication plan: A plan describing how, when, by whom, with which stakeholders, and for what purpose communication will take place, with the necessary costs and resources to do so.
Stakeholder engagement: The coordinated actions to effectively involve stakeholders to complete an initiative successfully.

INTRODUCTION

Engaging stakeholders is an important aspect of any project. Who are the people or parties that need to be heard? What are their interests and influence? How do we involve them in the project? How do we manage their expectations effectively?

Projects and the output of projects impact people and parties, but they also shape the project. They determine the scope, requirements, limitations and approach of the project and, to a significant extent, the risks related to the project.

A stakeholder is an individual, group or organisation who has or believes to have an interest or influence in an initiative. This goes beyond the formal people and parties involved in the project. A stakeholder could also be an environmental movement that believes that nature's interests could be harmed or a local community fearing the corruption of their neighbourhood. Many projects get into trouble if they do not take these stakeholders into account straight away.

POSITIONING

An initial stakeholder analysis should be carried out in the project preparation stage as this directly impacts the project organisation, the project outline, and who should be involved in preparing and reviewing the project management plan in the project definition stage. A more formal stakeholder analysis should be done in the project definition stage. Based on this, the stakeholder management strategy can be defined, and the communication plan for the project can be prepared.

Both strategy and plan can be part of the project management plan and separate documents. The latter is particularly recommended for environmentally sensitive projects. In such projects, the stakeholder management strategy and the communication plan are often separate discussion topics. The stakeholder management strategy and communication plan should be maintained during the project delivery and updated at least at each stage transition.

STAKEHOLDER ANALYSIS

- The stakeholder analysis includes:
- Identifying the stakeholders;
- Assessing their mutual relationships;
- Assessing their interest and influence towards the project;
- Assessing their attitude towards the project.

Identifying stakeholders

First, it is necessary to identify all project's stakeholders. Who are involved in the project assignment and the project funding, who will actually deliver the project output, who will use the project output, and who will be affected by or have an interest in the project output? If a project is part of a programme or a portfolio, these should also be identified as separate stakeholders (see Figure 4.02.01).

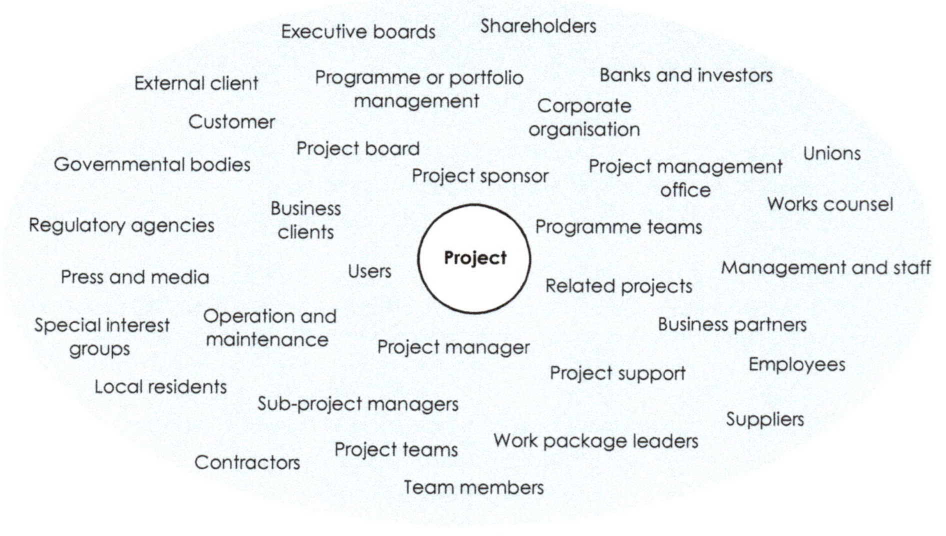

Figure 4.02.01 Project stakeholders

Stakeholders can be categorised in many ways. Categorisation helps prevent stakeholders from being overlooked. Stakeholders are often divided into internal-external, and primary-secondary stakeholders. In doing so, stakeholders simultaneously belong to different categories.

Internal stakeholders are those within the permanent organisation within which and or for which the project is implemented, such as management, staff and employees. External stakeholders are outside the permanent organisation, such as banks and investors, suppliers, external clients, press and media, local residents, and special interest groups.

Primary or direct stakeholders are those with a high vested interest in the project's outcome, such as the users and customers. Secondary or indirect stakeholders are stakeholders with a lower, more general level of interest, such as shareholders, governmental agencies, et cetera.

Assessing mutual relationships

After identifying stakeholders, it is essential to assess their mutual relationships. This can be visualised using a stakeholder map. In doing so, we should consider both formal and informal relationships. The connecting lines' thickness indicates the relationship's importance (see Figure 4.02.02).

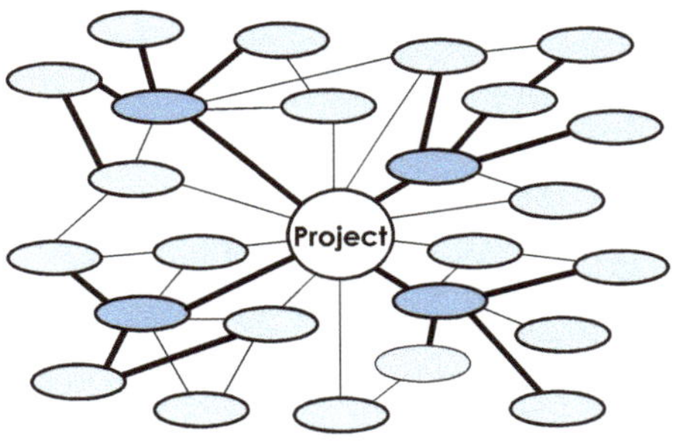

Figure 4.02.02 Stakeholder map

Based on the stakeholder map, it is relatively easy to distinguish which stakeholders are the 'spiders in the web'. We can distinguish between internal and external networks.

Assessing interest and influence

Based on the stakeholder map, an inventory can be made of the various interests and influences of the stakeholders. This is best visualised in an *interest-influence grid*. (see Figure 4.02.03). It basically distinguishes:

- Stakeholders with minimal interest and influence;
- Stakeholders with much interest but minimal influence;
- Stakeholders with minimal interest but much influence;
- Stakeholders with much interest and influence;

and all intermediate levels.

Assessing stakeholder's attitudes toward the project

In addition to the interest and influence on the project, it is also necessary to assess the attitude of the stakeholders towards the project. Is this positive or negative? Is there much or little trust in the relationship? Based on these two variables, six basic relationships can be determined (Groote, et al, 2011):

- *Coalition partner* – There is much agreement on content but little trust in the relationship. We now work together because this time, we agree on the content.

- *Ally* – There is a complete agreement regarding the content and much faith in the relationship. These parties often support each other through thick and thin, based on years of collaboration.
- *Opportunist* – There is a lack of clarity about the content. Furthermore, the opportunist has little faith in the relationship. The primary attitude is, 'What is in it for me?'
- *Doubter* – There is a lack of clarity about the content but trust in the relationship. Their position is unclear, but the primary attitude is positive.
- *Adversary* – Disagrees on content, and there is little or no faith in the relationship. The relationship is often emotionally determined by past experiences with the same people or similar situations.
- *Opponent* – Disagrees about the content, but there is much trust in the relationship. There is mutual respect.

ENGAGE STAKEHOLDERS

It is indispensable to engage stakeholders differently, depending on their interests and influence on the project. Basic possibilities are (see Figure 4.02.03):

- *Inform* – Stakeholders with little interest and influence are best informed through general communication channels such as newspapers and websites. Try to increase their interest. Ask them if they want to be on the mailing list or invite them to a community meeting.
- *Retention of interest* – Highly interested stakeholders with little influence should preferably be informed, specifically in those areas where their interest lies. They can become valuable supporters/ambassadors for the project. Informing them through blogs, newsletters, and community meetings are appropriate ways to get and keep them involved. Also, make sure they provide input.
- *Active consultation* – Stakeholders with little interest but much influence should be actively consulted in their areas of interest. Also, try to increase this. Try to connect their interests with the project output and the resulting change.
- *Active involvement* – Stakeholders with much influence and interest should be actively involved. These are key stakeholders in the project and desired project board members.

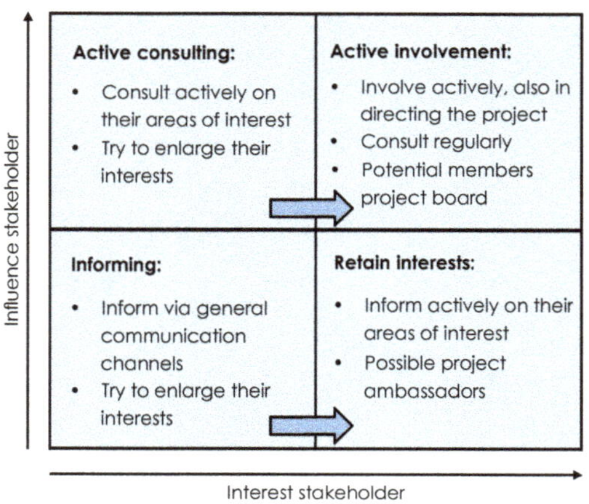

Figure 4.02.03 Interest-influence grid

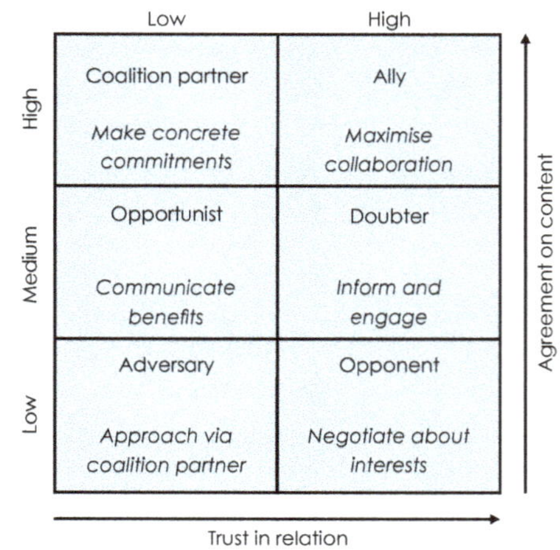

Figure 4.02.04 Managing expectations

Not informing/involving stakeholders is, obviously, also an option, but it should be a conscious choice. And this choice is risky. Stakeholders who are not involved can become your worst enemies. If you do not involve them from the outset, the process will quicken, but you will usually get less far or not get there at all.

> *In consultation with Ben van Buren, the project sponsor, the decision has been made to inform the staff through the in-house magazine. Shop managers will be notified by letter and invited to a company meeting. All executives will be consulted, and efforts will be made to enlarge their interests. The head of IT, Logistics and Marketing will be asked to participate in the project board.*

MANAGING EXPECTATIONS

Depending on their trust and their agreement on the content, stakeholders should be engaged differently (see Figure 4.02 04):

- *Coalition partner* – Make concrete agreements on collaboration and the results to be delivered.
- *Ally* – The more you cooperate, the better. Senior allies can be appointed as board members.
- *Opportunist* – Communicate clearly about the possible benefits.
- *Doubter* – They might have too little knowledge of the project; if possible, inform and involve them more.
- *Adversary* – Be clear about the goals and benefits to be realised, separate the business and emotional side, and, if possible, involve them through an ally or coalition partner.
- *Opponent* – Clarity is of great importance here. You can talk about the differences of opinion. Overlapping and conflicting interests can be negotiated.

> *Opinions among shop managers are divided. José is a strong supporter of the new webshop. He is also good friends with Ben. Marian decides to involve him actively in the project. What Julia thinks is still unclear. Furthermore, there is little trust between them. Marian realises it is necessary to highlight the advantages of the webshop to her. Richard is firmly against the webshop, and he and Ben dislike each other. Marian decides to keep in contact with him through José.*

When managing expectations, it is essential to determine how stakeholder input is incorporated into the project. Not pro forma but with an open mind. Up to when does their input still make sense, and can the project or parts of the project be changed without disrupting the process? Which input is requested, what is the latitude, and who makes the final decision? Clear process agreements should be made about this in advance. Nothing frustrates the process more than stakeholders feeling that decisions have already been made, that they are only involved pro forma, and that their input is meaningless.

STAKEHOLDER MANAGEMENT STRATEGY AND PLAN

The stakeholder management strategy is a high-level description of how stakeholders will be engaged in the project, including the procedures, roles, responsibilities, and techniques for involving them and managing expectations. What is the Communication

Department's role? Who is responsible for updating the project website? How does the project communication align with the communication policy of the sponsoring organisation? In which system is the stakeholder information recorded? Who manages the communication database? Who ensures that the agreements made are kept? But also, how will the stakeholder's feedback be taken into account, how will they be informed about it, and how will the effectiveness of the stakeholder management strategy be reviewed and the strategy updated?

The most commonly used approaches are a participative, informative or discursive approach. Less desirable approaches are restrictive and repressive approaches. A discursive approach focuses on resolving arguments through analytical reasoning. A restrictive approach focuses on discouraging stakeholders from acting. A repressive approach focuses on discouraging stakeholders from using force.

With a discursive approach, the focus is on the dialogues that take place between different stakeholders and the consensus that is achieved consequently, rather than on pre-defined objectives and priori assumptions. With a restrictive approach, you try to make stakeholders feel that objecting makes no sense or takes far too much effort with little chance of success. In a repressive approach, you want to make the stakeholders feel that objecting might have adverse consequences for them.

Communication plan

The communication plan describes for each stakeholder or group of stakeholders why, how often (when), to what detail (how), through which medium (where), by whom what should be communicated, and the estimated costs and resources. The communication plan should answer the following questions:

- What is the purpose of each communication activity?
- What are the key messages in the communication?
- Who are the target groups for the various communication activities?
- When are the various communication activities scheduled?
- Who should communicate what to whom?
- How much information is released, and at what level of detail?
- How will the information be released, and using what medium?
- How can stakeholders provide feedback, and how do we demonstrate that we have taken this into account?

Repeating key messages regularly and using different communication channels are both essential. Approach stakeholders actively but also allow them to review information at their convenience (passively).

SUSTAINABILITY

Stakeholder engagement and sustainability are closely linked. A sustainable approach will likely lead to identifying more stakeholders and a more proactive and open approach. These stakeholders may include environmental groups, human rights groups, and non-governmental organisations. The 'new' stakeholders will most certainly find more aspects to consider than the more 'ordinary' stakeholders.

According to ISO 26000, a company committed to CSR is accountable for its impact on society, the economy and the environment. It should be transparent in its decisions and activities affecting society and the environment and respect stakeholder interests and human rights. These principles directly affect stakeholder engagement in any project.

TAILORING

Agile development is characterised by strong interaction with users and other stakeholders. The product owner should ensure the product backlog is transparent, visible and understood. Developers and business people collaborate daily throughout the project. At the end of each timebox, the product owner, delivery team and stakeholders review what has been accomplished. The product backlog may be updated to reflect new opportunities. Since the work is done in restrictive timeboxes, adjustments are easily made.

While the Agile way of working may ensure strong stakeholder involvement, it also entails pitfalls. The product owner should have the trust of management, be able to represent all users, have insights into the work to be done, be fully committed, and has time to fulfil their role satisfactorily. Moreover, most of the focus of the delivery team is on the direct business people, and often less attention is afforded to the project sponsor, the sponsoring organisation and other stakeholders. Neglecting these parties jeopardises the project's success, as management left in the dark will feel the urge to somehow interfere with the project, and not always for the better. The project manager should collaborate closely with the product owner to ensure that stakeholder engagement is not weakened and grey areas are filled in effectively.

RESPONSIBILITIES

The project manager is responsible for conducting the stakeholder analysis and preparing the stakeholder strategy and communication plan. The project sponsor should approve these. The project manager and the sponsor are jointly responsible for engaging the stakeholders and managing their expectations.

4.03 PROJECT ORGANISATION

PURPOSE

The purpose of this chapter is to enable the individual to define, implement and manage the temporary project organisation effectively.

LEARNING OBJECTIVES

- Project governance;
- Customer-supplier relationship in a project;
- Separation between technique and management in a project;
- The various levels in the project management structure;
- The project governance and project organisation and the respective project organisation chart;
- The various roles and responsibilities in a project;
- The project meeting structure and the linking-pin principle;
- The project responsibilities matrix.

DEFINITIONS

Project governance: The principles, policies, and framework by which the project organisation is directed and controlled.
Project organisation: The temporary organisation in which the project output is realised.
Project sponsor: The individual accountable for the project's success to the sponsoring organisation or customer, and owner of the project's business case.
Project board: The highest governance board in the project responsible for the overall direction and management of the project within the constraints and directions set by the sponsoring organisation or customer.
Project manager: The individual responsible for the daily management of the project to achieve the project deliverables and enable project success.
Work package leader: The individual responsible for realising the products and services within a work package within the requirements and constraints agreed upon with the project manager.
Project support: A role within the project management team that supports the project manager in daily management by providing certain administrative services and specific tasks.
Project management team: The project manager and core team members leading the project.
Project team: A team that realises specialist products within a project.

INTRODUCTION

The project organisation is the temporary structure that includes project roles, responsibilities, levels of authority, and the reporting and communication lines within which the project output is realised. Project governance is the total of principles, policies, and frameworks by which the project organisation is directed and controlled. To be successful, it is of the utmost importance to create and maintain a high-performing project organisation throughout the project lifecycle.

POSITIONING

The sponsoring organisation appoints the project sponsor by issuing the project mandate at the start of the project preparation stage. The project sponsor appoints the project manager and sets up the project board. The project manager advises the sponsor herein and is responsible for setting up the project organisation. The project sponsor is accountable for the project organisation and should also ensure that the necessary resources are available. The assignment of all the individual roles should be confirmed by the sponsoring organisation. The project sponsor appoints the temporary project organisation and governance structures at the end of the project preparation stage at the authorisation of the project definition stage.

In the project definition stage, the project organisation is further specified, and the people/parties responsible for delivering specialist activities are selected and appointed or contracted. During project delivery, at best at the stage transitions, the project governance and the project organisation are assessed and updated if necessary. When the project is closed, the project manager dismantles the project organisation. Finally, the project sponsor grants a discharge to the project manager, terminates the temporary project governance structure and closes the project.

PROJECT GOVERNANCE

Project governance is the total of principles, policies and frameworks by which the project organisation is directed and controlled by the sponsoring organisation or customer and supplier side. It provides oversight for the policies, processes, and methods to be used, the management frameworks to apply, and the limits of authority for decision-making.

The responsibility for maintaining project governance is usually assigned to the project sponsor and other project board members. A permanent *Project Management Office* (PMO) may facilitate and assure the project governance set (see Chapter 9.04 Supporting Functions and Implementing PPP-management).

CUSTOMER-SUPPLIER RELATIONSHIP

In projects, there is always a customer and a supplier. The customer is the individual, group or organisation receiving the deliverables. The supplier is the individual, group or organisation that provides the products or services. The customer can be an internal department or someone of the external client. The supplier can be an external contractor but also an internal department.

The project sponsor and the project manager are usually not the individuals who enter into the agreement between the customer and supplier organisation about delivering the project output. These are authorised individuals within both organisations with power of attorney. At completion, the project output is formally handed over by the supplier to the customer and not by the project manager to the project sponsor.

SEPARATION OF TECHNIQUE AND MANAGEMENT

Managing a project is a different responsibility than delivering products or services. These are separate responsibilities that, if possible, should not be combined. However, in daily practice, this may not always be possible; projects are sometimes too small to justify a separate project manager. Furthermore, the project manager sometimes possesses specific expertise needed to deliver the products or services. The project manager may also fulfil the specialist or work package leader role in such situations.

However, when these responsibilities are combined, there is a risk that the project manager will become too preoccupied with the content and neglect their managerial role. This happens mainly because countless project managers were once specialists and still love that profession. Another disadvantage is that when conflicts over content arise, the project manager is no longer independent but part of the problem itself. In the context of the book, we only focus on the responsibilities and necessary competences of managing the project and not on combined positions.

PROJECT MANAGEMENT STRUCTURE

The project management structure distinguishes four levels of management:

- *Governance level* – The sponsoring organisation or customer;
- *Directing level* – The project sponsor with the project board;
- *Managing level* – The project manager and project management team;
- *Delivery level* – The project teams with individual team members.

The sponsoring organisation or customer is not part of the project organisation but is responsible for establishing and maintaining the overarching project governance, determining the business strategies, issuing the project mandate, coordinating between the different projects, and realising the ultimate business goals. They also appoint the project sponsor.

PROJECT ORGANISATION

The project organisation is the temporary organisation where the project output is realised. The project organisation comprises the project's roles, responsibilities, authorities and communication, and reporting lines. The project organisation consists of the project's directing, managing and delivering layers.

The project sponsor is responsible for obtaining the resources and making the executive decisions within the given mandate to enable project success. The project board supports the project sponsor in directing and controlling the project. The project sponsor/project board is the highest management level within the project.

The project manager is responsible for the daily project management within the framework given by the project sponsor/project board and ensuring that the project output is delivered successfully. The project management team are the project manager and core team members who assist in managing the project. Large infrastructural projects may consist of a construction manager, field engineering manager, contract manager, environmental manager, et cetera. In small projects, it may be the project manager, work package leaders, and project support.

A work package leader is an individual who is responsible for realising the products and services within a work package within the requirements and constraints agreed upon by the project manager. A work package is a group of related tasks and deliverables for which cost and duration are estimated and managed. A sub-project manager is responsible for the daily management of a sub-project and delivering the sub-project deliverables successfully. A sub-project is a project within the framework of the overall project with its own specific deliverables to the sponsoring organisation. A sub-project is a part of a larger project comprising two or more work packages. A sub-project may run through several project stages. Project support is a role within the project management team that supports the project manager in daily management by providing certain administrative services and specific tasks.

The delivery level consists of the project teams responsible for the actual performing of specialist activities to realise project deliverables.

Tailoring project organisation

The project organisation can vary greatly depending on the nature and complexity of the project and the project environment. In a small project, there may only be a project sponsor, project manager and team members, and no project board, project support, and work package leaders.

In a large and complex project, there is often a project board with separate user and supplier boards, a separate project assurance board, sub-projects and work packages led by sub-project managers and work package leaders, and a project support office (see Figure 4.03.01).

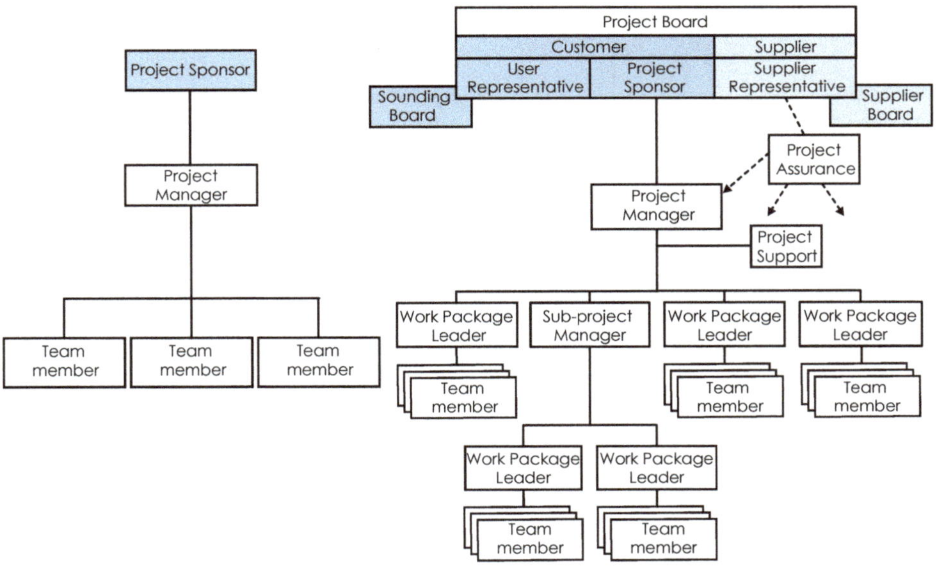

Figure 4.03.01 Tailoring of a project organisation

Project organisation chart

The project organisation chart is a schematic representation of the project organisation. There should be a direct line between the project sponsor/project board and the project manager, and between the project manager, the project management team, and the project teams. Reporting lines and consultation structures are not indicated.

It is essential to name the people for the various roles, not companies, organisational units or groups. You cannot address a group, but you can address a person. Individual team members are usually not indicated in the chart if sub-projects managers and work package leaders are.

Finally, it is important to distinguish between teams/people who support the project manager in daily project management and teams/people who are directly assigned to realising the project output. The supporting teams/people are indicated in a side branch, like the project support in Figure 4.03.01. The delivering teams/people are depicted in line under the project manager.

ROLES AND RESPONSIBILITIES

A role is a coherent set of tasks, responsibilities and authorities that one or more people can fulfil. It is essential that roles within a project are clearly described and do not overlap. Overlapping roles can cause much confusion.

Sponsoring organisation or customer – The organisation that commissioned and funds the work and makes the final go/no-go decisions in the project. The sponsoring organisation can vary greatly. They can be the corporate, programme organisation or an external client or can even consists of multiple organisations. Towards the project, they can be represented by a programme or portfolio manager but also by a director, council, or board of directors. The sponsoring organisation or customer establishes and maintains the project governance. Determining toll gates and making the go/no-go decisions are essential aspects of this.

Project board – The highest decision-making body within the project. A project board is appointed for most projects. In terms of composition and decision-making, the project board should consider the interests of the various stakeholders. In addition to the project sponsor, the project board consists of at least one or more user and supplier representatives (see Figure 4.03.02).

The project board should provide consistent direction and guidance for the project within the project governance set by sponsoring organisation. They should delegate daily management to the project manager and facilitate the integration with the functional units. The board should ensure the availability of people and other resources. They should ensure effective decision-making and provide visible and sustained support to the project manager. They should ensure that the interests of the participating organisations are served and assist the project sponsor with the strategic decisions. The project board communicates with the sponsoring organisation and senior stakeholders. Project board members should have authority and credibility and be available.

The project board's responsibilities may include further:

- Authorising the project definition and the start of the project delivery;
- Deciding whether and how to delegate project assurance responsibilities;
- Deciding whether to use a change authority and agree on the level of authority to delegate;
- Approving the applicable management strategies;
- Approving all major plans and making the necessary resources available;

- Providing overall guidance and direction to the project;
- Responding to requests for advice from the project manager;
- Making decisions on escalated issues and risks;
- Ensuring effective communication with all stakeholders;
- Approving the completion of stages and authorising the start of the next stage;
- Authorising any deviation that exceeds or is forecasted to exceed stage tolerances;
- Assuring that all products have been delivered satisfactorily;
- Confirming acceptance of the project output;
- Ensuring handing over documents are forwarded to appropriate bodies.

Among others, a project board may be referred to as a project steering committee, project steering board, or project management board.

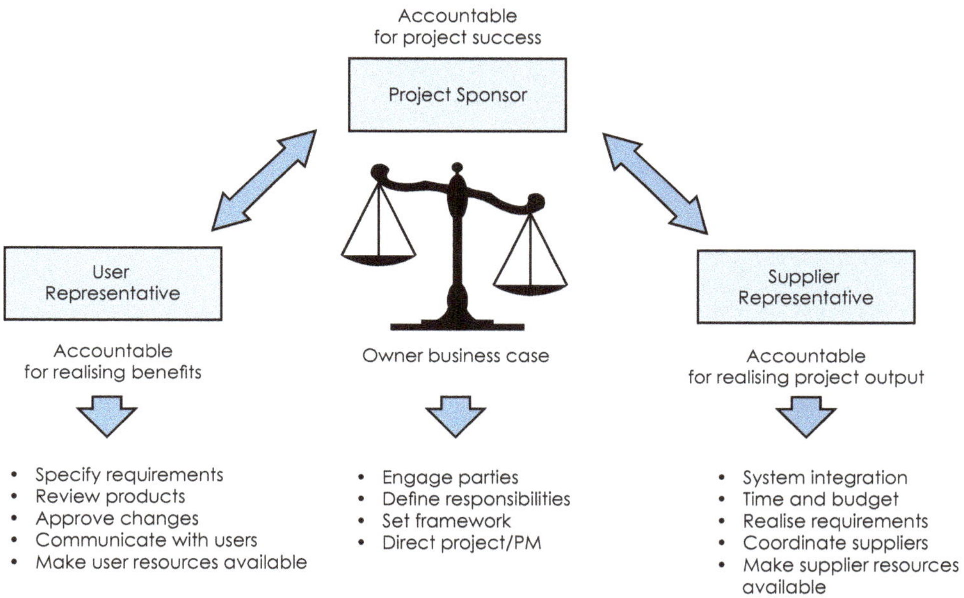

Figure 4.03.02 Roles, accountabilities and responsibilities on the project board

Project sponsor – Is accountable for the project's success towards the sponsoring organisation or customer and is the individual who takes the final decisions within the project board. The sponsor chairs the board and is the owner of the business case. The project sponsor represents the interests of the business and should ensure the balance between the user's and supplier's interests. Within a project, there is always only one project sponsor. The project sponsor is the highest change authority within the project.

In addition to the project board, the responsibilities of the project sponsor include:

- Appointing the project manager and the project management team;
- Approving the project outline and definition stage plan and authorising the project definition;
- Determining the goal, scope, approach, and result of the project;

- Ensuring that the project is embedded in and supported by the customer organisation;
- Securing the funding of the project and approving supplier contracts;
- Ensuring that the project remains justified throughout its lifecycle;
- Holding user representatives accountable for realising the benefits defined in the business case;
- Holding supplier representatives accountable for realising deliverables within requirements and constraints set;
- Ensuring a balance between users' and suppliers' interests;
- Shielding the project from its environment;
- Monitoring and controlling the project performance at a strategic level;
- Providing direction, advice and context to enable stated business needs;
- Making decisions within their delegated authority;
- Ensuring overall business assurance;
- Engaging senior stakeholders;
- Reporting to the sponsoring organisation;
- Escalating to the sponsoring organisation if project tolerance is forecasted to be exceeded;
- Deciding to whom the project deliverables will be handed over;
- Closing the project and granting a discharge to the project manager.

The project sponsor may delegate some of their tasks and authority to others but remains overall responsible. Among others, the project sponsor may be called the project executive, project owner, or project principal.

User representative – Represents the users' interests in the project board. The user representative is usually a manager of the user department accountable for ensuring that the forecasted benefits in the business case will be realised. Based on that responsibility, the user representative should specify the output requirements, approve change requests from the user's point of view, and (let) test and approve the products delivered.

Furthermore, it is the responsibility of the user representative to communicate with the users and make the necessary resources from the user organisation available for the project. In case of conflicting interests from the user side, the user representative takes the final decision. The user representative is often designated as the change authority within the project board. Within the project board, this role can be fulfilled by more than one individual.

Supplier representative – Represents the interests of the suppliers in the project board. The supplier representative is accountable for ensuring the project output is realised within the criteria set and will function as foreseen. The supplier representative is responsible for the technical feasibility of the products to be delivered. Also, they are responsible for making available the required resources and coordinating the suppliers. Within the project board, this role can be fulfilled by more than one individual.

The user and supplier representatives sponsor of the project within their own organisation.

The municipality had awarded the construction of the new football stadium to the consortium MBH. The project sponsor was Mrs Garcia, the municipality's sports and culture councillor. The user representative on the project board was Mr Gomes, the football club chairman that would rent the stadium from the municipality. The supplier representative on the board was Mr Hernandez, the director of the construction consortium. Mrs Lopez, the project manager, had been hired externally. She was responsible on behalf of the municipality for the construction of the football stadium and surrounding infrastructure. Mr Perez was the consortium's project manager, in charge of the actual construction of the stadium.

During delivery, Mrs Lopez noticed that, in order to save time, the work was not carried out as agreed. Mr Perez, however, had no intention of adjusting the work. Mrs Lopez brought this to the attention of Mrs Garcia, who spoke to Mr Hernandez. That helped. This simple intervention ensured that the work was corrected and continued as agreed.

Project assurance – Undertakes planned and systematic actions on behalf of the individual members of the project board to provide confidence that the project will be successful. Project assurance is, in principle, a responsibility of the project board members themselves. However, project assurance can be quite time-consuming and often requires specific qualities. That is why this responsibility is often delegated to third parties. However, the individual board members remain ultimately responsible for it.

For the project sponsor, the project assurance role is often performed by a financial controller. For the user representative, the project assurance role is often performed by a quality manager. For the supplier representative, the project assurance role is often performed by a financial controller and a quality manager from the supplier's organisation.

Under the principle of separation of duties, the project assurance role cannot be combined with the role of (sub-)project manager, work package leader, project support, or any project team member.

The municipality awarded the construction of the new theatre to the firm ABC. They are responsible for both the design and the construction. Mrs Collins, the councillor for culture, is the project sponsor. She reports on this project directly to the city council. The current theatre director is the user representative on the project board. The director of firm ABC is the supplier representative.

Since Mrs Collins knows nothing about building such a theatre, she has asked Mr Williams, the council's head of finance, to act as project assurance. He will review all financial reports the ABC project manager provides before these are forwarded to her. This way, she ensures that this project will not exceed the budget under her authority.

Project manager – Responsible for the daily management of the project on behalf of the project sponsor/project board to achieve the project deliverables and enable project success. Within a project, there should always be only one (overall) project manager. The roles of the project sponsor and project manager cannot be combined. Among other things, a project manager may be called a project director (large projects) or project leader.

The project manager's responsibilities may include:

- Agreeing with the project sponsor on the project's purpose, scope, output and approach;
- Establishing the project organisation in consultation with the project sponsor;
- Establishing the management approach per the agreed project governance;
- Preparing the project and stage baselines such as the project outline and project management plan;
- Supporting the project sponsor in preparing and monitoring the business case;
- Obtaining authorisation for the delivery of the individual stages;
- Establishing and managing the project procedures such as for communication and change control;
- Managing stages within the agreed tolerances and authorising work packages;
- Taking responsibility for overall progress and reporting against the project plan;
- Managing project procurement and supplier performance;
- Facilitating project board decision-making and advising on deviations from the plan;
- Managing issues and risks and taking corrective actions;
- Leading and managing the project (management) team;
- Ensuring stakeholder engagement and communication according to plan;
- Validating deliverables and outcomes provided by the project;
- Dismantling the project at closure and obtaining an official release of duty to perform work for the project.

Project support – Responsible for the administrative and specialist support of the project manager for the daily management of the project. The project support reports to the project manager. In small projects, project managers may carry out the project support tasks themselves. Among others, project support may be referred to as project office, project support office, or project support team.

Regular project support tasks are:

- Setting up and maintaining project files;
- Establishing document control procedures;
- Collecting actual data and forecasts;
- Assisting with the compilation of plans and reports;
- Administering and assisting with project board meetings and quality activities;
- Maintaining logs and registers and archiving records;
- Administering change control procedures;
- Maintaining configuration items records.

Work package leader – Responsible for realising the work package on time, within budget and according to the specifications as agreed with the project manager. The role of work package leader is optional. In small projects, team members may have to deliver the work packages by themselves without support from other team members.

The work package leader's responsibilities may include the following:

- Preparing the team plan and agreeing on the work package and team plan with the project manager;
- Planning, monitoring, and managing the work of the team and taking corrective actions when necessary;
- Informing the project manager of the progress of the work;
- Ensuring that quality activities related to the team's work are correctly planned and carried out;
- Liaising with any project assurance and project support roles;
- Identifying and advising the project manager on issues and risks associated with the work package;
- Managing issues and risks assigned by the project manager;
- Handing over the completed deliverables, including appropriate documentation, to the project manager.

Team members – Perform project activities and are responsible towards the work package leader or project manager for completing their assigned activities and the resulting deliverables.

The team member's responsibilities may include:

- Carrying out the assigned work according to plan;
- Contributing their expertise;
- Representing their department or interested parties;
- Taking joint responsibility for the performance of the team;
- Collaborating with other team members and stakeholders as agreed;
- Taking joint responsibility for the progress and performance of the work package.

MEETING STRUCTURE AND LINKING-PIN PRINCIPLE

The meeting structure comprises the framework of the various meetings. For proper decision-making within the project, these meetings should be linked to each other via the *linking pin principle*. This principle is put forward by Rensis Likert (1987). It presents an organisation as a series of overlapping units, with members of one unit in turn managing another unit. These individuals are the *linking pins* within the organisation. A similar model can be applied to a project. The *Project Sponsor* (PS) participates in the sponsoring organisation or customer management board meeting and chairs the project board meeting. The project manager participates in the project board meeting and chairs the project management team meeting. The individual work package leader participates in the project progress meeting and chairs the relevant team meeting (see Figure 4.03.03).

In addition to the regular meeting structure, large complex projects often have additional consultative bodies such as a sounding board, advisory board, policy board and or review board. It is essential to determine and agree on these consultative bodies' tasks, responsibilities and authorities in advance. They can only function well if they have delegated responsibility from one of the primary roles within the regular project organisation and if that role in question also directs them. For example, a sounding board can support the *User Representative* (UR) role, and a supplier board can support the *Supplier Representative* (SR) role. When the responsibilities of these boards are unclear or not supported by the various roles involved, it can have a strong negative impact on the effectiveness and success of the project.

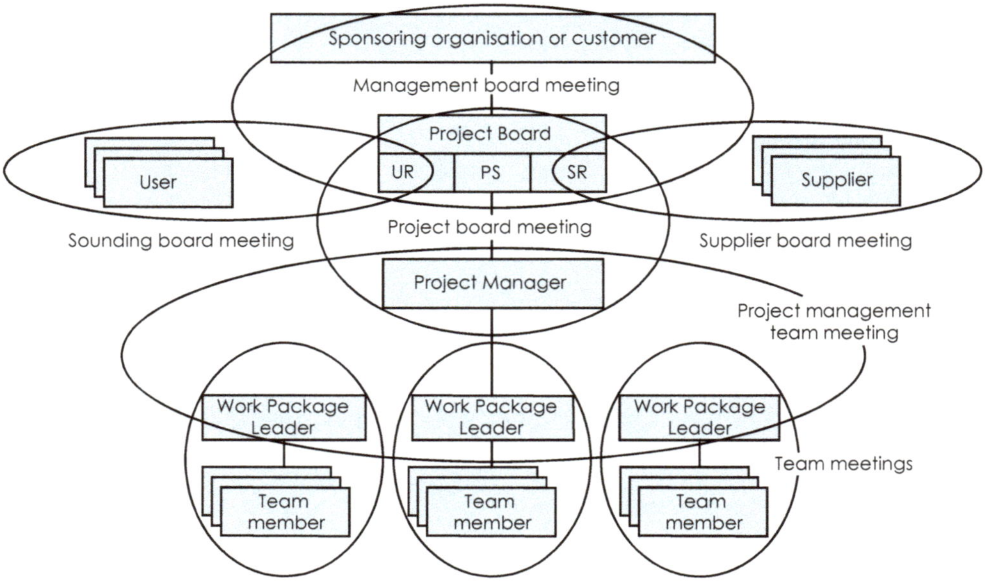

Figure 4.03.03 Linking pin

RESPONSIBILITIES MATRIX (RASCI MODEL)

The tasks and responsibilities of the various people within the project management structure can be made visible by drawing up a responsibility matrix. Therefore, the *RASCI model* is often used, see Table 4.03.01.

Code	Responsibilities	Description
R	Responsible	Responsible for realising the output
A	Accountable	Has to approve the output
S	Support	Support the one who is responsible
C	Consulted	Should be consulted
I	Informed	Should be informed

Table 4.03.01 RASCI model

For each task, only one individual can be responsible, and only one accountable. The responsible individual (R) reports the result to the accountable individual (A). The 'R' and the 'A' cannot be the same person. However, the responsible individual may be supported by more than one person (S), should consult more than one person (C) and or should inform more than one person (I) about a particular task. In more advanced matrices, additional roles can be assigned, such as the reviewing role.

SUSTAINABILITY

A sustainable approach will certainly influence the project. This can be done directly through input from customers, users, and suppliers and through input from environmental stakeholders in the opinion and decision-making processes within the project. Sustainability groups can participate in sounding boards that may even be set up specifically for this purpose. In sustainable project management, a positive and proactive attitude towards them is mandatory. From the sustainability perspective, assigning the corporate sustainability or CSR officer as project assurance is recommended.

TAILORING

Agile projects are characterised by self-managing delivery teams working collectively towards an agreed product goal. The team itself can carry out the work package leader role, who accepts and ultimately delivers the completed work package to the project manager.

However, without interfering with the responsibilities of the delivery team themselves, communication and reporting lines need to be established to enable the project sponsor/project board to fulfil their responsibilities. Project governance guidelines and regulations should be translated to the specific project conditions. The content and progress of the work packages should be managed within the needs and requirements of the project output as a whole. Obstacles that individual teams cannot resolve on their own should be swiftly removed to ensure that project objectives are met. In this respect, an effective project organisation can strengthen the performance of the self-directing teams and vice versa.

RESPONSIBILITIES

The project sponsor is accountable for the project's success on behalf of the sponsoring organisation or customer. The user representative represents the users' interests in the project board. The supplier representative represents the supplier's interests on the project board. The project manager is responsible for the daily management of the project on behalf of the project sponsor/project board to achieve the project deliverables and enable project success. The work package leaders are responsible for realising the work packages assigned to them.

4.04 REQUIREMENTS AND OBJECTIVES

PURPOSE

The purpose of this chapter is to enable the individual to establish the relationship between what stakeholders want to achieve and what the project is going to accomplish.

LEARNING OBJECTIVES

- Project deliverables, output, outcome, benefits, and goal;
- Project objectives, constraints, criteria and the SMART method;
- Need, expectations, acceptance criteria, requirements, and specifications;
- Functional and technical requirements of a product;
- MoSCoW technique;
- Requirement specification;
- 'Fit for use' and 'fit for purpose';
- Value management (advanced);
- Total cost of ownership and product cost management (advanced).

DEFINITIONS

Project deliverable: A tangible or intangible element to be realised by the project.
Project output: The total of the project deliverables that forms the project result.
Project objective: A target within which the project should be realised.
Project outcome: The result of a change enabled by the project output.
Project goal: The effect the sponsoring organisation or customer wants to achieve with the project output.
Quality expectations: A wish or statement about the quality expected from the project output.
Acceptance criterion: The value on a defined scale that the project output should meet to be acceptable.
Quality requirement: A condition or capability a product should meet to be acceptable.
Requirement specification: The documented total set of requirements the project output should meet.

INTRODUCTION

This chapter describes the 'why' of the project – which changes are to be implemented, which benefits to be realised and which goals to be achieved. They are derived from the needs, expectations, requirements and strategic goals of the sponsoring organisation and other stakeholders. You need to know these to determine the project output, requirements, and objectives and to deliver an output that is fit for use and fit for purpose. Without a good understanding of these, the chance of project success is limited.

POSITIONING

In the project preparation stage, the project goal, output, requirements and objectives should be established already, and an initial project assessment should be carried out. What is the change that needs to be realised with the project result? What are the requirements, wishes and expectations of the various stakeholders? What are the most important acceptance criteria of the project output to be delivered? And how does the project output contribute to the effect the sponsoring organisation or customer wants to achieve?

During the project definition stage, the requirements and objectives are further defined. During the project delivery, you should ensure that these requirements and objectives are met. At stage transition, the achievements are assessed, and the requirements and objectives are updated and further specified. At project closure, an account is made of the extent to which the requirements and objectives have been achieved.

PROJECT, OUTPUT, OUTCOME, BENEFITS, AND GOAL

Projects are initiated to solve a problem or seize an opportunity for an organisation. From these problems or opportunities, the project goals and benefits to be realised are derived. From these project goals and benefits, in turn, the project outcome, project output and project objectives are determined (see Figure 4.04.01).

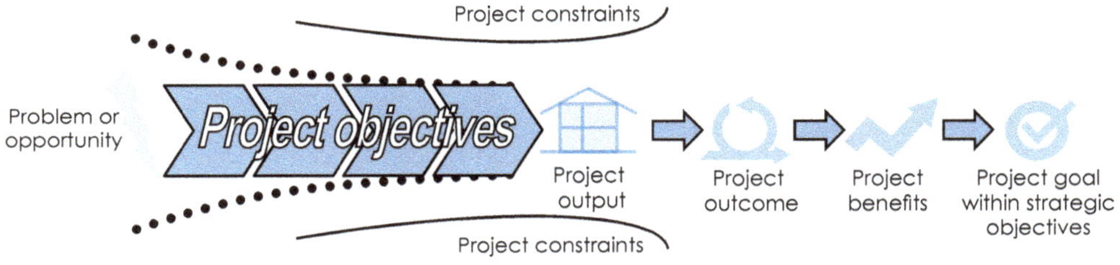

Figure 4.04.01 Project objectives, output, outcome, benefits, and goal

Goal analysis

The project goal describes the effect of *what* the sponsoring organisations wants to achieve with the project output. The project goal should support one or more strategic objectives of the organisation. The project mission statement is a brief description of *why* the project is needed (purpose). It explains the strategic reasons for starting the project.

From this project goal, a goal hierarchy with sub-goals is derived. This goal hierarchy is influenced and determined by contextual factors and specific stakeholder needs and requirements. Besides these immediate project goals, potential positive side effects (consequential benefits) can be defined too, such as gaining new knowledge, strengthening relationships, and experience with outsourcing.

Project deliverables, output, and result

Project deliverables are the tangible or intangible elements delivered by the project. The project output is the total of the project deliverables. The project deliverables can be products or services. The project output is sometimes also referred to as the project product.

Project outcome

The project outcome results from the change enabled by the project output. The project outcome occurs through the use of the project output. Therefore, the project outcome is not what the project delivers but what has been achieved with the project output.

Project benefits and dis-benefits

Based on this change, benefits can be realised that contribute to achieving the project goals. A project benefit is an advantage resulting from the project outcome. To realise these benefits effectively, a benefits owner should be assigned for each intended benefit. From this responsibility, they can act as user representatives within the project board.

Keep in mind that implementing changes can also bring dis-benefits. A dis-benefit is a disadvantage resulting from the outcome. These can seriously hinder the achievement of the project goal. In that context, it is recommended to also assign benefits owners to those dis-benefits, with a mandate to minimise the negative impacts.

Project objectives, constraints and criteria

Project objectives are the targets within which the project should be realised. Where the project goal is the effect that the customer wants to achieve with the project output, the project objectives comprise all the specific milestones within which the project output should be delivered. The project objectives are usually about delivering the desired project output on time, within budget, and conforming to specifications.

Project constraints are the limitations/restrictions within which a project should be carried out. Project criteria are the conditions a project should be meet. Constraints may be that overtime is not allowed, power cannot be switched off, or work cannot be interrupted. Criteria may be the quality procedures to be followed, that users should be involved, et cetera. Constraints are about what is limiting us from making progress; criteria are about how things should be done.

SMART

It is essential to formulate objectives *SMART*. SMART is an acronym for:

- ***S****pecific* – The objective is unambiguous.
- ***M****easurable* – Use measurable values to determine when the objective is achieved.
- ***A****chievable* – The objective is feasible under the circumstances.
- ***R****elevant* – The objective matters to you and aligns with the organisational goals.
- ***T****ime-related* – A precise moment in time when the objective should be achieved.

Constraints and criteria may be added to the SMART formulation of objectives. It is vital that the objectives are agreed upon by all parties involved and regularly reviewed and updated if necessary.

QUALITY EXPECTATIONS AND ACCEPTANCE CRITERIA

A quality expectation is a wish or statement about the quality expected from the project output. An acceptance criterion is a required value on a defined scale that the project output should meet to be acceptable with a clear pass/fail result. At least one acceptance criterion should be formulated for each quality expectation to determine whether that quality expectation has been met.

Quality expectations are, for example, not too long, user-friendly, safe, and so on. The associated acceptance criteria might be no more than 1.70 meters, with English instructions, in compliance with the health and safety regulations, et cetera.

MoSCoW technique

It is necessary to prioritise the requirements, wishes and expectations. Not everything is equally important. A subdivision into requirements, wishes and expectations is often not concrete enough. That is why the *MoSCoW* technique is often used nowadays. That makes it easier to select when not all quality expectations can be met due to, for example, budget or time constraints. This technique can also be used to prioritise change requests, tests, et cetera.

The acronym of MoSCoW stands for:

- ***M**ust-have* – Is essential; without this functionality, the output has no significance.
- ***S**hould-have* – Is highly desirable, but an alternative is also possible.
- ***Co**uld-have* (nice to have) – Only done if there is enough time and budget.
- ***W**on't have this time* – Not carry out now, perhaps later.

> - *If possible shorter than 1,65 meters (could-have), preferably no longer than 1,70 meters (should-have), but by no means longer than 1,80 meters (must-have).*
> - *If possible, everything is in English (could-have). If not, then still the user and system manual (should-have), but at least the user manual (must-have).*

REQUIREMENTS AND REQUIREMENT SPECIFICATION

A requirement is a condition or capability needed to solve a problem or achieve an objective. A quality requirement is a condition or capability a product should meet to be acceptable. Quality requirements should be defined for the individual deliverables of the project output. Quality requirements are derived from the quality expectations and acceptance criteria.

A requirement specification consists of all requirements to be imposed on the project deliverables and their development. An initial requirement specification is defined in the project definition stage. This requirement specification should contain just enough detail to prepare the project management plan. During project delivery, the requirement specification should be refined more and more. Detail the requirements as late as possible in the process to remain flexible for as long as possible.

It is unnecessary and often even undesirable to fully specify the requirements of all products right at the start of the project. That takes a lot of time, which is not always available. Moreover, it is yet to be determined. Techniques evolve, and insights and circumstances may change.

Functional and technical requirements

Quality requirements can be divided into functional and technical requirements. A functional requirement describes a specific function that a product should fulfil. A good functional requirement describes the desired function without prescribing the technical solution; see the format for user stories (see Chapter 9.05 Development Frameworks).

A technical requirement describes a characteristic or an attribute a product should meet. Technical requirements can include criteria for maintenance, reliability, availability, safety and health, performance or a specific technical solution for a function. In principle, technical requirements are derived from customer quality expectations but can also arise from the applicable regulations, norms, and standards.

> *With a mobile phone, you should be able to ring hands-free. This is a functional requirement. Technical requirements may include the mobile phone being equipped with a connection to a hands-free kit, that it does not easily break and that it has a battery that lasts at least 8 hours.*

Fit for use, fit for purpose

As a project manager, you not only should ensure that the project output meets the set quality criteria but also that the project output is fit for use and fit for purpose. A product or service is fit for purpose if it is suitable for the intended application. A product or service is fit for use if it is available when the customer needs it and can apply it. This can be even more important than the output meeting all the individual requirements.

The costume is suitable for tonight's party. It fits the prescribed dress code (fit for purpose). However, I cannot use it as it needs to be drycleaned first (not fit for use). The new CRM system is suitable for keeping track of our customers' data (fit for purpose). However, I cannot use it because it is not yet certified (not fit for use).

SUSTAINABILITY

Sustainability is about lifecycle orientation. From a social and environmental perspective, natural capital should remain intact. Requirements should be set that ensure the sustainable development, production, use and demolition of the deliverables to be achieved by the project. This should include criteria for the project output and the process to develop and produce this output. These criteria should cover using (renewable) resources and the waste produced. This is not easy and requires a thorough examination of the sustainable costs over the lifetime of the key products within an organisation. A project can contribute to this and also act as a catalyst in this respect.

TAILORING

The above-mentioned also apply to Agile projects. At the heart of Agile delivery is the product vision that describes the overarching goal the customer is aiming for and the key components to be delivered. This product vision is central to the product backlog to be developed.

The product backlog acts as a requirement specification and is initially specified only at a high level. Detail these backlog items as late as possible, preferably just before the start of the timebox in which they are developed. Focus as much as possible on functional requirements, which are enforced by describing the backlog items in user stories. Describe the requirements in technical stories where the 'user' is the system.

Business users are involved throughout the process to ensure increments are fit for use and fit for purpose. Features to be developed are prioritised for swapping when changes are needed or for choosing when time constraints require it. The less important backlog items are then dropped.

RESPONSIBILITIES

The project manager is responsible for ensuring the project goals, objectives, and requirements are captured, formulated SMART, and updated appropriately. Content-wise, the user representative is responsible for the requirement specification. The project sponsor is accountable for the project goals, objectives, and requirements set for the project.

ADVANCED

VALUE MANAGEMENT (ADVANCED)

Value management is the systematic approach to optimising costs and value for products or services to be delivered. The essence of value management is that first, the focus is on the functions that should be delivered and only then on the technical solution needed; you do not ask for curtains but sun protection. This prevents you from pursuing a specific solution too quickly without first looking carefully at the need, the necessary functions, and the alternatives. Let the team figure out the best sun protection in this case.

Value management distinguishes five steps:

1. *Describe the need* – Formulate the need as precisely as possible.
2. *Translate the need into functions* – Indicate what you want and not the solution you have in mind.
3. *Generate alternatives* – Determine alternatives with which the functions can be realised.
4. *Evaluate and choose* – Review the alternatives and submit your assessment to the management.
5. *Deploy* – Implement the preferred solution.

TOTAL COST OF OWNERSHIP (ADVANCED)

The design of the project output should consider not only the total production costs but the total costs of the product lifecycle: realisation, operation and maintenance, any future upgrades and finally, the costs of decommissioning and scrapping. This is called the *Total Cost of Ownership* (TCO) of a product.

It is important to find a balance between the initial investment and the total cost of ownership. Looking only at the investment costs is not enough. Focusing only on the total ownership costs is often not possible because project financing is limited.

Based on the concept of the total cost of ownership, a better choice can be made between different investments to achieve the same goal and between different versions of the same investment.

PRODUCT COST MANAGEMENT (ADVANCED)

For design projects, product cost management is very important. It helps to make design decisions and stay within budget. Traditionally, organisations receive manufacturer cost estimates after the completion of the initial design stages. If then the projected manufacturing costs are too high, design changes need to be made. However, opportunities to cut costs at that point in the process are limited. A cost-orientated approach from the start prevents repair work at the end. Here, we distinguish between:

- *Design-to-cost* – Costs are hereby a design criteria in the requirement specifications.
- *Target costing* – An approach under which the maximum production costs are set in advance. If they realise they cannot manufacture the product within that maximum, they will cancel the project.

4.05 RISK AND OPPORTUNITY

PURPOSE
The purpose of this chapter is to enable the individual to effectively handle risks and opportunities, including responses and overall strategies.

LEARNING OBJECTIVES
- Risk and opportunities;
- Risk management;
- Risk management strategy and response plan;
- Risk exposure, profile, capacity, appetite, aversion and tolerance;
- Probability, impact and proximity;
- Risk owners and risk action-holder;
- Various risk categories;
- Various risk responses;
- Inherent, residual and secondary risks;
- Risk register, risk matrix, and a risk tolerance line;
- Risk management framework, principles and processes, according to ISO 31000 (advanced);
- Various opportunity responses (advanced);
- Risk and opportunities identification techniques (advanced);
- Risk and opportunities assessment techniques (advanced).

DEFINITIONS
Risk: A possible event or situation that, if it occurs, might have a negative impact on the achievement of the objectives.
Opportunity: A possible event or situation that, if it occurs, might have a positive impact on the achievement of the objectives.
Risk source: An element that poses a risk.
Risk probability: The likelihood that a risk may actually occur.
Risk impact: An outcome of a risk, if it occurs, affecting objectives.
Risk owner: An individual responsible for managing a specific risk.
Risk register: A log used for recording identified risks and risk measures.
Risk matrix: A probability-impact grid to categorise risks by probability and impact.
Risk management: The aspect of management aimed at effective identification, analysis and evaluation of risks and the planning and implementation of risk responses.

INTRODUCTION
A project without risks and opportunities does not exist. Eliminating all risks is not an option. Maximising all opportunities is too expensive. The success of a project lies in managing the risks and opportunities. Ineffective project managers act reactively. Effective project managers look ahead and devise responses to reduce risks and exploit opportunities. Managing risks and opportunities is an essential responsibility of the project manager. It is paramount that this is not regarded as an administrative task but as an integrated part of project management.

Risks and opportunities are inextricably linked. Where risks are mentioned in this chapter, it basically means risks and opportunities.

POSITIONING

Risk management should be a continual process and not a one-off event. It starts in the project preparation stage and continues until the project's closure. A first risk analysis should be carried out during the project preparation stage. The key risks are identified and assessed based on the project mandate and the initial discussions with the project sponsor and other stakeholders about the project assignment. The project's viability is reviewed based on the identified risks and anticipated costs and benefits. The key risks and the key risk measures are included in the project outline and are input for the first project decision. How to anticipate risks can affect the project management approach.

In the project definition stage, an extensive risk analysis should be undertaken. The result of this analysis is input for the project plan and the business case to be developed. In this stage, the risk management strategy and risk response plan are also prepared, and the risk register is set up.

During project delivery, you should be continuously alert to possible (new) risks. This applies, in particular, to the allocation of work, the monitoring of progress, and any new issues. Risks should be part of every consultation and reporting. Do we identify new risks? What is the status of the known risks? Should we take additional risk measures? What is the effectiveness of the risk measures taken? Should we escalate the risk to the next level of management? The risk register should be updated accordingly.

At least at each stage transition, a new risk analysis should be carried out. This can have consequences for the next stage plan, the project plan, and even the business case. During a stage transition, the effectiveness of the risk management strategy should also be reviewed and updated if necessary.

At the conclusion of the project, identified risks that may occur during operation and maintenance should be transferred to the sponsoring organisation or customer. During the project evaluation, risk management should be evaluated, and any lessons learned should be transferred to the appropriate bodies.

RISKS AND OPPORTUNITIES

A risk is an event or situation that may occur that could have a negative impact on the project. An opportunity is an event or situation that may occur that could have a positive impact on the project.

Risk is usually expressed in terms of the risk source, the potential event or situation that may occur, and its consequences. A risk source is an element that, alone or in combination, has the potential to give rise to a risk. A consequence is the outcome of an event or situation that may occur, affecting objectives.

> *Due to the reorganisation (source), there is a good chance that the lead engineer will leave the organisation (event), causing a delay in the design (consequence). If that happens, we cannot complete the project on time (effect on an objective).*

The size of a risk is the likelihood times the expected impact. The risk source should indicate the root cause of why a risk might occur. By stating the root cause, you clarify the likelihood that the risk will occur. By indicating the possible consequence, you clarify the possible impact of the risk if the risk occurs.

People don't like risks and often try to find reasons to ignore them. The combination of root cause and possible impact is to clarify why paying attention to this risk is necessary. Describing a risk in terms of source, event, and consequence may prevent serious risks from being ignored.

Difference between risks and issues

A risk is a possible deviation from the expected that can affect objectives. In principle, it provides the opportunity to anticipate, contrary to an issue. An issue is an event or condition that has happened or almost certainly will happen and needs management attention. In the case of an issue, actions to prevent the event or condition are futile (see Figure 4.05.01). A risk that occurs becomes an issue.

Issue	Risk
Present	Future
It has happened or will almost certainly happen	May happen
Assess impact	Assess likelihood and impact
Often requires immediate action	Time to plan
The possibility of it happening again is a risk	The possibility that it occurs is the risk
Reactive	Proactive

Figure 4.05.01 Risk versus issues

> *Today we went on holiday to Paris. We were stuck in a traffic jam for hours. When we finally arrived at our hotel, our rooms were taken (issue). How do we solve this? Tomorrow we are going on holiday to Paris. There is a good chance that we will be stuck in a traffic jam, possibly arrive late at our hotel and that our rooms are taken (risk). How do we prevent this from happening?*

Difference between risk and uncertainties in estimates

An uncertainty in an estimate is not a risk either. Uncertainty of an estimate is, at most, the result of a risk, but it is not a risk as such. The uncertainty may simply be caused by insufficient information. Estimating focuses on the effort, cost and time required to carry out activities. Risk management focuses on managing the uncertainty of an event or condition that may occur and its impact on the project.

RISK MANAGEMENT

Risk management is the aspect of management aimed at the effective identification, analysis, and evaluation of risks and the selection, planning and implementation of risk measures. This process should be monitored, reviewed, recorded and reported continuously (see Figure 4.05.02).

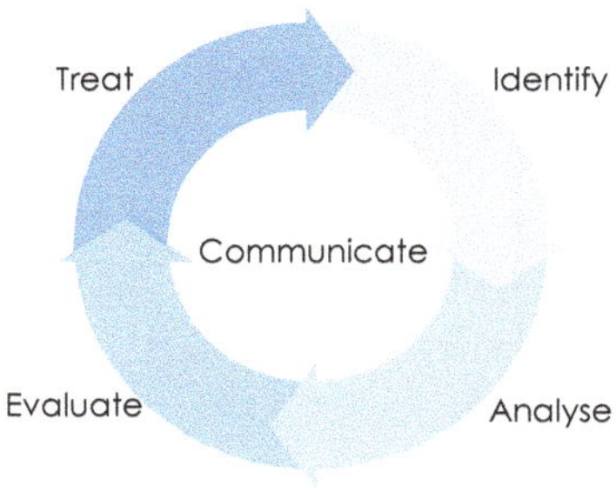

Figure 4.05.02 Risk management

- *Identify* – Identify individual risks and early warning indicators;
- *Analyse* – Estimate the probability, impact and proximity of the risks and the aggregated risk level;
- *Evaluate* – Assess if risk responses are necessary;
- *Treat* – Select, plan and implement risk measures, assess if the risk responses are effective and, if necessary, take further measures;
- *Communicate* – Monitor, review, record and report on the effectiveness of the process and outcome.

RISK MANAGEMENT STRATEGY AND RESPONSE PLAN

The risk management strategy is a high-level description of how risks will be managed on the project, including the intended outcome and the specific processes, procedures, techniques, standards, and responsibilities to be applied. The strategy also defines the project risk tolerance and the overall risk approach. The risk management strategy is derived from the risk management policy of the permanent organisation and is based on the risk profile, capacity, and risk appetite. Based on this strategy, a risk response plan can be developed covering the intended and planned actions for dealing with identified risks.

RISK DEFINITIONS

Risk exposure is the total extent to which an initiative or organisation is exposed to risks. A risk profile is the nature and exposure of risks an initiative or organisation faces. For example, the risk profile may show that at the start of a project, risks are mainly related to gaining support, during implementation to time and money, and at delivery and implementation to possible reputational damage. This makes a big difference in the risk management approach to be developed.

Risk capacity is the amount of risk an initiative or organisation can bear in achieving its objectives. Risk appetite is the amount of risk an initiative or organisation is willing to take in achieving its objectives. The risk capacity and risk appetite also depend on the nature of the risk. It is important to coordinate this with the project sponsor and other stakeholders. People prefer low-uncertainty outcomes to high uncertainty (risk aversion).

Risk tolerance is the limit value of a risk above which the risk has to be escalated to the next management level. Risk tolerances at the stage and work package level are included in the stage plans and the work package descriptions.

PROBABILITY, IMPACT AND PROXIMITY

The probability of a risk is the likelihood of a risk occurring. The impact of a risk is the expected negative consequence if the risk occurs. The size of a risk is the probability multiplied by the impact. The risk horizon or proximity is the period in which a specific risk may occur.

The risk proximity is essential to determine the risk responses more effectively. The risk proximity is usually subdivided into direct (next couple of weeks), this stage, one of the next stages, at the handing over, during the implementation and during the use of the project output. Realise that to manage risks, you should not wait until the period when the risks may occur but take risk measures earlier.

RISK OWNER AND RISK ACTION-HOLDER

A risk owner is an individual or entity responsible for managing a specific risk. A risk action-holder (risk actionee) is an individual who is responsible for taking a risk response when the risk owner cannot take that risk response by themself.

For each risk, a risk owner should be assigned. The project manager should avoid owning too many risks by themselves. If you do so, you take away the responsibility of others who will act accordingly. Also, the project sponsor and other project board members can be risk owners, especially for external and business risks.

The risk action-holder reports to the risk owner, and the risk owner reports to the project manager about that specific risk. This is to avoid the project manager implicitly taking over ownership of the risk from the risk owner when the risk action-holder directly reports to you.

> *Janet, the contract manager, is the risk owner for the risk that a supplier cannot fulfil its obligations. She may ask a team member (risk action-holder) to visit the factory to assess the supplier's progress. The risk action-holder should report to her about the visit. She can then report to the project manager on the risk of whether or not the supplier can meet its obligations.*

DIFFERENT TYPES OF RISKS

Furthermore, risks can be subdivided into project and business risks and internal and external risks. Internal risks are risks of which the cause lies within the scope and or within the responsibility of the project organisation. External risks are risks of which the cause lies outside the scope and or beyond the responsibility of the project organisation (see Figure 4.05.03).

Project risks are risks that may affect the project objectives. Business risks mainly affect the project goal, the effect that the sponsoring organisation or customer wants to achieve with the project output, but not on the project output itself.

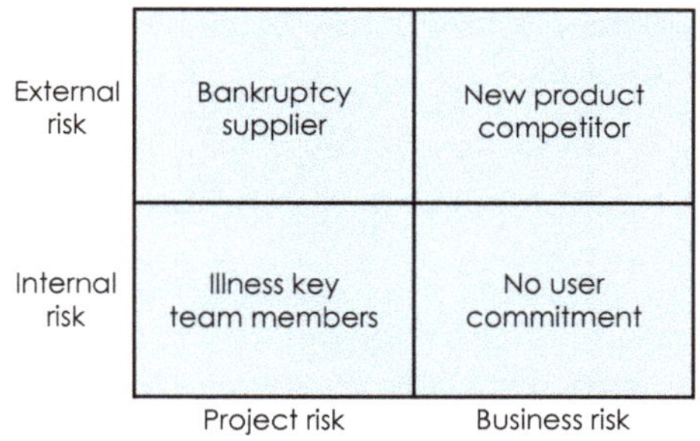

Figure 4.05.03 Example risk categories

The project manager should ensure that not only the internal project risks are managed but also the external and business risks. For project success, managing external and business risks is as important as managing internal project risks. At project closure, the remaining business risks should be transferred to the appropriate bodies.

RISK CATEGORIES

A list of risk categories can help to identify risks and avoid blind spots (see Table 4.05.01). For external risks, risk categories can be based on the *PESTLE analysis* (see Chapter 11.04 Power and Interests).

Risk categories	Example risks
Design	Design flaws
Finance	Lack of cash
Procurement	Bankruptcy of supplier
Staff	Job change key engineer
Political	New import/export restrictions
Economical	Inflation/fluctuation exchange rate
Social	Outbreak of contagious diseases
Technological	Artificial intelligence
Legal	New compliance regulations
Environmental	Chemical pollution

Table 4.05.01 Risk categories

RISK RESPONSES

Possible risk responses are:

1. Avoiding the risk by deciding not to start or proceed with the activity that gives rise to the risk;
2. Removing the risk source; this avoids the risk from occurring in the first place;
3. Reducing the likelihood of the risk;
4. Reducing the consequences/impact of the risk, including insuring the risk;
5. Sharing the risk with another party, including risk financing;
6. Preparing a contingency plan and implementing the plan as the risk occurs;
7. Accepting or even increasing the risk to pursue an opportunity;
8. Accepting the risk by an informed decision but staying informed.

Risk responses 1, 2, and 3 are preventive measures. Responses 4 and 6 are consequence measures. Response 5 can be both.

Define several risk measures for each risk so that a conscious choice can be made as to which measure can best be implemented. We also need to examine how we can combine measures for different risks.

A contingency plan is a plan that can be implemented to mitigate the consequences of a risk in case a risk occurs. A fallback plan is a special form of a contingency plan. It allows you to return to the original situation when a risk occurs. A fallback plan is regularly prepared when a new application is commissioned.

You should discuss the possible risk responses and expected effects with the relevant risk owner. If risk tolerances are likely to be exceeded, you should escalate the relevant risk to the project board for decision.

INHERENT, RESIDUAL AND SECONDARY RISK

An inherent risk is a risk before a risk response is taken. A residual or remaining risk is the risk that remains after taking a risk response. A consequential or secondary risk is a risk that arises by taking a risk response. It is important to realise that, by taking risk measures, new risks can arise. You should avoid going from a bad situation to an even worse one.

RISK TECHNIQUES

To keep an overview of all identified risks, a risk register is usually used, whether or not in combination with a risk matrix.

Risk register

A risk register is a log in which identified risks, including the associated status, history and responses, are recorded (see Figure 4.5.04). A risk register is a useful tool for managing risks. A risk register can also be used as a checklist when preparing for meetings.

- Risk identifier
- Risk author
- Date registered
- Risk description
- Probability, impact and expected value
- Risk horizon
- Risk response category
- Risk response
- Risk owner
- Risk action-holder
- Risk status

Figure 4.05.04 Risk register

Probability and impact classification

Usually, a five-point scale is used to classify the probability and impact of risks: very low, low, medium, high and very high (see Table 4.05.02). A finer subdivision often only gives a false sense of security. A three-point scale provides insufficient refinement to classify probability and impact with sufficient accuracy.

The scale for probability is usually not evenly distributed. A probability of less than 20% is often rated as low, but a probability of more than 60% is often already rated as very high or almost certain. Different scales can be agreed upon for different types of risks.

Impact	%	Class	Scale	Excepted size of risk					
	80	Very high	5	5	10	15	20	25	
	40	High	4	4	8	12	16	20	
	20	Medium	3	3	6	8	12	5	
	10	Low	2	2	4	6	8	10	
	5	Very low	1	1	2	3	4	5	
				1	2	3	4	5	Scale
				Very low	Low	Medium	High	Very high	Class
				< 5%	6-20%	21-35%	36-60%	>60%	%
								Probability	

Table 4.05.02 Scales of probability and impact

Risk matrix

A risk matrix visualises the probability-impact grid that has been agreed upon (see Figure 4.05.05). Within a risk matrix, the individual risks can be plotted. A risk matrix is usually used in combination with a risk register.

A risk matrix usually includes a *RAG code*:

- Red – Tolerance is exceeded: the risk should be escalated to the next management level;
- Amber – Tolerance threatens to be exceeded: risk measures are necessary;
- Green – No threat of tolerance being exceeded: no risk measures are required.

Risks with very low probability and impact are usually only monitored. Risk measures are taken only if possible at a very low cost or in combination with other measures. Risks with a very low probability but a very high impact are insured, if possible. For low and medium risks, risk measures are optional. For high risks, risk measures are mandatory. Risks, of which probability is almost certain, are usually treated as issues.

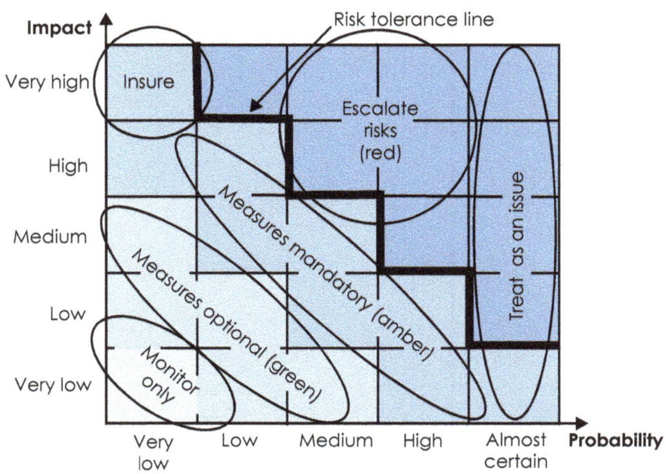

Figure 4.05.05 Risk matrix with a risk tolerance line

The risk tolerance line in a risk matrix is the boundary between which combination of probability and impact is and is not acceptable to the organisation. Risks above the risk tolerance line should be escalated to the next management level.

Finally, agree in advance on the criteria for the different categories of probability and impact and the different nature of risk. Does a low probability mean a particular risk will occur only once a month, once a year or even less frequently? Does medium impact indicate that, if a risk occurs, it will only affect one work package, the current stage, or the overall project? Such criteria are much easier to estimate and agree on than percentages. Finally, risks with a potential cost impact are very different than, for example, reputation or environmental risks.

TIME AND COST CONTINGENCY RESERVES

A contingency reserve is a reserve added to an estimate to address specific issues and risks. It is common to schedule extra time (and resources) prior to a milestone, a decision point and the agreed completion date to address specific risks. The same applies to the costs. A cost contingency reserve (risk budget) is different from a reserve for miscellaneous and unforeseen. The latter is a reserve for unexpected expenses (see Chapter 5.7. Finance).

SUSTAINABILITY

From a sustainable perspective, the project's long-term social and environmental impacts over the entire lifecycle of the products should be considered. This requires a broader-than-normal risk analysis. Such an analysis should also involve a broader range of stakeholders, probably from inside and outside the own organisation. Furthermore, a more precautionary approach should be considered, as environmental and social impacts are much more difficult to predict, and corrective measures usually require a lot of effort to be effective.

TAILORING

Many risk areas are already addressed with Agile, especially those related to delivery, assuming that Agile behaviours, concepts and techniques are well adhered to. If this is not the case, it is a risk in itself. Many organisations are not yet fully equipped for Agile working; strong leadership and visible support from management for Agile working are lacking, or they do not yet realise what is needed. This deserves the project manager's full attention during the initial assessment of whether to work Agile. Moreover, other risk areas remain unchanged. Therefore, risk management should remain a key focus area even in Agile projects, although it can be applied much more informally and low-tech. Risks and risk measures may simply be displayed on the information radiator. It is important to manage these risks in close collaboration with the Agile teams.

RESPONSIBILITIES

The project manager is responsible for risk management and establishing the risk management strategy. The project sponsor is accountable for the risk management in a project and should approve the risk management strategy. The project sponsor/project board is also responsible for coordinating the risks with the sponsoring organisation or customer and should inform the project manager about external risks.

The risk owners are responsible for managing individual risks. A risk action-holder is an individual who is responsible for taking a risk response on behalf of the risk owner when the risk owner cannot take that risk response by themselves.

ADVANCED

OPPORTUNITY RESPONSES (ADVANCED)

Possible opportunity responses are:

- *Exploiting* – Ensure that the opportunity is utilised; for example, accept an offer because a discount is offered now.
- *Enlarging* – Increase the probability or impact of the opportunity; for example, give an extra discount to increase the chance that you get the order.
- *Sharing* – Involve a third party; for example, submit a quotation with a qualified partner.
- *Ignoring* – Don't do anything with the given opportunity; the benefit is too small compared to the costs involved; stay informed.

ISO 31000 RISK MANAGEMENT (ADVANCED)

The ISO 31000-2018 Risk management standard contains principles, a framework, and processes for managing risks.

Principles risk management

To be effective, an organisation should comply with the following principles at all levels:

- It is an integral part of all organisational activities;
- It is applied structured and comprehensively;
- It is tailored to the context and objectives of the organisation;
- It appropriately and timely involves all stakeholders;
- It anticipates changes in an appropriate and timely manner;
- It is based on the best available information, as well as on future expectations;
- It considers human and cultural factors;
- It is constantly improved through learning and experience.

Risk management is not something you can do intermittently or delegate entirely to a separate risk manager. It is an integral part of managing a project: proactively and continuously in dialogue with your team and the stakeholders and in an open culture where uncertainties can be discussed freely.

Risk management framework

The purpose of the risk management framework is to assist the organisation in integrating risk management into significant activities and functions. The risk management framework encompasses integration, implementation, evaluation and improving risk management across the organisation.

Risk management processes

The risk management processes describe all activities necessary to manage individual risks (see Figure 4.05.06). The risk management processes should be an integral part of the project management processes. Managing risks includes:

Communication and consultation – Assist relevant stakeholders in understanding the risks, the basis on which decisions are made and the reasons why particular actions are required. Communication promotes awareness and understanding of risk, whereas consultation involves obtaining feedback and information to support decision-making. Communication and consultation should take place during all steps of the risk management process.

Scope, context and criteria – Customise the risk management processes to enable effective risk assessment and desired risk treatment. Scope, context and criteria involve:

- Understanding the external and internal context of the project;
- Specifying the amount and type of risk it may take in relation to the objectives;
- Defining the scope of the risk management activities;
- Defining criteria to evaluate the magnitude of the risk to support decision-making.

The scope, context and criteria should be established at the beginning of the risk assessment process, but they are dynamic and should be consistently reviewed and updated if necessary.

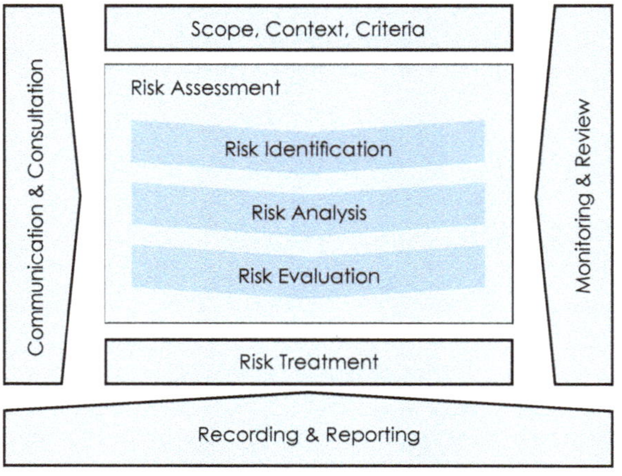

Figure 4.05.06 Risk management processes conform ISO 31000:2018

Risk assessment – The entire process of risk identification, analysis, and evaluation:

- *Identify risks* – Identify the individual risks. This is best done during a workshop with team members, other stakeholders and subject matter experts. Lessons learned, literature and a checklist can be used to avoid blind spots. Various risk identification tools can also be used.
- *Analyse risks* – Estimate the probability, impact and proximity of the identified risks and the overall aggregated risk level of the project. Once the magnitude of the individual risks has been determined, the aggregated risk level for the entire project can be assessed.
- *Evaluate risks* – Assess if risk responses are necessary. When evaluating risks, the identified risk levels should be compared to the risk criteria identified in the scope, context and criteria step. Based on this comparison, it can be considered whether risk measures are necessary and if the risk should be escalated to the next higher management level.

Risk treatment – Identify and assess possible risk treatment options; select, plan and implement the preferred responses; assess if the risk responses are effective and, if necessary, take further measures.

Monitoring and reviewing – Monitor and review the quality and effectiveness of the risk management process. Monitoring and reviewing should take place in all stages of the risk management process.

Recording and reporting – Document and report the risk management processes and their outcomes through appropriate mechanisms to provide information for decision-making and improve the risk management activities.

Besides this standard, various risk management models can be used.

RISK IDENTIFICATION TECHNIQUES (ADVANCED)

The *risk decomposition structure*, *fishbone diagram* and *pre-mortem* analysis are well-known risk identification techniques.

Risk decomposition structure

A decomposition structure is not just a perfect tool for determining the scope but also an excellent tool for identifying risks within a plan. A risk decomposition structure delivers an overview of the possible risks at the subsequent levels of detail.

Fishbone diagram

A cause-and-effect or fishbone diagram was initially used to categorise problems in production processes. Kaoru Ishikawa developed this method which is, therefore, also called the Ishikawa diagram. The first fishbone diagram had six categories of a standard classification of causes: *Measurement*, *Material*, *Machine*, *Mother Nature*, *Manpower*, and *Method* (see Figure 4.05.07). Nowadays, a variety of classifications is used. This diagram can be effectively applied to identify possible risk causes of a particular risk.

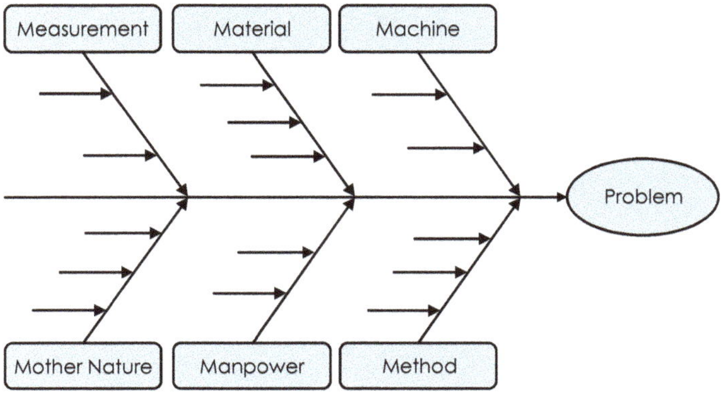

Figure 4.05.07 Ishikawa diagram

Pre-mortem analysis

A pre-mortem analysis is a risk identification technique based on the assumption that the project has completely failed. Each team member should spend 10-15 minutes determining for themselves how this could have happened. This often generates the most important risks that should be managed. An advantage of this technique is also that it prevents group thinking and group pressure. Finally, it encourages even the less critical thinker to look for possible risks that have not been faced before.

External environmental scanning

An external environment scan is an examination of external factors and trends that may affect its performance and decision-making. It helps identify opportunities and threats for the organisation to adapt strategies more effectively. The results of such a scan can directly impact the current projects but can also initiate new projects (see Chapter 11.04 Power and Interests).

RISK ASSESSMENT TECHNIQUES (ADVANCED)

The *Monte Carlo* technique, scenario planning, sensitivity analysis, decision tree, expected monetary value, probability calculations and statistical techniques are well-known risk assessment techniques.

Monte Carlo technique

The possible consequences of risks can also be approached from a statistical point of view. Based on many observations from the past, it can be determined how often particular outcomes occur. This produces a probability distribution, which is then used to estimate possible outcomes in the future. This approach is called the Monto Carlo technique because the same technique is applied in a casino.

Sensitivity analysis

Sensitivity analysis is used to examine the extent to which the results of a model depend on small changes in the input parameters. Sensitivity analyses are often used when preparing a business case using key figures to calculate the profitability of investments.

Scenario planning

Scenario planning involves defining and planning actions to anticipate possible scenarios adequately. The steps in scenario planning are:

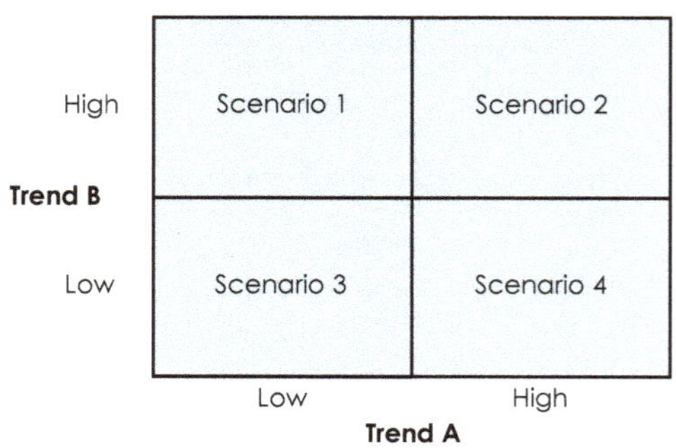

Figure 4.05.08 Trend matrix

- *Formulate a problem statement* – This can be either broad or narrow; 'Should we or should we not export to Australia?' (narrow) or 'What are the developments in the European Union?' (broad).
- *Research relevant trends* – This can be achieved through source research, in-depth interviews and workshops. Draw up a scenario matrix, choose the two most relevant trends, define the bandwidth for each trend and plot them in a matrix (see Figure 4.05.08).
- *Develop possible scenarios* – For each scenario, describe the expected future (what), the way to get there (how) and the logic behind that scenario (why).

- *Determine the implications* – Determine what the scenario means for the problem definition. What conclusions can we draw?
- *Prepare a roadmap* – What short and medium-term actions should we take to anticipate the scenarios adequately? What are developments that give clues about the direction of the future?

Probability-impact matrix

A probability-impact matrix provides an overview of the probability, impact and expected value of identified risks. The expected value is the probability multiplied by the impact. The expected values indicate the importance of the individual risks (see Figure 4.05.09).

Expected monetary value

A probability-impact matrix can also be created to show the effect on costs. The expected monetary value is the probability multiplied by the expected costs if the risk occurs (see Figure 4.05.10). The total of the expected monetary value can serve as a basis for the risk budget to be included in the project budget (see Chapter 5.07 Finance).

Risk	Probability	Impact	Expected value
A	3	2	6
B	4	1	4
C	2	3	6

Figure 4.05.09 Probability-impact matrix

Risk	Probability	Impact	Expected monetary value
A	40%	€ 50,000	€ 20,000
B	60%	€ 25,000	€ 15,000
C	20%	€ 100,000	€ 20,000
Total			€ 55,000

Figure 4.05.10 Expected monetary value

Decision tree

A decision tree is used to assess scenarios and risk responses (see Figure 4.05.11). Based on a decision tree, the total monetary value of individual scenarios can be calculated.

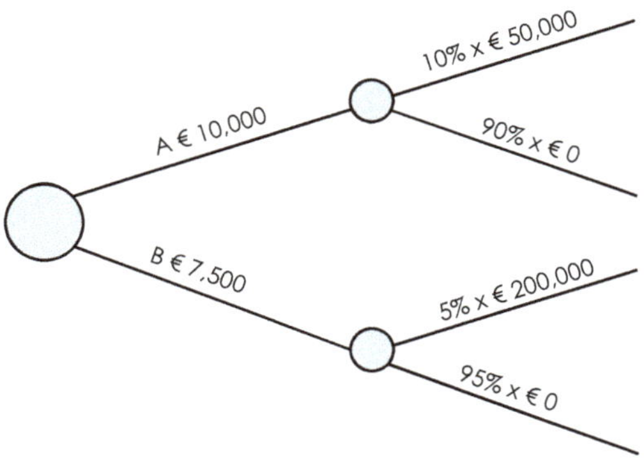

Figure 4.05.11 Example decision tree

In Figure 4.05.11, an assessment is made on whether it is statistically wise to opt for alternative A or B. In alternative A, the initial costs are € 10,000, and the risk of damage is 10%, with an impact of € 50,000. In alternative B, the initial costs are € 7,000, and the probability of damage is 5%, with an impact of € 200,000. Based on the decision tree, it is wise to opt for alternative A:

- Alternative A: € 10,000 + 10% of € 50,000 > the expected monetary costs are € 15,000.
- Alternative B: € 7,000 + 5% of € 200,000 > the expected monetary costs are € 17,000.

Probability calculations

Probability calculations are based on the extrapolation of past results toward the future. A person's life expectancy is determined by looking at the lifetime of other people in similar circumstances in the past, possibly with a trend correction.

But take note: probability calculations are always based on a model. A conclusion from a model that cannot be tested has little meaning, and a good outcome does not necessarily mean the model is valid. Only after repeated tests can a model be validated. And always check the assumptions and conditions on which the probability calculations are based. The claim that people with big feet are more intelligent than those with small feet is always true if you include babies in the study and determine intelligence based on the outcome of a written test. Always judge statistics with a modicum of scepticism. We call this having a 'sceptical view'.

Statistical techniques

There are various statistical techniques for calculating probabilities with one or more variables. One such technique is the PERT technique. The PERT technique calculates the likelihood of outcomes in an asymmetric distribution (see Chapter 5.05 Time).

5. PROJECT DEFINITION

This part focuses on the project definition stage. Its purpose is to lay a sound basis for the delivery of the project.

Chapter 5.01 – Project Definition Stage – describes the various actions that need to be carried out to develop a project management plan and get authorisation for the first delivery stage.

Chapter 5.02 – Project Design – Describes how to draft the project design based on the project success criteria and success factors.

Chapter 5.03 – Scope – Enables the project manager to define the scope and boundary of the project and prepare the related project decomposition structure.

Chapter 5.04 – Quality – Describes the quality planning, control and assurance to ensure that the products to be delivered meet the criteria set.

Chapter 5.05 – Time – Describes various ways of phasing a project and how to prepare a time schedule and determine the critical path.

Chapter 5.06 – Resources – Addresses the issue of capacity planning, including how to prepare estimates.

Chapter 5.07 – Finance – Focuses on budgeting and monitoring project costs. In addition, project accounting, procuration, and financial control are covered.

Chapter 5.08 – Business Justification – Focuses on assessing and monitoring the business justification for the project and preparing and updating the project's business case.

Together, these chapters form the basis for the delivery of the project. What is the scope, what are the quality requirements to be met, what is the planning, what are the resources and the budget required, and what is the business justification for the project?

5.01 PROJECT DEFINITION STAGE

PURPOSE

The purpose of this chapter is to enable the individual to develop and get agreement on the project management plan.

LEARNING OBJECTIVES;

- The activities to be undertaken in the project definition stage;
- The characteristics, reasons and goals of a project start-up workshop;
- The characteristics, reasons and goals of a kick-off meeting;
- The project management plan and supporting documents;
- The project decision at the end of the project definition stage;
- Set up the project support (advanced).

DEFINITIONS

Project definition stage: The first stage of the project in which a sound basis is laid for delivering of the project output.
Project management plan: The plan that describes how the project is being carried out and controlled.
Project start-up: A workshop with the project (management) team and other key stakeholders to develop a sound basis for the project or next stage.
Kick-off: The first meeting at the start of the project or stage to initiate an effective and efficient delivery of that project or stage.
2nd project decision: The decision to authorise the delivery of the project (decision to fund).

INTRODUCTION

The purpose of the project definition stage is to establish a sound basis for the project before the actual delivery of the project is authorised. Before starting the project delivery, it should be clear why the project is needed, what should be achieved with it, how the results will be realised and what the responsibilities are of all parties involved. But also how long the project delivery will take, the necessary budget, and the resources needed.

POSITIONING

The project definition stage is the first stage of the actual project. This stage starts with the authorisation of this stage by the project sponsor based on the project outline and the stage plan for this stage (see Chapter 4.01 Project Preparation Stage). In the project definition stage, the project outline is developed into the project management plan, and the stage plan for the first delivery stage is prepared. The project definition stage ends with the project assessment by the sponsoring organisation or customer. Based on this assessment, they may or may not authorise the project sponsor to deliver the project output. This is called the second project decision (see Figure 5.01.01).

ACTIVITIES PROJECT DEFINITION STAGE

The project definition stage starts with working out and deepening the project outline with the parties involved. These are not only the team members but also users and other stakeholders. This can be done through individual interviews but also in a joint session called a project start-up.

The project design is the 'charcoal sketch', blueprint or even high-level architecture of the project reflecting the project management approach. This design not only consists of the essential choices but also describes the reasoning behind these choices and the consequences of each choice for success. This design may include a high-level definition of the scope, quality, organisation, stakeholder engagement, resources, et cetera.

Based on the project design, first develop the project scope and boundaries in further detail. This can best be done by drafting a project breakdown in which both the scope and the demarcation are defined. Then determine the requirement specifications for the products to be delivered.

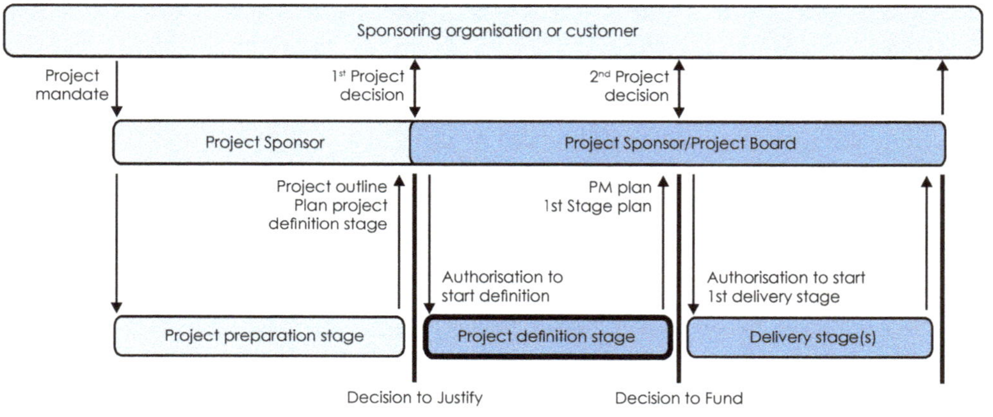

Figure 5.01.01 Positioning project definition stage

Do not get lost in details. The scope and requirements should only be worked out in such detail as is necessary to estimate the time, capacity and cost required to carry out the project. Any further detailing is pointless at this stage. It would be a waste of time and money, as things will change anyway. Furthermore, specifications developed in too much detail limit the possibilities of adapting the project to changing circumstances and insights. It is better to specify only the key points and detail them later.

Based on the scope and the requirement specification, the work can then be planned and budgeted, and a risk assessment can be carried out. Next, the business case, as included in the project outline, can be developed in further detail. The costs and envisaged risks can be derived from the project plan and the risk assessment. The benefits to be realised can be determined by the user representative. They should also indicate which negative effects (dis-benefits) should be included in the business justification. Have specialists from the sponsoring organisation or customer prepare the actual business case.

If everything still seems feasible, the stage plan for the first delivery stage can be prepared. This plan should obviously be planned in more detail than the project plan and should include the people and resources needed to carry out the work in that first stage.

In addition, the necessary procedures should be established: how shall we manage risks and issues? How will documents and configuration items be managed? How will the project's progress be monitored and reported, and to whom? For internal projects, these procedures may be derived from a project management handbook. For projects in a new environment, these procedures should be developed and agreed upon separately. Do not wait until delivery. Once there are problems, the procedures also become part of the problem.

Then, the project management plan can be put together. For small projects, all information can be assembled into one document. Sometimes, even a PowerPoint presentation will do. For larger projects, the project management plan is a summary of the underlying documents.

Finally, forward the project management plan and the stage plan for the first delivery stage to the project sponsor/project board for approval. The project sponsor will coordinate this with the sponsoring organisation or customer, as they have the final say in this. Upon a positive decision, the sponsoring organisation or customer authorises the project sponsor to deliver the project, and the project sponsor/project board authorises you to implement the first delivery stage. Ensure that with this authorisation, the project sponsor/project board also make the resources for this first stage available.

The main tasks during the project definition stage are:

- Refine the project outline into a project design;
- Detail the scope and demarcation and prepare the project breakdown structure;
- Draft the requirement specifications;
- Prepare the project plan and carry out a risk assessment;
- Develop the business case;
- Prepare the stage plan for the first delivery stage
- Establish the working procedures and reporting arrangements;
- Assemble the project management plan;
- Request approval and authorisation for the project and the first delivery stage.

Depending on the size and nature of the project, the amount of work in the project definition stage can vary greatly. Carry out the work together with the project management team. If project support is already set up during the project definition stage, involve them in preparing the work too.

PROJECT MANAGEMENT PLAN

The project management plan describes how the project will be delivered and controlled. It is prepared by the project manager and approved by the project sponsor/project board. In addition, the project management plan should be validated by the sponsoring organisation or customer.

• Management summary	• Business case
• Updated project definition	• Project organisation
• Project design	• Project management strategies
• Requirement specification	• Project control and reporting
• Key risk and risk measures	• Communication plan
• Project plan	• References

Figure 5.01.02 Project management plan

The project management plan includes more than just the project plan. It includes all relevant documentation to form a sound basis for the project (see Figure 5.01.02). Mostly, only the plan for the first delivery stage is kept separately. For the specification of the project plan, see Chapter 5.05, Time.

PROJECT START-UP WORKSHOP

It is recommended to develop the project design with the project team and involve the project sponsor and other key stakeholders. This is best done through a Project Start-Up (PSU). A PSU is a workshop with the project (management) team and other key stakeholders to develop a sound basis for the project or next stage. A good PSU results in a shared commitment to deliver the project successfully. Furthermore, it enables the team to build trust with the project sponsor and key stakeholders so that they may give them the space to deliver the project. Moreover, a PSU creates team building and, finally, saves time as the preparation is done more effectively (see Figure 5.01.03).

The nature, size and complexity of the project determine the topics, how they should be addressed, and thus also the duration of the PSU. Sometimes several sessions are needed. To keep a PSU manageable, in large projects, participation is limited to core team members.

A PSU starts with a mutual acquaintance after an initial introduction by the project manager. The project outline is discussed, followed by a joint intake with the project sponsor. The team then sets to work on the assignment. This is usually done in several rounds, with interim consultation with the sponsor. At the end of the PSU, the process is reviewed, and arrangements are made about the follow-up.

Project start-up	**Kick-off**
• Agree on project design and concept project management plan	• Info about the project authorised
• Building trust with project sponsor	• Who is doing what
• Accelerate decision-making	• Strategies and procedures
• Create commitment and teambuilding	• How to collaborate, working arrangements
	• Create commitment and teambuilding

Figure 5.01.03 Purpose PSU and kick-off

A PSU is usually held in the project definition stage. Sometimes an initial PSU is held in the project preparation stage (see Figure 5.01.04). A PSU may even be held at a stage transition to prepare the next stage plan.

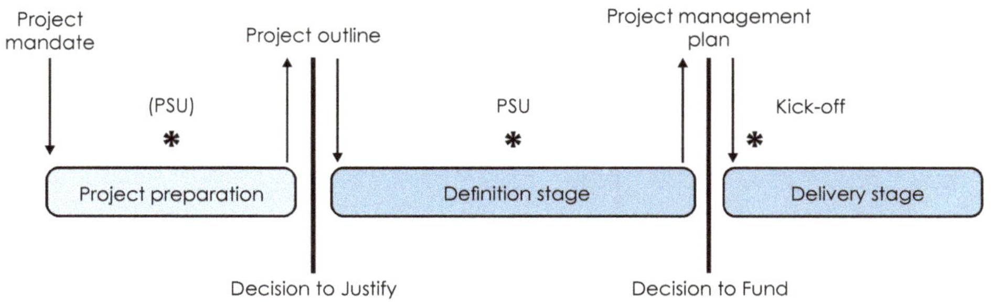

Figure 5.01.04 Positioning PSU and kick-off

It is advised to have the PSU chaired by an independent facilitator. This enables the project manager to focus on the content. The facilitator should ensure that all participants participate actively to guarantee that the outcome of the PSU is endorsed by all participants.

KICK-OFF

The kick-off is a meeting held after the authorisation to start the project delivery or a stage. The kick-off aims to create a flying start for the work. In addition to the members of the project (management) team, it may be useful that the project sponsor/project board members also attend, as well as key users, suppliers and other stakeholders with whom the project (management) team has to work regularly. However, the kick-off is explicitly meant for the team members (see Figure 5.01.03).

In the kick-off, the why, what, and how of the project are explained, the procedures clarified, and the first project activities are divided and coordinated. In addition, working arrangements are made, and it is agreed upon how the team members will collaborate. There also should be room for questions and suggestions.

A kick-off is also an excellent opportunity to get to know each other better, achieve team building and create further commitment among the individual team members. It can be useful to repeat the kick-off for successive stages.

PROJECT DECISION/ DECISION TO FUND

At the end of the project definition stage, a project assessment takes place based on the project management plan with the relevant business case. Based on this assessment, the sponsoring organisation or customer may authorise the project sponsor to carry out the project. Such authorisation automatically requires that they also ensure the necessary funds. This decision is therefore also called the 'decision to fund'. Based on this decision and the plan for the first delivery stage, the project sponsor authorises the project manager to start with this first stage.

SUSTAINABILITY

The project definition stage establishes a solid basis for the project delivery, enabling the sponsoring organisation and other key stakeholders to understand the work to be done AND the project's short- and long-term impact before the project delivery is authorised. Within a sustainable approach, this requires a broader examination not only of the project delivery but also of the environmental and social impacts of the project. This concerns the depth of the analysis and the stakeholders involved.

As long as sustainability is not an integral aspect of managing projects, preparing a separate *Sustainability Management Plan* (SMP) next to the regular project management plan is recommended. This SMP should be managed throughout the project lifecycle and updated at stage transitions and at project closure, also involving the corporate sustainability or CSR officer, if there is one.

TAILORING

In the project definition stage, it is decided which part of the work will be done Agile and which will be developed traditionally or in another way. For the Agile part, the product vision is worked out in the initial backlog. Based on the customer journey, a story map is developed, and the *Minimal Marketable Product* (MMP) is agreed upon. By setting priorities, the initial backlog is sliced into subsequent releases. Based on an estimated velocity, an initial road map is determined, with the number and size of the teams and the number and length of the timeboxes. Project and Agile roles are aligned, and individuals are appointed. The *Definition of Done* (DoD) is agreed upon, and the necessary facilities are set up. Finally, the expected benefits are reconfirmed to obtain authorisation for delivery.

RESPONSIBILITIES

The project manager is responsible for drafting the project management plan and the plan for the first delivery stage. The project sponsor should approve these plans and obtain approval from the sponsoring organisation or customer to implement the project and authorise the project manager to implement the first delivery stage.

ADVANCED

SETTING UP A PROJECT SUPPORT (ADVANCED)

Project support is the project management team's role, which supports the project manager by providing administrative services and specialist tasks such as planning and budget control. Depending on the size and complexity of the project and the context in which the project should be carried out, the project support can vary from a single individual working part-time to dozens of people who support the project manager and the project full-time.

The services of project support can vary considerably. However, the most usual services are setting up the project administration and filing structure, helping to prepare plans and budgets, administrative handling of the various processes and procedures, monitoring progress, and preparing reports.

- Set up and close-off project administration
- Prepare schedules and cost estimates
- Monitoring progress and preparing reports
- Administer and assist with project board meeting
- Assist with stakeholder communication
- Set up and maintain work procedures
- Information and document control
- Administer change control procedures
- Maintain logs and archive records
- Maintain configuration item records
- Resource management
- Procurement management
- Contract management
- Secretarial support

Figure 5.01.05 Possible services project support

Project support is sometimes also responsible for secretarial support, procurement, and contract management (see Figure 5.01.05). It is essential to agree on the services the project support will provide in advance. The project support is usually set up during the project definition stage or at the start of the first delivery stage.

5.02 PROJECT DESIGN

PURPOSE

The purpose of this chapter is to enable the individual to integrate all contextual and social aspects successfully and derive the most advantageous approach for a project to ensure buy-in and success.

LEARNING OBJECTIVES

- Project (management) approach and project design;
- Project success and project success criteria;
- Project success factors;
- Project management success;
- The use of lessons learned;
- Diamond model, according to Shenhar and Dvir (advanced).

DEFINITIONS

Project design: A 'charcoal sketch', blueprint or high-level project architecture.
Project success: The extent to which the completed project satisfies the relevant stakeholders.
Project success criteria: The aspects on which mainly the success or failure of a project is defined by the various stakeholders.
Project success factors: The aspects that strongly influence the success or failure of a project.
Project management success: The extent to which the project manager's performance satisfies the relevant stakeholders.
Project (management) approach: A high-level description of how the project will be realised and managed, including the main principles and essential choices for success.

INTRODUCTION

It is necessary to discuss and agree with the stakeholders in advance when they will consider the project a success, which factors contribute most to this, and what project design is best appropriate for it. In doing so, we should not only consider how best to produce the project deliverables under the given circumstances but also how to cooperate, how to engage stakeholders, how to create an open culture where issues can be freely discussed, how to stay true to our core values, how to take our social responsibility, et cetera.

POSITIONING

An initial analysis of the project's success criteria and success factors should be made during the project preparation stage. This should be based on lessons learned from previous projects, the project on hand and the project context. Based on this analysis, an initial project management approach is determined, which is then reflected in the project outline.

In the project definition stage, the project success criteria and factors and the project management approach are further elaborated and translated into a project design, which forms the basis for the project management plan.

At each subsequent stage transition, the success criteria and factors, the project management approach, and the project design are evaluated and updated if necessary. At project closure, the entire project is evaluated, especially on these aspects. The end-of-project report includes an account of how the project was managed. Lessons learned are passed on to the appropriate bodies.

PROJECT (MANAGEMENT) APPROACH AND DESIGN

The project approach describes how the project output will be realised; will we outsource the work?; will we work Agile or Waterfall, et cetera? The project management approach goes just one step further. It describes how the project output will be realised and the key points on how the project will be managed to achieve the highest probability of success, given the constraints and demands, the complexity of the project, the internal and external context, and the known success criteria. This approach may reflect on the scope, requirements and objectives, organisation, communication, documentation, planning, resources, et cetera. It reflects on how the project result will be realised; how the project will be organised and managed; how the support of top management will be secured; how users will be involved in the project, how you will ensure that the project team collaborate, and so on.

Based on this approach, a project design is developed at the beginning of the project definition stage. The project design is the ultimate 'charcoal sketch', blueprint or even high-level architecture of the project that reflects the project management approach. This design not only consists of the essential choices but also describes the reasoning behind these choices and the impact of each choice on its success.

The project design takes into account organisational governance, relevant standards and regulations, as well as cultural aspects and the positioning of the project within the organisation and broader context. This will result in a charcoal sketch that may be later developed into a blueprint and even a high-level architecture of how the project will be implemented, organised and managed. This is then translated into the individual plans and strategies.

> *To prepare the project management plan, the engineering department first drew up a production flow chart for the new plant to estimate the scope of work and what would be needed to realise it. This chart also gave the client an idea of the end result and the pros and cons of any choices. Based on this chart, the project design could be finalised and the project management plan completed.*

The project management approach and subsequent project design are partially based on the project success criteria as defined by the stakeholders involved. The project success criteria are the aspects against which the success or failure of the project is defined by the various stakeholders. On the one hand, these are the criteria formally stated by the sponsoring organisation or customer but they also include the criteria by which other interested parties evaluate the project results. These factors may include the real reasons why a project is started, supported, opposed or terminated. The basic for a sound project management approach and project design is therefore laid by a thorough stakeholder analysis and meeting with the relevant stakeholders right at the start of the project.

These success criteria play a crucial role in defining the project success factors, which in turn, determine the approach and project design. The project success factors are those elements in the implementation of the project that significantly enables the project to be successful. For an environmental project, It may be the involvement of local residents from the beginning. For an innovation project, it may be the involvement of partners in the development. These factors can be provided by the stakeholders you talk to and lessons learned from previous projects.

It is necessary to discuss and establish the project management approach and design with the project sponsor and other stakeholders right at the start of the project. It is important to regularly update this approach and design during the project's implementation as the work develops. However, the starting point is: what is a successful project, and what are the project success criteria and factors?

PROJECT SUCCESS

What is project success? This is not easily defined. The original definition was that a project is successful when the result is delivered on time, within budget and according to specifications. However, such a project can lead to much discontent. Is the project then still a success? We tend to disagree.

The opposite can also happen. Look at the Sydney Opera House. This project was certainly not completed on time, on budget, and according to the original specifications. Yet almost everyone was satisfied with the final result, and the project was seen as a huge success. It is, therefore, better not to speak of a successful project if the original goals have all been achieved but to speak of a successful project if the relevant stakeholders are ultimately satisfied. This may be because all the original project objectives have been met, but not necessarily. Project success is a subjective value.

> *Project success is the extent to which the completed project satisfies the relevant stakeholders. (Van Aken, 2014)*

This definition deliberately refers to the stakeholders and not only the sponsoring organisation or customer. How can we speak of a successful project if the users are unhappy, the suppliers have gone bankrupt, and or employees are burnout?

The sponsoring organisation or customer makes the final decisions but is usually not the most influential stakeholder. That are usually the users, but may also be local residents or interested groups. However, the users often have the most influence over others, including the project sponsor.

If the users are dissatisfied, they will hesitate to use the product or service delivered. It is even possible that they will not use the project result at all. Then the anticipated benefits will not be realised, and the sponsoring organisation or customer will also become dissatisfied with the delivered project result.

Therefore, you should focus on the user and other stakeholder satisfaction within the limits agreed with the project sponsor to ensure the sponsoring organisation's or customer's satisfaction.

Unfortunately, not everyone will be satisfied, whatever the project result. Moreover, that sense of satisfaction may change over time. This is true, but it does not make the definition of project success any less valid. It also makes managing a project such a challenging endeavour.

PROJECT SUCCESS CRITERIA

Multiple stakeholders thus determine the success of a project. Therefore, the criteria of all stakeholders should be taken into account, not just those of the sponsoring organisation or customer. These criteria may differ for each of them and may vary from project to project. Not meeting these criteria may lead to a loss of motivation and might be a reason for them to oppose the project or not even use the result.

For the sponsoring organisation or customer, the most important criteria are often that with the project output the intended changes can be implemented and the expected benefits realised. For the user, the most important criteria are often that the end result is fit for use and fit for purpose, but more importantly, that it is their solution to the problem. Suppliers have an interest in the continuity of their organisation. In the short term, profit-making is usually the most important criterion. In the long term, improving their image, strengthening customer relations, and gaining experience with a particular product or technology, or a combination thereof may be essential. For the project participants, it may be relevant that the work contributes to their development and social responsibility.

PROJECT SUCCESS FACTORS

Success factors should be distinguished from success criteria. Success criteria are the criteria by which the success of a project is measured. Success factors are those factors that contribute significantly to making the project a success.

Based on experience, certain success factors continually pop up. However, please realise that these factors differ between projects and that it is of utmost importance to discuss and agree on these with the project sponsor and other stakeholders ahead of the project on hand. Discuss the success criteria first, then determine which success factors contribute most to achieving them.

Usual success factors are:

- *Top management support* – Without a sponsor at the highest management level, the project will be sensitive to interventions, and necessary decisions are not taken or postponed.
- *User involvement* – Not involving users results in incomplete specifications, deliverables not fit for use and purpose, and growing resistance to the end result ('not-invented-here' syndrome).
- *Stakeholder engagement* – Keep them on board right from the beginning.
- *Competent staff* – Work cannot be done efficiently and effectively without skilled staff.

- *Clear goals and deliverables* – This provides direction and focus and also generates commitment.
- *Adhere to best practices* – Don't reinvent the wheel but tailor practice to the project and context.
- *Proper planning and short-term milestones* – SMART objectives that energise the team.
- *Agile approach* – Work flexibly with self-managing teams and be open to change.
- *Proactive risk management* – Anticipate what might happen instead of chasing problems.
- *Regular control and reporting* – This keeps the project on track and management informed.

PROJECT MANAGEMENT SUCCESS

Project management success is related to project success but is not the same. Project management success is about stakeholder satisfaction with how the project was managed. A project that had to be closed prematurely due to external circumstances may not be called successful. Still, the stakeholders may be extremely satisfied with the project manager because they picked up the signals on time and were able to close the project without too much loss. The reverse also occurs. The project was successful, but that was more despite than thanks to the project manager. Like project success, the satisfaction of the various stakeholders is decisive to project management success. Man is the prelude to everything.

Project management success criteria could include:

- Were stakeholders involved in the project to their satisfaction?
- Were the plans realistic?
- Was there no scope creep?
- Were we not faced with uncontrolled changes?
- Were there no unnecessary incidents?
- Were we not presented with a fait accompli?
- Were there no felt conflicts?
- Was the team result-orientated and motivated?
- Were the activities carried out according to the agreed procedures?
- Were the results tested and the test results satisfactory?

How did you contribute to the project's success? Did you do what was agreed upon? Did the stakeholders receive the agreed reports, was the website updated regularly, et cetera? This seems simple but is often forgotten in the hecticness of the day. A much-heard excuse is: 'I was too busy and already informed them verbally.' This is not an excuse; if they want to blame you, it will work against you.

PROJECT PERFORMANCE MANAGEMENT

During project implementation, the project performance needs to be checked regularly. This is not only about achieving the planned progress and expenditures but is about all kinds of performances resulting from the chosen design and the subsequent plans. These may relate to the number of drawings that would be delivered and the percentage of tests that should pass the first time, et cetera. Furthermore, it is necessary to check whether the project success factors are filled in and how we score with regard to the established project management success criteria.

These can all be warning indicators of risks that may arise in the near future. It is wise to establish such performance indicators at the beginning of the project, including the desired outcomes. Assign people to manage these values and measure and assess the performance regularly. What you measure gets attention. So for example also; are we involving the users sufficiently in the project et cetera.

LESSONS LEARNED

Learning from lessons is vital throughout the project's lifecycle. It starts right at the beginning of the project. What can we learn from previous projects? Lessons from previous projects can convince stakeholders to adjust their opinions and prevent a wrong approach to the project. At every milestone, but at least at every decision point, the work should be evaluated, and lessons learned should be incorporated into the next stage plan and passed on to the appropriate bodies, if relevant.

During an evaluation, discuss what went well and what could or should be improved, and then agree on one or two improvements until the next milestone. And don't forget to check whether the previous improvements have been implemented and were effective. If the previous improvements have not been carried out, there is no point in agreeing on new ones. Keep it small, but stick to it and evaluate regularly. A final evaluation should take place at the end of the project.

SUSTAINABILITY

Sustainability has a significant impact on project design, but project design also significantly impacts the project's sustainability. A sound project design strengthens the impact of the project on sustainability.

In a sustainable approach, It is essential to discuss and establish the project design with a broader range of stakeholders, not only to establish a sound design but also to ensure the cooperation and commitment of those stakeholders.

TAILORING

The Agile approach to projects is already established in many organisations. The question is often not if to work Agile, but how much Agile we want to apply in the project. Not every work package should or can be applied Agile. Finally, ensure that Agile behaviours, concepts and techniques are appropriately followed. Avoid the attitude: 'We are working Agile, so I can relax'. Look at lessons learned from previous projects and discuss how they can be incorporated into this project. Ensure that retrospectives are held at the end of each timebox and that important lessons are taken into account.

RESPONSIBILITIES

The project manager is responsible for reviewing, applying and exchanging lessons, determining the success criteria and success factors, and designing the project (management) approach. However, the project sponsor remains ultimately responsible for the project management approach and accountable for the project's success.

ADVANCED

DIAMOND MODEL (ADVANCED)

Shenhar and Dvir (2007) developed the *Diamond Model*, which recommends a project approach based on four dimensions: novelty, technology, complexity, and pace (see Figure 5.02.01).

Novelty – Reflects the product's level of innovation perceived by the project management team and future customers and users and is categorised into derivative, platform and breakthrough projects. Derivative projects provide an upgrade or improvement to an existing product. Platform projects focus on a new version of an existing product or a new line of products. Breakthrough projects focus on developing an unknown product that is totally new. The newer the developed product, the higher the level of ambiguity will be, and the later the specifications should be frozen.

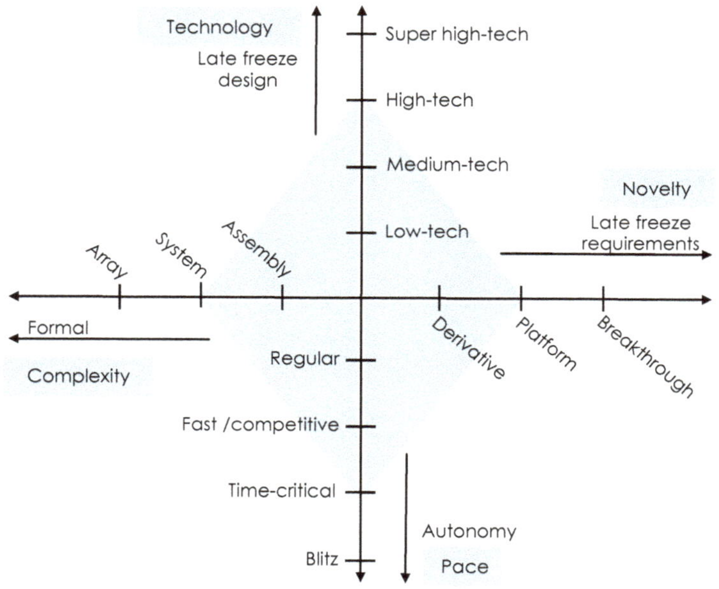

Figure 5.02.01 Diamond model (Shenhar and Dvir, 2007)

Technology – Covers the technical activities, including design, development, testing and prototyping. It ranges from low-tech projects, based on known and established technology, to super-high-tech projects, which are based on technology that is not yet available and is developed as part of the project. The more high-tech, the more design cycles are required, and the later the design has to be frozen.

Complexity – Represents the system scope of the project and influences the organisational structure and formality of project management. Complexity is categorised into assembly, system and array projects. Assembly projects focus on stand-alone products, system projects focus on products that cannot work in isolation, and array projects focus on a network of systems that interact through a platform. Assembly projects can be carried out by a single organisation using simple planning and control tools. System and array projects require sophisticated tools and refined 'soft skills' and should be organised more formally to keep all elements integrated.

Pace – Indicates the urgency to finalise the project, categorised into regular, fast/competitive, time-critical, and blitz projects. In regular projects, the time factor is not critical. In fast/competitive projects, the completion of the project is essential to achieve the organisation's competitive advantage. Procedures are structured, and top management is involved in approving key milestones. Time-critical projects focus on a specific window; any delay means the project has failed. Blitz projects are extremely urgent crisis projects. These projects are set up to manage natural disasters, acts of war and business crises. Because of the urgency, there is no bureaucracy and minimal documentation, but the top management is always involved. The more urgent a project, the more autonomy the team needs.

5.03 SCOPE

PURPOSE

The purpose of this chapter is to enable the individual to contribute to acquiring insight into what the boundaries of the project scope are, to manage this scope and to understand how scope influences (and is influenced by) decisions regarding the management and implementation of the project.

LEARNING OBJECTIVES

- Define the scope and the boundaries of the scope;
- Understand what scope creep is and its adverse effects;
- Develop a WBS and identify the necessary work packages;
- Apply the 100% rule in the WBS and set up a WBS dictionary;
- Prepare a product breakdown structure (PBS) and the respective product description;
- Draft a product flow diagram and make use of swim lanes;
- Scope (configuration) management;
- Position sub-projects in a WBS (advanced).

DEFINITIONS

Scope: The work and deliverables to accomplish.
Scope demarcation: A description of what does not belong to the scope to determine it more precisely.
Scope creep: A slow and almost unmarked scope change without recapturing the new scope.
Work breakdown structure (WBS): A delivery-orientated hierarchical breakdown of the work to be delivered.
WBS dictionary: A document in which every component in the WBS is described.
Product breakdown structure (PBS): A breakdown of the products to be delivered.
Product description: The description of a product, including the purpose, composition, quality criteria and by whom and how the product will be reviewed and approved.

INTRODUCTION

It is necessary to define and agree on the scope and deliverables of the project as early as possible, including what will not be done. By agreeing to this upfront and managing it during project delivery, the chance that the project will be successful increases significantly.

Who is not familiar with projects where during the implementation, a fierce difference of opinion arises between the customer and the supplier about what was agreed upon? The importance here is not only what is written on paper but also what the parties expect, whether or not fuelled by statements made during the acquisition.

Structuring a project is necessary to create order in the entirety of what should be delivered. Defining (intermediate) products makes it possible to assess them in the interim. In this way, you can establish whether the delivered products meet the quality criteria in an early stage. Desired changes can be identified, and, if necessary, a change procedure can be started.

POSITIONING

In the project preparation stage, the scope and the products to be delivered are agreed upon and laid down in the project outline. In the project definition stage, the scope is then further developed as a basis for time and cost estimates. During implementation, the scope should be controlled, and scope creep should be avoided. During stage transitions, the scope is further detailed as part of the relevant stage plans. Scope management should be evaluated at least during stage transitions and project closure.

SCOPE

The scope is the work and deliverables to accomplish. It is the total of the products and services to be delivered and the tasks to be carried out. The demarcation is a description of what does not belong to the scope, which determines the size of the scope more precisely. Scope and demarcation are inextricably linked. Without a good definition of one, you will not get a good definition of the other.

Scope gathering

Scope gathering is the process of gathering and defining all the information and requirements needed for the project. It involves gathering and understanding the project objectives, deliverables, features, functionalities, constraints and other relevant details from stakeholders and customers. The main purpose of scope gathering is to get a clear and complete understanding of what needs to be achieved in the project. Effective scope gathering is crucial for project success because it helps prevent misunderstandings, scope creep and project failure due to unmet requirements. By engaging stakeholders early and thoroughly understanding their needs, project teams can establish a well-defined scope that leads the project to successful completion.

Scope definition

You cannot estimate the work to be carried out with only a description of what will be delivered. You also need to know what work needs to be done and for which areas of work. Does the new kitchen's installation include removing the old kitchen? Does the installation only consist of the electrical connection, or should we also connect cold and hot water? For a complete description of the work, you should, therefore, not only determine what is to be delivered but also what work is to be done and for which areas (see Figure 5.03.01).

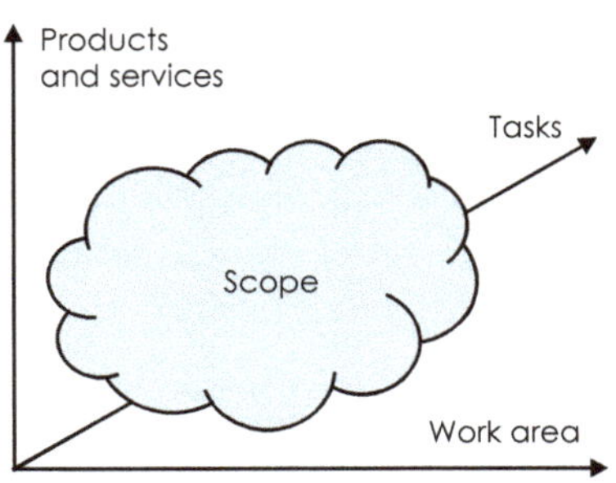

Figure 5.03.01 The three dimensions of the scope

Demarcation

In addition, you should also indicate what you are not going to do. This is particularly important for managing customer and other stakeholders' expectations and to avoid discussions afterwards.

Without proper demarcation, there is a good chance they also consider various matters to be part of the scope, even if they are not mentioned. Simply because, in their opinion, these matters are inextricably linked to the work or because they were discussed, although ultimately not included in the final assignment. This can happen unintentionally but also deliberately. Once the assignment has been accepted, many will try to include extra work within the assignment simply because they cannot get it done otherwise. The demarcation is also necessary to clarify in advance who will bear the costs for any additional work.

> *When the order for the new kitchen was placed, it was agreed that the residents would first remove the old kitchen and level out the floor themselves. The new kitchen will be installed and connected electrically and with hot and cold water. We will also remove the packaging materials. The reinforcement of the distribution board is not included. We have discussed this, but the residents will fix this themselves.*

However, describing what is not part of the scope should be done with care. Listing all kinds of nonsensical and obvious aspects should be avoided. The demarcation should only include those aspects that stakeholders might assume belong to the project's scope. Otherwise, the stakeholders will not feel they are taken seriously. A demarcation much longer than the scope description itself is (commercially) not very sensible.

Let's face it; if you want to name everything not part of the scope, you will end up with an endless list. And in that case, do all things not mentioned then belong to the scope? So be economical with it. Make sure you mention all essential matters, but no more than that.

Further, it is important to describe the demarcation separately from the scope. If the description is combined, there is a good chance that it is incomplete or omitted altogether. A separate list has the additional advantage that it cannot be overlooked.

Demarcation and interfaces

A specific point to pay attention to are the interfaces with other projects. This applies particularly to projects in a programme. Who does exactly what? And what products or services do other projects provide that you need in your project, and vice versa?

> *When the department moved, it was agreed that we would leave the previous office empty, clean and tidy, but that any repairs would be done by the project responsible for the move from the other department to our old office.*

The demarcation between the activities of different contractors in the same project is also often a source of conflict. Should the installation company cut the holes for its pipes, or is that the responsibility of the building contractor? Such interfaces should be precisely defined in the respective work packages before work starts.

SCOPE CREEP

Scope creep is a slow, and almost unmarked scope change without recapturing the new scope. Scope creep is created by small changes in the scope, which stay unnoticed or do not seem to justify a redefinition of it. However, all these small changes together may add up to a significant scope change. A well-defined demarcation forms a sound basis to prevent scope creep.

Scope creep often results in unforeseen overruns of project time and costs and undesirable consequences for other work packages and other projects or programmes. In this respect, made agreements are not only important but also what the expectations are of the customer and other stakeholders. In case of a supposed discrepancy, you should bring this up straight away to avoid scope creep.

Even if you accorded extra time and budget, expanding the scope is not always desirable. The larger the scope, the more difficult it becomes to manage. Stay focused on the initial goal and let the customer start a separate project for new work that is not essential for that purpose instead of adding it to your project.

PROJECT BREAKDOWN STRUCTURES

To be able to plan and monitor the implementation of the project, it is important to break down the work in more detail. This can be done in various ways, for example, by discipline, region, stage, responsibility, et cetera. These can also be combined.

Various techniques are available for this. The most well-known techniques are the *Work Breakdown Structure* (WBS) and the *Product Breakdown Structure* (PBS).

In the WBS, the project is broken down into work packages to be carried out. In the PBS, the project is broken down into intermediate products and deliverables. Both techniques are distinctive but also have many similarities.

WORK BREAKDOWN STRUCTURE (WBS)

A *Work Breakdown Structure* (WBS) is a hierarchical breakdown of the work to be performed. The work to be carried out is hereby defined by the work to be done and the products to be delivered (verb + nouns). A WBS should also include management activities.

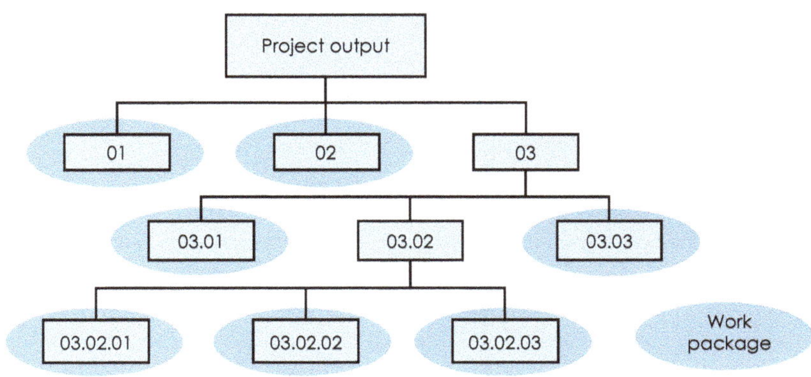

Figure 5.03.02 Example WBS with work packages

Work packages and components

All elements in a WBS are called components. The lowest component at each branch in a WBS is called a work package. Within a WBS, a work package is the smallest unit of work for which cost and duration are estimated and managed. The WBS in Figure 5.03.02 contains seven work packages.

WBS structure

The degree of decomposition depends on for whom the plan is intended. If the decomposition is part of the project plan, then it will be much less detailed than for a stage or team plan.

Each upper WBS component should include several underlying WBS elements (see Figure 5.03.03). A WBS does not have one-to-one relationships (A). Each WBS element should only be connected to one upper WBS element (B). Do not use arrows (C). A WBS is a work decomposition and not a flow diagram. Don't get lost in details. Focus on the decomposition first. This is to prevent work packages from being overlooked. Figure 5.03.04 shows the correct representation of the same WBS.

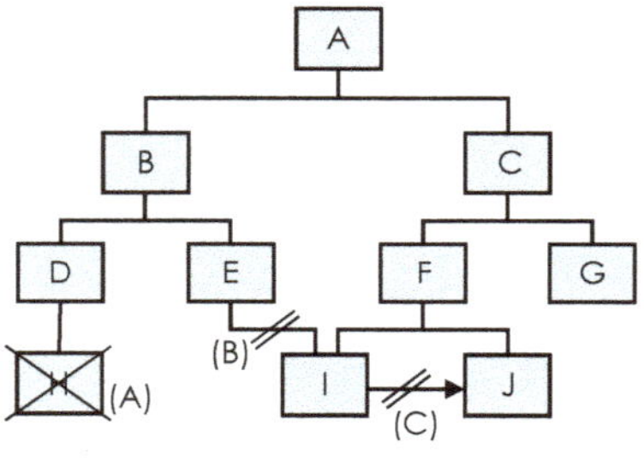

Figure 5.03.03 Incorrect structure WBS

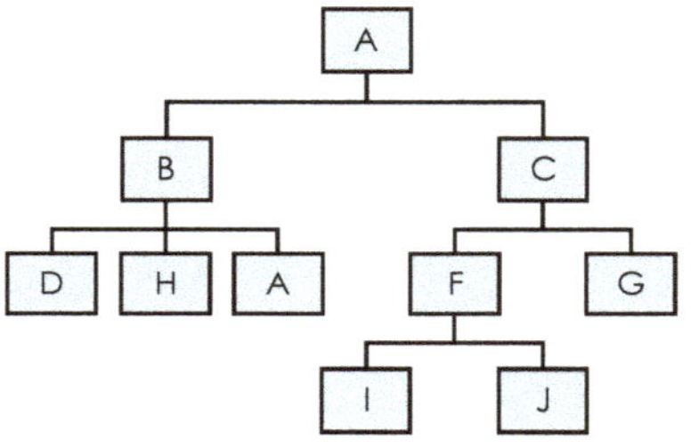

Figure 5.03.04 Correct structure WBS

100% rule and project coding structure

The WBS is the basis for the cost breakdown structure; therefore, the 100% rule applies. The 100% rule states that each WBS component should equal the sum of the underlying work packages. Furthermore, all components in the WBS should be given a unique identifier, which is a sub-number of the parent component.

If, due to lack of space, the breakdown has to be placed among each other, do not connect the single work packages but connect them only with the above component (see Figure 5.03.05).

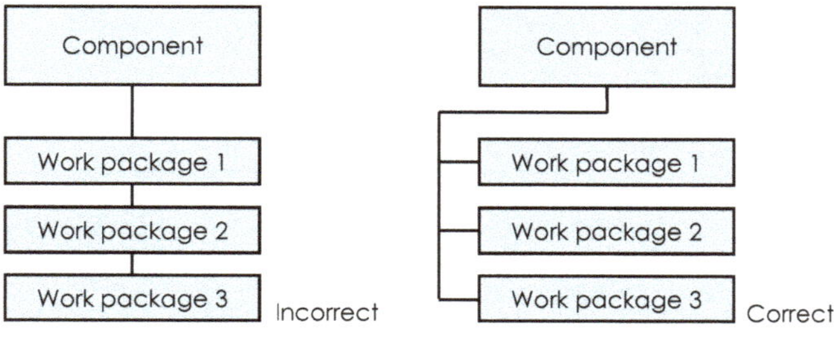

Figure 5.03.05 Presentation WBS

Finally, although each element has its own identifier, do not use the same titles for the different components and work packages in the breakdown, not even in the different layers or branches. This will inevitably lead to errors.

WBS dictionary

All components in the WBS should be described in a WBS dictionary. This should include at least the following:

- Identifier and title;
- Work description;
- Responsible organisation;
- Milestones;
- Tasks to be carried out;
- Products to be delivered;
- Dependencies with other work packages;
- Resources required;
- Cost estimates;
- Quality requirements;
- How and by whom the products will be tested;
- Technical references;
- Contract data.

PRODUCT BREAKDOWN STRUCTURE (PBS)

Instead of a work breakdown structure, a *Product Breakdown Structure* (PBS) can be prepared. A PBS is a breakdown of the products to be delivered. Therefore, the PBS contains only nouns, whereas the WBS describes work packages, i.e. verbs + nouns. A PBS does not include management products.

In addition to the products to be realised, PBS also includes external products. External products are products that already exist or whose realisation falls outside the project scope but are nevertheless necessary for realising the project deliverables.

Including the external products in the PBS itself prevents them from being forgotten. Distinguish them visually from the products that need to be realised within the project's scope. As with WBS, don't get lost in details.

> *The Purchasing department was supposed to provide us with the latest database of suppliers. However, when we loaded the database into our system, it turned out that the configuration of that database did not match the project database and also that much data was incomplete and incorrect. This caused much extra work and delayed our project considerably.*

Furthermore, it is possible to form subgroups of products for the sole purpose of obtaining a better overview. The 100% rule does not apply to PBS. To avoid confusion, subgroups should be distinguished in colour and or shape from the products in the PBS (see Figure 5.03.06).

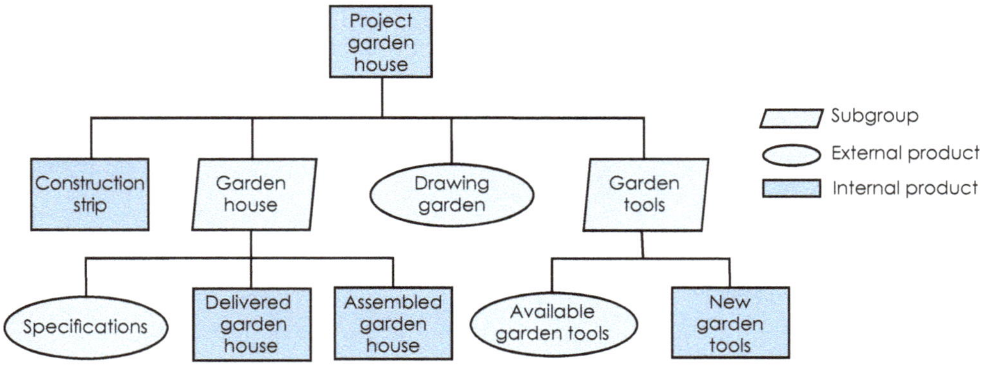

Figure 5.03.06 Example PBS with external products and subheadings

Product description

A product description should be written for each product in the PBS. It gives the team a clear picture of what they need to deliver. The product description indicates the purpose of the product, who should realise the product and the sources from which the product is to be produced. These may be the materials from which the specific product should be assembled, but also the documents describing how the product will be produced. Furthermore, the product description contains the composition of the product. For a book, this may be the arrangements of the chapters; for a machine, the main machine parts.

You also need to indicate how the product will be delivered (format and presentation). For example, a document should be delivered according to a certain template, on A4 and bound. A machine should be delivered, packaged, and ready for transport. Furthermore, the product descriptions should include the quality criteria and quality tolerances, how the product will be reviewed and by whom, and finally, who ultimately approves and releases the product (see Figure 5.03.07). The set of product descriptions is laid down in the requirement specification.

Product description

- Product identifier and title
- Purpose product
- Responsible organisation
- Derivation
- Composition
- Format and presentation
- Quality criteria and tolerances
- Quality review method
- Quality review responsibility

Figure 5.03.07 Product description

Time and budget constraints are not part of a product description. These details are added in the work package description of the product to be realised.

A product description should be written as soon as it is confirmed that the product in question will be used or realised within the project. The product description should be frozen as soon as the stage plan for the stage where the product will be used or produced is approved. The product description may not be changed without the (formal) approval of the same individual that approved the original product description.

The strength of a product description lies in its simplicity. Keep the product description short: one or two pages are usually sufficient. Furthermore, involve the people who will deliver or develop the products and who will use the products. Finally, a product description should also be written for the external products so that it is clear to all parties, including those who have to supply these products, what they should meet before they can be used in the project.

Product flow diagram

To make a time schedule (see Chapter 5.05 Time), it is important to know the order in which the products should be realised. For this purpose, a product flow diagram is drawn up as the last step in product-based planning. In this diagram, all products as defined by the PBS, are displayed in their mutual sequential relationship.

The rules for drawing up a product flow diagram are simple. The flow diagram is drawn from top to bottom or left to right. All products from the PBS are displayed with the same names used in the decomposition. Arrows indicate the order of realisation of the products. Products are, in principle, only drawn one after the other or in parallel. In the flowchart, both internal and external products are included. The flowchart ends with the project output to be delivered (see Figure 5.03.08).

When drawing up a product flow diagram, it is advisable to draw it from the beginning to the end (start to finish) and from the end back to the beginning (finish to start). This gives the best results. It is also advisable to involve the individuals doing the work in preparing the product flow diagram.

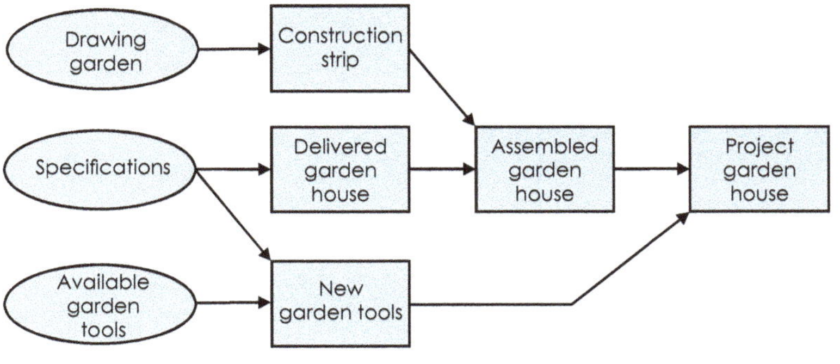

Figure 5.03.08 Example product flow diagram with external and internal products

It regularly occurs that new products are identified while drawing the flow diagram. These products then have to be added to the PBS to ensure that both diagrams remain consistent.

Swim lanes

If appropriate, the product flow diagram can be subdivided according to the different responsibilities; all products produced by a specific team are then drawn in a separate 'lane' in the flow diagram, the so-called *swim lane* (see Figure 5.03.09). By drawing swim lanes, the transitions of responsibilities from one team to another are immediately visible. During the implementation of the work, you should pay special attention to these transitions.

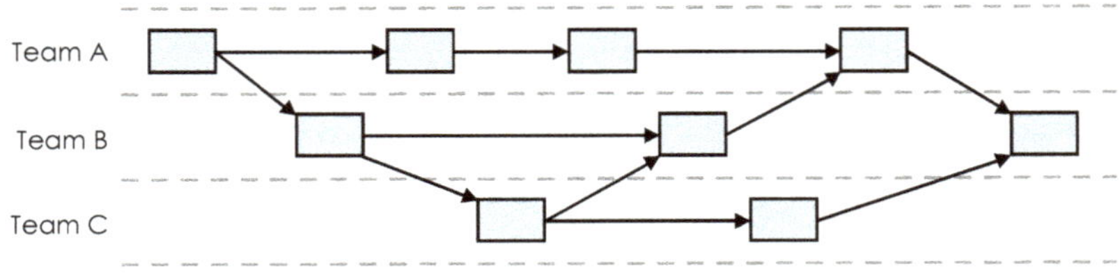

Figure 5.03.09 Example swim lanes

SCOPE (CONFIGURATION) MANAGEMENT

The scope configuration is the arrangement of the scope in a particular combination. This applies to the configuration of the scope into different sub-projects and work packages and the configuration of the products and services to be delivered.

Scope (configuration) management is the aspect of management to ensure that the scope is aligned with agreed stakeholder needs and requirements and that the creation of the deliverables to achieve the stated objectives can be realised effectively. The scope configuration should be an integrated part of each plan.

Scope management is directly related to change control (see Chapter 6.02 Change Control) and document management (see Chapter 6.03 Information and Documentation). The first ensures that product baselines cannot be changed without authorisation. The second ensures that all resources assigned to the project work with the correct baseline versions.

SUSTAINABILITY

The scope needs to be redefined when social and environmental perspectives are considered, recognising the broader context and impact of the project approach and deliverables. How do we ensure deliverables are easily maintained, repaired, improved, decommissioned and disposed of? How do we ensure that materials can be reused or recycled after disposal? How do we avoid a hostile environment? How do we achieve a positive social impact? How do we prevent the depletion of resources and unnecessary waste? This will not only affect the defined work but will, in all likelihood, also lead to new and different work packages to be carried out and products to be delivered.

TAILORING

Scope and a scope breakdown are also important topics within Agile. Unlike traditional projects, however, scope is described in functions (user stories) rather than deliverables. Moreover, scope prioritisation is much more important, as progress control is achieved by dropping the lowest-priority features when necessary to meet agreed deadlines. Additionally, what needs to be delivered is much more flexible. The highest priority in

Agile is to satisfy the customer. Higher-priority changes are traded for lower-priority backlog items. The project scope is defined in the product backlog, initially in large chunks of work, later more in functions and eventually even in features. The sprint scope is defined in the spring backlog.

RESPONSIBILITIES

The project manager is responsible for defining and managing the scope in coordination with the project team members, users and other relevant stakeholders. The project sponsor should approve the scope as part of the project plan and the subsequent stage plans. The work package leaders are responsible for the further decomposition of the work packages within the various team plans.

ADVANCED
POSITION SUB-PROJECTS IN A WBS (ADVANCED)

A sub-project is a project that is part of a larger project. A sub-project has its own deliverables to be realised and handed over to the sponsoring organisation or customer within predefined requirements and constraints. The financial risk of non-compliance lies primarily with the responsible supplier. It has its own profit and loss account. The sub-project holder can be an external contractor but also an internal department. The planning and control of the work to be performed lies with the sub-project manager and on the account of the supplier. From the position of the project manager, the work will only be controlled based on the work package agreement. In the WBS, a sub-project is a WBS component that is separately controlled and reported on. A sub-project contains two or more work packages (see Figure 5.03.10). To define part of a project as a sub-project is not a technical but an organisational decision.

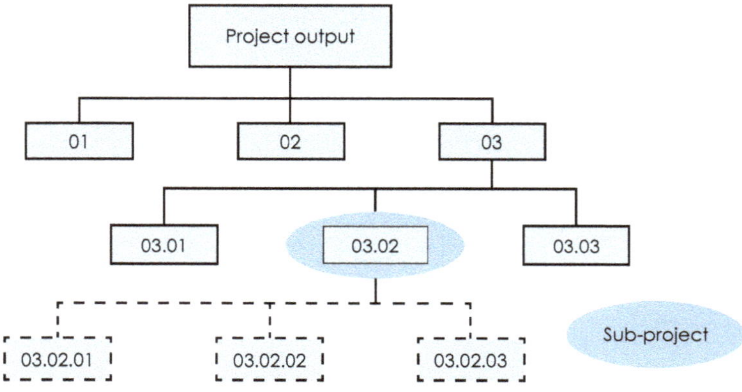

Figure 5.03.10 Example of a sub-project within a WBS

5.04 QUALITY

PURPOSE

The purpose of this chapter is to enable the individual to establish and manage the quality of the service/product to be delivered and the delivery process being managed.

LEARNING OBJECTIVES

- Process and product quality in a project;
- Validation and verification;
- Quality management;
- Quality management strategy and quality management plan;
- Quality management cycle (Deming cycle);
- Standards, norms and regulations;
- Quality reviews, audits and evaluations;
- Quality tools;
- Quality/test register;
- Some additional quality tools (advanced);
- Inspection methods and techniques (advanced);
- Various test concepts and test plans (advanced);
- Quality costs (advanced).

DEFINITIONS

Quality: The extent to which a set of features and characteristics of a product, service or process satisfy stated or implied needs.
Process quality: The quality of the process undertaken.
Product quality: The quality of the product delivered.
Quality criteria: The set of features and characteristics that can be tested and measured to confirm that the quality objectives have been met.
Verification: The confirmation that the set requirements have been fulfilled.
Validation: The confirmation that the requirements and deliverables meet the need of the customer and other stakeholders.
Quality management: The aspect of management aimed at directing and controlling an organisation regarding quality.
Quality register: A log used for recording planned and conducted quality activities.

INTRODUCTION

Quality is the extent to which a set of features and characteristics of a product, service or process satisfy stated or implied needs. This makes quality one of the most important control aspects of a project. If the project result does not meet the quality criteria, the product cannot or will not be used as intended. In the worst case, the customer is entirely unable or unwilling to use the project output. The project has then completely failed. Therefore, it is essential to ensure the quality of the products throughout the project. Also, the opposite is possible; delivering features and characteristics that the user has not asked for and does not satisfy the user's demands. That would be a waste of effort.

POSITIONING

Quality management starts in the project preparation stage, as part of the project assignment, by identifying the customer's quality expectations and acceptance criteria.

In the project definition stage, these quality expectations and acceptance criteria are elaborated into an initial requirement specification for the individual products to be delivered at project completion. In the project definition stage, the quality management strategy is also established, and, if applicable, the quality register is set up.

At stage transitions, the requirements of the individual products to be developed in the next stage are specified as part of the preparation of the respective stage plans. The planned quality activities are recorded in the quality register. The quality management strategy is also reviewed and, if necessary, updated.

During the implementation, the planned quality activities are carried out. All developed products should be checked to ensure they meet the requirements and are fit for use and fit for purpose. The results are recorded in the quality register, and any corrective actions are taken.

At project completion, if all goes according to plan, the acceptance of the users, operation and maintenance of the project output can be confirmed, and the project output can be handed over to the customer.

PROCESS AND PRODUCT QUALITY

Quality requirements can be imposed on the output to be delivered (product quality) and on the process to achieve this result (process quality). In projects, we have to deal with both. The project itself can be seen as a process. The deliverables are the products of that process. Process quality can relate to the use of specific development standards, testing methods, the involvement of stakeholders, the project management method to be applied, and so on. Process quality management frameworks are, for example, *Kaizen* (see Chapter 8.05 Result Orientation) and *Lean Six Sigma* (see Chapter 9.05 Development Frameworks).

STANDARD OPERATING PROCEDURES

A *Standard Operating Procedure* (SOP) describes *step-by-step a process to correctly perform a routi*ne. SOPs are an effective tool to ensure process quality in specialist work and management. Within projects, SOPs are used to achieve repeatable results and track progress consistently. In projects, SOPs are primarily defined to comply with the organisation's governance. SOPs are particularly valuable for recurring projects. Ensure that the SOPs are complete and clear, as well as fit for use and fit for purpose to the project scope. SOPs can also be a project deliverable to ensure that the customer can use the project output correctly.

VERIFICATION AND VALIDATION

Verification is the confirmation that the set requirements have been met. Validation is the confirmation that the requirement specifications and deliverables meet the need of the customer and other stakeholders; that the products and services are available for use and suitable for the intended application.

It would not be the first time the project output is built entirely according to the specification, but the customer is unhappy because the output is not available for use (fit for use) and or not suitable for the specified application (fit for purpose). In that respect, validation is often even more important than verification.

To realise the project result, the customer demand is translated into a system specification. The system specification is then divided into a product specification, which in turn is divided into a component specification. Subsequently, based on these specifications, successive designs are made, based on which the project output is finally realised (see Figure 5.04.01).

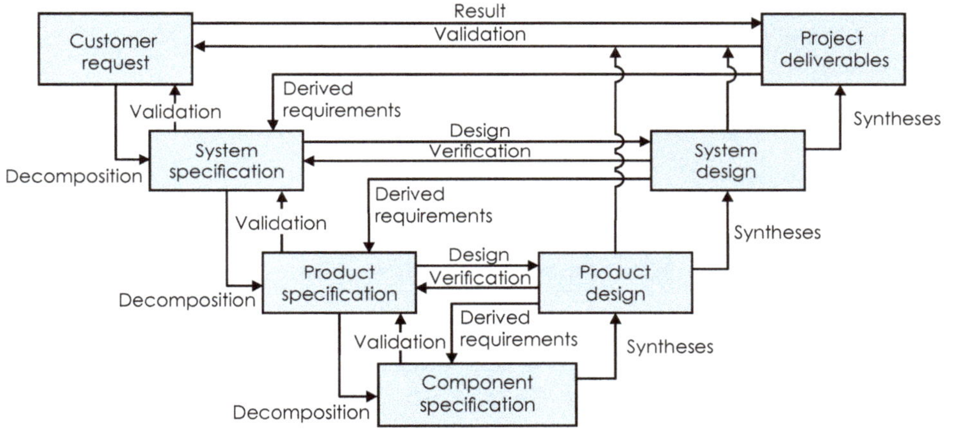

Figure 5.04.01 Verification and validation

To ensure that the system, product and component specification will deliver the desired output, these specifications should be validated against the higher levels. In particular, translating customer demand into a system specification is critical. Does that system specification actually reflect what the customer wants? Because if it does not, you can make a beautiful product based on those specifications, but the customer will still not get what they had in mind. How often do customers despair when they see what they get and wonder: 'Is this what we ask for?' A good way to avoid this is to build a mock-up or model first.

Finally, all intermediate products and deliverables should be checked to ensure they meet the requirements (verification) AND are fit for use and fit for purpose (validation). It is your responsibility to ensure that this verification and validation actually takes place throughout the development of the project deliverables.

QUALITY MANAGEMENT

Quality management is the aspect of management aimed at on directing and controlling an organisation regarding quality (ISO/TC176, 2015). The quality management system comprises all policy guidelines, standards, procedures, responsibilities and objectives to direct and control an organisation with regard to quality. Quality management consists of quality assurance, planning, control, and improvement.

Quality assurance
Quality assurance is that part of quality management aimed at ensuring compliance with quality requirements. It is the establishment, maintenance and monitoring of the quality management system for the project.

Quality planning
Quality planning is that part of quality management aimed at establishing quality objectives and identifying the necessary processes and associated resources to achieve those quality objectives. It is about defining quality requirements and planning how and when compliance with these quality requirements will be verified.

Quality control
Quality control is that part of quality management aimed at meeting quality requirements. It is about evaluating whether products are being delivered according to the specifications and taking action to eliminate the causes of unsatisfactory performance.

Quality improvement
Quality improvement is that part of quality management aimed at increasing the ability to meet quality requirements. Quality improvement includes improving the efficiency, effectiveness and traceability of the quality management system.

QUALITY MANAGEMENT STRATEGY AND PLAN
A quality management strategy is a high-level description of how quality will be managed on the project, including the intended outcome and the specific processes, procedures, techniques, standards and responsibilities to be applied. The quality management strategy can be derived from both the customer's and supplier's quality management system. If the existing standards and procedures are modified for the project, this should be explicitly mentioned in the strategy. The project's quality management strategy is usually referred to as the project's quality management system or quality management approach. The quality (management) plan comprises the basic requirement specification and the project's quality management strategy.

The project's quality management strategy should include the following:
- When audits will be held by the sponsoring organisation or customer.
- Applicable quality techniques and standards, such as certain types of inspections or quality reviews.
- Quality records that will be maintained.
- Form and composition of the quality register.
- Quality reports: purpose, frequency, form and recipients.
- Times when quality activities such as inspections and reviews will be carried out.
- Quality responsibilities within the project.

DEMING CYCLE
The *Deming cycle* describes the quality management cycle through which improvements can be implemented. Its cyclical nature ensures constant attention to

quality improvement. The four activities in the Deming cycle are:

- ***Plan*** – Review the current work, set objectives and draft a plan to improve it.
- ***Do*** – Implement the planned improvements.
- ***Check*** – Measure the performance and check it against the set objectives.
- ***Act*** – Adjust the activities based on the results.

This cycle can be applied at any level within the organisation and the project.

STANDARDS, NORMS AND REGULATIONS

Standards, norms and regulations are terms often used in the context of quality but are regularly mixed up. However, these terms have different meanings:

Standard – A set of responsibilities, processes, procedures and techniques for general and repeated use to create order. Standards are often set in the field of technology but also in the field of performing activities such as project management. The use of standards is optional, and different standards can coexist. Well-known standards are HTML and JPEG. Organisations can also apply internal standards.

Norm – A set of rules parties voluntarily agreed on about their products, services, or processes. Such agreements are usually made through a national or international body, such as the International Organization for Standardization (ISO) in Geneva.

Regulation – A mandatory provision with a legal basis issued by an administrative authority. This can be done at local, national and international levels. Many norms are thus converted into regulations.

The difference between a norm and a regulation is that the user is obliged to apply the regulation but is free to apply the norm. However, a generally recognised norm does exert a certain degree of coercion.

QUALITY REVIEW, AUDIT AND EVALUATION

There are quantitative quality assessments, such as tests and inspections, and qualitative quality assessments. Qualitative assessments can be divided into audits, reviews and evaluations (see Figure 5.04.02).

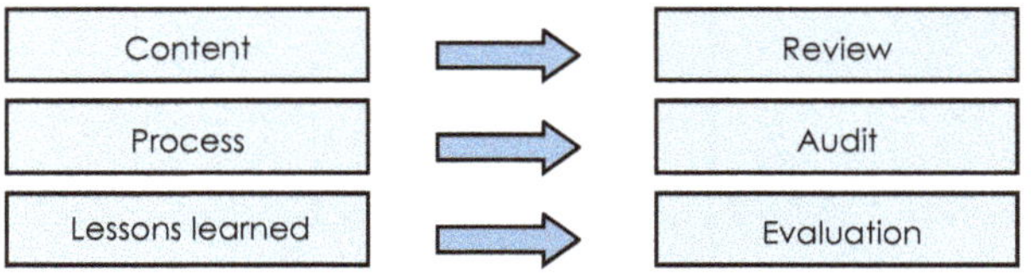

Figure 5.04.02 Quality review, audit and evaluation

Quality review

A quality review is an assessment of a product by a team of stakeholders to determine whether it meets a set of quality criteria. When assessing an intermediate product, the assessment also involves determining whether the product in question is a good baseline for developing the desired output. Reviewers are often fellow specialists and users affected by the final product.

A quality review is often conducted to assess deliverables in the design stage, such as drawings, models, et cetera. Such a review has many advantages. It enables an objective assessment of quality and early detection of defects. It also creates a platform for quality improvement and support among stakeholders and ensures objective progress control and effective decision-making.

Audit

An audit is a systematic, independent and documented process to determine whether the implementation processes comply with the quality guidelines, standards and procedures and are efficient and effective.

Auditors are usually performed by individuals outside the project organisation and sometimes even by bodies outside the respective permanent organisations. If audits are to be carried out, it is essential to determine in advance what information is required for this purpose and how this information will be retained.

Evaluation

An evaluation or retrospective is an assessment of activities carried out and their results to identify areas of improvement: what went well and what can or should be improved. An evaluation takes place to identify learning points and implement process improvements. An evaluation can best be carried out together with the whole team.

It is recommended to evaluate after each milestone, but at least at each stage transition and at the conclusion of the project. It is more effective to do a brief evaluation regularly rather than extensive evaluations occasionally. Making many small steps forward is more effective and also easier to implement than trying to make a large improvement every now and then.

QUALITY REGISTER/TEST REGISTER

A quality register is a register used for recording planned and conducted quality activities. A quality register contains the dates of when the assessments were planned and performed, the products being reviewed, the type of review, who is performing it, the result, and a reference to the relevant quality records (see Figure 5.04.03). A quality register is used to facilitate the quality control process.

Quality register

- Quality identifier
- Product(s) to be reviewed
- Method of assessment
- Performer quality activity
- Planned, forecast and actual date assessment
- Result assessment (passed or failed)
- Date sign-off
- Reference to quality records (test plan, test results)

Figure 5.04.03 Quality register

The quality register is set up in the project definition stage or right at the beginning of the first delivery stage. Dates of the intended quality activities are taken from the successive stage plans. The results of the assessments are extracted from the quality records.

A test register is a special form of a quality register. A test register is a quality register specially for tests performed. Quality assessments, such as a quality review, are not included. A test register is usually set up when a separate test manager is appointed for a project.

QUALITY TOOLS

There are many quality/problem analysing tools available. The *histogram, Pareto analysis, fishbone diagram,* and *flow chart* are often used. These are four of the seven quality analysis tools introduced by Dr Kaoru Ishikawa (1986), the first total quality management guru (the seven basic quality tools):

Histogram

A histogram is a diagram where the frequency of outcomes of a process, given a varying input value, is displayed in corresponding lengths of bars. By visualising the values, a histogram can help analyse a process (see Figure 5.04.04).

Pareto chart

A *Pareto chart* is a histogram in which the input values are sorted by frequency of occurrence (see Figure 5.04.05). A Pareto chart is used to analyse deviations and to prioritise corrective actions. The Pareto chart is related to the Pareto principle that 20% of the causes cause 80% of the effect.

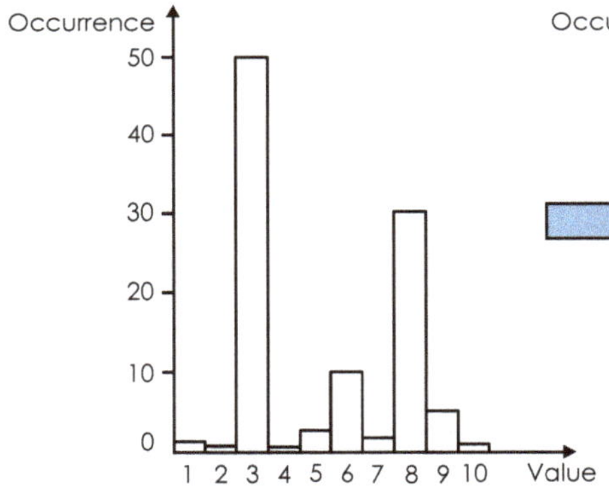

Figure 5.04.04 Example histogram

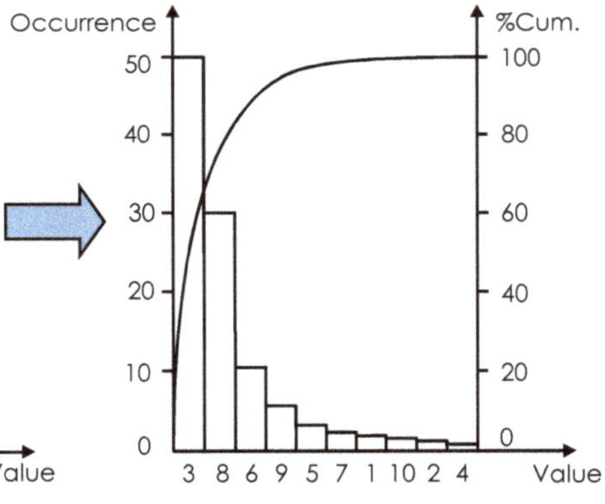

Figure 5.04.05 Example Pareto diagram

Fishbone diagram

The cause-and-effect or fishbone diagram, also called the *Ishikawa diagram*, is a tool to map and evaluate all the inputs to a given process. This diagram helps you to determine possible causes of deviations from specifications (see Chapter 4.05 Risk and Opportunity).

Flowchart

A flowchart is a visualisation of a process. A flowchart often uses separate symbols for activities, decision points, documents, storage and input and output (see Figure 5.04.06).

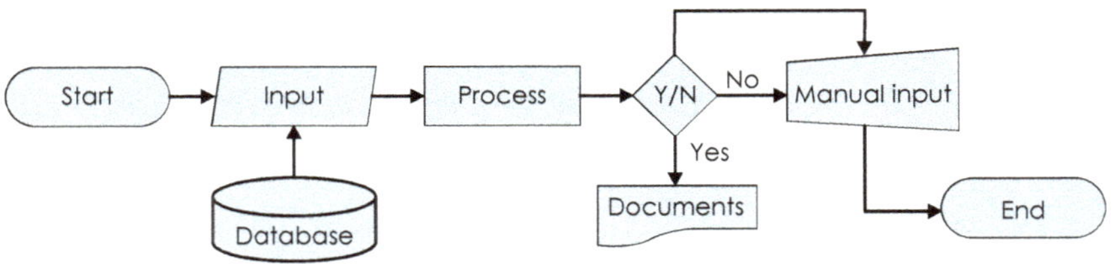

Figure 5.04.06 Example flowchart

SUSTAINABILITY

The lifecycle orientation of sustainability implies that the acceptance criteria of the project output and the project's quality management should be more goal-orientated than deliverable-orientated and include environmental and social perspectives.

In recent years, various instruments have been developed to assess the sustainable impact of projects. These range from rudimentary checklists to a more structured sustainability impact assessment and certification (see Chapter 11.02 Sustainability). Ensure support from the corporate sustainability or CSR officer, if any.

TAILORING

Quality is the extent to which the output satisfies the customer. This makes quality an essential aspect of Agile. Quality in Agile is defined by the purpose of each user story. In Agile, quality is tested throughout development and reaffirmed in the reviews at the end of each timebox. Validation is the first priority here.

Numerous testing concepts apply. Determine in advance how items will be tested. Test as early as possible. Make use of models and mock-ups. Repeat tests, preferably automatically, involve users in early testing, and prioritise tests based on probability and impact of failure. If backlog items are delivered incrementally, test the new features/functions in conjunction with what has already been delivered. In fact, these testing concepts should be the credo in most projects.

Although a working application takes preference over documentation, regulations may require recording test results. Setting up a test register can be very useful in this regard. Include in the Definition of Done (DoD) which test results should be recorded.

RESPONSIBILITIES

The project manager should prepare and agree to the quality management approach. You can apply the user and supplier quality management systems. You should also ensure that the quality criteria are established, quality standards are met, and quality assessments are conducted.

The project sponsor is ultimately responsible for obtaining quality in the project. The user representative is responsible for setting the quality criteria. The supplier representative should ensure that quality standards are applied, and the quality criteria are met.

The work package leaders should initiate individual quality activities and ensure appropriate entries in the quality register. The project support is responsible for maintaining the quality register and archiving the quality records.

ADVANCED
ADDITIONAL QUALITY TOOLS (ADVANCED)

Three more sophisticated quality tools out of the seven basic quality tools are the scatter diagram, run diagram and control chart (Ishikawa,1986).

Scatter diagram

In a scatter diagram, the values of two variables are plotted along two axes. (see Figure 5.04.07). A scatter diagram can be used to reveal any correlation present.

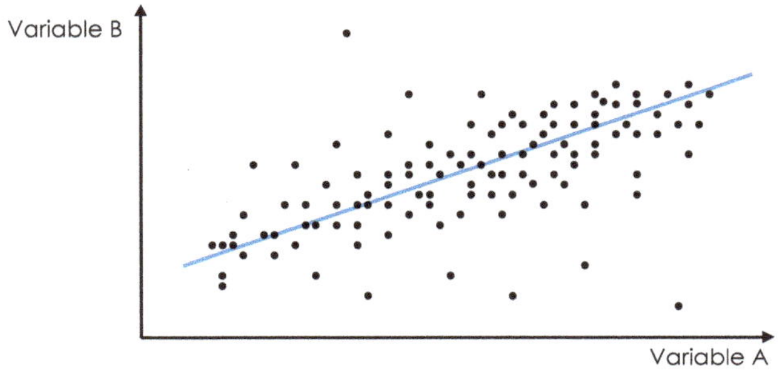

Figure 5.04.07 Example scatter diagram

Run chart

A run diagram visualises observations over time (see Figure 5.04.08). A run chart can be used to follow the process's outcome over time and to assess the effect of process changes. A run chart can also be easily used to perform trend analyses. When results deviate below or over the norm value more than seven times in a row, this is referred to as a 'run' or a trend deviation.

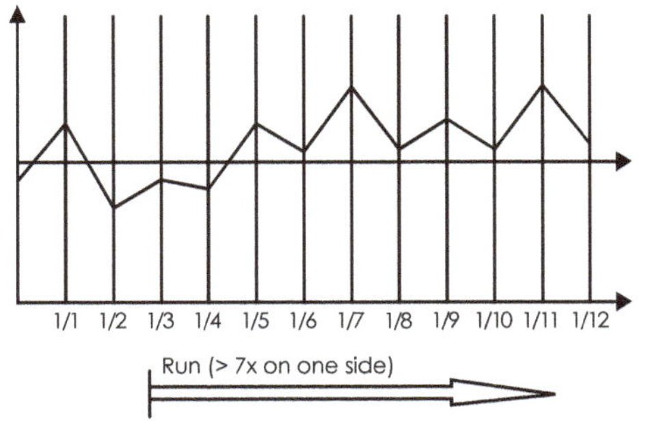

Figure 5.04.08 Example run diagram

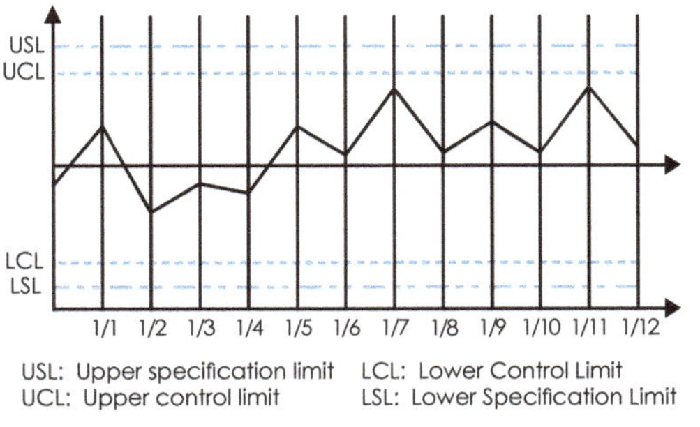

Figure 5.04.09 Example control chart

Control chart

In addition to a run chart, a control diagram visualises observations over time in relation to agreed specification limits and established control limits (see Figure 5.04.09).

Control limits should be set within the agreed specification limits to ensure timely action can be taken in case of any deviation. A slip chart (see Chapter 6.04 Control and Reporting) is an example of a control chart.

INSPECTION METHODS AND TECHNIQUES (ADVANCED)

An inspection is a systematic assessment of a product or process by one or more specialists to determine whether it meets the specifications. A test assesses whether a product meets the requirements under different circumstances. You inspect the thickness of the coating, but you test the braking distance of a vehicle.

Inspection techniques can be distinguished into destructive and non-destructive techniques. You can measure the paint thickness of a pipe by cutting the pipe and physically measuring the thickness (destructive). You can also use an ultrasonic thickness gauge (non-destructive). More and more inspections are done using non-destructive inspection techniques.

Most inspections are carried out visually. Sometimes it is just a matter of checking that what has been delivered is also what has been ordered. Many products already have an inspection plate or label with all the relevant data. Then it is just a matter of verifying whether the data complies with the requirements.

In other situations, the system already registers the required data itself. Then you only need to check the recorded data. Take, for example, a tachograph in a truck. By reading the tachograph, inspectors can easily check whether the driving and rest times regulations are met.

TESTING AND TEST CONCEPTS (ADVANCED)

Testing assesses whether a product meets the requirements under different circumstances. We can distinguish different test concepts:

- *Test-based design* – Determine in advance how and under which circumstances the test will be carried out and base the design on it. It makes quite a difference whether you test in a laboratory or in situ.
- *Early testing* – Test as early as possible to avoid wasting time and resources by developing a system that does not meet the requirements from the start.
- *Repeatable testing* – Perform the same test periodically, preferably automated, during development.
- *Independent testing* – Ensure that the individual performing the test is not the same as the individual developing the product.
- *Collegial testing* – Perform a peer review first before the product is released for final testing.
- *Testing together* – Involve users in early testing to reduce the overall testing costs and to incorporate the input from the users as early as possible.
- *Risk-based testing* – Test in priority of probability and impact of failure.

Within a project, different types of tests are applied. Well-known types of tests are:

- *Unit test* – Test the individual components.
- *Integration test* – Test the interfaces between the individual components.
- *System test* – Test all components together.
- *Regression test* – Test whether a system still functions appropriately after an adjustment.
- *Acceptance test* – Test by users, operation, and maintenance.

- *Performance test* – Test the processing speed of a system.
- *Stress test* – Test a system at peak load.

For construction and installation projects, we further distinguish:

- *Factory Acceptance Test (FAT)* – To test a product before it leaves the factory. This is often the responsibility of the supplier.
- *Site Acceptance Test (SAT)* – To test a product after on-site installation. This is often the responsibility of the main contractor.

Software test management tools are available to help you plan, run, and report tests by managing test cases, requirements, and defects.

Automated testing is a testing application that tests software automatically on each system version, i.e., without human initiative or effort. This is also known as continuous integration.

QUALITY COSTS (ADVANCED)

Quality costs are the costs caused by achieving and securing the desired quality and the losses incurred when the desired quality is not achieved. In the *Quality Control Manual*, J.M. Juran (1988) distinguishes conformance and non-conformance costs. Conformance costs are prevention and assessment costs; non-conformance or failure costs are replacement and repair costs.

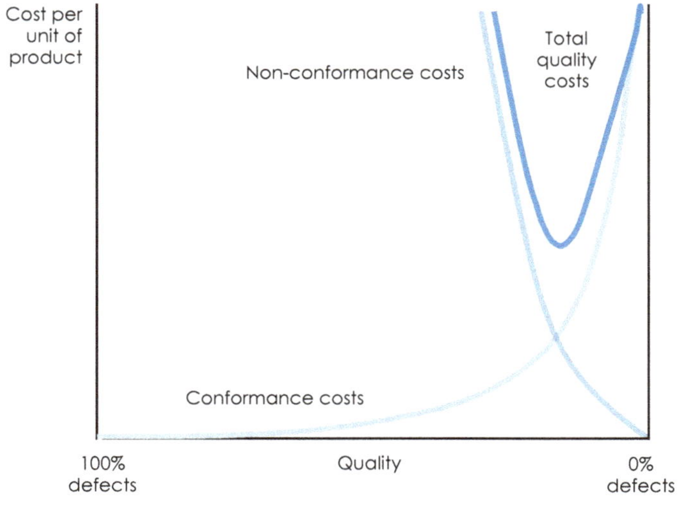

Figure 5.04.10 Quality costs (Juran, 1988)

According to Juran, total quality costs are lowest when conformance and non-conformance costs are roughly equal. (see Figure 5.04.10)

5.05 TIME

PURPOSE

The purpose of this chapter is to enable the individual to define, sequence, optimise, monitor, and control all components to delivering the agreed project output of the project.

LEARNING OBJECTIVES:

- Identify and divide a project into milestones, stages, and decision points;
- Project stages and phases;
- Apply a suitable phasing model in the project;
- Draw a Precedence chart with the critical path and total float of the individual activities;
- Prepare a Gantt chart with milestones, stages, and decision points;
- Record the progress of the work in a Gantt chart;
- Shorten the lead time with crashing and fast track;
- Apply other planning restrictions and calculate the free float in a Precedence chart (advanced);
- Apply statistical calculations based on the PERT method (advanced).

DEFINITIONS

Phasing model: A widely used phasing that serves as a reference for the phasing of future projects.
Precedence chart: An activity network with a schematic representation of dependencies over time based on activities on node.
(Total) float: The period by which an activity can be delayed from its earliest start without delaying the plan's completion, assuming that all other activities are performed according to plan.
Critical path: The longest chain of activities to be carried out in a plan.
Gantt chart: A graphical depiction showing the duration of activities along a time bar.

INTRODUCTION

Project output usually have to be delivered before a predetermined end date. Controlling time is, therefore, an essential management aspect of projects. This is impossible without a proper time schedule. You should be able to prepare a realistic and supported time schedule with the parties involved. Proper staging is essential for interim decision-making at the board level.

POSITIONING

Plans are prepared throughout the entire lifecycle of a project. Time planning is an essential part of this. In the project preparation stage, a time estimate is made of the total project, and the stage plan is prepared for the project definition stage.

In the project definition stage, the staging for the project delivery is determined, and the project plan and the stage plan for the first delivery stage are prepared. During the stage transitions, the project plan is updated, and the stage plan for the next stage is prepared. At the latest during delivery, team plans are prepared for the individual work packages.

PLANNING TYPES

Within projects we mostly distinguish between the project, stage, team, and exception plans. In principle, all plans have the same structure (see Figure 5.05.01). However, the final layout of a plan can differ depending on the type of project and the project context.

- Plan description
- Plan prerequisites
- External dependencies
- Plan assumptions
- Delivery approach
- Project breakdown structure (WBS/PBS)
- Requirement specification/product descriptions
- Budget and time schedule
- Product flow diagram/activity network
- Resources required/assigned

Figure 5.05.01 Composition of a plan

Project plan

The project plan describes how, when and by whom the project objectives will be realised. The project plan provides the project board with a baseline against which the project's progress can be monitored. The project plan identifies the decision points and stages of the project and defines the projected project costs and time schedule for the business case. The project manager prepares the project plan in the definition stage and updates it at stage transitions. The project board has to approve the project plan. The project plan is part of the project management plan (see Chapter 5.01 Project definition stage).

Stage plan

The stage plan is the basis for the project manager's daily management of that stage. The stage plan for the next stage is created at stage transitions. For projects with only one delivery stage, the delivery stage plan can be combined with the project plan, but each of its own level of detail. The project manager should prepare the stage plans and get them approved by the project board.

Team plan

The team plan includes the work of a work package. The team plan is optional. If necessary, it is prepared during the preparation of the relevant stage plan, at the latest when the work package is assigned. The team plan should be prepared by the work package leader and approved by the project manager. With an external supplier, the team plan submitted to the project manager for approval may contain only the necessary data to enable the project manager to monitor the progress of the work package.

Exception plan

The exception plan replaces the plan in which tolerances are (or threaten to be) exceeded. The format of the exception plan is the same as the plan it replaces. The exception plan encompasses the remaining period of the plan it replaces and is approved by the next higher management level (see Chapter 6.04 Control and reporting).

BASELINES

A baseline is an agreed status that serves as a reference for the remaining work. We roughly distinguish specialist and management baselines. A specialist baseline can be an approved design. Management baselines are, for example, approved plans, strategies, and work packages (see Chapter 6.04 Control and Reporting). Expired baselines should be preserved to trace successive versions of the baselines afterwards. Baselines are also a reference for change and progress control.

PROJECT STAGES AND PHASES

Within projects, we distinguish project stages and project phases. Project stages are linked to decision points, and project phases to milestones.

Project stages

A project stage is a period within a project, separated from other periods, with a predetermined output, and concluded with a go/no-go decision. The project can only continue after the sponsoring organisation has issued explicit authorisation. A decision point (gate) is a (usually predetermined) control point where the project is reviewed to decide whether or not a project can proceed and, if so, the budget for the next stage is released.

Every project has at least two stages: the project definition stage and the project delivery stage. The project preparation stage takes place before the start of the actual project. The delivery stage in a project is often divided into sub-stages.

Project phases

A project phase is a period within a project with its own characteristics and a predetermined output, such as engineering, tender, and construction. A project phase concludes with a milestone. A milestone is an important event that provides visible evidence of progress.

Project phases can overlap, and project stages do not. Project phases can coincide with project stages, but they don't have to. The same applies to milestones. A milestone can coincide with a decision point, but it does not have to. Decision points and milestones should be included in the project plan (see Chapter 3 Project Orientation).

Pros and cons of staging

Staging has several advantages. It concretises the end result in time steps, reduces uncertainties, stimulates decision-making, increases manageability, and creates ownership among those involved. Staging makes the project's progress also more transparent. The stage transition allows those involved the opportunity to check whether the project is still on track, needs to be adjusted, or closed prematurely.

Furthermore, a stage transition allows the project manager to account for the current stage, be discharged from the work performed, and ensure that the required deployment of people and resources for the next stage is guaranteed. A stage transition also stimulates the evaluation of learning points and simplifies the interim adjustment of the project organisation.

However, staging can also act as a straitjacket. Staging also creates extra paperwork and costs extra time and money due to the associated decision-making. However, this is a necessity to avoid mistakes. Running to the end in one go is quicker if everything goes as planned the first time. However, that rarely happens, which is why staging is a wise thing to do. Mind you: too many stages is also undesirable.

PHASING MODELS

A phasing model is a widely used phasing that serves as a reference for future projects. We distinguish *linear*, *parallel*, and *cyclic phasing* (see Figure 5.05.02). Cyclic phasing can be further divided into *version*, *development phasing* and *timeboxing*. The choice of phasing depends on the type, complexity and degree of uncertainty of the project. The project staging can be linked to those phasing models.

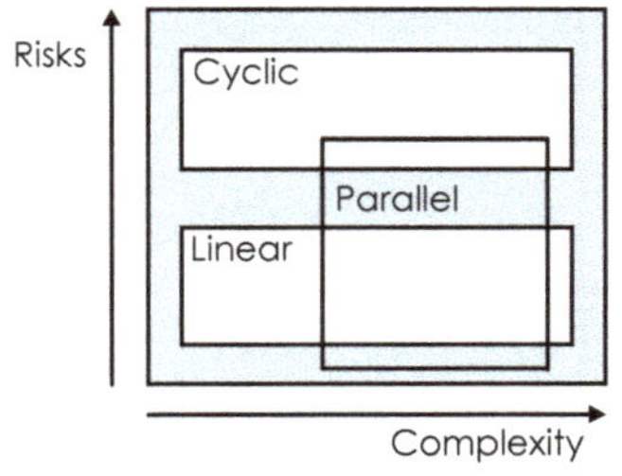

Figure 5.05.02 Phasing models (Groote, et al, 2011)

Linear phasing

In linear phasing, the different phases are performed sequentially. Each phase is carried out once after the previous phase has been completed and the associated decision-making by the project sponsor has taken place. This phasing is also known as *Waterfall phasing*. Just like a waterfall, in linear phasing, you don't return to a previous phase after that phase has been completed (see Figure 5.05.03).

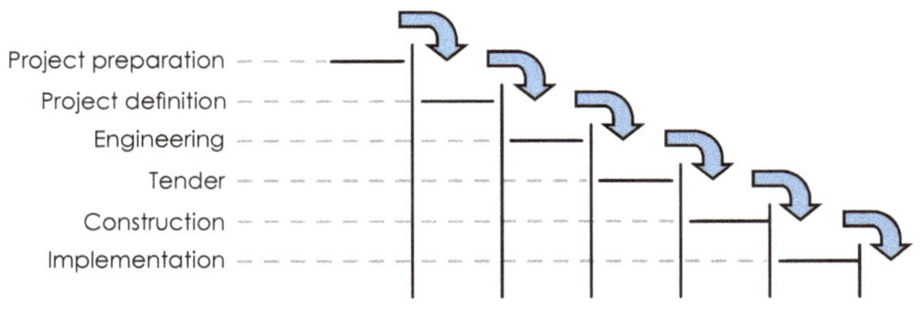

Figure 5.05.03 Linear or Waterfall model

Linear phasing is used for simple and unambiguous (not uncertain) projects. In such projects, the question is clear at the start, and the input from the users is limited. The environment is stable. These are often single engineering and maintenance projects.

Parallel phasing

Parallel phasing is best suited for complex but limited ambiguous projects. These are often divided into sub-projects after the basic design has been approved. The various sub-projects are then initiated, each with its own characteristics, phases and lead time. After completing the last sub-project, the total project output is completed and handed over, and the project is concluded.

Parallel phasing is also known as sub-project phasing. Due to parallel phasing, the engineering, preparation, and realisation phases overlap at project level (see Figure 5.05.04).

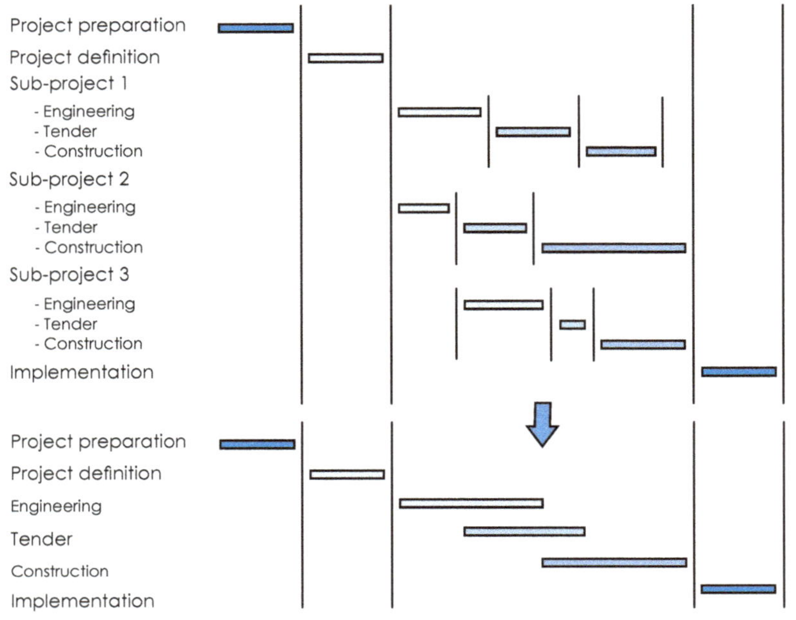

Figure 5.05.04 Parallel or sub-project model

Development model

The development model is appropriate when it is unclear at the start what the specifications should be. In this type of project, the specification and design process is repeated several times.

A solution is designed and tested based on an initial specification. If this solution is unsatisfactory, the specifications will be adjusted based on the outcome of the first cycle. A new solution is then developed and tested again. This process is repeated until a good solution is found. Only then will the remaining phases be started (see Figure 5.05.05). Examples of such a development phasing can be found in Research and Development projects (hence the name).

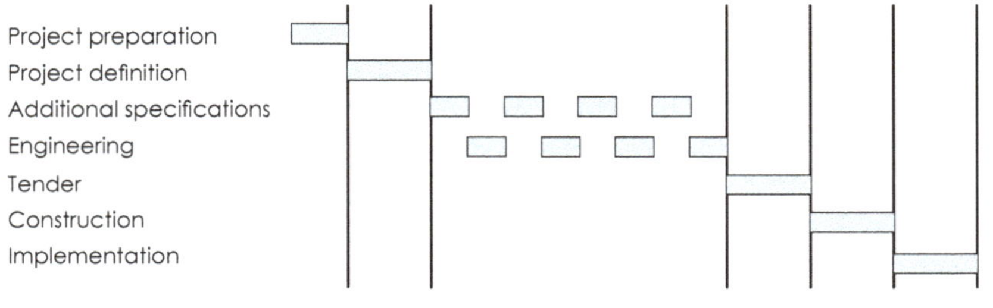

Figure 5.05.05 Development model

Version phasing

Version phasing is best suited for projects in which benefits depend strongly on the judgement of the end users, and several similar models should be developed and launched. In such projects, the standard model will be developed and launched first. Based on the feedback from the market, the other versions are developed and launched (see Figure 5.05.06).

Examples of version phasing can be found in the automotive industry. First, the standard model is launched, and only when this model is successful will the other models be developed. If necessary, the standard model is also slightly modified. Version phasing is also often used in software development. First, one application is developed and tested, and the following applications are developed only after a successful operation.

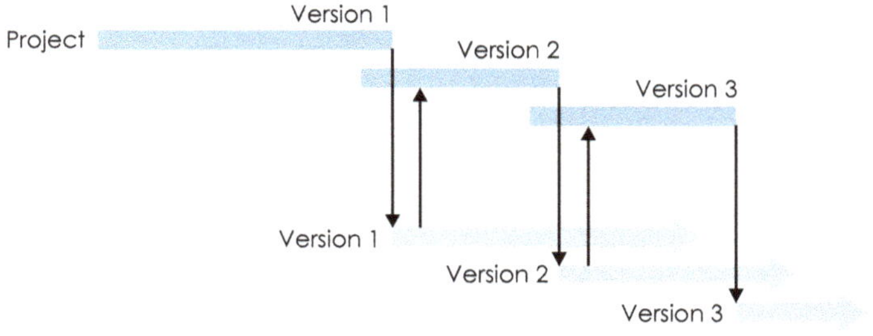

Figure 5.05.06 Version model

Timeboxing

Timeboxing is best suited for projects that rely heavily on user interaction and allow incremental delivery. With timeboxing, the output is delivered in fixed time periods. A timebox is a pre-agreed period within which a predetermined result should be realised. Any task with a deadline is actually a timebox. However, a timeboxing model has a fixed rhythm in which shippable products are delivered.

Timeboxing is widely used in Agile, whereby a self-organising team develops a shippable product per timebox (see Chapter 9.05 Development Frameworks). This can be a new product or an extension of an existing product (see Figure 5.05.07).

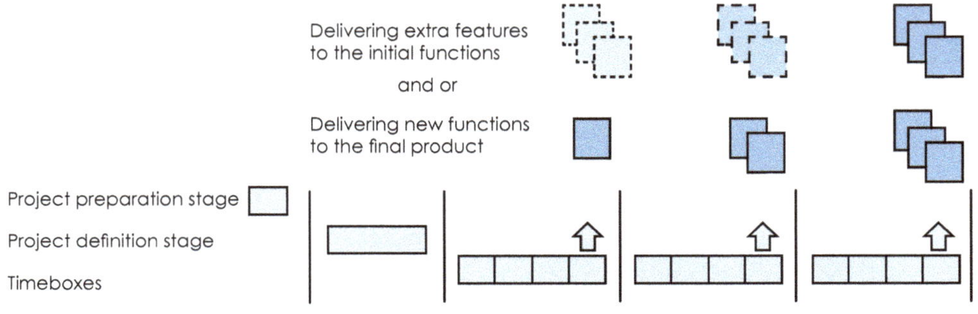

Figure 5.05.07 Timeboxing

Highly complex and ambiguous projects often consist of a mix of parallel, development and version phasing combined with timeboxing.

SCHEDULING METHODS

Various techniques are available for drawing up a time schedule. Common techniques include network diagrams, Gantt charts and planning tables. Sometimes even a simple activity calendar is sufficient as long as the agreed dates are clear and easy to read.

A network diagram is a good and quick means to analyse various alternatives. This is more difficult with a Gantt chart. A Gantt chart has the advantage of being easy to understand. This is essential for stakeholders' involvement and acceptance of the time schedule. Also, the work progress can be visualised more effectively in a Gantt chart. Therefore, a network diagram is often prepared first to analyse the various alternatives and is then converted into a Gantt chart.

PRECEDENCE CHART

A *Precedence chart* is a network diagram with activity on nodes and is easy to use for network analysis. With this method, (1) the earliest possible start and finish of all planned activities are determined. Then, (2) the latest possible start and finish of all activities within the earliest plan completion is determined. Next, (3) the (total) float of the individual activities is determined. Finally, (4) the critical path of the plan is determined. The critical path is the longest chain of activities in the plan, as it determines the earliest possible completion time of the plan.

The (total) float of an activity is the time that the activity can be delayed from its earliest start without delaying the plan's completion, assuming that all other activities are performed according to plan. The float is zero for all activities on the critical path since a delay of an activity on the critical path immediately delays the completion time of the plan. For all other activities, the float is greater than zero.

Activities

The activities in the Precedence chart are displayed in nodes. Per activity is recorded (see Figure 5.05.08):

- *Earliest Start (ES)* – The earliest possible start time of the activity in the plan;
- *Latest Start (LS)* – The latest possible start time of the activity in the plan;
- *Earliest Finish (EF)* – The earliest possible end time of the activity in the plan;
- *Latest Finish (LF)* – The latest possible end time of the activity in the plan;
- *Activity* – The name of the activity;
- *Duration (D)* – How long the activity takes;
- *Float* – The total float of the activity.

ES	Duration	EF
	Activity	
LS	Float	LF

Figure 5.05.08 Notation activity block Precedence chart

All start and finish dates in the chart are indicated at the end of the day. Therefore, the first activity starts not on day 1 but on (the end of the) day 0. This is not how we would indicate it ourselves, but it makes calculating the Precedence chart easier.

Relationships

A simple Precedence chart consists only of end-start relationships; as soon as one activity finishes, one or more other activities can start. In reality, the relationships are often more complicated, but simple end-start relationships are often more than sufficient for preparing an overview.

Drafting the chart

The steps to draft a Precedence chart are as follows:

- Identify the activities;
- Identify the sequence of activities;
- Define the duration of the individual activities;
- Draw the network chart;
- From start to finish, determine the earliest start and finish per activity and the shortest completion time of the total plan;
- From finish back to start, determine the latest finish and start per activity;
- Define the total float per activity and the critical path of the total plan.

Calculating the chart from start to finish determines the fastest possible start dates for the individual activities in a plan (*As Soon As Possible (ASAP)*). By calculating the chart from the finish back to the start, the latest possible start dates for the individual activities in a plan are determined (*As Late As Possible (ALAP)*).

Except for the first and the last activity, any activity in the network should be connected to other activities at the front and back. Loose ends in an activity network should not occur.

The Earliest Start (ES) of an activity is determined by the sum of all Durations (D) of the longest combination of activities leading to that activity. The Earliest Finish (EF) of an activity is determined by adding the Duration (D) to the Earliest Start (ES) of that particular activity: EF = ES + D (see Figure 5.05.09).

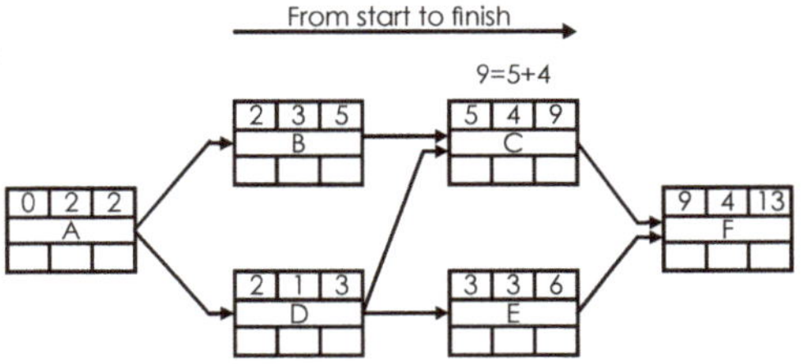

Figure 5.05.09 From front to end

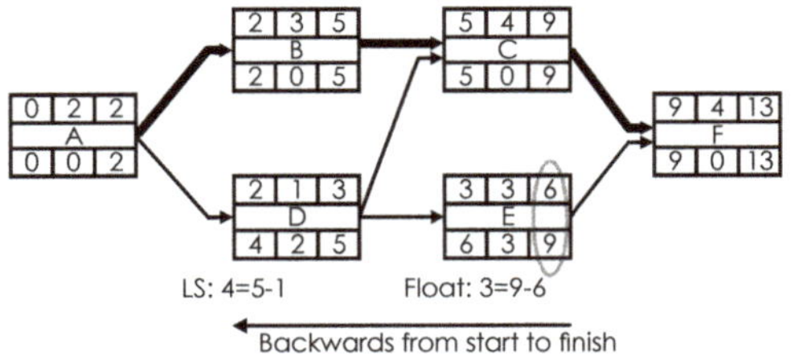

Figure 5.05.10 From end to front

When calculating the network back from the finish to the start, the same principles are followed, but in reverse. The Latest Finish (LF) of an activity is determined by subtracting from the plan's completion time the sum of all Durations (D) of the longest combination of consecutive activities to be performed after completing this activity. The Latest Start (LS) of an activity is determined by subtracting the Duration (D) from the Latest Finish (LF) of that activity: LS = LF – D (see Figure 5.05.10).

Subsequently, the total float per activity can be determined and thus also the critical path. The total float per activity is the difference between the latest finish (LF) minus the earliest finish (EF) of that activity in the chart: Float = LF – EF.

The critical path is the chain of activities where the float of each activity is zero. The other activities are on sub-paths. The critical path is indicated in the chart with a thick line. There may be multiple critical paths in a plan.

An alternative way of notation is to record the start of an activity not by the end of the previous day but at the start of the day itself. The implementation of activity A is then: start day 1+ duration of 2 days = finish end of day 2. This corresponds to our normal way of speech but is more difficult to calculate. However, both notations are accepted and are applied.

GANTT CHART

Based on the network diagram, we can then draw up a Gantt chart. A Gantt chart is a graphical depiction showing the duration of activities along a time bar. If necessary, linking arrows between the activities can be included. The float of the individual activities can also be visualised (see Figure 5.05.11). If the sequential relationships between the activities are clear, you can directly draft the Gantt chart and skip the Precedence chart.

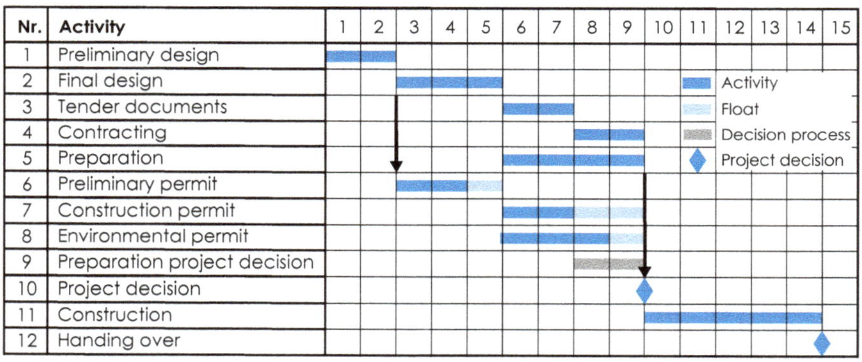

Figure 5.05.11 Example Gantt chart

Decision points

Decision points should also be included in a Gantt chart. Decision points have a theoretical duration of zero (D=0). In practice, however, decision points can cause significant delays because preparing such a decision takes time. Sometimes it is even wise to include the various steps of the decision-making process and the time needed for them in the Gantt chart.

Please note: activities cannot continue over a decision point. New activities cannot start until the relevant decision has been made. Decision points form nodes in a time schedule.

Recording progress

It is easy to visualise progress at successive decision points in a Gantt chart. This can be done by colouring the finished work or drawing progress lines; draw a vertical line down at the control point and move this line forward or backwards if a particular activity, at that moment, is ahead or behind schedule. The advantage of progress lines is that the progress made per period remains visible.

In Figure 5.05.12, at the end of period 4, Activities 2 and 6 are behind schedule. At the end of period 5, Activity 2 is still somewhat behind schedule, and Activities 3 and 5 are ahead of schedule. At the end of period 6, Activity 5 is ahead of schedule and Activity 8 is behind schedule.

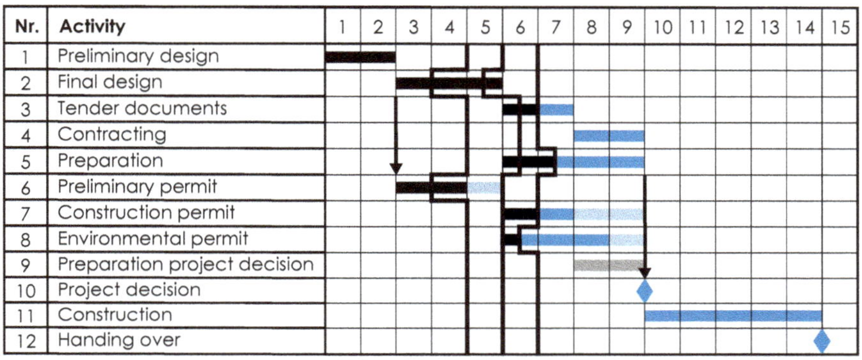

Figure 5.05.12 Example recording progress

SHORTEN THE TIME SCHEDULE

The plan's lead time can be reduced by shortening the duration of the activities on the critical path (crashing) or by partial overlapping of critical activities (fast track).

Crashing

Crashing is the deployment of extra resources on the critical path to shorten the lead time of the total plan. We should do that for those activities on the critical path with the lowest cost and the smallest resource claim per unit of time. Note: shortening the critical path can cause other activities to become critical, creating a new critical path.

Fast track

Fast track is the partial overlapping of critical activities to accelerate progress. Fast track is only possible between activities not separated by a decision point. A fast track can be achieved by starting the next activity based on the preliminary results of the previous activity. Of course, this brings additional risks. Analyse which action will have the most effect with the least risks. With fast track, keep in mind that you may have to adjust the succeeding work once the previous activity is completed.

SUSTAINABILITY

Sustainability challenges the project team to think beyond how things are typically done. Consider CO2-neutral working methods, prefabricated and modular construction methods, et cetera. This offers sustainable advantages and less waste. It also allows for reduced costs, better use of scarce resources, improved working conditions, and use of economy of scale.

However, sustainability goes beyond infrastructure and construction projects and affects all types of projects. Meet online more often, print only when necessary, use public transport, et cetera. Sustainable project management also implies running the project as efficiently as possible, combining work items and building in buffers to accommodate inevitable deviations from the plan without causing inefficient corrections.

TAILORING

At project level, it is advised to use a more traditional planning approach, such as a Gantt chart, and a more Agile approach, such as a task board within timeboxes. For the roadmap, determine the number and size of the teams and the number and duration of the timeboxes. Then determine any releases and go/no-go decision points required by management (stages). Make use of the experience of the developers (empiricism). Within the individual timeboxes, apply planning techniques such as Planning Poker.

RESPONSIBILITIES

Within the project, the project sponsor/project board decides on the staging and decision points to include in the project plan. The project manager advises them in this regard. The project manager is responsible for preparing and controlling the time schedule for the project and the individual stages. The work package leaders are responsible for preparing the team plans for the individual work packages. Time schedules should always be approved by the next higher management level, i.e., the team plans by the project manager and the project plan and stage plans by the project sponsor/project board.

ADVANCED

OTHER SCHEDULING RESTRICTIONS (ADVANCED)

In addition to the traditional finish-start relationship in a Precedence chart, start-start relationships, finish-finish relationships and start-finish relationships can also be applied (see Figure 5.05.13):

- *Start-start relationships* – Activity B can only start after Activity A has commenced. You cannot start serving the dishes before they start plating them in the kitchen.
- *Finish-finish relationships* – Activity B cannot end until Activity A has been completed. You cannot finish clearing the dishes before guests have finished dinner.
- *Start-finish relationships* – Activity B can only be finished once Activity A has commenced. You cannot finish a shift until the next team has arrived.

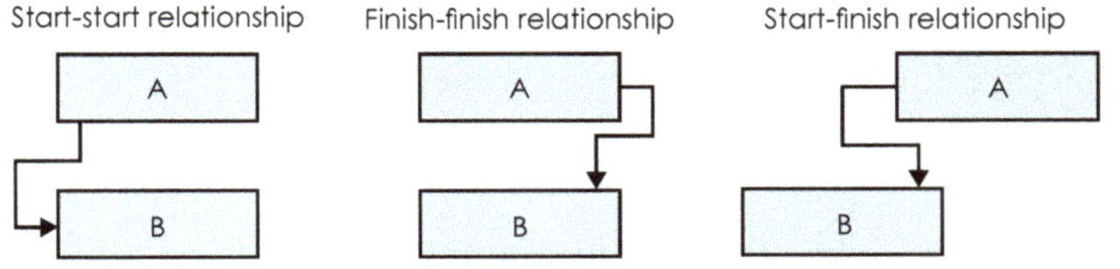

Figure 5.05.13 Other scheduling relationships between activities

Lead and lag

A lead accelerates the successor activity; the successor can start earlier. A lag delays the successor activity, so the successor should start later.

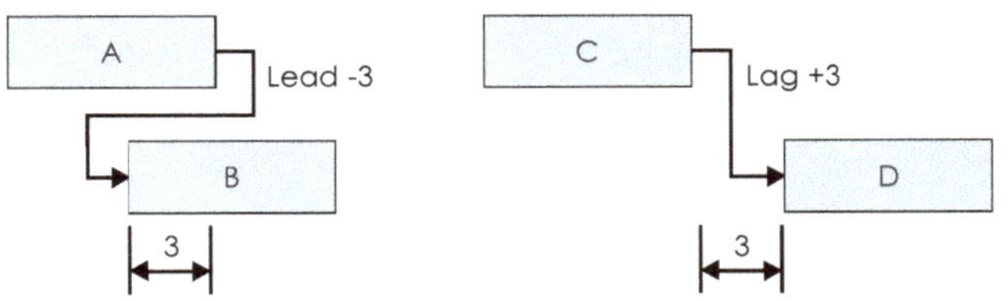

Figure 5.05.14 Lead and lag

In the chart, the lead (-) and the lag (+) duration are noted right next to the connecting arrow. In Figure 5.05.14, Activity B can start 3 weeks before Activity A ends; Activity D can only start 3 weeks after Activity C ends.

Free float

In addition to the total float, there is also a free float:

- The total float of an activity is the time that this activity can be delayed from its earliest start without delaying the plan's completion, assuming that all other activities are implemented according to plan.
- The free float of an activity is the time that this activity can be delayed from its earliest start without delaying the earliest start of any successor activity, assuming that all other activities are implemented according to plan.

When calculating free float, an extended notation block is used, including an identification number and the team responsible (see Figure 5.05.15).

Nr.	Resp.	Duration
Activity		
ES	Total Float	EF
LS	Free Float	LF

Figure 5.05.15 Extended notation activity block.

In Figure 5.05.10, the total float of Activity D is 2 days, but the free float is 0; if Activity D delays, Activity E has to start later. Free float is especially important if different teams perform the various activities in the chart.

Not earlier than

Last but not least, the earliest start dates can be set for individual activities, independent of the earliest finish dates from the predecessors in the chart. These earliest start dates are due to dependencies on other initiatives or constraints set by the sponsoring organisation or customer.

THREE-POINT ESTIMATES (ADVANCED)

In practice, the duration of an activity differs. It may take longer or shorter than usual. However, the probability that the activity will take longer than planned is often much greater than the probability that the activity will take less than planned. The overrun is usually much greater than the time saved if the work is completed more quickly. This results in an asymmetric probability distribution, where the average duration is higher than the most common duration (see Figure 5.05.16). It is, therefore, wise not to plan with the most common duration but to calculate an average duration first and plan accordingly.

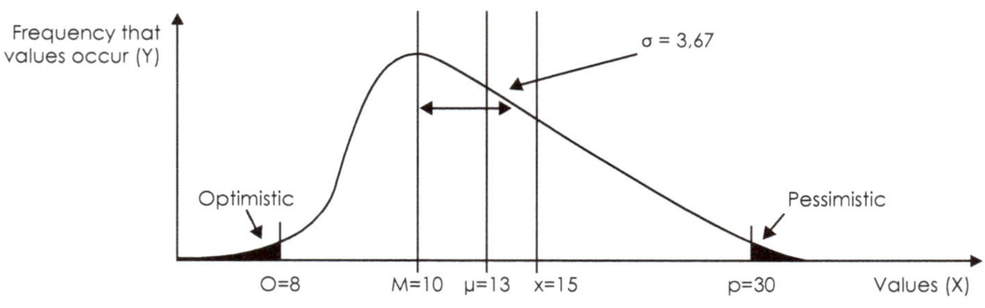

Figure 5.05.16 Asymmetric probability distribution

Average duration

For calculating the critical path, it is important to calculate with the average duration instead of the most common duration (modus). Conforming to the PERT method, the average duration can be calculated with the formula:

$\mu = (O + 4 \times M + P) / 6$

With:
- *μ = Expected or average value.*
- *O = Optimistic value.*
- *M = Most common value (mode).*
- *P = Pessimistic value.*

Whereby:
- Optimistic value – The value which is undercut only in 10% of the situations.
- Pessimistic value – The value which is exceeded only in 10% of the situations

In the example in Figure 5.05.16, the $\mu = (1 \times 8 + 4 \times 10 + 1 \times 30) / 6 = 13$ days.

This technique can be used if sufficient statistical data is available to calculate the necessary key figures, but you can also ask an expert to give a pessimistic, most common and optimistic estimate.

Spread of the duration

The probability that an activity can be completed on time depends not only on the average duration but also on the spread (dispersion) of the duration. The dispersion is the extent to which the current durations deviate from the average duration (see Figure 5.05.17).

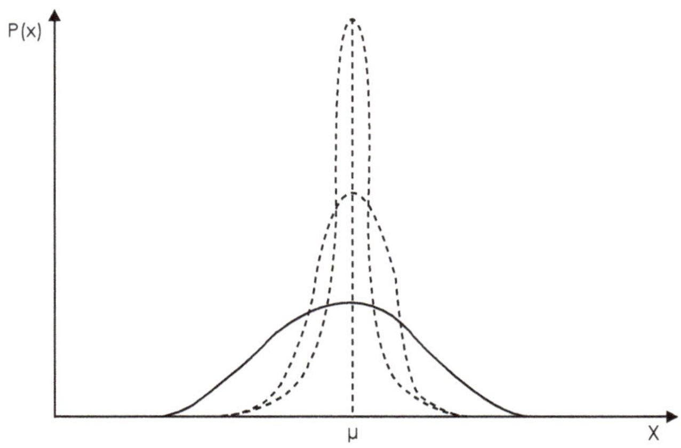

Figure 5.05.17 Different dispersions in a probability distribution

Common measures of statistical dispersion are the standard deviation and the variation. The standard deviation is the distance on the horizontal axe between the average value and the point where the bulge of the probability distribution turns into a cavity (see Figure 5.05.18). The variation is the standard deviation squared.

According to the PERT method, the standard deviation can be calculated by the formula:
$\sigma = (O - P) / 6$

In the example in Figure 5.05.16, the standard deviation is $\sigma = (30 - 8) / 6 = 3.67$.

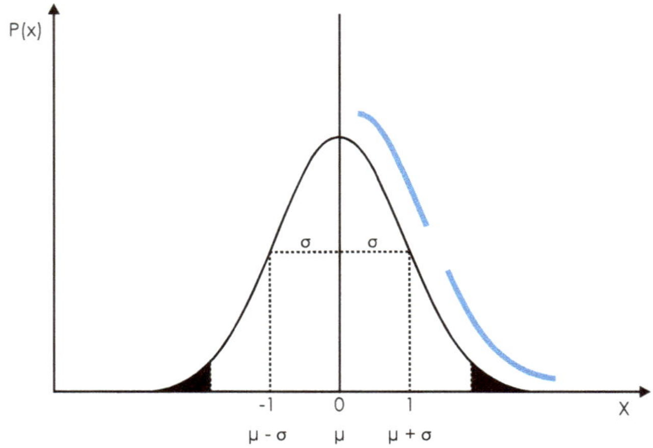

Figure 5.05.18 Average value and standard deviation in a standard probability distribution

Probability to complete an activity on time

The probability of completing an activity within a specific period (X) can now be calculated with the formula:
$Z = (X - \mu) / \sigma$

For the different (positive) Z-values, you can find the probability of completing an activity within a specific period (X) in the attached Z-table. At a negative Z value, the table shows the probability of exceeding (see Table 5.05.03).

The probability that the activity in Figure 5.05.16 lasts less than 15 days:
$Z = (X - \mu) / \sigma = (15 - 13) / 3.67 = 0.545$

According to Table 5.05.03, the probability is about 70.7% that the activity lasts less than 15 days (somewhere between the value 70.54% (Z=0.54) and 70.88% (Z=0.55).

Probability to complete a plan on time

If we want to calculate the probability that a plan can be completed on time, we should, of course, calculate the average duration and the standard deviation of the whole plan first.

The average duration of a plan is just the sum of the average durations of all activities which are on the critical path.

μ total = Σ *μ activities on the critical path*

For the standard deviation of a plan, however, we should first calculate the variance of the individual activities on the critical path. We can then add those values up to the variance of the total plan and then take its square root to calculate the standard deviation of the total plan.

$VAR = \sigma^2$
VAR total = Σ VAR activities on the critical path
σ total = √ VAR total.

Activities A, B, C and D are on the critical path with the average durations and standard deviation below (see Table 5.05.01). How likely is it to complete the project within 38 days?

The average duration of the plan can be calculated by adding the average durations of the individual activities on the critical path together: 10+8+4+12=34.

Var = σ^2

Activity	μ	σ	Var
A	10	4	16
B	8	2	4
C	4	5	25
D	12 +	6	36 +
Plan	34	9	81

$\sigma = \sqrt{\text{Var}}$

Table 5.05.01 Activities critical path

	Second decimal					
Z	**.00**	**.01**	**.02**	**.03**	**.04**	**.05**
0.0	.5000	.5040	.5080	.5120	.5160	.5199
0.1	.5398	.5438	.5478	.5517	.5557	.5596
0.2	.5793	.5832	.5871	.5910	.5948	.5987
0.3	.6179	.6217	.6255	.6293	.6331	.6368
0.4	.6554	.6591	.6628	.6664	.6700	.6736
0.5	.6915	.6950	.6985	.7019	.7054	.7088

Table 5.05.02 Z-table with Z-value 0.44

The standard deviation of the plan can be calculated by calculating the variance of each activity, adding up these values together (81), and then taking the root square of this total (9).

Using the Z-table, it is then possible to calculate the probability that the total plan can be delivered within 38 days: $Z = (X- \mu)/\sigma = (38-34)/9 = 0.44$, i.e., the likelihood that the project can be completed within 38 days is 0.67, or 67% (see Table 5.05.02).

A condition of this calculation is that the dispersion of the various activities on the critical path is independent of each other. If, for example, the probability of exceeding the activities on the critical path depends on one and the same risk, for example, the availability of certain resources, this calculation cannot be used. Then the standard deviation of the total plan is the sum of the standard deviations of the individual activities.

Z	.00	.01	.02	.03	.04	.05	.06	.07	.08	.09
0.0	.5000	-5040	.5080	.5120	.5160	.5199	.5239	.5279	.5319	.5359
0.1	.5398	.5438	.5478	.5517	.5557	.5596	.5636	.5675	.5714	.5753
0.2	.5793	.5832	.5871	.5910	.5948	.5987	.6026	.6064	.6103	.6141
0.3	.6179	.6217	.6255	.6293	.6331	.6368	.6406	.6443	.6480	.6517
0.4	.6554	.6591	.6628	.6664	.6700	.6736	.6772	.6808	.6844	.6879
0.5	.6915	.6950	.6985	.7019	.7054	.7088	.7123	.7157	.7190	.7224
0.6	.7257	.7291	.7324	.7357	.7389	.7422	.7454	.7486	.7517	.7549
0.7	.7580	.76111	.7642	.7673	.7704	.7734	.7764	.7794	.7823	.7852
0.8	.7881	.7910	.7939	.7967	.7995	.8023	.8051	.8078	.8106	.8133
0.9	.8159	.8186	.8212	.8238	.8264	.8289	.8315	.8340	.8365	.8389
1.0	.8413	.8438	.8461	.8485	.8508	.8531	.8554	.8577	.8599	.8621
1.1	.8643	.8665	.8686	.8708	.8729	.8749	.8770	.8790	.8810	.8830
1.2	.8849	.8869	.8888	.8907	.8925	.8944	.8962	.8980	.8997	.9015
1.3	.9032	.9049	.9066	.9082	.9099	.9115	.9131	.9147	.9162	.9177
1.4	.9192	.9207	.9222	.9236	.9251	.9265	.9279	.9292	.9306	.9319
1.5	.9332	.9345	.9357	.9370	.9382	.9394	.9406	.9418	.9429	.9441
1.6	.9452	.9463	.9474	.9484	.9495	.9505	.9515	.9525	.9535	.9545
1.7	.9554	.9564	.9573	.9582	.9591	.9599	.9608	.9616	.9625	.9633
1.8	.9641	.9649	.9656	.9664	.9671	.9678	.9686	.9693	.9699	.9706
1.9	.9713	.9719	.9726	.9732	.9738	.9744	.9750	.9756	.9761	.9767
2.0	.9772	.9778	.9783	.9788	.9793	.9798	.9803	.9808	.9812	.9817
2.1	.9821	.9826	.9830	.9834	.9838	.9842	.9846	.9850	.9854	.9857
2.2	.9861	.9864	.9868	.9871	.9875	.9878	.9881	.9884	.9887	.9890
2.3	9893	.9896	.9898	.9901	.9904	.9906	.9909	.9911	.9913	.9916
2.4	.9918	.9920	.9922	.9925	.9927	.9929	.9931	.9932	.9934	.9936
2.5	.9938	.9940	.9941	.9943	.9945	.9946	.9948	.9949	.9951	.9952
2.6	.9953	.9955	.9956	.9957	.9959	.9960	.9961	.9962	.9963	.9964
2.7	.9965	.9966	.9967	.9968	.9969	.9970	.9971	.9972	.9973	.9974
2.8	.9974	.9975	.9976	.9977	.9977	.9978	.9979	.9979	.9980	.9981
2.9	.9981	.9982	.9982	.9983	.9984	.9984	.9985	.9985	.9986	.9986
3.0	.9987	.9987	.9987	.9988	.9988	.9989	.9989	.9989	.9990	.9990
3.1	.9990	.9991	.9991	.9991	.9992	.9992	.9992	.9992	.9993	.9993
3.2	.9993	.9993	.9994	.9994	.9994	.9994	.9994	.9995	.9995	.9995
3.3	.9995	.9995	.9995	.9996	.9996	.9996	.9996	.9996	.9996	.9997
3.4	.9997	.9997	.9997	.9997	.9997	.9997	.9997	.9997	.9997	.9998
3.5	.9998	.9998	.9998	.9998	.9998	.9998	.9998	.9998	.9998	.9998
3.6	.9998	.9998	.9999	.9999	.9999	.9999	.9999	.9999	.9999	.9999
3.7	.9999	.9999	.9999	.9999	.9999	.9999	.9999	.9999	.9999	.9999
3.8	.9999	.9999	.9999	.9999	.9999	.9999	.9999	.9999	.9999	.9999

Table 5.05.03 Z-table

5.06 RESOURCES

PURPOSE

The purpose of this chapter is to enable the individual to ensure that the resources required are available and assigned as needed in order to meet the objectives.

LEARNING OBJECTIVES

- Manage the resources in a project;
- Different estimation techniques;
- Calculate the gross and the net capacity of the people to be deployed in a project;
- Draft a resource plan;
- Optimise the capacity deployment using levelling; and smoothing;
- Understand the impact of student syndrome, Parkinson's law and multitasking (advanced);
- Apply the critical chain method with project and feeding buffers (advanced).

DEFINITIONS

Resource management: The aspect of management aimed at the identification, analysis, acquisition, planning, deployment, monitoring and adjustment of resources required.
Resource plan: A plan for allocating resources (except money).
Resource-time variance graph: A graph showing planned resources in successive periods.
Resource levelling: The optimisation of allocating resources, which may affect the critical path.
Resource smoothing: The optimisation of allocating resources, without affecting the overall duration of the plan.

INTRODUCTION

Resources include the necessary people, materials and required facilities, services, information, and equipment, as well as the ability to travel, an internet connection, et cetera. Here,' people' include your own people as the personnel of contractors and suppliers. Hereby, it is essential to consider not only the number of people but also the competences needed to carry out the work, both in terms of content and the ability to collaborate (see Chapter 8.03 Teamwork). Although money is also a resource, it is not discussed in this chapter. The competence to manage the finances for the project is discussed separately (see Chapter 5.07 Finance).

POSITIONING

Planning resources actually begins before the project starts and ends only when the project is completed. In the project preparation stage, the plan for the project definition stage is prepared, including the necessary resources to carry out the work in that stage. In the project definition stage, the project plan and the stage plan for the first delivery stage are prepared. During delivery, team plans and, if necessary, exception plans are drawn up. At stage transitions, the stage plan for the next stage is prepared, and the project plan is updated.

For all these plans, each at its own level of detail, the deployment of people and other resources should be planned and agreed upon with the permanent organisation or hired. During delivery, the deployment and availability of people and other resources should be monitored and controlled. At stage transitions and project closure, management thereof should be evaluated, and lessons learned should be implemented or passed on to the appropriate bodies.

RESOURCE MANAGEMENT

Resource management is the management of the available and needed resources in a project and includes the entire control cycle:

- *Plan* – Develop an initial resource plan. Determine the quality and quantity of resources required, identify potential sources of resources, assess the available resources, negotiate the availability of the necessary resources, and optimise their allocation over time.
- *Do* – Ensure that allocated resources are actually made available and distribute them according to the identified need.
- *Check* – Verify that the allocation of resources is still on track, that resources are being applied efficiently and effectively, and that their deployment is producing the planned results.
- *Act* – Take the necessary corrective actions and escalate if the agreed tolerances are likely to be exceeded.

Resource assessment Is the process of gathering information about available resources to meet a specific need. The availability of resources is not evident either in terms of quality or availability. If employees have to be assigned internally, the actual availability can be significantly lower than expected. Hiring of outside staff may be subject to final approval of the required budget.

RESOURCE UTILISATION

Once the required capacity has been established, you can determine how many people you need. Keep in mind:

- The theoretical number of working days per year (which is usually: 52 weeks × 5 days = 260 days)
- The regular number of holidays and public holidays.
- The number of hours team members work on average per week (usually 36 or 40 hours).
- A reduction rate for administrative and operational work, as well as for sickness and special leave.

RESOURCE ALLOCATION

The required resources per time unit can be determined based on the time planning and the estimated productivity. The required resources per time unit per activity is the total required resources for that activity divided by the planned lead time. The necessary total resources per time unit is the sum of all resources needed for that period. The required resources are usually displayed in a resource-time variance graph (see Figure 5.06.01).

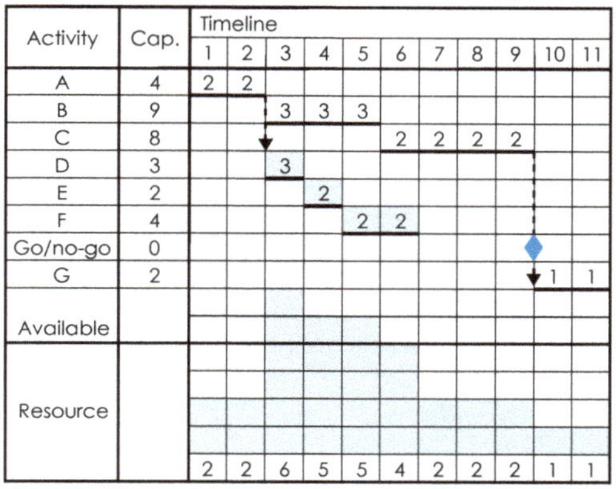

Figure 5.06.01 Resource-time variance graph

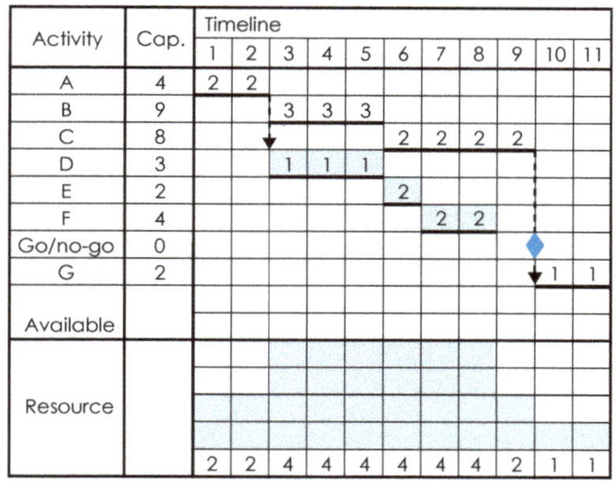

Figure 5.06.02 Resource graph after smoothing

Levelling and smoothing

Levelling is optimising the allocation of resources, which may affect the overall duration of the plan. *Smoothing* is optimising resource allocation without affecting the plan's overall duration. Levelling is applied when an even deployment of resources is critical. Smoothing is applied when the time constraint takes priority. Possible techniques include:

- *Shifting* – Examining whether non-critical activities can be moved without jeopardising the plan's completion date.
- *Splitting* – Splitting non-critical activities to avoid peaks.
- *Stretching* – Increasing the lead time of non-critical activities, reducing the resource demand per time period. This option is applied in Figure 5.06.02.

If these actions do not lead to the desired result, then you need to adjust the scope or postpone the delivery date of the plan. This should always be agreed upon with the project sponsor/project board.

ESTIMATING TECHNIQUES

Known estimation techniques are decomposition, single and multi-expert estimates, equal bet analysis, planning poker, velocity technique, analogous and parametric estimates, and using historical data.

Decomposition

The simplest method to improve estimating is to divide the work into smaller units, each of which is easier to estimate. This can be done using the WBS or PBS that has already been set up. These smaller units may also occur more frequently in the project, so the estimates can become more and more accurate as the project progresses.

Single expert estimates (three-point estimates)

Of course, you can also ask an expert. But is their estimate positive, neutral or negative? That makes quite a difference. Therefore, it is better to ask them explicitly for a positive, a negative and a most frequent value and then take a weighted average of these three estimates. Such a weighted average is important because negative values are often more extreme than positive values. A well-known calculation rule for this is the PERT analysis (see Chapter 5.05 Time).

Equal bet analysis

The term 'equal bet' comes from the gambling world, whereby a bookmaker does not bet on a particular outcome but only makes money from the commission paid by the gamblers to bet. In making estimates, an 'equal bet' is an estimate in which the involved parties see an equal advantage and disadvantage if the outcome is higher or lower than the estimate. With this estimate, the probability of over- or underperformance is not only considered but also the impact of the over- or underperformance in question. This is actually a further refinement of the three-point analysis. Not only do you include the positive and negative values, but also the impact that these values have on the project.

Multi-expert estimate

Another approach is the multi-expert approach. Instead of asking one expert, you ask the opinion of several experts. You can do this in an open conversation in the hope of reaching a joint understanding. This is often very time-consuming and far from successful. Therefore, a more structured approach is usually chosen. This consists of at least two rounds. After explaining the works to be done, there is a first round in which everyone makes the first estimate. The individual with the lowest and the highest estimate explains their estimate. The others may ask questions. This is followed by a second round. In the short version, the average of all estimates in the second round is taken as the final estimate. In the extended version, several rounds are made until all estimates are equal. This rarely works in practice, as the experts' estimates rarely become entirely equal. All estimates should be made independently. You can arrange this by having all participants record their estimates first, after which they are all revealed simultaneously.

Delphi analysis

In a multi-expert estimate, if you are afraid that a specific expert will be a dominant factor, it is best to use the Delphi method. This is basically a standard multi-expert method with the difference that the participants cannot see and hear each other. Information is exchanged only in writing or online. This forces the participants to react to the content of the others' comments without being able to consider the status of the individual who made the estimate or comment.

Group planning

This is a variation of the multi-expert technique. Here, it is not a team of experts requested to make an estimate but the project team itself. This may seem strange because some team members will do entirely different work, but this is usually not a problem. Team members are generally quite capable of estimating the duration of colleagues' work because they have often worked on projects where similar work has been done. This way of estimating usually works well as long as the estimates are made independently.

Velocity technique

In the velocity technique, work is not estimated in values but relative to each other. For example, in Agile, user stories are estimated in story points, where a story point is the amount of work needed to develop a simple user story that counts as a reference value. All other user stories are estimated relative to this reference value. Often, a fixed set of multipliers is used. In the T-shirt multiplier, values are classified into XS, S, M, L, XL and XXL relative to the reference value (S).

If the team knows how many story points they can develop per timebox, they can estimate the work they can do in a timebox. The reference value may vary from team to team and assignment to assignment, as well as the number of story points a team can develop per timebox. Usually, the team's velocity improves as the project progresses. The velocity technique is also used outside Agile. In those situations, the reference value is linked to the time and cost required to achieve such a reference value.

Planning Poker

This combines group planning and a velocity technique whereby a derived Fibonacci sequence is used as a fixed set of multipliers (see Figure 5.06.03). Since, like the regular multi-expert method, all values should be revealed at once, this approach is called Planning Poker, where the cards are not initially revealed either. Planning Poker is widely used in the Agile world. This technique has many variants but also a registered version. There is even a deck of cards and an app for this available.

Figure 5.06.03 Derivative Fibonacci sequence used in the registered version of Planning Poker

Analogous estimates

Analogous estimates use information from similar previous projects (top-down). For example, what did the previously built hospital cost per bed? What did a comparable house cost per m2? Analogical estimation is used when only a limited amount of information is available, usually during a feasibility study in the pre-project stage.

Parametric estimates

In parametric estimation, parameters are applied to work clusters (an approach between top-down and bottom-up). This technique is widely used. Parametric estimates have been developed for a wide range of work, such as building dormers, making drawings, drafting a requirement specification, and so on. Function point analysis in software development is also a form of parametric estimation.

Historical data

Many estimates are made based on experience gained over time. You can build this data yourself, or you can store it in a shared database. In doing so, it is important first to eliminate previous wastage and to record the circumstances under which the work was carried out. Some companies have built up very detailed post-calculation databases. These organisations can make very accurate estimates for the work to be carried out.

SUSTAINABILITY

The selection of resources should consider the price/quality ratio AND the sustainability impact of the materials used both during the project delivery and the use and eventual demolition of the project deliverables. Where are the materials coming from? Herewith, the whole supply chain of the materials should be considered. For the latter, the materials' potential reusability and recyclability should be taken into account. Special emphasis should be given to the use of hazardous substances, prevention of pollution, and energy consumption.

Another aspect is the deployment of people in the project. In particular, fair wages, workload, and working conditions are important, but social considerations such as cultural differences, equal treatment, inclusiveness, equal opportunities, and personal development also deserve attention. Aspects such as commuting distance, digital/hybrid work opportunities and work-life balance should also be considered.

TAILORING

Resource management includes planning and deploying people in the project and the necessary equipment and facilities, such as a test and user environment. The latter is for users to experiment with using the delivered products. This should be arranged well in advance, preferably in the definition stage, to avoid delays and frustrations.

Furthermore, stick to small teams, preferably no larger than nine people. This prevents the formation of subgroups within teams. If more team members are needed, splitting them into several teams is better. Ensure a good mix of disciplines and experience within the teams. Keep the teams stable. Avoid adding new team members to avoid peak loads. This is often counterproductive (see Chapter 8.03 Teams).

RESPONSIBILITIES

The project manager is responsible for managing the resources at project and stage level. The work package leaders are responsible for managing the resources within their respective work packages. The user and supplier representatives should ensure the required user and supplier resources are made available. The project sponsor is accountable for the availability of the necessary resources for the entire project.

ADVANCED

CRITICAL CHAIN METHOD (ADVANCED)

Theory Of Constraints (TOC) is a management philosophy developed in 1985 by E.M. Goldratt. This philosophy focuses on production units. As a follow-up to the TOC, Goldratt developed the *Critical Chain Method* in 1997. Goldratt defined a critical chain as the longest chain of activities in a plan, given the planned lead times, dependencies and required and available resources. The critical chain differs from the critical path in this respect. The critical path is not based on required and available resources, while the critical chain is.

The Critical Chain Method seeks to address the many project time overruns that occur despite the extensive planning that has been done. Together with the TOC, the critical chain method forms a holistic approach to project management that provides an effective risk-orientated focus for planning and monitoring the project, managing people and resources, and minimising dependencies between projects.

Hidden reserves

When professionals have to give an estimate of how long work will take, they usually claim more time than they need. They know that many things can go wrong and consider this when they give an estimate because they are held to their estimates.

Human behaviour

Goldratt further noted that based on normal critical path time planning, work is hardly ever delivered ahead of schedule. People tend to start work only when it has become critical (*student syndrome*). And people tend to prolong their work if they have too much time (*Parkinson's Law*). Moreover, in the regular approach, there is no incentive to finish earlier than planned.

Creating joint buffers

To overcome this, a network diagram is first drawn up based on non-conservative estimates of the duration of activities. Then the availability of the required capacities is added. Finally, buffers are added per chain of activities. This replaces the hidden reserves in individual activities with a joint reserve per chain of activities. Instead of managing the start and end dates of the individual activities, the critical chain method focuses on managing the buffers and the deployed capacity.

Start non-critical activities as late as possible

Whereas the critical path method aims to start all activities *As Soon As Possible* (ASAP), the critical chain method aims to start implementing non-critical activities *As Late As Possible* (ALAP). In this way:

- Maximum attention can be focused on the critical activities at the start;
- The work can mostly be carried out without interruptions;
- Fewer adjustments need to be made due to increased knowledge and insight;
- Expenses are made only when necessary.

No multitasking

Work in most projects is carried out in a multi-project environment. This means that most team members work on several tasks simultaneously. However effective this may seem, it is not. In the *Critical Chain Method*, the next task only starts after the previous task has been fully completed. Constantly changing tasks takes extra time, there is a higher probability of making mistakes, and working on several tasks simultaneously ensures more tasks are completed later than when you complete one task first before starting on a new one.

In the example on the left in Figure 5.06.04, five different tasks are worked on each week. In this situation, the tasks are completed on days 11, 12, 13, 14 and 15. The same tasks are completed without multitasking on days 3, 6, 9, 12 and 15.

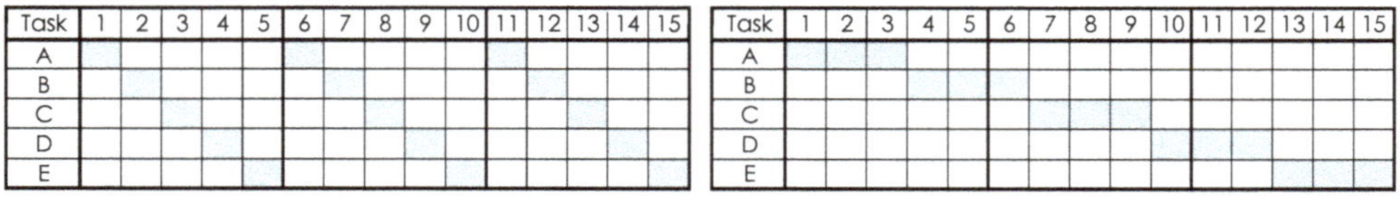

Figure 5.06.04 Example multitasking

Planning with non-conservative estimates

Since, in the traditional approach, work package leaders have to guarantee the turnaround times they issue, each task contains a margin to accommodate the uncertainty of performing that activity. These margins are often of the same order as the duration of the activity itself. Agreeing on a ten-day lead time for a five-day activity is common.

Therefore, Goldratt uses non-conservative estimates that are half of the normal estimates given by team members under the conditions that:

- All necessary information is available;
- The work can be done without interruption;
- No surprises occur or changes take place.

This is often made possible by starting as late as possible and not multitasking.

Setting up project and supply buffers

A buffer is added at the end of each chain of activities:

- Project buffer – A buffer at the end of the critical chain of activities;
- Supply buffer – A buffer at the end of each non-critical chain of activities.

Each buffer is equal to 50% of the total duration of that chain, based on the non-conservative estimates. Assuming that a non-conservative estimate of activities is only 50% of the usual conservative estimate, the lead time of each chain of activities within the Critical Chain Method plus buffer is only 75% of the duration of that same chain of activities in traditional planning:

- The initial conservative estimate is 100%.
- The non-conservative estimate is 50%.
- The buffer is 50% of the non-conservative estimate or 50% × 50% = 25% of the initial estimate.
- The non-conservative estimate plus buffer is 50% + 25% = 75% of the initial estimate.
- The time saved in respect of the initial conservative estimate: 100 – 75 = 25%.

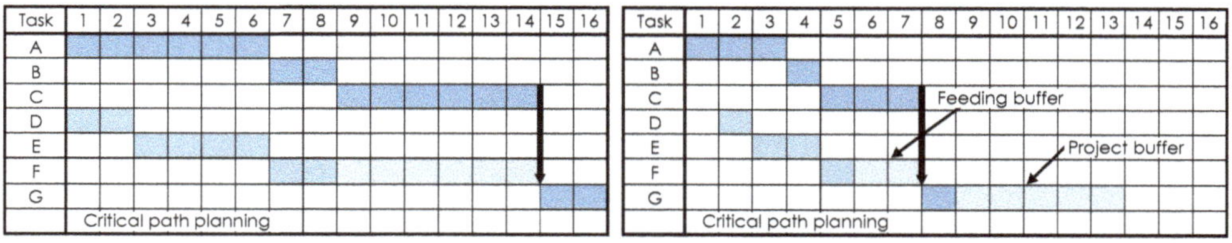

Figure 5.06.05 Critical chain versus critical path method

Hereby, the activities on the critical chain start as soon as possible and the activities on the non-critical chain start as late as possible. This ensures that non-critical activities in the Critical Chain Method can usually start later than in the Critical Path Method, even with this shorter lead time (see Figure 5.06.05).

Relay approach to delivery

Normally, work is carried out and followed up like a railway timetable, based on planned start and finish dates. In the Critical Chain Method, however, work is carried out based on a relay approach. Each subsequent activity starts as soon as the previous one is finished. This principle is very challenging and also requires each team to keep the next team informed of their progress.

Management of buffers

Within the Critical Chain Method, monitoring the project and supply buffers is the key to progress control. Instead of monitoring the individual activities against planned start and finish dates, each chain of activities is only monitored to what extent the respective buffer is decreasing or increasing. Each buffer is divided into three zones: green, amber and red (see Figure 5.06.06).

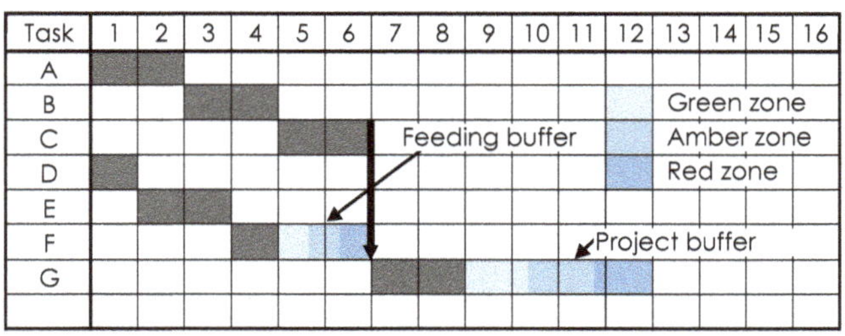

Figure 5.06.06 Management of buffers in critical chain method

If the foreseen completion date of a chain of activities falls in the:

- Green zone – No actions are necessary.
- Amber zone – The situation is assessed, and possible corrective actions are planned.
- Red zone – The planned corrective actions are carried out.

5.07 FINANCE

PURPOSE

The purpose of this chapter is to enable the individual to ensure that enough financial resources are provided to the project at any time, that the financial targets of the project can be met and the financial status is monitored, reported, and properly used for adequate management of financial resources.

LEARNING OBJECTIVES

- Cost estimating, budgeting and cost control of a project;
- Cost breakdown structure (CBS) with cost objects, cost items and cost categories;
- Reserves and margins;
- Reporting standards;
- Power of attorney;
- The link between project and business accounting;
- The link between WBS, CBS and OBS (advanced);
- Financial control and cash flow planning (advanced);
- The various forms of project financing (advanced).

DEFINITIONS

Cost estimating: Forecasting financial resources needed for a particular purpose.
Budgeting: Allocating financial resources to a particular purpose.
Cost control: Controlling expenditures and outstanding financial obligations against the available budget.
Project accounting: The extra compatible accounts to be kept by the project in addition to the business accounting.
Cost breakdown structure: A hierarchical cost breakdown into cost objects, items, and categories.
Management reserve: A reserve for unforeseen issues and risks (unknown unknowns).
Contingency reserve: A reserve for foreseen issues and risks (known unknowns).

INTRODUCTION

Money is often one of the most important control aspects of a project. Sponsoring organisations and customers often have a funding limit. Suppliers often have fixed-price contracts. That makes budgeting and cost control key aspects of managing projects(see Chapter 6.04 Control and Reporting).

POSITIONING

Costs and finances play an important role throughout the project lifecycle and even before. In the feasibility study, a first estimate of the project costs is made. In the project preparation stage, this estimate is refined, and a budget is also prepared for the project definition stage. In the project definition stage, the budget and, if necessary, a cash flow plan are prepared for the project, and a detailed budget is prepared for the first delivery stage. The project accounting is set up during the project definition stage or, at the latest, at the start of the first delivery stage.

During delivery, costs and finances are monitored, and budgets are prepared for additional work. At stage transitions, costs incurred to date are evaluated, the budget and the funding required for the remainder of the project are updated, and a detailed budget is prepared for the next stage. At stage transitions and project closure, budgeting and cost control are evaluated, and, if possible, post-calculation data is generated.

ESTIMATING, BUDGETING AND COST CONTROL

When managing costs, a distinction is made between cost estimating, budgeting and cost control.

Cost estimating

Cost estimating is forecasting financial resources needed for a particular purpose.

In cost estimating, the following steps can be distinguished:

- Make an inventory of the cost objects, cost items and cost categories;
- Determine the quantities to produce and to be used;
- Determine the costs of the cost items, including charges and margins;
- Determine the relevant cost trends;
- Conduct a risk analysis and agree on the level of uncertainty;
- Include a reservation for miscellaneous and foreseen and unforeseen expenses;
- Determine the total cost price and record the assumptions made;
- Schedule the costs in time.

In finance, a charge is a pass-through of indirect costs, such as overhead and general office costs. A margin is a provision to cover inaccuracies in the estimates. A reserve is a reservation set aside to cover additional costs.

Preparing a cost estimate is not easy. At the stage when information is still scarce, we have to make the most important decisions (see Figure 5.07.01). Involve team members and subject matter experts. Use historical data. Don't lose yourself in the details at the beginning because much is still unknown, but make sure you cover the whole scope. And don't forget to include charges, margins and reservations.

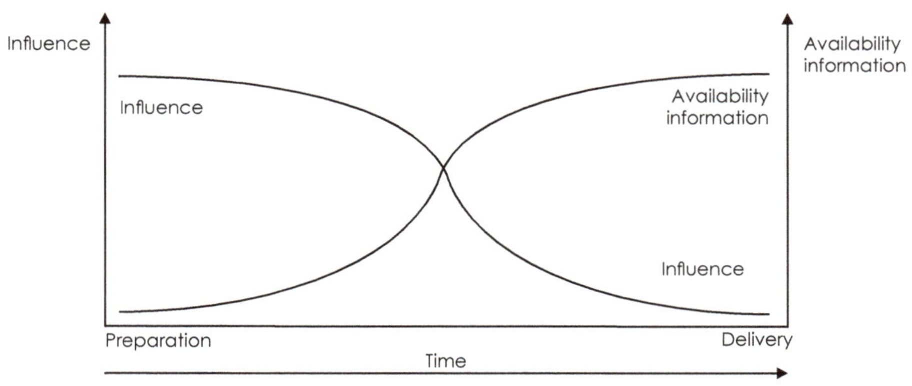

Figure 5.07.01 Influence and availability of information in time

Budgeting

Budgeting is allocating financial resources to a particular purpose. The budget can equal the cost estimate but does not have to; it can be more or less. In the latter case, a shortfall is built in, and the project management team has a challenge in advance.

In budgeting, the following steps can be distinguished:

- Allocate budgets to the defined budget items, including charges and margins;
- Allocate budgets to the individual budget holders;
- Include a budget for miscellaneous and unforeseen expenses;
- Include a risk budget and a change budget, if applicable;
- Determine the overall budget and record starting points made;
- Agree on tolerances (for both over- and underruns).

A budget can have the same structure as the cost estimate but does not have to. A budget should first be subdivided into individual work packages and then subdivided into various cost objects and cost items. This can make it necessary to reallocate cost objects and cost items. For example, if, for some cost objects, certain cost items are taken care of by one team or supplier and other cost items are taken care of by another team or supplier.

The budget should also be condensed to allow for meaningful cost control. While a cost estimate can be hundreds of pages long, the budget breakdown is often much smaller. If you only want to control a budget at the level of a responsible department or contractor, it makes no sense to break down the budget at that level further (see *Sub-projects* in Chapter 4.02, Scope). That level is also where you receive the invoices from contractors and or internal departments.

Cost control

Cost control is controlling expenditures and outstanding financial obligations against the available budget. Cost control also includes determining the necessary funds to implement change requests, taking corrective measures where necessary, and escalating in case it is forecasted that the agreed cost tolerances will be exceeded.

In cost control, the following steps can be distinguished:

- Check expenditures and contracts against the available budget;
- Measure the actual expenditures and outstanding financial obligations;
- Determine the necessary funds for implementing change requests;
- Estimate the expected costs to complete;
- Compare the expected cost at completion with the available budget;
- Take corrective measures where necessary;
- Escalate in case the agreed cost tolerances are forecasted to be exceeded.

COST BREAKDOWN STRUCTURE

The *Cost Breakdown Structure* (CBS) can be set up based on the WBS. The CBS defines relevant cost items and associated cost categories for each cost object (see Figure 5.07.02).

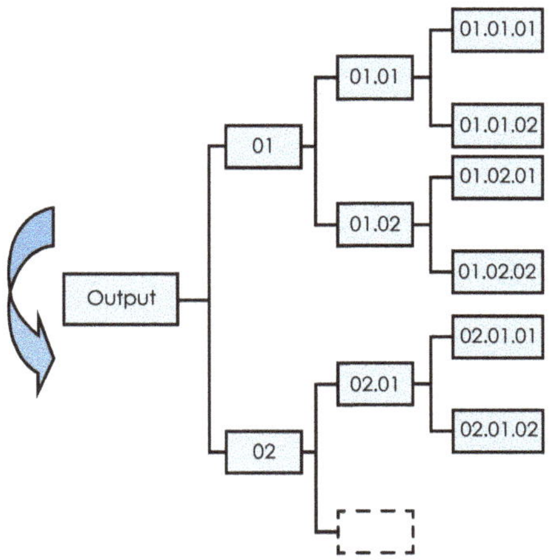

Cost Breakdown Structure (CBS)				
Cost objects	Cost cat.			
	Cost category	Cost category	Cost category	....
01. Main category				
01.01 Subcategory				
01.01.01 Cost item				
01.01.02 Cost item				
....				
01.02 Subcategory				
01.02.01 Cost item				
01.02.02 Cost item				
....				
02.Main category				
02.01 Subcategory				
02.01.01 Cost item				
02.01.02 Cost item				
....				
Contingencies				
Total				

Figure 5.07.02 Link between CBS and WBS

A cost object is a financial term used in management accounting that represents any object for which costs are separately allocated and controlled. Cost items are the various expenditures to realise a cost object. Cost categories are the different types of resources used to realise the cost objects, such as manhours, materials, and contractors (see Figure 5.07.03).

Cost Breakdown Structure				
Cost objects	Cost cat.			
	Cost category	Cost category	Cost category	....
01. Main category				
01.01 Subcategory				
01.01.01 Cost item				
01.01.02 Cost item				
....				
01.02 Subcategory				
01.02.01 Cost item				
01.02.02 Cost item				
....				
02. Main category				
02.01 Subcategory				
02.01.01 Cost item				
02.01.02 Cost item				
....				
Contingencies				
Total				

Cost Breakdown Structure				
Cost objects	Cost cat.			
	Manhours	Materials	Contractors	....
01. Office building				
01.01 Structural				
01.01.01 Window frames				
01.01.02 Masoning				
....				
01.02 Interior				
01.02.01 Plastering				
01.02.02 Paintwork				
....				
02. Infrastructure				
02.01 Pavement				
02.01.01 Earthwork				
02.01.02 Asphalt				
....				
Contingencies				
Total				

Figure 5.07.03 Example cost breakdown

RESERVES AND MARGINS

In finance, a reserve is money set aside to cover additional costs. Reserves can be differentiated into contingency and management reserves. A management reserve is a reservation for unforeseen issues and risks (unknown unknowns). A contingency reserve is a reservation for foreseen issues and risks (known unknowns). Examples of a management reserve are the budget for miscellaneous and unforeseen expenses and a change budget. An example of a contingency reserve is a risk budget

A project budget may include a change budget, a risk budget and a budget for miscellaneous and unforeseen expenses. This is independent of the margins included in the individual cost estimates. (see Figure 5.07.04).

The project sponsor is responsible for the overall project budget. The project manager is responsible for the operational project budget. The project manager cannot spend change and risk budgets without the prior approval of the change authority and or the project sponsor.

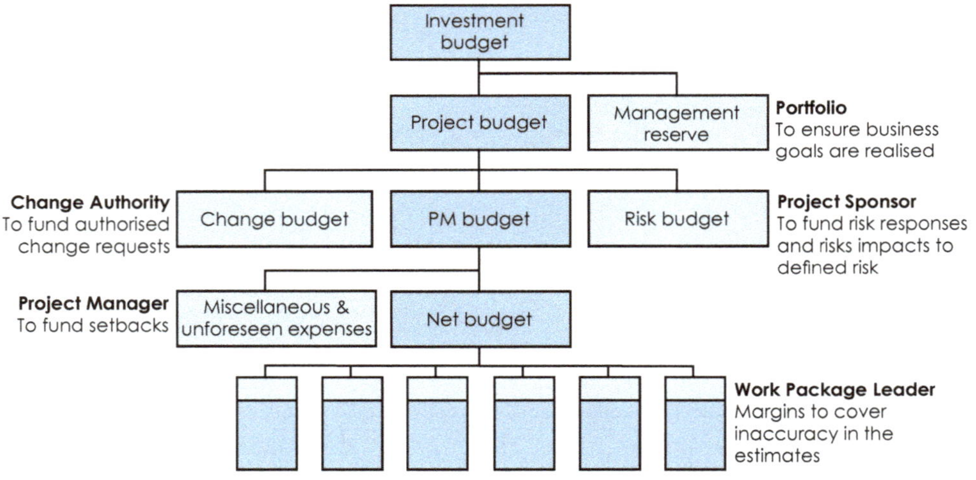

Figure 5.07.04 Budget breakdown

A breakdown into multiple reserves is preferable to one joint reserve. With one joint reserve, parties often want to secure 'their' share, which is why such a reserve is usually used earlier and more often than when each party has its own reserve.

Margins

A margin is a provision to cover inaccuracy in the estimates. Normally, the margins are included in the cost estimates of the individual cost items and not separately budgeted. The margin of uncertainty can differ per cost item and per project. However, a 10% add-on to the net cost estimate is usually used.

Reserve for miscellaneous and unforeseen expenses

The reserve for miscellaneous and unforeseen expenses reduces in the successive stages as we better understand the work to be done. At stage transitions, the unused portion of the previous stage's reserve can be released in the next stage plan (see Figure 5.07.05).

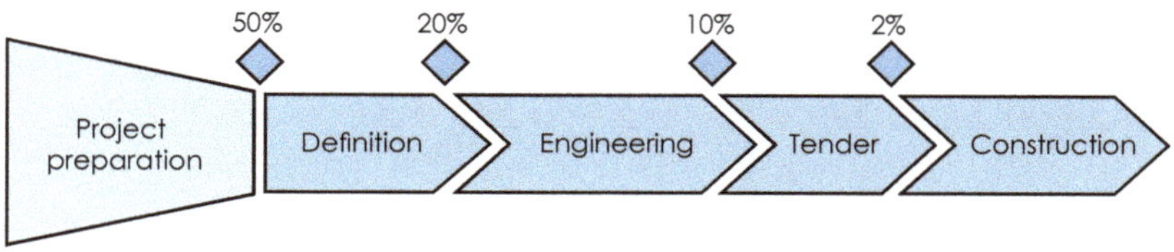

Figure 5.07.05 Possible decrease reserves during project lifecycle

Risk budget

A risk budget is a reserve for identified risks, such as the risks of contaminated soil, whether or not a permit will be received on time, or possible cost increases due to inflation.

It is advisable to include these reserves separately in the budget. This may explain why the budget is higher than foreseen. By allocating the risk budgets directly to the individual teams, there is a risk that these budgets will be used regardless of whether the risk occurs. Risk budgets should fall under the project sponsor's responsibility, as depicted in Figure 5.07.04.

The reservation for cost increases due to inflation deserves particular attention. A forecast is usually based on the actual price level, and funds are made available accordingly. If, during the course of the project, the project faces (much) higher costs due to price increases, it always leads to much fuss because additional funds have to be acquired. Stating that the forecast was based on the price level at that time does not help.

Change budget

This budget is intended to finance approved change requests. If there is no separate change budget, the changes are usually paid for from the budget for miscellaneous and unforeseen expenses, which is undesirable. It tempts users to implement changes as quickly and as much as possible to make maximum use of this budget. When the implementation is finally in full swing, and this budget is needed, there is often no more budget left. It is, therefore, better to give the users a separate change budget from which they should finance desired changes. A separate change budget also creates a psychological buffer to limit the number of change requests.

An alternative is, of course, to apply the exchange principle for changes. New functionalities are added only when less important ones are dropped (see Chapter 6.02 Change Control). However, this is not always possible.

Tolerances

Please note that tolerances are not reserves, and reserves are not tolerances. Tolerance is a permissible deviation above or below the plan's target without having to escalate the deviation to the next management level. Tolerances can be positive AND negative. You should also escalate to the next management level if you don't need the total budget. They need to be informed. With that extra budget, the sponsoring organisation or customer can start new initiatives.

A reserve is a budget. Tolerance is the mandate within which you can decide. Usually, the tolerance is smaller than the reserve. You need to inform the project sponsor before the total reserve is exhausted. Otherwise, they can no longer act effectively.

COST AND BUDGET CONTROL

A cost reporting standard is a tool to control and report on costs. Well-known methods are *variance analysis* and earned *value analyses* (see Advanced, Chapter 6.04, Control and Reporting). In the variance analysis, both the budget and costs can be controlled (see Figure 5.07.06).

Cost and Budget Control										
Budget items	Budget				Costs					
	Original budget	Approved budget	Approved RFCs	Current budget	Spent	Outstanding obligations	Free budget	Estimate to complete	Estimate at completion	Balance
Cost carrier 1										
Cost carrier 1.1	O	A	B	C=A+B	D	E	F=C-D-E	G	H=D+E+G	K=C-H
Cost carrier 1.2										
Cost carrier 2										
Cost carrier 2.1										
Cost carrier 2.2										
Contingency										
Total										

Figure 5.07.06 Cost and budget control

In the left half of the figure, the development of the budget is controlled:
O. Original approved budget at the end of the project definition stage;
A. Approved budget at the last stage transition;
B. Approved change requests (RFCs) in the current stage;
C. Current available budget (C = A + B).

In the right half of the figure, the development of the costs is controlled:
D. Costs spent so far;
E. Outstanding work subcontracted;
F. Free budget still available (F = C – D – E);
G. Expected cost to complete;
H. Expected cost at completion (H = D + E + G);
K. Balance: the difference between the budget and the expected cost at completion (K = C – H).

If required, additional columns can be included on the cost control side to control cost at completion within the current stage or the current fiscal year.

Budget control or reporting should be carried out periodically. Usually, the project manager receives the current expenditures from the controller, the outstanding financial obligations from Finance, the actual data from project support and the forecasts from the sub-project managers and work package leaders. However, the project manager remains responsible for accurate and timely cost and budget control.

PROJECT AND BUSINESS ACCOUNTING

Project accounting is the extra compatible accounts to be kept by the project in addition to the business accounting. The project accounting is responsible for the following:

- Managing the budget based on the initial budget plus approved change requests;
- Managing expenses, outstanding commitments and forecasts versus the last approved budget.

Business accounting usually records the available budget, expenses, commitments, invoices and payments. Furthermore, it controls the commitments and expenses versus budget, the invoices versus the commitments, and the payments versus the invoices. It also makes the actual payments (see Figure 5.07.07). Before these payments can be made, the project manager should approve the invoices first.

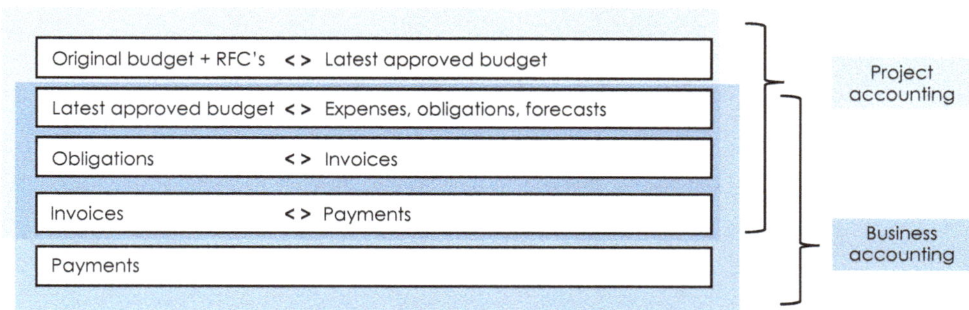

Figure 5.07.07 Project and business accounting

POWER OF ATTORNEY

A *power of attorney* is the legal authorisation that gives an individual the authority to enter into financial commitments for another individual or company. A power of attorney can be registered with the Chamber of Commerce. However, a power of attorney can also be issued by means of a signed statement from someone who already has a power of attorney. A power of attorney should describe the acts to which it applies.

It is best to include the power of attorney of all responsible individuals in the project directly in the agreements to be concluded. As a project manager, you are usually only allowed to make appointments within the agreement but not to agree on additional work and make payments. Usually, this is not a problem. You just need to consider the extra procedural steps required. This is also an extra built-in check to avoid errors.

SUSTAINABILITY

The lifecycle orientation of sustainability implies that cost estimation should consider not only the direct investment but also the total cost of ownership of the project deliverables. In addition, costs should be regarded as part of the more comprehensive multi-criteria assessment based on the *Triple Bottom Line* concept. Finally, non-financial costs should also be examined, especially regarding the environmental and social aspects.

TAILORING

To calculate the costs per timebox, multiply the team member's rate by the total weekly working hours. Then multiply this by the number of weeks in a timebox. Since Agile projects usually work with fixed teams, a fixed burn rate can be maintained for the project's duration, in addition to the cost of materials, equipment, licences and facilities needed. Usually, the latter are one-offs and do not need to be recalculated for each timebox. Since project costs are usually directly related to lead time, cost tolerances can also be set to zero.

RESPONSIBILITIES

The project sponsor is accountable for the project budget and for obtaining the necessary funds for the project. The project manager is responsible for preparing the project budget and for the budget and cost control of the project and the respective stages. The work package leaders are responsible for the estimating and cost control of the respective work packages. Project support should assist the project manager in collecting up-to-date data and forecasts. A separate project controller will often assist the project manager in setting up the financial project administration and with cost and budget control.

ADVANCED

LINKING WBS AND CBS WITH THE OBS (ADVANCED)

The WBS and the CBS can be linked to the organisation via the *Organisation Breakdown Structure* (OBS) and a *Responsibility Assignment Matrix* (RAM). The OBS is a hierarchical breakdown of the project organisation. The OBS is derived from the project organisation chart. The OBS lists the various work package leaders and sub-project leaders. The RAM then visualises which work package leader and sub-project manager is responsible for which work package and sub-project (see Figure 5.07.08). Using RAM makes it easy to see who is delivering which product or service in the project. The RAM is the basis for the project control at the subsequent management levels within the project.

RAM New Office	Work Breakdown Structure							
	Building				Infrastructure			
	Construct		Finishing		Road		Garden	
Organisation Breakdown Structure	1.1.1 Windows	1.1.2 Brickwork	1.2.1 Plastering	1.2.2 Paintwork	2.1.1 Earthwork road	2.1.2 Roadwork	2.2.1 Earthwork garden	2.2.2 Landscaping
Maison		■						
Carpenter	■							
Painter			■	■				
Earth worker					■	■	■	
Gardener								■

Figure 5.07.08 Example Responsibility Assignment Matrix

FINANCIAL CONTROL & CASH FLOW PLANNING (ADVANCED)

Financial control includes planning, monitoring and optimising the required financial resources over time. A cash flow plan is set up to plan and control the necessary financial funds. The income and expenses are plotted over time with a correction due to the applicable invoicing and payment terms. Down payments and interest payments should also be included. In some organisations, the negative cash balance is charged with an internal interest by the corporate organisation. For convenience's sake, this is often 0.5% per month or 6% per year.

Even projects with positive revenues can run into cash flow problems. This is usually due to delayed payment from the client and direct payments to be made for wages and purchases. Clients can usually be sent invoices for work performed only monthly in arrears. The final payment is typically another month later because there is usually a 30-day payment period. This means that payments for work done are ultimately received two months later, while salaries and supplies are generally payable in the same month (see Figure 5.07.09). With a return of 30%, this project still runs into serious cash flow problems. A possible measure is to agree on a down payment (see Chapter 6.01 Procurement).

Calendar	Jan	Feb	March	April	May	June	July	Aug	Sept
Progress	10	30	40	40	30	20	10		
Invoice send		10	30	40	40	30	20	10	
Bank receipts			10	30	40	40	30	20	10
Wages	-5	-15	-20	-20	-15	-10	-5	0	0
Payments	-2	-6	-8	-8	-6	-4	-2	0	0
Cash flow	-7	-21	-18	2	19	26	23	20	10
Cumulative cash flow	-7	-28	-46	-44	-25	1	24	44	54

Figure 5.07.09 Example of cash flow planning

PROJECT FINANCING (ADVANCED)

A project can be financed both internally and externally.

Internal financing

Internal financing occurs when management decides to use part of its profits to fund a new investment. A distinction can be made between funding by the central organisation (central financing), by one or more operating companies (decentralised financing), or a combination of both (hybrid financing).

External financing

Concerning external financing, a distinction is made between risk-bearing and non-risk-bearing financing. Risk-bearing forms are shares, bonds and, for example, subordinated loans and crowdfunding. In the case of non-risk-bearing financing, there is always some form of collateral:

- *(Bank) loan* – An individual or company that serves as collateral. For people, this is often based on their salary and, for companies, on the expected revenues. Before a loan is granted, banks usually assess the company's cash flow, solvency, and profitability.
- Mortgage – A fixed asset that serves as collateral. This may be a house or office, but also movable means of production.
- *Assignment of claims* – The transfer of claims to a lender by an act of assignment. This gives the lender the right to collect these receivables.
- *Pledge* – A collateral security that encumbers a movable item or claim. The right of pledge is established in order to receive the sales price of that movable or claim in priority in the event of bankruptcy.

Reduction of external financing needs

An attempt can also be made to reduce one's own financing needs. Well-known forms of this are factoring and leasing. They are usually also considered as a form of financing.

Factoring – A factoring company takes over the collection of receivables against a certain fee. This saves a lot of paperwork but usually also ensures that the total of outstanding receivables is often much lower than when they try to collect the outstanding receivables themselves. This increases the company's available resources and decreases the company's financing needs.

Leasing – Renting movable or immovable properties from third parties via specific financial constructions. In the case of a lease construction, the positions change: the sponsoring organisation becomes the user representative, and the lease company is the new sponsoring organisation. A distinction can be made between operational and financial leases:

Operational lease – A terminable lease whereby the costs of insurance and maintenance are borne by the lender or lessor. The lease period is shorter than the economic lifetime. This makes the total lease smaller than the total investment. The economic risk of the residual value at the end of the lease lies with the lessor. The difference between operational leasing and renting is that operational leasing offers a purchase option. Operational leasing is primarily used for commodities such as photocopiers, cars and so on.

Financial lease – A non-cancellable lease contract where the costs of maintenance and insurance are usually borne by the lessee. The lease term is usually about the economic lifespan of the product. Since the contract cannot be cancelled, the risk of economic obsolescence lies with the lessee. The leasing company holds legal ownership. Financial leasing is used, for example, when a company needs a special machine that other companies cannot use The decision to use such a form of leasing is often based on fiscal motives.

5.08 BUSINESS JUSTIFICATION

PURPOSE

The purpose of this chapter is to enable the individual to ensure the ongoing validity of the business/organisational justification of the project.

LEARNING OBJECTIVES

- The content and the characteristics of a business case;
- When and by whom a business case is prepared and updated;
- The baseline measurement, baseline scenario, and delta measurement;
- The link between a feasibility study and the business case;
- Benefits review and the post-investment review;
- The difference between customer and supplier business cases.

DEFINITIONS

Business case: The business justification to invest.
Project benefit: An advantage resulting from a project outcome.
Project dis-benefit: A disadvantage resulting from a project outcome.
Feasibility study: A research into whether a desired outcome is realistic and feasible.
Benefits review: An assessment of whether the envisaged benefits are or have been realised.

INTRODUCTION

The business case describes the justification for investing. Based on the business case, the sponsoring organisation or customer authorises the project sponsor to initiate the project. No project should start without a valid business case. To ensure that the project remains valid during the implementation, the business case should be continuously monitored during the project. The project sponsor is the owner of the business case.

However, the business case is not about making money, although the name suggests this. Of course, it can be about making money, but more generally, it is about justifying an investment in light of the organisational objectives and strategies. Is this the best way to achieve our goals? Is it in line with our mission, vision, and corporate values? Does it contribute to our broader social responsibilities? But also, can we afford it, given our other needs and wishes? This also makes the business case an indispensable tool for governments and NCOs.

POSITIONING

In the feasibility study, an outline business case is prepared for each alternative to realise an initial idea. Based on that, the best alternative is chosen, and the project mandate is issued. In the project preparation stage, the outline business case of the selected alternative is evaluated. In the project definition stage, the business case is further elaborated. During the implementation, the validity of the business case is continuously monitored. At stage transitions and project closure, the business case should be reviewed and, if necessary, updated.

A benefit review plan is prepared in the project definition stage and is also updated at each stage transition and project closure. Benefit reviews and a post-investment review should take place during the period of use when it can be assessed whether the expected benefits have been or will be realised.

CHARACTERISTICS BUSINESS CASE

The business case is essential for a good investment assessment. Without a good business case, the decision whether or not to initiate or continue a project (go/no-go decision) is made based on emotional and political grounds only. However valid these grounds may be, without a good business case, the investments in the project will not have a solid basis, and there is a chance that the wrong project will be started. Without a good business case, there is often insufficient management support when resources need to be released. Without a good business case, there is often also insufficient support amongst users to accept the changes that the project in question will inevitably entail.

Business case and statutory regulations

It is often suggested that a business case is only necessary for business investments. This is not correct. The term business case originates from the British government. It is intended to obtain a more objective assessment of investments. A business case is even necessary for implementing statutory regulations. When implementing a legal regulation, there are always several options to be considered: do we opt for a golden, silver or bronze solution? The remaining budget can be used for other purposes.

Realistic benefits

In addition, it is important to work with realistic benefits. If every employee saves five minutes a day when using a new application, that is fine, but it will not provide a financial benefit unless staffing cuts can be made as a result thereof. Be aware of wishful thinking. Avoid bias. Often, people are prepared to promise you the moon to get approval for the desired investment. Have a manager sign for each benefit to be achieved, have it counter-signed by the financial department, and have them reconfirm it at any stage transition and project closure. Some organisations have even issued guidelines for defining benefits used to justify an investment.

Continued business justification

The time when the business case was only used to support the initial investment decision is over. Nowadays, the context and circumstances in which a project is to be carried out change so rapidly that it is necessary to monitor the viability of the business case throughout the implementation of the project. If, under the given circumstances, there is no longer a valid business, it is better to change the objectives and direction of the project or terminate the project prematurely.

BUSINESS CASE DOCUMENT

The business case describes the investment justification. The business case should, as a minimum, include:

- *Reasons* – Why should the project be carried out, and why has this become so urgent?
- *Purpose* – What changes need to be accomplished, and how does it fit our strategy?
- *Business options* – The other alternatives considered to achieve the organisational goals and why they were not chosen.
- *Benefits* – Expected advantages and the metrics to determine their created value.

- *Dis-benefits* – Expected negative consequences and metrics to determine their degree.
- *Costs* – The expected costs of the project and implementation and the possibility of financing.
- *Time* – The planned lead time of the project and the period of use of the project output.
- *Resources* – The human and material resources to be used.
- *Risks* -The key risks that can impact the project, the realisation of the benefits, and the occurrence of dis-benefits.
- *Investment appraisal* – Compares the project's costs, benefits and risks of the project and assesses whether it is justified to start or continue the project on this basis.

Each business case should be accompanied by advice on whether it is wise to initiate or continue the project and any measures to be taken. Business options should always include the option not to invest. This 'do nothing' option should be the basis for qualifying the other options.

The total costs, resources and lead time of the investment can be extracted from the project plan. The breakdowns of these themselves are not included in the business case. The expected costs should include the costs required to realise the project result and the costs incurred by taking the project output into use after delivery.

Financial AND non-financial benefits and dis-benefits should be included in the business case. A responsible individual should be designated for each of these. Without management attention, negative consequences often skyrocket, which can seriously backlash the project. The loss of revenue and increase in operational costs are not investment costs but dis-benefits.

Various techniques can be used to assess the financial component of the investments. Commonly used techniques are the *Net Present Value* (NPV) method, the *break-even point calculation* and the *payback period calculation*. For a long-term investment, usually, the NPV method is used (see Chapter 10.03 Financial Management). The actual calculations are usually done by the financial specialists of the sponsoring organisation.

BASELINE MEASUREMENT, BASELINE SCENARIO AND DELTA MEASUREMENT

The baseline measurement reflects the current status quo. The baseline scenario is the anticipated development if no investment is made. The delta measurement is the difference in development between the baseline scenario (do nothing) and the development based on the planned investment.

To calculate the benefits forecasted in the business case, the outcome based on the planned investment should be compared with the baseline scenario and NOT with the actual status quo.

We have to establish the baseline measurement, baseline scenario and delta measurement every time we update the business case to avoid the conditions from being changed unnoticed.

THE BUSINESS CASE IN THE PRODUCT LIFECYCLE

The project's business case is usually part of the business justification throughout the product lifecycle (see Figure 5.08.01).

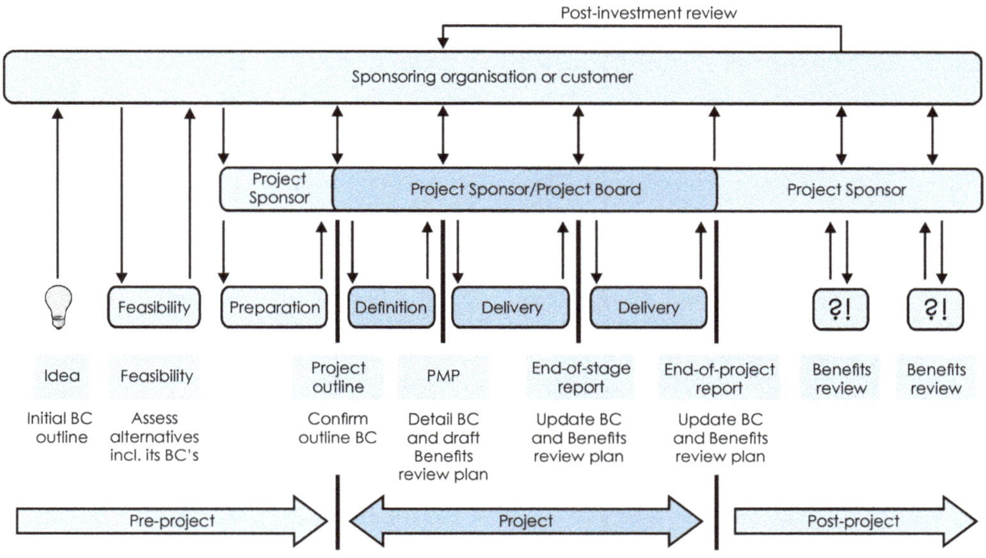

Figure 5.08.01 Business case in the product lifecycle

Initial business case

An outline business case is often prepared before the actual project starts. This may occur during the annual business planning process, when preparing the business case of a programme, or the result of a feasibility study. Sometimes the initial idea already includes an initial outline business case.

Feasibility study

To support a sponsoring organisation or customer decision, a feasibility study is often carried out first, examining several business options before initiating the project. For each alternative to realise the original idea, an outline business case is prepared, and the management is advised on whether or not to invest and, if so, the best option. A feasibility study is a project in itself.

Project preparation stage

In the project preparation stage, the outline business case is included in the project outline. The outline business case should include: (1) the reasons and purpose for initiating the project; (2) the other business options considered and why they were not chosen; and, if possible, (3) an initial estimate of the anticipated benefits and dis-benefits.

Project lifecycle

In the project definition stage, the business case is further elaborated. This elaborated business case forms part of the project management plan. During this stage also, the benefits review plan is prepared.

At change requests and other project issues, you also have to assess the consequences of these issues on the business case for decision-making. In case it is forecasted that the project tolerances will be exceeded, you have to escalate this to the project sponsor by means of an exception report. In this exception report, you should also assess the impact on the business case. However, you should not update the business case yet. Only if the sponsoring organisation or customer decides to proceed with the project, usually in another form or direction, should you, based on these new conditions, update the business case.

Before each decision point, you should update the business case as input for the project decision by the sponsoring organisation or customer. At the end of the project, you should update the business case for the last time. While updating the business case, you should also update the benefits review plan.

Benefit reviews and benefits review plan

Only when the project result has been in use for some time, can it be checked whether the anticipated benefits have or will be realised. This is usually a couple of months after the completion of the project. In the case of a staged delivery, this can sometimes already be done during the project's lifetime. Benefits reviews after the completion of the project are not part of the project's scope. Benefit reviews during the project's lifetime can be included in the project's scope at the sponsor's request.

It is essential to agree early on when, by whom, and how the expected benefits will be measured and reviewed. This is stipulated in a *benefits review plan*. This plan should be prepared in the project definition stage and updated at the end of each stage and the end of the project. As the benefits reviews are usually carried out after the completion of the project, the benefits review plan is usually not included in the project management plan but kept separately.

In the benefits review plan, you also record the management activities that still need to be done by the customer after the project's completion to ensure that the planned changes can be implemented and the expected benefits realised.

Post-investment review

Based on the benefits reviews, a *post-investment review* can be carried out. A post-investment review assesses whether the original investment decision at the end of the project definition stage (decision to fund) was justified and whether the investment is worthwhile. This assessment serves as a learning point for the sponsoring organisation or customer for future investment decisions.

The business case is not updated during the benefits and the post-investment reviews. A post-investment review can be combined with one of the benefits reviews. In the case of a project being part of a programme or portfolio, the programme or portfolio organisation usually carries out the post-investment review.

CUSTOMER AND SUPPLIER BUSINESS CASES

If the sponsoring organisation or customer and the supplier belong to different organisations, both parties have their own business case based on their own cost, benefits and risks. Staff departments within the sponsoring or customer organisation do not have their own business case. Their business case is part of the business case of the sponsoring organisation or customer.

The supplier's business case may be based on the anticipated profit of the work itself, but it may also be based on, for example, the expected benefits of entering a new market. If the supplier's business case is based on the profit of the contract itself, then its business case is usually much easier to identify and realise than the business case of the sponsoring organisation or customer, which is generally based on the long-term effects of changes that need to be implemented. When discussing the project's business case, we refer to the customer's business case.

SUSTAINABILITY

From a sustainable approach, the investment justification should be assessed from an economic perspective AND an environmental and social perspective based on the *Triple Bottom Line* concept. This should include the financial and non-financial costs, (dis-)benefits and risks. A multi-criteria approach is essential in this context. Such an assessment should also examine the environmental and social consequences of the alternative solutions, what happens if we do not invest, and how the investments match the organisation's sustainable ambitions.

TAILORING

In a mature Agile environment, a business case is created in some form before the start of a project. This may be part of creating a product vision or a feasibility study. Since time and costs are known in advance, the focus is on the deliverables' best, worst and expected scenarios combined with the envisaged benefits. The *Minimal Marketable Product* (MMP) describes the product with the smallest possible set of features that creates the desired user experience and can be successfully marketed.

Note that incremental delivery directly impacts the business case, both in terms of costs and benefits to be realised. Due to the incremental delivery, benefits can be realised earlier, but also, don't forget the additional costs of putting the deliverables incrementally into use. Finally, include the feedback you receive in the interim assessment of the business case.

RESPONSIBILITIES

The project sponsor is the owner of the business case. The project manager is responsible for preparing, monitoring and updating the business case. However, the sponsor can also delegate this responsibility to a third party, for instance, project assurance.

The project manager is also responsible for preparing the benefits review plan. The project sponsor is responsible for the actual benefits and post-investment reviews.

6. PROJECT DELIVERY AND CLOSE-OUT

This part focuses on the project delivery. In this stage of the project, the project manager works with the team to deliver and hand over the project output.

Chapter 6.01 – Procurement – Provides considerations for the choice between make or buy, purchasing or outsourcing, how to develop a procurement strategy, and how to prepare a procurement plan. Also, various contract forms and tendering methods, legal aspects of contracts, and tendering rules and securities are discussed.

Chapter 6.02 – Change Control – Provides guidance on how to manage change requests, off-specifications and other project issues. It also indicates how the configuration of project deliverables should be managed.

Chapter 6.03 – Information and Documentation – Outlines how information and documentation should be managed for the benefit of the project and the various stakeholders.

Chapter 6.04 – Control and Reporting – Starts with several management theories. Subsequently, the daily management, managing work packages, managing stage boundaries, and escalating exceptions are discussed, as well as various control instruments. Finally, various techniques are discussed, such as the slip chart and earned value analysis.

Chapter 6.05 – Change and Transformation – Deals with how organisational changes can best be implemented. What needs to be considered, and how to deal with resistance.

Chapter 6.06 – Project Closure – Provides the project manager with tools for careful closure. Important themes are the handing over of the project output decommissioning, evaluation and closure of the project, and obtaining an official release of the duty to perform for the project.

Together, these chapters outline the most important aspects the project manager faces during the delivery and conclusion of the project.

6.01 PROCUREMENT

PURPOSE

The purpose of this chapter is enable the individual to obtain the best value possible from the chosen suppliers or partners and thus deliver the best value for the buyer and the organisation.

LEARNING OBJECTIVES

- Make or buy, and purchase or outsource decision;
- Procurement process, including longlist and shortlist;
- Selection and award criteria;
- Best-effort and performance agreements;
- Contractual terms and conditions;
- General terms and conditions and 'battle of forms';
- Procurement roles and responsibilities;
- Procurement strategy and procurement plan (advanced);
- Types of procurement contracts (advanced);
- RFI, RFS, RFQ and RFP (advanced);
- Letter of intent and pre-contractual arrangements (advanced);
- Bank guarantees and letter of credit (advanced);
- Contract and claim management (advanced);
- Various partnerships (advanced);
- Supply chain management (advanced).

DEFINITIONS

Procurement: The process of buying or obtaining goods and or services from external parties.
Purchase: The actual act of buying goods and or services from external parties.
Longlist: A list of potential qualified external parties to submit a proposal or quotation.
Shortlist: A list of external parties to be invited to submit a proposal or quotation.
Selection criteria: Criteria based on which parties are selected to submit a proposal or quotation.
Award criteria: Criteria based on which a proposal or quotation is awarded.
Contract: A legally binding agreement setting out mutual obligations and rights.
Best-effort agreement: An agreement to perform specific tasks to the best of their ability.
Performance agreement: An agreement to deliver an output within predefined terms and conditions.

INTRODUCTION

Project success depends largely on the availability of resources. Purchasing and outsourcing are becoming increasingly important as organisations concentrate on their core activities and make more and more use of external parties to carry out (parts of) projects. For the project manager, procurement is not just an extra activity but is often the key to project success.

Besides purchasing as activities within a project, purchasing and in/outsourcing can also be the project's purpose. The project is then initiated and implemented entirely to purchase a product or service or to in/outsource business activities.

POSITIONING

Procurement may take place throughout the project. It often starts even earlier. In the project preparation stage, the decision has mostly already been taken on whether the work will be done in-house or outsourced (project approach). Parties are contracted for the project definition stage.

In the project definition stage, the procurement strategy is determined, and the procurement plan is prepared. The parties involved in the first delivery stage are contracted. During the individual delivery stages, key parties may be contracted for the next stage. Other parties may be contracted during the individual stages themselves. At the end of the project, parties may be contracted to operate and maintain the project output in the usage stage.

MAKE OR BUY

An important decision in many projects is: will we do the work ourselves, or will we purchase or outsource it? Purchase is the actual act of buying goods and services (including hiring). Here, the responsibility for the work to be carried out remains with us. Outsourcing is transferring a business function to a third party. Here, the function's responsibility is transferred to a service provider.

Arguments for purchasing or outsourcing the work are:

- *Competence* – We don't have the competence to achieve the desired quality.
- *Capacity* – We don't have the people, or the project will burden the organisation too much.
- *Flexibility* – To cope with workload peaks and the absence of staff.
- *Costs* – To reduce costs as third parties can do it cheaper.
- *Sustainability* – As well with respect to the work and the deliverables.
- *Risk* – To transfer risks.
- *Acceptance* – To legitimise internal decisions.
- *Control* – To know in advance what the costs will be.
- *Performance* – To ensure that work is done as planned.
- *Licences* – We don't have the required licences and accreditations.
- *Creativity* – To find new solutions, third parties may bring new insights.

Procurement policies and strategic considerations should also be taken into account. These policies and considerations are often imposed top-down and cannot be ignored.

In many organisations, there is a surcharge on direct costs to cover the organisation's indirect costs. Under normal business conditions, comparing the quotations received with the internal cost estimate based on the internal rates is appropriate. In case of severe understaffing, it is better to look at out-of-pocket costs only.

PROCUREMENT PROCESS

In general, procurement involves the following steps, sometimes very formal and procedural, sometimes informal and short-cycle:

- *Describe the work package* – The work to be performed;
- *Conduct a market survey* – Carry out a market survey and prepare a longlist;
- *Define selection and award criteria* – Can be carried out at the same time as the market survey;
- *Define the selection process* – For example, based on a call, contest or tender;
- *Carry out a pre-selection* – Shorten the longlist to a shortlist based on the selection criteria;
- *Ask for quotations* – It is advised to add the general terms and conditions beforehand;
- *Review the quotations* – Compare the offers based on the award criteria;
- *Make a decision* – The final decision usually rests with the project sponsor;
- *Enter into a negotiation* – Refine the offer to meet the actual project conditions;
- *Sign the contract* – Record the agreement made.

A longlist is a list of potential qualified suppliers. A shortlist is a list of suppliers who will be invited to submit a proposal or quotation.

SELECTION AND AWARD CRITERIA

Selection criteria are criteria based on which external parties are selected to submit a proposal or quotation. *Award criteria* are criteria based on which a proposal or quotation is awarded.

Important selection criteria are often:

- *Knock-out criteria* – Such as supplier in the suspension of payments or with a conviction.
- *Professional criteria* – Such as having certificates and membership in professional associations.
- *Financial-economic criteria* – Such as liquidity, profitability and solvency.
- *Core values* – Including Corporate Social Responsibility.
- *Turnover* – The order should be proportionate to the annual turnover (mostly < 15%).
- *Technical criteria* – Such as experience with similar projects, qualified staff, et cetera.
- *Customer appreciation* – Churn, references but also aspects such as reputation.
- *Competition* – The supplier may or may not work for a direct competitor.

Input on selection criteria can usually be obtained mainly from websites and other public sources.

Important award criteria are often:

- Price and quality;
- Delivery time;
- Maintenance costs;
- Durability deliverables;
- Sustainability of the work and the deliverables;
- Fits the (project) organisation;
- Services and after-care;

- Warranty period;
- Duration availability of spare parts.

An application of goods or services by another operating company of the same legal entity can be assimilated into an invitation to tender. In such cases, the application should be treated as if it is between independent parties and subject to the same degree of control.

BEST-EFFORT AND PERFORMANCE AGREEMENTS

Contracts can be divided into best effort and performance agreements.

Best-effort agreement

A best-effort agreement is an agreement to perform certain tasks to the best of one's ability. Such an agreement is usually made based on hours x fixed rate and reimbursement of expenses. The risk of whether the result will be achieved according to plan lies with the customer.

Performance agreement

A performance agreement is an agreement to deliver an output within predefined terms and conditions. Such an agreement is usually made for a fixed price and with a fixed completion date. The risk of whether the result will be achieved according to plan lies with the contractor.

Best-effort agreements are generally made in the preliminary stages of a project. Consultancy agreements are considered best-effort agreement. Performance agreement are usually made in the project delivery stages, as the output is sufficiently measurable and predictable.

CONTRACTUAL TERMS AND CONDITIONS

A *contract* is a legally binding agreement setting out mutual obligations and rights. The purpose of a contract is to clarify what has been agreed, in order to avoid conflict, and to be able to enforce it in court should the need arise.

Contracts come in many shapes and sizes; some are simple and short, and others are very elaborate. Most contracts also declare certain general terms and conditions applicable. Which articles are included in the actual contract and which in the general terms and conditions varies per organisation, type of contract and country to country. However, the performance, price and delivery time should always be specified in the actual contract (see Figure 6.01.01).

General terms and conditions are a set of recurring supporting conditions that can be referred to so that they do not have to be included in the contracts themselves. If you want to make different agreements about these, you should include them separately in the actual contract. The agreements in the actual contract always take precedence over the general terms and conditions.

Actual contract

- Terms of definitions
- Preamble
- Activities to perform
- Results to be delivered
- Quality expectations and acceptance criteria
- Required resources
- Other requirements parties
- Liaisons
- Contract sum and unit prices
- Terms of delivery
- Hand over/acceptance procedures

General terms and conditions

- Quality activities and reports
- Guarantees and insurances
- Change procedure
- Payment terms
- Licences and authorship
- Secrecy / relations third parties
- (No) take over staff
- Force majeure
- Dissolution agreement
- Penalty clauses / incentives
- Four corner clause
- Disputes / arbitration
- Applicable law / regulatory

Figure 6.01.01 Customary contract clauses

Preamble

The will and the expression of the will should correspond to be valid (see Chapter 11.03 Laws and Legislation). It is, therefore, important that a preamble ('Whereas...') is included at the beginning of a contract, setting out the background, reason and what the parties intend to achieve by the agreement. The clearer this preamble is, the more guidance it provides in interpreting the contract. This can also be very important in case of a dispute later on.

Four Corners Clause

To prevent sales pitches and lapsed arrangements of earlier drafts from becoming part of the final agreement, the *Four Corners Clause* is often included in a contract. This clause stipulates that all arrangements relating to the agreement are included in the current contract and that all other (previously made) arrangements no longer apply. In other words, only what is 'between these four corners of the contract paper' is valid and nothing else.

Payment conditions

Every contract should include a payment schedule. A supplier who manufactures goods specifically for the project doesn't want to wait to invoice until all goods have been delivered. Especially as it often takes an extra (couple of) month(s) before they get paid after submitting the invoice. It is then customary to agree on a payment schedule. A typical schedule is as follows:

- 20% when the order is issued;
- 40% upon start of the work;
- 40% at completion.

Sometimes it is agreed that a final 5 or 10% of the contract is only paid after all the remaining issues have been dealt with or after satisfactory performance during an initial period of use. For the supplier, this can create quite a payment risk. As a counter-security, the supplier can demand a bank guarantee from the customer. When a consultancy assignment requires the submission of a final report, it is often agreed that the final invoice can be submitted after a one-off adjustment to that report.

Dispute resolution

Each contract should also determine which legal system applies and how disputes are dealt with. It is usually stipulated that disputes are to be submitted to a specific court. However, such litigation is often time-consuming, expensive, and more focused on establishing the truth than on the (possible) continuation of the relationship.

Other forms of dispute resolution are:

- *Free advice* – Non-binding advice by external subject-matter experts.
- *Mediation* – An independent third party which focuses on de-escalating the conflict and developing an acceptable solution by the parties themselves.
- *Conciliation* – Is usually led by neutral lawyers and aimed at further collaboration.
- *Binding advice* – Whereby each party usually appoints one advisor who jointly appoint a third advisor.
- *Arbitration* – This follows a strict procedure and focuses heavily on the legal interpretations of the contract and the applicable law.

If free advice does not provide a solution, and mediation or conciliation fails, parties can still go to court. This is not possible with the last two forms of conflict resolution.

Do's and don'ts when drawing up contracts

- Draw up simple contracts, with the exception of some legal provisions, and in 'ordinary' language.
- Plan enough time for the contract negotiations.
- Do not be distracted by statements such as, 'Our working relationship is based on trust'. Record the things that need to be arranged.
- Object to unreasonable provisions. The meaning of the words 'we understand each other' is lost in the event of a conflict.
- Object to superfluous clauses. In the event of a conflict, the judge will still give meaning to them.
- Ensure all documents referred to in the contract are also provided with the contract.
- Always thoroughly read a contract and ask what you do not understand.
- Ensure the contract answers all the obvious 'what if' questions.
- Ensure reciprocity. Obligations should be reciprocal, in addition to a penalty clause.
- Include in the contracts provisions on changes, how to measure results, how to report, and how to deal with irregularities.

GENERAL TERMS AND CONDITIONS

Using general terms and conditions saves both parties time and costs. However, do not assume that the general terms and conditions are reasonable and balanced. They can be very one-sided and deprive you of any right if there are irregularities. In a growing number of countries, legislators have already stipulated that companies may no longer use certain terms and conditions in contracts with individuals.

Battle of forms

Depending on the jurisdiction, different rules may apply to the question of which terms and conditions apply if both parties have issued or referred to their own general terms and conditions when negotiating the contract.

Depending on the jurisdiction, who has the 'first shot' or who has the 'last shot' wins. In the first situation, the general terms and conditions of the party that first declared them applicable will apply unless the other party explicitly rejects these and declares its own general terms and conditions applicable. In the latter situation, the general terms and conditions put forward lastly apply. In practice, this means that when a buyer places an order on a standard purchase form containing its general terms and conditions and receives an acceptance order from the supplier containing its own terms and conditions, the supplier does not actually accept the order but makes a counter-offer. If the buyer then agrees when and how the supplier should deliver the goods, the buyer effectively accepts the counter-offer, and thus the general terms and conditions of the supplier, as they had the 'last shot'.

Often, both parties will try to get their last offer accepted by the other party to ensure that their own general terms and conditions apply to the final contract. This process of submitting proposals back and forth is known as the 'battle of forms'. It is better to put both general terms and conditions on the table, sort out the differences, agree on them, and include the adjustments in the actual contract.

SUSTAINABILITY

Procuring materials and equipment and subcontracting the works are ideal for setting sustainability and social criteria. In doing so, do not focus solely on the use within the project but on the total supply chain. Consider also the sustainable performance of the supplier. Furthermore, concentrate also on the tendering process itself. Make sure the valuation of potential suppliers is fair. Beware of bribery. Ensure there are enough alternatives so you are not obliged to make unattractive choices.

TAILORING

Agile work also requires contracts. However, the focus should be more on the changes to be realised (outcome-based) and less on precisely what is to be delivered (output-based). Determine the level of user participation. Specify who on the customer side acts as product owner and their mandate. Agree on a release schedule and which core elements should be delivered per release. This isn't necessarily a ready-to-use product but can also be a model or a prototype. Additional points of attention are:

- Buy timeboxes with deliverables;
- Relate incentives to value delivered or throughput;
- Avoid detailed requirements;
- Prioritise requirements and identify a minimum marketable product;
- Handle changing requirements by trading off the less important ones;
- Build a contract from an absolute minimum;
- Enable early closure of the project.

RESPONSIBILITIES

Purchases may be carried out by the project or the procurement department. In all cases, the procurement department should ensure the organisation's procurement policies are followed. In all cases, the project manager remains responsible for the following:

- The specifications set;
- That the contract terms fit within the project objectives;
- The fit of the supplier/contractor to the project organisation;
- The integration of the supplier/contractor's work with the other work within the project;
- The contract management.

It is essential to make clear arrangements with the procurement department, in consultation with the project sponsor, before the start of the work.

Within public bodies, international tendering procedures should also be respected. The consequences can be serious if parties do not comply with these procedures. For consumables, the project manager should usually use the framework agreements concluded.

ADVANCED

SOURCING STRATEGIES (ADVANCED)

Sourcing strategy includes planning, designing and building a reliable and competitive supplier base, defining sourcing strategies, pricing strategies and supply chain requirements. Sourcing strategies are closely related to the company's vision, strategies, core values, sustainability policy, et cetera. Many organisations follow different strategies to find the necessary resources for their activities and projects. Strategies may depend on the type of source available.

The first decision to be made is which items to manufacture in-house and which to outsource (make or buy). The latter can come from one or more sources via a preferred supplier, an exclusive supplier or even a partner in the supply chain. Aspects such as reliability, value for money and reputation should be taken into account. Finally, should the items be outsourced locally or to another country? This includes aspects such as boosting the local economy, reducing transport distances, reducing dependency, or exploiting economies of scale, et cetera. Each choice has its advantages but also its disadvantages.

SUPPLIER DEVELOPMENT METHODOLOGIES (ADVANCED)

Supplier development is an approach to work more closely with suppliers to improve product performance. A company needs to build a network of competent suppliers to compete effectively in the global market. Supplier development aims to create and enhance such a network.

Projects are heavily influenced by supplier development strategies. By involving suppliers early in the development process, you typically get the best value for money, as nearly 80% of product costs are determined during the engineering and design phases. It will also increase the speed of product development, improve problem-solving abilities, build firm partnerships, and increase competitive advantage. Develop supplier best practice guidelines and assess the supplier development process throughout the project. Involve the project owner/project board and relevant bodies within the permanent organisation in this process.

PROCUREMENT STRATEGY AND PLAN (ADVANCED)

When procurement affects a significant part of a project, a procurement strategy should be determined and developed into a procurement plan at the project definition stage. These should be reviewed and updated at least at each stage transition.

The *procurement strategy* is a high-level description of how procurement will be managed on the project. This includes, at the very least, the main contracting structure, types of contracts to be used, roles and responsibilities, and supplier selection standards and procedures.

Main contracting structure

The main contracting structure provides a schematic overview of all contracts to be concluded and their mutual coherence. Possible combinations are:

- One main contractor with subsequent sub-contractors;

- All separate contracts;
- All separate contracts with an obligation to coordinate for one of them.

The advantage of one main contractor is that the entire responsibility for implementation lies with one party. This makes the assignment of responsibilities unambiguous. The downside is that this limits the number of qualified contractors and that they still might have to subcontract specific work packages to other parties, which you have no insight into.

The advantage of working with separate contractors is that each contractor can be deployed to its own strengths. However, the downside is that responsibilities between contractors are not unambiguously covered, and the liability between the contractors is often unclear. Without a qualified project manager and procurement department, this is not desirable.

An intermediate solution is to make one of the contractors responsible for the coordination between the different implementing parties; e.g., the architect is responsible for the coordination with the construction, electrical and mechanical engineering companies, and the building contractor is responsible for the coordination with the electrical and mechanical installation companies. It is important to consider this early on in the project and include it in the procurement strategy.

Procurement plan

The procurement plan is drafted based on the procurement strategy. This plan comprises:

- The work packages to be contracted;
- The method of tendering, public or limited, with or without pre-selection, or singular;
- The contract form, such as a fixed-price or an incentive contract;
- The selection and award criteria to be used for the tendering of the various contracts;
- The time schedule in which the various contracts should be concluded;
- The roles and responsibilities for the selection and tender of the individual contracts;
- The necessary resources for the selection and tender of the individual contracts.

TYPE OF CONTRACTS (ADVANCED)

Depending on the degree of control by the customer and the transfer of risks, different contract types can be distinguished. With complete control by the customer, there are maximum opportunities to tailor the work. With the complete transfer of all delivery risks, there is absolute price certainty (see Figure 6.01.02):

- *Brochure plan* – A fixed-price contract for a concept developed by the supplier. The customer does not run any price risks but has hardly any possibilities for customisation.
- *Turn key* – A fixed-price contract based on customer specifications to deliver a complete product that is fully ready for immediate use. After approving the overall design, including the fixed fixtures and fittings, there is little possibility of making changes, or only at a considerable cost.
- *Fixed-price contract* – A contract with a fixed price based on a precise specification. Changes can only be made based on an official change procedure. However, distinctive elements can be tendered over time, whereby the customer still has the opportunity to specify their vision in more detail.

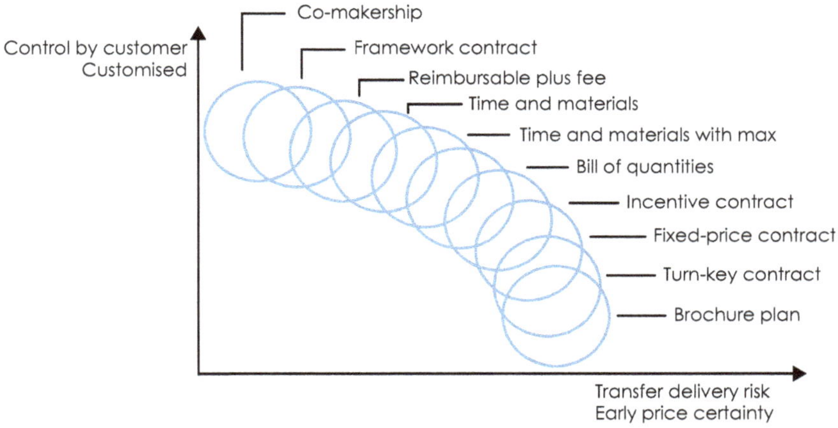

Figure 6.01.02 Different contract forms

- *Incentive contract* – A fixed-price contract with an incentive for early delivery. These contracts often also include a penalty clause in case the project is delivered late. The bonus is usually lower than any penalty. This is a variant of fixed-price contracts.
- *Bill of quantities* – A contract based on fixed rates for all work to be carried out.
- *Time and materials* – A contract with fixed rates for hours spent and materials delivered.
- *Time and materials with max* – The same as the previous contract but now with a task-setting maximum. The maximum can only be exceeded if there are exceptional circumstances.
- *Reimbursable plus fee* – A contract based on actual costs of hours and materials with a fixed fee per period or for the entire project
- *Framework contract* – A contract to deliver specific products and services during a predetermined period at pre-agreed prices and conditions. Within a framework contract, separate agreements are made for individual assignments. Framework contracts are often concluded for consumables.
- *Co-makership* – The project is carried out at the shared risk of the customer and the supplier. Co-makership assumes long-term strategic cooperation.

RFI, RFS, RFP, RFQ (ADVANCED)

Common concepts within procurement are RFI, RFS, RFQ and RFP:

Request for Information (RFI) – A questionnaire to ask suppliers about their products and services. An RFP is often used to collect background information and solution ideas for planning purposes. An RFI is usually made at the start of large tenders when there are multiple options to meet the customer's needs.

Request for solution (RFS) – A request to potential suppliers to indicate possible solutions to a defined problem. An RFS is more focused on submitting innovative solutions than providing information for preselection. An RFS is much more open to innovation than an RFP.

Request for Proposal (RFP) – An invitation to make a comprehensive offer for a specific service or product. Often, interviews are then held with some or all of the suppliers so they can explain their proposals. Sometimes some or all of those are then asked to submit a *Best And Final Offer* (BAFO).

Request for Quotation (RFQ) – An invitation to submit a bid based on fixed specifications. Sometimes an RFQ is also used to request unit prices from suppliers, after which the final supplier is selected based on an RFP.

SUPPLY AND DEMAND CONCEPT (ADVANCED)

The supply and demand concept describes how price changes affect supply and demand and vice versa. When the price goes up, supply also goes up and demand goes down. When the price goes down, the supply goes down, and the demand goes up. The extent to which price changes affect the demand or supply is called *price elasticity*. Products with high price elasticity are subject to greater fluctuations in demand due to price fluctuations. Conversely, prices for basic necessities will be relatively low. Of course, there are exceptions. For goods that are considered inferior, a lower price can lead to lower demand as buyers turn to higher-quality alternatives. For goods that are considered exclusive, a higher price can even increase the demand.

TENDER PROCEDURES AND PRACTICES (ADVANCED)

Specific tender procedures are:

- *Public tender* – All suppliers are invited to submit a quotation via a public announcement.
- *Public tender with pre-selection* – After a public announcement, a pre-selection is first carried out.
- *Limited tender* – A limited number of suppliers is invited based on an existing shortlist.
- *Limited tender with pre-selection* – A limited tender based on a long list and a shortlist.
- *Single tender* – An invitation to a single supplier to submit a quotation.

Public tender – The request for a tender is published, usually via a website. Everyone can apply. The advantage is that all suppliers have equal opportunities. However, when a considerable volume of work is available in the market, qualified suppliers might choose not to apply due to the limited likelihood of success. If there is little work on the market, a public tender can provide a very competitive offer, but with the risk of poor performance.

Public tender with pre-selection – After an open call for tender, a selection is first made as to whether a supplier is qualified. The selected suppliers are then offered the opportunity to submit a tender. This prevents unqualified candidates from submitting a complete bid and the contracting firm from assessing them in the bid review. The latter can be very costly and time-consuming.

Limited tender – A limited number of suppliers are invited to submit a tender. Often, these are well-known suppliers who worked for them before or who have emerged from an initial market survey.

Limited tender with pre-selection – A limited number of suppliers are given the opportunity to participate in a pre-selection, after which one or more of them are invited to submit a tender.

Single-tender – The intended supplier is directly invited to submit a tender one-on-one. This does carry the risk that the supplier may not offer the most competitive price. Therefore, in such cases, the supplier is usually asked to submit a cost specification. Furthermore, it is of utmost importance that the supplier signs a waiver before the first negotiation takes place. If the customer and the supplier cannot reach an agreement, the customer can switch to another supplier.

The advantage of the latter option is that the customer can quickly enter into negotiations with the supplier and also involve them in preparing the specifications and finding creative solutions. This also makes it more likely that the supplier will be interested in making an offer, even when there is much work on the market. The supplier may even be willing to reserve capacity before the contract is actually concluded. In all situations, the supplier should indicate how long their offer stands.

The method of tendering depends on many factors, such as:

- *Structure of the market* – Are there many suppliers, or is the market dominated by one or a few major players?
- *Pace* – If little time is available, a pre-qualification is impossible, and a limited or even a single tender will often be chosen.
- *Level of specification* – If the specifications are only narrowly specified, the supplier's quality becomes essential, and a pre-selection or single tender is usually chosen.
- *Seller's or buyer's market* – In a seller's market, there is a surplus of buyers, and the sellers dictate the market. In a buyer's market, there is a surplus of sellers, and the buyers dictate the market. In a seller's market, the selection is more often based on a limited or single tender. In a buyer's market, a public tender will usually be chosen with or without pre-selection.
- *Risk transfer* – If significant risks are to be transferred to suppliers, larger suppliers should be invited based on a pre-qualification. A single tender is then less obvious as the possible cost impact of these risks may then be fully factored into the price and thus passed on to the customer.

LETTER OF INTENT AND PRE-CONTRACTUAL ARRANGEMENTS (ADVANCED)

For larger contracts, a *letter of intent* or a *pre-contractual arrangement* may be concluded separately from the main contract.

Letter of Intent

A *Letter of Intent* (LOI) is a document that sets out the plans and agreements between two or more parties before entering into a contract. An LOI is also called a *Memorandum of Understanding* (MOU).

An LOI is used to quickly agree on the basic terms before significant resources are devoted to concluding the final agreement. It is also used to officially state that the parties are currently negotiating, such as in a merger, but also to provide safeguards in case the agreement fails during negotiations.

Although an LOI is not binding on the parties in its entirety, many LOIs contain binding provisions, such as those on non-disclosure, non-solicitation, exclusivity, copyright, recoverable costs, negotiating in good faith, as well as the compensation to be paid if the negotiations fail.

Pre-contractual arrangements

When the contract negotiations are complex and lengthy, sometimes a pre-contractual arrangement is made to allow for preparatory work or ordering materials with a long delivery time. A pre-contractual arrangement is a contract in itself. It is especially effective if the first part of the work takes a fair amount of time, is limited in value, and can easily be separated from the rest of the work. For example, site preparation can easily be assigned separately for the new office building to gain more time to negotiate the contract to construct the office building itself.

SECURITIES (ADVANCED)

Various securities of payment can be included in a contract. Besides down payments, the most common security is a bank guarantee. For export purposes, a letter of credit or an export credit guarantee can be issued.

Bank guarantees

A bank guarantee is a contract whereby the bank of the liable party guarantees payment to the other party if the debtor defaults. There are different forms of bank guarantees, ranging from unconditional to bank guarantees where the bank pays only on court order. A buyer may provide a bank guarantee as security for payment. Conversely, a supplier may provide a bank guarantee to the buyer as security for a down payment. Bank guarantees have a maximum validity. The credit facility of the payer decreases with the amount of the bank guarantee.

Letter of credit

A Letter of Credit (LOI) is a bank letter that guarantees that payment will be received on time and in the correct amount according to the terms of the LOI. Banks require collateral or cash from the buyer before issuing a LOI. There are different types of LOIs, ranging from commercial to confirmed LOIs. In a commercial LOI, the issuing bank makes the payment directly to the beneficiary. In a confirmed LOI, a confirming bank transfers the payment under the LOI if the buyer and the issuing bank default. The buyer's bank is usually the issuing bank. The seller's bank is usually the confirming bank. The LOI is an important tool in international trade. This is of particular interest when trading large shipments to new customers in new areas.

Export Credit Guarantee

In specific cases, the government may issue an Export Credit Guarantee to ensure that an exporter is paid for goods shipped abroad in case of customer default. The possibilities and conditions for such a guarantee vary per country.

CONTRACT MANAGEMENT (ADVANCED)

Contract management includes agreeing on the terms and conditions of contracts, monitoring compliance with these terms and conditions, and agreeing and recording contract amendments.

Concluding a good contract is no easy task. But once the contract has been concluded, the real work begins. The project manager should ensure that the desired result is delivered on time, within budget and according to specifications and that all the administrative provisions of the contract are met.

Immediately after the conclusion of the contract, the contract management should summarise the specific contract obligations, who is responsible for what, and the timeline for the subsequent obligations. Also, it should record how this will be reported, how contract changes are approved and implemented, how results are to be assessed, how products are to be delivered and how invoices and payments are to be approved.

Contract manager

Many organisations have separate contract managers. The contract manager in the customer organisation is the one who is responsible for managing all supplier contracts and for drafting and maintaining procurement standards. This contract manager usually works in the procurement department. The contract manager in the supplier organisation is the one who is responsible for managing the contracts with one or more customers.

Within a project, the project manager is responsible for contract management. In large projects, a separate contract manager may be appointed. This contract manager is then responsible for the daily management of all contracts during the implementation of the work and should ensure that all administrative provisions of these contracts are complied with. This contract manager reports to the project manager.

CLAIM MANAGEMENT (ADVANCED)

Claim management includes all activities necessary to enforce justified claims against third parties and avert unjustified claims from them. Deviations from agreed contracts in projects are often difficult to prevent. Therefore, developing and agreeing to a claim strategy in advance is wise. Depending on the circumstances, a defensive or offensive claim strategy can be chosen. The choice of the claim strategy can be influenced by the permanent organisation's policy.

Defensive claims strategy – The emphasis is on concluding equivalent agreements, accepting justified claims, offering generous compensation, and only claiming compensation if one has actually suffered damage and is fully within one's rights.

Offensive claiming strategy – The emphasis is on the search for unilaterally advantageous contracts, categorically rejecting all claims at all times, always trying to build up a counter-claim, and immediately demanding the absolute maximum from third parties at every apparent deviation from the contract.

Management of project claims should always be done in close cooperation with the in-house legal department/legal specialists and in consultation with management.

VARIOUS PARTNERSHIPS (ADVANCED)

Assignments are often carried out in collaboration with other suppliers or contractors. Different forms of cooperation can be used, such as:

Consortium

A consortium is a collaboration between two or more parties to carry out a project, whereby each carries out its own part of the total contract at its own expense and risk and retains its own profit. Often, one of the parties acts as a principal towards the customer. Many large infrastructural projects are offered and carried out in a consortium. The advantage of a consortium is that the strengths of each of the participating parties can be utilised while still making a joint offer. A consortium is often a one-off incidental cooperation.

General Partnership

A general partnership (GP) is a cooperation under a common name and risk, in which each partner is liable for all debts and obligations of the GP. A GP has its own capital, usually a joint account, and employs its own staff. A GP is registered under its own name in the Chamber of Commerce Trade Register but is not a separate legal entity. Unless the partnership agreement states otherwise, each partner is authorised to act on behalf of the GP. Setting up a general partnership is relatively simple. A disadvantage is that personal assets aren't protected, and partners are liable for each other.

Joint venture

A joint venture is a business venture by two or more parties that otherwise retain their own identities. In a joint venture, the parties share ownership together with risks, profits, losses, and governance. A joint venture may be entered into to develop a new product or enter a new market. Companies also enter a joint venture to carry out highly complex, long-term projects. With a joint venture, the risk of each participating party is limited to their share in the joint venture.

Back-to-back agreement

A back-to-back agreement is an agreement whereby the contract is entirely carried out by a sub-contractor under the main contractor's responsibility and whereby the rights and obligations of the main contractor are passed on one-on-one to the sub-contractor. A back-to-back agreement is a special form of subcontracting. This relieves the main contractor and provides additional control by the subcontractor, but also effectively closes any liability gaps in the contractual chain.

The main contractor does not have to pay the subcontractor until it has been paid itself. Schedule and deadlines with possible penalties for the main contractor apply one-on-one to the subcontractor. The same applies to dispute resolution procedures. Terminating the main contract automatically means terminating the contract with the subcontractor.

Co-makership

Co-makership is a long-term collaboration with a limited number of suppliers to gain a mutual business benefit. Co-makership is based on trust. It usually strives to deliver an outstanding product at minimal costs based on reliable just-in-time delivery. Co-makership is particularly interesting for the leading party if the suppliers each have their own development expertise.

SUPPLY CHAIN MANAGEMENT (ADVANCED)

Supply Chain Management (SCM) is the coordinated management of goods and services from raw materials to the delivery of the finished product or service by the retailer to the end user. However, each link in the chain retains its own management.

SCM covers everything from manufacturing, product development, logistics, marketing and sales to the systems needed to manage the supply chain. By managing the supply chain, companies can reduce costs and deliver products to consumers faster and more efficiently. SCM includes manufacturers, wholesalers, and retailers. Depending on the power of its position in the chain, each can fulfil the function of the chain director (see Figure 6.01.03).

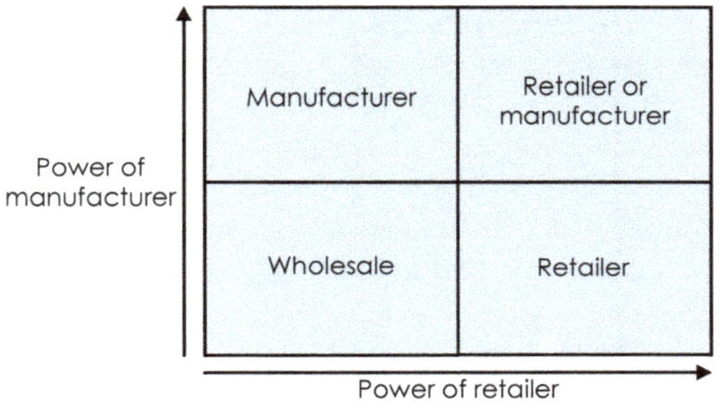

Figure 6.01.03 Position chain director in supply chain management

SCM requires trust, and trust takes time. Transparency is essential. The parties involved should have insight into each other's activities, open accounting and clear agreements on profit sharing. The supply chain works best when a limited number of suppliers is involved. Partners should have a strategic and cultural fit, capability, industry know-how, experience, and an outstanding price-quality ratio.

6.02 CHANGE CONTROL

PURPOSE

The purpose of this chapter is to enable the individual to assess, get agreement on and implement project changes.

LEARNING OBJECTIVES

- Change requests, off-specifications and other issues;
- Change control strategy and issue register;
- Change authority and change budget;
- Urgency and priority of issues;
- Configuration and configuration items within a project (advanced);
- Configuration item records and the configuration management database (advanced);
- Configuration management process and plan (advanced);
- Ordinary and configuration baselines (advanced);
- Relationship between change control and configuration management (advanced).

DEFINITIONS

Issue: An event or condition that has or almost certainly will occur, was not foreseen, and needs management attention to be resolved or dealt with.
Issue register: A log used for recording information on issues that need to be formally addressed.
Change request: A request for approval to change a product or service.
Off-specification: A product or service that should be delivered but currently is not or is forecasted not to be.
Change control: A process used to ensure that changes to a product or service are controlled and coordinated.

INTRODUCTION

Projects and project outputs are always subject to change. This may be due to advancing insight and or changing circumstances. Therefore, a predefined and transparent change control process is an essential element of project management. Without proper change control, we do not know which changes have been approved and implemented and their impact on the initiative. We may not even know if, and if so, what changes have occurred.

In the context of this chapter, we also describe how to manage off-specifications and other issues that require management attention, as these may impact the product and services to be delivered. Finally, we describe configuration management in the advanced section.

POSITIONING

In the project definition stage, agree on the change control approach and create an issue register. Make sure that these processes are agreed upon before the actual implementation of the project starts. This is to avoid the change procedures becoming subject to discussion when the first changes are assessed. Changes are not just factual adjustments but are often sensitive issues on which stakeholders may have strong differences of opinion.

During the implementation of the works, changes should be identified, described, classified, assessed, rejected or approved and, in the latter case, implemented in a controlled and coordinated way. The change control processes should be evaluated and, if necessary, updated during stage transitions. At project closure, any outstanding issue should be transferred to the appropriate bodies, and the issue register should be closed.

CHANGE CONTROL AND CHANGE MANAGEMENT

A distinction should be made between change control as part of project management and change management to implement organisational change (see Chapter 6.05 Change and Transformation). The latter may lead to changes within the project but is not part of change control.

This still does not make change control a straightforward process. In change control, it is important not only to deal with the actual changes in the project but also with all situations and circumstances that could lead to a change. A test that fails or a simple question raised could reveal a major problem that needs management attention. On the other hand, it would lead to too much administration to deal with all these issues formally. It is better to handle some issues informally. Furthermore, different issues require different processes.

THREE TYPES OF ISSUES AND OTHER ISSUES

Within change control, we can distinguish three types of issues, all of which can lead to changes, but each of which requires a different procedure. Here, an issue is defined as any relevant event or circumstance that has happened or almost certainly will happen, that was not foreseen, and requires management attention to be resolved or dealt with. We differentiate:

- Change requests
- Off-specifications
- Problems and concerns ('problems and concerns')

A change is an alteration of a product or service, a condition or a situation. A change request for approval is a request to change a product or service; within a project, a change request is a request to change a deliverable. Requests to change a condition or situation, such as a change of staff or the permission to work overtime, are categorised as 'other issues'. An 'other issue' can also just be a question or a concern. An off-specification is something that should be delivered but currently is not or is forecasted not to be.

> *A request for a different carpet colour is a change request. A product that does not meet the specifications is an off-specification. The late delivery of a shipment is an 'other issue'.*

These three different issues can be tracked separately. Nowadays, they can also be recorded in a common issue register.

CHANGE CONTROL STRATEGY AND CHANGE REGISTER

A change control strategy is a high-level description of how changes will be managed in the project, including the intended outcome and the specific processes, procedures, techniques, standards, and responsibilities to be applied. This strategy should also define which changes can be handled informally, who the change authority is, and what its mandate is.

A standard change procedure is:

- Record the change request in the change register, plus assign a first priority and urgency;
- Analyse the consequences (impact analysis) and determine the final priority and urgency;
- Draft a *Request for Change* (RFC) and get approval from the change authority;
- After approval, implement the decision taken and inform the applicant and relevant stakeholders.

Small changes that do not compromise the quality and do not change the functionality to be delivered can often be addressed informally. However, the line between what can be addressed formally and informally remains tricky.

> *A request not only to register students via the website but also to release exam results via the website is an extension on a previously determined scope and should therefore be formally dealt with. A request to also include a help function button on the home screen is likely just a further extension of the agreed functionality and can probably be dealt with informally.*

Also, agree on how to deal with these informal changes. Although they do not require formal administration, someone should decide on them. Avoid that role. Before you know it, you will end up in the middle between proponents and opponents of seemingly minor changes. Within Agile, this role is assigned to the product owner (see Chapter 9.05 Development Frameworks). For other projects, this should be agreed upon separately.

Formal change requests should be recorded. This is usually done in a change register (see Figure 6.02.01). This register provides an overview of RFCs filed. The RFC identifier also serves as a reference to the relevant RFC. When preparing an RFC, a template is usually used.

Change register

- RFC identifier
- Date raised
- Description
- Raised by
- Priority and severity
- Impact outline
- Decision
- Approved by
- Date decision

Figure 6.02.01 Change register

OFF-SPECIFICATIONS AND OFF-SPECIFICATION REGISTER

Most off-specifications come from tests that have failed. This is noted in the quality or test register, with reference to the relevant off-specification note. The off-specification note (corrective action or non-conformance note) describes the off-specification and indicates the corrective actions to be taken. After implementation of the corrective actions, a retest should be carried out. This retest should be recorded as a separate entry in the quality register. After approval of the result, the off-specification note is signed off. In large projects, a separate off-specification register is usually set up.

If it is impossible to correct the off-specification within the agreed tolerances, then the off-specification is forwarded to the change authority for a decision. An off-specification accepted by the change authority without corrective action is called a *concession*. If the change authority accepts the off-specification but also decides to remove a particular requirement entirely, this is called a *waiver*. This only happens when it is clear that the specific requirement cannot be met and is not necessary (anymore) to achieve the stated quality objectives.

OTHER ISSUES AND ISSUE REGISTER

Many 'other issues' can be handled informally. It is simply part of the daily management of the project. You make a note in the minutes of meeting or your daily log and deal with it accordingly. However, there will always remain 'other issues' that you need to address formally, as they could have serious consequences for one of the project parties involved or agreed objectives. Those issues should be officially recorded in a decision or issue register. An initial priority and urgency should be established, and the individual who raised the issue should be notified of the registration. Then, the issue's impact should be analysed, potential measures determined with their implications for the project and the final priority and urgency set.

Potential risks should be registered in the risk register. If the measures can be implemented within the agreed tolerances, you can implement them on your own authority. If the issue threatens to exceed tolerances, you should escalate it to the project sponsor/ project board for decision-making (see Chapter 6.04 Control and Reporting).

Issue report

For issues that require formal handling, it may be necessary to prepare a separate issue report. This is in addition to the registration in the issue register. Such a report contains the issue description with cause and effect, the actual impact analysis with the various options considered and the recommendation with consequences.

CHANGE AUTHORITY AND CHANGE BUDGET

A change authority is an individual or entity authorised to approve change requests and off-specifications. The project sponsor is the highest change authority in the project. Usually, the user representative is designated as change authority on behalf of the sponsor. The user representative may, in turn, delegate this authority to a subject matter expert for operational changes.

For major changes, however, the decision should be referred back to the user representative and possibly even to the project sponsor. A change budget is a budget allocated to the change authority to finance changes. The changer authority and the change budget should be agreed upon before the start of work.

In most cases, if there is no separate change budget, change costs are charged to the reserve for miscellaneous and unforeseen expenses. However, there is a risk that this will deplete this reserve early in the project, as many will want to use it. This immediately leads to a budget overrun later in case of unforeseen expenses. Therefore, it is advisable to assign a separate change budget to cover the costs of necessary changes (see Chapter 6.04 Control and Reporting).

An alternative is to introduce an exchange procedure. The change authority is then empowered to make changes within the agreed mandate on the condition that other less important features are dropped. In this way, the overall duration and cost of the project do not change while the change authority can still adapt the project output to the evolving insights of users and developers.

PRIORITY AND URGENCY

A priority and urgency should be established for each change request. Priority is the measure of the importance of a fact or condition in respect to others. Urgency indicates how swiftly an issue should be responded to. The priority is generally classified according to the MoSCoW principle (see Chapter 4.04 Requirements and Objectives). This allows a low-priority requirement to be exchanged for a new high-priority requirement to maximise project value (see the exchange procedure above).

SUSTAINABILITY

Changes in a project are inevitable as the project output becomes clearer during the project itself and adapts to new insights on how to make the project output better fit for use and fit for purpose. From a sustainable perspective, an effective change control procedure can better align the project and the project output with the intended sustainable benefits. Change control should always include all sustainable aspects laid down in the project preparation and definition stage

TAILORING

Agile embraces change. Changes are the basis for adding extra value to deliverables. Features are specified as late as possible, limiting the number of changes. The frequent releases of deliverables usually limit the impact of the requested changes. Changes are resolved directly between the product owner and the delivery teams. Only fundamental business model adjustments (pivots) need to be escalated to the project board in coordination with the product owner authority. Therefore, it is essential to agree to the product owner's mandate in advance and keep in close contact with them.

All deliverable features and change requests are prioritised. A change budget doesn't apply here because changes outweigh the minor ones. The product owner acts as change authority and reports on this to the user representative, who acts as the product owner's representative on the project board.

RESPONSIBILITIES

Changes can arise at any time. Anyone can submit change requests. The project manager is responsible for effective change control. The supplier is responsible for correcting any off-specifications. The change authority is authorised to approve change requests and off-specifications. Project support may administer the change control procedures and set up and maintain the change and issue register. The project sponsor is accountable for change control towards the sponsoring organisation.

ADVANCED

CONFIGURATION MANAGEMENT (ADVANCED)

According to ISO 10007:2017, Configuration management is the aspect of management aimed at technical and administrative control of a configuration item, and its associated configuration information, over its period of use. Configuration management originated in the defence industry for complex systems to establish and maintain consistency of a product's performance throughout its lifetime. Today, it is widely used in a variety of industries. Lack of configuration management can cause serious problems in maintaining and updating systems. What is a filter's ID number, which gasket and type of bolts belong to it, and when was the filter last replaced? This kind of information should be accurately recorded.

Configuration management is quite different from scope (configuration) management. The latter should ensure that the scope is aligned with agreed stakeholder needs and requirements and that the configuration of the scope enables effective realisation of the deliverables. The scope configuration is the classification of the scope into a particular combination, usually defined in a WBS or PBS.

A *Configuration Item* (CI) is a component that satisfies an end-use function and of which configuration information should be controlled. A *Configuration Item Record* (CIR) is the registered information of a configuration item. The *Configuration Management Database* (CMDB) is the database that contains all configuration item records.

If a system is to be developed or modified, it should be determined right at the beginning whether the system is or will be subject to configuration management. This should be determined no later than the project definition stage. If so, a configuration management approach should be determined, and a configuration management plan prepared. During project implementation, the required configuration information should be captured and maintained. At project closure, the updated CMDB should be handed over to the customer at the same time as the project output. However, this does not apply to every project or to all deliverables. For example, it is required for the installation in the transformer house, but not for the building itself.

> *Configuration management should be distinguished from asset management and document management. Asset management is the process of developing, operating, maintaining, and selling assets in a cost-effective way to maximise value for an organisation. Document management is the process of recording, storing, amending and releasing documents in a controlled manner and ensuring that correct documents are used (see Chapter 6.03 Information and Documentation).*

Configuration item records

At the minimum, a configuration item record should include the product identifier, product name, version number, status, location, who is responsible, product description, and interfaces to other CIs should be recorded. When a CI changes, often, other CIs should also be changed. Therefore, it is essential that these interfaces are also recorded in the configuration item record (see Figure 6.02.02).

• Project identifier	• Item type
• CI title and identifier	• Item attributes
• Current version	• Location
• Product status	• Variant
• Date of last status change	• Producer/supplier
• Product owner	• Brand/type
• Interfaces with other CIs	• Serial/licence number
• Cross-reference to relevant issues	
• Cross-reference to relevant documents	

Figure 6.02.02 Example composition configuration item record

Configuration management strategy

The configuration management strategy is a high-level description of the configuration management processes, procedures, techniques, standards, and responsibilities to be applied to the project.

The configuration management process consists of five basic functions:

- *Planning* – Define the configuration architecture and the information to be recorded;
- *Identification* – Identify the current CIs and record their status and characteristics;
- *Change control* – Manage all CIs through an authorised change procedure;
- *Status accounting* – Report on the status of the CIs and the changes made;
- *Verification* – Ensure that the current status of all CIs corresponds to the status in the CMDB.

It is essential that the configuration architecture, the items under configuration management, and the configuration information to be recorded are agreed upon with the customer and supplier.

With effective configuration management:

- Everyone works with the right products;
- All products are easy to trace;
- The current status of the various products is known;
- These products are not modified without authorisation.

Configuration management plan

To enable configuration management, a configuration management plan should be prepared. A configuration management plan should include the following:

- Why configuration management is applied in the project;
- Which products are covered by configuration management;
- The procedures, methods and techniques to be applied;
- What information is stored in the CI records;
- The required resources, responsibilities, and authorities;
- A reference to the customer and supplier configuration management systems.

The configuration management procedures for the project are often derived from the customer or supplier configuration management system. If we deviate from these procedures, we should indicate this and the reason why in the configuration management plan.

Configuration baseline

A configuration baseline is the approved configuration information at a point in time that serves as a reference for activities throughout the lifecycle of a product or service. A configuration baseline is thus a special type of baseline. Expired baselines should be preserved. This makes it possible to trace successive versions of the baselines afterwards. This also makes it possible to fall back on an earlier version if necessary.

Product status account

To verify the status of the CIs and associated configuration baselines, it is recommended that a product status account is prepared regularly. This account provides an overview of the status and version of all products developed during the project. Usually, a product status account is prepared at stage transitions and project closure.

Change control and configuration management

With each approved change to a configuration baseline, the appropriate CI record in the CMDB should be updated. Approved change requests should be recorded in the appropriate CI records. Change control and configuration management are, therefore, inextricably linked.

Roles and responsibilities

The project manager is responsible for configuration management in the project, if applicable. Project support may assist in establishing the CM process, preparing the CM plan, setting up the CMDB, maintaining CI records, and preparing product status accounts. The supplier is responsible for delivering and updating the configuration information. The project sponsor is accountable for the configuration management towards the sponsoring organisation.

Configuration management can also be assigned to a separate configuration manager. This may be a separate individual or a configuration manager from the customer or supplier organisation. Configuration management in an IT project is often managed by the configuration manager of the customer's IT department.

6.03 INFORMATION AND DOCUMENTATION

PURPOSE

The purpose of this chapter is to enable the individual to establish infrastructure, processes, and systems for information and documentation flow.

LEARNING OBJECTIVES

- Information versus data;
- Information versus document management;
- Information and document management systems;
- Information management strategy and information management plan;
- Quality and security requirements;
- Project file structure;
- Document tracking matrix.

DEFINITIONS:

Data: The bare figures, numbers or graphs.
Information: The assumed meaning given to data received or provided.
Document: A written, printed, or electronic matter that provides information or evidence or serves as an official record.
Information management: The aspect of management aimed at the effective identification, collection, storage, and exchange of information.
Document management: The aspect of management aimed at the effective identification, collection, storage, and sharing of documents.
Project filing structure: The structure of folders in which project documents are stored.

INTRODUCTION

Managing information and documentation is not very exciting, but it is a necessary aspect of project management. The use of expired documents and, for example, the simultaneous use of different versions of the same document can seriously jeopardise project success. Failure to preserve original baselines and changes can lead to annoying stakeholder disagreements. Redundant information can disrupt the efficient and effective implementation of the project.

POSITIONING

In the project definition stage, the information management approach should be determined, the information management plan prepared, the information management systems set up, and the project filing structure established. During implementation, regular checks should be made to ensure that information management functions correctly and everyone in the project team receives and uses the correct documents.

At stage transitions, information management should be evaluated and, if necessary, updated. At project closure, the existing files should be cleaned up, closed and handed over to the appropriate bodies. Information and document management should be reviewed as part of the project evaluation.

INFORMATION VERSUS DATA

Data are the bare figures, numbers, or graphs. Data are, in themselves, meaningless. Information is the assumed meaning given to data received or provided. The information obtained based on the same data may vary per individual.

In projects, we are often overwhelmed with vast amounts of data that we cannot use, which only takes time to scan and put aside. It is even worse when we try to use it and draw the wrong conclusions, or discard all the data we have received, because we received so much of it, overlooking the fact that they contain some valuable information. In this context, 'less is more'.

INFORMATION VERSUS DOCUMENT MANAGEMENT

Information management is the aspect of management aimed at the effective identification, collection, storage, and exchange of information. Document management is the same but is primarily focused on documents. In this context, a document is a written, printed, or electronic matter that provides information or evidence or serves as an official record. This comprises not only the various specialist and management documents but also e-mail correspondence and could even include WhatsApp and Twitter accounts. These can be particularly relevant in politically sensitive environments.

However, information is more than that. It also includes information exchanged at meetings, presentations, workshops and stand-ups, what is displayed on an information radiator, what is posted on the websites, narrated in interviews and articles, et cetera. In this context, information management refers to both formal and informal information.

The information needs and associated processes and infrastructure depend on the project itself, the organisation's governance, the broader context in which the project has to be implemented, the roles and responsibilities of those involved, and the interests and influence of stakeholders. To set up effective information management processes and infrastructure, thoroughly examining these is paramount.

INFORMATION MANAGEMENT INFRASTRUCTURE

Information management infrastructure also includes the meeting and reporting infrastructure and any structured way of communicating with stakeholders outside the direct project organisation. The latter should be carefully designed and coordinated with the project sponsor/project board and the communications department.

The project's document management system is usually a computerised system used to store and manage documents. The purpose of such a system is to ensure that documents can quickly be found and it is always clear what the latest version is. Furthermore, that information/ documentation is only accessible to those who need it and are entitled to it and that there is a correct basis for subsequent reviews and audits.

To enable this, it is advised to make one individual responsible for document management within the project. This can be a separate document manager or a project support officer. This individual is usually also responsible for setting up and maintaining the project's document management system and liaises with the service department about the system's functioning.

INFORMATION MANAGEMENT STRATEGY

The information management strategy is a high-level description of how the information will be managed on the project, including the intended outcome and the specific processes, procedures, techniques, standards, and responsibilities to be applied. Information management describes the planning, identifying, approving, tracking and monitoring of information.

Planning information management

Determine who should supply what information to whom, who should review and approve it, and how it should be stored. What procedures apply? How are the documents coded, and what is the filing structure? Which information systems and techniques are used? What are the required resources and costs to manage the information during the project? And last but not least, what are the quality and security requirements and how are they met?

Identify, record and store information

Agree on a uniform document coding system for the whole project. Based on this, each document should be given a unique identifier. This code should preferably include the project number, item code, item name, version number, date of issue, and status.

Individuals/teams need to keep track of the information they receive and send. The storage of documentation can be centralised or decentralised. Information can also partly be stored on paper and digitally. Furthermore, storing documents at different locations is advised to prevent loss of information in case of calamities. If a shared platform is used, this system will automatically track when information has been shared, used and updated.

Approve, change and distribute information

Who should review and approve what and how should be determined in advance. Management documents should always be approved by the next higher management level. Changes should be approved by the same individuals that approved the original document. Distribution should be made only to those individuals who are entitled to receive a copy.

To ensure that approval, changes and distribution take place in a controlled manner, it is recommended to include a colophon in the relevant documents stating:

- Who is the author;
- Who should review or have reviewed the document;
- Who should approve or has approved the document (signature);
- What is the latest version, and why was the change;
- Who will receive a copy or is entitled to have access;
- Identification code, place of storage, and date of issue.

If a document management system is used, it should be determined beforehand who has certain rights. People can then view the documents at their convenience. When documents are posted or updated, it is useful to have a notification sent with the desired action per individual. For critical documents, it is advisable to send documents to them personally. This has a higher attention value; thus, recipients are more likely to take immediate action.

Tracking of information

In addition to managing the most up-to-date information, it may be necessary to retain previously approved versions. This applies especially to baselines, contracts and decision documents. Not only should previous versions be retained, but also the comments received, based on which the changes were made.

Monitoring and control

The collection, recording, storage, distribution, and use of information do not automatically go well. This should be checked regularly: are the right people receiving the correct information and in time, are changes authorised by the right people, and is everyone working with the latest approved version? At least at every stage transition, information management should be evaluated and adjusted if necessary.

Avoid overload of redundant information.

It is important to limit/avoid unnecessary information flows in the project. Limit the number of people who get a copy of sent e-mails. Inform stakeholders through pre-agreed contacts. Do not distribute all incoming documents to all team members automatically. Apply the linking pin principle. Above all, ensure that responsibilities correspond to the project roles and that the provision of information matches them. If possible, apply management by exception. Providing information and participating in meetings elicit input, leading to mandatory follow-up, et cetera. Is that always necessary?

INFORMATION MANAGEMENT PLAN

The information management plan describes the information systems, the information procedures and the required resources and budget to manage the information during the project.

Information system

The information system specifies which information is to be stored centrally and de-centrally and how. It specifies which documents are to be kept, the filing structure within which they are to be stored, the information that certain documents should contain, the format and form of those documents, and how they are to be identified and registered.

Information procedures

The information procedures specify who is responsible for identifying, recording, storing, reviewing, approving, updating and distributing the information and how monitoring and control will take place. The procedures also specify the routing of the document flow and the time available for the individual steps within that routing; for example, 'drawings for approval should first be registered by project support before they can be forwarded' and 'drawings should be reviewed within two weeks'.

Required capacity and costs

Finally, it includes time and costs required for information management, such as the time and costs of the information manager, project support and possibly the secretariat, and the costs of setting up and maintaining the various information management systems.

QUALITY AND SECURITY CRITERIA

Good information management is essential in every project. We need to avoid losing documents, information getting into the wrong hands, not knowing what the latest version is, and whether the content of documents and data files is still up to date. Unfortunately, this is a common nightmare in many projects. It is, therefore, essential to define the quality and safety requirements in advance, to design the information system accordingly and to keep checking whether these requirements are being met:

- *Compliance* – Are the procedures per the internal corporate procedures and the official regulations and legislation, such as the statutory retention periods and the General Data Protection Regulation (GDPR) (see Chapter 11.03 Laws and Legislation)?
- *Reliability* – Are the procedures effective? Are the information systems reliable? Do we always have the correct version of the documents? Is the information consistent with each other?
- *Actuality* – Has the latest data been processed? Have changes in one document already been incorporated into the others?
- *Confidentiality* – Is information protected against theft and unauthorised access? Does distribution take place according to the agreed clearance levels?
- *Availability* – Do people have access to the information they need? Is all information available? Can the required information be found quickly? Is the relevant historical information retained? But also: has information that is no longer required or is outdated been deleted?

PROJECT FILING STRUCTURE

The project filing structure is the structure of folders in which documents are stored. It is recommended to use the same filing structure in all projects. It is hereby important to distinguish between the following:

- *Specialist documents* – Documents for realising the project output;
- *Quality documents* – Management documents to control the quality of the project output;
- *Other management documents* – Documents other than quality documents to control project performance.

A common project filing structure is divided into specialist files, quality files, and other management files, which in turn are divided into project files and stage files.

Project files

The project file contains all management documents, except quality documents, which relate to the entire project, such as:

- Project start-up documents such as project mandate and project outline;
- Project management plan;
- Business case and benefits review plan;
- Risk register;
- Project management structure;
- Communication plan;
- Contract documentation;
- Project accounting;

- Stage approvals;
- Lessons learned log;
- Project closure documents, such as the protocol of delivery, statement of acceptance, and the end-of-project report.

Stage files

A stage file contains all management documents that are not part of the project and quality files and which relate to a particular stage, such as:

- Stage organogram with contact details of the various participants;
- The different versions of the stage plan and any team plans and exception plans;
- Management documents such as progress reports and exception reports;
- Minutes of meetings and correspondence, such as letters, memos, notes, e-mails and the like.

Quality files

The quality file contains all management documents directly related to (the control of) the quality of the project deliverables, such as:

- Project quality plan, including the requirement specifications;
- Configuration management database;
- Inspection documents, such as test plans, inspection reports and test results;
- Quality register with the status of the quality activities to be carried out;
- Change register with all the formal change requests filed.

Specialist files

The specialist file contains all the specialist documents. These include documents to be handed over to the customer at completion and documents needed to realise the project deliverables, such as designs, flow charts, and so on. It is recommended that specialist files be classified according to the WBS structure.

DOCUMENT TRACKING MATRIX

To visualise the order in which different documents should be prepared, a document tracking matrix can be created. Such a matrix shows who is responsible for preparing the various documents, who should approve them, to whom they should be distributed for follow-up, who should archive them, and so on. For an example, see Figure 6.03.01.

Document tracking matrix	Supervisor	Engineer	Building contractor	Mechanical contractor	Support
Floor drawing	A	O	I	I	F
Installation drawing	A	I	I	O	F
Cut-out drawing	A	I	O	I	F

Legend	
A	Approve
O	Output (drafting & distribution)
I	Input (receive document)
F	File (archive)

Figure 6.03.01 Document tracking matrix

These matrices can be very useful in providing an overview of the sequence of documentation to be developed. Similar overviews can be created to link, for example, requirements to test cases or deliverables (requirements traceability matrix), et cetera.

SUSTAINABILITY

Information and documentation can have a significant impact on the project's sustainability. It enables communication, monitoring and reporting on sustainability, as well as extracting lessons learned on sustainability within the project. Information management should also ensure that all relevant information is available for CSR reporting. It is recommended that environmental and social aspects are recorded and reported separately. What gets attention grows.

In addition, sustainability requires that information and documentation are managed as efficiently as possible and that printing of documents is kept to a minimum.

TAILORING

According to Agile, face-to-face communication is the most effective way of conveying information. Furthermore, in Agile, deliverables take precedence over comprehensive documentation. This sometimes leads to the idea that documentation is no longer needed, which is not true. Test results should be kept, and system and user documentation should be prepared. The product backlog needs to be determined and updated. A CMDB may need to be set up and maintained, and so on. The project manager needs to ensure that the applicable governance requirements are translated into Agile delivery. This should be agreed upon in the definition stage and ensured during development.

At work, an information radiator can be used to ensure that all necessary aspects are visible to those responsible for the deliverables. A wide range of Agile project management software is available nowadays for remote development.

Collaboration between developers and business users is already firmly embedded within most Agile frameworks. Ensure you also keep the project sponsor/project board and other stakeholders informed.

RESPONSIBILITIES

The project manager is responsible for the information and document management of the project. The project support is responsible for setting up and maintaining the document control procedures, the information management systems, and the project filing structure under the overall responsibility of the project manager. Work package managers are responsible for ensuring that agreed procedures and processes are followed. At project closure, the project manager should ensure the various files are tidied up and handed over to the appropriate bodies.

6.04 CONTROL AND REPORTING

PURPOSE

The purpose of this chapter is to enable the individual to establish and maintain a balanced and integrated view about the management of a project and report about it accordingly.

LEARNING OBJECTIVES

- Deming's control cycle (Plan-Do-Check-Act);
- The alignment of the different control and reporting levels within a project;
- The characteristics of MBO and the meaning of the acronym SMART;
- The characteristics of MBE and the principle of tolerances;
- The different project management products and project controls;
- Applying daily management;
- Managing a stage transition and preparing an end-of-stage report and stage plan;
- Escalating an exception and preparing an exception report and exception plan;
- Making use of various reports in a project;
- Analysing progress using trend analysis;
- Analysing progress using Earned Value Analysis (advanced).

DEFINITIONS

Management By Objectives (MBO): A management philosophy that focuses on the joint setting of clear goals and monitoring progress.

Management By Exception (MBE): A management philosophy that only requires escalation to the next management level if it is predicted that the agreed tolerances are to be exceeded.

Work package: The work and the associated conditions assigned to an individual or team.

Tolerance: The permissible deviation above or below the plan's target without the need to escalate the deviation to the next management level.

Exception report: A report detailing the cause and consequences of an exception and options to continue.

End-of-stage report: A report at stage transition detailing the project status, stage performance, and updated project management plan to obtain authorisation for the next stage.

Project controls: The set of activities to ensure the implementation of the project in a controlled way.

INTRODUCTION

Controlling a project is one of the core responsibilities of the project manager. Controlling is the process of ensuring that work is performed according to plan. Controlling consists of analysing the situation, monitoring progress, estimating the expected work to be completed, taking corrective actions, and escalating to the next management level if agreed tolerances are forecasted to be exceeded. Reporting is the process of giving an account of something one has observed, heard, done, or investigated. Reporting should occur periodically to inform the addressee about the work's progress, to enable them to take on their responsibilities.

POSITIONING

Controlling and reporting are typically activities that take place during the project implementation. However, these activities should also take place at the project start and closure to control the implementation of these phases too. During project delivery, this process ensures that the work is carried out in a controlled manner. During stage transitions, this process aims to provide the project sponsor/project board with sufficient information to evaluate and close the current stage, decide whether the project should continue, and, if so, approve the updated project management plan and next stage plan.

CONTROL CYCLE

The basis for project control is the Deming cycle (PDCA):

- ***P**lan* – Draw up a plan for the work to be carried out;
- ***D**o* – Direct the work to be carried out;
- ***C**heck* – Monitor and review the work carried out;
- ***A**ct* – Take necessary corrective actions.

The Deming cycle is originally a quality management cycle but can be applied in all situations where performance needs to be controlled. Control covers the *Check* and *Act* steps within this cycle.

Start checking the work progress early on so that if deviations are found, there is still time to take corrective actions. The first action should be to check whether work is, in fact, commencing on the scheduled start date. Start by asking the responsible people in advance if they have everything they need actually to start on time.

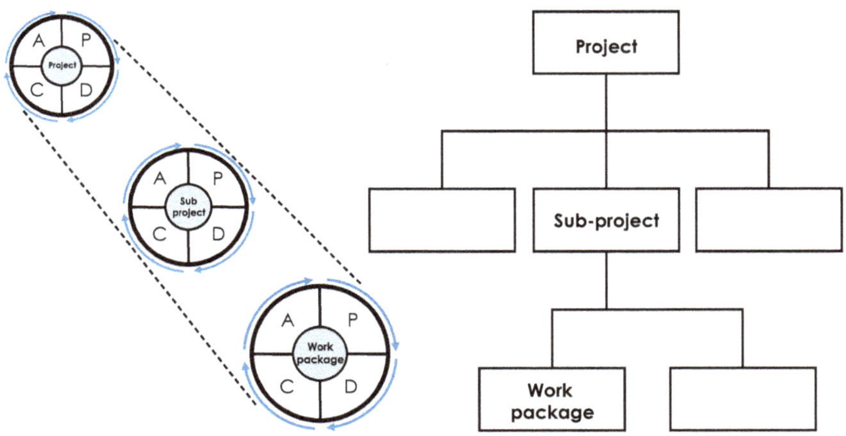

Figure 6.04.01 Different control and reporting levels

MANAGEMENT AND REPORTING LEVELS

The control cycle makes it possible to report it to the next management level. The frequency of controlling and reporting should be tailored to the duration of the work and the associated risks. The work package leader controls the progress of the work package and reports about it to the project manager. The project manager controls the progress of the stage and reports about it to the project sponsor/project board. The project sponsor/project board oversees the project's performance and reports it to the sponsoring organisation or customer (see Figure 6.04.01).

MANAGEMENT BY OBJECTIVES

There are basically two different approaches to controlling the implementation of the work with all the variations in between; Management by Objectives and Management by Exception.

Management By Objectives (MBO) is a management philosophy where managers and staff jointly set and monitor objectives to improve the organisation's performance.

An important aspect of MBO is the formulating of SMART objectives:

- *Specific* – The objective is unambiguous;
- *Measurable* -Measurable values determine when the target is realised;
- *Achievable* – The objective is feasible under the circumstances;
- *Relevant* – The objective matters to you and aligns with the goals;
- *Time-related* – It is clear when the work should be completed.

Within MBO, it is important that objectives are set together. Within this approach, it is also important to regularly report on the progress of the work, not through progress reports but in the form of coaching and problem-solving. At MBO, objectives are not used as a means of assessment but as a means of development.

MBO places great emphasis on teamwork, openness and communication between management and staff. Creating an open climate and paying attention to the personal and career wishes of those involved are of great importance. MBO can be applied between the project sponsor and the project manager but is applied more often between the project manager and team members. MBO leads to regular consultation between the parties involved.

MANAGEMENT BY EXCEPTION

An entirely different control philosophy is *Management By Exception* (MBE). MBE is a management philosophy based on an agreed mandate within which the delegate carries out the work independently. MBE is also based on the joint formulation of objectives. However, progress is not monitored in regular feedback of coaching and problem-solving but based on periodic progress reports. The idea behind MBE is that as long as everything is done within pre-agreed limits (tolerances), there is no need for consultation except at stage transitions.

In doing so, management by exception ensures effective use of senior management time by reducing time-consuming meetings that typically burden projects. Between stage transitions, you only report to the project sponsor/project board via periodic status reports, in addition to ad hoc consultation whenever that is needed. Board meetings only take place at stage transitions and when it is forecasted that the agreed stage or project tolerances are exceeded.

However, this approach requires a high degree of maturity of the project manager and the confidence of the project sponsor/project board in the project manager. Finally, it entails the risk that you are on your own and losing the support of the project sponsor due to its limited involvement in the project implementation. You need to ensure that the project sponsor continues to feel ownership of the project.

DAILY MANAGEMENT

The project manager is responsible for the daily management of the project. This includes managing work packages, issues and risks and assessing and reporting stage status. A work package is the work and the associated conditions assigned to an individual or team.

Managing work packages

Managing work packages includes authorising and reviewing work packages and accepting completed work packages. Work may only be carried out if authorised by the project manager. Otherwise, there is a risk that it will commence while changes still need to be made, conditions have changed, or (a certain part of) the work is no longer needed.

When authorising the work, the project manager and the work package leader should discuss the work package to be carried out in advance; what needs to be delivered, what the specifications are, what the available budget and the duration are, but also what the procedures to be followed are, and so on. When authorising a work package, do not assume that the work package leader knows all the latest ins and outs of the work to be carried out and the conditions that apply. Discussing the upcoming work package before authorising the work has proven to be a very valuable use of time.

When applicable, the work package leader should draft a team plan first. At best, the team plan is prepared when the relevant stage plan is also prepared, at the latest, when the work package is assigned. Team plans should be approved by the project manager. With an external supplier, the team plan submitted to the project manager may contain only the necessary data to enable the project manager to monitor the progress of the work package.

The work package description records all the agreements between the project manager and the work package leader that are relevant for the implementation of the work package, the assessment of the products to be delivered, the reporting on progress and the delivery and closure of the work package as a whole (see Chapter 5.03 Scope). The work package description usually includes the following:

- *Date – The date the work package is agreed upon between the project manager and the work package leader.*
- *Responsible for implementation – The name of the work package leader or supplier with whom the work package is agreed upon.*
- *Work package description – A description of the work to be performed (scope and demarcation).*
- *Product and product descriptions – The products and the product descriptions of the products to be delivered within the work package. This is normally added as an appendix to the work package. The product descriptions include, inter alia, the applicable specifications and how and by whom the quality assessments will be carried out.*

- *Techniques, processes and procedures to be applied – The techniques, processes and (quality) procedures to be applied for the realisation and the assessment of the products to be delivered in this work package.*
- *Interfaces – Interfaces of the deliverables with other products outside the work package. These can be products from other work packages and other projects, but also with products and systems within the business organisation.*
- *Dependencies on other work – The necessary coordination with other work during the implementation of the work package.*
- *Configuration management – This concerns agreements about which products fall under configuration management, the configuration coding to be used, the configuration item records to maintain, and the applicable configuration procedures.*
- *Key elements of the project or stage plan – A summary of the relevant parts of the project or stage plan for the work to be carried out.*
- *Start and finish date, budget, planning and deployment of people and resources – All agreements relevant to the work package, including any tolerances.*
- *Preconditions – All frameworks and regulations within which the work package should be carried out. These include safety regulations that should be complied with.*
- *Progress reports – The agreed dates and format of the reports that should be prepared, and dates, times and locations of the progress meetings.*
- *Change control and escalation procedure – The change control procedure and the procedure if work package tolerances are forecasted to be exceeded.*
- *Approval of deliverables – The individual approving the work package products.*
- *Work package delivery – How the completed work package should be delivered, how and by whom the completed work package should be signed off and how the handover of products after delivery should occur.*

Furthermore, you should periodically review the progress of the individual work packages. This can be done based on the work package leader's progress reports, supported by the data and forecast collected by the project support. At all times, you remain responsible for having an accurate insight into the status of the work in progress.

At completion, you have to assess if all the work as stipulated in the work packages has been completed and handed over and whether all the necessary documents and inspection reports have been signed off and received. Only then can you accept the completed work package and formally release the supplier/work package leader from their duties.

Managing issues and risks

Managing issues and risk include capturing and assessing issues and risks and taking preventive and corrective actions. All new issues and risks should be recorded and analysed. That could be in minutes of meetings or on an information radiator, for example. Project support may help you keep any formal registers. Don't just react to issues and risks brought to your attention, but actively look for potential issues and risks.

Take preventive and corrective actions as necessary. Change requests should be forwarded to the change authority for decision. If the stage or project tolerances are forecasted to be exceeded, escalate this to the project sponsor/project board via an exception report.

Reviewing and reporting stage status

The project manager and the team should also periodically evaluate the status of the stage as a whole. In doing so, you should look at the progress of the individual work packages and how they affect each other. You should also include the possible impact of the issues and risks identified and look for new ones.

Based on this, corrective actions can be taken, new work packages can be authorised, and issues and risks may need to be escalated to the project sponsor/project board. Such a periodic review ensures that the focus remains on the products and services to be delivered and that we look ahead rather than just solve problems.

Finally, you have to inform the project sponsor/project board and other stakeholders regularly about the status of the work and the issues and risks on hand. Stick to the highlights. Effective reporting keeps them informed and involved in the project without getting lost in details. Without regular updates, they will become nervous and will interfere.

MANAGING STAGE TRANSITION

A stage transition is an ideal moment for the project sponsor/project board to assure the project's continued viability and to decide to continue, redirect or close the project prematurely (go/no-go decision).

To enable the project sponsor/project board to exercise their responsibility, you should report on the performance of the current stage, update the project management plan, including the business case, project plan and the risks involved, and prepare the next stage plan. Based on this, you can request discharge from the current stage and authorisation to start the next stage.

Report on current stage

To conclude the current stage, you need to report on the stage status and the work done. Which products were realised and, if possible, delivered and transferred to the users? How did the work and the cooperation go, what issues occurred, how were they addressed, and how did these arise? The status of the current stage and the work done should also be compared with the original stage plan. Finally, any lessons learned should be indicated.

Update the project management plan

The project management plan, including the applicable procedures, needs to be updated based on the actual results and the above lessons learned. However, the most important thing is to update the project plan, the business case and the risks based on the latest insights about the project and the environment. What are the total expected costs and total lead time? What are the key risks? Do we need to change our approach? Is there still a business justification to continue the project in its current form, or should we redirect it or close it prematurely?

Prepare the next stage plan

Next, we should prepare the next stage plan; which products should be delivered, what requirements should they meet, and how, in what way, by whom, and when should the work be carried out. The global requirement specifications, as laid down in the project management plan, should be worked out in more detail. The resources needed should be determined. Involve the work package leaders responsible for carrying out the work in this next stage.

Close-off the current stage

At the end of a stage, teams may change. Perhaps some will also leave the project. A stage closure and recognition and appreciation of the work done are therefore very important. This is best done together with the project sponsor. Celebrate any successes. This can be done on a separate occasion or be combined with a joint evaluation of team performance and a review of lessons learned.

If lessons learned are also of interest to the permanent organisation, a lessons learned report should be forwarded to the appropriate bodies. At stage transition, deliverables may also be handed over to the customer. For these deliverables, a similar process should be carried out as described at project closure (see Chapter 6.06 Project Closure).

Obtaining authorisation to carry out the next stage

Finally, you need authorisation from the project sponsor/project board to carry out the next stage. They will do this in consultation with the sponsoring organisation or customer, who has the final say. This requires the previous information to be clearly presented to them for decision-making. This is best done through an end-of-stage report (see Figure 6.04.02).

End-of-stage report

- Status to date
- Stage performance
- Review quality activities
- Review team performance
- Major issues and risks
- Update project plan
- Update business case
- Update benefits review plan
- Outline next stage plan
- Lessons learned (if applicable)
- Project manager's summary report

Figure 6.04.02 End-of-stage report

Make sure this report is short and to the point. Sometimes even a PowerPoint presentation will do, or a combination of both. The report is then used as a reference document, the PowerPoint, to lead the discussion during the meeting. For details, you can always refer to the underlying documents. Make sure that, at the same time, the relevant budget is made available for the next stage and that the project sponsor/project board actually commits to the resources needed to carry out the work. Finally, ensure that you get an official release of the duty to perform work concerning the previous stage.

ESCALATING EXCEPTIONS

Tolerance is the allowed deviation above or below the plan's objectives without the need to escalate to the next management level. Tolerances can be agreed upon on all management aspects, such as time, costs, quality, scope, risks and benefits, but also on health, security, sustainability, and so on. An exception is a situation where it is forecasted that there will be a deviation beyond agreed tolerances. In case of an exception, the situation should be escalated to the next management level.

The tolerances can be either positive or negative. Also, if the project is carried out much quicker than expected, it should be escalated. In that case, the sponsoring organisation or customer can/should start other projects earlier. Tolerance is thus not extra time or budget made available but the mandate within which you can operate according to your own insights, as agreed.

If the agreed work package tolerances are forecasted to be exceeded, the work package leader should escalate this to the project manager. If the agreed stage or project tolerances are forecasted to be exceeded, the project manager should escalate this to the project sponsor/project board. In case project tolerances are forecasted to be exceeded, the project sponsor should escalate this further to the sponsoring organisation or customer.

The work package leader can escalate an exception to the project manager via an issue. The project manager should always escalate an exception via an exception report. This report also includes possible options and a recommendation how to proceed (see Figure 6.04.03).

Exception report

- Exception plus cause of exception
- Consequences of the exception
- Options and their consequences
- Recommendations inclusive reasons
- Lessons learned (if applicable)

Figure 6.04.03 Exception report

Based on the exception report, (1) the project sponsor/ sponsoring organisation or customer takes a preliminary decision. (2) Based on this, the project manager will prepare an exception plan and update the business case. (3) The management then makes the final decision as to whether or not to proceed and, if so, in what way. The exception plan encompasses the remaining period of the plan it replaces. It has basically the same format as the plan it replaces.

Premature project closure

If a project has to be terminated prematurely, it should be done carefully. Usually, it is impossible to simply pull the plug on a project. Ongoing contracts should be completed or dissolved. Partial deliverables have to be completed somehow. Already implemented changes should be secured or reversed. Therefore, In case of premature closure, it is also often necessary to compare various options, as in an exception report, and escalate it with advice to the project sponsor for decision-making.

PROJECT CONTROLS

Project controls are the set of activities to ensure the implementation of the project in a controlled manner such as:

- *Stakeholder management* – A procedure for engagement of stakeholders;
- *Risk management* – A procedure for managing risks and opportunities;
- *Quality management* – A procedure for controlling and securing quality;
- *Change control* – A procedure for handling change requests and off-specifications;
- *Configuration management* – A procedure for controlling configuration items;
- *Information management* – A procedure for managing information;
- *Control and reporting* – A procedure for control and reporting progress;
- *Escalation procedure* – A procedure for escalation exceptions.

PROJECT MANAGEMENT PRODUCTS

Project management products are products specially designed to control the project. These can be divided into strategies, baselines, registers/logs, and reports:

- *Strategy* – An outline description of how an individual, group or organisation wants to achieve its goals;
- *Baseline* – A status that serves as a reference for the further implementation of the work;
- *Register/log* – To record and maintain information on certain topics for further reference;
- *Report* – An account referring to a particular matter, usually in the form of an official document.

Management strategies

A management strategy is a high-level description of how some management aspects will be applied, including the intended outcome, processes, procedures, roles, responsibilities, and techniques. Management strategies should be developed for all management aspects within a project, such as risk, quality, stakeholder, information management and change control.

Management baselines

Often used project management baselines are:

- *Project outline* – Used to describe the project assignment, which serves as the basis for the project definition stage.
- *Project management plan* – Used to describe how the project is being carried out and controlled and is used by the project sponsor/project board to direct the project as a whole.
- *Business case* – Used throughout the project to monitor the viability and business justification of the project. The business case is part of the project management plan.
- *Project plan* – Used by the project sponsor/project board to control the project stage by stage. The project plan is also part of the project management plan.
- *Stage plan* – Used by the project manager for the daily management of a stage.
- *Exception plan* – Used by the project manager to correct the works according to directions from the project sponsor/project board after an exception.
- *Work package* – Used by the project manager to assign work to a work package leader.

Management registers and logs

Management registers and logs are:

- *Issue register* – A record of all project issues that should be formally handled;
- *Risk register* – A record of the identified risks, including their status, history and measures;
- *Quality register* – A record of all planned and conducted quality activities in a project;
- *Lessons learned log* – A record of lessons learned during the implementation of the project;
- *Daily log* – The personal diary of the project manager, used to record actions and issues that can be dealt with informally.

Management reports

Management reports are:

- *Progress report* – Prepared periodically by the work package leader to inform the project manager about the progress of the work package;
- *Status report* – Prepared periodically by the project manager to inform the project sponsor/project board and key stakeholders about the status of the stage;
- *End-of-stage report* – Prepared by the project manager at stage transition detailing the status and performance to date and the updated project management plan;
- *Exception report* – Prepared by the project manager to report about the cause and consequences of an exception and options to continue;
- *End-of-project report* – Prepared by the project manager at the end of the project detailing the project results and performance;
- *Lessons learned report* – Prepared by the project manager to pass on any lesson learned to the appropriate bodies for further reference.

The reports to inform the project sponsor/project board and key stakeholders about the status of the project includes a summary of the underlying progress reports. In these reports, we often use RAG-codes. RAG is an acronym for Red, Amber, and Green, which function as traffic lights to indicate the status of a particular aspect and whether action needs to be taken (see Figure 6.04.04). Trend analysis can also be used.

Status report

- Code and name project
- Reporting period:
  - Work packages, budget performance + RAG-code and Remarks
  - Work packages, progress performance " "
  - Deliverables status and performance " "
  - Quality control activities performance " "
  - Actuals about issues and risks " "
- Next reporting period:
  - Work packages to start/to continue/to be completed
  - Quality actions planned
  - Corrective actions planned
- Lessons learned (if applicable)
- Project manager's summary report

Figure 6.04.04 Status report

Please note: you are not automatically a good project manager if you use all the above project management products. This can lead to an enormous bureaucracy. Determine which management products you need and stick to those. Information can also be captured in e-mails, on a shared portal or an information radiator, or sometimes simply conveyed verbally or presented in a PowerPoint.

TREND ANALYSIS

To analyse progress, you should not just assess the project's status at a particular point in time but also its development over a series of control points. Common tools are the Cost Trend Analysis (CTA) and Time Trend Analysis (TTA). In these trend analyses, we commonly apply traditional and relative slip charts/burn down charts.

Traditional slip charts

In a traditional slip chart, one axis shows how much time has already elapsed or what has already been spent at the successive control points. The other axis shows the estimated work still to be done to finish work at control points (see Figure 6.04.05/6).

The straight solid line from top left to bottom right represents the planned time/costs to complete at the successive control points: at the start of the work, this is 100%, and at the scheduled completion, it is 0%. The dotted lines on both sides of the solid line represent the tolerance levels above and below the planned values.

In a time slip chart, the steps on the horizontal axis between the successive control points are equal, as the period between the control points is equal (see Figure 6.04.05). In a cost slip chart, the steps on the horizontal axis differ between the successive control points because the costs incurred in each period are different (see Figure 6.04.06).

In Figure 6.04.05, the slip chart shows that the work can be completed increasingly earlier. In Figure 6.04.06, the slip chart shows the costs are increasingly out of line. In both slip charts, the forecasts exceed the agreed tolerances.

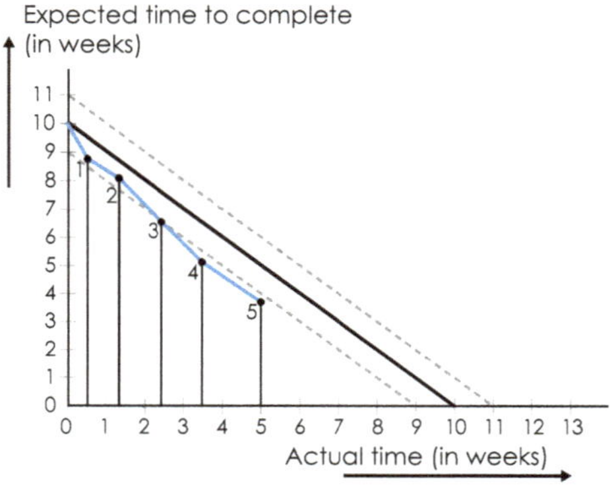

Figure 6.04.05 Traditional time slip chart

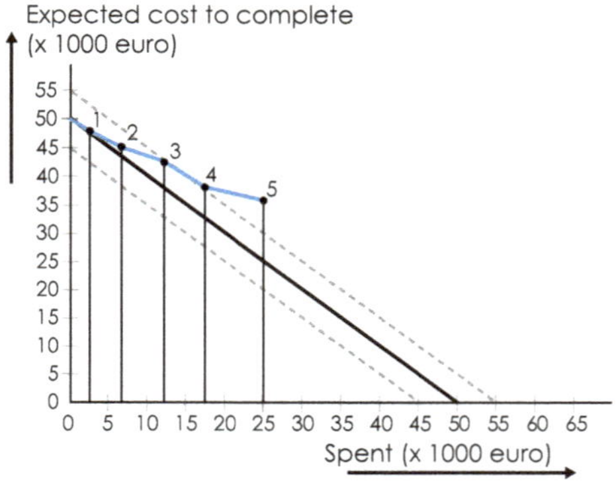

Figure 6.04.06 traditional costs slip chart

Traditional slip charts are often drawn to visualise the expected completing time and costs at various control points. However, these slip charts can also be used to visualise various trends, such as the outstanding number of drawings or the remaining user points to develop during the present sprint.

Relative slip charts

In a relative slip chart, the values on the horizontal and vertical axis are a percentage of the total value of the original plan (see Figure 6.04.07 and 6.04.08). The rest remains unchanged.

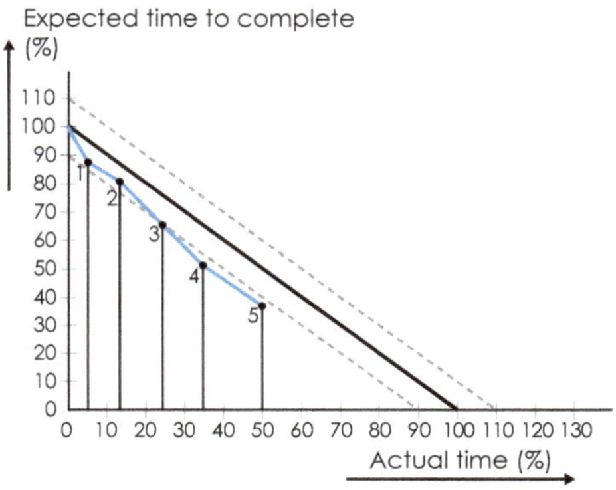

Figure 6.04.07 Relative time slip chart

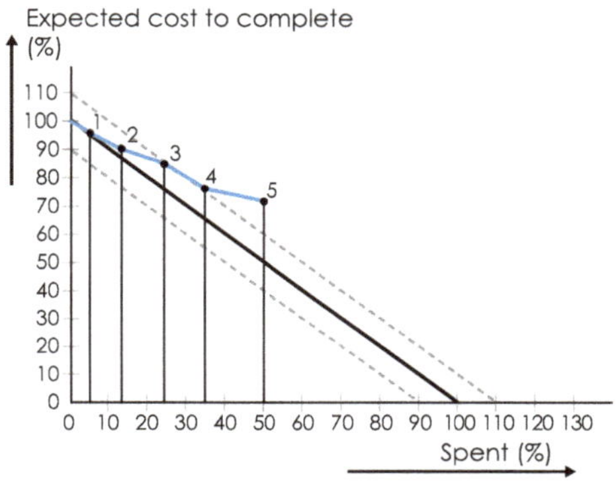

Figure 6.04.8 Relative cost slip chart

MILESTONE TREND ANALYSIS

Another type of trend analysis is the *Milestone Trend Analysis* (MTA) The MTA is a powerful tool for tracking overall project progress. It visualises the expected completion dates of the different milestones at successive control points (see Figure 6.04.09). Together with the underlying reasons for the different forecasts, it provides a good picture of the project's health.

The initially planned completion dates of the individual milestones are the weeks indicated at the vertical axe; in the example, milestone A at the end of week 3, milestone B at the end of week 6, and milestone C at the end of week 9. The expected completion dates at the control point at the end of week 4 were for milestone A at the end of week 5, for milestone B at the end of week 7, and for milestone C at the end of week 10.

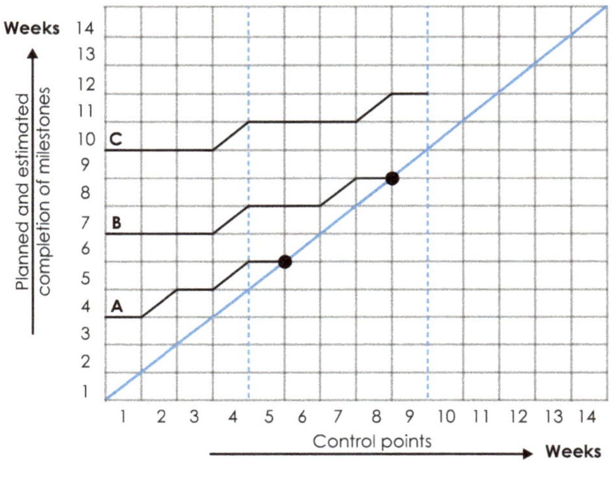

Figure 6.04.09 Milestone slip chart

Upon completion of a milestone, the expected completion date equals the current date, i.e., when the line of the expected completion date touches the diagonal; in the example, milestone A is completed at the end of week 5; milestone B is completed at the end of week 8.

SUSTAINABILITY

Sustainability implies proactive and open communication about the project, including its status and progress. This should also include the environmental and social aspects of the project. To this end, key performance indicators and acceptance criteria for these aspects should be established so that they can be reported on. For this, the Triple Bottom Line method can be used. If benefits are already realised during the project, they should also be reported on.

TAILORING

In Agile, completed deliverables are the primary measure of progress, whereby controlling progress is achieved by prioritising what will be delivered. This is accomplished by prioritising the features to be delivered and developing them in that order.

Velocity is the most important measure of productivity. Velocity is the rate of progress a team makes during a timebox. The velocity is determined relative to a reference feature. The work to develop that feature is called a *story point* or *point value*.

Within timeboxes, progress is monitored with task boards and burn down charts. The task board shows the work not yet started (To Do), work in progress (WIP) and work completed (Done). The burn down chart shows the number of story points of the work not yet started on the consecutive stand-ups. Individual developers update the task board as work progresses. The team updates the burn down chart prior to the daily stand-up.

At timebox reviews, the product owner discusses the current product backlog and the likely completion date of the work in total. Therefore, the end of a timebox is an ideal moment to provide a project status report to the project sponsor/project board and other stakeholders.

Ensure that arrangements are made in advance on how progress will be monitored, not only within but also across the timeboxes, how progress information is collected and how the project sponsor/project board and other stakeholders will be informed. For the latter, the project manager should play a leading role.

RESPONSIBILITIES

The project manager is responsible for the managing and controlling the project, managing stage transitions, and escalating to the project sponsor/project board if it is forecasted that the stage or project tolerances will be exceeded. The work package leader is responsible for accepting, implementing, reporting and delivering the work package to the project manager. The project sponsor is accountable for the project's success towards the sponsoring organisation. If the project tolerances are forecasted to be exceeded, the sponsor should escalate this to them for a decision.

ADVANCED

EARNED VALUE ANALYSIS (ADVANCED)

The *Earned Value Analysis (EVA)* is an effective way to gain insight into the project's cost and schedule performance. The method answers whether expenditure and progress are still according to plan and indicates the consequences for the project if current performance continues. With the EVA, it is possible to estimate the total expenditure and throughput time of the entire project based on the present performance.

Basic concepts

To prepare an EVA, you need to know the planning and budget of the entire work, as well as the percentage of completion and the costs at a given moment in time. With this knowledge, you know (see Figure 6.04.10):

- Budget At Completion (BAC) – The approved budget for the entire work;
- Planned Duration (PD) – The approved time schedule of the entire work;
- Actual Time (AT) – The time passed at the moment the EVA is carried out;
- Percentage Complete (PC) – The realised percentage of work to date;
- Planned Value (PV – The budgeted costs of planned work to date;
- Earned Value (EV) – The budgeted costs of actual work carried out to date;
- Actual Costs (AC) – The actual costs of the work performed to date.

Earned value analysis

- BAC = Budget at Completion
- PD = Planned Duration
- AT = Actual Time
- AC = Actual Cost
- PC = Percentage Complete
- CV = Cost Variance = EV – AC
- CPI = Cost Performance Index = EV / AC
- SV = Schedule Variance = EV – PV
- SPI = Schedule Performance Index = EV / PV
- VAC = Variance at Completion = BAC - EAC

- PV = Planned Value = Budget Cost Work Scheduled (BCWS)
- EV = Earned Value = Budget Cost Work Performed (BCWP)
- EAC = Estimate At Completion
- ETC = Estimate To Complete

Multiplicative extrapolation:

- EAC = AC/PC or BAC/CPI
- ETC = EAC – AC or AC.(1-PC)/PC

Additive extrapolation:

- EAC = BAC + (AC – EV) or BAC – CV
- ETC = EAC – AC or BAC – EV

Figure 6.04.10 Formula Earned value analysis

Based on these data, the progress of the work and the cost performance to date can be easily calculated, both in absolute values and as a percentage.

Did we spend less or more than the budgeted costs:

- In absolute value: *Cost Variance* (CV) = EV – AC.
- In percentage: *Cost Performance Index* (CPI) = EV/AC x 100%.

Are we ahead or behind schedule:

- In absolute terms: *Schedule Variance* (SV) = EV – PV.
- In percentage: *Schedule Performance Index* (SPI) = EV/PV x 100%.

If the variance <0, then the index is <1, and the work is behind schedule, or we have overspent.

If the variance > 0, then the index is > 1, and the work is ahead of schedule, or we have saved costs.

If we extrapolate these values to the future (linear extrapolation), an estimate can be made of the total expected costs up to when the work has been finalised:

- *Estimate At Completion* (EAC) = AC/PC or BAC/CPI.
- *Estimate To Complete* (ETC) = AC x (1-PC)/PC or EAC-AC.

The difference in costs at completion relative to the original budget is:

- *Variance at Completion* (VAC) = BAC – EAC.

For an example, see Figure 6.04.11.

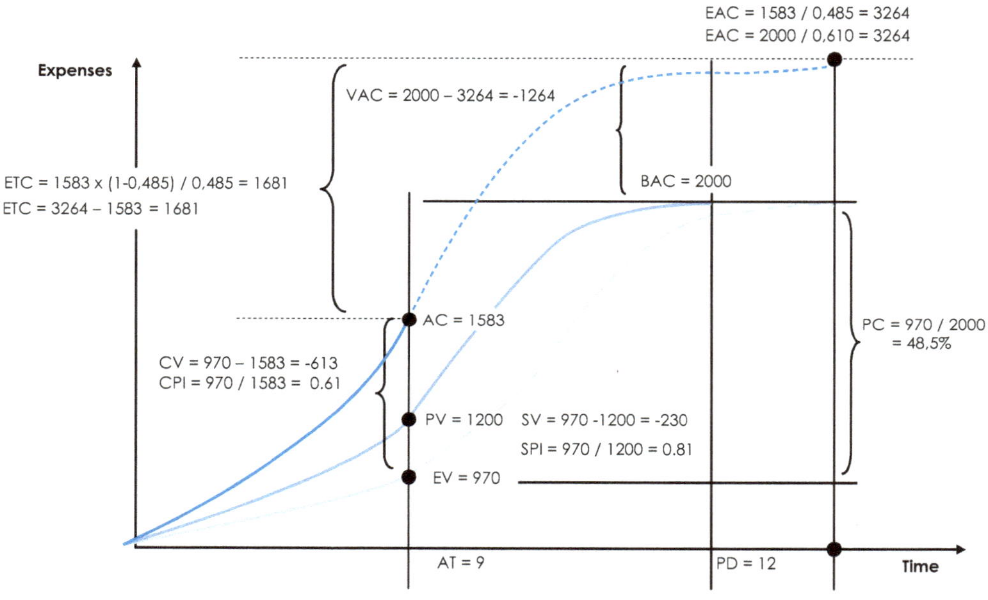

Figure 6.04.11 Example Earned Value Analysis

If we argue that the backlogs so far are only start-up losses and that from now on, progress will go according to plan (additive extrapolation), we get a completely different situation. Then:

- Estimate At Completion (EAC) = BAC + (AC – EV) or EAC = BAC – CV.
- Estimate To Complete (ETC) = EAC – AC or ETC = BAC – EV.
- Variance at Completion (VAC) = CV.

If we state that we will catch up on the backlog in the remainder of the project, we have to accelerate twice: once from current performance to planned performance and then even quicker to catch up. That's not easy. That is why, after 10-20% of the work, the EVA usually gives already a very reliable prediction of the project's final results.

Earned Value Analysis versus Earned Value Management

Unlike the CPI, towards the end of the project, the SPI no longer gives a valid value, as the SPI then always tends towards 1. That is why alternatives have been developed, such as Earned Value Management, which distinguishes between project duration, actual time and earned schedule.

Earned Value Analysis versus slip chart

The direct advantage of the slip chart is that it is based on the expertise of the responsible manager. The disadvantage, however, is that the slip chart also depends on it. The EVA is merely an extrapolation of current performance into the future. It does not consider future circumstances, and it is quick and easy to carry out. The EVA is, therefore, often used as a contra-expertise to provide an independent reference of whether the project will be completed on time and within budget based on the current performance.

6.05 ORGANISATIONAL CHANGE AND TRANSFORMATION

PURPOSE

The purpose of this chapter is to enable the individual to help people, organisations and societies to change or transform, achieving intended benefits and goals.

LEARNING OBJECTIVES

- Change management and change management approach;
- The principles of leading change, according to John Kotter;
- Group dynamics (advanced);
- Kübler-Ross' change curve (advanced);
- How innovations spread over time in a social system, according to Rogers (advanced);
- The five disciplines of a learning organisation, according to Senge (advanced);
- Transformational learning, according to Schein (advanced).

DEFINITIONS

Change: An alteration of a product, service, condition or situation.
Transformation: A change in core beliefs and sustained behaviour to achieve intended benefits and goals.
Organisational change: The change in an organisation's characteristics and or configurations, whereby the organisation's behaviour also changes sustainably.
Change management: The aspect of management aimed at helping people, organisations and societies to change or transform, achieving intended benefits and goals.

INTRODUCTION

Projects deliver an output that enables new capabilities. However, only when these capabilities are applied, can value be added and benefits achieved. This almost always requires changes in people's and organisations' behaviour, which is challenging.

Change often provokes resistance, especially if the people themselves do not initiate the change. This can lead to changes not being sustainable or project outputs not being used at all. Therefore, you need to understand how changes can be implemented and design your project accordingly to be effective, whether or not you yourself are responsible for implementing the project output within the organisation.

POSITIONING

People usually do not object to change – they object to being changed. Therefore, it is essential to involve people in the project straight from the start. Resistance to the intended changes can have a devastating impact on the project itself.

Assess the adaptability of the organisation(s) involved to change. Identify change requirements and opportunities. Develop a change strategy and change management plan, and prepare for the change; build support, address resistance and develop the required knowledge and ability to implement the change right from the start. When change management is performed satisfactorily, people feel engaged in the process and work collectively towards a common goal, realising benefits and delivering results.

CHANGE MANAGEMENT

Change management includes all management tasks aimed at helping people, organisations, and societies to change or transform, achieving intended benefits and goals. This can range from replacing an application with a newer version (change) to adjusting core beliefs and sustained behaviour of the people involved (transformation).

The first may involve simply training the people involved and helping them adapt to the new working method. The latter involves a much longer process. This will also encompass influencing a leading coalition and other psychological and psychosocial interventions. Change is improving a current situation, keeping the past in mind. Transformation is the emerging development of new situations based on a future-orientated vision.

The level of change and transformation management required will largely depend on the degree of disruption created in the daily lives of individuals and groups, plus aspects such as culture, value system and history with past changes. Change and transformation do not happen mainly 'by design' and are usually not linear. The change capacity and capabilities of people and organisations should also be considered. Often, a project will trigger and organise change but ends before the resulting benefits are realised.

CHANGE MANAGEMENT APPROACH

Implementation of the project deliverables requires changes to the user environment. People are generally prepared to change but do not want to be changed. You can remove much resistance by allowing them to influence their own future. People will resist when they feel their interests are in danger.

Implementing change should be carefully planned, and the process for doing so is already an essential part of the change process itself. It is advisable to plan this separately from the plan for delivering the project output; otherwise, the change process will likely become secondary to the technical approach to delivering the output. Change management is about people and less about content.

Asses the adaptability to change

Assess the ability to adapt to change. People and organisations have a limited capacity, capability and willingness to change. This is influenced by, among other things, the success of previous changes, the perceived need for this change, the organisational culture and atmosphere, and the perception of favourable or unfavourable perspectives. In many cases, resistance does not come from those directly affected by the change but from those who direct them. This step can be carried out in parallel with the stakeholder assessment.

Identify change requirements and transformation opportunities

For business-orientated projects, you need to analyse the requirements to determine which transformation or business change needs to take place and when. For more societal-orientated projects, you also need to identify which social groups the project can and should impact. This can be done through interviews, gathering knowledge, analysing data or workshops.

Develop a change or transformation strategy and plan

Develop a change strategy to address the anticipated changes or transformations. The strategy should be based upon the impact of the change and the ability and willingness to change by the people, organisation, or society. The timing of changes needs to be considered. The plan should be developed through consultation and should be updated regularly.

Implement the change or transformation management strategy

Plan a series of interventions. These may include workshops, training, information sessions, and pilots. However, also plan interventions focused on dealing with resistance. Practice what you preach. Once a changes has occurred, take measures to sustain the change, helping people not fall back into old behaviours.

LEADING CHANGE – KOTTER

Various authors have developed approaches to implement change effectively. A well-known approach is that of Prof. J.P. Kotter (2012), who defined eight steps to implement significant organisational changes.

1. Create a sense of urgency

Without urgency, there is no drive for change. What remains are merely good intentions. Establishing a sense of urgency is crucial to bringing about the desired cooperation. If this sense of urgency does not permeate all layers of the organisation, transformations usually come to nothing because people are not even interested in collaborating. Many changes are verbally supported but not supported by actions. Spend significant time and energy creating a sense of urgency before moving on to the next step.

2. Build a guiding coalition

Radical change cannot be achieved from middle management alone or with only one sponsor at the organisation's top. It requires strong leadership and visible support from key people in the organisation. Managing change is not enough; it should be led. To do this, you need to build a guiding coalition of influential people whose power comes from different sources within the organisation. This requires emotional commitment and work on team building. Once formed, the team should continue to build urgency and momentum for the need for change.

3. Form a strategic vision

Without an attractive vision, the change will be unfocused and uncoordinated, which is counterproductive; One result neutralises the other. An appealing vision of the desired future is needed to focus energy in one direction. Communicate this vision regularly.

4. Enlist a volunteer army

Large-scale change can only occur when many people rally around a common opportunity. At an individual level, they should want to contribute actively. Collectively, they should be unified in their pursuit of achieving the goal.

5. Removing barriers

Give the guiding coalition an official mandate to remove barriers. Often, the most significant obstacles are existing structures and systems, the lack of new skills and the middle managers themselves, who are stuck with the current status quo. A real mandate for the change teams is essential to actually implement changes. Nothing is more frustrating than to be held back by the organisation itself.

6. Generate short-term wins

Do not wait for success; generate it. This is the fuel for change. Without short-term wins, the energy quickly drains from the change. Short-term wins do not prove that the desired vision will be realised, but they do show that the movement can implement changes, which is quite an achievement. Moreover, short-term wins often provide the resources to finance the rest of the change. Therefore, you should not only celebrate short-term wins but also generate them.

7. Sustain acceleration

Ensure that the change becomes an integrated part of the organisation's processes, procedures and governance, down to the roles and responsibilities of staff. Remove old legacy systems, and look for additional improvements. You need to prevent that if the focus of the change is on other issues, the new way of working evaporates, and people fall back into old habits.

It is one thing to achieve short-term successes; the real challenge is to make continuous and sustained progress towards the organisation's longer-term goals. Achieving real success is sometimes the greatest enemy of change. The feeling arises that the initial threat has been easily overcome. The sense of urgency ebbs away. Complacency creeps back into the organisation. Ongoing changes are suddenly viewed with suspicion, and before you know it, the energy is gone. Keep the sense of urgency high, keep the leading coalition on board, and make sure the change teams stay empowered.

8. Institute change

Embed the implementation of change in the culture of the organisation. Make continuous efforts to ensure that the implementation of change throughout the organisation is viewed as an opportunity to improve. This creates a more Agile organisation and makes it easier to realise new strategic initiatives in the future. However, there's still a long road ahead. This is an issue far beyond the scope of the project

As long as the management's full attention is focused on change, it seems this is already the case. However, as soon as the management changes and attention wanes, it appears that change itself as a new way of working has not yet become a core value of the organisation, and the organisation falls back into its old beliefs. This is the prelude for new major threats emerging.

SUSTAINABILITY

The lifecycle orientation of sustainability implies a goal-orientated focus of the project. This implies that the organisational and societal change required to achieve these goals should already be taken into account during the project itself.

In case of an organisational or societal change, the human and group processes that arise should also be considered. An informative and or discursive approach is then not enough. Desired choices do not always produce immediate visible effects. Behavioural changes for the future may not presently appeal. A well-thought-through approach, together with your project sponsor, is therefore necessary. However, realise that the sponsoring organisation/project sponsor is ultimately responsible for the required change and transformation.

TAILORING

Agile is an ideal approach to implementing change if the work can be delivered incrementally. Business people are involved from the start. Changing requirements are welcomed, even later on in development. Benefits can be realised early on by immediately using what was delivered incrementally.

However, realise that much more is needed to bring an organisation into transition. Blockers are often not the operational people but the management. Therefore, even with Agile delivery in transition, a thorough change management approach is mandatory.

RESPONSIBILITIES

The project sponsor is accountable to the sponsoring organisation or customer for achieving the benefits and goals intended by the project results. The user representative is usually responsible for actually implementing the changes and realising the projected benefits.

In many projects, however, the project manager is not only responsible for delivering the project output but also for implementing the output in the organisation. In all cases, with the right approach and design of the project, the project manager should at least support the change process.

ADVANCED

KÜBLER-ROSS' CHANGE CURVE (ADVANCED)

According to Kübler-Ross (2014), people go through five stages of grief when coping with personal loss: denial, anger, bargaining, depression and acceptance. This model also applies to organisational change, as it disrupts people's status quo in their workplace. Each phase triggers different emotional responses. If we understand these stages, we can provide people with the necessary guidance and support and prepare them for success (see Figure 6.05.01).

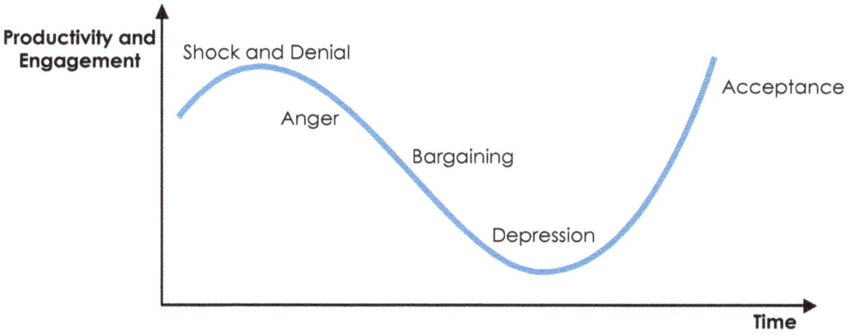

Figure 6.05.01 Kübler-Ross, Change Curve (2014)

Denial – The first reaction will likely be shock and denial. They don't accept that the change is needed and is taking place. They may even try to avert it. This may result in a decline of productivity. You need to help them to understand why this change is needed and how it can help.

Anger – Once reality hits them and they realise the seriousness of the situation, they may become angry and look for who is to blame. They may begin to fear what awaits them. This can lead to resistance. The forthcoming change may undermine their position. Provide clear communication, support and focus on the future.

Bargaining – They regain their composure and may start thinking about ways to delay the inevitable or try to negotiate so they don't have to compromise too much. They may try to learn only what they think is important. Ensure everyone gets the best training to suit different learning styles.

Depression – They realise they have to accept the situation. This initially leads to resignation and regret that things have changed, leading to a loss of energy at work. They may feel sadness, anxiety, guilt and other negative emotions. The more exciting the training and adapting to the new situation are, the easier it is for them to move on.

Acceptance – People are finally beginning to embrace the change. They come to terms with the situation and develops new hopes and aspirations. They recognise, understand and embrace the importance of the change, some for lack of another option, others in a positive way.

The Kübler-Ross' change curve helps to understand the process people go through when adjusting to a significant change at work and the emotional moods associated with it. It also helps to tailor communication and guidance accordingly.

DIFFUSION OF INNOVATION – ROGERS (ADVANCED)

Evert M. Rogers is the author of Diffusion of Innovations (2010). His book explains how and at what rate innovations spread over time in a social system.

Diffusion is the communication process that a new idea or product should go through to be accepted by the market. The diffusion rate is the pace at which a new idea or product spreads from one consumer/user to another. Adoption is the psychological decision-making process of an individual user.

The adoption process of the innovation depends on the relative advantage gained by the innovation and the extent to which it fits in with current thinking. It also depends on the difficulty of the innovation, the opportunity to experiment and the visibility of the results.

The personal acceptance of a new idea or product proceeds as an S-curve as the product matures, moving from knowledge to persuasion, decision, implementation and finally, confirmation (see Figure 6.05.02).

Rogers also distinguishes five adoption groups, each with its own characteristic size, which ensures that the acceptance of a new idea or product in a social system also proceeds like an S-curve (see Figure 6.05.03):

Innovators – Are educated and entrepreneurial, have access to multiple information sources and show a greater willingness to take risks. They appreciate technology in a raw form and are motivated by the idea that they are viewed as innovators in their own peer group. They are prepared to accept the teething problems of a new product.

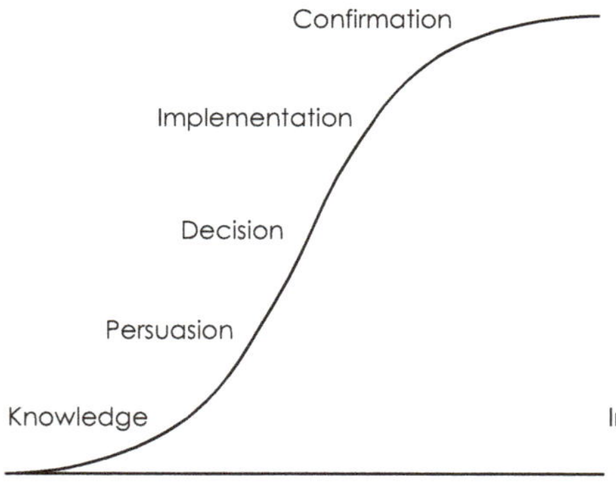

Figure 6.05.02 Adoption process innovation

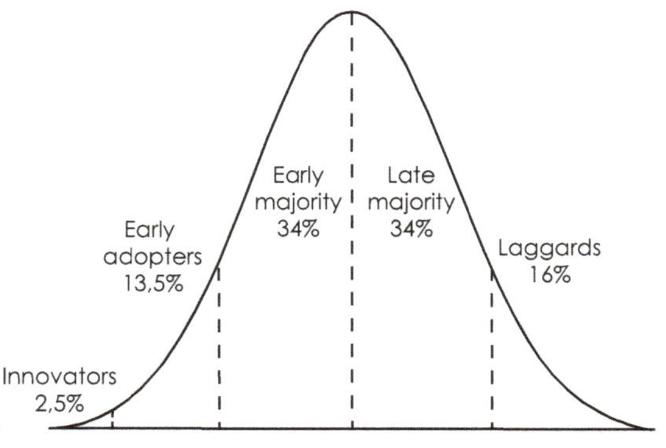

Figure 6.05.03 Adoption groups innovation

Early adopters – Are social leaders. They are popular and well-educated. They are visionaries in their field and are interested in applying new technologies to create revolutionary breakthroughs and competitive advantages for the organisation.

Early majority – Make informed decisions and have many informal social contacts. They are driven by evolutionary rather than revolutionary change. When they decide on a new product, they do so almost simultaneously. This also explains the sudden increase in demand.

Late majority – Are sceptical about change, value tradition, and often have low social status. They are very price-conscious and need integrated, mature and guaranteed solutions. They buy new technologies to stay one step ahead of the competition and base their decisions on a reliable advisor who accompanies them in the decision-making process.

Laggards – Are sceptical about technology and prefer to keep the status quo. They often believe that technology cannot increase productivity. They shy away from buying new technologies.

Rogers' innovation theory shows that innovators and early adopters should first be convinced before innovation can reach full maturity. Rogers' innovation theory can be used to determine the size and market approach of the target group in the various phases of an adoption process.

LEARNING ORGANISATIONS – SENGE (ADVANCED)

A learning organisation is an organisation that constantly expands its capability to shape its future. This requires the willingness to learn by individuals, but that alone is not enough. Together, even very reasonable people can make entirely wrong decisions due to existing social structures and processes. Senge (2006) distinguishes five coherent disciplines a learning organisation needs to develop.

1. Personal mastery – Implies a high level of mastery. People with a high level of mastery can consistently shape ideas they consider to be really important. They do this through lifelong learning. This makes personal mastery a key element for a learning organisation.
2. Mental models – These are deeply rooted beliefs that affect how we perceive and react to things. True organisational learning only occurs when supported by shared mental models.
3. Team learning – A process by which a team develops the skills needed to perform specific tasks effectively. Without these shared competences, teams can act very incompetently, while all team members are highly competent. This is the paradox that team learning aims to resolve. Team learning starts with a dialogue where team members learn to think together without starting from their own prejudices. The latter requires the certainty that individuals will not be judged for wrong decisions as long as they take well-considered risks.
4. Develop a shared vision – Create a shared identity and purpose. People perform and learn, not because they are told to but because they want to. Without a shared vision, the other disciplines of the learning organisation are directionless and, therefore, ineffective.
5. Systems thinking – An approach in which the organisation is viewed as a system in which the individual parts influence each other and the organisation is seen as part of a larger whole. Systems thinking enables management to recognise the

underlying patterns and thus implement change more effectively. Systems thinking is consistent with the concept of double-loop learning (see Chapter 10.02 Personnel Management).

Applying all five disciplines is essential for a learning organisation, as all five disciplines are interrelated. Therefore, the fifth discipline, systems thinking, is considered the central discipline of learning organisations.

Various recommendations can be formulated based on systems thinking:
- Beware of treating the symptoms. By denying the fundamental cause, the problem will return with increased intensity later. Any long-term solution should be aimed at strengthening the system's ability to bear its own burdens.
- Do not keep repeating familiar solutions. The more we revert to these, the worse the problem becomes.
- Pay attention to delayed feedback. The effects of an intervention often only become visible in the long term, which creates the risk that the intervention is carried out too intensively and or for too long. Be patient or make the system react more directly.
- Do not force growth but remove growth-limiting factors. Note: there are always new growth-limiting factors to be tackled. A one-off intervention is insufficient.

TRANSFORMATIONAL LEARNING – SCHEIN (ADVANCED)

Edgar H. Schein (2002) describes transformational learning as a meaningful and constructive learning process that challenges deeply ingrained assumptions about business strategies and processes. This results in fundamentally different thoughts and actions. To enable a transformational change in an organisation, transformational learning is required.

According to Schein, three sub-processes play an essential role in this process: the subversion of our expectations by real events, the emergence of survival anxiety, and overcoming the fear of learning. Survival anxiety can arise when the change process is perceived as threatening.

Transformational learning requires that the fear of surviving is greater than the fear of learning. This can be achieved by increasing the sense of urgency and creating a safer learning environment.

Learning anxiety arises when people fear that something new will be too difficult or that they will be laughed at if they put what they have learned into practice. They fear they will have to give up their core values and beliefs and become outsiders.

So it makes sense that learning usually starts in a small group and gradually spreads across the organisation and then to the top. In fact, it's rather common that individuals or small groups make learning leaps before the rest of the organisation does.

Ultimately, if the organisation as a whole is to learn, top management should enforce the new company policy and methods among all employees. In addition, it is important to bring new people into the organisation with the new mindset to avoid the need for a painful period of coercion.

It is also necessary to distinguish between forcing people to learn something they can see the need for and asking them to learn something they question. Therefore, in addition to a sense of urgency, it is also essential to always be transparent about where the organisation is heading (vision) and how new learning contributes to that transformation.

Finally, a distinction should be made between forcing people to learn something they feel they need and asking them to learn something they question. Therefore, in addition to the sense of urgency, it is also important to be transparent about where the organisation is going and how new knowledge contributes to this transformation.

6.06 PROJECT CLOSURE

PURPOSE

The purpose of this chapter is to enable the individual to effectively hand over the project deliverables and formally evaluate and close the project.

LEARNING OBJECTIVES

- Handing over the project output;
- De-commissioning the project;
- Evaluating the project;
- Closure and discharge.

DEFINITIONS

Handover: The legal and physical transfer of the project output to the customer organisation.
De-commissioning: The systematic and controlled close-down of the project, including dismantling the facilities, and closure of the project records and contracts.
Project evaluation: The assessment of the activities undertaken and the associated results to identify areas of improvement for future projects.
End-of-project report: The report at the end of the project detailing the project results and performance to obtain release of duty to perform.
Project discharge: The official release of the project manager's duty to perform by the project sponsor in relation to the project.

INTRODUCTION

Since the project is a temporary endeavour with a formal start, it should also be formally closed. We should prevent the project from slowly drifting into operational use. A formal closure ensures that the ownership from the project management team is transferred to the customer and that the project management team is subsequently released from its responsibilities.

Before this can happen, the project output should be handed over to the customer, the project facilities dismantled, the project evaluated and documented for future reference, and the project records closed. Where formal contracts have been signed, these should be finalised, the warranty period confirmed, and final payments invoiced. Recommendations for follow-up actions and lessons learned should be passed on to the appropriate bodies.

Controlled project closure is not an easy job and should be planned carefully. Cost, time and resources to close a project should be incorporated in the last stage plan.

Of course, whether you act on behalf of the customer or the supplier and whether the supplier is an external party or an internal department within the sponsoring or customer organisation makes a difference. In the remainder of this chapter, we will assume that you act on behalf of the sponsoring organisation or customer and that the supplier is an external party.

POSITIONING

Project closure is preferably scheduled shortly after the completion of the project output or when it has been confirmed that the project has nothing more to contribute. Prevent the closure from dragging on. Obviously, some time is needed to carry out the activities associated with project closure but limit this as much as possible. The project output can be delivered in stages or even incrementally in the case of an Agile approach.

It is also possible that a project may have to be closed prematurely when, according to the opinion of the project sponsor/sponsor organisation, the business justification has disappeared, or other projects take priority. Even then, the closure should be planned and agreed upon. The work should not simply be abandoned. Update the project plan with the most recent status, and secure or finish products that may be useful. Decommission the project, close the administration and evaluate the process for future reference. Finally, prepare an end-of-project report and request a formal discharge and closure by the project sponsor.

HANDING OVER THE PROJECT OUTPUT

The supplier is responsible for the delivery of the project output. First, they have to ensure that the users and Operation and Maintenance accept the project output. Next, they should hand over the project output to the customer. Furthermore, the agreed as-built documents with the associated *Configuration Management Database* (CMDB) should be passed on to the appropriate bodies, and the residual items should be resolved. Finally, depending on the assignment, they have to take care of or assist with implementing or commissioning the project output in the user organisation. You should ensure that all this is done correctly.

Statement of acceptance and residual items list

A statement of acceptance is the explicit statement that the product to be delivered meets the acceptance criteria and is fit for use/purpose. It is strongly recommended that the user and Operation and Maintenance issue a separate statement of acceptance.

These statements usually include a *list of residual items* the supplier still needs to resolve. The statements of acceptance should be signed off by the representative of the users, Operation and Maintenance and the supplier.

Handover and protocol of delivery

Based on the signed statements of acceptance, the project output can be handed over to the customer. A distinction should be made here between the physical and legal transfer. Both should be formally confirmed.

The legal transfer takes place first. For the legal transfer, a *protocol of delivery* should be drawn up and signed by both parties with reference to both statements of acceptance. As soon as the delivery protocol is signed, the (legal) ownership of the project output passes from the supplier to the customer.

Then the physical transfer takes place. This could, for example, be handing over the keys. Both parties should sign for this as well. A receipt should also be signed to transfer additional items such as documentation, as-built drawings, permits, et cetera.

Handover documents are all official documents drawn up when the project result is handed over to the customer. Handover documents are the statements of acceptance with the list of residual items, the protocol of delivery and the receipts of the physical transfer of the various products.

The supplier is responsible for handing over the project output and all associated documents. They should also ensure that the agreed as-built documents are completed, and the CMDB is updated. Finally, depending on the contract, the supplier should facilitate or arrange the commissioning.

You should ensure that this process runs smoothly. Ensure that all handover documents are signed in duplicate by representatives of both sides. Assure that the host site can support the products handed over. Finally, ensure that the supplier resolves the residual items as specified in the residual items list.

Early commissioning
Commissioning normally takes place after the handover. A legally unclear situation arises if the customer takes the project output into use before the handover. In case of a defect, who caused it? Such discussion points should be avoided.

Should early commissioning nevertheless be necessary, it is wiser to hand over the relevant parts in advance and to record the work still to be done as residual items rather than the user taking an uncompleted part into use.

Service level agreement (SLA)
Sometimes, the supplier is also responsible for the service and maintenance of the project output after delivery. A so-called *Service Level Agreement* (SLA) is usually concluded for this purpose. In such situations, the project output should first be formally handed over to the customer, after which the service level agreement begins. In some industries, it is customary to set up separate operational companies, especially for this purpose.

Second handover
Projects in various sectors schedule two handovers. The aim is that at the second handover, all residual items agreed upon during the first handover have been resolved to the customer's satisfaction. The date of the second handover should, if possible, be agreed upon at the first handover.

Implementation and commissioning
Implementation and commissioning of the project output are sometimes part of the project and sometimes not. Should a working or a running system be delivered? This makes a big difference. Ensure that this is laid down unambiguously in the contract and that the stakeholders' perception corresponds to this. Sometimes the agreements go so far that the supplier is responsible for operations for the first few months after delivery to demonstrate that the new system will deliver a specific performance. In that case, a second handover should be scheduled after the end of the operational period.

Maintenance period
The maintenance period is the period after the first handover, during which defects arising during use are still the supplier's responsibility. In other words, during this period,

the supplier is responsible for repairing all defects at their expense unless they can prove that the defect has arisen due to improper use or causes beyond their control. The maintenance period may be a fixed period or linked to a situation. For example, for heating installations, the maintenance period may be linked to the end of the first heating season. Sometimes the second handover is also linked to the end of the maintenance period. This is, of course, possible, but should only happen when appropriate.

Hidden defects

After the end of the maintenance period, the normal period of usage begins. Here, the roles are reversed. Defects that occur are then the customer's responsibility unless the customer can prove that this is due to incorrect delivery by the supplier.

In this context, the concept of hidden defects plays an important role. A *hidden defect* is a defect, damage or imperfection that is not recognisable on reasonable inspection at the time of delivery. Within projects, the supplier should repair or replace the good or product in case of a hidden defect, even after the maintenance period has expired. However, the supplier only has to repair hidden defects that prevent the normal use of the project output.

Warranty period and conformity principle

Often, a supplier will issue a guarantee for a certain period. This is usually a limitation of the customer's legal rights. A customer may expect the output to function for a period corresponding to the price and the normal technical life expectancy of that product. This principle of conformity is often enshrined in legislation. The customer can then still make a claim, even if the (limited) guarantee period has expired.

DECOMMISSION THE PROJECT

At the end of the project, you should ensure that the workplaces are cleared, the facilities dismantled, and the project team is released. Furthermore, make sure the project documentation is updated, closed, and passed on to the appropriate bodies.

Update, tidy up, close and transfer project files

Have the project files updated, tied up, closed, and transferred. The project files may still be needed for audits and as a reference for similar projects. Legal regulations may also stipulate that certain documents should be retained. Periods of 5 or 10 years often apply.

Prepare as-built documents and update CMDB

Have *as-built documents* prepared and the CMDB updated. As-built documents and the CMDB are essential for properly operating and maintaining project deliverables in the usage stage. The CMDB is the database that contains all the recorded configuration information of the configuration items (see Chapter 6.02 Change Control).

As-built documents are specialist documents used during the realisation of the project output that have been updated to show how the project output was actually built. These are, for example, drawings with the final dimensions and details.

Identify recommendations for follow-up actions

Have recommendations for follow-up actions prepared. Hardly any project is concluded without outstanding actions. Often, outstanding change requests at the end of the project are pushed through to the usage stage because there is no time left to implement them before handover. It is also common to make recommendations to the customer on using and maintaining the project output to ensure no defects occur and to maximise the added value. Significant project issues can even be a reason to start a new project.

All these issues should not go to waste. If they do, this may even lead to a negative perception of the project. Therefore, it is advised to document all these issues, include them in a list of *recommendations for follow-up actions*, and pass them on to the sponsoring organistation or customer at the project's conclusion.

Update business case and benefits review plan

Have the business case and the benefits review plan updated. Based on the delivery of the project output, the customer will implement the changes and should realise the intended benefits. To work on this realistically, it is necessary to update the business case for the last time. This business case should also include the benefits already realised during or upon project delivery. In addition, the benefits review plan should be updated with the latest insights on how and when benefits reviews should be held and the management actions to be taken to ensure that the planned changes can be implemented and benefits realised.

Dismantle project and release project team

At project closure, the project facilities should be dismantled, and the project team released. The project office should be vacated, and any remaining assets disposed of, sold or returned to the owners.

Besides the formal side, you should also pay attention to the emotional side of project closure. Often, people have shared their ups and downs over a long period and will see much less of each other after that. When a period of sometimes intense work ends, people may fall into a void. A good closure can enable team members to complete the project emotionally as well. The closure can also mark the transition to new work. Therefore, celebrating successes together is very important. This can be done in a separate event, linked to the handing over of the project output or in combination with the project evaluation. Recognition and appreciation for the team's services are very important and are best done directly by the project sponsor.

Finally, pay attention to the transition of project members to new positions. The end of a project can create much uncertainty. The transition of them to a new project or back to the permanent organisation should be prepared. The timing and any transitional arrangements need to be agreed. It is often also desirable to hold a final performance review or an exit interview. If necessary, a redundancy scheme should be drawn up. In any case, the transition of project members to their new future often deserves more attention than it currently receives.

PROJECT EVALUATION

Performance should always be evaluated. How did we implement the project, and will we repeat this again next time? Did we deliver what was agreed upon, and did we meet the objectives, and if not, why? Both questions should be put forward during an evaluation at the end of a project. However, both questions have different angles.

Project retrospective

Answering the question, 'How did we implement the project, and will we repeat this again next time?', provides valuable lessons for the team members, customers, supplier organisations, and other stakeholders. These lessons should be recorded in a *lessons learned report* for future reference.

The lessons recorded in the lessons learned log can be used. In addition, a separate retrospective should be held at the end of a project. Such a retrospective is also an excellent means to close of the project with the project team. Preparing individual lessons learned reports for the various parties may be necessary.

Project accountability

Answering the question, 'Did we deliver what was agreed, and did we meet the objectives, and if not, why?', provides project accountability. This accountability is recorded in the *end-of-project report* (see Figure 6.06.01). Among others, the end-of-project report may also be referred to as a close-out report or closure report.

People easily forget what happened and why things turned out the way they did. If you don't record it yourself, someone else will do it for you, or even worse; it won't happen at all. That can be much worse than doing it yourself. An end-of-project report is, therefore, not only an accountability from you to the project sponsor but also an important tool to maintain the support built up during the project. It is advisable to prepare this report in such a way that the project sponsor and other stakeholders can also use it for their own accountability.

The recommendations for follow-up actions, the lessons learned report and the benefits review plan can be recorded in separate documents and included in the end-of-project report.

End-of-project report

- Confirmation product handover + list of residual items
- Review project objectives
- Updated business case
- Outstanding issues
- Review qualities activities
- Review team performance
- Summary recommendations follow-up actions
- Summary benefits review plan
- Summary lessons learned (if applicable)
- Project manager's summary report

Figure 6.06.01 End-of-project report

CLOSURE AND DISCHARGE

In consultation with the sponsoring organisation and based on the end-of-project report, the project sponsor formally closes the project. This consists of a formal notification to all suppliers and other stakeholders that the project has ended, the dissolution of the project board, and granting the project manager and project team an official *release of the duty to perform*. Ensure timely closure of project time and cost records.

SUSTAINABILITY

The post-project phase largely determines the ultimate success of the project. Are the anticipated benefits realised, but also what are the long-term environmental and social impacts? Does the intended change also deliver the environmental and social benefits? This requires thoughtful implementation of the necessary changes and careful monitoring of the foreseen social and environmental impacts. These should be included in the benefits review plan. Unresolved environmental and social issues and risks, lessons learned and recommendations for follow-up actions should be passed on to the appropriate bodies. The latter may even include initiating follow-up projects.

TAILORING

Formal closure of a project is also vital for Agile projects for the same reasons as for 'traditional' projects. We have to prevent the project from slowly and inconspicuously drifting into operational use. Project documentation is lost, responsibilities are not transferred, and project costs continue.

At project closure, the remaining product backlog and responsibility for continued development should be transferred to one of the customer's continuous development teams. Also, ensure that the other handover documentation, such as the CMDB and records required by regulators, are correctly passed on to the appropriate bodies.

It is also recommended to organise a formal workshop with the delivery teams to conclude the project, review the final status, determine any lessons learned (retrospective), and make recommendations for follow-up actions. The workshop may also include a final product review.

RESPONSIBILITIES

The supplier is responsible for delivering the project output to the customer. The project manager should facilitate this process and is responsible for dismantling the project and releasing the project team. The team members, project support and the configuration manager, may support the project manager. The project sponsor is responsible for formally closing the project, dissolution of the project board and granting the project manager and project team an official release of the duty to perform work.

PEOPLE COMPETENCES

7 MANAGING YOURSELF

The central theme of this part of the book is managing yourself. Here, project management is considered from the perspective of the project professional. How can the project professional deepen and strengthen personal behaviour to cooperate more effectively with third parties?

Figure 7.01 elaborates on the key elements with which people present themselves to the outside world. When presenting oneself, behaviour and skills are the visible elements, whereas beliefs, values and personal attitude form the inner elements. Although not directly visible, they do reflect in one's behaviour and skills. To achieve a smooth flow in 'your being in professional situations', reflective attention to the behaviour, skills, beliefs, values, and personality is necessary. That is the essence of managing yourself and, as mentioned in Chapter 2, the basis for competence development.

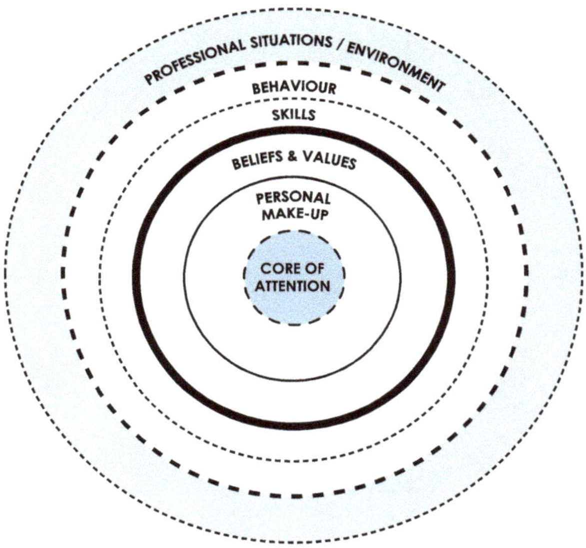

Figure 7.01 The project professional in their environment

Chapter 7.01 – Self-reflection and Self-management – Focuses on how to reflect on yourself and effectively manage your own actions. Self-reflection puts you on track with the goals you want to achieve. This is important for personal time management and for maintaining a good balance between stress and workload.

Chapter 7.02 – Personal Integrity and Reliability – Focuses on developing a basic attitude anchored in ethical principles. The IPMA Ethical Code of Conduct, also part of this chapter, provides a framework to carry out your work professionally and ethically. Within this framework, respect for the environment and social relationships are important concerns.

Chapter 7.03 – Personal Communication – This chapter covers what communication is and how to communicate in speeches, documents, meetings, and presentations. Organising workshops is also covered in this chapter.

7.01 SELF-REFLECTION AND SELF-MANAGEMENT

PURPOSE

The purpose of this chapter is to enable the individual to control and direct his or her behaviour by acknowledging the influence of your personal set of emotions, preferences and values.

LEARNING OBJECTIVES

Self-reflection and self-analysis:

- Emotional intelligence;
- Johari diagram;
- Big Five;
- Core quadrants;
- Rational Emotive Behaviour Therapy (advanced).

Effectiveness theories:

- Self-motivation;
- Seven habits of highly effective people;
- Personal time management;
- Steps in goal-setting (advanced).

Stress management:

- Eustress and distress;
- Triggers and symptoms of distress;
- Reducing distress;
- Intervention techniques for reducing distress (advanced).

DEFINITIONS

Emotional intelligence: The ability to recognise one's own emotions and those of others and to handle these emotions well in social relationships.
Self-motivation: The ability to put oneself into action and pursue stated goals.
Personal time management: The ability to create focus by making conscious decisions and organising your personal schedule accordingly.
Eustress: Tension that provides creativity, energy and motivation, and positively influences behaviour.
Distress: Tension caused by a prolonged or sudden severe imbalance between load and load capacity and, as a result, negatively influences behaviour.
Stress management: The whole of techniques and treatments aimed at reducing stress.

INTRODUCTION

Effectively managing yourself is only possible if you have sufficient self-awareness. This self-knowledge is acquired chiefly by carefully reflecting on situations in which you have or have not acted effectively. Self-reflection is the ability to acknowledge, reflect on and understand your own emotions, behaviours, preferences, values and their impact. Based on the insights of reflection, personal choices can be carefully weighed. You need the competence of self-management to make your choices come true. Self-management requires the ability to set personal goals, check and adjust progress, and cope with daily work in a disciplined and systematic way. Self-management will prevent you from ending up in a stressful situation.

SELF-REFLECTION AND SELF-ANALYSIS

Self-reflecting and analysing your behaviour, skills, beliefs, values, and personality is valuable. Such reflection gives insight into how you act and the patterns that cause these actions. It provides a good basis for strengthening your personal qualities and presence in work environments. Various methods are reviewed within this chapter.

Emotional intelligence includes the aspects you need to consider to recognise your emotions and handle them well in social relationships. *The Johari diagram* shows you how to bring your blind spots and hidden and unknown self into the open. The *Big Five* provides a blueprint for understanding the key dimensions of personality. The *Core Quadrants* help you understand your core qualities, pitfalls, challenges, and allergies and how to get into your inner strength. *Rational Emotive Behaviour Therapy* (advanced) enables you to explore the relationship between your thoughts, feelings and behaviour in concrete situations and transform irrational beliefs into positive beliefs and feelings to achieve your goals.

EMOTIONAL INTELLIGENCE

Goleman (2005) defines emotional intelligence as the ability to recognise your emotions and those of others and to handle these well in social relationships. According to Goleman, emotional intelligence is visible in personal and social skills. It consists of self-awareness, self-management, self-motivation, social awareness, and social skills.

Self-awareness: recognising, knowing and acknowledging your own emotions – Self-awareness concerns recognising and acknowledging your own emotions and having a real insight into your personal qualities. Self-insight arises by understanding the origin of your emotions and examining their effect on your actions. Finally, deepening your self-awareness creates space for managing your emotions more effectively.

Self-management: learning to regulate your emotions – Self-management means that you can regulate and handle your own feelings, making it easier to control yourself and stay true to the values and norms vital to you. An important skill is to perceive and precisely describe your emotions. In this way, you learn to distinguish them from behavioural options you can apply to deal with others. The emotion itself is an important signal. It indicates how you experience the situation. You manage yourself by choosing the proper behavioural response to this emotion, setting personal goals, checking progress, and coping with daily work in a disciplined and systematic way.

> *In a study on self-control (Goleman, 2005), children were given sweets but forbidden to eat any of them until the researchers returned. The children were promised that they would get double the number of sweets if they did not eat the sweets until their return. Many children could not resist the temptation and ate the sweets. A smaller part of the group restrained themselves. A later study showed that this group was, on average, more successful in later life than the group that could not control itself.*

Self-motivation: motivating yourself – By being aware of your emotional impulses and not directly giving in to them, you calm your mental and emotional turmoil. This creates a basis for exploring choices and actions, leading to self-motivation: the competence to get yourself to act and pursue stated goals. To be thoroughly successful in making use of your social awareness and skills.

Social awareness: empathic recognition of another's emotions – The essence of social awareness is empathising with the other person's feelings, needs and concerns. This process starts with understanding the other person. What is their perspective view of the world? What needs to be achieved in terms of interest? Which concerns need to be addressed? A sincere attitude to understanding the other creates space for opportunities that serve common interests. Therefore, you need social skills to utilise these opportunities.

Social skills: dealing effectively with relationships – Social skills focus on consciously exerting influence to evoke mutually desired responses. The ability to be attuned to the other individual and yourself also ensures that you can regulate possible conflicts more easily. This, in turn, strengthens the ability to work together effectively, which is the basis for realising project results and related goals.

In professional situations, emotional intelligence makes it easier to discuss issues, provide and receive feedback, and reveal yourself in difficult situations.

JOHARI DIAGRAM

The *JOHARI Window* (Blackburn, 2022) is a technique that helps you bring your blind spots and your hidden and unknown self into the open for discussion. The four quadrants of the Johari Window are Open Self (or open area/arena), Blind Self (or blind spot/ blind area), Hidden Self (façade/hidden area), and Unknown Self (unknown area), see Figure 7.01.01.

Arena – Attributes in this area are known to yourself and known to others. These can be discussed openly, revealing strengths and weaknesses. It provides space for learning and is good for both personal and team development. In theories on learning organisations, openness is a basic value.

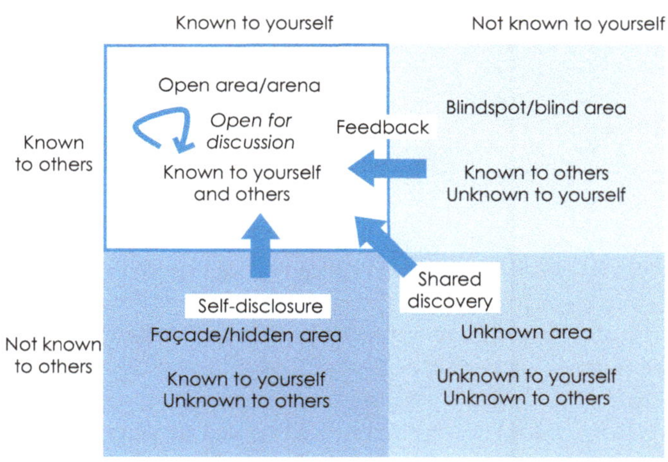

Figure 7.01.01 Johari window (Blackburn, 2022)

Blind spot – Attributes you don't recognise yourself but which are recognised by others. These are unconscious characteristics, feelings, external perceptions, et cetera with which you don't identify. They come into the open area by soliciting feedback.

Façade – Attributes you know about yourself but which are unfamiliar to others. These are characteristics, feelings, experiences, perceptions, et cetera, that influence your behaviour. With self-disclosure, you reveal what is on your mind to others. It is an exciting and vulnerable process because you do not know how other people will react. Nevertheless, in many group processes, self-disclosure is valuable. It gives insight into what group processes do to people and what is needed to stay effective and cooperative.

Unknown area – Attributes unknown to yourself and unknown to others. These are feelings, skills, experiences, et cetera, stored deep in our subconscious. They can be brought to light through shared discovery during intense group work. The unknown area can also shift to the blind or hidden area first. Discovering unconscious hidden feelings and experiences can be an emotional process. Take the opportunity to investigate and try new insights without adding pressure on yourself to succeed.

BIG FIVE

The *Big Five* personality theory provides a blueprint for understanding the key dimensions of personality. These dimensions are universal and provide an accurate picture of human nature. The Big Five model helps people put names to their characteristics to understand better how they compare to others and explore relationships between their personality and other life indicators. A Big Five personality test can measure a person's key personality characteristics and which roles fit them best.

The Big Five personality theory divides personality into five dimensions. Each dimension reflects two polarities which characterise people. Somewhere between these polarities, you can position yourself or someone else. The five positions together give a picture of a person's personality. The five personal dimensions that the Big Five distinguishes are (see Figure 7.01.02):

- Extraversion <> Introversion
- Agreeableness <> Disagreeableness
- Conscientiousness <> Unconscientiousness
- Neuroticism <> Emotional stability
- Openness to experience <> Preserved

Figure 7.01.02 Big Five

Extraversion – The ability to deal with the environment in a positive, active, ambitious and lively manner or to work from inner calmness and self-reflection. Extraverts like to seek other company and openly display their emotional commitment. Making contact is easy for them, and they take the lead in conversations. Introverts keep more distance. They are often reserved and modest. They like to choose their own path and need fewer stimuli than extroverts to feel comfortable and useful. Introverts feel comfortable within themselves.

Open-Mindedness – The ability to act creatively, artistically and imaginatively. Or conversely, to work using a down-to-earth mentality based on facts and abstractions. People who score high on having an open attitude to experience are curious, creative and complex. They are open to change and are resourceful in implementing these changes. People at the other end of the scale like to keep things as they are. They deal with things in a realistic, practical and conventional manner. They analyse the world based on observable facts and then define the best course of action.

Agreeableness – The ability to work together tactically, sympathetically and in a relationship. Or conversely, to be decisive, critical, harsh, logical, analytical and consistent. People who score high on agreeableness can adapt flexibly to what the environment requires of them. They empathise with others and give them space by listening to them. They are more accommodating and cooperative than people who score lower on this aspect. People with low scores are more dominant, can stand up for themselves, and can quickly create more space for themselves. They dare to make decisions and challenge the steps needed to achieve their goals. They exert an active and targeted influence and often take the lead.

Conscientiousness – The ability to act responsibly, in an organised, systematic, and reliable manner, or conversely, to act spontaneously and creatively without a plan. People with high scores work in a planned and conscientious way. They like clear rules and agreements, stick to them, and often react rigidly and reluctantly to new events. People with low scores respond more spontaneously and know how to improvise. They trust themselves and are unfazed about details. Everything will be fine because the environment offers all the possibilities they need.

Emotional stability – People with high scores are calm and relaxed and often have an even temper. They remain calm in stressful situations and are stable. Conversely, people with low scores react more violently to emotional situations and are more easily irritated. They are passionate and tackle things with enthusiasm.

For the composition of and cooperation within project teams, it is essential to recognise and acknowledge the personalities in the team. Everyone has their own specific qualities. By knowing and appreciating the qualities of yourself and others and taking them into account when assigning tasks, you lay a solid foundation for both personal and team effectiveness. The core quadrant method offers good support in naming and discussing each other's core qualities.

CORE QUADRANTS

The *Core Quadrant Theory* was developed in the mid-nineties by Daniel Ofman. This model helps you understand your core qualities, pitfalls, challenges and allergies. If you are aware of these, you can strengthen your core qualities, avoid pitfalls, and come into your power. If you help others become aware of their core quadrants, you can empower them.

Figure 7.01.03 shows how a core quadrant is constructed. A core quality is a quality others genuinely value you for. The pitfall is showing too much of this quality. Others will resent you for it. Don't show less of your core quality but add a positive competence. That is your challenge. This challenge is the opposite of your pitfall. It is what you admire in others and what you miss in yourself. Finally, your allergy is what you can't stand in others. This confronts you with your own shortcomings and is the negative opposite of your core quality. If one of your core qualities is that you are modest, your pitfall may be that you are invisible. Your challenge is to give a better presentation of yourself, and you can't stand arrogance.

As an individual, you can construct such core quadrants for yourself, especially if certain relationships in the project are strained. By thinking about your own core qualities and those of the other individual, you can make decisions about approaches that might be more effective. When giving feedback to others, it is often more effective to first name someone's core qualities before pointing out someone's pitfalls. Name challenges rather than just indicating their pitfalls.

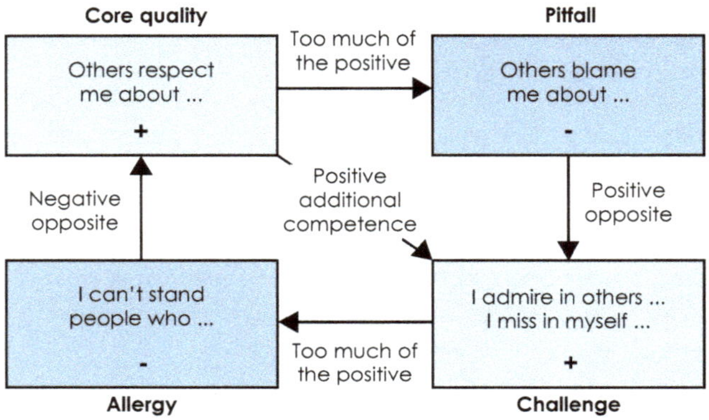

Figure 7.01.03 Core Quadrant example

To explore possible collaboration and avoid potential clashes, you can use the double quadrant (see Figure 7.01.04). Collaboration can clash because one person's allergy is the other's pitfall. By using the double quadrant, the two people involved learn to understand each other better. This creates a working atmosphere where people challenge each other to do their best and achieve goals that suit the individuals they are. This also increases their self-confidence.

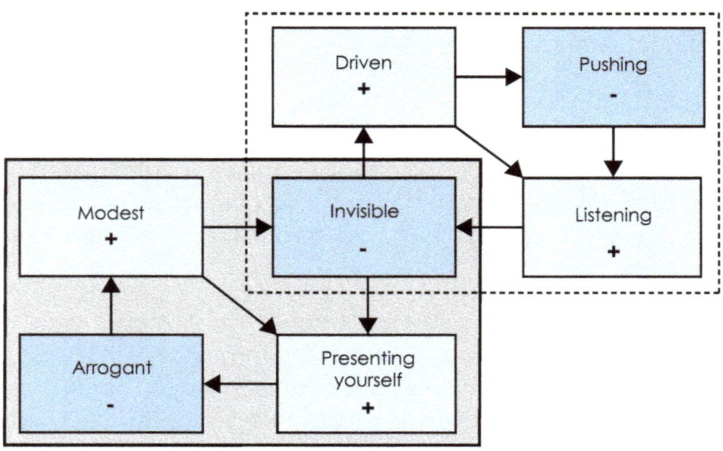

Figure 7.01.04 Dual Core Quadrant example

EFFECTIVENESS THEORIES

The effectiveness of the team starts with your own effectiveness. The latter has been the subject of many studies. Various methods are reviewed within this chapter. Self-motivation is about putting yourself into action to pursue stated goals. Next, we focus on how to be effective and then zoom in on personal time management. Some time management techniques are addressed in the advanced section. Steps in goal-setting (advanced) explain how you can work in a disciplined way to achieve your personal goals.

SELF-MOTIVATION

Self-motivation is the ability to put oneself into action and pursue stated goals. This ability is often linked to what you see and experience in the environment. When the external trigger evokes meaningful and positive thoughts and feelings, it stimulates your creative tension. You are willing to set goals and take action to reach them because they contribute to the development of yourself and the environment in which you live.

> *In a project team, a team member worked with great enthusiasm. He was competent, quick and effective. During breaks, however, he frequently spoke about the sluggishness and incompetence of his colleagues. He got angry about actions that were not performed efficiently, and in conversations with his superiors, he was constantly focused on demonstrating his superiority over others.*
>
> *During a training session, one of his colleagues confronted him with this behaviour and said, 'Frank, if everyone were as good as you, the world would surely be perfect. However, I would appreciate it if you refrain from judging me, and focus on your own area of expertise. Some of my colleagues are starting to rebel. They damaged your work glasses and are bullying you. It is very annoying, and I don't condone it, but somehow I understand them. Please focus on your own job and stop interfering with us. It drives us crazy!'*
>
> *The trainer asked, 'Frank, what does this tell you?' Frank answered, 'My professionalism is appreciated, but my meddling is unappreciated!' 'And', the trainer asked, 'are you going to do anything with that knowledge?' ... 'I am going to focus on what I am good at. I love this work and know I contribute to a great product. Sorry everyone, but my esteemed colleague is right. It is neither my job nor my role to force my own standards on you!'*

People who perform through self-motivation work from creative tension. They have developed the ability to transform feelings of fear, anger and or sadness into feelings of belonging, justice and purpose (Cornelis, 1999). They can turn feelings of dependency, powerlessness and inferiority into feelings of commitment, self-confidence and creativity (Senge, 1992). By changing this, you create a basis for self-motivation. The connection and involvement with the environment are strengthened because personal choices are no longer linked to dependence, powerlessness, or feelings of inferiority. You can use the theory of Stephen Covey to see how to work on developing your self-motivation.

THE SEVEN HABITS OF HIGHLY EFFECTIVE PEOPLE

In his book *The Seven Habits Of Highly Effective People*, Covey emphasises the development of an attitude that focuses first on personal independency and then connects with others based on the awareness that we are mutually dependent. The development of seven habits is central to his thinking (see Figure 7.01.05).

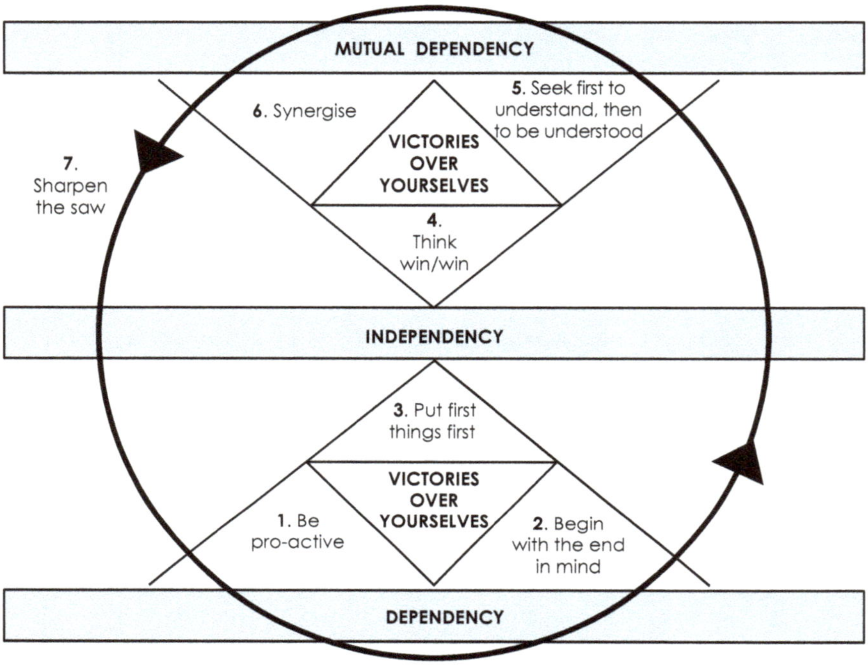

Figure 7.01.05 Seven Habits of Highly Effective People (Covey, 1989)

1. *Be proactive* – Proactive people *do not* criticise, compare themself to others, complain, compete or argue. They dedicate their time and attention to positive energy; from that positive energy, they influence their environment through their strengths and convictions. They consciously and actively focus on matters within their sphere of influence and mind their own business. See *Circles of influence and concern* in Chapter 8.02, Leadership.

A project manager had a meeting with the project sponsor and the user representative about the project output. The meeting was a bit chaotic. When the discussion had gone on for a while, the project manager made a few essential interventions. She asked the user representative how he intended to implement the project output in his organisation and whether the users felt it was urgent. She asked the project sponsor which organisational goals he wanted to achieve by implementing the project. Both interventions aimed at consciously moving with and strengthening the other two roles.

After listening carefully to the answers, she proposed how to deliver the project output and specified the conditions to do so. With this intervention, she did precisely what she was hired to do; she demonstrated she was there to ensure that the intended results would be achieved! This acting out of her role created the trust necessary to authorise the start of the project by the project sponsor.

2. *Begin with the end in mind* – Highly effective people know which core values and life principles their personal choices and behaviour are based on. They are aware of the contribution of their actions to themselves and the people they work with. They answer the question, 'Why do I do what I am doing?' with clarity. This answer gives meaning to their lives.
3. *Put first things first* – Now that you know your core values or life principles, you can pay attention to your personal agenda. You know what to prioritise, and you create focus in your work through conscious scheduling. You are reliable regarding the agreements you have made with yourself and others. While working on your chosen themes, you balance different areas of life well. This balance ensures you live your life however you want rather than being busy with stressful survival.

With these first three habits, you create your personal independence and distance yourself from your flight, freeze or fight behaviour. It is, however, important to realise that we depend on each other and natural resources, liveable temperatures, clean water, sufficient food, reliable suppliers, et cetera. A personally independent attitude becomes effective if mutual dependency is fully considered. With the fourth, fifth and sixth habits, you interact carefully with the environment, creating a healthy interdependence.

In an organisation, a project was started to improve the cooperation between the software development and the service department — two departments within the company that are strongly dependent on each other but operate independently. The head of the software development department gave a fierce speech about how good his department is (and it is!) but, in doing so, implicitly criticised the user support staff.

One of these staff members said: 'You have such a wonderful strong department, but your speech comes across as very arrogant. You say all sorts of things about us, but you don't really understand us. You want to collaborate, but only on your terms. That's unfair because even though we work differently, we are also competent and professional. We have different roles for a reason. We are not creative builders but reliable support officers who solve the questions and problems that the users of our systems encounter. Accepting, appreciating and understanding our different roles creates a foundation for trust and cooperation.'

4. *Think win-win* – As proactivity is the basic attitude to becoming independent, a win-win or no-deal attitude is necessary to reach essential mutual dependency. Win-win or no deal reflects an open attitude towards other people. It focuses on a genuine desire to know where the other person's interests lie. With this knowledge, it's much easier to find opportunities that serve the mutual interest of all parties. People who only want to win at the expense of others do not see these possibilities. In the short term, this can be lucrative. In the long term, however, they often dig their own grave.
5. *First understand, then want to be understood* – Highly effective people realise that listening to others is essential for realising win-win agreements. You will gain insight

into their perspective if you fully prepare to listen to the other individual first. Because genuinely listening is often rewarded by being heard, you can express your own views in return. This is the foundation for mutual understanding, trust and win-win agreements.

6. *Synergise* – Synergy occurs when team members are in tune with each other. They know what, when, how and by whom things need to be done. Communication and collaboration are necessary to achieve this alignment. Communication creates insight, trust and awareness of what needs to be done. Collaboration ensures that team members learn to fulfil their roles professionally. In moments of synergy, the team works as if in a flow. The work is effortlessly accomplished, and the team experiences what it is like to work as a whole.
7. *Sharpen the saw* – To conclude the theory, Covey describes the seventh habit. This habit reflects life as a process of learning and continuous improvement. All sorts of things can cause mutual dependency to break down. Keeping the saw sharp means taking time and space to reflect on what you do and what passes your way. Take your time and rest to make new choices to find a new balance and adapt your resources and energy to create a healthy, sustainable, long-term, effective lifestyle.

Being faithful to and disciplined in following your choices brings us to the principles of personal time management.

PERSONAL TIME MANAGEMENT

Personal time management focuses on making your own choices and taking them seriously. This creates focus. If you don't, result-orientated work will degenerate into an accumulation of ad hoc actions: urgent actions that need to be realised immediately. This creates distress and problems. Personal time management is aimed at avoiding this.

The practical principles of personal time management are simple:

- Identify words that motivate you, words that reflect 'Begin with the end in mind.';
- Determine the concrete results you want to spend your energy on;
- Enter these results into your daily schedule and when they should be completed;
- Link a motivating 'end in mind' word to this result;
- Reserve time in your daily schedule to do the necessary work to realise these results;
- Follow your schedule decisively and consistently (discipline means to follow).

Pace of work

The pace of work is the rate at which you complete tasks and duties. Change positions regularly, switch tasks and alternate tasks with a co-worker, and take breaks. These strategies can help maintain both your productivity and health. But alternatively, don't be distracted by all kinds of temptations and unimportant matters, and complete your current task before moving on to the next.

The Eisenhower Quadrant

The *Eisenhower quadrant* can be used to apply personal time management in a structured way. This quadrant is based on Eisenhower's statement, 'I have two kinds of problems, the urgent and the important. The urgent are not important, and the important are never urgent.' With this sentence, he contrasted these two issues, and the message was clear: focus on the important issues that are not urgent. Four fields are created by contrasting importance and urgency on two axes, as illustrated in Figure 7.01.06, the Eisenhower quadrant.

	URGENT	**NOT URGENT**
IMPORTANT	Quadrant I: *Has to be done now* • Crises • Firefighting • Meet impending deadlines • Pressing problems • Stressful behaviour **Do it now: to-do-list!**	Quadrant II: *Attention based* • Prevention • Relationship building • Strategic planning • Long-term opportunities • Balanced behaviour **Schedule: stay in focus!**
NOT IMPORTANT	Quadrant III: *It is me again* • Reactive actions • Short-term activities • Victim behaviour • Resolve interruptions • Dependent in the relation **Delegate: stay out of it!**	Quadrant IV: *Temptations* • Give into temptations • Be easily distracted • Impulsive activities • Pleasant activities • Avoiding responsibilities **Limit: learn to say NO!**

Figure 7.01.06 Eisenhower Matrix

Your behaviour becomes visible in the four quadrants when applying the Eisenhower Matrix. In Quadrant I, you live life in the fast lane. You are working on tasks that require your attention. This often creates stressful situations. When do you intend to start planning? In Quadrant III, you respond reactively to the environment's requests to support or cooperate with them. Your focus is primarily on the short term, and you have a short concentration span. When do you learn how to say no? Matters in Quadrant IV distract you from your fundamental responsibilities and personal goals. How do you stay focused?

Reflecting on this, you can consciously change your focus to essential but non-yet-urgent matters. As a result, Quadrant II will take a more central role in your life. If you stick to Quadrant III and Quadrant IV matters, there is a big chance that Quadrant I will become a dominant factor, situations that you will have to deal with but then under pressure. This can be stressful.

STRESS MANAGEMENT

Stress is a prolonged or severe disruption of the load and workload capacity balance. It is, unfortunately, a common occurrence in projects. Stress management is the process of acquiring and practising various cognitive and behavioural techniques to manage and cope with stress. Within stress management, the distinction between eustress and distress is important. Furthermore, we look into triggers and symptoms of stress, how to reduce stress within yourself, and intervention techniques to reduce stress in others (see Advanced section).

EUSTRESS AND DISTRESS

Hans Selye introduced the concept of eustress and distress. In complex collaborative processes in projects, tension is constantly present. Usually, this tension has a positive effect on you. It creates energy and motivation. This is called eustress. But if the pressure becomes too great or reoccurs too often, it will have a negative impact on you and your performance. This is called distress.

Stress can occur suddenly. A serious incident or event requires fast, effective action. Distress may also build up during the project and take on a structural character. If it persists, you may even suffer burnout.

Burnout is when one is physically and or emotionally exhausted and is unable to perform adequately. Burnout is characterised by exhaustion (extreme fatigue), cynicism (distancing oneself from work or colleagues), and low self-esteem. Burnout requires professional help.

TRIGGERS AND SYMPTOMS OF DISTRESS

To prevent distress in projects, it is necessary to recognise triggers and symptoms of distress. Many factors can cause distress. These include monotonous work, authoritarian leadership, continuous heavy workloads, insufficient information to make decisions, dependency on others, insufficient decision-making power, lack of stimulation, harassment, poor communication, unclear tasks and responsibilities, poor relationships, political games, work-life imbalance, conflicting interests, et cetera.

Robert Karasek's *Job Demand and Control Model* is one of the leading stress models. Karasek hypothesises that the extent to which employees control job demands determines whether or not distress arises (see Figure 7.01.07).

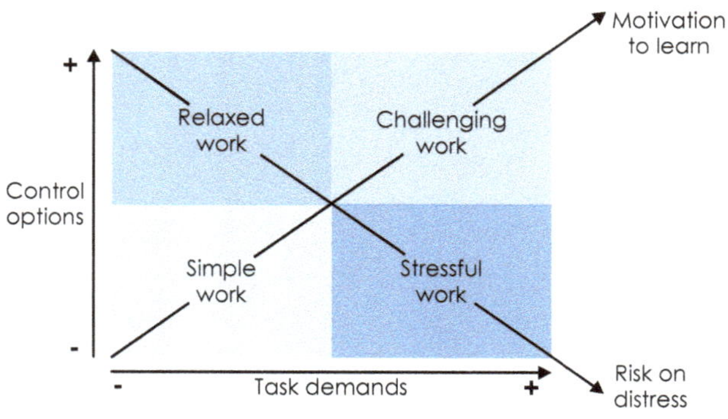

Figure 7.01.07 Job Demand and Control Model (Karasek, 1992)

Symptoms that may indicate distress include fatigue, sleeplessness, headaches, muscle aches, emotional outbursts, panic, complaining behaviour, withdrawn attitude, absentmindedness, change in natural behaviour, tenseness and more. The symptoms vary per person (see Figure 7.01.08).

METICULOUS, RATIONALISING PEOPLE Cold and calculating Icy and distant Unfeeling	**GOAL AND ACTION-ORIENTATED PEOPLE** Aggressive Insensitive On the attack
ATTENTIVE AND CAREFULLY LISTENING PEOPLE Heavily offended Full of resentment Victimised	**PEOPLE WITH A HOLISTIC MINDSET** Emotional outbursts Verbose Headless chicken

Figure 7.01.08 Symptoms of distress

If symptoms of distress occur, you need to discuss them and find out what is causing them. In addition, appropriate techniques and interventions may be applied to reduce the stress and achieve a new, manageable balance between load and load capacity.

REDUCING DISTRESS

To avoid distress, it is necessary to discharge this tension regularly so that you can relax. A state of balance and calm will then emerge. There are various techniques for achieving this relaxation.

Physical relaxation techniques

- *Exercising* – Exercising is an excellent way to calm your mind and emotions. A walk through the park or an hour of sport creates peace of mind. It shifts your attention from thinking and feeling to your body.
- *Breathing* – Conscious breathing in and out provides a direct form of relaxation. Emotions directly affect breathing and vice versa. Concentrating on your breathing helps you relax and focus on the here and now. Your mind is unburdened. This way, you can create space for new useful thoughts and feelings.

> *Breathe in and feel your stomach expand. If this doesn't work, place your hand on your stomach. It will move upwards beneath your hand. Hold your breath for seven seconds and then slowly exhale while once again counting to seven again. While exhaling, feel your stomach contract. Hold for a moment and repeat.*

- *Loosening muscles* – Various stretching exercises allow tense muscles to relax.
- *Healthy and varied food and drink* – Make sure your body regularly receives good nutrients, which provide a healthy balance and will supply you with enough energy to perform the necessary tasks.

Mental relaxation techniques

- *Reframing* – Being negatively judged can cause negativity and stress. Instead of focusing on the negativity and stress you are experiencing, reframe your thoughts in a more positive direction: 'How can I respond positively to the negative judgement I have experienced?' As you think about an answer, you reformulate your thoughts, and the associated emotions will adjust accordingly. The essence of reframing is to change your perspective. It helps you to open up to other possibilities and outcomes.

- *Examining and reversing judgements* – You can also reverse judgements. First, reverse the judgement and then ask yourself whether the reversal feels equally valid, less valid or more valid than initially meant.

> *An example of a judgmental accusation is: 'My boss is an egotist because he concentrates solely on himself.' When you reverse the judgement, such as: 'I am an egotist because I want to be the centre of his attention.' or 'My boss isn't an egotist because he is attentive to others.', you change your thinking perspective. Being judgemental causes destress. It can make you believe that you have insufficient influence on the situation. Examining and reversing a judgment bring the initiative back to yourself. It paves the way for finding new opportunities you can take up from your motivation.*

- *Autogenic training* – In autogenic training, by repeating a 'positive formula (affirmation)', the attention is focused on eliciting a desired physical response, e.g., calmness, relaxation, and coolness.

> *Sit in a comfortable upright position, eyes closed.*
> - *Focus on a 'formula', for example, 'My arms and legs are heavy.' and repeat this six times, followed by the formula 'I am calm.' Repeat this cycle a few times. End the session by moving your arms, taking a deep breath, and opening your eyes. The effect of this mental training is a physically relaxing response.*
> - *After the exercise, you can replace the formula with formulas like 'My forehead is pleasantly cool.', 'I accept myself.', 'I am strong and confident.', et cetera.*

Emotional relaxation techniques

- *Having fun: laughing, humour* – A simple and widely used technique to achieve relaxation is humour. It makes people laugh (emotion and breath), which relaxes the body and creates new thoughts and perspectives.
- *Reliving emotions, visualising, discharging, positive affirmation* – If a situation has evoked strong emotions and you cannot break free from the negative thoughts they have caused, it may help to visualise the situation and re-feel the sentiments it generates consciously. When doing so, you may experience having emotions and not being them. With that, you can consciously say goodbye to your negative thoughts. This reduces the intensity of your feelings.
- *Meditation* – During meditation, sit or lie quietly on a flat surface and relax. Whilst consciously breathing, let your thoughts come and go. By welcoming each thought, possibly smiling at it and letting it go, you automatically becomes calm inside your head.

Whatever relaxation techniques you apply, it is important to realise that there should always be a delay between the stimulus that comes from the outside and your response. You can use this time to find a careful, relaxed and emotionally intelligent response (see Figure 7.01.09).

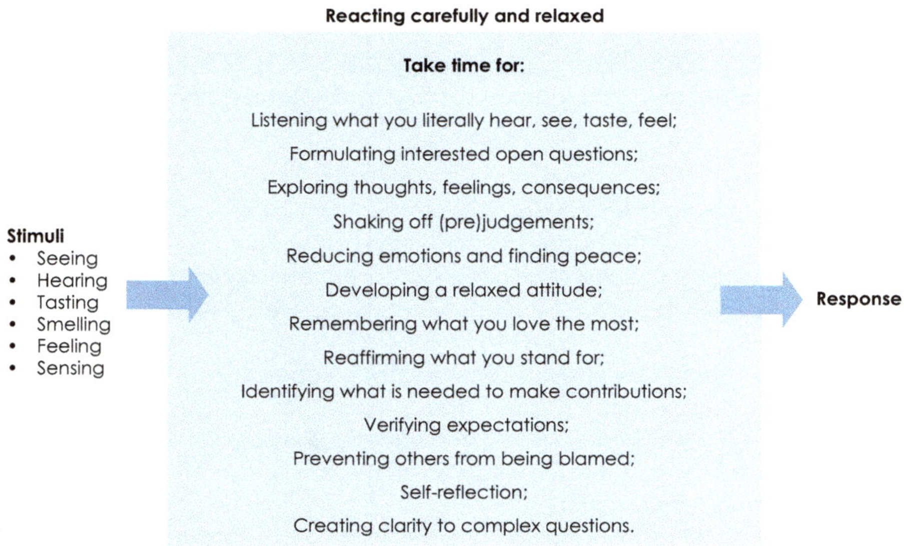

Figure 7.01.09 There is a moment between stimulus and response

ADVANCED

TECHNIQUES PERSONAL TIME MANAGEMENT (ADVANCED)

Various time management techniques, such as GTD, 20/80 rule, and Time Surfing, are available.

Getting Things Done

Project environments are often hectic. You are constantly exposed to various issues, such as emails, WhatsApp messages, and questions. How do you manage all this? In *Getting Things Done* (GTD), Dave Allen advices consistently following the decision tree below, which helps you to organise stuff that comes your way. 'Stuff' is everything you have to deal with:

1. What is it? Pay attention to the specific information coming in.
2. Is it an action for me?
   2a. NO! Delete the email or archive it in a retrievable folder for later reference or assessment;
   2b. YES! Define your next action:
      - Take action if it is immediately solvable within a short space of time.
      - Delegate it, if possible, and leave it to the other person.
      - Postpone it: consciously put the action or series of actions on your agenda.

By consistently following this decision tree, you ensure that the distracting thoughts of 'whether or not to take action' disappears from your mind. The 'decision tree' creates order in your daily business.

The 20/80 Rule of Pareto

The 20/80 rule was developed by the economist Pareto: 20% of customers generate 80% of sales. You can apply the same rule within time management:

» 20% of my project work leads to 80% of the intended results > focus.
» 20% of my tasks take 80% of my time and add little value > unlearn.
» 20% of my goals for the coming year really contribute to what I want to achieve > choose.
» 80% of my time, I spend on the 20% goals I really want to achieve > organise and stay focused.

The last line of reasoning focuses on the question: 'What do I want to focus on in my life?' Whereafter, you can ask yourself: 'How do I stay focused on the things that matter to me?'

Focused time surfing

In his book *A Manual For Time Surfing*, Loomans (2017) defines seven principles to help you maintain your focus:

1. *Focus* – Pay attention to what you are doing. Don't get distracted. If you get distracted, stop immediately and ask yourself: 'What do I actually want to achieve?' This question helps you to focus again.
2. *Satisfaction* – Start paying attention to things that you enjoy. This way you can concentrate on doing what you love most. Steve Jobs said this in his speech to students at Stanford University: 'You're lucky if you know what you love early on. If you don't, keep looking until you find that happiness!'

3. *Balance* – Rest. Take a break. Do something physical to clear your mind and get enough sleep.
4. *Avoid noise* – avoid things that cause stress or that distract you. Consciously plan a '20% white space' in your diary. If you're not careful, your mind will start to wander.
5. *Intuition* – Regularly choose what 'your mind' is telling you. What comes up in those quiet moments that make you feel 'This is what really makes me happy?'
6. *Let go* – Ask for help if you can't figure something out. Find out why you are resisting something.
7. *Declutter* – Give up your resistance! Are you afraid, angry, or sad? Allow yourself to be in touch with these emotions. If you don't, fighting them will cause you much stress and unhappiness. Allowing these emotions creates space to find a way out and a goal to focus on.

RATIONAL EMOTIVE BEHAVIOUR THERAPY (ADVANCED)

Rational Emotive Behaviour Therapy (REBT) is a method for examining the relationship between thoughts, feelings and behaviour in actual situations. As illustrated in Figure 7.01.10, the situation and the goals you want to achieve influence your thoughts, feelings and behaviour. Beliefs are thoughts that are strongly anchored within yourself and determine to a large extent, how you perceive the world around you. They influence your feelings and behaviours. This behaviour determines whether you achieve your goals. Achieved goals provide experiences of success and, in the process, strengthen the corresponding positive beliefs and feelings.

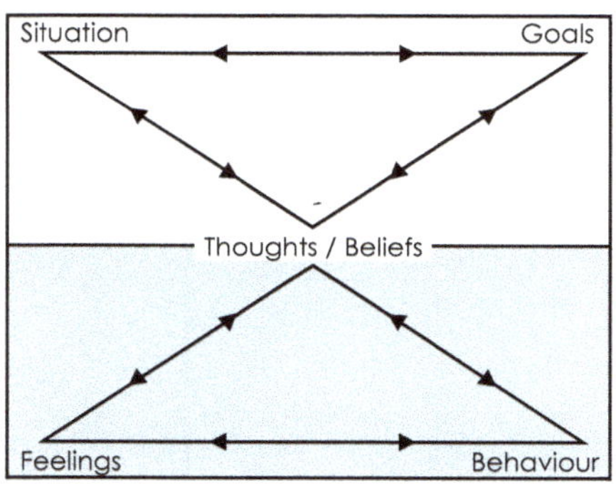

Figure 7.01.10 REBT (Jacobs, 2009)

Irrational beliefs

Irrational beliefs often lead to ineffective feelings and dysfunctional behaviour. You can recognise them by (Jacobs 2009):

- *Demanding or compulsive attitudes* – Thinking in terms of, 'I have to...', 'The boss has to...'
- *Judging yourself or others* – Thinking in terms of 'good/bad' and or 'right/wrong'. It is about being too quick to link a judgement to a concrete situation.
- *Low frustration tolerance* – Thinking in terms of, 'This has to be better or different ... you losers.'
- *Disaster thinking* – Thinking in terms of, 'This is the worst thing that has ever happened to me.'

- *Exaggerated generalisations* – Thinking in terms of, 'It's always like this', 'Everyone knows!'

ABCDEF method

REBT offers good starting points for breaking through irrational beliefs and finding beliefs that positively stimulate personal behaviour. The ABCDEF method can be used.

A. *Activating event* – This can be an external situation or an inner event, such as a thought or feeling.
B. *Beliefs* – The explicit and implicit meanings and assumptions about the events. The stories you tell yourself. If these stories are rigid, dysfunctional, against or fictional, it will negatively impact your behaviour.
C. *Consequences* – The emotional and behavioural effect of such beliefs.

> - *Project manager: 'I am furious with supplier X for not involving me in the work he does for us. I find it extremely frustrating. He only does what suits him.'*
> - *Coach: 'Well, why don't you terminate his contract?'*
> - *Project manager: 'If only that were possible, but no other supplier is as experienced!'*
> - *Coach: 'Oh, that's why he gets free rein?' So, those with knowledge have free reign?*
> - *Project manager: 'Well, I could really use some help managing this partner.'*

In REBT, the beliefs (B) are the most important. You should examine these beliefs if they hinder you from functionally dealing with situations. By becoming aware of them, you can clarify the causes of your inadequate feelings and behaviour. You can explore these causes using the letters DEF.

Reflective Dialogue (D) – Here, you ask yourself questions about the thoughts linked to the situation. Questions such as: 'Why does the other or why do I act this way?'; 'What could happen if what I want doesn't happen after all?'; 'Why is the other person's behaviour wrong?'; 'In what way does my behaviour evoke unwanted behaviour?' et cetera.

> - *You can support this reflection process by asking yourself four questions about your judgement:*
> - *Is it true that 'the supplier only does what suits him?' Yes or No?*
> - *Can you be absolutely certain that it is true that 'the supplier only does what suits him?' Yes or No?*
> - *How does the thought 'The supplier only does what suits him!' affect your behaviour? Reflect on your behaviour and write down your answers. This can be a very enlightening process.*
> - *Who would you be without the thought, 'The supplier only does what suits him?'*
>
> *After this reflection, you can establish if it's possible to reverse the thoughts:*
> - *Can you reverse the thought? For example: 'I only want the supplier to do what suits me!'*

> - *Is this reversal more true, equally true or less true? Be honest when you ponder the question, and you will discover that judging others says much about yourself.*
>
> *It is important to literally write down those thoughts because thoughts quickly turn to solutions. Working out your judgements and answering them on paper creates a deeper understanding of your part in the story. That is the basis for making reversals.*

New Effects (E) – Such reflective questions lead to other views and thoughts. By becoming aware of these views and thoughts and naming them explicitly, new perspectives on reality emerge. This almost immediately leads to different thoughts and feelings.

Feeling good in your new world (F) – By making choices based on those more positive thoughts and feelings, you take responsibility for them. By implementing these choices, you develop more appropriate behaviour for the situation.

> - *Coach: 'OK, it's good that you say that. Do you have any ideas on how you can manage him?'*
> - *Project manager: 'Hmm, I will let his knowledge be a more significant guiding factor during our meetings. Instead of imposing timetables on him, I will approach him more as a partner.'*

This confrontational way of thinking directly impacts your actions. By making choices based on those positive thoughts and feelings and consciously following those choices, you can achieve your desired goals.

STEPS IN GOAL SETTING (ADVANCED)

Goals are guiding focal points you can work towards in a disciplined way. The *Goal Setting Theory* by Locke and Latham (2017) provides insight into a coherent set of necessary factors for realising goals (see Figure 7.01.11). These factors apply to realising the personal goals and goals of a group or team.

Set challenging but achievable goals – Formulate challenging goals that are specific and ambitious. As long as you accept those goals and can achieve them, there is a positive relationship between the difficulty of the goal and the innate drive to achieve them. The achievability of challenging goals is partly determined by goal-promoting and goal-supportive factors.

Goal-promoting factors – When you are competent and committed to specific and ambitious goals, it will be easier for you to reach them. Competence is increased by training your skills. Commitment is increased by developing an intrinsic engagement with the goals set. By asking for feedback, you acquire external help realising the challenging goals. Dealing with the complexity involved in achieving goals means you align your goals and clearly say no to activities that do not contribute. You can also break down challenging goals into intermediate ones and make a realistic time schedule. Finally, don't allow yourself to be distracted by situational factors. This means accepting your choices' consequences and defying your environment's opposition.

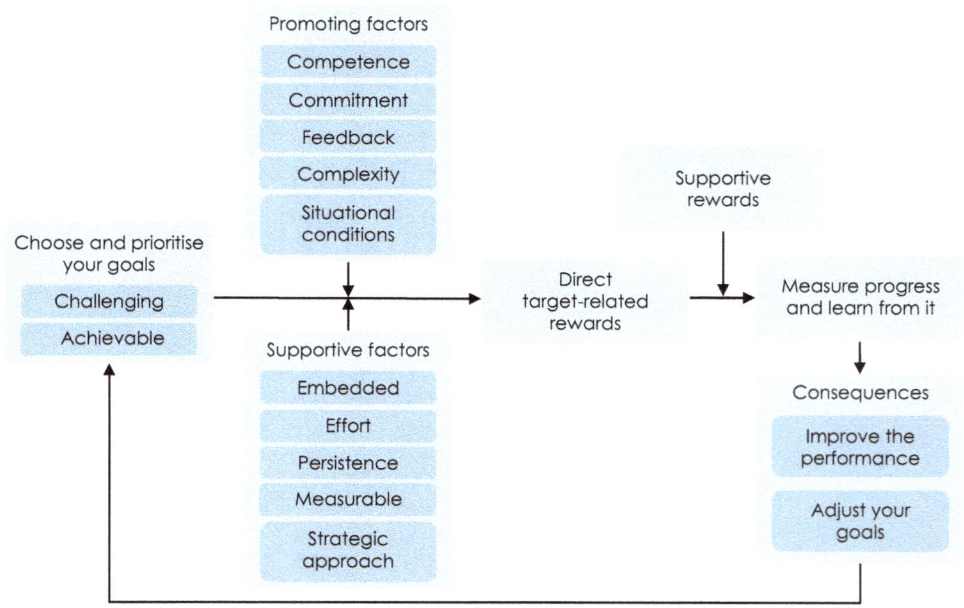

Figure 7.01.11 Goalsetting theory (Locke and Latham, 2017)

Supportive factors – Ensure the challenging goals are anchored in core values. They should suit you. Also, assure yourself that you can handle the effort. If achieving a goal requires too much effort, you become exhausted. Embedded goals and achievable actions strengthen your perseverance. Set intermediate targets. Reaching these confirm that you are on the right track. Formulate these intermediate targets SMART. SMART stands for Specific, Measurable, Achievable, Relevant and Time-bound. Finally, don't just get started. Make a plan to affirm that 'This is how I intend to realise the challenge!'

Direct goal-related rewards – Reward yourself for having realised intermediate targets. Allow yourself to receive such rewards. Share your achievements with colleagues and friends and celebrate the progress made.

Supportive rewards – Also, be open-minded about rewards that encourage you. Receiving a compliment or being asked to lecture on your work are examples. Positive reactions from your immediate surroundings reinforce your sense of purpose. Be attentive when receiving these reactions. They confirm the direction you are taking.

Measure and learn from progress – Reflect on the significance of intermediate results achieved and what these results have set in motion, both directly and indirectly. Also, look back at the interim results you experienced as difficult and how you handled them. This makes you mentally strong and provides insight into pitfalls and learning points.

Process the consequences – If necessary, improve or revise your strategic approach based on the results you have achieved and the lessons you have learned, and adjust any intermediate targets.

Achieving challenging goals often puts you in exciting and sometimes stressful situations. Reducing distress is necessary to persevere.

TECHNIQUES FOR REDUCING DISTRESS (ADVANCED)

Creating a sustainable balance between load and load capacity requires careful interventions. Possible interventions are:

- *Relaxed responses* – Everyone knows the saying: 'First count to ten.' If you want to achieve a relaxed response, it is important to take the time to formulate a careful and relaxed one.
- *Talk about stress* – This is the simplest and perhaps the most widely used intervention. As soon as too much stress arises, it is important to discuss it. This discussion focuses automatically on creating a better balance between load and load capacity.
- *Intervision* – Intervision is a technique in which colleagues support each other to explore difficulties and remove blockages they experience at work. Intervision is an excellent technique to strengthen mutual trust in teams. However, especially in the beginning, intervision requires some process supervision.

The general structure of intervision/guided intervision:

1. *The introducer brings in an issue and formulates the problem.*
2. *The other participants investigate the background of the problem by first writing down open questions and then choosing three open questions to ask. The introducer notes these questions.*
3. *The introducer categorises these questions into warm, neutral and cold and answers the warm and neutral ones.*
4. *The other participants formulate creative advice for the introducer in the form of: 'I would ...'*
5. *The introducer indicates which advice is experienced as valuable and ends with: 'I shall ...'*
6. *The introducer formulates several realistic, achievable actions. The intervision ends.*
7. *Evaluate the process and, if necessary, formulate learning points for next time.*

- *Problem-orientated work consultation* – You can often solve a problem through informal consultation. Sometimes, however, an issue has too many dimensions. At these moments, it is important to involve the team and find an answer to the issue together.
- *Teambuilding* – Teambuilding is a collective term for a series of group activities in which collaboration is fundamental. These can be project-related activities, such as the project kick-off, and activities outside the project, such as a social outing. Good team building improves collaboration. This creates better results and a better atmosphere.
- *Relaxation rituals* – To maintain the balance between workload and load capacity, it is important to have relaxation rituals. Think of starting the day together, eating lunch together, going for a walk, Friday afternoon drinks, et cetera. In a healthy working environment, such rituals arise naturally.
- *Performance interviews* – During these interviews, the work and how it is perceived

are central. At the same time, you look for solutions to strengthen the balance between load and workload capacity.

- *Coaching/supervision* – Whereas the performance interview is mainly about functioning and how people perform their tasks, coaching focuses on developing awareness and responsibility. GROW is a useful method to use for this. GROW stands for coherently examining Goals, Reality, Opportunities and the Way Forward (See section Advanced, Chapter 8.02, Leadership).
- *Revitalising* – Revitalising is about positively stimulating, energising and strengthening the will to go for it. It is about making what is possible and achievable visible and restoring their faith in it. Furthermore, it is also about positively encouraging them to take good care of themselves through quality sleep, good nutrition and relaxation techniques.
- *Escalating/delegating* – Involves consulting at a higher hierarchical level to discuss a stressful situation or delegation the problem to a team member who can better deal with the issue.

7.02 PERSONAL INTEGRITY AND RELIABILITY

PURPOSE

The purpose of this chapter is to enable the individual to make consistent decisions, take consistent actions and behave consistently in projects.

LEARNING OBJECTIVES

- Aspects of reliability;
- Ethics school of thoughts;
- Social equity and sustainability principles;
- Professional Standards IPMA Code of Ethics;
- Ethics test (advanced);
- Personal ethics versus business ethics (advanced);
- UN Universal Declaration of Human Rights (advanced).

DEFINITIONS

Personal integrity: Acting per their own moral and ethical values and principles.
Reliability: Acting dependably, according to expectations and or agreed behaviour.
Ethics: Moral principles that control or influence a person's behaviour.
Utilitarianism: The ethical approach which states that the best action is the one that maximises the well-being of the participants.
Deontology: The ethical approach that focuses on the normative ethical position based on rules.
Virtue ethic: The ethical approach where the best action is determined by 'How should I live?'
Care ethic: The ethical approach where the interest and care of others determine the best action.
Professional ethics: The ethical approach to making conscious choices to comply with standards and values in implementing your profession.

INTRODUCTION

The effectiveness of the project manager stands or falls with personal reliability. We first discuss different aspects of this. Personal integrity means the project professional acts according to moral and ethical values and principles. We discuss four ethical schools of thought and the IPMA code of ethics. The latter provides a clear professional standard for acting professionally and conforming to ethical values and principles. You can mirror your personal responsibility to it to take the right decisions and to stay in line with it.

ASPECTS OF RELIABILITY

Reliable means that you are consistent, transparent, consequent and predictable.

- *Consistent* – Being consistent means that your actions are coherent and contradiction-free. The logic you use and your attitude can be followed and understood by those around you.
- *Transparent* – Being transparent means that you are open-minded and clear to others. You have no secret agendas and are sincere to those around you. This does not mean that you always speak your mind. After all, political and social sensitivity is also an important competence for the project professional. It does, however,

mean that you can openly and honestly justify why you do what you are doing to yourself and others.

- *Consequent* – Being consequent means you show the same behaviour in similar situations. Being consequent also means that, in principle, you continuously behave per the agreed arrangements.
- *Predictable* – Being predictable means that you are dependable to other parties. There are no unpleasant surprises in store, and if things go differently than agreed upon, those involved are informed in good time.

ETHICS

It is essential to justify your own choices carefully. You may have to compromise your morals when you cannot find that justification. We discuss four ethical schools of thought for reflecting on your personal actions.

Utilitarianism or consequentialist ethics

In utilitarianism, the contribution to the common good is central. You ask yourself: 'Will I, by my intended actions, contribute to the well-being and happiness of all people?' Project professionals regularly face dilemmas in finding a correct answer to this question. After all, in the short term, a choice may adversely affect some people. You can brush this away by hiding behind the assignment. You can also take responsibility by standing up for adversely affected people. In this way, the complexity of goal-setting takes on a substantiated meaning. Project professionals who do this consciously make a stand. They do not shy away from dialogue about forward-looking trade-offs. Instead, they dare to enter into dialogue and are open about the consequences of their choices.

> *A project manager in the insurance industry focused his team on realising and implementing a workflow management system. By organising and controlling the flow of documents, a considerable efficiency gain could be achieved — a criterion for choosing the project. At the same time, for 30% of the people, the project would mean losing their current job — a criterion to veto the project.*
>
> *Everyone feels this is an unfair choice for the people who will lose their jobs because of it. For that reason alone, it is a difficult 'take it or leave it' message to communicate if you choose to lead the project.*
>
> *The project leader articulated this message: 'I have realised workflow management solutions in organisations for ten years. I am passionate about how collaboration across departmental boundaries improves by digitally managing the document flow. People are no longer drowned in paperwork and focus more on the work they were hired to do. Personally, I experience this as valuable. However, at the moment, you are a victim of the implemented innovation. But I have only one goal for you: finding a new job in which you can make a meaningful contribution again. Fortunately, this project also has created space to realise this objective, to which I am fully committed.'*

Virtue ethics

Virtue ethics focuses on how an individual should live to experience happiness. Aristotle defines virtue as the '*middle ground between excess and deficiency*'. Virtue is an attitude that enables us to think about a possible course of action, which together will take us forward and in which common sense is a leading factor. Possible steps to resolve a dilemma can be determined by searching for the wisest option.

The cardinal virtues are 'courage', 'justice', 'wisdom' and 'moderation'. These virtues give direction to the intended actions. In short: acquire a moderate attitude when searching for fair solutions for all parties involved and dare to take that step.

Deontology or ethics of principle

Deontology focuses on acting per moral principles. It is about absolute acceptance of moral rules. If you do not follow these rules you expect everyone else to follow, you are not acting ethically, even if they have positive consequences. This sets deontology against utilitarianism, which focuses on the consequences of your behaviour. Deontology is also called duty ethics.

Care ethics

The French philosopher Levinas already spoke about the basic principles of care ethics. He describes a human being 'as *an inescapable ethical sensibility, who as such experiences responsibility towards the other*'. By taking the Other into account, (Levinas writes Other with a capital letter), ethics becomes relational.

Care ethics does not focus on utility, virtues or principles but on values that are important for maintaining relationships and allowing them to flourish. Joan Tronto (1993), the founder of care ethics, defines caring as *an activity that includes everything we do to maintain, continue and restore our world so that we can live well.* It is not just about a reciprocal care relationship between people but especially about care focused on what Tronto calls the life-supporting web. It starts with tuning in to what needs care, followed by conscious choices and actions to take responsibility for this. The construct of Corporate Social Responsibility can be viewed from the perspective of care ethics. To keep the life-supporting web strong and healthy, you need to see the whole picture, feel and know what needs care, and take responsibility for that within your power.

> *'In my role as a project support officer, I always coordinate with the project teams I support and ensure that the project follows the guidelines we set together as much as possible. This support is different in every project. All clients differ. Some project teams work more independently than others. I keep a close eye on the project's progress and actively bring up any points of attention that seem to be neglected. In this way, I take my own responsibility. In this way also, I meet my own needs, those of the project managers and their teams, our own organisation and those of the client organisation.'*

SOCIAL EQUITY AND SUSTAINABILITY PRINCIPLES

Social equity refers to fairness, justice and equal opportunity in society. In project management, social equity principles ensure that project benefits and opportunities are distributed fairly to all stakeholders, regardless of their background, identity or status.

Sustainability principles relate to balancing economic, environmental and social aspects to achieve long-term viability and minimise negative impacts. In project management, sustainability principles ensure that projects integrate sustainability considerations throughout the project lifecycle. This includes assessing and mitigating environmental impacts, promoting resource efficiency and considering the social and economic implications of the project.

By incorporating social equity and sustainability principles into project management practices, you take into account the broader societal implications of projects. This approach aligns with the global shift towards more justice and sustainable development, ensuring that projects positively contribute to society while minimising harm to the environment and disadvantaged communities. The core of sustainable business is integrating value chain impacts into your thinking and doing (see Chapter 11.02 Sustainability).

PROFESSIONAL ETHICS AND IPMA CODE OF ETHICS

Professional ethics is about making conscious choices for norms and values you uphold in your profession's performance. To develop an ethical professional attitude, project professionals can assess their behaviour against codes of conduct appropriate for their profession. IPMA offers a code of conduct for project professionals: the IPMA Code of Ethics and Professional Conduct, a set of values, rules, standards, and principles outlining what the IPMA expects from project professionals' behaviour. It focuses on trust, integrity and respect, care and responsibility towards relations, society and the environment. The IPMA code provides guidelines for the following:

Professional ethics – IPMA professionals avoid conflicts of interest and bribery, continuously work on their personal competence development and only accept assignments they can correctly and adequately carry out. They are realistic and reliable in their offers, give an accurate picture of progress and make reasonable forecasts.

Commitment to project sponsors and other stakeholders – IPMA professionals value their stakeholders and faithfully honour agreements that have been made with them. They handle confidential information with care and share it with those with authority. In dealing with stakeholders, awareness of the possible consequences of one's work on others' interests plays an important role. The aim is to minimise negative impact. Unethical behaviour and illegality are non-existent traits in the conduct of the IPMA professional. IPMA professionals inform stakeholders correctly and encourage them to reflect critically on expectations and possible ethical consequences of project results.

Commitment to colleagues and employees – IPMA professionals hire people for projects, programmes and portfolios suitable for the job. IPMA professionals stand for a safe and healthy working environment and are trained to fulfil standards in this area. IPMA professionals prefer working conditions that are sustainable. They show high cultural sensitivity and respect people's rights and culture. They do not tolerate child labour or other forms of forced labour. Mental and physical punishment and sexual harassment are not condoned. IPMA professionals don't withhold employees from joining a trade union. They ensure that salaries equal the statutory minimum wage and that this is paid fairly overtime. IPMA professionals don't discriminate based on gender, ethnic origin, religion, sexual orientation, age, or other grounds.

Responsibility to society – IPMA professionals adapt to the culture in which they work. Mutual respect is central. IPMA professionals do not work in environments that harm or undermine local communities. Instead, they abide by international treaties and the laws of the countries where they operate. IPMA professionals take social responsibility and develop their profession accordingly. They maintain high ethical standards, even in complex and conflict-ridden environments.

Sustainability and the natural environment – IPMA professionals strive to minimise the potential environmental damage resulting from a project. They actively demonstrate their awareness of taking responsibility for this environment within teams, organisations, and society.
IPMA professionals do everything in their power to prevent waste and stimulate circularity. Instead, they make corporates aware of the measures they can take to benefit the environment.

The educational mission – IPMA professionals continuously develop their awareness of the Code of Ethics and Professional Conduct principles. They share their knowledge about technology, science and the management of projects with their direct colleagues and other project professionals, including, of course, IPMA members. Their focus is on developing better projects for a better world.

Professional codes provide a framework for practising the profession. Understand that the code should never stand above the meaning of ethics. Every situation is unique and requires a consciously considered ethical approach. This approach can be based on the four ethical schools of thought discussed:

- Do personal actions contribute to the common good (utilitarianism)?
- Is personal action anchored in virtues (virtue ethics)?
- Does personal action comply with universal principles (deontology)?
- Do I develop personal actions from 'caring' for other interests (care ethics)?

Each individual obviously replies differently to these questions. That is precisely the essence of the ethical dialogue you conduct with other stakeholders. By engaging in this dialogue, you develop a moral, reliable basis for collaboration.

ADVANCED

ETHICS TEST (ADVANCED)

It is not always easy to determine whether an action is ethical or not. Various ethics tests have been developed to provide a handle on this. A well-known ethics test is that of Kaptein (2011):

- *Spectacle test* – How do you judge the action from the point of view of the different parties involved?
- *Frontpage test* – Would you also act like this if it appeared in the newspaper?
- *Shoe test* – What would my role model do? Is your role model Nelson Mandela? What do you think Nelson Mandela would have done in this situation?
- *Mirror test* – Can I still look myself in the eye? Is this action in line with my own internal compass?
- *Slope test* – What would be the social and ecological impact if everyone behaved like this? Would this behaviour still be acceptable?

If others do not act in accordance with ethical standards, careful communication is required. The question is how to address those others in such situations. Does their behaviour jeopardise the success of the project? If so, state the consequences of their behaviour for the project. Is the ethical code not respected? Discuss compliance with the ethical standard. Does the behaviour conflict with your own values and standards? Tell how their behaviour affects you and discuss it together (see *Giving feedback* in Chapter 7.03, Personnel Communication).

PERSONAL ETHICS VERSUS BUSINESS ETHICS (ADVANCED)

Business ethics studies values and norms that can influence a company's moral choices. The main ethical views that companies may follow are:

Transactional ethics – An enterprise needs to act economically to survive. If a company fails to do so, various stakeholders will be affected. For example, shareholders receive lower dividends, consumers have to pay higher prices, and employees lose their jobs. Transactional ethics are determined by law, decency and reliability.

Ethics of recognition – These ethics assume that a company is obliged to accommodate the rights of weaker parties and the public interest in certain situations. They recognise the problem and take the responsibility to help them. An energy company, for example, doesn't directly cut off defaulters but brings them into contact with debt assistance beforehand.

Change ethics – This ethical line of thinking stipulates that companies also actively and deliberately work toward a better society. For example, a statement such as 'The polluter pays.' is insufficient. It is not only about payment but also about taking responsibility for removing the source of pollution.

All schools of thought are concerned with taking responsibility. Corporate social responsibility (CSR) is becoming increasingly central in this respect. According to John Elkington, the essence of corporate social responsibility is to create a good balance between profit, people and a liveable planet, with welfare as a guiding principle. For example:

- Consciously developing and producing products that do not harm humanity, stimulate the quality of life and support sound profitability;
- Not producing products in countries where human rights are violated;
- Creating space for disadvantaged people and developing social capital;
- Taking responsibility for environmental protection and or improvement.

To underline their ethical responsibility, companies draw up codes of conduct. In these, the company certifies:

- Its mission with regard to people, planet, and profit;
- The core values it adopts to do business;
- How it takes responsibility toward the various stakeholders in and around the company;
- The standards set for the behaviour of employees and what rules should be followed by them in order to comply with these standards.

Determining how you relate to the organisations you belong to is essential. Ethical choices made by the organisation are not necessarily your choices. Sometimes you will face dilemmas and need to ask yourself: 'Can I still work for this organisation?' Or: 'Will this organisation undergo an internal transition to be more compatible with my values and standards?' Ethics never absolve you from taking responsibility for your own choices and actions. Ethics tests can help you make the right decisions.

UN UNIVERSAL DECLARATION OF HUMAN RIGHTS (ADVANCED)

Shortly after the Second World War, the United Nations was founded (24 October 1945). The organisation was established to prevent future generations from ever having to experience another war. Because of the objective of establishing peace, a document was drawn up to capture human rights. This document is recognised as the United Nations Universal Declaration of Human Rights. This declaration serves as a benchmark for moral principles. However, this does not relieve you of your responsibility to ask yourself whether these principles are consistent with your own.

Universal rights

1. *All human beings are born free in dignity and rights.*
2. *Everyone is entitled to all the rights and freedoms set forth in this Declaration, without distinction of any kind.*
3. *Everyone has the right to life, liberty and security of person.*
4. *No one shall be held in slavery or servitude.*
5. *No one shall be subjected to torture or cruel.*
6. *Everyone has the right to recognition everywhere as a person before the law.*
7. *All are equal before the law and are entitled without any discrimination to equal protection of the law.*
8. *Everyone has the right to an effective remedy by the competent national tribunals for acts violating the fundamental rights granted him by the constitution or by law.*
9. *No one shall be subjected to arbitrary arrest, detention or exile.*
10. *Everyone is entitled to a fair, public and independent trial.*
11. *Everyone is innocent unless proven guilty.*
12. *Everyone has a right to privacy.*
13. *We all have the right to move freely.*
14. *Everyone has the right to seek and to enjoy in other countries asylum from persecution.*
15. *Everyone has the right to a nationality.*
16. *Every adult has the right to marry and start a family. These rights are the same for men and women.*
17. *Everyone has the right to own and share property*
18. *Everyone has the right to freedom of thought, conscience and religion.*
19. *Everyone has the right to freedom of opinion and expression.*
20. *Everyone has the right to freedom of peaceful assembly and association.*
21. *Everyone has the right to participate in the government of their own country.*
22. *Everyone has the right to social security, to housing, medical care, child care and medical assistance as far as resources allow.*
23. *Every adult has the right to exercise a profession at a reasonable wage and to be a member of a trade union.*
24. *Everyone has the right to play, to rest from work and relax.*
25. *Everyone has the right to a standard of living adequate for the health and well-being of himself and of his family.*
26. *Everyone has the right to education.*
27. *Everyone has the right freely to participate in the cultural life of the community, to enjoy the arts and to share in scientific advancement and its benefits.*
28. *Everyone is entitled to a social and international order in which the rights and freedoms set forth in this Declaration can be fully realised.*
29. *Everyone has duties to the community in which alone the free and full development of his personality is possible.*
30. *Nothing in this Declaration may be interpreted as implying for any State, group or person any right to engage in any activity or to perform any act aimed at the destruction of any of the rights and freedoms set forth herein.*

7.03 PERSONAL COMMUNICATION

PURPOSE

The purpose of this chapter is to enable the individual to communicate efficiently and effectively in a variety of situations to different audiences and across different cultures and to support others in doing so.

LEARNING OBJECTIVES

- Communication;
- Communication levels;
- Active listening;
- Asking the right questions;
- Giving and receiving feedback;
- Meetings;
- Facilitates workshops;
- Features workshops;
- Written communication;
- Presentations;
- Elevator pitch (advanced);
- Bad news conversations (advanced).

DEFINITIONS

Communication: Exchange of information.

Miscommunication: The situation where the receiver interprets the message differently than intended.

Communication channel: Manner how to convey information.

Active listening: A technique in which the listener adopts an active and encouraging attitude.

Feedback: Reaction provided to someone about their performance or behaviour, and desired performance or future behaviour.

Meeting: A gathering within a specific timeframe to discuss subjects to reach a judgement or decision.

Workshop: A gathering where participants interactively participate in contributing to an intended result.

Written communication: Transmission of information through written, printed or electronic symbols, signs or words.

Presentation: An oral transmission of information to a group, typically supported visually.

INTRODUCTION

Communication concerns the exchange of information between parties. Communication should be consistent, relevant, clear and timely. Effective personal communication is vital to the success of any project.

In this chapter, we will first discuss several concepts of communication itself. In the second part, we will focus on practical themes that every project professional has to deal with, such as conversation skills, organising meetings and workshops, written communication, and presentation.

COMMUNICATION

The exchange of information is necessary for understanding each other. It is a decisive factor in cooperation because, without good communication, people would not understand why, what, how and when things have to be done.

Criteria for good communication

Good communication is the result of interaction between sender and receiver. It is about getting a message to the receiver that is understood as intended by the sender.

Criteria for assessing the quality of communication are:

- *Effective* – The extent to which a sender succeeds in communicating a message clearly and unambiguously.
- *Comprehensible* – Besides conveying the information clearly, the target group should also fully understand it. The message should not be too difficult and not too simple. The first can cause misunderstanding, and the latter creates false expectations. The information should be clear, understandable and complete.
- *Efficient* – The ease with which the communicative process proceeds and the energy it takes to get a message across or received.
- *Accepted* – The extent to which communication meets ethical and social standards. When not, parties involved will show resistance and be suspicious. When communication is carefully built up and tuned to involved parties, there is a significant chance that they will accept the information.
- *Timely* – Information should, of course, not come as a complete surprise. Parties should have sufficient time to absorb the information. With good timing, you activate attention for a message at the right moment. If not, parties will be reluctant or unresponsive when they receive the information, preventing it from coming across.

For communication to be effective, the communicating parties should understand each other well. This understanding arises from the interaction between the sender and the receiver.

Communication model

Communication can be done verbally, through a gesture, in writing, via a video message or podcast, et cetera, and via symbols and behaviour. It is important to realise that communication is almost always disrupted by noise. Noise is everything that disrupts communication. Noise can occur during the transmission of the message. The noise causes can be found in the message, the channel, the sender and the receiver (see Figure 7.03.01).

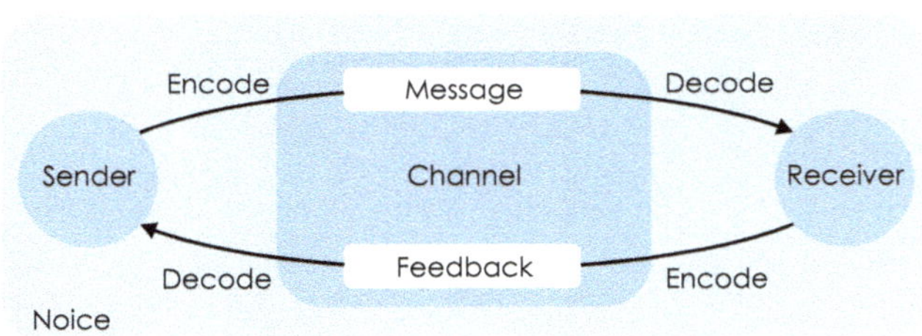

Figure 7.03.01 Communication model

The sender can ask the receiver whether the information has been adequately understood and summarise the message. The given feedback can be enhanced with additional information. The receiver can also ask for further details. Feedback and clarification prevent the receiver from misinterpreting the message. Interaction is necessary to understand each other well.

Communication channels

Communication channels are manners of conveying information. It is essential to choose channels and codes that suit the recipients of the information. This also implies that you may give the same message differently to different recipients. Channels you can use are:

> *They wanted to transfer relatively simple tasks from the technical department to the operators in a factory. The aim was to deepen and broaden this group's capacities so that they could solve simple malfunctions themselves. Initially, staff training was used for this. However, the technical department staff felt they had to explain the same thing too often. During a discussion with the production staff, the idea arose of depicting the relatively simple actions on large boards mounted on the factory ceiling. From then on, the operators understood the message's content well, evidenced by the fact that they asked far fewer questions and began to perform the actions correctly and on their own accord.*

Oral or verbal communication – The spoken word is central. The content spoken and heard is essential for the effectiveness of the communication. You can play with intonation, speed, volume, pauses and accents. This is the para-verbal part of verbal communication. If the para-verbal does not match the content of the message, it reduces the effectiveness of the communication.

Non-verbal communication – Non-verbal communication is communication through body language (expression, posture or gestures) and how you dress. When non-verbal communication is consistent with verbal communication, it reinforces the message. The reverse is also true. When non-verbal communication does not match verbal communication, it reduces the effectiveness of the message or may even negate it altogether. A threatening message with a timid attitude does not match. Inconsistency in communication always reduces the effectiveness of the message.

Written communication – The content, structure, style and tone are important aspects for successfully conveying the message. Written communication may include billboards, (electronic) newsletters, reports, journals, books, newspapers, letters, electronic messages, internet sites, folders, et cetera.

Communication through film/video, images and or sound – This is an important option because you can give the content both a realistic and emotional touch. Think about 3D videos and images. They show a 'realistic' future, whereby music and or voice-overs enhance the message and evoke emotions.

When conveying a message through multiple channels, you need to coordinate the messages well. Mixed messages confuse recipients and cause multiple or even false interpretations of a message. Choosing the most suitable combination of form and channel is difficult. Communication professionals know better which channel is best for conveying consistent messages. Involve them when necessary.

Body language

Body language largely determines non-verbal communication. It includes facial expressions, body posture, gestures, eye movement, touch and the use of space. Negative body language examples are arms folded in front of the body, minimal or tense facial expression, body turned away, and maintaining minimal (eye) contact. Positive body language examples are having an open posture, being relaxed, not slouching, sitting or standing upright and placing your hands by your sides. Avoid standing with your hands on your hips, as this can communicate aggression or a desire to dominate. Use a firm handshake. Maintain eye contact. Avoid touching your face while answering questions, and show a friendly face.

Rhetoric

Rhetoric is the art of persuasion through an effective combination of verbal and non-verbal communication:

- Structure your story logically, including the use of substantiated arguments (logos);
- Touch the audience's feelings and emotions (pathos);
- Ensure the audience trusts you by being authentic, adopting a confident posture, speaking with conviction, and using reliable sources to support your arguments (ethos).

Communication technologies

Communication technologies refer to all the tools used to send, receive, and process information. Think of mobile phones, messaging systems, websites, laptops, computers and even data centres. Communication technologies are becoming progressively more important because they are so convenient. You can reach more people at the same time and can easily repeat the message over and over. However, be aware of the threats it encompasses. Feedback is delayed, and visual feedback is often limited. Retrieving messages from the receivers is almost impossible, and they can be manipulated.

Miscommunication and noise

There is miscommunication if the receiver interprets the message differently than the sender intended. This can happen due to internal or external noise.

Internal noise – Internal noise means that the communication is disturbed by the inner state of (one of) the communication partners. Two forms of internal noise are selective perception and cognitive dissonance.

- With *selective perception*, the receiver only hears what appeals to their own feelings and convictions. As a result, (large) parts of the sender's message are often lost in the interpretations made by the recipient. In short, I only want to hear what suits me.
- In the case of *cognitive dissonance*, the receiver experiences an uncomfortable mental state due to contradictory thoughts within oneself. The sender's message is weighed against this internal contradiction, often causing doubt and resistance. In short, I don't agree with myself yet.

External noise – External noise includes any interference in communication channels that affects the actual communication. Poor connections and high ambient noise are examples.

The communication wall shows what internal and external noise can lead to (see Figure 7.03.02). To avoid noise, feedback and clarification are essential. The message you want to convey is not always what you say. What you said is not what they heard. What they heard is not what they understood. What they understood has not yet been agreed upon. And finally, what they agree upon is not always what they will do. One option is to close the loop and ask them what they have understood and will do at the end.

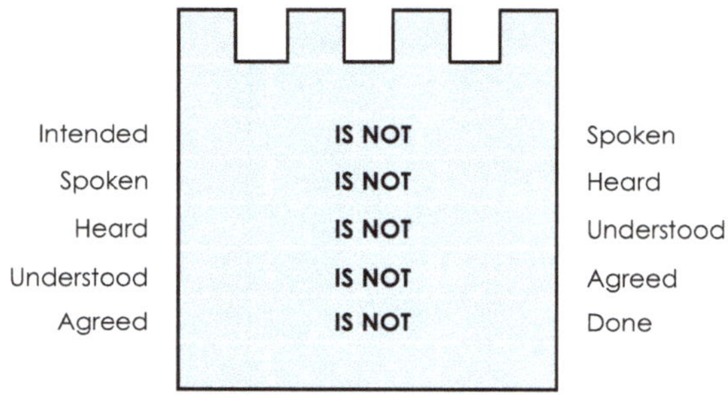

Figure 7.03.02 The communication wall

LEVELS OF COMMUNICATION

Every communication consists of multiple messages. By paying balanced attention to these communication levels, the effectiveness will increase. Friedemann Schulz Von Thun recognises four levels of communication (see Figure 7.03.03):

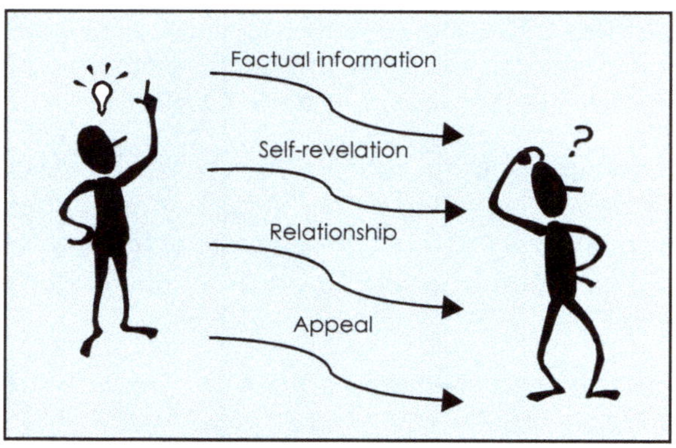

Figure 7.03.03 Communication levels

- *Factual information level* – The factual message consisting of the literal text that you say or write.
- *Self-revelation level* – How you say or write something it expresses your feelings and shows how you experience things that happen. The expressive aspect is visible in how people intonate words, gestures, facial expressions, et cetera.
- *Relational level* – The relational level includes how the sender sees and judges the

other. Do you regard the other individual as your equal? Do you look up to them or disqualify them? This affects the tone and content of the message too.

- *Appealing level* – The appealing level includes your expectations of the other person. Even without always expressing this explicitly, communication contains a wish or demand for what the other individual should do next.

The expressive and relational levels give charge to both the content and appealing levels. That charge can mean the difference between participating or opposing. That is why it is necessary to recognise, acknowledge and discuss emotions and relational issues.

> *After testing, it turns out that the design does not meet the customer's requirements. When the project manager sees his designer, he approaches him angrily: 'This is the SECOND time you have delivered the wrong design. The entire production has come to a standstill!'*
> *The project manager's messages are:*
> - *Content: 'This is the second time you have delivered the wrong design. The entire production has come to a standstill.'*
> - *Expressive: I am angry and outraged.*
> - *Relational: I can't rely on you.*
> - *Appealing: Immediately improve your design and do a better job next time.*

ACTIVE LISTENING

Active listening is essential to understanding the message clearly. Active listening focuses on wanting to understand the other person. Do not listen passively, but ask questions about what you hear and see. You can use various techniques to do this. Well-known techniques are the LSQ formula, paraphrasing, and mirroring.

LSQ formula – LSQ stands for listening, summarising and asking questions. Listen to what the sender says, summarise the message to check whether you have understood it correctly and ask further questions to understand it better.

Paraphrasing or parroting – By paraphrasing, you summarise in your own words what the sender has said, conveying to the sender that you have understood the intention of their message. By parroting, you repeat the words verbatim, letting the sender know you have perfectly understood what was said and are not twisting their words. Decide what best suits the situation.

Mirroring – Mirroring is copying the sender's posture and gestures, creating a non-verbal connection between one another. With children, crouch down to the same eye level. If someone slumps in their chair, do the same, et cetera. But you can also mirror a person's clothing and words. Dress in the same style as the other person. Use the same words.

The LSQ formula, paraphrasing or parroting, and mirroring can be combined quite well. Together they form a powerful tool to really enter into a conversation with another person.

Building rapport

Building rapport goes one step further. Building rapport is developing mutual trust, friendship and affinity with someone. It helps you to establish good interpersonal relationships. Communication becomes fluid, people are more likely to adopt your views, and it can open many doors. That can happen straight away. It may also need more effort. Ensure an excellent first introduction, tune in carefully to the other individual, listen actively, ask engaging questions, find commonalities, share experiences, and lead with empathy and respect.

ASKING THE RIGHT QUESTIONS

Questioning allows you to check whether your interpretations are correct and helps you to explore more deeply. By using open questions, the other individual can express themselves more clearly. Closed, suggestive and rhetorical questions may cause the conversation to become stagnant or one-sided.

Open questions – An open question is a question you cannot answer with a yes or no, does not guide, and invite the other to provide more information. An open question often starts with a W or an H: who, what, why (curiously expressed), with which, where, when and how. Take note: a question beginning with 'why' can come across as an accusation. Figure 7.03.04 provides examples of open questions.

Statement	Question
• They never deliver on time.	• Who never delivers on time?
• John has not programmed it correctly.	• How would you have programmed it?
• We cannot work like this.	• What would you like to do differently?
• We want to start tomorrow.	• Why do you want to start tomorrow?
• This is the wrong spot for our meeting.	• Where would you like to meet?
• We are starting far too late.	• When would you like to start, and why then?

Figure 7.03.04 Examples of open questions

Closed questions – A closed question is a question that can be answered with a yes or no or by selecting one of the provided options. This may be the intention if you want to ask a control question. A multiple-choice question is a particular form of a closed question. If you want more information, it is better to ask an open question.

Suggestive questions – A suggestive question already contains the direction of the desired answer. The sender's opinion and or intention is locked into the question. The recipient can no longer give a free answer but has to consider the sender's opinion. 'Don't you agree that we should have done a better check on the supplier?' First, outline the situation, after which you can freely give your opinion without answering the question with a direct yes or no.

Rhetorical questions – Rhetorical questions are questions to which you do not expect an answer. Rhetorical questions are often used to emphasise a previous statement ('Can fish swim?'), or an opinion (Have you lost your mind?'), or to initiate an action ('Can you get your books?').

GIVING AND RECEIVING FEEDBACK

You give feedback if the usual transparency during normal social interaction doesn't work. 80-90% of our time is spent on transparency and recognition. What gets attention progresses. If that does not work, give feedback. Feedback is not meant to confront: 'Adapt or...' Feedback is an intermediate form, but it isn't easy.

The rules for good feedback are basically simple. Do not give feedback in public, present it on neutral grounds, don't wait too long, refer to your own observations, and also indicate the desired behaviour. Make use of the four feedback steps:

- *Observation* – Describe the behaviour you have observed;
- *Feeling* – Describe your own feeling about it;
- *Consequence* – Describe the effect their behaviour has on the project;
- *Desire* – Tell what you desire in this respect.

> *John is increasingly withdrawing from the team; this behaviour was noticeable again yesterday. Today you give him feedback: 'John, yesterday you left early without saying anything (observation). I am disappointed (feeling). This way, we will never become a team (consequence). Next time I would like you to inform me if you have to leave early (desire).'*

Don't try to interpret why: 'You obviously don't take our team seriously.' If you do, you will immediately get caught up in a discussion, making John defensive. This is not the result you seek; perhaps there's another reason for his behaviour. By limiting yourself to literal observation and your own feelings, you might maintain an open dialogue. What you have seen is true. What you feel is true. By expressing that first, you increase the chance that John will be responsive to your feedback.

Besides giving feedback, receiving feedback is never easy, either, even if the feedback is positive. When receiving feedback, some simple rules also apply:

- Do not see feedback as an attack on you as an individual but as a comment on your behaviour. Focus on the content.
- Listen first before replying. Do not jump to the defence, but ask what the other individual means first.
- Show appreciation for the feedback. For many, giving feedback does not come easy; for you, it is an opportunity to learn. You show respect by thanking the feedback giver, and the relationship can only improve.
- Assess the feedback. Is it justified or not? Have you been told this before?
- Indicate what you will do with the feedback and why. If you find it difficult and want to think about it first, say so and tell the feedback giver that you will come back on it.

MEETINGS

A meeting is a gathering within a specific timeframe to discuss subjects to reach a judgement or decision.

Success factors of a meeting

Pay attention to the following issues to have effective meetings:

- Timely sending of invitations, agenda and underlying documents.
- Define the goal of the meeting so participants know why this meeting is important.

- Make expectations clear so everyone knows what to provide and how to prepare.
- Only invite the necessary people; people's time is scarce.
- Schedule sufficient time for the various agenda items.
- Work with a clear agenda structure. Start with informative items and reserve enough time for decision-making. Schedule opinion-forming items in the final stages of the meeting or a separate meeting.
- Make sure that the meeting runs smoothly. Do not deviate unnecessarily from the established agenda. Give everyone space to contribute their bit. Ensure that participants stick to the subject and listen to each other. Don't let differences of opinion escalate. Maintain a good atmosphere.
- Formulate and record decisions concisely.
- Ensure that the meeting does not linger.

The meeting should be prepared appropriately, held and followed up to meet these success factors.

Preparing the meeting – While preparing the meeting, determine its purpose, the agenda items, where and when the meeting will be held, and who will be invited. Prepare the agenda, decide the order and approach for each item, and collect the necessary documents. If participants want to introduce specific agenda items, discuss the terms of content, approach and time allocation with them in advance. Send the agenda, notes and underlying documents to the participants on time so they can prepare for the meeting.

Actual meeting – During the meeting, the chairman is in charge. He or she opens the meeting and sets the agenda. The minutes of the previous meeting are reviewed and approved, and incoming correspondence is briefly discussed. Official announcements are made. The meeting subjects are then addressed according to the agenda. The secretary writes the minutes and notes the action points. The participants concentrate on their contribution to the opinion-forming or decision-making process. At the end of the meeting, the secretary summarises the decisions and conclusions and the main action points agreed upon. If applicable, the location and time of the next meeting are agreed upon or confirmed.

Follow-up – The secretary prepares the minutes, gets them approved by the chairman and distributes them to the participants and the agreed copyholders. Don't delay until shortly before the next meeting. If the minutes cannot be distributed at short notice, send out an action list first to ensure the agreed actions are implemented on time.

Where appropriate, the minutes may also be confirmed and approved at the end of the meeting, thus avoiding discussing and approving the minutes at the next meeting. Another option is agreeing that participants respond to the minutes within a certain time; otherwise, the minutes are considered approved.

Agenda and agenda items

Usually, official meetings have a fixed agenda:

- O – Opening and agenda
- M - Minutes of the previous meeting

- I – Incoming correspondence
- A – Announcements
- S – Subjects of the meeting
- A – Any other business or questions
- C – Closure

Meeting subjects

Meeting subjects can be categorised into opinion-forming and decision-making subjects. Both subjects need their own approach. When these subjects intertwine, it affects the quality of the outcome.

Opinion-forming subjects – Require an open atmosphere where participants encourage each other to share insights, opinions and judgements. This allows them to analyse a situation or develop ideas for new approaches, et cetera. When opinions are conflicting, it is necessary to write the minutes carefully and to inquire about the precise wording of specific passages after the meeting. For future meetings, these subjects require extra attention from the chairman to prevent standpoints from escalating into unbridgeable situations.

The reverse also occurs, meaning consensus is reached on a particular topic. In that case, the opinion-forming topic leads to a decision. The chairman should mark such moments well, carefully formulate the intended decision and ask the meeting to record it in the minutes for approval.

Decision-making subjects – Decision-making subjects require a firm structure. A structured decision ensures that the decision is based on criteria and information that accurately reflect what the stakeholders have discussed and ultimately produces the best decision. Steps in a structured decision-making procedure can be found in Chapter 8.04, Resourcefulness.

Minutes

Minutes should at least record the date and location of the meeting, who was present and absent, the subjects on the agenda and any action and decision agreed upon. If possible, the minutes can also record the next meeting's date, time, location and other particular subjects.

In principle, there are three types of minutes:

- *Action and decision list* – Only the agreed actions and decisions are recorded.
- *Summary minutes* – Point-by-point recording of the results, including a summary of the considerations that led to these results.
- *Detailed minutes* – Includes the input from the individual participants in the discussions.

An action and decision list is best suited for a progress meeting. Summary minutes are best suited for capturing positions, such as in a project board meeting. Detailed minutes are best suited for a meeting in which the exchange of information is central. Keeping a list of outstanding actions and decisions taken on a common platform is recommended. This makes it clear to everyone what the status of the various subjects is.

Roles and responsibilities in meetings

In meetings, we distinguish the role of the chairman, secretary and participants.

Chairman – Determines the meeting's purpose and agenda and who is invited. They ensure that facilities are booked, participants are invited, and necessary documentation is sent to participants on time. They ensure that the meeting runs smoothly and that minutes are taken. After the meeting, the chairman ensures the minutes are properly prepared and distributed to the participants and copyholders on time. Finally, they need to ensure that the agreed actions are carried out.

Secretary – Prepares the meeting with the chairman, invites the participants and sends the agenda with the underlying documents. During the meeting, they take the minutes. After the meeting, the secretary prepares the minutes, approves them by the chairman and distributes them to the participants and copyholders.

Participants – Effectively prepare for the meeting by reading the agenda and underlying documents received. For items where a participant has substantive input, they may prepare a presentation. During the meeting, they should provide input, listen actively and stick to the subjects. After the meeting, they need to check the minutes received, act according to the decisions taken, and take the agreed actions.

In project team meetings, the project manager is often the chairman of the meeting, and one of the members of the project support office is the secretary. In a more informal meeting, one of the participants may alternately take the role of the chairman or secretary.

FACILITATED WORKSHOPS

A workshop is a gathering where participants interactively participate to contribute to an intended result. In projects, workshops are held for various activities, such as project start-up, risk analysis, and creative problem-solving.

Characteristics workshops

A workshop is characterised by the following:

- *Active participation* – A workshop is about gaining insight into issues through active involvement. The facilitator should ensure that each participant actively contributes.
- *Activating methods* – To achieve active participation, activating methods are used. These are methods in which the attendees are challenged to discuss subjects and find solutions actively.
- *Concrete results* – The workshop is focused on concrete results. For all participants, these results should reflect, answers to the questions with which the workshop started.
- *Shared meaning* – By collectively contributing, the results will most probably become meaningful for all participants.
- *Collective decision-making* – Because a workshop is based on active engagement and shared meaning forming, the workshop can be seen as a collective decision-making process.
- *Process-orientated facilitation* – Active participation and collective decision-making occur through a collaborative and interactive process. The facilitator guides the process that participants go through.

UBUNTU is the collective decision-making culture that is still common in countries such as Botswana and South Africa. It is a matter of conducting a joint dialogue on an issue at hand. The facilitator has an important role. They ensure that every story is heard and that dialogue occurs instead of discussion. Also, they encourage people to share their own stories (see Figure 7.03.05).

Principles UBUNTU – (Lekgotla = common meeting place)	Core values
1. Everyone has the right to attend the Lekgotla 2. Every voice is heard and counts 3. There is trust in the dialogue 4. There is mutual respect 5. Stories are a means of communicating a message 6. Truth is shared 7. There is observational or literal, non-interpretive listening 8. A decision always follows	Humanity Dignity Respect Trust Dare Entrepreneurship

Figure 7.03.05 Principles and core values UBUNTU

Setting up and running workshops

Gaining the maximum benefit from a workshop requires a careful process. In general, the following steps are taken.

Defining the subject – Various issues in and around projects qualify for the workshop approach. Examples of issues are: what is the most effective approach for this project? How do we concretise the project result, and with which work packages will we achieve this result? What risks can be identified, and with what measures do we prevent these risks? How do we create optimal collaboration between the project teams? How can we set up an engaging acceptance test for all users? Searching together for answers to such open-ended questions stimulates the project process positively.

Determine results and objectives – The workshop owner and facilitator then determine the results the workshop should deliver and which goals they are pursuing. For example, this can be a breakdown of the work packages to be delivered so that the project teams know what, when, and how they will accomplish their part of the project. It can also be an effective user acceptance test so that users will apply the project result in their daily work.

Establish outline – The workshop owner and facilitator then determine the workshop format and approach. These outlines are established by answering the following questions: who will participate, and why? Where and when will everyone be expected? Which activating working methods are central? Which key questions should be answered at the end of the workshop? What are the concrete results of the workshop? What are the intended goals of the workshop? How will the programme be structured?

Make script – The workshop facilitator then creates a script with the stakeholders directly involved. This script is a more detailed elaboration of the programme. It gives the workshop owner, the facilitator and the participants a complete picture of the duration and results of each workshop component. The script should be assessed based on feasibility, effectiveness, efficiency, attractiveness and challenge criteria.

Invite participants – Send the participants an appealing invitation. They should understand the reason for the workshop, why they have been invited, and the relevant preparations needed. The selection of the participants should be based on the commitment to, the knowledge and skills required for, and experience with the topic, including the balance within the team. It is important to invite relevant stakeholders, even if you know some will probably decline. The composition should be such that the results and objectives of the workshop can be achieved. Notable participants, such as guest speakers and the external facilitator, should be mentioned explicitly in the invitation. They reinforce the importance of the workshop.

Arranging the workshop area – The setting of the workshop space is important. Adequate space for movement and a pleasant atmosphere are important. A U-shaped table arrangement already creates an atmosphere of openness. A circle of chairs enhances this even more. For larger groups, you can opt for a café setup. The work tables are placed irregularly in the room, with most chairs facing the stage.

Flip charts, bulletin boards, and audio-visual equipment are needed to organise the workshop correctly. One of the flipcharts should at least contain the broad outline of the programme. The main questions discussed during the workshop can also be displayed in the workshop room. Depending on the questions, the facilitator may put together wall charts to elaborate on the question.

Interactive performance – The workshop owner welcomes the participants. They give a brief introduction about the why, the purpose and the intended outcomes of the workshop. The workshop owner then introduces the facilitator (and their team) who leads the workshop. The facilitator explains the programme, followed by a meet and greet, the rules of the day, the matching of the expectations and finally, a first general warming up on the subject of the workshop itself. The facilitator activates the participants and oversees the atmosphere in the group. They should take the liberty of deviating from the script if necessary. At the end of the workshop, the participants should also evaluate the workshop process. Learning points are essential to improve the workshop process next time, but it also strengthens the buy-in of the substantive result.

Follow-up results – Finally, it is important that the participants know that the workshop results will be put to good use. For good aftercare, sharing the workshop results, preferably within 48 hours, is necessary.

The role of the facilitator can sometimes also be fulfilled by a senior team member, but then the team should have already set and agreed on its own working standards. This takes time and can usually only be done in teams that have been together for a considerable period.

Roles and responsibilities workshops

In facilitated workshops, the following roles are distinguished:

- *Workshop owner or problem owner* – The individual who wants the result and decides whether and how the workshop results will be applied in the further course of the project. During the workshop, the owner is either absent or just a participant. There should be no hierarchy in the room.

- *Facilitator* – Independent workshop leader who ensures the smooth running of the workshop process. A good facilitator guides the process and takes the participants through the core questions of the workshop in an inspired way.
- *Secretary or workshop assistant* – Assistant to the facilitator who ensures all necessary facilities and materials are in place, supports the process during the workshop and prepares the workshop report.
- *Participants* – Contribute to the workshop's outcome with their expertise and representation.

Advantages workshop

The main advantage of a good workshop is that informed decisions can be made quickly. They give the individual participants extra energy. Uncertainties are resolved, and misunderstandings are prevented from occurring. A high degree of consensus and commitment is often obtained about the decisions taken. Last but not least, the team's commitment and collaboration are built up. This is certainly not unimportant in today's projects, where the team is often under considerable pressure to perform.

WRITTEN COMMUNICATING

Written communication includes letters, reports, emails, and other digital means of communication. It is essential to realise that non-verbal communication is missing.

Communicating effectively in writing

Jan Renkema (2010) compares writing with composing. Like a composer, a writer wants to convey a message to the reader. The text should be understandable, precise, concise and attractive to them.

- *Understandable* – Text becomes understandable when you tailor the message to the target group, make short sentences, use logical summaries, preferably presented as a bullet list, and avoid difficult words and uncommon abbreviations.
- *Accurate* – Text is considered accurate when the message does not raise questions. Specify what you compare it with when using the superlative clause and make clear references.
- *Concise* – Text becomes concise if you write effectively, avoid superfluous words, and, if possible, express the meaning in one word or sentence. The following words in italics are superfluous: The progress report shows the *quantitative amount of* hours spent per activity. The project manager and the supplier signed a *mutual* agreement.
- *Attractive* – Text becomes attractive when you make the text more personal, use recognisable examples, and vary sentence structure and word choice.

Document design and structure

The design and structure of the text are important for both the reader and the writer. It helps the writer to articulate his or her intention logically. It helps the reader to understand the text. Some tips:

- Create a clear picture of who the readers are;
- Establish what the important issues or concerns around the topic are;
- Determine the structure to organise the information in a logical and readable way;
- Ensure an even structure per chapter;

- Use, preferably, no more than three layers in the layout: chapters, paragraphs and sub-paragraphs;
- Have others review the structure before you write;
- Ensure a balanced scope of the text;
- Describe the topic and purpose of the text right at the beginning of each chapter;
- Make sure the text is understandable, accurate, concise and attractive;
- Have your text reviewed by others before distributing it.

Standards

Based on available examples, templates can be designed for future use, such as for a project outline, project plan, progress report, et cetera. If standards for certain documents are unavailable and a comprehensive report still needs to be created, the following layout can be used:

- Foreword
- Colophon
- Management summary
- Table of contents
- List of illustrations and abbreviations
- Introduction
- Actual content divided into chapters
- Conclusions and recommendations
- References to other documentation
- Attachments

PRESENTATIONS

Presenting is orally transmitting information to a group and is usually supported visually. As a project manager, you will probably have to give presentations regularly. Effectiveness is achieved through proper preparation, performance and visual support.

Ensure that the presentation is tailored to the subject and the audience. Who is the target group? Why are they attending the presentation, what are they particularly interested in, and which questions would they like to have answered? And, obviously, what message do you want to convey?

Performance

Be mindful of your pace and loudness of voice, vary your tone, articulate, and limit the use of gap words. Choose the right moments for a short silence. Interact with the audience from the beginning. Ask questions at appropriate moments. Avoid making it a one-way show. Make eye contact with people in the audience.

Build your presentation like a sandwich. Tell what you're going to tell, tell it and tell what you have told. Show the structure of your presentation at the beginning. Make sure the audience always knows where you are in your story. Keep track of time or have someone do it for you.

Match your verbal and non-verbal behaviour. Present your presentation. Do not just read the text on the slide out loud. Ensure the audience can see the slides but don't hide yourself in the corner.

Realise that the quality of the speaker determines about 70% of the impact of the presentation and that often less than 10% of the information is remembered by the audience. Therefore, at the end of the presentation, it is important to summarise your story to reiterate the main message you want to convey.

Visual support

Important considerations for the outline of your presentation include:

- The visual presentation is there to support, not to be read out loud. Avoid long texts.
- Use images that support your message. An image says more than 1,000 words.
- Limit the number of slides. You need at least 3-6 minutes per slide.
- Be careful with bullet points. Bullet points are boring. Use them only when listing coherent facts.
- The complete enumeration should begin with a verb if you start with a verb.
- Preferably one topic per slide and not more than six bullet points per slide.
- Avoid too much colour, italics and underlining in the text.
- Make sure the text is visible from the rear of the room.
- Show examples that are recognised by your audience.

Presentations are a powerful tool to get your message across.

ADVANCED

ELEVATOR PITCH (ADVANCED)

An elevator pitch is a very short verbal presentation to sell yourself and your idea. The name is linked to the image of an elevator. To pitch your idea, you have about 60 seconds, the average amount of time you would typically spend with someone in an elevator. What can you tell about yourself when you only have 60 seconds?

The basic structure for an elevator pitch is:

- *Purpose* – The future-orientated opportunity or solution we offer you.
- *Picture* – See and enjoy what's in it for you.
- *Plan* – You can get there by following the next steps.
- *Part to pay* – Your role in this exciting plan.

> *I am John from ABC*
> - *Purpose: We provide highly energy-efficient and customised mechatronic solutions.*
> - *Picture: It saves 30% of your operating costs, unique worldwide.*
> - *Plan: We first make a 3D design so you can envisage what it would look like in your factory. The final implementation takes a weekend in most cases.*
> - *Part to play: I would like two hours of your time to demonstrate the feasibility of our systems in your factory.*

Six tips for your pitch:

- Write out the pitch in advance;
- Practice the pitch out loud;
- Ask others for their opinion;
- Tailor the pitch to those you want to address;
- Be enthusiastic;
- Always end with your goal (an appointment or decision).

BAD NEWS CONVERSATION (ADVANCED)

Delivering bad news is something that we all have to do at some point, and it is never easy. How you communicate bad news directly impacts how the recipient perceives and reacts to the situation and how your approach will be remembered, not only by the individual who receives the bad news but also by the others who remain in the team. This can have a substantial impact on your effectiveness in the future. That is why delivering the bad news honestly, empathetically, and structurally is essential. When delivering bad news, getting the message across clearly and capturing the recipient's emotions is important. An effective structure is:

- *Deliver the bad news* – Outline the context briefly, then announce the bad news and follow up by delivering the message; do this clearly and without sugarcoating it. Sugarcoating things only sends mixed signals and leads to misunderstandings.
- *Capture the emotions* – Give room to respond, listen and sympathetically summarise their feelings.
- *Support the message* – After capturing the emotions, explain the rationale behind the decision. Speak confidently and avoid negative body language.

- *Recapture any released emotions if necessary* – Employees may want to vent their feelings. As long as they remain respectful, venting is fine, but avoid a debate and don't defend yourself.
- *Discuss the follow-up* – The recipient should speak out about the consequences for themself and what possibilities they see for tackling these consequences. Only when the recipient leaves room for recommendations can options be offered. If possible, agree on actions and deadlines to be followed up.

Prepare yourself well before delivering bad news. If the decision comes from higher management, ensure you are familiar with their rationale; be more than a middleman. In the follow-up, work proactively to bring beneficial outcomes for both parties because these interests should never be mutually exclusive.

8 CONNECTING WITH OTHERS

The central theme of this part of the book is connecting with others. Project management is primarily a social profession. Entering into relations, showing leadership, and problem-solving together ask for competences related to connecting with others.

Chapter 8.01 Relationships and Engagement – Creating openness in working relationships, creating networks, carefully building arguments, and motivating people. What moves people, and how to respond to it? In the advanced section, we look at the role of the consultant and how to use it in our relationship with various stakeholders.

Chapter 8.02 Leadership – Explains the differences between leadership and management. Which leadership style best suits the many different circumstances? How to be assertive and to work from your circle of influence. In the advanced section, we look at how to stay strong in your role and different leadership styles.

Chapter 8.03 Teamwork – Explores the phases of team development, how to move the team to higher performance levels, and how to deal with resistance. In the advanced section, we examine the different team roles.

Chapter 8.04 Resourcefulness – This is about structured and creative problem-solving. We look at different methods and techniques for solving problems and a structured way of decision-making.

Chapter 8.05 Results Orientation – Focuses on the principles of continuous improvement and the conditions under which these principles can be applied. This strengthens results orientation in all steps of the project process. In the advanced section, we describe the five principles of result-orientated project management according to Laufer and how entrepreneurs get their results.

Chapter 8.06 Negotiation – Covers negotiation strategies, like achieving win/win agreements with others. In the advanced chapter, we look at the different phases of the negotiation process and how to influence the negotiation by focusing on various aspects of the negotiation process.

Chapter 8.07 Conflict and Crisis – Explores the different conflict styles you can use in conflict situations. You will learn about the different levels at which conflict can occur and how to de-escalate conflict at these levels. The advanced section looks at the different roles of the project manager in a conflict and how to act during a crisis.

8.01 RELATIONSHIPS AND ENGAGEMENT

PURPOSE

The purpose of this chapter is to enable the individual to build and maintain personal relationships and to understand that the ability to engage with others is a precondition for collaboration, commitment and, ultimately, performance.

LEARNING OBJECTIVES

Openness:
- Aspects, characteristics and policies on openness;
- Building networks;
- Creating an open business culture (advanced).

Advising:
- Building arguments;
- Behavioural patterns/Rose of Leary (advanced);
- The role of the project manager as a consultant (advanced).

Motivation theories:
- Hierarchy of Needs;
- Motivation and hygiene factors;
- Differences between X and Y managers;
- Self-determination theory (advanced);
- Spiral Dynamics (advanced).

DEFINITIONS

Openness: An attitude that is open to new ideas, opinions or arguments and actively encourages exchanging ideas, opinions and arguments.
Culture of openness: A culture where people are encouraged to interact and discuss complex issues openly, helping to become more innovative, creative and responsive to change.
Motivation: The inner desire and determination to work in a disciplined way towards concrete results.

INTRODUCTION

Building relationships and strengthening their commitment to the project is a necessary competence to achieve project results. This chapter focuses on developing these relationships so parties feel engaged and motivated by the project. Openness is hereby an important factor. It strengthens relationships and makes sharing visions, setting goals, and discussing problems much easier.

ASPECTS, CHARACTERISTICS AND POLICIES ON OPENNESS

A policy concerning openness means that, besides paying attention to the project output and the formal procedures, you also consciously and actively pay attention to the collaboration process: how do people work together? Do they take each other's opinions and concerns seriously and recognise that success depends on their collaboration?

Aspects of openness

Aspects of openness are frankness, accessibility, participation and introspective:

- *Frankness* – You talk honestly and effortlessly about your feelings and concerns.
- *Accessibility* – You are accessible but also interested in the opinions of others.
- *Participative* – You allow others to give advice or make decisions.
- *Introspective* – You have a genuine willingness to listen to the insights of others and consciously incorporate them into your own thinking and actions.

The above aspects are visible in organisations that actively and consciously create space to discuss issues.

Characteristics of openness

Projects are constantly faced with issues that need resolving. An open culture is crucial to resolving such issues properly and sustainably. In situations where a culture of openness prevails, the following characteristics are visible (Senge et al., 1992):

- Mutual appreciation;
- Collective thinking and decision-making;
- Introspective culture;
- Complexity is always open for discussion;
- Pure motives and subordinating personal interest.

Mutual appreciation – Mutual appreciation is essential for a good working relationship. Give each other explicit compliments, be enthusiastic and informative, and actively listen to each other's insights and visions.

Collective decision-making processes – Different interest groups play a role in projects. Each interest group gives meaning to the project from their perspective and interpretation. It is precisely these interpretations and the associated meanings that lead to different perceptions of reality and also to differences in determination. This regularly drives interest groups apart.

To arrive at a more shared picture, it is necessary to carefully exchange perspectives, interpretations and the associated meanings with each other. This can be achieved by entering into dialogue in a safe environment and carefully listening to each other as equals:

- Share opinions and criteria and ask others open questions;
- Discuss alternatives and perspectives that offer possibilities to work toward a solution;
- Take stock of support for the alternatives;
- Decide; see *Decision making process* in Chapter 8.04, Resourcefulness.

Doing this creates a deeper and shared understanding of the issue and the decision to be taken. That insight is the basis for decisions the management can finally confidently endorse.

Introspective culture – A culture in which employees, staff and decision-makers solve problems by actively listening to each other and are willing to understand issues from each other's perspective. This goes beyond a participatory culture, in which employees have the right to advise on or agree to decisions.

> *Within the company, there is a strong culture of dialogue and reasoning, with managers openly discussing situations they experienced as being problematic. It was a conscious decision not to solve such issues unilaterally from the hierarchy but to opt for dialogue and discussion with the supporting staff and the executive team members.*
>
> *During these discussions, participants ask each other about the facts and the convictions locked up in the solutions put forward, offering a picture from different perspectives. Decisions are based on these.*
>
> *In the production unit of the company, this culture is fully implemented. Operators raise their problems for discussion with management and each other. This creates a clear impression of the current situation and jointly supported decisions. These are laid down in procedures and or converted into feasible projects. The company is decisive and efficient mainly because all perspectives are consistently considered and included in the approach.*

Complexity is always open for discussion – Once a decision is made, it does not mean it can never be changed. New facts often complicate the daily work situation. In an open culture, there is always room for discussion. By doing so, you increase the likelihood of project success.

Pure motives and subordinating personal interest – In companies, it is about service to the company's goals. It is not about you but the organisation you have chosen to work for. A political game where parties balance interests based on personal gain generates a counterbalance. Openness requires a basic ethical attitude in which pure values are central. Jane Clarke (2001) applies a decision model to determine if personal behaviour is ethical:

- Am I not driven by personal motives which are incompatible with the interests of the company?
- Am I acting justly and fairly?
- Do I respect the interests of other stakeholders?

Openness policy

An organisation needs to develop a policy on openness. Openness sometimes seems to conflict with the necessary confidentiality and security, but it shouldn't. Openness is an attitude of genuine willingness to listen and understand each other; it does not mean confidential information should be shared or left unprotected. Policy on openness focuses on how stakeholders make decisions, solve problems, and deal with change.

Openness policies should focus on getting to know each other better, valuing and respecting each other, and developing core values that encourage collaboration. In doing so, openness requires carefully building arguments.

BUILDING ARGUMENTS

Toulmin (2013) distinguishes six aspects in building arguments: facts, conclusion, justification, substantiation, rebuttal, and qualifier. A rebuttal can be further broken down into reservation and exception (see Figure 8.01.01).

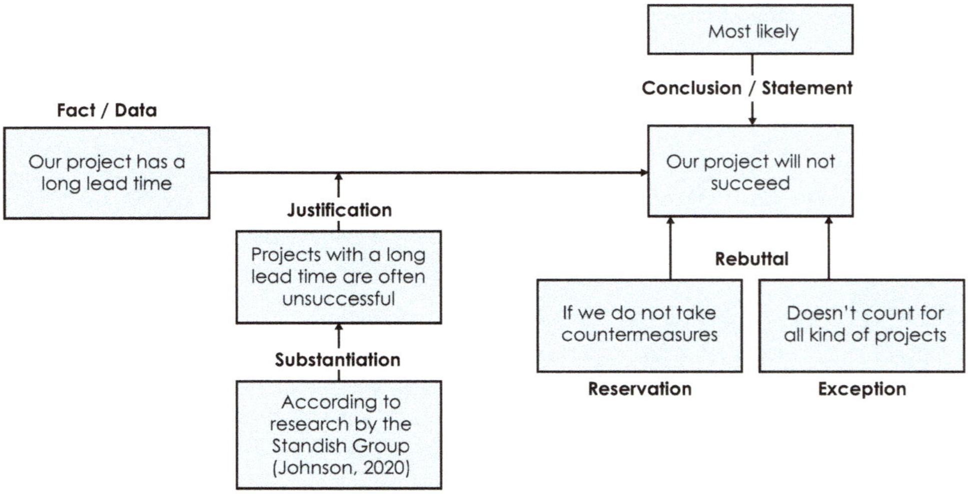

Figure 8.01.01 Example of building arguments, according to Toulmin (2013)

- *Fact* – The description of the factual situation;
- *Conclusion* – The statement you want to make;
- *Justification* – The information that justifies the conclusion based on the observed facts;
- *Substantiation* – The authoritative sources that strengthen the justification;
- *Rebuttal* – An exception or reservation to the conclusion;
- *Reservation* – The condition or limitation under which the conclusion is valid;
- *Exception* – The situations for which the conclusion does not apply;
- *Qualifier* – A word or phrase to assign a quality to the conclusion; for example, 'most likely' or 'probably'.

Openness and dialogues based on substantiated arguments are important to develop quality in business networks.

BUILDING NETWORKS

Building networks is important for project professionals. When you have a broad network, it is easier to find people who can support the development of the project output. Granovetter (1973) distinguishes open and closed networks and strong and weak ties (see Figure 8.01.02).

John has a relatively closed network. Most of his business relations are acquainted (straight lines). Caroline's network is reasonably open (dotted lines). Her business relations are not or are only vaguely acquainted. She is in contact with several groups. This can interest experts, who often function in more closed networks. A business relationship is strong if you maintain direct communication and weak if people only vaguely know each other through another person.

According to Granovetter, the development of networks starts by distinguishing three complementary core qualities, which bring valuable new connections closer: connectors, knowledge sharers, and salespeople.

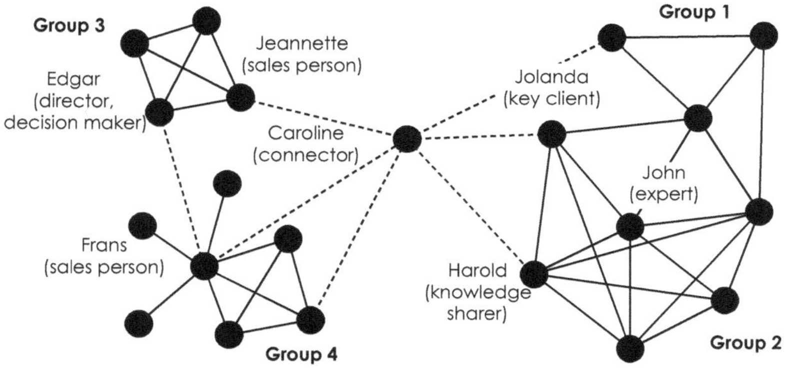

Figure 8.01.02 Open and closed networks

> ***LinkedIn***
> *Granovetter's theory corresponds to the idea of social networks such as LinkedIn. If you share your knowledge, others will notice it. They will share this with their networks if this knowledge makes them enthusiastic. This way, valuable ideas spread to other groups, even those you haven't met. Salespeople in these groups will make their relations aware of the needs the new knowledge meets.*

Connectors – Connectors are people with various business contacts in the broader business environment. You name it, and they will know someone who can help you or who can make good use of your knowledge and skills. These people are part various groups and thus can ensure you create new contacts. They quickly bring together people or groups who can be valuable to one another. In Figure 8.01.02, Caroline is a connector. Access to other networks is possible through connectors like Caroline.

Knowledge sharers – To connect with others, you need to have something to say. Knowledge sharers are content-driven people in social networks. They know what experts are concerned about and share this knowledge by actively writing about it. They exert their influence by skillfully and actively demonstrating how certain things really work. In Figure 8.01.02, Harold may be such a knowledge sharer. Whereas John, as an expert, has a more internally focused attitude toward the group, Harold conveys this expertise to the outside world. Without Harold, the knowledge within this group is likely to remain hidden. When Harold writes about John's expertise, Caroline can, if she wishes, share this knowledge within her network. This way, knowledge of John's expertise is spread through Harold and Caroline to other networks.

Salespeople – Salespeople know how to get people excited about the content of the knowledge sharers. They are sensitive to latent needs in groups. Their engaging stories ensure that initially resistant and sceptical people adjust their insights or become aware of new possibilities. In doing so, they create an atmosphere of openness and motivation to the ideas substantiated by knowledge sharers, which connectors make visible in new groups. In Figure 8.01.02, Jeannette and Frank may be representatives of this group.

> *Through a business relationship, a director of a medium-sized company came into contact with the sustainability network of Utrecht University (the connector). He met a person within this network who had for some time been concerned with the*

sustainability of products and materials by applying tensile and compressive forces to them. This individual (a knowledge-sharer) told him that inspection institutes need professional machine designers to make product quality measurable. The director took a chance by saying, 'That is exactly our area of expertise.' and immediately asked: 'Can you put me in touch with these testing institutes?' (actively looking for salespeople). The carousel is now in full swing. Excellent test installations have already been placed at various companies. They are technically in order and measure things accurately. The connector gets adequate compensation for bringing in new networks. The knowledge sharer receives fascinating guest lectures on measuring the sustainability of products. This is a win-win-win that came about through valuable meetings.

MOTIVATION THEORIES

Motivation is the inner desire and determination to work in a disciplined way towards concrete results. Self-motivation is having the ability to stimulate yourself and pursue stated goals. Insight into what motivates people is essential. You can use that insight to activate people positively.

In his *Hierarchy of Needs,* Maslow states that our actions are motivated by certain physical and psychological needs. In his *Two-factor Model,* Herzberg distinguishes motivation factors that increase motivation and hygiene factors that help prevent dissatisfaction. In the *Theory X and Y manager,* McGregor establishes that how managers treat their employees is partly based on their own view of people. In the *Self-Determination Theory,* (advanced) Deci and Ryan explain the link between intrinsic and extrinsic motivation. *Spiral Dynamics* (advanced) reveals how people are motivated differently and how they develop.

MASLOW HIERARCHY OF NEEDS

In his theory of the *Hierarchy of Needs,* Maslow suggests that people's motivation is stratified in a certain hierarchy, with the most basic needs at the bottom and the higher-level needs at the top (see figure 8.01.03). According to Maslow's theory, people tend to focus on fulfilling lower-level needs first before moving on to higher-level needs. When a need is met, it no longer serves as a primary motivator, and attention shifts to the next level.

People residing in challenging circumstances focus first on survival and then look for safety. When those needs have been satisfied, they focus on love and belongingness. Then they look for recognition and respect and finally to self-fulfilment.

The hierarchy from bottom to top:

1. *Physiological* – The basic needs for survival, such as food, water, air, and sleep.
2. *Safety and security* – Look for safety, health for yourself and your family, and basic welfare.
3. *Love and belongingness* – Look for friendship, family, and community.
4. *Self-esteem* – Look for recognition, respect, self-esteem, and a sense of accomplishment.
5. *Self-actualisation* – Pursue personal growth, creativity, and self-fulfilment.

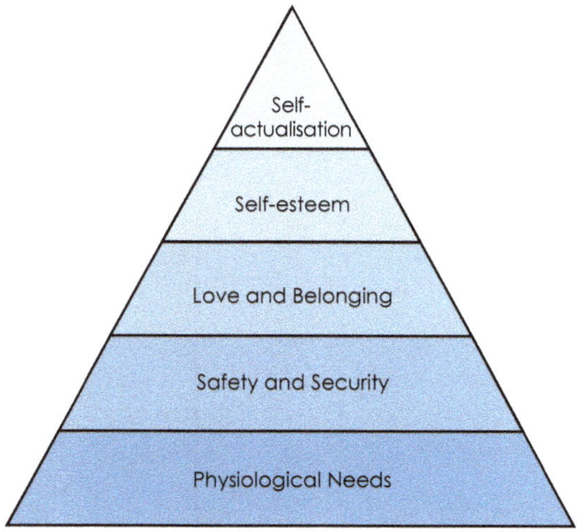

Figure 8.01.03 Pyramid of Maslow

The hierarchy is not rigid. Individuals may pursue different needs simultaneously or in a different order based on their cultural, social, and personal circumstances. However, this theory makes clear that people may have a very different focus depending on the circumstances in which they consider themselves.

MOTIVATION AND HYGIENE FACTORS

In his two-factor model, Herzberg (2003) distinguishes motivation factors that increase motivation and hygiene factors that help prevent dissatisfaction.

Motivation factors are factors that are related to workplace satisfaction. They cover intrinsic needs such as achievement, recognition, the meaningfulness of the job, assigned responsibilities and learning opportunities. Motivation factors allow employees to be content in their jobs and promote growth. Motivation factors are also called satisfiers, as their presence leads to satisfaction and intrinsic motivation.

Hygiene factors are unrelated to workplace satisfaction but necessary to prevent dissatisfaction. Hygiene factors cover extrinsic needs such as company policy, supervisor relationships, salary and benefits, working conditions, work environments, relationships with peers and subordinates, and job security. Hygiene factors are also called dissatisfiers, as their absence leads to dissatisfaction and complaints.

If you want to motivate your team, you should provide satisfiers. If you want to avoid complaints, you should remove dissatisfiers. Realise that this classification does not always apply to everyone in all circumstances. Personal circumstances can play a role. Money can motivate you, especially if you need it for your livelihood and family.

THEORY X AND Y MANAGER

As a project manager, knowing how to view people's motivation is essential. If you think people won't do anything of their own accord, you are more likely to be directive. But is that absolutely necessary? And vice versa: if you are of the opinion that people motivate themselves, you are more likely to leave it to them. But what if they need direction? According to McGregor (1960), how managers treat their employees is partly based on their own view of people. He describes two management views which he calls theories X and Y.

Theory X manager

In theory X, the manager assumes that employees naturally want to do as little as possible. Ideally, they don't want to work at all. They wait to see what work needs to be done, and nothing is done when not indicated. The X manager gives instructions to them and controls their work.

The theory X manager expects employees to:

- Wait for problems to arise until someone comes and fixes them;
- Constantly question the authority of the management.

Managers who believe that theory X is correct:

- Have many 'unmotivated' employees in their department;
- Do not expect constructive input from the employees;
- Need much authority and power to manage the employees;
- Need opportunities to punish and reward employees.

Theory Y manager

The Theory Y manager believes employees are motivated when they come to work. They expect employees to want to work, take initiative, be self-directed, and ask for help when needed. The Y manager gives space to perform the work independently.

The Theory Y manager expects employees to:

- Feel connected to their own goals and ambitions and those of the organisation;
- Work independently and accept that managers have their own responsibilities.

Managers who believe that Theory Y is correct:

- Are attentive to what motivates the employee at work;
- Have a keen eye for the conditions and resources the employee needs to excel at work;
- Have a supportive attitude towards employees;
- Pay attention to adequate working conditions, such as a well-appointed workplace.

McGregor's Theory X and Y establishes that people act according to their presuppositions and assumptions. They guide how leaders work with their teams and, at a broader level, shape the culture of organisations. The usefulness of this theory is that we realise that what we perceive in the environment, including how our team members operate, is primarily determined by our own assumptions.

ADVANCED

SELF-DETERMINATION THEORY (ADVANCED)

Deci and Ryan (2013) distinguish intrinsic and extrinsic motivation their *Self-Determination Theory*. Intrinsic motivation is driven by a person's personality, values, and beliefs. This form of motivation determines a person's behaviour based on their inner will. Extrinsic motivators are external influences to which a person responds to avoid negative consequences or punishments or to receive expected rewards. This form of motivation leads to behaviour based on meeting expectations.

In their theory, they distinguish:

1. The basic needs: autonomy, competence and belonging;
2. How intrinsic motivation can be influenced (cognitive evaluation);
3. How people internalise behaviour (organismic integration);
4. The effect of personality on the degree of self-determination (causality orientation).

1. Basic needs

According to Deci and Ryan, people possess three innate basic needs: autonomy, competence and connectedness. Conscious attention to these basic needs strengthens intrinsically motivated behaviour:

- *Autonomy* – The feeling that you can determine what you do and how you do it. Many professionals put autonomy at the top of intrinsic motivators. They take inner responsibility to add value where their responsibility comes into its own.
- *Competence* – The feeling that you are good at what you do and also of having opportunities to improve yourself. By improving yourself, you can take on more complex challenges and vice versa. This makes life exciting and challenging.
- *Connectedness* – The feeling of being part of a team, family or group. When you work toward goals that are truly meaningful to your family, the organisation and society, you will find that those around you respond positively.

2. Cognitive evaluation

The cognitive evaluation assesses the extent to which external factors affect intrinsic motivation. In general, factors that negatively affect autonomy reduce intrinsic motivation. Factors that positively appeal to competence development enhance intrinsic motivation.

3. Organismic integration

Organismic integration indicates how people internalise behaviour. People regulate their motivation differently in different situations. In one situation, they are intrinsically motivated; in another, they only do what others ask. Deci and Ryan distinguish between a-motivation, external regulation, introjection, identification, integration and intrinsic regulation (see Figure 8.01.04).

Type of motivation	A-motivation	Extrinsic motivated				Intrinsic motivated
Organismic integration	Non-regulation	External regulation	Introjected regulation	Identified regulation	Integrated regulation	Intrinsic regulation
		MUST		CONFORM	WANT	
Characteristic behaviour	You can't change	The other decides	The other decides	The other decides	We decide	I decide myself
	It don't care It will be unsuccessful	I do what you say	I follow your values & standards Am I doing it correctly?	I derive my Identity from my position and what I do	I have integrated the position that I have in my personal behaviour	I do things because it makes sense, I like it and it fascinates me
Causality orientation	Impersonal orientation	Controlled orientation			Autonomous orientation	

Figure 8.01.04 Self-Determination Theory (Deci & Ryan, 2013)

- *Non-regulation* – There is no personal intention. What happens around you happens because it happens. You experience no autonomy. Life is determined for you.
- *External regulation* – You do what the environment asks of you. There is nothing wrong with this form of regulation because the work will be done. It is even 'normal' in various cultures to do so: 'You do what the boss says!'
- *Introjection* – You follow the prevailing values and norms, even if they are not yours. This behaviour is common in many organisations and groups. People want to excel, and the introjection definition of doing well is adapting to the values and norms of the system in which they live and work.
- *Identification* – You derive your feelings of self-esteem from the working environment. Your motivation is stimulated by how you identify with your job and the self-esteem you associate with it. It is the level at which you think/feel, 'I am my job!'
- *Integration* – You have integrated your work and the work environment into your personal actions and being. To work with motivation, you no longer depend on the approval of the working environment. Your work is a source of joy for you. You can envisage the feeling of loss when it ceases to exist for whatever reason.
- *Intrinsic regulation* – You do things because they are meaningful, fun and exciting. Your path is no longer tied to one place but is linked to an intrinsic desire to do what you want. You have made something your own that you fully enjoy, and you share that enjoyment with others. Compliments are still welcome, but they do not polish your personality. You receive them as a gift for the choices you have made, and they encourage you to continue on the path you have taken.

4. Causality orientation

Deci & Ryan distinguish three types of self-determination or ways in which people orientate themselves in specific situations:

- *Impersonal orientation* – People who think they cannot influence the outcome of an action; they just do what others tell them to do.
- *Controlled orientation* – People who require guidance and clarity and tend towards external and introjected regulation.

- *Autonomous orientation* – People who actively and creatively regulate their behaviour based on their own interests and personal values. They are more inclined towards integrated and intrinsic motivation.

How you see yourself can vary per situation. For example, some people are autonomously orientated at work, while at home, they feel dependent. It is valuable to explore the cause of such differences in orientation. You learn to discover yourself and the motivations from which your behaviour arises. From that insight, you can take steps towards situations where autonomy, competence and connectedness are increasingly in balance.

> **From extrinsic to intrinsic motivation**
> *Marian was not happy with herself. She no longer wanted to engage in creative design work. Even though she was creative, an inherited trait, she felt she preferred to work with groups. A coach helped her make a breakthrough. During the first session, she realised she always did what her family suggested. This felt safe and secure, but she had never fully identified with her work. After the third coaching session, she clearly understood what she wanted. She applied to art school for a job where she could work with students to develop their artistic skills. Straight away, she felt at home. Instead of designing and creating herself, she was now helping others develop their creative talents. Finally, she was doing what she loved.*

BEHAVIOURAL PATTERNS/ROSE OF LEARY (ADVANCED)

Timothy Leary developed a communication model for interpreting relational behaviour and enhancing mutual interaction called the *Rose of Leary*. It clarifies human behaviour and the interaction between people. The rose distinguishes two axes (see Figure 8.01.05):

Horizontal axis – This axis represents 'together' (collaboration) versus 'against' (opposition). Usually, behaviour aimed at collaboration evokes collaboration, and behaviour aimed at opposition evokes opposition.

Vertical axis – This axis represents the above behaviour (dominance) and the under behaviour (submission). The behavioural tendencies here are often opposite: dominant behaviour evokes submissive behaviour, and submissive behaviour evokes dominant behaviour.

The four basic attitudes that arise are: leading (together-above), following (together-under), attacking (against-above) and defending (against-under). These four basic attitudes have been split into eight positive (light blue) and eight negative-orientated (dark blue) behaviours as featured in Figure 8.01.05.

In communicating with others, it is first important to recognise negative behaviours in yourself; try to avoid them. Switch to the positive opposite variant in yourself. From there, it is a matter of communicatively working towards positive equality in the relationship. When communicating from this perspective, always keep in mind people's different values.

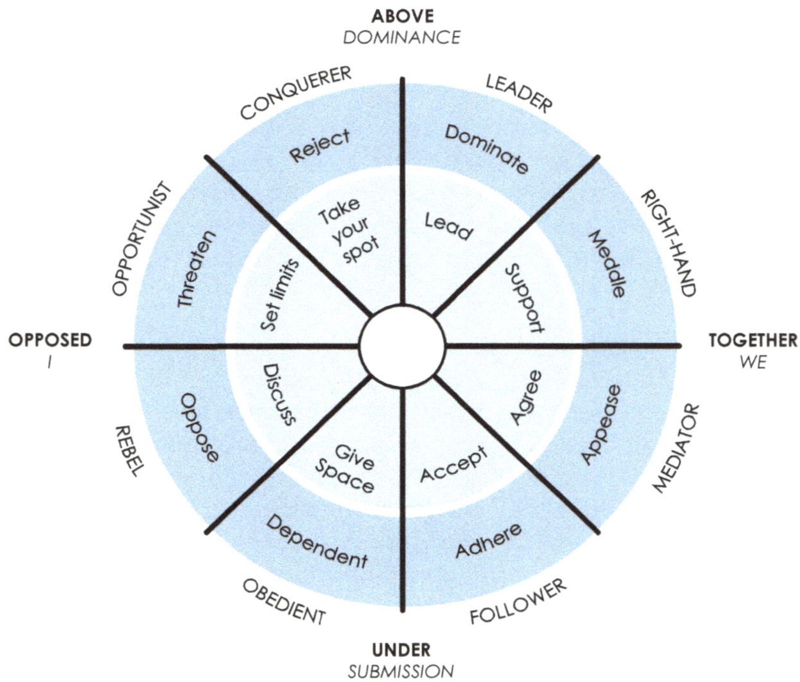

Figure 8.01.05 Rose of Leary

> *To a proposal to register all change requests in a logbook, John replied fiercely: 'Nonsense; we are not doing that.' (negative opposed-above). Instead of directly opposing this: 'It is not up to you to decide' (negatively against-under), you can also respond positively from together-under: 'I understand that you do not see anything useful in this proposal. Perhaps we can look for a solution we can all agree on?' In doing so, you challenge John and others to find a solution together.*

SPIRAL DYNAMICS (ADVANCED)

Collaboration in projects is focused on creating outputs that organisations can use to achieve their goals. The underlying value systems of people in this collaboration can be very different. Where one individual may seek the safety and security of the group, another may seek the intellectual challenge embedded in the project. Why are there such differences between people? *Spiral Dynamics* provides an answer.

Graves (1974) defines the meaning of Spiral Dynamics as follows: 'The psychology of the adult human being is an unfolding, emergent, oscillating spiral process characterised by gradual subordination of older, lower-order behavioural systems to newer, higher-order systems as people's existential problems change.'

Knowing how and why you do what you do in situations and the underlying values that 'drive' that behaviour means you can adapt your behaviour to the situation. You can give your own behaviour a new twist, allowing yourself to unfold dynamically. In doing so, you gradually transform old behaviour systems into new behaviour systems, allowing you to respond better to the complexity of life that comes your way. Figure

8.01.06 shows this unfolding spiral, including people's underlying focus on values or drives. The different drives can be described as follow:

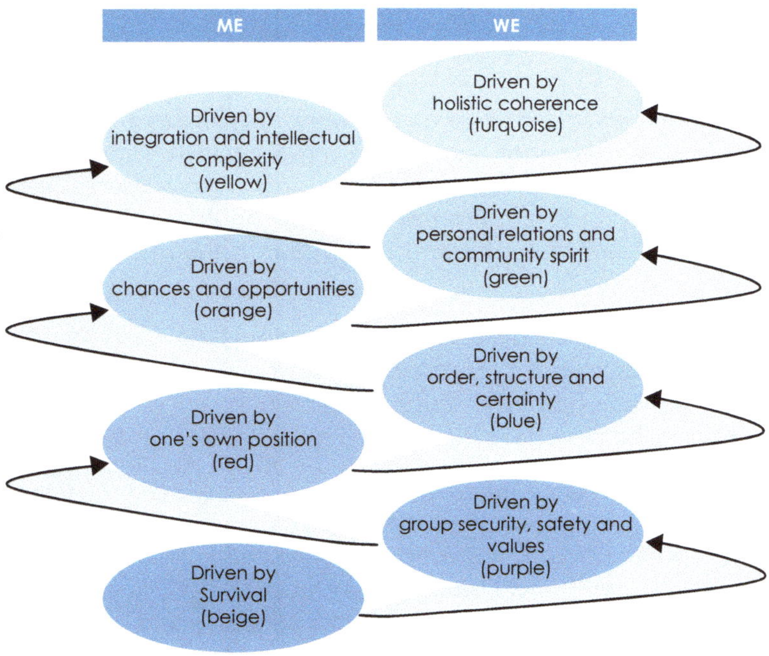

Figure 8.01.06 Spiral dynamics

Driven by survival (beige) – This drive focuses on doing everything to survive in challenging circumstances. In these particularly difficult situations, people fight or flee. They often build up traumatic memories they carry with them for the rest of their lives. When these traumas are processed carefully and courageously, the experiences form a strong foundation under a person's inner being.

Driven by group security and safety (purple) – This drive is focused on seeking the safety and security that a group can provide. People with this drive experience the value and unity of the group as an important support in their life. They surrender to the customs and rituals that come with it. By confirming, they know, feel and trust that they are included, similar to a safe, loving family.

Driven by one's own position (red) – This drive is focused on will and power. It's all about your position. People with this drive are forceful when they need to be. They guard their own boundaries well and assertively defend them. They act with self-confidence and are clear to others about the division of roles and, of course, their own position within them.

Driven by order, structure, and certainty (blue) – This drive is focused on order and systems that enable people to live their lives and do their work in a structured way. People with this drive love to build strong structures and normative systems through which order and law can be maintained. It is about dutifully and loyally honouring the agreements made and the rules laid down.

Driven by chances and opportunities (orange) – This drive is focused on competition and winning. People with this drive are competitive and want to be the best at what they were born to do. They are focused on standing out from others and see risks as opportunities to be seized. To this end, they weigh up the opportunities and do whatever it takes to excel.

Driven by interpersonal relationships and community spirit (green) – This drive focuses on social connectedness and a sense of community. Together we make a society which requires caring for each other and everything that procreates. People with this drive love equality, harmony, commitment, learning together and a good atmosphere between people. They have an eye for feelings and the social aspect of working together.

Driven by integration and intellectual complexity (yellow) – This drive focuses on analysis and getting to the bottom of things. People with this drive are free thinkers who base their decisions on knowledge and insight. They love to look at issues from a broader perspective, creating well-thought-out solutions to complex problems.

Driven by holistic coherence (turquoise) – This drive focuses on solutions consciously anchored in the living community. People with this drive look at things from a committed distance and do not get lost in the madness of everyday life. By consciously attuning to the bigger picture, opportunities arise that can benefit everyone. It involves asking questions that stimulate an intuitive awareness of seeing and caring for the bigger picture. This drive reflects that everything is interconnected.

By recognising and acknowledging these differences, they can become part of the conversation. This conversation makes visible the patterns of behaviour and thinking of individuals and the differences between them. By valuing the importance of each drive completely, developmental steps can be taken that allow individuals and the team to flourish. Beige removes the fears that keep people from taking action. Purple provides a safe culture. Blue provides a practical and strong structure. Red gives each individual a valued place. Orange creates results and purpose for the team to align around. Green creates team cohesion and focuses on working together. Yellow integrates so that all facets of complexity are considered and well understood. Turquoise is attuned to the environment as a holistic whole and works from an awareness that everything is interconnected.

THE ROLE OF THE PROJECT MANAGER AS A CONSULTANT (ADVANCED)

Projects aim to realise concrete results with which organisational goals can be achieved. In doing so, solutions to issues should be sought with diverse stakeholders. The project professionals' consultancy skills are regularly called upon during this joint search. Edgar Schein (2005) provides three models and ten principles of helping.

Models for consultancy

Schein describes three models for consultancy:

- *Expertise model* – You choose to convey your content expertise. You state what you know and what should be done to achieve success. Important in this model is that you are sure that your advice is essential to the individual seeking advice. This means that you should first connect with the underlying question. Based on that, you offer the knowledge to help solve the question. If you don't make this contact with the underlying question first, it will diminish excellent advice. This model comes into its own in situations where your knowledge directly applies to the client's situation.

- *Doctor-patient model* – In this model, first, an accurate diagnosis of the situation is made. Based on structured research, you diagnose and suggest solutions. In doing so, you need to be able to gather sufficient information to make an accurate diagnosis. Hereby, it is important to clearly indicate what effort the client organisation has to make to provide you with that information. This model comes into its own in situations where independent, methodical research is needed to gain insight into the situation, including possible directions for improvement.
- *Process consulting model* – In this model, you position yourself as someone who will guide the process of examining the situation and defining possible solutions. You go through a process with the client organisation that enables them to identify causal factors and suitable alternatives. This model comes into its own when the expertise to solve problems need to be sourced from within the client organisation.

In all three models, knowing which interests should be considered is necessary. The most important is the client with whom the first contact has been made and the users directly affected by the advice. You should also observe the people who can provide you with the correct information. Finally, to avoid resistance to the advice, it is important to think carefully about the parties not directly involved in drafting the advice but who will be affected by it when it is put into practice. In all three models, building a relationship of trust is essential. This is necessary to ensure that your advice is accepted.

Principles for consulting

To go through the advisory process properly, Schein describes ten principles of helping.

Principle 1: Be careful, make sure what you do is helpful – Consulting work is not obligation-free. You find yourself in a situation where the other individual encounters a problem that needs to be solved. The first principle expresses that you are there for the client organisation. Maintaining your independence will define the helper's attitude. Don't act like a henchman of the client or a distant advisor. What matters is that you, as an equal partner, contribute meaningfully to the problem.

Principle 2: Stay in touch with reality – Base your advice on facts. People are often tempted to indicate solutions without research. Some do this with beautiful, visionary stories. Others with simple linear reasoning, such as: 'If the supplier has twice delivered incorrectly, it does not have its work processes in order!' The real issue may, however, be how the client organisation calls for the deliveries.

Principle 3: Recognise your ignorance – It is important to remain curious. Dare to scrutinise and continually ask questions to understand what is really going on. Ask people who are not involved in the process but are affected by it. Re-read the books and thoroughly verify the conclusions you draw from the situation. In short: don't make the mistake of assuming you already know things.

Principle 4: Recognise that everything you do is an intervention – When you are asked to contribute as a consultant, it is important to recognise that the words you use, the books you mention, the questions you ask, the notes you take, the suggestions you make, et cetera, are all interventions. By doing so, you exert influence on the thinking and feeling of the other. From this awareness, being conscious of your behaviour and how your surroundings react to it is important.

Principle 5: The client owns the problem and the solution – Getting caught up in the helper's attitude is sometimes tempting. Clients can, in an instant, shrug off responsibility and saddle the consultant with tasks that are not theirs. Realise that you are being employed as a consultant, not a task performer, to offer solutions as the client sees them.

Principle 6: Go with the flow – Don't get caught up in negative attitudes and judgements. Always search for areas where people want to think constructively. Engage with them by asking questions. This will help you understand the situation better, which will benefit your advice.

Principle 7: Watch your timing – It is often good to be temporarily silent, sometimes longer. There comes a moment when the message falls into place. Dare to wait for that moment.

Principle 8: Be constructively opportunistic – When a group is open to your input, dare to be confrontational so that the group really experiences what is needed to move forward. Then search for areas where you can build on the group's strengths and positive motivation. This way, it can easily integrate the result into daily work.

Principle 9: Everything provides data – Mistakes are inevitable: learn from them. Things always happen that provoke unexpected reactions in the group. Avoid shaming and blaming. You can learn a lot from feedback about how things can be done differently.

Principle 10: When in doubt, raise the issue – This elaborates the third principle. You don't have to know everything, and if you are unsure about something, say so, so that it can be included in examining the issues.

CREATING AN OPEN BUSINESS CULTURE (ADVANCED)

Openness can be stimulated by being open about your own actions and about the situation. You create situations in which dialogue about complex issues is possible. You work with methods for collective decision-making and create frameworks in which people can and want to support each other. You prevent political power games and take cultural differences into account. Action science shows how to do so.

Action Science

Action Science is a strategy for enhancing the skills and confidence of individuals in groups to promote long-term effectiveness. Argyrus, Putnam and McLain Smith (1985) distinguish two types of organisations in their book Action Science:

Model I organisations – Focus on rationalising measurable goals and standards and maximising solutions within the framework of these goals. If people do not realise the set goals and standards, they fall back on defensive reasoning. They demonstrate that they have done everything possible to realise the set goals and standards. Therefore, the cause of not achieving the goals should lie outside their sphere of influence. They tend not to discuss underlying convictions and principles for one's own behaviour, which hinders learning processes. Characteristics of Model I organisations are:

- People do not want to give up control of the goals for which they are responsible. Typical arguments are: 'Why should we discuss this? I know my area of expertise better than anyone. Stop meddling!'
- Sharing problems is seen as a weakness. As a result, complex issues remain undiscussed for too long.
- Negative emotions related to problems are suppressed. As a result, important cues for recognising issues are lost.
- People explain away problems and look for quick solutions to visible symptoms. The deeper layers of the issues are not explored and exposed.

Model II organisations – Have incorporated the characteristics of openness into their actions. People can conduct an open dialogue about the facts as they occur in the here and now. As a result, they can better identify the causes of issues and take action based on insight. Characteristics of Model II organisations are:

- Making choices based on information without a predetermined solution direction.
- A strong commitment to problem-solving together.
- Learning in groups by identifying and correcting gaps between what is officially described and what actually happens in practice.

Model II organisations make decisions involving subject matter experts, product and process designers and implementation experts. As a result, decision-making is not a unilateral responsibility of management. It arises from an open dialogue between parties who are actually capable of realising solutions, removing causes and creating conditions.

8.02 LEADERSHIP

PURPOSE

The purpose of this chapter is to enable the individual to lead, provide direction and motivate others, to enhance individual and team performance.

LEARNING OBJECTIVES

- Differences between leadership and management;
- Styles of leadership;
- Situational leadership;
- Circle of influence and circle of concern;
- Assertiveness;
- Role content, interpretation and expectation (advanced);
- Coaching (advanced);
- Servant leadership (advanced);
- Sense-making and sense-giving (advanced);
- Dimensions and levels of leadership (advanced);
- Decision model and decision styles (advanced).

DEFINITIONS

Leadership: Directing and motivating others in their role and task to realise goals.
Management: The whole of all managerial tasks necessary to realise a planned result. This includes planning, organising, controlling and directing an individual, group or organisation.
Leadership style: How a leader accomplishes their team's objective by motivating them to work towards the common goal and focusing on their well-being.
Situational leadership: Adapting your leadership style to circumstances as they arise.
Assertiveness: Standing up for one's own opinion, needs or interests in a non-abusive, tactful way.

INTRODUCTION

Leadership is actively moving people to achieve goals based on a clear vision. It focuses on the correct thing to do and, even more importantly, why it needs to be done. Expressing a compelling vision and motivating others to be assertive in their own roles are important leadership qualities. Assessing a situation well, knowing what motivates other people, adapting your style and behaviour accordingly, and influencing and encouraging them, makes leadership situational.

DIFFERENCES BETWEEN LEADERSHIP AND MANAGEMENT

As a project professional, you need both leadership and management skills to exert your influence and get people on board. Management is the set of supervisory tasks required to achieve an intended result. Leadership is about motivating others in their role or task to realise goals.

Both approaches are necessary to achieve the desired result on time, within budget and according to specifications. They are two sides of the same coin, but there is a big difference between the two approaches. The core difference between leadership and management can perhaps best be depicted as 'doing the right things' versus 'doing things right' (Bennis, 1999).

Leaders love to inspire groups with meaningful and visionary stories. They are motivational in personal contact. They emphasise what should be achieved and the added value for the organisation and its environment. Managers are most effective when they direct and control the performance of the work. They are good at distributing tasks and responsibilities and challenging team members to do their work correctly and on time (see Figure 8.02.01).

Leadership	Management
• Do the right things	• Do things correctly
• Implementing changes	• Continuous business operations
• Focus on what and why	• Focus on how and when
• Attention for purpose, direction and effectiveness	• Attention for speed, efficiency and quality
• Influence individuals, most effective in personal contact	• Most effective at controlling plans and specifications
• Focus on meaning, what should be achieved, and added value	• Focus on tasks, processes, and delivery

Figure 8.02.01 Differences between Leadership and Management

Leadership and management are thus clearly different. But there is more to it than meets the eye. A good leader also pays attention to management, such as planning and controlling progress. A good manager also pays attention to leadership, such as directing and motivating others. Thus the two roles are complementary to each other. Still, the tone of voice is different.

In both roles, you should focus on people and the results you want to achieve. The situation determines which intervention and leadership style is most appropriate to motivate people to do their work correctly.

STYLES OF LEADERSHIP

In Goleman's (2017) research, six dominant leadership styles emerge. We describe these styles in the order of the positive correlation between style and team climate.

Authoritative style – With this style, the leader communicates a clear situational vision. This clarity gives team members a strong sense of direction, which creates a willingness to follow. Authoritative leaders trust their vision and make it concretely measurable through, for example, critical performance indicators. The authoritative style is very different from the authoritarian style. The authoritarian leader gives strict orders to be performed. They play the big boss. The authoritative leaders do not prescribe how teams should realise the vision. They trust in the direction they have set and dare to delegate its performance.

Relational style – This style suits those leaders who are good listeners and can easily share their personal experiences. This creates a shared understanding of the situation and what is needed to achieve results. The style requires a high degree of emotional intelligence, as the leader is willing to actively align their own direction and ideas with those of the team members. The style sometimes lacks concreteness, causing the team to underperform.

Democratic style – This style suits those leaders who want to involve stakeholders in the search for solutions. Their support, knowledge and experience are necessary for developing a successful approach. These leaders can facilitate processes so that people feel heard and involved. They listen to the content and the undercurrent and translate these into decisions that people can identify with. In this way, they patiently work on the needed course, which can only arise from and with the people themselves.

Coaching style – This style assumes that people are aware of their personal performance in concrete situations and are receptive to development. The leader as coach ensures that people see where development opportunities lie and how they can include these in their personal responsibility. Stimulating awareness is the core of the approach. This requires good listening and asking open questions, enabling the coach to investigate his or her GROW, an acronym for *Goals, Reality, Opportunities and Way (Forward)*. What are the goals you wish to achieve? What is really going on? What opportunities do you see to make possible breakthroughs? What are decisions which are going to help you on your way forward?

Pace-setting style – This style is best applied within a motivated and professional team working on a challenging task together. The leader sets challenging goals. They expect quality and lead by example. If necessary, they roll up their sleeves to save the situation. These leaders give few instructions. They expect their team to know what to do. This can be successful in the short term, but it can lead to exhaustion and declining results in the long term.

Coercive style – This style can be used effectively in a crisis when immediate and effective action is required. In such situations, you should direct people on what to do and how to do it. In many other cases, the directive or authoritarian style harms the working climate of a team. It deprives people of the opportunity to take the initiative and responsibility, making the style feel more like a straitjacket.

Leadership aims to direct individuals and teams effectively to arrive at set objectives jointly and with agreed results. The effectiveness of the used style differs per situation.

CONTINGENCY THEORY

Contingency theories state that effective leadership is contingent upon the situation at hand. Someone can be an effective leader in one circumstance and an ineffective leader in another. Such theories focus on matching the leadership traits to the situation. According to Fiedler's Contingency Theory (1971), a task-orientated leadership style is appropriate in situations where the relationship between leader and co-workers is good, the tasks are well structured, and the leader has a strong positional power base. A more relation-orientated style is needed when the power base is weak and the task complex and unstructured, but the relationship between the leader and co-workers is strong. When you are a leader with a natural task-orientated attitude, you will prefer, in the last case, better-structured tasks and a stronger positional power base. If this is possible, you influence the situation towards your favourite personal leadership style. Adapting your leadership style to the situation is also possible to better deal with the given contingency.

SITUATIONAL LEADERSHIP

Situational leadership emphasise that leaders can adapt to the situations they face. Hersey, Blanchard & Johnson are key representatives of this way of thinking. Based on their research (2008), they developed a model for situational leadership, which is based, on the one, on the task capability and, on the other hand, on the willingness and or the confidence of employees to carry out their work.

Performance readiness

Performance readiness is a combination of the employee's ability to perform their tasks and the level of confidence and or willingness to do so. Based on this premise, Hersey, Blanchard & Johnson distinguish four areas of performance readiness (see Figure 8.02.02):

- Performance readiness level 1: Unable and Insecure or Unwilling;
- Performance readiness level 2: Unable but Confident or Willing;
- Performance readiness level 3: Able but Insecure or Unwilling;
- Performance readiness level 4: Able and Confident or Willing.

A lack of relevant knowledge, work experience and insufficient understanding of the specific task can cause low ability. Lack of willingness may be caused by sheer unwillingness but also by uncertainty about the performance of the task or a lack of self-confidence.

Performance readiness level 1 (R1) – An employee with low task capability and willingness performs the task unacceptably, causes delays, doesn't finish, is defensive, avoids work, and often feels uncomfortable. Competence development should focus mainly on increasing the ability to fulfil tasks properly.

Performance readiness		Typical behavioural indicators
R1	Unable and insecure or unwilling	If insecure: delays work, is afraid to make mistakes; feels uncomfortable. If unwilling: avoids work; performs tasks unacceptably; doesn't finish work; is defensive
R2	Unable but confident and willing	Enthusiastic, eager to proceed: 'Yes, I already know, and I can do it'; talks about the end result but omits essential steps; delivers moderate work; is not fully concentrated on the task to be done.
R3	Able but insecure or unwilling	If insecure: doubts about own qualities; seems confused; seeks confirmation; is afraid to finish. If unwilling: demonstrates resistance; complains about too many obligations; withdraws from the team.
R4	Able, confident and willing	Works autonomously, is pro-active and result-orientated; is willing to provide support; delivers quality; keeps management informed; is concentrated on the task; is honest about matters that are difficult.

Figure 8.02.02 Indicators for performance readiness (Hersey, Blanchard and Johnson, 2008)

Performance readiness level 2 (R2) – An employee with a low task ability and high willingness sees his or her task as a new experience and is interested, but because of their moderate ability, will not always realise that they don't have enough knowledge. Competence development should focus on improving task competence and creating awareness of how things were done, ineffective or wrong.

Performance readiness level 3 (R3) – An employee with high task ability and low willingness has proven knowledge and experience but resists performing their task under current conditions. Competence development should focus mainly on the relationship to enhance willingness and or self-confidence.

Performance readiness level 4 (R4) – An employee with a high level of competence and willingness can work autonomously, focus on tasks, and deliver quality. Competence development should focus mainly on keeping the relationship strong. By entrusting challenging tasks to these employees and involving them in discussions about complex situations, the task capability and willingness to perform will remain high.

Situational leadership styles

It is a leadership task to steer for performance. What styles can the leader apply in different situations to do this effectively? Hersey, Johnson and Blanchard distinguish four leadership styles linked to the employee's performance readiness (see Figure 8.02.03):

1. Telling – High focus on directing task performance and low focus on relational support;
2. Selling – High focus on directing task performance and high focus on relational support;
3. Participating – Low focus on directing task performance but high focus on relational support;
4. Delegating – Low focus on directing task performance and low focus on relational support.

Telling (S1) – This style is most appropriate in situations where you have to lead employees with a low-performance readiness (R1). It is mainly about directing a task performance to increase confidence and willingness. Telling may also be referred to as directing.

Effective leadership behaviours are:

- Provide clear information about how the task should be performed;
- Give step-by-step support/instructions;
- Reinforce confidence to carry out the work by giving minor tasks;
- Check the progress and performance frequently;
- Give clear corrections if the performance deviates from the stated standard;
- Point out the consequences if a task is performed incorrectly;
- Discuss uncertainty and or unwillingness so that they no longer interfere with task performance;
- Give compliments when a specific task has been performed correctly.

Selling (S2) – This leadership style is most appropriate when employees have low to moderate capability and a high willingness to perform the task (R2). They are not fully capable of doing their jobs satisfactorily, but they think they can. The leader is focused on both task performance and relational support. Selling may also be referred to as explaining or persuading.

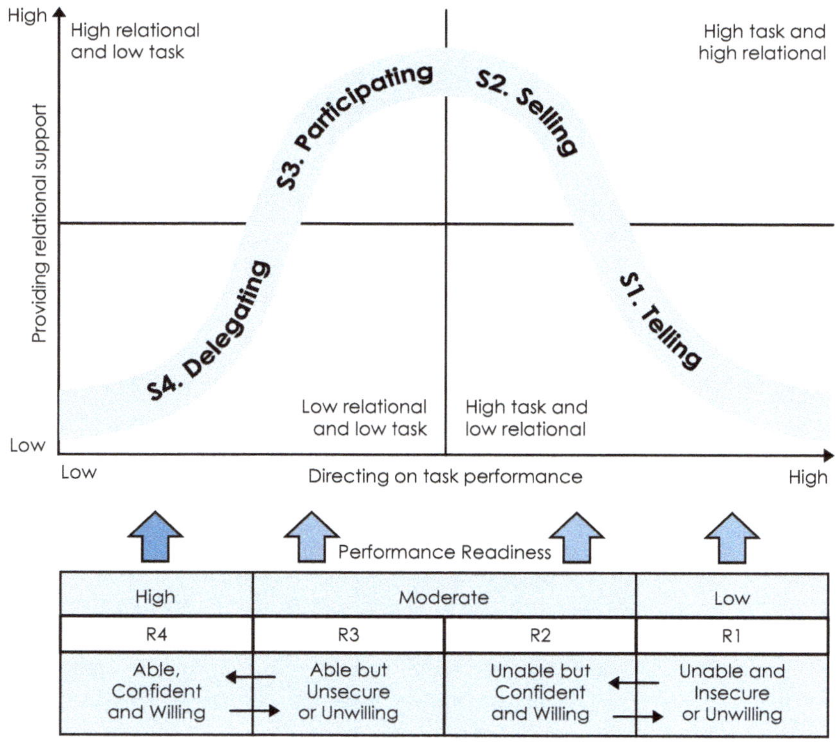

Figure 8.02.03 Leadership styles and performance readiness (Hersey, et al, 2008)

Effective leadership behaviours are:

- Keep the power distance as small as possible;
- Explain the concept of the task and how it needs to be done;
- Actively check if the task content is well understood;
- Be interested, show understanding, and encourage two-way conversation;
- Give attention to ideas and suggestions from the employee;
- Align project and employee interest;
- Convince that specific actions are necessary to achieve a good result;
- Give clear and convincing feedback when things need to be done differently;
- Find out what resistance the employee still has;
- Take and explain the final decisions.

> *Susan has been working in the department for a fortnight. She is a very enthusiastic management trainee. However, Susan is also quite stubborn because she thinks she is already well-trained for this job. Ensuring she listens to the more experienced staff members supervising her is challenging.*

Participating (S3) – This leadership style is most appropriate when employees have moderate to high capability to perform the task but a low willingness (R3). They know what they should do, but somehow, they have lost their motivation. In these situations, you need to give relational support. Participating may also be referred to as supporting, empowering or encouraging.

Effective leadership behaviours are:

- Listen and show understanding; take personal circumstances into account;
- Optimise the conditions under which the employee is performing the task;
- Try to solve the problems together but leave the role of expertise with the employee;
- Facilitate but leave the responsibility with the employee;
- Create an atmosphere of trust;
- Facilitate the development of self-confidence;
- Be clear about the consequences if tasks can't be done and discuss how to deal with this together;
- Make sure they agree with the decisions taken.

> *John has just returned from sick leave. He had a burnout. Last week he was added to the team. However, he is not yet fully functional, although he knows exactly what needs to be done. During our conversation this morning, he told me he fears having another burnout. I agreed that he starts later in the morning and that Mary would support him with the correspondence.*

Delegating (S4) – This style is primarily appropriate when the workers are both highly skilled and highly involved (R4). In these situations, the leader should be reluctant to give both task-orientated guidance and relationship-orientated support. This does not mean leaving the staff member to their fate but giving them the confidence and freedom to perform their tasks independently and professionally. Delegating may be called entrusting and assigning.

Effective leadership behaviours are:

- Delegate responsibilities;
- Give the employee the space to do the job in their own way;
- Agree in advance on the applicable procedures (concerning, e.g., changes and reporting);
- Act as a sounding board for the employee; listen, understand, and show interest;
- However, let the employee solve their own problems, don't pursue your solutions;
- Maintain some distance, but do not neglect the employee;
- Give the employee a coaching role to support less experienced colleagues.

> *The progress meeting went well today. The team was a bit behind schedule. However, Harold said that he had simplified the design somewhat so that the engineers could complete the work drawings more quickly. It has become a professional team.*

CIRCLE OF INFLUENCE AND CIRCLE OF CONCERN

Covey's first habit, see Chapter 7.01 Self-Reflection and Self-Management, is 'be proactive'. Being proactive is more than taking the initiative. It means taking charge of your own life, no matter what. Our behaviour depends more on our decisions than the circumstances we find ourselves in. Taking responsibility for your decisions, however difficult at times, is 'being proactive'.

Reactive people are considerably influenced by circumstances and their social environment. If things are going well, they feel good. They feel unhappy and blame the environment if things are not going their way. Proactive people are guided by their values and principles. Reactive people are guided more by their beliefs and emotions. You can become aware of your pro-activity by looking at where your attention is focused. Is it mainly focused on what you feel involved in or on factors you can influence and change yourself?

Reactive people depend on the circles of concern they are part of. They are busy with others and what others should do to make them happy. As a result, they neglect what they can influence, which lessens their circle of influence. Proactive people, on the other hand, focus on factors they can influence and thus strengthen their circle of influence. Achieved results give them extra energy, leading to a growing circle of influence (see Figure 8.02.04).

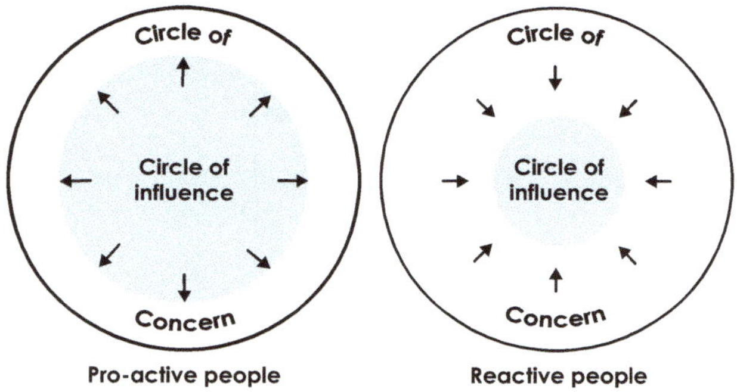

Figure 8.02.04 Circles of Influence and Concern (Covey, 2010)

Direct, indirect and no impact

The problems you face in exerting your influence fall into three categories:

- Direct influence – Problems you can solve by yourself;
- Indirect influence – Problems you can solve by involving or influencing others;
- No influence – Problems you cannot do anything about.

Take direct action for the problems you can solve yourself. Problems in the 'indirect influence' category can be solved by changing your approach to exerting influence. Problems in the category of 'no influence' are those you should learn to live with. You have to accept the situation, and learning to let go is the best thing you can do.

Strengthening a proactive attitude is essential in organisations. It ensures that people learn to focus on their own tasks and not interfere with the work assigned to others. They can call others to account for their behaviour, only to indicate what is needed from them to perform their own task well. And conversely, situationally, they inquire from others about what they need to do their task effectively, so they will know what and when to deliver. However, complaining and interfering are not part of the vocabulary of proactive people; assertively standing up for themselves is.

ASSERTIVENESS

In projects, there will be moments the project manager should assertively state what he or she needs and stands for. It may be a team member who fails to deliver their contribution on time or a supplier who does not deliver per the specifications. At such moments, you should tactfully and attentively stand up for your opinions, needs, and interests.

Assertiveness can be distinguished from sub-assertiveness and aggressiveness. Sub-assertiveness is not standing up for your own interests and letting others violate your rights and limits. By this, you will not accomplish what is agreed upon. Aggressiveness is standing up in a threatening or angry manner for your opinions, needs and interests, with little regard for the interests of others, thus crossing the boundaries of what is decent and acceptable. Both behaviours have a negative influence on the collaboration process.

You can be skillfully and powerfully assertive while being fair and respectful. It is about creating harmony between your and other people's interests. Always be clear about your needs to do your job successfully. Don't hide!

When others exhibit these behaviours, give the aggressive person clear feedback to calm down. Invite the sub-assertive person to put forward their opinions and questions more actively.

ADVANCED

ROLE CONTENT, INTERPRETATION AND EXPECTATION (ADVANCED)

The project manager is responsible for the daily management of the project and should ensure the successful delivery of the project output. This determines the project manager's role content. Role interpretation is how the individual in charge performs their role. Each project manager has their own personal role interpretation and gives substance to it from there.

At the same time, the environment has explicit and implicit expectations about your role and how it should be performed. This is called role expectation. Tensions arise as soon as the role content, role interpretation, and role expectations are not aligned.

Important focus points are:

- Immersing yourself in the culture of the environment you will be working in;
- Adapting to the culture where you find yourself in;
- Adjusting your approaches to the environment;
- Being aware of the reactions to your behaviour and subtly changing it to maintain contact;
- Explaining why you are doing what you do and what effect you are aiming for;
- Staying true to your values, standards and behaviour without imposing them on others;
- Exerting your influence from your role and not interfering with how others fulfil theirs.

In all cases, you should continually ask yourself how to give form and content to your role in specific situations and environments. How and with which attitude you realise the project result is strongly linked to the role content the environment expects from you. Therefore, you should learn to communicate in a role-appropriate manner.

Role-conscious communicating

The core of the project manager's role is to 'ensure that the project result is realised successfully'. This is the starting point for professional communication with the environment. Consider, for example, that a team member from department X has absented herself from the project meeting for the second time. Start acting from your role content and your circle of influence. Role-conscious communication always starts from one's own role.

> *Marian has absented herself from the project meeting for the second time. You are worried because you know she has to provide information for Peter, but so far, she has failed to do that. Now he cannot fulfil his task. With this in mind, you first ask Peter what he has done to get the correct information from Marian on time. You then ask him to contact her to ensure he still receives the information on time. Peter reaches out to Marian and asks her: 'You weren't at the meeting this morning. I'm worried because I can't continue my tasks without your input. As a result, the project is in danger of running out of time. When can I expect to receive your information?'*

> *The problem only falls back on you when she doesn't deliver the information on time. Your communication to Marian could then be as follows: 'What is preventing you from contributing to the project? What do you need to complete your task so that Peter can complete his and we can successfully complete the project?*

By communicating in a role-conscious manner, you remain at the centre of your own role. You work from your circle of influence. Communication can still go in different directions, but the facts are on the table, and no personal accusations have been made. From there on, together, you can look for solutions. Knowing your role and the responsibility that goes with it is crucial for starting constructive conversations about solutions that will work.

COACHING (ADVANCED)

Coaching is a method where, through dialogue, the coach helps the coachee, through self-discovery and self-awareness, correctly set goals, find the best way to achieve them and reveal the hidden inner potential to enhance their productivity or overcome a problem.

A project manager who chooses coaching leadership allows team members to reflect on situations via open-ended questions actively. These questions are meant to develop awareness about the situation and one's role and take responsibility for it.

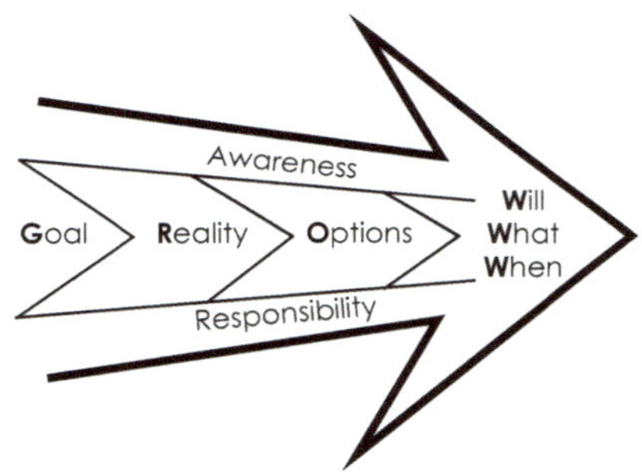

Figure 8.02.05 GROW as an acronym to organise coaching sessions

GROW (see Figure 8.02.05) is an acronym for organising coaching sessions in a structured way.

- *Goal* – What do you most want to achieve in this situation? What goals do you have in mind and why?
- *Reality* – What does the situation look like? What are you good at? What can't you do yet? What motivates you? What factual aspects of the situation are you finding difficult? What thoughts, feelings and behaviours does this lead to? How does this affect the goals you want to achieve?
- *Options* – Which alternatives do you see to help change your behaviour? What support can you organise to get where you want to go?
- *Will or Way Forward* – What decisions will you make? What concrete steps will you undertake to take disciplined responsibility for achieving your goals?

Coaching encourages the coachee to think carefully about the real situation and link the choices that can be made to concrete behaviour. This 'reality check' can trigger a range of emotions. If you move away from these emotions too quickly, the person may not feel properly heard. Another pitfall is that you start filling in the options for the person so that taking responsibility is not embedded in the person. You cannot force the birth of a butterfly. Emering from their cocoon takes time. So, the coach needs to be patient when supporting people by developing their personality. Being encouraging is okay, but don't force it.

On the other hand, new insight into how work could be done creates a basis for new decisions around doing the work correctly. Before coaching can be effectively applied, proper training is required.

SERVANT LEADERSHIP (ADVANCED)

In 1970, Robert Greenleaf wrote an essay entitled, *The Servant Leader*. He wrote: 'The servant leader is servant first. It starts with the natural feeling that one wants to serve, wants to serve first! Then a conscious choice leads one to aspire to lead. This style of leadership is strongly promoted within the Agile way of working.

To check whether your servant leadership is optimally functioning, Greenleaf developed a 'best test'. This test works as follows: *'Do those being served grow as a person? As they are served, do they become healthier, wiser, freer, more autonomous, or more inclined to become servants themselves? And what is the effect on the least privileged in society? Are they better off or at least not further disadvantaged?'* So, servant leaders put the needs of others first. They demonstrate moral behaviour with 'the best test' as the guiding ethical perspective in their thinking and being.

Based on Greenleaf's theory, Spears (1998) describes ten characteristics of servant leaders. What characteristic behaviours do servant leaders display when they serve and create an environment where people feel respected, valued and appreciated? Those characteristics are:

- *Listening* – They listen very carefully to the needs of those they serve. They offer an attitude of presence and listening with full attention to needs. It is not about what they want but literally hearing what is being said and what not. They are good observers; as they hear and see, they gain insights into what is happening.
- *Empathy* – They care about team members. They consider and understand the perspective of others on an emotional level. They empathise with feelings of pain and gain and can truly understand how a situation affects someone's needs and preferences.
- *Healing* – They know that people's and teams' problems need to be solved first. They have a keen eye for problems that prevent people from doing what they want. They do not push through the achievement of intended goals if the right environment to do so is not yet in place. They ensure that problems are solved and that the team has the support and resources necessary to excel.
- *Self-awareness* – They can look at themselves and reflect on the causes and consequences of their own emotions and behaviour. They dare to show their own vulnerability and are honest about their weaknesses and strengths. They can also

support others in exploring their feelings and discovering personal strengths and weaknesses. In this way, they help teams to grow.

- *Persuasion* – They are very good at explaining and persuading. They are active listeners and, at the same time, good communicators. They make you feel heard and, almost simultaneously, explain why it makes sense to make a particular choice. They never make that choice for you, but you feel deeply understood of what is happening and see the possibilities arising from those insights.
- *Conceptualising* – They show that it is not about them or the other person. They can see the bigger picture. In this way, they do not oversimplify questions but amplify insights. They make it possible to understand the complexity you are dealing with. It is this insight that helps you to find the right way forward.
- *Foresight* – They help teams understand why things are how they are now. They draw lines from the past to the present so that everyone can understand how certain things have developed. This way of thinking often leads to the root causes of the problems you are facing now. This makes it easier to make the right decisions for the future. Servant leaders always gather facts and information to formulate a strong vision and make the best decisions. And if they don't know, they ask for feedback and hold meetings with the whole team.
- *Stewardship* – They take their own responsibilities in the team seriously. They know they have a role as a leader in the team and as a figurehead of the team. Their leadership is value-driven, and when it comes to getting things done together, they roll up their sleeves and are not afraid to do operational work.
- *Commitment to growth* – A key attitude is the desire to help others grow. They are always looking for ways to develop the individual, the team, and the organisation. They dare to give challenging assignments because they focus on personal growth and goals that motivate people.
- *Building community* – They encourage collaboration and engagement. They like to engage in collective dialogues that make sense to help make the best decision.

SENSE-MAKING AND SENSE-GIVING (ADVANCED)

Sense-making is focused on understanding and interpreting ambiguous or confusing issues or events. It is more about gaining insights and understanding rather than directly creating solutions. This approach starts by deeply investigating and empathising with the problem/desire of the customer/user and understanding the needs and motivations of all the people involved. It often uses techniques like storytelling and collaborative discussion. This way of innovating is characterised by extreme customer focus. From there on, sense-giving is about providing direction and meaning to others to influence their perceptions and actions. Both concepts are essential in organisational settings. Sense-giving allows leaders to really support and guide people towards a shared vision. Sense-making helps individuals and groups make informed decisions.

For this approach, an open leadership style and adaptability, active listening, the willingness to consider diverse perspectives, and delay any judgement are essential. It is a challenging but rewarding style of leadership.

THREE LEVELS OF LEADERSHIP (ADVANCED)

Scouller's *Three-level leadership* model is about cultivating your own leadership attitudes and behaviours (level 1) and influencing the behaviour of others in individual (level 2) and group situations (level 3). In doing so, Scouller focuses on four dimensions: setting challenging goals, achieving results, maintaining group unity and cohesion, and encouraging individual commitment. In these four dimensions lies the core responsibility of the leader. It requires the deployment of both leadership and management qualities.

Setting challenging goals – A leader should be focused on providing clear direction. In doing so, they create a goal- and result-orientated focus for both individuals and groups. Through this focus, team members know what needs to be achieved as a team. It is the basis for working together.

Achieving results and progress – A leader is also responsible for assigning tasks and tracking individual and group achievement. By managing the realisation of tasks and monitoring progress, you can see to what extent defined results and set goals have actually been achieved.

Maintaining group unity and cohesion – A leader is the group's figurehead. How they represent the group to the outside world reinforces its sense of direction. A leader is also responsible for group cohesion. They should ensure that group members listen to each other and seek approaches that promote progress. A leader also dares to stand in the middle of the group and discuss situations perceived as really difficult.

Attention to the individual – The leader works with individuals to focus on their roles and tasks in the group and enhance their personal effectiveness. This part of leadership includes attention to task distribution, discipline and personal development.

Three levels of leadership

These four dimensions require concrete behaviour from the leader. This behaviour occurs on three levels: the inner, the 1-on-1, and the 1-on-group (see Figure 8.02.06). The first level concerns the cultivation of one's attitude. From this cultivated inner attitude (inner level), the leader interacts with individuals (outer level 1) and groups (outer level 2). Each level requires the use of specific skills aimed at improving the four dimensions.

Public Leadership (Outer level 2)

Public-level leadership first focuses on setting prioritised goals that reinforce a sense of direction and feasibility. You work with the group to organise and distribute the tasks that should be accomplished to reach these goals. When resolving issues, you actively involve the group so that the group can follow up and support decisions. During the realisation of the work, you are a stimulating presence.

In addition, you also pay attention to the atmosphere and cohesion within the group. You create an atmosphere where people listen to each other, resolve conflicts and coordinate their work. Further, this role also focuses on representing the team externally. When the team is in trouble, the leader stands up for the team and protects it from the outside world.

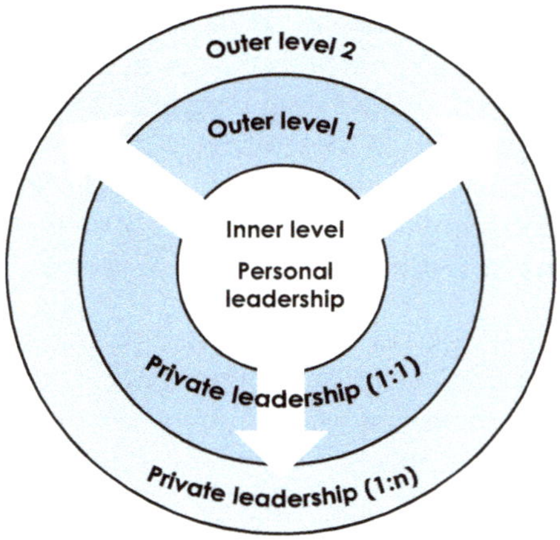

Figure 8.02.06 Three levels of leadership (Scouller, 2011)

Private leadership (outside level 1)

Your attention on a public level is also relevant on a one-to-one level. After all, what the group has to achieve affects the individuals within the group. Focus, team spirit, and group results are, therefore, also issues on an individual level. How team members deal with each other interpersonally, actively solve group issues, follow decisions and carry out planned work is part of the conversation with each group member.

As a leader, you also work at this level on how team members position themselves within the group. You redirect team members if they show sub-assertive or aggressive behaviour so that individual points of view can really be heard within the team. You act assertively and, in doing so, clearly set the direction. By setting clear boundaries, individual team members can excel within the set frameworks.

With the individual team members, you also work on formulating short, challenging, attainable and motivating personal goals. In doing so, you will be tuned to the individual's load capacity so that objectives are both challenging and achievable.

Personal leadership (inner level)

To adequately perform leadership tasks at the public and private levels, the leader needs to develop personal leadership skills and techniques, their attitude towards others, and development of psychological self-control.

Leadership skills and techniques

At the skill level, leaders should focus on developing their personal time management, knowledge of people and group dynamics. A leader should be skilled in building relationships and managing groups. This management should be anchored in clear guiding and motivational goals to which the leader is personally committed in word and deed.

Attitude towards others

Determining your attitude towards others concerns the moral side of leadership. Your approach to others is aimed at gaining each other's trust. Connecting with people is strongly embedded in how they value your leadership. Scouller describes the right attitude towards others as one in which the leader:

- Makes mutual dependence central;
- Shows appreciation for the other;
- Makes support for each other concrete;
- Clarifies the mutual service to each other;
- Clarifies the tasks to be done;
- Discusses the balance you experience in the work that is being performed.

The two main reasons this attitude is not always visible are the lack of a shared vision and inner self-confidence. For the development of both these aspects, attention to the development of personal self-awareness is necessary.

Developing personal self-control

With self-development, it is important to realise that we are all a centre of self-awareness, will and imagination. To fully manifest that centre, called 'Self' by Scouller, you should develop your identity. This identity, formed by your psyche, fills itself with beliefs, thoughts, feelings, wishes and habits. Realise that from now on, 'You have them, but you aren't them!', so you can change them.

It is essential to examine the underlying thoughts consciously, especially when they lead to feelings of fear, anger and or sadness, such as the fear of being rejected or not being good enough or less forceful. Which experiences cause these thoughts and feelings? How real are they? To what extent do they determine your professional behaviour? This self-analysis enables you to establish your personal competence in a given situation. With this, you learn to recognise your own patterns and redirect your thoughts and behaviour to be more effective (see Figure 8.02.07).

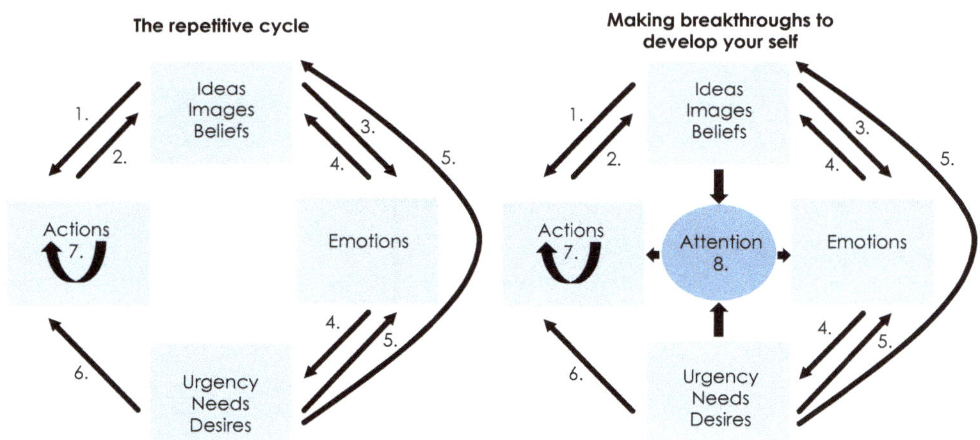

Law 1: Ideas, images and beliefs lead to actions
Law 2: Actions reinforce beliefs, images and ideas
Law 3: Beliefs, images and ideas evoke emotions
Law 4: Emotions intensify both beliefs and needs
Law 5: Needs justify emotions and beliefs
Law 6: The pursuit of needs is reflected in actions
Law 7: Repetitive actions easily become habitual

Law 8:
Attention to reversals of beliefs, emotions, needs and actions and confirming them makes them stronger
Or vice versa:
Less interest in old thoughts, emotions, needs and actions weakens them

Figure 8.02.07 Breaking patterns by giving attention to them (Scouller, 2011)

To achieve breakthroughs, focusing on how actions, thoughts/beliefs, emotions and needs/desires interact is necessary. You can only make explicit reversals towards different and more appropriate behaviour from a conscious focus on these interactions.

Individual learning

The more you repeat this breakthrough cycle, the more experienced you will become at recognising and seeing through the source of limiting beliefs, emotions, desires and the behaviour linked to them. By consciously making reversals, you strengthen the authenticity of your personal leadership and your ability to see others from the perspective of their undistorted selves. It is a compelling form of individual triple-loop learning (see Chapter 10.02 Personnel Management). Both your one-to-one leadership and your attitude and influence in one-to-group situations gain strength as a result.

VROOM AND YETTON DECISION MODEL (ADVANCED)

Making decisions is an important part of a leadership role. In doing so, you should always ask yourself, 'Can I make this decision on my own, or do I need to involve other people?' To answer this question, Vroom and Yetton (2010) developed a decision tree, which helps you to identify when and how to involve others by making high-quality decisions.

They ask seven questions to determine this. Three of these questions are focused on the quality of the decision to be made. Four of them are related to the team accepting the decision.

Quality related questions are:
1. Does the best solution matter?
2. Do you have all the information you need?
3. Do you know what information is missing and how to get it?

Relational related questions are:
4. Is the acceptance of others essential for effective implementation?
5. Will the team accept your decision without their active involvement?
6. Is the team aligned with the organisation's goals?
7. Is there likely to be disagreement within the team about alternatives?

Decision styles

From these questions, you go through Vroom and Yetton's decision tree (see Figure 8.02.08) to explore which style to choose to make the decision. Vroom and Yetton distinguish five decision styles.

Vroom and Yetton distinguish five decision styles:

A1. Autocratic 1 – It is not necessary to involve the team. Especially when there is little time to make the decision, and you feel confident acting alone, you decide based on your information.

A2. Autocratic 2 – You have enough information to decide independently, but the team's commitment to the decision is important. That's why you ask team members for specific information so that you can sharpen your decision. The decision will be better, and the team members will feel involved.

C1. Consultative 1 – You consult your team members individually and ask them for their opinions. Because of the complexity of the problem and or the time factor, you don't gather the entire team. You make the final decision yourself.

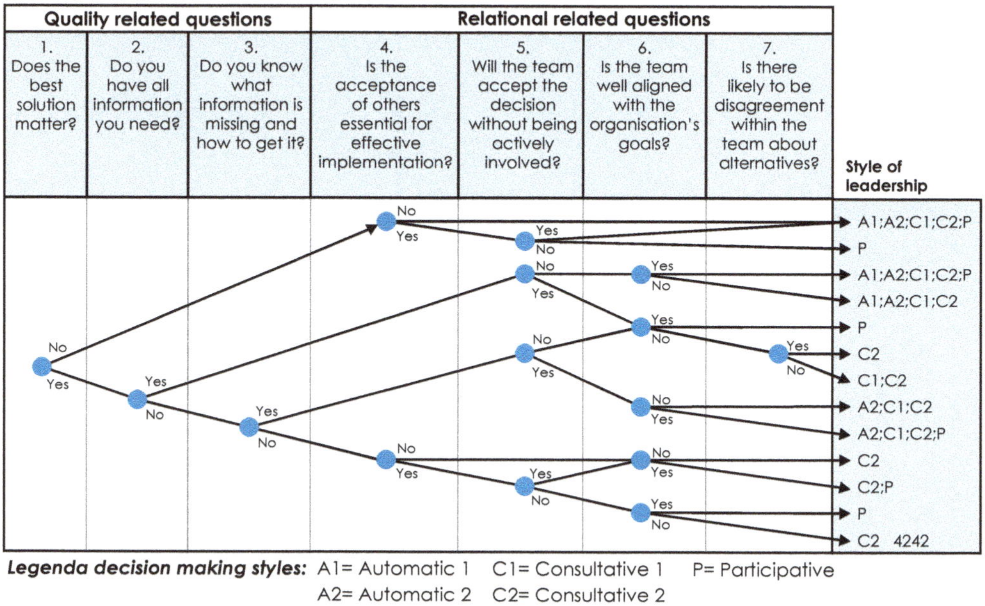

Figure 8.02.08 Vroom and Yetton's decision tree (Vroom, Yetton, 2010)

C2. Consultative 2 – You gather the whole team to discuss the complex problem. You listen carefully to their opinions and suggestions, but you still make your own decision.

P. Participative – You use the participative or collaborative style when you don't have enough information and know the team is well-aligned with the organisation's goals. Using the participative style, you motivate team members to solve these complex problems together. They will support and fully understand the decision because they have been involved in the process.

8.03 TEAMWORK

PURPOSE
The purpose of this chapter is to enable the individial to select the right team members, promote team orientation, and effectively manage a team.

LEARNING OBJECTIVES
- Team lifecycle;
- Situational leadership in relation to team development;
- Interventions at phase transitions;
- Teambuilding;
- Dealing with resistance;
- Team composition (advanced);
- Developing a project culture (advanced);
- Team roles (advanced);
- Group thinking (advanced);
- Dealing with difficult people (advanced);
- Managing virtual teams (advanced).

DEFINITIONS
Team: A group of people working together to achieve a common goal or result.
Teambuilding: A collective term for a series of group activities to promote cooperation in a team.
Team development phases: Successive steps in the group development of teams to effectively implement cooperation.
Resistance: The hesitation or refusal to accept, comply or agree with something.

INTRODUCTION
Throughout the lifecycle of a project, people work intensively together in teams to define and create the project result. Good team composition is a prerequisite for creating a well-functioning team. Such a team consists of people who understand their profession, complement each other and can work together.

To develop a team, you need to recognise the dynamics in team phases and make the right interventions in every phase so that the team can grow. Teambuilding sessions are meant to improve teamwork. Discussing resistance is necessary for maintaining a solid team.

TEAM DEVELOPMENT PHASES
A team is a group of people working together to achieve a common goal or result. To achieve result-orientated collaboration, a team goes through several development phases. Groups are unique in terms of their dynamics and complexity. However, teams almost always go through the same phases to develop towards team maturity. Psychologist Bruce Tuckman (1965) distinguishes five phases in team development: Forming, Storming, Norming, Performing and Adjourning. Each phase has its own dynamics, and if you want to grow as a team, you have to recognise the phases and make the right interventions to promote team development.

Forming phase – In the first phase of team development, team members look for their roles and what is expected of them. They are also exploring how they want to organise their cooperation. Social contacts are often limited to one or two other team members. People are still waiting to see which way the wind is blowing. Team members in this phase are:

» Reticent and waiting to see how the situation develops;
» Uncertain about what exactly is expected of them;
» Take a dependent attitude towards the leader of the team;
» Show personal interest to know each other somewhat better;
» Task-orientated, partly due to uncertainty about what exactly is required of them;
» Polite to each other.

Storming phase – Due to discrepancies between expectations and daily reality, team morale may decline. Several factors can cause this, such as clashing personalities, unbalanced dividing of tasks, conflicts with responsibilities, differences in role interpretation, varying core values, formation of sub-groups, et cetera. Any conflicts that may arise in this phase should be discussed. If these conflicts are not dealt with effectively, the turmoil within the team will increase, and the team cohesion will come under pressure or even disappear. Team members in this phase:

» Distrust and compete with each other;
» Fight internal conflicts in which distinct subgroups reinforce themselves;
» Challenge a position, role and or responsibility;
» Doubt the purpose, plan and approach of the project.
» Even challenge the position of the team leader;
» Are recalcitrant and interfere with other people's positions and roles;
» Question whether they still want to be part of the team.

Norming phase – From the contradictions and differences between the team members and the discussions they generate, a common understanding of the teamwork and how they will collaborate develops. In this phase, information is shared more openly with the other team members, and a sense of joint responsibility arises. Collaboration among team members is now central, and the focus shifts from individual to common goals. A jointly developed pattern of cooperation becomes an accepted norm by the whole team. Decisions are made using collective decision-making methods and are usually based on consensus. Team members in this phase:

» Share common goals regarding content and cooperation;
» Perform their work based on agreements laid down in procedures;
» Accept their own task and the group agreements;
» Trust each other basically;
» Show willingness to improve personal skills;
» Show willingness to learn from each other;
» Work together, but productivity is still not optimal.

Performing phase – Only when the team has gone through the previous phases can it reach the phase of effortless performance. Each team member with their own specific talents has established their place within the team and is valuable to the team. The team deals effectively with changing organisational conditions and demonstrates a self-learning capacity. They go with the flow, each knowing exactly what to do and how to do it without being distracted by peripheral issues. Team members in this phase:

- Have fully accepted each other's roles;
- Solve their own problems professionally;
- Take decisions as an independent team;
- Monitor and control the work as a team;
- Cooperate respectfully and professionally;
- Are motivated and show a high work ethic.

Adjourning phase – No team lasts forever. Transferring team members to other workplaces is important when the team is dissolved. Especially in well-functioning ones, the grief of dismantling the team can be significant. Therefore, it is essential that you acknowledge this and, together with them, earnestly search for new challenges that match their capabilities and personal goals.

Intermittently, team members may leave, and new ones will join. A change in a team's composition means the old team ceases to exist. The new team composition entails going through the team phases, starting from scratch. The rate of this process depends on the extent of the change, the newcomer's personality and the acceptance by the team members who remain. Newcomers come with their own peculiarities and core values, requiring a renewed alignment with and among the other team members.

You should make the right interventions to lead a team smoothly to higher maturity levels.

SITUATIONAL LEADERSHIP AND TEAM DEVELOPMENT PHASES

To consider which interventions to apply, you can use situational leadership styles. The four team development phases can be managed using the four styles of leadership identified by Hersey, Johnson and Blanchard (see Figure 8.03.01).

Each situation requires a different style, bringing the team performance to a higher maturity level.

- *Forming phase* – Needs a style focused on defining the tasks to be performed to achieve the results and objectives. (*Telling*)
- *Storming phase* – Needs a more convincing and involving style to align differences in approaches and to work towards acceptable agreements with each team member. (*Selling*)
- *Norming phase* – Shifts the team focus toward developing team cohesion. How does the team work out the procedures and agreements they have made professionally? (*Participating*)
- *Performing phase* – Offering the team enough space to develop. In addition, the team leader should adequately represent the team in the broader environment. (*Delegating*)

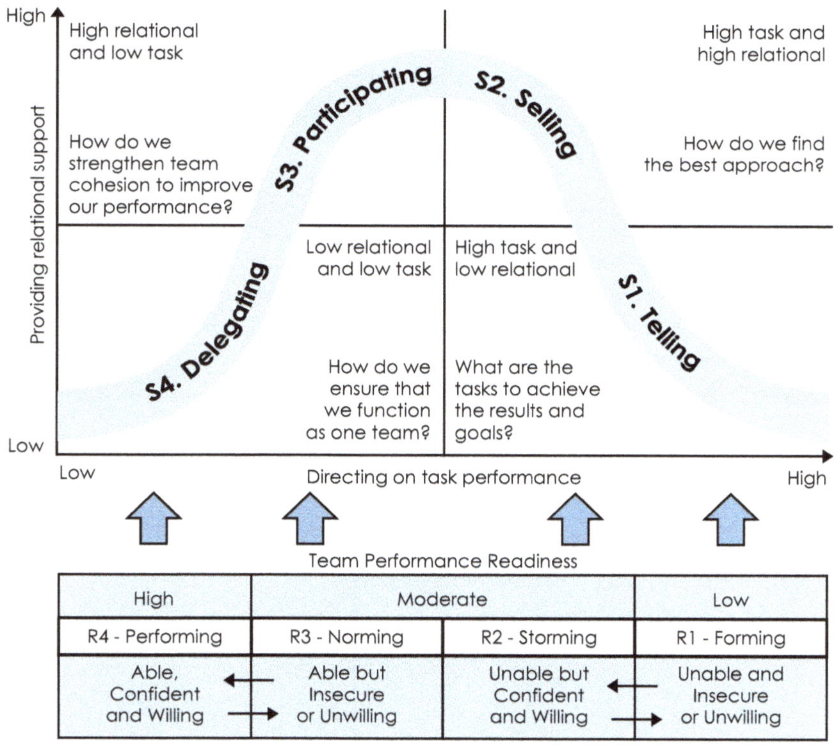

Figure 8.03.01 Team phases and situational leadership (Hersey, et al, 2008)

TEAM INTERVENTIONS AT PHASE TRANSITIONS

Interventions to smoothly lead a team from one phase to the next are important for team development. In the case of misguided interventions, there is a good chance that the team will remain in the present phase or even fall back to a previous one (see Figure 8.03.02). So, what interventions should be used to lead a team to the next phase?

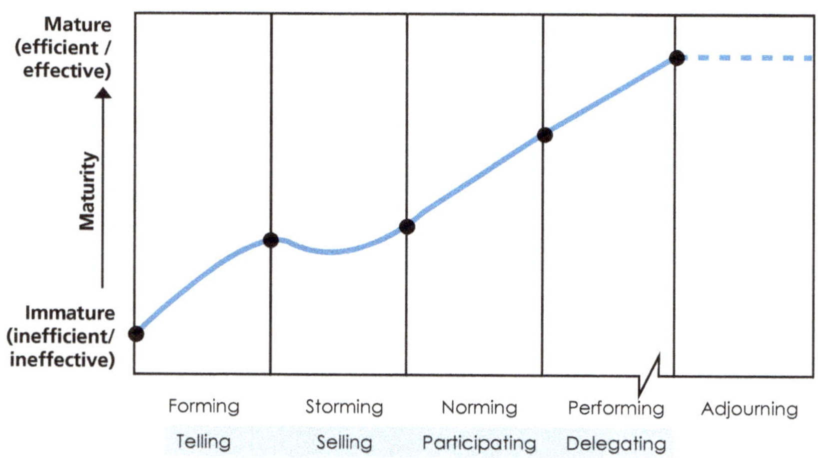

Figure 8.03.02 Phase transitions

From Forming to Storming – In the forming phase, the focus is on the goal and result-orientated teamwork. Team members are busy understanding their own tasks and how to work together. When a team gets stuck in this phase, team members remain too dependent on the leader and are not receptive to collaboration. They do not proceed beyond: 'Just tell me what to do.' or 'I do what I have to do because you told me to do so!'

When you want to lead a team to the next phase, you need to pay attention to the joint team responsibility and the interdependency between tasks. This way, team members discover the meaning of the team task. They learn to understand their task better and why, when and how they need each other to fulfil the team task. By consciously creating a 'storm' around issues that team members experience as challenging, you enable team members to discuss these issues.

The interventions in this phase are thus intended to shift the focus from the individual task to the team task and how to handle the difficulties that the team might have to deal with. Serving interventions are:

- Clarifying the project needs;
- Forming a common goal;
- Focusing on results and objectives;
- Discussing difficulties and possible contradictions;
- Stimulating collaboration.

From Storming to Norming – The willingness of team members to meet the needs of others determines the intensity of the storming phase. The art is to carefully discuss oppositions and differences of opinion so the team can further develop. If you don't bring the differences to light and don't encourage discussion, you risk the team members becoming bitter and subgroups polarising among themselves. Obviously, this will not create a close-knit team.

Many feelings may remain under the radar if this phase is not practiced correctly. These will come back to haunt you in the team development process. Therefore, paying serious attention to the team process is essential. Paying genuine attention to the team dynamics leads to a team spirit wherein team members discuss contradictions quietly and professionally, resulting in broadly supported agreements and commonly shared standards. Serving interventions are:

- Stimulate structured dialogues to discuss contradictions and differences in views;
- Encourage to share insights;
- Respect underlying feelings and create space to discuss what causes them;
- Establish clear agreements how to collaborate;
- Continue to clarify the distribution of tasks and how they are interrelated;
- Let the team discuss how to fulfil the tasks together.

From Norming to Performing – When cooperation towards results is more complicated than expected, and the agreed rules do not appear to be the solution, a team can get stuck in its development. A reaction can be that the team continues to discuss rules, procedures, and norms that should be followed. This puts pressure on the joint results to be created, resulting in the falling back into the storming phase.

To avoid the fallback, you should first reach a deep consensus on the objectives and implement the joint approach effectively. Learn together by doing. Shifting the focus to the external context is also important. How do the customer, the users and other stakeholders view the team? What can the team do better, viewed from their perspective? This creates a close-knit team towards the outside world and the will to serve that world well. When the team eventually learns to evaluate the processes it has gone through and celebrates its successes, it will perform as one. Serving interventions are:

- Achieve consensus on goals and approach;
- Work on shared responsibilities;
- Keep the focus on the external context;
- Celebrate successes together, share rewards;
- Continuously evaluate the results of the team as a whole.

Figure 8.03.03 gives an overview of the team phases and effective interventions. Most of these interventions can be viewed as team-building activities.

Stages team development	Characteristics of the team	Interventions to move to the next stage
Forming (telling)	• Uncertainty, wait and see • Who is the boss? • What do they expect from me? • Introduction / are the people friendly? • Am I able to carry out my task?	• Clarify the need of the project • Form a common goal • Focus on results and objectives • Stimulate collaboration
Storming (selling)	• Distrust, rivalry, internal conflicts • Question results and objectives • Project plan and approach are challenged • Challenge position PM, recalcitrant • Do I still want to be a member of the team?	• Stimulate discussions • Encourage to share insights • Agree on targets and performance indicators • Establish collaboration agreements
Norming (participating)	• Acceptance of one's own tasks and group standards • Start trusting each other, cooperate, solve problems together • Productivity not yet optimal	• Achieve consensus on goals and approach • Work on shared responsibilities • Keep the focus on the external context • Celebrate success together, share rewards • Continuously evaluate results of the team as a whole
Performing (delegating)	• Accept each other's roles • Important decisions are taken together • Shared goal and responsibilities • Everyone assists each other • The team achieves the required results independently, solves their own problems • High productivity	

Figure 8.03.03 Team characteristics and interventions per team phase

TEAMBUILDING

Teambuilding is an umbrella term for a series of group activities to promote cooperation in a team, all aimed at the team's growth. These can, for example, be about organising:

- An introductory game during a kick-off meeting so that the team members get to know each other and each other's qualities and motives for participating in the project.
- Group training in which you learn skills such as cooperation, discussion, negotiation, giving compliments, and feedback.
- A simulation game in which future or current cooperation is imitated and insight is

gained into the meaning of different roles.

- Periodic retrospectives to gain insight into success and failure factors of teamwork and improve working methods and collaboration.
- Periodic discussions about the progress of the work as a whole.
- Intervision sessions to thoroughly discuss issues team members have to deal with.
- Moments of relaxation, to get to know each other from a different perspective. To fulfil this need, regular coffee-corner meetings, daily lunch walks and a monthly drink are customary in many projects.
- Excursions to places where the team can see and learn from inspiring examples.

Include a definition of fun in your team charter. It helps to set borders and create space for moments of relaxation. Teambuilding is essential during the entire project lifecycle. Only the form and content may differ depending on the team development and project phase. Even if a project team has been together for a long time, the team may be in the forming or storming phase due to changes in the team or undermining behaviour. You, therefore, need to keep a close eye on where the team is in its development. Resistance is always an issue that has to be discussed.

DEALING WITH RESISTANCE

Every project faces resistance, both from within and outside the project. Resistance can be caused by a lack of understanding, differences of opinion, values , norms, interests, et cetera. In itself, this is not wrong. A critical attitude means that people are involved in the issue one is trying to find a solution for. In any case, critical behaviour or resistance should not be ignored. Making critical behaviour and resistance negotiable often also leads to better solutions and collaboration.

When doing this, though, you should always stay true to yourself. If you start playing a role, people will see through that sooner or later, and you will be even worse off. That is why it is vital to approach resistance from within when working towards the other person.

Working from within:

- *Work from your own role* – Realise that you need other people's help to do your job. If someone's resistance affects your role, they should understand this and know what you need them to do and why. This will provide a framework for the conversation.
- *Be clear about your limits and choices* – This will ensure that others do not take advantage of you. It should be clear why you face limitations so the other individual understands your choices. This also makes it possible to discuss them.
- *Be reliable in your actions* – Be consistent, transparent, consequent and predictable.
- *Make sincere contact* – First contact, then contract. Standing up for yourself without making genuine contact first makes you come across as only being concerned with yourself and your veracity from your perspective. With a question such as 'Can I ask you to ponder on an issue with me that I find difficult?', you create a breeding ground to work on solutions together.
- *Adjust your behaviour and remain flexible* – People differ from each other.

Working towards the other:

- *Observe* – Carefully state what you literally see and hear. Don't judge. Mention only the visible facts. This provides a clear context.
- *Present* – Briefly explain what you think about these facts and how and why they affect your emotions and concerns.
- *Connect* – Ask what the other individual means by using words and what triggers their emotions. Show respect and ensure you fully understand the cause of the other person's resistance.
- *Put things in motion* – From this point on, discuss what motivates and the options for removing the resistance.

ADVANCED

TEAM COMPOSITION (ADVANCED)

In teamwork, team members have multiple responsibilities. They are responsible for their own efforts and expertise and the team's efforts as a whole. They should also coordinate their efforts with team members who realise the work. Finally, team members sometimes also have to represent their organisational unit and might be the ones who need to communicate with their backers.

When assembling a team, you should ensure that the team and the individual team members can bear this broad responsibility. When assembling the team, you should take into account the following:

- The size and complexity of the task;
- The team's role within the whole of the organisation;
- The necessary professional knowledge and experience;
- The availability and motivation of individual team members;
- The ability to collaborate;
- The representation of the various stakeholders.

The success of the teams ultimately depends on the fulfilment of several factors. Figure 8.03.04 illustrates the aspects of effective teamwork. On the one hand, they focus on the task and the other, on collaboration. Awareness of these two sides of teamwork is essential for building an effective team. Without collaboration, there is no joint result. Without focusing on a joint result, there is no need for collaboration. Both aspects require full attention.

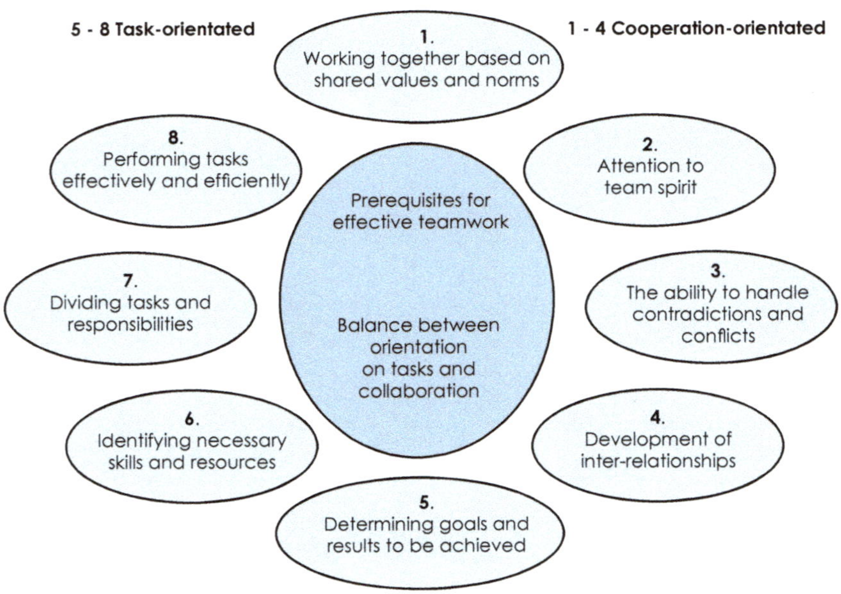

Figure 8.03.04 Factors that enhance teamwork

Collaboration-orientated aspects

Teamwork is all about working together towards agreed results and goals. For professional collaboration, you need the following:

Shared values and norms – By agreeing on core values, a team creates a basis for holding each other to account. For example, an agreed core value is a 'simultaneous representation of interests.' You can ask, 'Does your decision and or action serve the interests of all stakeholders?' Core values define the principles underlying collaboration.

Norms are concrete agreements about collaboration and how the work should be performed. They may be laid down in procedures and are meant to be followed up entirely. For example, a norm in a team could be that when your work for the other individual is completed, you consult with them to ask whether the work (1) complies with the agreements you made beforehand and (2) whether they can proceed. Adhering to these guidelines prevents the result from being thrown over the wall. The professional application of such rules prevents negative emotions from escalating within the team and promotes team spirit.

Team spirit – Getting to know each other well often does wonders for team spirit. You can promote this togetherness in various ways. Think of company visits, team outings, fixed break rituals, workshops aimed at collaboration and getting to know each other, and so on. Such actions strengthen mutual respect and thus contribute to team building.

Dealing with contradictions and conflicts – Not everyone thinks and acts similarly. Causes may lie in differences of vision; analysis of the situation; approach to content questions; personality; experiences with and judgements about each other, et cetera. How the team discusses these contradictions determines its ability to learn. Insufficient elaboration of these contradictions lifts the conflicts to a higher level. Emotions then come into play, and a process-based approach is needed to resolve the conflicts and to flourish as a team.

Development of interpersonal relationships – People each have their own character traits. This should not compromise our ability to work together. However, it is common for feelings of inferiority or superiority to emerge among team members, leading some to consider themselves less or more important than others. Having a deeper knowledge of yourself helps to break through such considerations and to understand that each contribution is valuable for the collective team's performance. Such insights keep people away from limiting convictions and strengthen their ability to stay connected and collaborate effectively.

Harmonising mutual role perceptions and acting role-compliantly also strengthen mutual relationships. Project management methods are beneficial in supporting and defining the content of roles and help a project team to understand these properly. This enhances the collaboration within and around the project.

Goal- and task- orientated team factors

To strengthen a team so they can focus on goals and results, it is necessary to pay attention to the following:

Goals and results – A team gains focus by concentrating on a concrete result and the goals that can be achieved with this result. For project teams, the project result is leading in their joint work. It is the value they deliver to the customer's organisation and, thus, the foundation on which the team is built. Creating project results motivates most people because making new products to achieve customers' goals is challenging. The fact that the personal task contributes to valuable customer goals ensures that many team members experience their work as motivating.

Skills and resources – The team's work determines the skills and resources you need. You can work on skills development in various ways, such as training, on-the-job coaching, peer reviews, introduction procedures for new team members, et cetera. Resources should be sought in and around the organisation. Are the right tools and instruments available to do the job efficiently and effectively? Does a project team member get enough time from their department to do their project work? Teamwork is negatively affected if the right resources are not available.

Dividing tasks and responsibilities – It should be clear to everyone what their task is and when it should be done. However, rotating tasks leads to an enrichment of these tasks. The division of work also includes collaboration in its performance so that the team stays focused on the joint result and team members do not get bogged down in the details or complexity of their own tasks. Collaboration can be organised hierarchically but also through self-management

Effective task approach – While performing a task, details are often essential. Delivering and receiving each other's work requires careful communication about the specifications of the work. By consciously performing the task according to the specifications, you can improve your personal contributions to the team. Furthermore, it is fine if people can choose their own performance method, which often enhances their motivation. However, by discussing the preferred manner of performance, the team can improve its collective skills.

The development of effective teamwork can be seen and heard in the behaviour and words of the team members. Figure 8.03.05 shows the behavioural characteristics of effective and stalled teams.

Effective teams	**Stalled team**
• Members work together for clear results	• Everyone works in isolation
• Trust and respect prevail	• Distrust and division prevail
• Different feelings exist side by side	• Resistance is experienced mutually
• Conflicts are made explicit	• The adage: seeing is believing
• People dare to share their stories	• Caution is the order of the day
• Team members act from their own strengths	• Team members act reactively
• Team members dare to be themselves	• Team members keep the façade high
• Leadership emerges	• It is expected of the leader
• Decision-making is an open process	• Decision-making follows formal lines
• The division of roles and tasks is flexible	• The division of tasks and roles is rigid
• The team collaborates	• The hierarchy coordinates

Figure 8.03.05 Effective and ineffective behaviour in teams

Recognising these behavioural factors is essential while developing teamwork. The team's development phase can be deduced from it. Ultimately, the team should develop into a mature entity in which collaboration and task orientation go hand in hand. Creating a project culture is an important competence for project managers.

DEVELOPING AN EFFECTIVE PROJECT CULTURE (ADVANCED)

Project culture can be defined as the project team's shared norms, beliefs, values, and assumption. This requires your full attention right from the start. If you falter, people will develop their own ways of working, harming the development of an effective project culture. Understand that creating project work is a shared task that requires a shared project culture to collaborate efficiently and effectively.

It is first and foremost important that the project team experiences the priority and importance of the project to the organisation. A temporary team needs to be grounded in their work and feel that together they are essential to delivering an output that is of value to the sponsoring organisation. The official decision to start the project, granted by an external authority, gives the project team its own status. By carefully integrating this mandate into the project work, you create a strong foundation for building the project culture you want.

Secondly, you need to answer the question: 'How do we function as a team within the governance set by the permanent organisation?' Developing a project culture means that the team agrees on translating the governance into their project work. In this, also the culture and values of the individual team members come into play: 'How do we position the project from a strategic point of view?'; 'How do we involve key stakeholders?'; 'How do we apply the chosen project methodology?'; 'How do we create a focus on delivering high-quality work on time and budget?'; 'How do we deal with change?'; and so on.

By aligning the team with the answers and the 'why' behind them, the team creates a value base for the project work to be done. If the team flexibly and consciously follows the procedures resulting from these answers, a strong project culture will result.

Then, it becomes important to agree with the team on how to collaborate professionally between team members. For example: try to do your utmost to attend the agreed meetings and you share daily/weekly progress. When you agree on work to be done by one of the other team members, always let a colleague review the work first before you share it with others, and so on.

By agreeing to this upfront, you can return to the external mandate provided, the agreed procedures within the applicable governance, and the agreed ways to collaborate when the work is done differently. By being open and respectful, you may develop an efficient and effective team culture that also considers the different cultures and values of those involved. Team-building exercises are also an important tool to apply. And don't hesitate to put project culture regularly on the agenda of the project team meetings. Finally, always realise that each team member fulfils specific team roles to develop a team into a mature whole within a healthy project culture.

TEAM ROLES (ADVANCED)

Some teams are more successful than others. This success appears to depend heavily on the composition of the team and the behaviour, contribution and interrelationship of the different team members towards each other.

Dr Meredith Belbin studied teamwork for many years and observed that team members tend to adopt different 'team roles'. In his book Team *Roles at Work* (Belbin, 2017), he defines a team role as '*a tendency to behave, contribute and interrelate with others in a particular way*'. He identified nine team roles that underpin team success. Each team role has its value to the team process. These roles are:

Chairman/Coordinator

- *Role in the team* – The Coordinator or Chairman sets the agenda for the team. They use procedures and conversation techniques to ensure that team members can express what is important to them. They summarise and reflect on the process followed. This assures support for the decisions to be made.
- *Core beliefs* – A good process brings calm to the team.
- *Strengths* – Ability to command respect and generate enthusiasm; a sense of timing and balance; good communication skills, such as listening, summarising and connecting.
- *Challenges* – Developing flexibility towards new insights and questions; giving space to creativity.

Resource Investigator

- *Role in the team* – The Resource Investigator is the one who searches outside the team for information, ideas and interesting developments. They are externally focused and have a keen eye for new ideas and their applicability. When innovation is needed, the Resource Investigator takes the lead and points out the opportunities available to the team. Their insight, outward-looking attitude and input of useful and stimulating ideas keep the team moving forward. Group thinking is not likely to occur with a Resource Investigator on the team.
- *Core beliefs* – Improvements and innovations are there for the taking; learning pays off.
- *Strengths* – Extraverted personality; inquisitive mind; entrepreneurial; willingness to see opportunities in anything new.
- *Challenges* – Learning to temper over-enthusiasm; paying attention to aftercare and follow-up activities; staying focused.

Team Worker

- *Role in the team* – The Team Worker is sensitive to the atmosphere and relationships in the team. A Team Worker knows what each member needs and what bothers them. They are loyal to the team, which does not mean they cannot take sides when necessary. The Team Worker supports colleagues and uses others' ideas and input positively.
- *Core beliefs* – We are in this world to care for each other.
- *Strengths* – Empathetic; friendly; good listener; understanding; connecting; loyal, and above all, supportive.
- *Challenges* – Dare to confront and make clear decisions at critical moments.

Implementer

- *Role in the team* – The Implementer is about acting effectively and efficiently. Their main contribution is to convert team plans into operational tasks. They ensure that decisions and strategies are translated into concrete work plans. The Implementer needs these plans to keep an overview and do what they have been told to do. They know better than anyone else what has been decided and how the tasks have been distributed.
- *Core beliefs* – Just do your job; hard work never killed anyone.
- *Strengths* – Controlled and disciplined; persistent; realistic; practical; effective; systematic and structured based on common sense.
- *Challenges* – Being open to others, exploring and substantiating new possibilities or ideas.

Shaper

- *Role in the team* – The main role of the Shaper in a team is to give direction to the team's efforts. They look for certain discussion patterns and combine visions, ideas, goals and practical considerations into a manageable whole. Achieving results and goals gives the Shaper satisfaction. They head straight for their goal. This is why the Shaper is sometimes experienced as restless. However, most people love their drive.
- *Core beliefs* – Teamwork is performance; I value the colleague who values me.
- *Strengths* – Driven; visionary; action-orientated; entrepreneurial.
- *Challenges* – Learn to slow down and listen to summarise and ask questions; give space to others; be diplomatic.

Finisher/Completer

- *Role in the team* – The Finisher makes sure things are performed correctly. They never do things half-heartedly. The agreed quality is delivered. They check everything perfectly and are confident that no detail has been overlooked. Sometimes the Finisher is too precise and is seen by others as obsessive.
- *Core beliefs* – The work is finished when completed; it is all about the finishing touch.
- *Strengths* – Conscientious; accurate; a sense of detail; ability to finish; disciplined and planned.
- *Challenges* – Working from tolerance without giving up the natural desire for perfection; being confident; skilful delegation.

Monitor/Evaluator

- *Role in the team* – Having a Monitor in the team is valuable. The Monitor reaches informed decisions based on information they peruse, process and evaluate. They substantiate their statements. Monitors have a keen eye for proper analysis and assessment. This keeps the team on its toes. The Monitor does not readily show their enthusiasm, but their objectivity is often highly appreciated. If the Monitor becomes too critical, it can negatively affect the team's atmosphere and enthusiasm.
- *Core beliefs* – Risks require action. Things can always go wrong.
- *Strengths* – Ability to analyse critically and objectively; to see through the complexity of proposals.
- *Challenges* – Remaining constructive and giving space to others; creating a breeding ground for own insights; acting and communicating more tactfully.

Plant/Idea Generator

- *Role in the team* – New solutions and possibilities to persistent problems come through the Plant. As a result, the team does not get stuck. The Plant comes up with original ideas and suggestions. They have a high level of imagination and intelligence. The Plant is inspiring because of their original ideas and sharp eye for alternatives, likes to stand out and is sometimes prone to showy behaviour. The Plant also tends to separate itself from the team and choose its own solutions.
- *Core beliefs* – I see what no one else sees; work should inspire; work is art.
- *Strengths* – High intelligence; independent in their opinions; imaginative; inspiring; creative.
- *Challenges* – Making creativity practical, remaining realistic and daring to put their own ideas into perspective, structuring the wealth of ideas for communication with others.

Specialist

- *Role in the team* – Assumes that everyone will follow the Specialist's lead and performs the assigned role competently. Then, every team member does precisely what needs to be done. That is the power of the Specialist. They know what to do and act accordingly based on professional standards. In their own field, the Specialist is a source of inexhaustible knowledge. Often, Specialists are able and willing to contribute to developing new talent in their field. In doing so, they propagate their profession and craftsmanship.
- *Core beliefs* – I love my work; I am a master in my field of expertise.
- *Strengths* – Skilled, knowledgeable, dedicated.
- *Challenges* – Staying out of defensive patterns. Increasing sensitivity in the working environment. Showing interest in the underlying needs of others and broadening communication skills.

Team composition

According to Belbin, a team member can fulfil several team roles as long as the team roles are complementary and do not compete. Beware of a high proportion of the same roles in the team. A 'group resonance' can then develop, causing people to agree with each other and develop blind spots quickly. Effective team members pay attention to their own roles and invite others to complement them. The project manager should wisely lead by example in this respect.

To achieve complementary roles, team members may agree to let someone fulfil a role that differs from their 'ideal' one. A good briefing is then needed to understand the nature and content of this role. Team members can also fill in a missing role together by asking how a Monitor would assess this situation or what they would do at the moment if they had a Team Worker in their midst.

Project types and team composition, according to Belbin

Belbin distinguishes four types of projects. For each particular project, certain specific team roles should be represented. In addition, it is always valuable to have a Coordinator and Team Worker on board. Keeping an overview and a good atmosphere is vital for any project team. Belbin distinguishes between:

People-orientated projects – These projects focus on the connection between people and the project output. For example, a project that focuses on redesigning a work process. In these projects, the Coordinator ensures that the objectives and intended direction are maintained and that any contradictions between parties are bridged. The Team worker ensures that team members release tensions and enjoy the collaborative process towards the project result.

Implementation-orientated projects – These projects involve delivering a concrete result, such as a building or refurbishing a factory hall. The Implementer focuses on the planned and structured completion of the project. The Shaper provides input for practical ideas. Both won't hesitate to intervene if the project threatens to stall.

Innovative projects – These projects involve the realisation of an innovation and or novelty, such as projects to establish a new corporate image or explore the possibilities of using renewable energy sources. The Plant comes up with original ideas. The Source Investigator assesses their potential and compares them with environmental developments. The Coordinator provides direction and overview so that ideas do not get lost in the abundance of creativity.

Control-orientated projects – These projects involve flawless delivery of products – for example, redesigning a business application. The Monitor provides a considered analysis of the situation, reviewing all risks and developing a sound plan. The Finisher ensures the accurate, detailed and precise performance of that plan.

GROUP THINKING (ADVANCED)

Intensive teamwork can lead to a team becoming isolated from its environment. Group thinking can occur in these situations. Group thinking is the symptom of when a team is too internally focused on its functioning and ignores environmental signals to be effective.

Symptoms – Group thinking can be recognised by how team members distance themselves from their environment. In their actions and thinking, their own team is entirely central. They consider the environment irrelevant to their work and their team indispensable. They feel that the environment should adapt to them! When you try to change the team and the processes within, you will hear things such as 'It doesn't work in the way you suggest; we always did it this way, and it pays off; we don't have time for new things; we will never do that.', et cetera.

Causes – An important cause is the freedom given and taken to carry out their own task independently for an extended period. The work has become a fixed routine for the team members in which they feel comfortable. An inward-looking attitude almost automatically arises if regular attention to the changing environment is not included in the team process. The fixed routine becomes an ingrained, immutable habit.

Consequences – The team becomes inaccessible to its surroundings and ends up isolated. This is detrimental to the well-being of the team and its environment, as well as to the collaboration with other teams and the quality of the results to be delivered together.

Preventing – Group thinking can be prevented by carefully involving the teams early on in opinion-forming and decision-making discussions about changes, the reasons for these changes, and the consequences for the team's tasks. It is an excellent idea to organise this process in a way that transcends the team so that it experiences being part of the bigger picture. You can strengthen this process by organising workshops with the team. During these workshops, you discuss the meaning of necessary changes within the team and practice new working methods. In this way, the team can adapt to perform tasks differently.

Ending – Group thinking can be ended by changing the team's composition and making decisions about the team's work outside the team.

DEALING WITH RESISTANCE (ADVANCED)

Resistance within teams can be differentiated according to different causes and forms of how the resistance manifests itself (see Figure 8.03.06). By recognising these, you can deal with them more effectively.

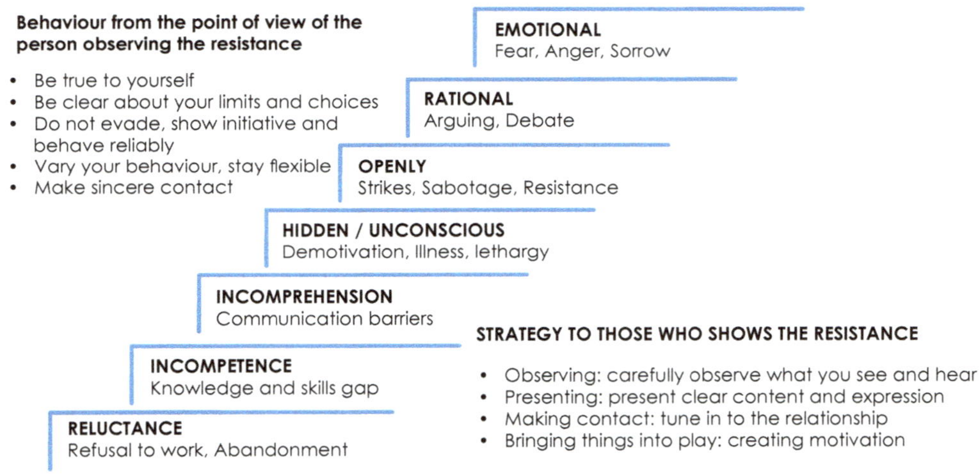

Figure 8.03.06 Forms of resistance and basic intervention strategies

Dealing with reluctance – There is often a meaningful story behind the reluctance. By finding that meaning and including it in the project approach, you can turn the reluctance into a more proactive and motivated attitude. Another way is to simply leave the reluctant team member alone for a while and trust in the positive impact of the teamwork and the project result.

Dealing with incompetence – Incompetence evokes feelings of uncertainty in people. Can I do the job? Incompetence can turn into reluctance if you overlook these feelings or play down the uncertainty. The best method to deal with incompetence is to let people experience that they can carry out the assigned tasks. To that end, make the steps leading to the result smaller, and coach, guide, and support them to do the work properly.

Dealing with comprehension – Team members often do not immediately understand or see through the meaning of an intended change. Persuasion can lead to degenerating into yes/no games. Providing more information and or engaging them in the solutions may help create understanding. Strengthening matching attitudes, inner beliefs, and feelings may also be effective. As a result, users experience a more intrinsic connection with the project result and the goals to be realised.

Dealing with hidden resistance – It is difficult when people hide their feelings of resistance. Show an overall interest in everyone. If you feel that something is not right, discuss it. 'How are you doing? Do you still feel happy with the project? What makes working on this project difficult for you at the moment?' At the point that people literally withdraw, showing genuine interest in the situation is essential. In case of illness, be attentive. In case of absence, do not judge but enter into a conversation, 'I missed you yesterday. Too bad, what kept you busy?' The answers allow you to understand the resistance and tailor your approach accordingly.

Dealing with open resistance – Don't hesitate to pick up on it. Resistance happens, and some people are not afraid to show it. It will often grow and negatively affect the situation, or become invisible to the naked eye if ignored or trivialised. It is more effective to go along with it in the first instance, 'Why are you so opposed to the project or the project approach? What would you like to change? Which ideas need to be improved?' When the open resistance continues, an open form of unwillingness arises. The key is to isolate their reluctance and disconnect them from the project. This may very well mean saying goodbye to the employee within the project so that you can focus your energy on the +20% group.

Dealing with rational resistance – Rational resistance stems from people's beliefs about situations. People judge the situation as wrong and use arguments to say that it can never amount to anything. In such cases, it is best to use dialogue sessions. Most importantly parties experience that they have your full attention. In addition, you should include every available perspective. Dialogue sessions can be worked out in workshops.

Dealing with emotional resistance – Fear, anger, and sadness are the three main drivers of emotional resistance. Recognising and acknowledging these emotions creates space to discuss them. This discussion is necessary because suppressed emotions surface sooner or later and can significantly disrupt constructive processes at those moments. Empathy is essential in reducing such emotions. Only then can you ask sincere questions like, 'I see and hear that you are very angry/disappointed? It affects me to the extent that it worries me and makes me feel uncertain. Can you explain to me what exactly causes this anger/disappointment? What can I do for you in this regard?' By providing enough space, the resistance becomes visible, and only then can possible solutions be discussed.

The value of 'difficult people' in projects

Resistance is often associated with the words, 'Don't be so difficult!' However, in many situations, resistance is useful. It reveals issues that need attention. Making these issues visible gives insight into how things are done and experienced. Therein lies room for improvement. Addressing resistance creates meaningful conversations about subjects that need to be discussed. Teams with the skill to engage in such discussions will deepen their collaboration and often achieve better results.

MANAGING VIRTUAL TEAMS (ADVANCED)

Virtual teams are teams where members perform their personal group tasks from different locations, sometimes even from other countries or time zones (see Figure 8.03.07). In virtual teams, it is necessary to pay attention to the following:

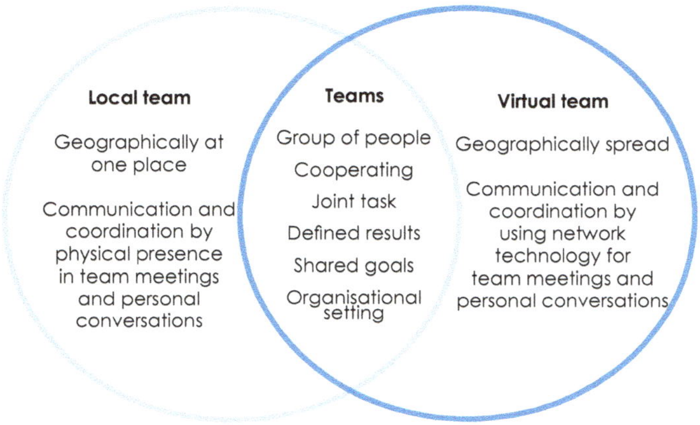

Figure 8.03.07 Virtual versus local teams

Clear task descriptions – Working remotely makes it difficult to refine task descriptions during work. It is also more difficult to occasionally give simple feedback on team members' results. That is why it is essential to formulate clear task descriptions beforehand and discuss them thoroughly with all involved.

Effective understanding and use of technology – Use a shared digital workspace. Within that virtual workspace, team members can share documents and track progress. This requires the availability of technology and the ability of all team members to make good use of it. They should feel safe and confident. Working with new technology and teamwork-sharing platforms requires specific skills. Training on how to work with the latest technology boosts team members' confidence.

Team members can work independently and are self-supporting – Much more than in traditional teams, team members in virtual teams should be able to work independently and be self-supporting. Asking for help remotely is much more complex than asking your neighbour, especially if there is also a significant time difference between geographical locations. Team members have to solve all kinds of practical problems independently. The deployment of easy-to-use tools on the virtual network increases the professionalism of teamwork. Organising remote support does this too.

Remote progress monitoring – Managing virtual teams while 'on the move' is practically impossible. Progress reports, therefore, have to be set up formally. Logging in for a short call is not that easy. It is, therefore, better to strictly regulate progress reporting so that communication on progress becomes a regular, predictable habit. This also strengthens mutual trust. It prevents team members from letting their individual contributions lapse, knowing there are fixed moments when realised work and problems are discussed within the team.

Most virtual systems today have tools that support the team in visualising planned and distributed tasks. This supports effective monitoring of progress by the whole team. On the other hand, this can be experienced as an intensive social control. Therefore, scheduling enough time for sharing problems is important so everyone understands why specific tasks are complex and overrun.

Understanding cultural differences – How people interact differs per country and company. Focusing on these cultural differences during training sessions and physical meetings is good. This conscious attention strengthens mutual understanding and ensures team members gain insight into each other's customs. During workshop sessions, team members can exchange what they experience as practical, successful and suitable. Together they can make concrete behavioural agreements that consciously consider cultural differences and preferences. The basis of these agreements will always have to be mutual respect and, at the same time, clearly express that the agreements are intended to achieve a meaningful project together. The joint work and its environmental significance should be clear and serve as a guide and inspiration for all team members.

With only one remote location, it is also possible to exchange team members so that one member from one location is always present at the other. This makes communication much easier. In that case, alternate regularly. For a few weeks, one of their team members will be on your site, and then someone from your team will be on their site.

Obstacles come in many shapes and sizes. Some tips to prevent them:

- Establish a clear, shared vision of what the team should deliver and what the organisation wants to achieve with that result;
- Appoint a facilitator whose primary responsibility is facilitating communication and collaboration between team members;
- Provide good technical support so that technical problems can be solved quickly;
- Organise regular contact moments between the different locations;
- Provide a shared platform for working together and storing all files.

You should eliminate any problems hampering the work as quickly as possible. Nothing is more demotivating for a virtual team than to experience that nothing is done to remove obstacles.

8.04 RESOURCEFULNESS

PURPOSE

The purpose of this chapter is to enable the individual to effectively handle uncertainty, problems, changes, limitations and stressful situations by systematically and continuously searching for new, better, and more effective approaches and or solutions.

LEARNING OBJECTIVES

- Thinking methods;
- Analytic problem-solving;
- Creative problem-solving;
- Methods of decision-making;
- Analytic and creative problem-solving techniques;
- Problem-solving in standardised processes (advanced);
- Additional divergent creativity techniques (advanced);
- Converging creativity techniques (advanced);
- Decision-making procedure (advanced);
- Innovation processes and techniques (advanced);
- Effective realisation of organisational innovation (advanced).

DEFINITIONS

Analytic problem solving: A structured and methodical approach to solve a particular problem or issue.

Creative problem-solving: A problem-solving approach using creative techniques in order to come up with new and original solutions to a particular problem or issue.

INTRODUCTION

Projects are initiated to solve problems or exploit opportunities. In addition, problems and opportunities also often arise during the implementation of the project itself. Projects constantly seek new, better and more effective approaches and solutions. Solving problems and exploiting opportunities is, therefore, an important competence in projects.

THINKING METHODS

There are different ways to generate ideas, solve problems and make decisions. Which one you use depends on the situation and your own preference. It can be useful to change approaches if a chosen approach does not produce the desired results. Several methods can be combined.

In the first section, we look in particular at analytical and creative problem-solving approaches and decision-making methods. In the advanced section, we look at problem-solving in a standardised process, describe some additional problem-solving techniques, and a decision-making procedure. Finally, we discuss techniques commonly used in innovative projects and how organisational innovations can be realised.

Convergent and divergent thinking are discussed as part of the creative problem-solving approach. Systems thinking and lateral thinking are discussed as advanced techniques. Some other methods are:

Strategic thinking – Strategic thinking is a cognitive process that analyses complex situations and considers long-term implications. It focuses on developing long-term positions, goals, and approaches to accomplish the overall mission and vision of individuals, organisations and even countries. It includes environmental analysis, long-term perspective, adaptability, risk assessment, resource allocation, possible collaborations and continuous learning. It plays an important role in anticipating and navigating long-term challenges, seizing opportunities and determining direction and path within the overarching vision.

Conceptual thinking – Conceptual thinking is the ability to see and experience interrelationships in many abstractions and facts and to create a meaningful picture or a coherent concept from them. These images of the future often serve as powerful metaphors, providing a horizon point towards which a team can move. Nelson Mandela expressed a powerful conceptual vision, stating: *Education is the most powerful weapon that can change the world.* A completely different example of conceptual thinking is spatial planning. Such high-level plans show at a glance what is possible for parties who want to realise beautiful projects in that space.

Abstraction thinking – Abstract thinking is a cognitive process in which complex ideas or concepts are simplified by focusing on essential characteristics. It enables us to understand complex ideas, solve problems and communicate effectively. Abstract thinking is going back to the essence of the problem and the reasons behind it and developing new ideas and concepts from there. Within abstract thinking, we like to use symbols to understand and communicate underlying problems and present ideas and solutions.

Synergy and holistic thinking – Synergy and holistic thinking are closely linked. Synergy emphasises that the combined strength of people is more than the total strength achieved by each individual. Holistic thinking is a way of thinking that sees the parts as inseparable from the whole. Synergistic thinking focuses on finding solutions through cooperation, integration and interconnectedness. Holistic thinking looks at the bigger picture rather than just individual elements. Synergistic and holistic thinking focus on collaboration, breaking silos and creating value through combined efforts. It focuses on the root cause, continuous improvement and long-term effects. It lends itself to flexibility, with a tolerance for contradictions and paradoxes. Keep an open mind, an open heart and an open will. See what is actually happening. Suspend your judgement.

Design thinking – Design thinking is an approach that puts users' needs and preferences at the heart of the design process. It starts by observing and interacting directly with users, conducting interviews and other research methods to understand their experiences and perspectives in order to arrive at a clear and focused problem statement that guides the rest of the design process. A final solution is then developed through creative processes and prototyping. By combining a user-centred approach and creativity, design thinking makes it possible to develop innovative, relevant and user-friendly solutions to various challenges.

ANALYTIC PROBLEM-SOLVING

Analytical problem-solving is a structured and methodical approach to tackling complex problems and challenges. This is necessary to avoid looking only at the symptoms and not the underlying causes and to avoid jumping to conclusions. Therefore, a structured approach in which the individual phases are completed in their entirety is important.

Problem identification – First of all; what is the problem? This phase describes the current and desired situation and the standards used by the interest groups.

Data collection – Next, we can look at the relevant data. What happened when, where, why and by whom. What was the sequence of events? When did it first happen? What were the first signs, et cetera? This can be done by collecting existing data from research, interviews, et cetera.

Analyse – Here, the focus is on analysing the available information. This can be done through statistical analysis, Pareto analysis, and fishbone analysis, as well as by using matrixes, decomposition, and analysing trends over time.

Identify root causes – After analysis, we know where the problem is, but not yet what causes it; 'Most tests fail at the beginning of the week, but why?' This may involve using literature and one or more experts, possibly in a Delphi setting. This phase can end by restating the problem definition, preferably in a solution-orientated question statement.

Generate possible solutions – Beware of jumping to conclusions. Take time to generate multiple solutions first. This can be done analytically and creatively, and every conceivable manner in between.

Evaluate solutions – This includes selecting the most promising ideas, deepening these solutions and finally evaluating the best options. This can include SWOT analysis and multi-criteria analysis.

Decision-making – Take this as a separate step. Usually, the final decision is also made by someone not involved in the problem-solving process on a daily basis.

Planning implementation – Work out the chosen solution in a detailed plan and submit it to the decision authority for final approval. Based on the elaboration, adjustments may be needed.

Test and refine – Implement the solution, where possible, in a constrained environment that allows for refinement.

Implement and continuously improve – Eventually, full implementation of the solution can take place. Track performance and effects. Use the results and feedback for continuous improvement.

CREATIVE PROBLEM-SOLVING

Creative problem-solving is an approach to solving problems using creative techniques to generate new and original solutions to the formulated issues. The essence of such an approach is not to formulate several possible alternatives based on an extensive problem analysis but first to generate as many ideas as possible and, only then, based on analysis, to see if any of them are promising.

Creative problem-solving is usually conducted by a team in a workshop setting. It is wise to have an independent facilitator head such a session. Someone who can lead the process in such a way that everyone feels free to speak and contribute ideas. A creative workshop session consists of an analysis, divergence, convergence and decision phase. It is a specific workshop approach (see Chapter 7.03 Personal Communication).

Analysis phase

In the analysis phase, you define the question. You collect relevant information and determine the workshop's result and what you want to achieve with it. In this phase, it is also essential to determine who owns the problem. You should also determine whether the problem suits a creative approach and who you will involve in the creative process. Suitable creative problems can always be defined as solution-orientated questions. Finally, you plan the workshop and invite the participants in coordination with the problem owner.

The problem owner is the individual who wants and needs the result of the workshop. A good problem owner is:

- Involved – Is affected by the problem itself;
- Willing – Actively supports the dissemination of good ideas;
- Authorised – Can and may take decisions;
- Competent: – Can actually initiate the solution of the problem.

Divergent phase

The divergent phase is the 1st phase of the workshop and focuses on creating as many ideas as possible. The facilitator should ensure that all participants feel safe to make this possible. This requires agreeing on some ground rules from the very beginning. The most important ground rules for a creative session are:

- Postpone judgment. Any criticism has a paralysing effect.
- Be open internally but guarantee privacy to third parties.
- Go along with others' ideas.
- No hierarchy or arrogance. The boss's idea is no better than that of the youngest servant.
- Focus on quantity; quality comes later.
- Bold ideas are welcome. It may be the basis for the final brilliant solution.
- Ideas belong to the group. One person's idea stems from another's.
- Challenge the thinking and let go.

The team often needs to warm up before the session starts. How varies from team to team. You can have an association exercise or ask the team members to choose from pictures and say something about them. There are as many possibilities as there are teams. Then the actual session starts.

Research shows that teams generate the most ideas when participants write down their thoughts for a few minutes, each for themselves. During this individual time, each person independently focuses on the creative question. This way, they are not distracted by the others and the personal perspective of each individual is included in the session. It is best to use moderation cards. When everyone is ready, ask them to present their ideas and post them on a large whiteboard, or large sheet of brown paper. A central point where all ideas are collected is handy because it gives everyone an overview of which and how many ideas have been generated. In addition, other people's ideas help generate new ones. After all, the divergent phase is all about generating as many ideas as possible.

To increase the number of ideas, a brainstorming session can be organised. You can encourage participants to develop more ideas using analogies, mind-mapping and other divergent creativity techniques.

Convergent phase

This phase is about sensing which ideas have the most potential and then developing these ideas into promising concepts for the final selection of the best ideas for decision.

Organising – The central question is: what do you choose, and how? Before making a choice, however, the creative team should first refocus on the starting question it was based on. The team may have lost focus on the goal because of the freedom of thought in the divergence phase. Is the starting question still relevant, even with the new insights gained? Are we still as motivated? Are the criteria still the same? Next, the 3-5 most promising ideas are selected. This can be done by giving each participant a number of stickers they can use to indicate their preference. If no clear group preference ensues, a 2nd round can be held at group level.

Developing – After this initial selection, the creative team develops the selected ideas into realistic concepts. You can do this with the help of mood boards, mirror interviews, et cetera.

Selecting – Finally, the best concepts should be selected. You can do this by multi-criteria analyses, SWOT analysis, et cetera.

Following this, it can be forwarded to the problem owner for a decision.

METHODS OF DECISION-MAKING

Lastly, a decision has to be made as to which idea will be implemented or presented to the decision-making body, such as the project board. This is not a decision to be taken lightly. There are several ways you/they can make the final decision. You might consider the following options:

Majority – Majority decision-making means that a group decides based on the most counted votes: 50% + 1, or even with a two-thirds majority. The risk with this form is that the minority no longer feels heard and understood. This can lead to polarization and resistance. Power should consider the powerless.

Compromise – This is a decision made by those involved based on differing views. They have sought a middle ground that they can live with. Such a decision leads to reasonable support, but usually, the time taken is often too short. The result is mostly not the ideal solution, and not all parties will be satisfied.

Consensus – This decision is reached actively and collaboratively by the parties involved. You organise a decision-making process in which interested parties can actively participate. Through dialogue and discussion of contentious issues, an acceptable result is agreed upon, partly based on criteria. This decision provides a large support base but is usually time-consuming.

Delegation – In delegation, the power to make decisions is transferred to one or more persons. Delegation is used when authorised stakeholders do not have the time or expertise to make and implement decisions carefully. This power is then delegated. Usually, conditions are attached to this delegated power, and the formal decision-makers retain the right to veto or control.

Unanimity – Unanimity means 'without a difference of opinion', i.e., everyone should agree. These decisions usually take a long time due to lengthy discussions before a solution is reached to which all parties can agree. Decisions that have to be taken based on unanimity are, for example, decisions on increasing the number of Member States of the European Union. It forces the parties to consider all perspectives.

Authority – This often applies to operational decisions in organisations. For this, an extensive decision-making process is ineffective and takes too long. As long as these decisions are well-founded, they will not lead to objections, but if they are taken arbitrarily, resistance will result. People want to understand the decisions made.

CAUSE IDENTIFICATION AND ANALYSIS TECHNIQUES

A large number of problem identification and analysis techniques have been developed. Commonly used techniques are tree structures, network diagrams, matrixes, and root-cause analysis. For cause-and-effect or fishbone diagrams, see Chapter 4.05, Risk and Opportunity. For flow charts, histograms, and Pareto charts, see Chapter 5.04, Quality.

Tree structure

By breaking down the problem into sub-problems, insight is gained into the factors that make up the problem. The tree structure shows the decomposition. A commonly used decomposition is the product breakdown structure for specifying the work to be carried out (see Chapter 5.03 Scope). When the problem has been carefully dissected, the smaller parts can be studied and solved with attention.

Network diagram

A network diagram allows you to visualise the interrelationships of elements concerning each other. Well-known networks are, for example, a product flow chart (see Chapter 5.03 Scope) and the Precedence chart (see Chapter 5.05 Time). Stage transitions often cause delays. By mapping out the decision process in a network diagram, they can be discussed and scheduled early.

Matrix

A matrix allows you to relate different aspects to each other and determine the best approach for each combination. A well-known matrix is the interest-influence grid (see Chapter 4.02, Stakeholders).

Root cause analysis – 5xWhy

A more intuitive root-cause analysis is the 5xWhy. By asking the why question repeatedly, a lot of valuable information is gathered. That's how the root cause can be found.

> *An organisation has failed the audit. Why did we fail?*
> - *Because the packaging department had too many red cards. Why?*
> - *Because the teams did not give the right answers. Why?*
> - *Because they were not trained well enough in the audit procedure to be followed. Why?*
> - *Because the team leaders built and implemented the procedure without involving them. Why?*
> - *Because it has always been done that way without getting into trouble. Why? …*

SOLUTION IDENTIFICATION TECHNIQUES

After determining the cause, you can identify solutions. Various techniques are also available for this. Common analytic methods include literature review, expert opinion, and Delphi.

Literature review

A literature review is a method to collect existing knowledge about your topic or problem. You find this knowledge in various sources, such as scientific journal articles, professional journals, books, papers, theses and archival material.

Expert opinion

In principle, this method is simple. Ask an expert if they have a solution. But who is an expert? Is it a theoretician who can discuss all the options but has never applied them? Is it a professional with practical experience who only views the problem from their own frame of reference? To what extent is their opinion valid? And if you ask several people for an opinion, to what extent is the opinion of the one not influenced by the opinion of the other? A valuable alternative is to apply the Delphi method.

Delphi method

With this method, you consult several experts and then submit the proposals of each to the others. In this approach, however, the experts do not know who submitted which proposal. Hence this method is named after the *Oracle of Delphi*. They hear the oracle speak but don't know who said what (see Chapter 5.07 Resources).

DIVERGENT CREATIVITY TECHNIQUES

Divergent creativity techniques help to create an open, creative atmosphere in which ideas are expressed without hesitation. Frequently used techniques are solution-focused formulation, brown paper sessions, brainstorming, analogies, and mind mapping.

Solution-focused formulation – Solution-focused formulation means that instead of formulating the problem, you describe the situation you want to achieve. This is an excellent way to create an open mind and let one's imagination have free reign. A good solution-focused question invites you to think about what might be possible in the future. An example of a solution-focused question is, 'What does our future knowledge platform for customers look like?'

Brown paper sessions – A brown paper session is an interactive meeting where participants first write down ideas for solving a problem individually on moderation cards or post-its and then share these ideas on a central wall or, as the name suggests, on a strip of brown paper. It strongly activates the creative thinking process. The brown paper session technique combines well with many other creative techniques.

Brainstorming – Brainstorming is a creativity technique in which a group generates as many new ideas as possible about a particular topic. Make sure that participants postpone any judgement on the ideas generated until after the session. They should not reject or comment on ideas. Additions, however, are allowed. Brainstorming is often the core of the divergence phase. The process facilitator should ensure everyone participates and activates participants through interventions.

Analogy – An intervention could be the introduction of an analogy (see Figure 8.04.01). This surprising image changes the participant's mind during the creative process. The image activates a person's ability to associate. You can project such an image or circulate an object or picture.

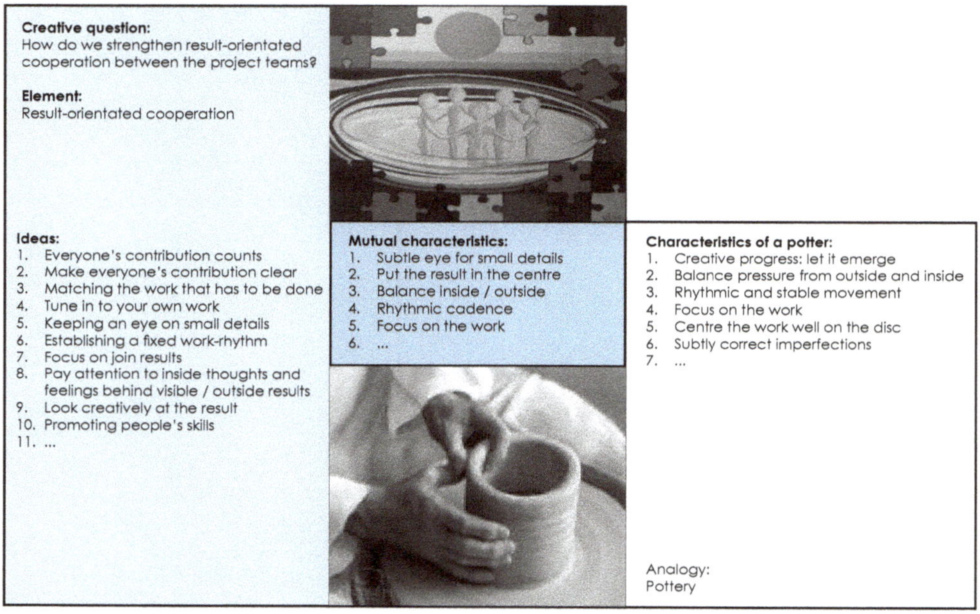

Figure 8.04.01 Analogy, activating the flow of ideas with stimulating images

Mind mapping – Another frequently used technique is a mind map. A mind map is a graphical representation of ideas organised around a solution-orientated question. It helps a group to give voice to their ideas randomly. The mind map is visualised on a large whiteboard or wall. The fact that everyone can see it makes them react to each other almost automatically. One person's ideas evoke associations in others, which initiate a new flow of ideas (see Figure 8.04.02).

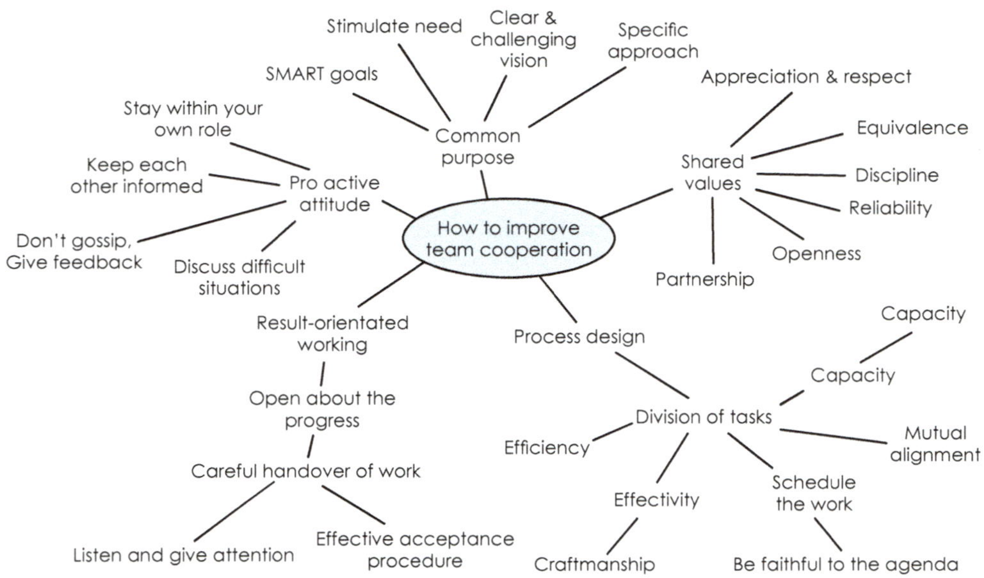

Figure 8.04.02 Example mind map

SOLUTION ASSESSMENT TECHNIQUES

It is good to assess the preferred solutions carefully. You want to avoid choosing the wrong solution after all. Well-known techniques for assessing solutions are modelling and prototyping, 3D design, and virtual reality concepts. With these techniques, you lay a solid foundation for deciding which solution is best to implement.

Modelling and prototyping

Prototyping involves creating a model or prototype to evaluate a solution. A model is a simplified representation of reality. A prototype is a simplified version of the result to be delivered. A map or a scale model is a model. A show house is a prototype.

Fast modelling is the approach to quickly create a physical part, model or assembly using 3D Computer-Aided Design (CAD). to get feedback on key design choices right from the start or even before the actual development begins.

3D design

With 3D software, the future reality can be made transparent to the customer on the screen. You can show the to-be-developed product from all perspectives and its functionality. This gives the customer a realistic picture of what will be produced and how it will fit into the existing environment.

Virtual reality

Virtual reality even goes one step further. With VR glasses, customers can fully experience the future environment. Virtual reality also benefits training skills because you can see and feel what to do in certain situations.

SOLUTION EVALUATION TECHNIQUES

Commonly used techniques are multicriteria analysis and SWOT analysis. For the SWOT analysis see Chapter 9.01, Strategy.

Multicriteria analysis

A multicriteria analysis is a common technique for prioritising options. This technique offers a systematic approach to complex decision-making based on predetermined criteria and objectives. This analysis can be used to compare options on several qualitative criteria. The different criteria are usually rated: ++, +, 0, -, – - (see Table 8.04.01). Various criteria can be used for different situations.

	Pace	Feasibility	Efficiency	Flexibility	Effectiveness
Project A	++	0	++	+	-
Project B	-	+	0	+	0
Project C	0	-	--	+	++
....					
Project N	+	+	0	+	++

Table 8.04.01 Example multi-criteria analysis

ADVANCED

PROBLEM-SOLVING IN STANDARDISED PROCESSES (ADVANCED)

Shiba & Walden (2007) describe in their book *Four Practical Revolutions In Management* the VVV-model (see Figure 8.04.03), a model for problem-solving in standardised processes. They distinguish corrective, reactive, and proactive problem-solving and project planning:

Corrective problem-solving – This often concerns simple problems, usually identified through the daily process control routine. These problems can be solved straight away: (4b) implement the solution, (5) evaluate the effects, and (6) standardise the solution. The data gathered during this process is collected and recorded.

Reactive problem-solving – This refers to more complicated problems. These usually become apparent when certain incidents occur more frequently than usual. It is then necessary to look at the underlying problem. First, (1) select the theme, (2) collect and analyse data, (3) analyse the causes, and (4a) plan the solution, after which the same steps as in corrective problem-solving can be followed. At each step, the gathered data is collected and recorded. Finally, (7) the whole problem-solving process is evaluated.

Proactive problem-solving – This refers to problems which do not arise from repeated incidents. These are issues or problems that may occur in future. This requires a change. The most important step here is (0.1) becoming aware of the problem itself, then (0.2) investigate the situation, and (0.3) delineate the problem, after which the same steps as reactive problem-solving can be followed. Also, the gathered data should be collected and recorded at each step, and (7) the whole process should be evaluated.

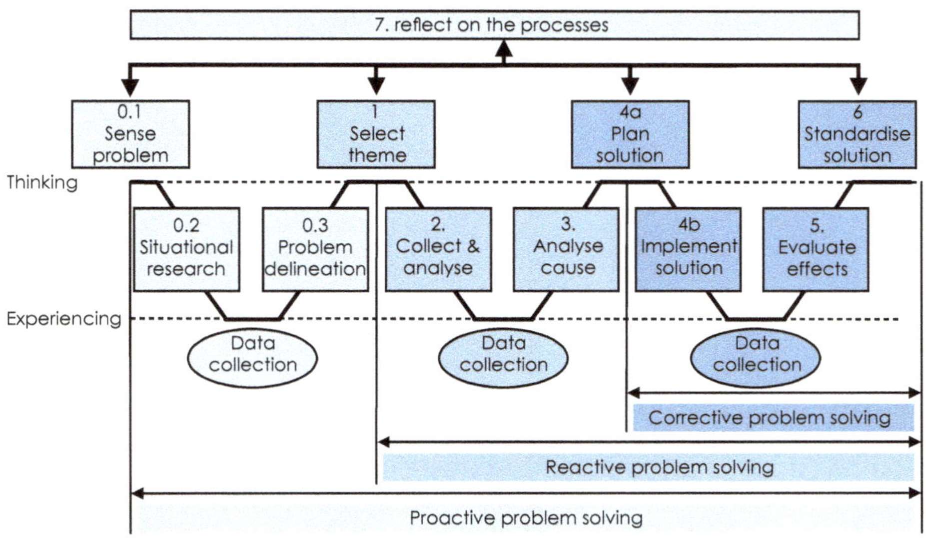

Figure 8.04.03 VVV problem-solving model (Shiba & Walden, 2007)

In the model of Shiba and Walden, corrective problem-solving requires only one 'V', Reactive problem-solving requires a double 'V' (VV), and proactive problem-solving requires a triple 'V' (VVV). Each 'V' consists of a thinking and experience level, and data collection. In reactive and proactive problem-solving, the process should also be evaluated. That is unnecessary for the corrective problem-solving process, as this is a straightforward repair.

> *What is going on?*
> - *The lamp is broken. The janitor has replaced the bulb (corrective/incident).*
> - *We now discover that the same lamp broke three times this week. There is more to this and it needs to be sorted out first (reactive).*
> - *During the last meeting, it was mentioned that all the lamps consume much energy which will become very expensive in the future. Perhaps replacing these lamps with LED lighting (proactive/change) may be an option.*
> - *The Head of Facilities notes that the entire electrical installation is quite old. The whole installation has to be replaced sometime in the future (project/something new).*

Project planning: working on something new

If the problems cannot be solved within the existing processes, something new should be created. This is usually done by initiating projects. This is a nine-step approach; slightly more detailed than the seven-step proactive problem-solving approach. Figure 8.04.04 places the seven steps of reactive problem-solving alongside the nine project planning steps.

The nine steps of project planning are:

1. *Define the project* – Based on the situation analysis, you define the project. Formulate in one clear sentence what you want to achieve with the project.
2. *Research the essentials and prepare a step-by-step plan* – Specify why the project is needed, which project results you want to realise, the goals you want to achieve with it, and what the scope and boundaries of the project are. Determine the successive steps in the project.
3. *Determine what you will deliver per step* – Establish what should be delivered at the end of each step and what the individual results should satisfy to be approved. Also, determine per step if there are any restrictions.

PDCA	Project planning	Reactive problem solving
Plan	1. Define the project 2. Research essentials and prepare step-by-step plan 3. Determine results to be delivered per step 4. Select the best approach 5. Develop optimistic project plan	1. Select the theme 2. Collect and analyse data 3. Analyse causes
Do	6. Design and implement a detailed plan per step	4. Plan and implement solution
Check	7. Evaluate results per step	5. Evaluate the effects
Act	8. Standardise the solution 9. Reflect on the processes	6. Standardise the solution 7. Reflect on the process

Figure 8.04.04 Proactive project planning versus reactive problem-solving (Shiba & Walden)

4. *Select the best approach* – For each step, determine alternatives for achieving the results of that step. Select the best approach.
5. *Develop an optimistic plan* – Based on the chosen approach, develop an optimistic but feasible project plan. Setting this plan will strengthen the focus of the team. Analyse possible risks and define measures to control these risks.
6. *Design and implement a detailed plan per step* – Make a detailed plan per step: who does what, why, where, when and how (5W/1H method, see Chapter 8.05 Result Orientation). Visualise the work in a bar diagram, implement the plan and monitor progress.
7. *Evaluate the results per step* – Assess per step to what extent the set objectives have been realised with the way the work has been carried out.
8. *Standardise the solution* – Implement the result and standardise the new working method.
9. *Reflect* – Review how the nine steps were completed and identify learning points for the next project.

ADDITIONAL DIVERGENT CREATIVITY TECHNIQUES (ADVANCED)

Additional convergent techniques are listening inside out, lateral thinking and Thinking Hats.

Listening inside out – The aim here is to capture all the thoughts that come to mind when listening to an argument. A helpful tool for this is to take a sheet of paper with a vertical line in the middle. On the left, you write down the keywords from the speech (listening outside); on the right, you write down the associations, thoughts and feelings that come up due to that speech (listening inside). This way, the story behind the argument is recorded. This could possibly help solve the problem.

Lateral thinking (De Bono) – According to De Bono (1973), the intermediate position between YES and NO is essential for stimulating thought. He uses the word PO, which stands for *POssible*. It makes you approach a problem from a different perspective or laterally: from the sidelines. You can actively and continuously stimulate this intermediate position by provoking. For example: 'If we don't know how to turn our most popular handbag into a small fridge, we will lose our market share!' By approaching this provocative thought 'PO', a diversity of possibilities can arise, such as a handbag in which a light turns on when opened; a handbag with space for a cooling element; a handbag with different compartments; et cetera. The most important aspect of lateral thinking is your attitude: you do not say yes, you do not say no, but you think: this idea offers possibilities! This way, you keep your mind open for unexpected and surprising opportunities and insights.

Thinking hats (De Bono) – The six thinking hats are a specific technique to keep thinking of new or different possibilities. Each thinking hat has its own colour, and when you put on that coloured hat, you think only from that coloured hat's perspective.

- *White thinking hat* – Represents facts and figures. Which facts play a role in this situation?
- *Red thinking hat* – Represents emotions and intuitions. With the red thinking hat on,

information is brought in by feeling and intuition without the need for explanation.

- *Black thinking hat* – Makes markedly clear why something does not work or is unfeasible because it does not correspond to daily practice or the most recent research.
- *Yellow thinking hat* – Shows the positive aspects of the idea and expresses hope. It assesses ideas for the value they can bring. Yellow offers concrete suggestions and shows how they can be implemented.
- *Green thinking hat* – Stands for creative thinking. It offers other perspectives, leaves the beaten track and provokes new angles, logic and words that seem unrelated to the issue. It is a hovering technique: you float away from the existing reality and add ideas from other sources to solve the issue independently.
- *Blue thinking hat* – Controls the thinking process. This thinking hat brings the team back to the problem on which the creative thinking is focused, intervenes when the process becomes too chaotic, suggests putting on a different coloured hat and summarises the discussion. They are the guardians of the process.

It is fascinating to hear naturally positive thinkers suddenly voice their pessimism or, conversely, to hear pessimists suddenly offer various possibilities.

CONVERGENT CREATIVITY TECHNIQUES (ADVANCED)

A *COCD box* is used when organising many ideas. Sensory exploration can be used for developing the selected ideas. Value analysis and scenario analysis can be used to select ideas.

COCD box (organise) – The COCD box (see Figure 8.04.05) was developed in 1997 by Mark Raison for the Centre for Developmental Creative Thinking. The box is a practical tool to help you organise countless ideas quickly and effectively. By sorting the ideas in the COCD box, you prevent the team from making rapid decisions for ordinary feasible ideas and putting aside original ideas that are not yet feasible. The grouping provides an overview and differentiation of the ideas. This focus is necessary to retain potential ideas and arrive at the right approach to the ideas submitted.

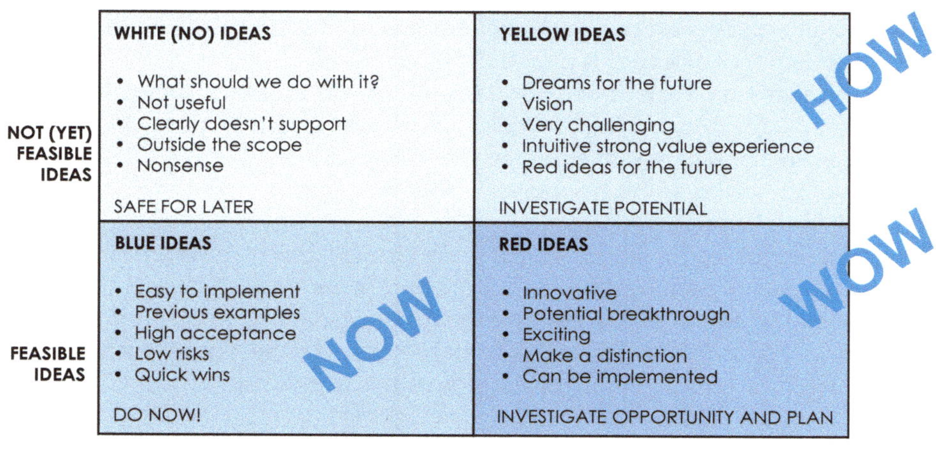

Figure 8.04.05 COCD box (Raison, 1997)

Deepening the senses (develop) – Deepening the senses ensures you appeal to all the senses to reinforce the ideas. You can use questions such as:

- What will the world be like after this idea is realised?
- What do you hear people say, or what sounds do you hear when this idea is realised?
- What happens if you make this idea tasty, spicy or sweet?
- What associations do you have when the idea is realised and delicious smells fill the air?
- What positive feelings does the idea evoke in you, and what can you do with the idea to reinforce these feelings?

Value analysis (select) – A value analysis prevents identified ideas from being too expensive, too complex or over-specified. A value analysis aims to systematically eliminate costs that do not contribute to the functional value of a product, process or service. Value is everything that makes a user want the product or service. You can depict a picture of the actual value and costs by asking why the user wants the function and how it can be realised (see Chapter 4.04 Requirements and Objectives).

Scenario analysis (select) – Scenario analysis examines the feasibility of an idea under different circumstances (scenarios). It is a future-orientated analysis examining the possible consequences of different ideas. For this investigation, you can ask questions such as, 'What is the worst/best thing that could happen to us if we choose this idea?' or 'What are the advantages/disadvantages of choosing this idea?' The idea with the most promising scenarios and the least risky consequences can be implemented.

DECISION-MAKING PROCEDURE (ADVANCED)

Many decisions are made during the project lifecycle. A structured procedure gives teams confidence and control over this process. Such a procedure also leads to a good justification of the decision, which also improves the quality of the decision. The following procedure structures the process of decision-making very well:

1. Determine the decision goal. Recognise that a decision goal may already have decisions locked in. For example: 'book a vacation' is a different decision goal than 'plan a vacation trip'.
2. Define criteria against which you weigh the choice to be made. This is a creative process. Ensure that all interests are considered.
3. Divide the criteria into Requirements and Desires. Give the desires a weighting factor on a scale of 1-10. For example, the maximum budget level may be a requirement, and the entire travel time to the desired destination a wish.
4. Determine alternatives. This is, again, a creative process. Don't limit yourself to finding alternatives.
5. Assess the alternatives. If it does not meet a requirement, drop it. For each alternative, for each weighting factor, determine a score on a scale of 1 – 10. Multiply the scores by the weighting factor and determine the total score for each alternative.
6. Make a risk analysis for the two or three alternatives with the highest score.
7. Make a definitive choice. Inform all the stakeholders involved.

The different roles of the leader and team members in decision-making procedures

In preparing for this process, the leader involves the team in formulating the precise decision question, taking into account the interests of the team members. At the beginning of the meeting, the leader opens the meeting and sets the procedure. Team members react and ask questions. It should be very clear what will be decided and how the decision will be taken. The leader facilitates the dialogue during the opinion-forming phase by structuring the process. Team members form opinions, share criteria, and generate ideas. Sometimes they need space to consult their backbenchers. The leader should provide this space. At the end of the opinion phase, the ideas are compared with the criteria. The leader summarises the results and formulates the decision. This final decision can be made in different ways as described before: majority, compromise, consensus, delegation, unanimity or authority.

INNOVATION PROCESSES AND TECHNIQUES (ADVANCED)

Innovative projects have a specific heartbeat. More often than usual, it is necessary to examine whether the proposed idea or solution is (still) feasible and valuable to proceed with to avoid wasting expensive investments. To repeatedly examine new ideas the following methods are used:

Minimal Viable Product (MVP) – In his method *Lean Startup*, Eric Ries (2011) defined the *Minimal Viable Product* (MVP) as the simplest form of a product in order to test it against potential consumers. An MVP should be created as early as possible in the project to test hypotheses.

Guided trial – A guided trial is a self-service model for experiencing a product idea at the beginning of the product development. It is considered a low-cost alternative to a Proof of Concept (POC).

Proof of Concept (POC) – A POC is a small-scale demonstration to determine whether an idea can become a reality. A proof of concept aims to help decide whether the idea is feasible and works as intended.

Prototype – A prototype tests a working model's usability, functionality and design. It is a concept version of the final product. A prototype allows developers to determine how best to develop the product ready for full production.

Pilot – A pilot is a small-scale implementation used to demonstrate the viability of a project idea. A pilot is a scaled-down version of an innovation or change a company wants to implement. Pilots allow you to assess potential obstacles or needs before implementing the change in its entirety.

For each innovation, you need to determine which innovation processes and techniques can best be applied. These processes and techniques should always be aligned with what you want to achieve and the broader context.

ORGANISATIONAL INNOVATION (ADVANCED)

Organisational innovation requires an integrated approach to develop new ideas that serve the organisation's survival. Keely (2013) describes ten points of leverage to implement innovative ideas successfully:

- *Profit model* – A potential profitability ensures that financiers are willing to contribute, enabling investment.
- *Network* – The ability to collaborate with other parties is crucial for developing innovative ideas. A large number of small innovations creates a successful innovative product. 'Don't do it alone!'
- *Structure* – Be clear in identifying the issues you seek a solution for. This provides the collaborating companies insight and direction in the challenge.
- *Process* – Innovation breaks through existing processes. It is important to know how. Dialogue should become a habit.
- *Product performance* – Ensure the core products you make are continuously improved.
- *Product system* – Core products can often be enriched with complementary products. A strong product can lead to valuable by-products.
- *Service systems* – Additional services can also lead to valuable innovations. During the Corona epidemic, ASML realised an ingenious remote service system using camera set-ups.
- *Sales channel* – What are the opportunities to improve sales channels effectively? Streaming services have rendered music shops and video stores obsolete.
- *Branding* – The brand also adds value to the product. By marketing the product and or service attractively, positive interest in the product is created.
- *Customer engagement* – Involve the customer in innovation processes. By involving them, you have insight into their needs and gain loyal customers.

As a project manager, it's important to keep the bigger picture in mind when working on innovative projects.

8.05 RESULT ORIENTATION

PURPOSE

The purpose of this chapter is to enable the individual to focus on the agreed outcomes and drive towards making the project a success.

LEARNING OBJECTIVES

- Efficiency, effectiveness and productivity;
- Continuous improvement;
- Entrepreneurship (advanced);
- Efficiency improvement techniques (advanced);
- Results-orientated project management (advanced);
- Political and social sensitivity (advanced).

DEFINITIONS

Effectiveness: The extent to which the desired outcome is achieved.
Efficiency: The ratio of yield to use of resources.
Productivity: The amount of work done per period.
Kaizen: A philosophy which encourages continuous improvement in all aspects of result-orientated collaboration.

INTRODUCTION

Result orientation is the core of every project. Projects are meant to deliver results with which the organisation wants to achieve its goals. To achieve that result, efficient and effective action is a prerequisite. This is partly based on the principles of continuous improvement. At the same time, you need political and social sensitivity for dealing with internal and external relationships and decision-making processes in and around the organisation.
Entrepreneurs know better than anyone how to achieve results in concrete situations. Strengthening the project manager's entrepreneurship enhances their resourcefulness and result orientation.

EFFICIENCY, EFFECTIVENESS AND PRODUCTIVITY

Result orientation requires attention to achieving project results efficiently and effectively. Efficiency is the degree to which resources are used to achieve a particular goal. A process is called efficient if few resources are used compared to a set standard. Working efficiently means minimising the costs of delivering what you have promised. This means having a keen eye for avoiding waste and adopting an attitude of doing the job right the first time.

A process is effective if it delivers the desired output and allows the customer to realise the intended goals. The degree of effectiveness can best be measured using the formula: Effectiveness = Content × Acceptance. Sometimes Quality is used for Content: Effectiveness = Quality x Acceptance.

Productivity is the amount of work done per period. However, this may be done with too many resources, and the output may not meet the desired goals. Therefore, all or part of it has to be redone. Focusing on productivity alone is a dangerous road.

Focus on productivity should always go hand in hand with a focus on efficiency and effectiveness.

Keeping a close eye on the efficiency and effectiveness of the work and implementing necessary or desired improvements should be an ongoing process.

CONTINUOUS IMPROVEMENT (KAIZEN)

Kaizen means continuous improvement. This philosophy encourages continuous improvement in all aspects of result-orientated collaboration. The development of Kaizen went hand in hand with the development of all kinds of quality techniques but was not limited to this.

Objectives of Kaizen

Kaizen (Imai, 2012) aims to improve work processes with due regard to result orientation and the role of the people. The objectives of Kaizen are to eliminate waste (Muda) and to prevent overload (Muri) and irregularities (Mura). In Japanese culture, the cradle of Kaizen thinking, the most prestigious awards go to teams that work visibly and with an initiative on continuous process improvement.

> *Staff at a company canteen were puzzled by the use of tea during the breaks. On some tables, jugs of tea remained half full; on others, they were always empty. They started keeping statistics on the use per table and its reasons and found that while the number of people at the table was often the same, one team drank more tea than the other. They adjusted their tea offerings per table accordingly and reduced tea consumption by 50%. The team received the Presidential Gold Medal for correctly applying KAIZEN's principles.*

Waste (Muda) – Muda stands for preventing waste. This includes wrong products, unused products, unnecessary distribution time and distances, waiting times, excess stock, unnecessary operations, delivering more than the customer requires, unused manpower, sub-optimal machine deployment, et cetera. In particular, the employees who do the work should be trained to recognise and prevent Muda.

> *In many projects, checks are made on the realised time, costs and quality delivered. Various departments need this information to carry out these checks. Many project managers have to prepare several management reports. By carefully studying such a process and looking at what information needs to be delivered to whom and combining it, much time can be saved on delivering management information.*

Overload (Muri) – Muri is about making the best possible use of people and machines. To this end, you can standardise the process in such a way that it meets the delivery of predefined quality in the most efficient way. To realise Muri, it is necessary to thoroughly analyse the process steps towards a (sub-) product, optimise them and fine-tune them to the other process steps.

To avoid Muri, it is also important to develop pull processes. This means that the process or the customer who needs the product determines when this product is delivered. When bottlenecks occur, which you can often recognise by growing stocks before a specific process step, you know that this part of the process is overloaded. You can solve this by adding more capacity to the process, developing a more efficient working procedure, training people to work smarter, and or reducing the speed of the preceding processes. If you try to solve the problem by putting pressure on the team members and or the machine, this will work for a short period of time, but in the long run, the problem will worsen. Never overload people or machines!

Irregularities (Mura) – Mura stands for irregularities, imbalance and unevenness in processes. The goal is to balance the daily routine so that it becomes possible to get a lot done without stress with lean processes. Irregularities are caused by various factors, such as different ways of working, different visions on how to fulfil the work optimally, deviations from the requested product, lack of communication on dealing with these deviations, et cetera. To address such anomalies, you can train teams, reduce the complexity of the process, standardise the process, use real-time monitoring systems, et cetera. Everything you do aims to develop a smooth process, from supplier to end user and all process steps in between.

Principles of Kaizen

KAIZEN's five key principles are:

Know your customer – The acceptance of the result by the customer plays an important role within KAIZEN. Within KAIZEN, the next process is the customer, i.e. 'the process that receives and accepts your output'. The question is always: 'With my product, can my customer/next team continue with their process?' If not, communication is needed!

Quality first – In KAIZEN, quality has absolute priority over costs and delivery. If the quality is not good, the customer's processes do not function optimally, irregularities arise, waste occurs, and work has to be repeated, leading to overloading. All these side effects make the process unnecessarily expensive and customers dissatisfied. It is better to mutually agree to postpone the delivery for a while than to find out later that the customer cannot proceed with the delivered product.

Improving the process improves the result – A well-designed process ensures that all crucial steps and handovers can be carried out correctly. Well-designed processes ensure that:

- Processes are more manageable;
- Tasks can be clearly allocated;
- The transfer of work to other people is easier;
- Fewer mistakes are made;
- Communication about improvements has a basis;
- The organisation increases its learning capacity;
- Better results are achieved.

Acceptance of delivery based on specification is important for processes to run smoothly. The 'next process' should be able to continue effortlessly with the input it has received from the previous process. Communication between subsequent teams is necessary for delivery according to specification (see Figure 8.05.01). Careful communication between these teams determines the success of the entire process and serves the customer: the next process.

Analysing problems based on facts – Based on KAIZEN, you conduct structural improvement by analysing well-recorded factual events. When incidents occur, you record them in the statistics. In this way, you create a basis for further analysis and real improvements.

Separating maintenance from improvement – Implementing improvements is different from carrying out maintenance. Maintenance focuses on maintaining the existing processes to the best of their ability. Improvement focuses on implementing new processes and requires jointly analysing facts and thinking about possible improvements and how to realise them.

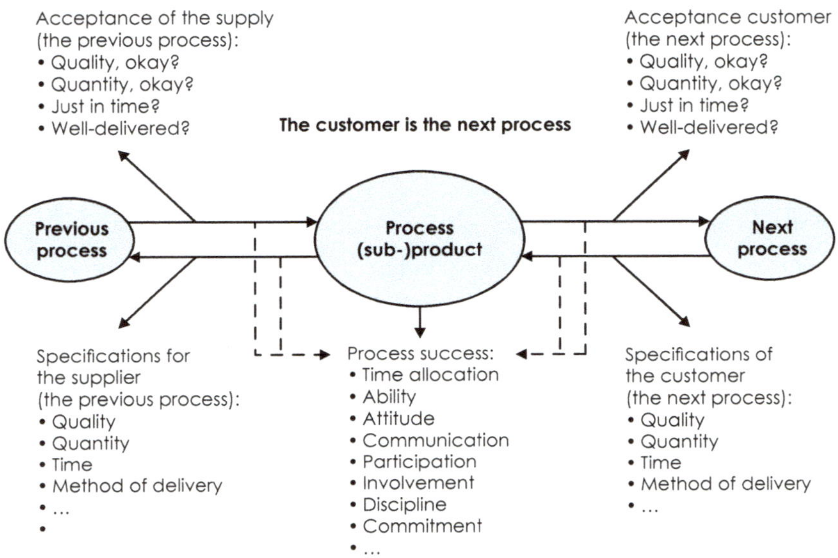

Figure 8.05.01 Continuous improvement

Conditions for applying Kaizen

According to Kaizen, the most important conditions to prevent waste, overload, and irregularities are:

Continuous attention to improvement – Employees and managers adopt an attitude that is constantly focused on finding opportunities for improvement. The actual process is central to their thinking and acting. Considering this process as a whole and the will to deliver according to specifications creates insight into opportunities for improvement.

Personal discipline – The process cannot be improved just by optimising it. Employees should also keep to their agreements. Without personal discipline, there is no optimal process.

Teamwork – Kaizen organisations realise that achieving quality is teamwork. They realise that the links in the overall process should be appropriately aligned. Employees have the task of properly substantiating their ideas for improvement. Management has the task of taking up these ideas, discussing them across team boundaries and reporting back on what has been done with them.

Quality circles – Because improvement can come from any step in the process, quality circles are essential. Quality circles are small groups of workers who do similar types of work and meet regularly to attempt to identify and solve work-related issues.

Improve morale – Continuous improvement takes time and attention and is not something you do overnight. It requires the will to persevere and the flexibility to constantly learn new capabilities. Managers should be positive about the training and employability of employees and take improvement proposals from the teams constructively.

ADVANCED ENTREPRENEURSHIP (ADVANCED)

Hisrich, Peters, and Shepherd (2013) describe the characteristics of entrepreneurs and how they build successful organisations. In situations with many uncertainties, entrepreneurs display a natural attitude characterised by structural thinking, working with what is available, making the best use of available opportunities and cognitive adaptability. These competences are also valuable for project managers.

Structured thinking – Structured thinking is thinking about the capabilities of a product or technology rather than just looking at its current applications. Most people think about how to meet the current market's needs with the current applications. This prevents breakthrough ideas for new markets or how to serve user groups differently. Entrepreneurs intuitively sense the structural capabilities of a particular technique. This also comes in handy in many projects. Regularly ask yourself, 'What existing technology can we use differently to meet users' needs?'

Working with what is available – Entrepreneurs are well aware that they have to make do with the resources they have. They determine the effect that you can achieve. Entrepreneurs don't complain about the lack of resources but make clever combinations of what they have. If it cannot be done the way it should be, it should be done the way it can be.

Making the most of opportunities – If realisation is more complicated than expected, they always know how to find parties willing to seize opportunities and can convince them of the future they envisage.

Cognitive adaptation – Cognitive adaptation is the ability to absorb and process knowledge and information. Entrepreneurs constantly reflect on themselves and the situation. By doing so, they enable themselves to adapt effectively to the situation. Their reflections are not about the details but the patterns that maintain the situation. They then focus on breaking these patterns to pave the way for the opportunities they see.

> *On a small tropical island, a solar park has been operated, providing 25% of the island's energy needs. The panels are placed two metres above the ground. The entrepreneur behind this idea will grow vegetables under them. That way, the surface will be used twice. At present, vegetables are still imported at a high cost.*
>
> *That this is an entrepreneur is evident by the plans to build another park and to use the sun's energy to pump water from the sea into the volcano's crater on the island during the day. At night, the water can flow back out of the crater to provide the island with electricity from hydropower.*

EFFICIENCY IMPROVEMENT TECHNIQUES (ADVANCED)

To achieve improvements, KAIZEN provides several techniques to identify and analyse opportunities:

- 5 S improvement approach
- 5xW and 1xH focus areas
- 4 M checklist
- 7 Statistical tools (see Chapter 5.04 Quality)

5S improvement approach

The 5S improvement approach consists of Sorting (Seiri), Arranging (Seiton), Cleaning (Seiso), Standardising (Seiketsu), and *Systematisation (Shitsuke)*. The elements are also very useful for structuring project work.

Sorting (Seiri) – Sorting here means distinguishing between necessary and superfluous. You bring order by eliminating unnecessary steps and removing broken items. When you work Seiri, you first collect and sort out everything you need and then carry out the work.

Arrange (Seiton) – Seiton means you store things in an orderly way. You give tools a fixed place and store documents according to a fixed structure. The result is that everyone can find what they need for work quickly and easily. A good example of Seiton is the drawn contours of tools on the walls in the workshops for hanging tools. You know exactly where to store a particular tool; if you miss one, it is immediately visible.

Cleaning (Seiso) – Clean up, and keep clean. Workplaces that are cluttered or dirty result in efficiency losses. A neat workplace prevents breakdowns and provides peace of mind.

Standardise (Seiketsu) – Standardising makes the previous three steps sustainable. Seiri, Seiton and Seiso become a habit by standardising processes and storage systems. By following these standards in a disciplined way, peace and order are created in work.

Systematisation (Shitsuke) – Systematisation means securing the other four pillars through checklists, reviews, audits and or evaluations.

5xW and 1xH

The 5xW and 1xH model supports mutual deepening, strengthening and improving collaboration and optimising the division of tasks. With each W and H, critical questions are asked, which answers lead to ideas for improvement:

» *Who?* – Who is doing the work? Who should do it? Who can do it? Who will do it in the end?
» *What?* – What is being made? What should be made? What can be made differently? What should be made differently?
» *Where?* – Where are the results created? Where should it be created? Where can they be created? Where should they be created in the end?
» *When?* – When is a product made? When should it have been made? Can it be made at a different time? Should it be made at a different time?
» *Why?* – Why do we do what we are doing? Why should we do it? Can there be another reason to do it? Why should we make it in the end?
» *How?* – How do we make it? How should we make it? How can we improve how we make it? How will we make it in the end?

Project professionals can make good use of 5W/1H during workshops and daily work management. By consciously working through the six question areas, project professionals clearly understand who should do what, where, when, why and how.

4M checklist

The 4M checklist is used to make process criteria conscious and discussable. The 4M checklist verifies that what should be done according to the agreement is done (see Table 8.05.01). The 4M checklist can also be used in projects.

4m	Possible control questions
Mankind/ Members	• Do people keep to the standards? • Do people work efficiently/cost-consciously? • Do people understand the problem before they start working? • Are the people adequately trained? • Does the work to be done suit the people? • Are people willing to improve? • Do people take responsibility for their work? • Do people take the initiative for improvement? • Do people maintain good interpersonal relationships?
Machinery/ Equipment	• Can the products be produced efficiently with the equipment? • Does the equipment support the process effectively? • Does the equipment deliver accurate results? • Is the equipment well maintained and managed? • Is the use of the equipment well-supported? In the context of office environments, computer networks, computer equipment, applications running on them, and data storage facilities are the most important facilities for optimising the process.
Materials	• Are the right materials supplied in the correct quantities and quality? • Are the materials properly processed? • Are materials and machines well-matched? • Are the materials easily accessible? For office environments, it is mainly about the materials necessary for equipment and software to work correctly. Information is an important material in this line of thought. • How is the information organised and made accessible? • How is the information processed, stored and made accessible? • Does the processing of information produce the correct documents?
Methods	• Are the work instructions adequate? • Is the quality of the product to be delivered guaranteed by the working method? • Are the work instructions adequately maintained? • Does the working method promote efficiency, effectiveness and mutual learning? • Does the work method lead to the use of a proper work sequence?

Table 8.05.01 4M control questions

RESULTS-ORIENTATED PROJECT MANAGEMENT (ADVANCED)

An effective and efficient approach to projects is essential for achieving project success. Alexander Laufer (2009) identifies five principles for result-orientated project management, each with three guidelines for applying them.

Principle 1 (green) – Plan and manage to embrace change

» *Setting objectives while examining available resources* – This should not be a theoretical exercise. An initial assessment of the available resources should be included immediately. This is why Laufer recommends including an outline project plan when preparing the project outline. It prevents you from thinking all too easily about feasibility.

- *Apply a learning-orientated style of planning and control* – A rigid plan does not work. Leave room for adjustments. Build in retrospectives at all milestones. Discuss progress and what makes certain parts of the work difficult. Make sure you know from each other what you are working on and how far everyone has progressed.
- *Include sufficient redundancy* – Include margins and ensure that activities can be done as much as possible in parallel. This allows you to start new activities while some previous ones are not completed. Also, ensure you have a backup for resources and contingency plans to manage risks.

Principle 2 (Brown): Create a result-orientated focus

- *Ensure focus* – Do not be tempted to produce more than agreed upon, even at extra cost and time. Dare to say no. The project does not run out of its original framework by saying no.
- *Think in terms of delivery* – Be product-orientated. Deliver incrementally. This leads to strong customer engagement and focuses on the project team's work.
- *Be agile* – Do not specify everything in detail at the start. Only determine the outline upfront. This leaves room for interpretation and allows new insights to be incorporated flexibly during implementation.

Principle 3 (Yellow): Develop the 'will to win'

- *Know and feel your mission* – Teams and organisations need a sense of direction and meaning for a purpose that is bigger than themselves. Such a team solves problems not from command and control but from the will to make the project succeed.
- *Challenge the status quo* – It is sometimes good to go against prescribed procedures. Trusting professionals gives them the motivation to harness their full potential. It also requires the courage and boldness to make morally sound decisions that transcend conventional norms.
- *Persevere, but know when to stop* – Even if it doesn't go well the first time, learn to persevere when you feel the solution is near. When your intuition tells you to stop, stop and discuss it. Acknowledge that some of the paths you take are dead ends! Be honest about that.

Principle 4 (red): Work together by promoting interdependence and trust

- *Take the selection of team members very seriously* – The team composition should focus on the whole. Qualities should complement each other in technical and professional terms and regarding the team member's ability to work together. The most important criterion should not be having experience but a committed attitude to the work to be carried out.
- *Build a network based on trust* – Developing trust requires an attitude of genuine attention. Conversations about trust and safety are necessary to comprehend what is needed to work together based on mutual trust. These conversations create space for vulnerability and the courage to discuss difficult things.
- *Assess the team's performance and create new energy* – Project results are made together. Every link in the team is needed to achieve success. Addressing and complimenting each other strengthens the sense of interdependence. By celebrating partial achievements, people discover the importance of their task as a whole. This has a motivating effect.

Principle 5 (grey) – Connect through intensive communication

- *Acquire and provide information regularly* – Informing each other is not routine. It should stem from a deep awareness that the other individual needs to know what you are working on and what information you need to do so. You know how things are going if you keep each other informed frequently. It keeps you involved and creates space to support each other where necessary.
- *Use all means of communication, with personal face time as a top priority* – Direct contact covers the full spectrum of human interaction. This ensures that messages are better understood. At the same time, it also provides opportunities to clarify, ask questions, give feedback and learn from each other.
- *Use informal 'management by walking around' communication style* – By being actively present on the work floor, you see and hear what is happening, and problems can be solved quickly and directly.

Laufer's principles clarify the importance of the collaboration process behind the content. By truly being part of that process, result-orientated work gains common ground. This should also be the inner attitude when deploying your political and social sensitivity.

POLITICAL AND SOCIAL SENSITIVITY (ADVANCED)

Political and social sensitivity are important competences for project professionals. Decisions have to be made many times and at many levels. Knowing how these decisions are made is very important (political sensitivity). Negative relationships within the broader context can seriously impact the project, but we should be conscious of the fact that we can also influence this (social sensitivity).

Political sensitivity

Political sensitivity is sensitivity to relations within organisations. It makes you aware of how the decisions are made. It is important to observe the formal rules of the game. However, to get a difficult decision approved, you can, for example, ask a senior user to collaborate to emphasise the importance of a change. Doing so involves someone with a higher formal position in the organisation. They may not be authorised to make the decision, but they can tip the balance towards a favourable decision.

Since your project is likely to be one of the many projects being implemented within the organisation, it is necessary to positively keep the project in the attention of business and portfolio management. Its importance should be clear to them and evoke a strong positive response. You can also influence the distribution of resources. Political sensitivity means knowing when decisions are made and when exerting influence is most effective.

To strengthen your political sensitivity, you can use the interest matrix as part of stakeholder management (see Chapter 4.02 Stakeholders). Who are the influencers, and what is their attitude towards the project? What is their interest and influence? What are the positive and negative consequences of the project for them and their position? In addition, insight into the power play in the customer organisation is very important. What type of organisation is it, what kind of coordination mechanisms are dominant, and how do people with power make decisions? See Chapter 10.01, Organisation Theories and Chapter 11.04, Influence and Interest.

Social sensitivity

Social sensitivity also refers to sensitivity to internal relationships, now especially related to social, cultural, and interpersonal differences between different groups and people. It makes you aware of the potential resulting discrimination and more subtle adverse mechanism. This may negatively impact those people and the project's ability to succeed. All team members and other stakeholders around the project should feel safe and valued, feel that their qualities and contributions are appreciated, and that they can also move with the changes resulting from the project.

You can strengthen your social sensitivity by:

- Approaching those groups and people in an open, unprejudiced and respectful way;
- Empathising with the feelings, thoughts and behaviour of others, especially at times when they are having a tough time;
- Maintaining your respect for the authenticity of each individual instead of stereotyping them;
- Adapting to the (cultural) diversity within the team;
- Contributing to an organisation in which everyone feels at home, including yourself;
- Discussing frustrations;
- Appreciating the individual qualities of employees and the collective qualities within the team.

Social sensitivity contributes to an organisation where people feel at home and experience that the project has been set up in a social and safe working environment.

8.06 NEGOTIATION

PURPOSE

The purpose of this chapter is to enable the individual to reach satisfactory agreements with others by using negotiation techniques.

LEARNING OBJECTIVES

- Negotiation strategies;
- Positional negotiation;
- Best Alternative to a Negotiated Agreement (BATNA);
- Principled negotiation/Harvard method;
- Phases in a negotiation process (advanced);
- Aspects of Negotiation (advanced);
- Negotiating tactics (advanced).

DEFINITIONS

Negotiation: A consultation aimed at reaching an agreement.
Negotiation strategy: The approach you take when negotiating.
Positional negotiation: A negotiating style which focuses on taking positions to achieve goals.
Principled negotiation: A negotiating style which focuses on achieving a win/win agreement.
BATNA: The best alternative to a negotiated agreement.

INTRODUCTION

In projects, various interests need to be coordinated to achieve deliverables successfully. Negotiations underpin this process. Some of these negotiations will be conducted formally between parties, but many negotiations take place on an interpersonal level as part of the daily management of the project. Negotiating is, therefore, a key competence of the project manager.

NEGOTIATION STRATEGIES

Two aspects are central in negotiations: concern for the outcome and concern for the relationship (Thomas & Kilmann, 2002). Attention to those aspects determines the negotiation strategy parties can employ (see Figure 8.06.01).

Accommodating – In this strategy, you can, at certain points, give in to the other party's wishes to maintain the relationship. This can also come from the knowledge that the other party has a strong position in the negotiation. You can also use this strategy, for example, to create a situation of mutual dependence, to show others that you are working with a strong partner, to gain knowledge from the collaboration, or to build up credit for the future.

Competing – In this strategy, you strive for a favourable negotiation outcome for yourself and your supporters at the expense of the relationship. In a rock-solid position, you can push through your self-interest. However, this strategy generates all sorts of counterforces that can work against you in the long run.

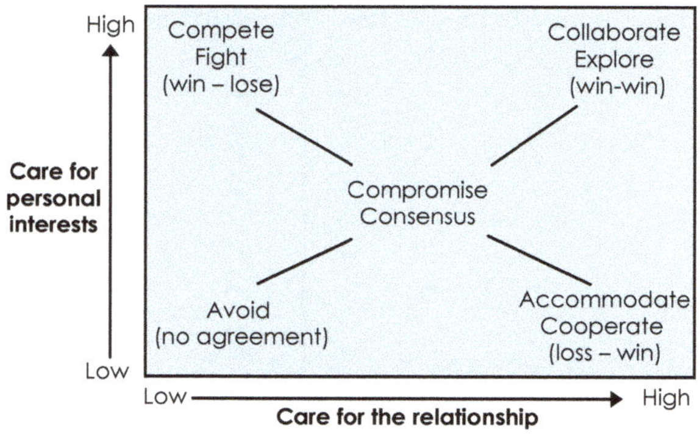

Figure 8.06.01 Negotiation strategies (Thomas & Kilmann, 2002)

Avoiding – With this strategy, you immediately opt for an alternative that eliminates the need to negotiate with that party. You may choose this if you expect the negotiations to go unfavourably and a good alternative is available. However, this can also be a strategy to bring the other party to the table eventually.

Compromising – This strategy is somewhere between competing and accommodating. Both parties make certain concessions that they consider acceptable for the result achieved. A compromise strategy is particularly effective when swiftly reaching such an agreement is possible. It is essential that both parties feel that the compromise is balanced and truly reinforces mutual interests. If not, resistance will arise sooner or later with the same negative effects as the competing strategy.

Collaborating – This strategy aims to achieve an outcome that satisfies the essential interests of both parties (win-win). Creating such a mutual gain requires an open attitude, carefully identifying the interests of both parties and pursuing alternative solutions that meet those interests.

Competing, compromising and accommodating are complementary strategies based on positional negotiation. It is like a tug of war (see Figure 8.06.02): whoever pulls the hardest wins. When the forces are balanced, compromise is reached. Cooperation is of a different order. It requires principled negotiation.

POSITIONAL NEGOTIATION

Positional negotiation focuses on taking positions to achieve results. What opening offer is most effective; what is the desired target point; what is your outcome expectation; what is your best alternative to a negotiated agreement, what are your resistance and breaking points; and what are your opponent's? An open search for alternatives that benefit both sides is not central. The question is: how do you get the best out of it?

Figure 8.06.02 Position-based negotiation

- *Opening offer* – The offer with which you start the negotiation.
- *Target point* – The outcome you want to achieve in the negotiation.
- *Outcome expectation* – The result of the negotiation, as you envisioned.
- *Resistance point* – The outcome just before the breaking point that you are still willing to accept.
- *Breaking point* – The point at which you break off the negotiation and look for another solution.
- *BATNA* – Best Alternative to a Negotiated Agreement.

It is important to discuss the outcome expectation with the backers as well. In complex negotiations, you negotiate simultaneously at two tables, with the opponent on the one hand and with the backers on the other.

BEST ALTERNATIVE TO A NEGOTIATED AGREEMENT

Having a *Best Alternative To a Negotiated Agreement* (BATNA) is an important lever. The BATNA is the best thing you can do if negotiations do not lead to an acceptable outcome. The BATNA largely determines the breaking point in the negotiation. The *Zone Of Possible Agreement* (ZOPA) lies between the breakpoints of the negotiation parties.

Positional negations are about the actual facts and figures and the other party's expectations. What do they think your BATNA is? Do they think you will use it? How hard do they think you want to play the game? At what point do they think you will break off negotiations and vice versa?

It is best to have a plan B ready for important negotiations in case you do not reach an acceptable agreement. It is wise to think this through before entering the negotiations.

PRINCIPLED NEGOTIATIONS

A very different approach is principled negotiation. Principled negotiation aims to achieve a win-win agreement. The Harvard method of negotiation is one such principled negotiation. The Harvard method describes four principles that facilitate win/win negotiation processes (Fisher, et al, 2011).

Principle 1: Separate the individual from the problem – Negotiations often occur when people already have a history with each other. This may significantly affect the opportunities to enter into a win-win agreement. In complex situations, it may even be necessary to focus the first meeting(s) on creating an open atmosphere in which people are willing to discuss their interests and are curious about the interests of others instead of focusing on positions only. People are not the problem. They have legitimate interests, needs, fears and desires from their individual perspectives.

Principle 2: Negotiate with a focus on interests instead of position – One way to get to the core is to focus on the real content-related interests that people bring to the negotiating table. When you separate the people from the problem, you foster an open atmosphere in which you can discuss these perspectives, often by asking open-ended questions, such as, 'Which of your interests will be served during this negotiation?' or, 'What is your loss if this negotiation fails?' Listening to the answers gives confidence and the feeling of really being heard. The ultimate art will be to develop a joint desire that includes both parties' legitimate interests.

Exploration phase

After the solution-orientated question has been accepted, the parties can proceed with exploration. Much information has already come to light during the question formulation process. In the exploration phase, giving substance to this information by asking open questions is important. This allows parties to clarify, substantiate and deepen their positions and interests. The other parties learn to see the situation from someone else's perspective and also learn to understand why specific priorities and or adopted positions are essential to that party. This strengthens everyone's commitment to solving the question at hand.

Implementation phase

By asking open questions, a picture emerges of the entire situation. In this phase, parties look for solutions that serve their interests. Parties first formulate criteria against which solutions can be tested. They then explore options. The parties should recognise the criteria as logical and perceive the options as positive, authentic and valuable.

Completion phase

In the concluding phase, the parties work on the agreement. They make a final choice, lay down the agreement and define in outline how, by whom, where, when, why, and with what it will be concretised.

Negotiations are not always successful. This means that talks may fail because the parties cannot agree. They can reconsider the actual situation, the solution-orientated question and ways to solve it. They can also ask a third party to mediate, seek arbitration, et cetera (see *Dispute resolution* in Chapter 6.01, Purchase).

To make negotiation processes run smoothly and avoid impasses, negotiators can focus on different influenceable aspects.

INFLUENTIAL ASPECTS OF NEGOTIATION (ADVANCED)

Willem Mastenbroek (2012) identifies five aspects you can use to influence negotiations: content, procedures, power balance, atmosphere, and playing field (see Figure 8.06.03).

Influence content – Influencing content is about limiting, extending or changing the topics on the table. Do salary negotiations include working conditions or not? Aspects for which there is a weak negotiating base are best taken into account when negotiating the bigger picture.

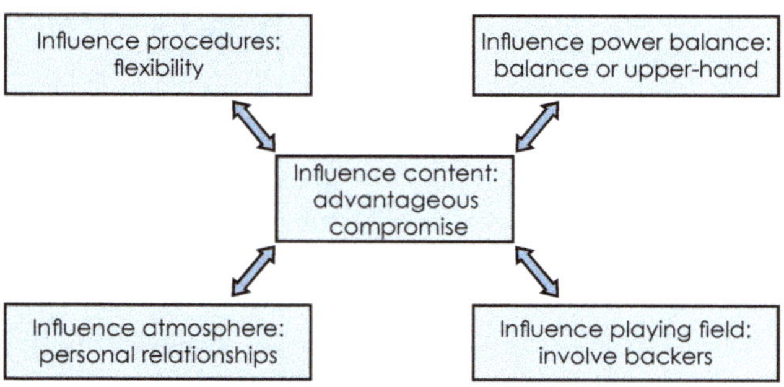

Figure 8.06.03 Influenceable aspects of negotiation (Mastenbroek, 2012)

Influence flexibility – Flexibility can be influenced by choosing an exploratory or rigid stance. From an exploratory style, you actively seek mutually beneficial solutions. With an uncompromising stance, you stand by your own viewpoints. When conducting an exploratory style, a flexible, inquisitive attitude is recommended. The exploratory style usually leads to a better relationship and results that benefit both parties.

Influence power balance – Parties can strengthen their position by taking the initiative and consciously deploying their power sources, such as substantive insight, decision-making power, acquired support from third parties and the already discussed BATNA. It is important not only to have a substantiated BATNA but also to present them and convince your opponent that you are prepared/forced to use it if the result is unfavourable.

Influence atmosphere – You can create a positive climate by getting to know each other informally and casually, with humour, showing interest in personal matters, acting consistently, and displaying an attitude of mutual dependence so that the other party knows, 'We need each other!' Maintaining a positive atmosphere for everyone involved is also necessary to avoid losing face. A climate wherein parties do not overrule or get too familiar with each other can make this attainable.

Influence playing field – The playing field largely determines the room to manoeuvre. You can consciously create more or less room to manoeuvre by referring to the space your backers have given you. If the talks do not offer enough room to meet these demands and wishes, the time has come to suspend the negotiations to consult your support base.

NEGOTIATION TACTICS (ADVANCED)

Negotiation is about influencing the other party to reach an agreement that moves the project forward without alienating or angering them. When negotiating, you can use several tactics to influence the other party to get them on your side.

- *The foot-in-the-door tactic* – Start with a small request, such as a discount on a cheap item, and if the other party responds, ask for the same discount on a second more expensive one.
- *Yes, and ...'* – Add some benefits and possibilities, when you accept a proposal. 'Yes, that's a good approach, and if we actively involve the supplier, it will be even better.'
- *Take it or leave it* – This tactic is possible if you have a good BATNA. You force them to take or leave it because you have a good alternative. Make it clear that you cannot pass the BATNA.
- *Big Brother* – You clarify the boundaries by pointing out that your backers will never agree to certain proposals. If you agree to such proposals, these will surely be nullified by the backers.
- *Compare with potential competitors* – Show the benefits of working with you and convince them they will never get a better offer elsewhere.
- *Good guy, bad guy* – On the one hand, explain clearly why your offer is very advantageous to the other party. This shows that you have their best interests at heart. On the other hand, tell them that you are very disappointed with their offer

and why. You may find their offer almost indecent. It is wise to do this together with someone else.

- *Offer a bogey* – Make it clear how much you sacrifice to drop a stated condition. If you give in, they will feel you have done something for them. This gives them a reason to do something for you.
- *Show your personal commitment* – Let the other individual know why you are committed to reaching an agreement so they will choose to work with you for the greater good.
- *What goes around comes around* – To accept a proposal, what do you get in return?
- *Counterclaim* – Negotiation is also about listening carefully. What is the other party really trying to achieve? Once you have heard that, you can give in to specific demands and immediately state what you want in return. After all, there has to be a balance.
- *Price anchor* – If you are the first party to state a price, this becomes an anchor in the minds of others and, therefore, in the negotiations.
- *Give in the first time* – Accept the other party's offer the first time without bargaining. This opens up room for bargaining on every subsequent issue.
- *Submit your own proposal* – This yields better results than commenting on theirs.

8.07 CONFLICTS AND CRISES

PURPOSE

The purpose of this chapter is to enable the individual to take effective action when a crisis or clash of opposing interests/incompatible personalities occurs.

LEARNING OBJECTIVES

Conflict management:

- Functional and dysfunctional conflicts;
- Types of conflicts;
- Conflict management styles;
- Conflict phases;
- Conflict deregulation mechanisms;
- Project manager in various roles in conflicts (advanced).

Crisis management:

- Crisis and desired style of Leadership in managing crises (advanced);
- Crisis plan (advanced).

DEFINITIONS

Conflict: A disagreement between parties with opposing interests, values or goals.
Functional conflict: A conflict that contributes to improving decisions or cooperation.
Conflict phase: A distinctive gradation of severity and depth of a conflict.
Conflict de-escalation: Interventions in order to resolve a conflict.
Conflict management style: A specific behaviour for resolving a conflict.
Crisis: A situation of intense difficulty requiring a quick response.

INTRODUCTION

Conflict is sometimes unavoidable. However, they are not always dysfunctional. Resolving conflicts can lead to better resolution and understanding, benefiting the project. However, they should be managed effectively to prevent them from becoming destructive to those involved and the project. In such situations, the conflict can even develop into a crisis.

You should always be alert to possible crises and include them in your risk analysis. You should take measures to prevent it and plan measures in case of a crisis. You need to know how best to act in case of a crisis. A crisis will hopefully not occur, but if it does, it could endanger human lives and threaten the project's continuity. From your responsibility as project manager, you need to prepare for this.

FUNCTIONAL AND DYSFUNCTIONAL CONFLICTS

Conflicts can be distinguished into functional and dysfunctional conflicts. We speak of functional conflicts when the conflict leads to better solutions and or collaboration. Parties disagree, for example, about how they receive work from another party or the time they are given to perform the work. Such conflicts can be recognised and discussed in the open space. An attentive approach usually ensures that the conflict ultimately has a positive effect on the team's performance.

However, if a conflict continues to fester, dysfunctional conflicts arise. These are conflicts where the content is pushed aside, and personal annoyance and dissatisfaction arise. The clash arising from the initial disagreement becomes relational and personal. These conflicts no longer contribute to functional decision-making and collaboration processes between parties. To do so, the dysfunctional tensions that arise between the conflicting parties should first be resolved.

TYPES OF CONFLICT

Conflicts are about contradictions that people experience or have experienced. However, not every difference of opinion or point of view is a conflict. Essential to a conflict is that the people actively work to resolve the disagreement in their favour. This can lead to overt or concealed tensions that affect functional collaboration. To de-escalate or resolve these conflicts, it is important to distinguish different types of conflicts. Each type of conflict requires a different approach. Four types of conflict are generally distinguished:

Instrumental or business conflicts – These include differences in diagnosis and approach to problems, differences in priority setting, and so on. In such conflicts, conflicting parties should agree on an approach that is satisfactory to both parties. This calls for open, informal discussions in which different approaches are balanced against each other based on arguments.

Conflicts of interest or scarcity – These involve the distribution of scarce resources. These resources can be tangible (money, goods, machines) and intangible (powers, time, information). Such conflicts directly affect the interests of the parties involved and may even endanger the survival of organisations. These interests, therefore, should be secured. Negotiations are important in such situations. They make it possible to align interests and agree on measures that serve mutual interests.

Power or dependence conflicts – These are conflicts that arise when people strive or risk losing autonomy and control. Such conflicts are about the distribution of power and influence. As viewed from the perspective of the power holder, it is important to involve others in the decision-making process. Acting too directly, dominant and suppressing creates counterforces that want to change the political framework of the game. The key is to create a healthy balance between the parties involved.

Social-emotional conflicts – These refer to differences in values, beliefs, culture, style, personality and identity. Such conflicts are about conforming to the prevailing norms or being appreciated for the individual you are and your qualities. With such conflicts, it is important to respect people's dignity. By focusing on the content, you can discuss people's qualities concerning that content. In this way, you gain insight into the value of each person's contribution to the whole. Focusing on the relationship creates space for dialogue about what conflicting parties find difficult and how this can be overcome.

These conflict sources often influence each other, reinforcing and deepening the conflict. The best way to prevent this escalation is to distance yourself from the conflict, allowing room to reflect on the emerging situation. This provides insight into the conflict behaviour of others and yourself and its effects. You can choose an appropriate style to resolve the conflict from this insight.

CONFLICT MANAGEMENT STYLES

Thomas & Kilmann distinguish five conflict styles (see Figure 8.07.01). These styles reflect, on the one hand, the assertive ability to stand up for yourself and, on the other, the ability to give space to others. These styles correspond to negotiation strategies discussed in Chapter 8.06, Negotiations. This is not surprising, as negotiation issues are, in fact, conflicts of interest.

Competing – Competing is imposing your will on the other party without really considering what they want. You can do this by blocking decisions, deciding for the other party, portraying them negatively, withholding information, forming coalitions, threatening sanctions, et cetera. A negative effect of competing is that the other party starts using counter-power based on resistance.

The positive side of competing is its effectiveness and speed. If swift action is needed, you are sure you are right, you have the power, and vital issues are at stake, be bold, decide, and go for it. You can gain sympathy by briefly informing others of the benefits and necessity of the decision. Even if other means have failed, you can use competing as an approach. The party with the power to force the decision decides. Again, a clear vision and explanation usually reinforce success.

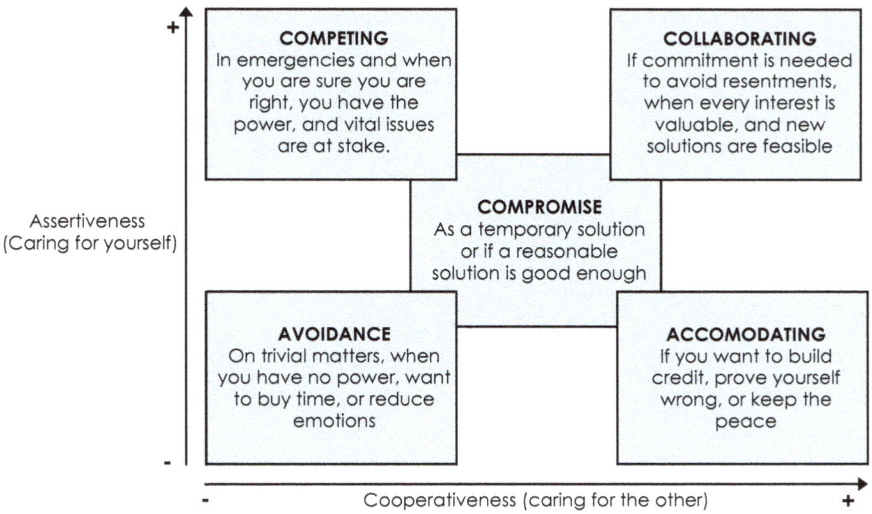

Figure 8.07.01 Conflict styles according to Thomas & Kilmann (Thomas, 2002)

Accommodating – Accommodating means giving space to the other individual and letting go of your own perspective for a while. You can choose this style when the other person's power pressure is high or what they want is real. You can also use this style to build credit or prevent escalation. But beware: accommodating can give the impression of weakness.

Avoiding – Avoidance means leaving the conflict for what it is. Examples of avoidance are: diverting attention, remaining silent, qualifying contradictions as irrelevant, not taking sides, literally walking away, choosing your own solution, et cetera. By avoiding, you avoid the confrontation. That is both the strength and the weakness of this style. It is effective when the situation is not important enough to fight for. Letting go is a skill! You can also use this style if you have no power, want to buy time or reduce emotions.

Compromising – In a compromise, conflicting parties seek a middle ground. They share differences. Compromise holds the middle ground between competing and accommodating. The problem is quickly and directly addressed, but the depth of the collaborating style is lacking.

There may be a sense of disappointment if one party feels it has fallen short. There may also be a remaining level of mistrust, reinforcing the need for control. In such situations, collaborating would have been a better style. Compromise is effective when there is not enough time to resolve the conflict by collaborating or if there is already some trust between the conflicting parties. People know each other and understand what they can expect from each other. This trust makes a quick deal possible.

Collaborating – Collaborating means entering into a dialogue with the other party to find a mutually satisfactory solution. By working together, you tackle the conflict with the underlying idea that both parties (can) benefit. You explore common and or overarching interests and base alternatives on clear criteria.

Positive effects are that the conflict is usually resolved to the satisfaction of both parties, the relationship between the parties is not disrupted, and the parties get to know each other better. This reduces the likelihood of new conflicts. It may even strengthen the collaboration. This style is particularly effective when the interests of both parties are high and collaboration is valued. A prerequisite is that both parties are motivated to solve the conflict together.

PHASES IN A CONFLICT

A conflict phase is a distinctive gradation of the severity and depth of a conflict. Louis Pondy (1992) distinguishes four conflict phases and aftercare. It starts with latent irritations, which then develop into rational disagreements, after which emotions take over and finally become a real battle. Without aftercare, conflicting parties might slip back into old habits after resolving the conflict, partly because they had also affected the teams. During aftercare, you should ensure that it does not simmer in the team.

Latent phase (zero phase) – There is no actual conflict yet. However, parties do signal that a conflict is latent by how they communicate. They have a fierce tone, repeat arguments, occasionally exhibit harsh behaviour in debates, and do not listen to each other. When they don't feel heard, they may express dissatisfaction. As a result, latent conflicts surface or remain hidden and flare up later. In many cases, latent conflicts have already been detected by others. However, they are still dismissed by them as something that will pass.

Perceived phase (rational phase) – In this phase, parties realise they have a conflict. They contradict each other and express their dissatisfaction. The other is to blame, and parties are no longer willing to concede. Debates polarise. Due to poor listening, opinions become distorted, and a mutual suspicion ensues that the other is no longer willing to pursue a common course of action. Others become involved and are brought into the coalitions of conflicting parties, making these conflicts more complex.

Felt phase (emotional phase, conflict) – If a conflict is not addressed in the previous phase, negative emotions will increase. Conflicting parties focus their attention on the other party's mistakes, clumsiness and personality. The other party becomes an antagonist, characterised as unreliable or worse. Parties use harsh words, start blaming people directly and strengthen the relationship with coalition partners to reinforce their own opinion and position and to have their feelings confirmed. Those who are not with me are against me. Resolving the conflict is no longer the first priority; they just want to win.

Manifest phase (battle phase) – If the conflict has not been adequately addressed in the previous phase, it automatically enters the manifest phase. In this phase, parties no longer speak to each other at all. Respect is completely lost, and they only want to destroy the other party; they want the other to move, leave or disappear. In this phase, the conflict manifests itself to its full extent. Intrigues and destructive actions dominate behaviour. When coalitions are strongly forged, the team is also fragmented. However, as you have already reached the felt phase, you will often notice that others have distanced themselves from the conflict and wish to see it resolved.

DE-ESCALATION IN THE DIFFERENT CONFLICT PHASES

Each phase needs an appropriate style to solve and de-escalate the conflict (see Figure 8.07.02).

Latent phase

It is important to recognise latent conflicts. The situation has not yet taken root in negative beliefs or emotions and, therefore, is not yet heavily charged. Name what you see and invite parties to listen to each other. A team in which members can open up, give each other feedback and discuss contradictions can be very effective. In such teams, conflicts can improve collaboration. In a team where conflicts remain hidden and unspoken, conflicts will build up and eventually surface.

Perceived phase

At this phase, simply inviting the parties to listen to each other no longer works. You should first restore trust and respect between them to resolve the conflict and develop possible win-win solutions. The best way to do this is by sitting down with them and having them convey how they view a future collaboration. Let them listen attentively to each other. By giving them this space, the parties start listening to each other again, leading to a solution being found that all parties can agree on.

At this stage, creative and scenario techniques can be used to reach an acceptable solution. Brainstorming and envisaging different scenarios can help. The essence is developing a solution-orientated question before looking for possible solutions. In effect, you turn the conflict into a search for mutual gain.

If all goes well, this solution will positively affect the team. If some people have already been involved in a coalition and show that they are still harbouring negative feelings about the conflict, discuss this with them and explain that a solution has been worked out with the conflicting parties.

Phase	Characteristics	Deregulating actions
Latent	• Fiercer tone of voice • Repeating arguments • Parties don't listen	• Appoint what you see and hear • Invite them to listen to each other
Perceived	• Contradicting each other • The other is to blame • Don't want to give in	• Appoint feelings • Conduct round table discussions • Develop mutually agreed solutions • Support collaboration
Felt	• Hard 'you' words • Search for coalition parties • Avoiding contact with the other • Only wants to win • Resolving conflict no longer 1st priority	• Mediation • Use pendulum swing strategy • Let emotions be expressed
Manifest	• Refuse to communicate • Respect is completely gone • Only wants to destroy the other party	• Deploy independent mediator • First let off steam • Eventually, use position to make tough decisions

Conflict After care

Figure 8.07.02 Characteristics and deregulation actions conflict phases

Felt phase

At this phase, sitting directly around the table with the parties involved no longer works. Emotions run so high that you cannot explore the situation and its origins. An initial pendulum swing strategy is needed. Now is the best time to call in a mediator. At this stage, the conflict often has a strong psychological dimension. Mediators are trained to be sensitive to this level. Sometimes, you can take on this role yourself. The latter is only possible if both parties still see you as genuinely independent, and you can also carefully factor the personal level into your approach. First, you hear the parties separately and check the heard message with the other party. Never take sides here. Make it clear that you only want to understand both stories first and will only seek and formulate solutions together, i.e. in the presence of both parties. You often need to undergo professional training to act appropriately as a mediator.

Once the situational background is understood and the intentions of both parties are clear, a triangular discussion can be initiated. The context should be outlined in which the conflict arose and the parties' story about the disrupted cooperation. Situations that cause irritation or disappointment should be laid on the table. By channelling the emotions, you can work with the parties to find solutions that benefit both sides.

If the team is greatly affected by the conflict, it is good to let them know, without passing judgment on anyone or anything, that the process of finding a suitable solution has begun. Talk with the team members you know who were affected by the conflict. Concentrate, for example, on your own personal responsibility and let go of things that are someone else's responsibility.

Manifest phase

Prompt intervention is important at this phase; otherwise, the conflict will spill over to the entire project team. Mediation by a professional, independent third party is mandatory. In this phase, you should remain outside of the conflict. Dealing with the often intense emotions felt by those involved in this phase is not without risk. The use of trained professionals is necessary.

First, the mediator should give the parties space to 'unload' their emotions from the conflict. Then, they can start with a pendulum swing strategy, as described in deregulating the conflict in the felt phase. Finally, all parties can sit together and try to reach a joint solution.

> ***From the TV programme 'Arguing with the Neighbours'***
> *The neighbours love music, but their youngest son practices on the drum kit for hours, even in the middle of the night. 'We have often complained about this, and now the atmosphere is completely ruined. We no longer speak to each other, only through the police. All we want now is for the housing association to evict them.'*
>
> *The presenters, coached by a professional mediator, first talks to the parties individually. They make sure that both parties feel heard and let off steam first. This is followed by a second round of talks in which they explore the situation and its origins.*
>
> *They then sit with both parties. Both parties express their anger, but the presenters know how to channel it and connect it with stories they have heard in their preparatory conversations with them. These interventions allow them to listen to each other once more and finally reach a joint solution.*

The mediator should consider whether mediation can lead to success given the situation and available time and resources. If success is not achievable, they should return the assignment, and decisive intervention, such as a court order, replacement, or dismissal of one or both parties, is inevitable, which will obviously affect the team. Aftercare is necessary for both the conflicting parties and the team that worked with them.

Aftercare – When the solution is to move forward with both parties, keeping a finger on the pulse is important. A relapse should be avoided. This can be achieved by checking with both parties on how the cooperation is going and offering support if necessary. When doing this, ensure the work situation is central to the discussion and the atmosphere is friendly. Based on the tone, attitude and mutual contact, you can assess the extent to which the parties get along. If tensions are rising again, dare to discuss this by inviting them for a constructive conversation in a friendly environment, for instance, such as a lunch meeting.

In situations where one or both parties should be replaced, careful counselling of those remaining in the project is essential. They should understand the motives behind the replacement. This will nip personal interpretations in the bud. You can also involve them in the replacement process. 'What support do you need to complete the project successfully?' This will help them end the conflict and reduce the likelihood of unpleasant surprises resulting from their colleague's departure.

Take note: when the removed conflict partner was in the project to represent a particular interest and has to be replaced for that interest by someone from the same group or organisation, there is a high risk that the conflict will reoccur. After all, the conflict has not yet been resolved, and those involved may still experience anger and pain. Those remaining in the project team will easily bombard the newcomer as 'just another one of those'. On the other hand, the project team's expelled conflict partner may have already shared their views on the conflict with their colleagues. The colleague replacing them thus begins their work with a certain prejudice. You will, therefore, have to carefully supervise the newcomer's introduction and pay particular attention to establishing open communication with the people involved in the conflict who may still be in the project team. Both attention to task and relationship are essential here.

ADVANCED

VARIOUS ROLES IN CONFLICTS (ADVANCED)

As a project manager, you can be part of the conflict and also be involved as a mediator between conflicting parties. Both roles require special skills.

Project manager as participant in a conflict

You need to be especially alert to any conflicts of your own with others and know when mediation by a third party is necessary. Reflection enables you to place the conflict at the proper phase and choose an appropriate approach:

- *Latent phase* – carefully examine your own position and view it from the other's perspective. Listen to the other individual and create understanding and space for jointly accepted choices.
- *Perceived phase* – Explain how the other person's attitude affects you and invite them to do the same. This increases mutual understanding, from where you can work towards more effective collaboration.
- *Felt phase* – Reduce your own emotions through reflection, putting the issue in a more genuine and often fairer perspective. Suggest bringing in a third party as a mediator. Inform the project sponsor and consult them on how to proceed. Discuss the potential consequences this can have on the project.
- *Manifest phase* – Engage a professional mediator, and escalate the conflict to the project sponsor. Accept the other person; reflecting on emotions and judgements made about each other is important. These often say more about yourself than you think. Dare to be truthful about yourself. From that vulnerability, you will develop insight and better understand your role in the conflict. That makes you more conscious and authentic, ensuring you can also approach others from a new perspective.

Roles of the project manager as a third party in a conflict

As a third party in conflicts, you can assume various roles, such as expert, authority, arbitrator, advocate, process facilitator or mediator. The situation depends on which role you can take on and how you can fulfil it.

Expert – In the role of expert, you provide a substantive solution to the conflict. You may also involve a third party as an expert. The expert role can be applied, especially if the conflict is still functional. But be careful because the conflict may have already developed into an inner conflict. If you focus only on the substantive solution, the conflicting parties may feel they are not being heard. This may worsen the conflict.

Authority – In the role of authority, you decide on a conflicting issue and supervise its implementation. This role is legitimised based on your position as project manager. Again: it is important to recognise that many conflicts have a psychological dimension. If you rate this dimension highly, attention to the human factor is important. Inner conflicts need to be listened to. The conflict will progress to a higher conflict phase if you don't. At the same time, conflict parties need to realise that an organisation as a whole has its own role to play, which counts when making decisions about the conflict.

Arbitrator – In the role of arbitrator, you take a binding decision. In this role, parties should recognise your expertise and decision-making authority. In this role, holding the conflicting parties to the arbitrator's decision is important. As a project manager, you are mostly not in a position to be the arbitrator for the conflicts in your own project.

Advocate – In the role of an advocate, you support one of the parties involved in the conflict. In such a situation, it is important that you clearly state your role, that you are not unbiased, and explain why you support the individual in the conflict. This may be because of the vulnerable position of the individual being supported or because a particular task needs to be firmly defended in the project's interests.

Process facilitator – In the role of process facilitator, you are focused on preventing conflicts. The role of process facilitator is especially important when conflicts are expected in advance, requiring someone to manage the process that parties are entering into.

Moderator – As a moderator, you direct the conversation and discussion between the conflicting parties. You invite them to the discussion, set the agenda, ask questions, grant or deny participants the floor, summarise the conclusions, and so on. You act as the discussion leader.

Mediator – You act as a mediator when parties seek a substantive solution under someone else's guidance. You actively support the parties in resolving the conflict and finding an acceptable solution. The role of mediator in a conflict of one or more of your own team members requires special care. In this role, the parties should recognise your expertise and independence. It is desirable to undergo special training to act as a mediator.

The project manager as the third party: temptations and conditions

A project manager who becomes involved in a conflict as a third party should consider their role in it and the strategy to follow. An analysis of the conflict situation and the conflict process should precede this. Important points and conditions here are:

- When you become involved as a third party in a conflict, establish by whom and with what motives. Is it to strengthen one's position, limit one's own loss of face, make a good impression on the outside world, or work seriously at finding the best solution to the conflict? Never allow yourself to be used for purposes that lack integrity!
- Explore the conflict by speaking with the people involved about the causes and effects of the conflict individually, the emotions it evokes and the options for resolving it. Look at the differences and similarities in how participants define the conflict and the willingness to find a solution.
- Identify the nature of the conflict. You should also identify the conflict phase and tailor your approach accordingly.
- The contribution you wish to make to resolving a conflict can vary. The role you choose and are given is essential to your approach.
- Ensure you are accepted in your role as a third party in the conflict.
- Your formal decision-making authority primarily determines the extent you can take charge in a conflict. Never take on roles that do not suit your authority.

- It is imperative to remain neutral; otherwise, your contribution as a third party is more likely to escalate the conflict than resolve it. In situations where you act as an advocate and choose to support one of the parties, you should justify this very clearly in advance.

CRISIS AND DESIRED STYLE OF LEADERSHIP (ADVANCED)

A crisis is a situation of intense difficulty requiring a quick response. It can endanger human lives and threaten the continuity of the business or project.

Types of crises

Ury Rosenthal (2013) distinguishes crises according to their different causes, such as:

- Natural disasters, such as floods, forest fires, famines and outbreaks of pandemics;
- Explosions and fires, such as fireworks disasters and explosions at chemical plants;
- Transport accidents, such as aeroplane crashes and oil tanker accidents;
- Riots and disturbances, such as riots around football matches and other major events;
- Terrorism and hostage-taking, such as hijackings and attacks;
- Psycho-crises, such as the assassination of politicians or well-known world or national figures;
- Administrative crises, such as court rulings that conflict with implemented policies;
- Economic crises, such as credit crises, commodity crises and hyperinflation.

Crises can occur instantly or gradually. In the first case, it is a calamity, such as a flood, an outbreak of a pandemic, or an unexpected bankruptcy of a key supplier. In the second case, an accumulation of events leads to a crisis, such as an escalating conflict that results in the demand for project closure. Realise that most crises in a project arise within the project itself.

Desired style of leadership in a crisis

When managing a crisis, it is important to use different leadership styles. For direct management, instructing is essential; for coordination with other responsible parties, the ability to chair meetings is important; while for others to perform tasks, a careful delegation of responsibilities is necessary. Always maintain an overview and do not get lost in detail.

Having crisis plans ready is a form of good leadership. Good leaders know that a crisis can always occur and are prepared for it by preparing a crisis plan in advance and practising what is in the crisis plan. If a crisis arises, everyone will know who is in charge and what to do. Depending on the circumstances, you can rely on the crisis plan of the permanent organisation or should prepare your own plan for the project.

Necessary competences of a crisis manager

A crisis manager should be analytical, stress-resistant, decisive and result-orientated, but should also be able to develop initiative, know the right people, understand the environment, be a leader and be bold. The most important style during the crisis is 'keeping an overview' and directing the crisis team confidently, based on information gathered from this team. The messages should be precise and comprehensible when communicating to the outside world.

Most importantly, a crisis manager anticipates crises that may arise. They analyse potential risks and ensure that plans are in place and specialists are trained to implement them so that when a crisis does occur, it can be effectively controlled.

CRISIS PLAN (ADVANCED)

A crisis plan describes how to act in a crisis and ensures you are prepared. These focus mainly on a crisis with a physical component, such as a disaster or riots. But crisis plans are also developed on dealing with fraud, what to do if your systems are hacked or when sensitive information is accidentally disclosed. What scenarios has your organisation developed for dealing with resource shortages? Et cetera.

A common format for a crisis plan is:

- Objectives and policies on how to deal with a crisis.
- A representative range of possible scenarios. It is essential to consider multiple scenarios that may occur. Also, to differentiate between the scale of the disaster.
- Clear roadmaps for the different scenarios and classifications.
- Criteria that determine when there is a crisis and of what magnitude, and who makes that decision.
- Composition of the crisis team and their individual roles and responsibilities.
- Command structure and a backup if the relevant roles cannot be fulfilled.
- Roles and responsibilities of other involved parties.
- Signals informing those involved that the crisis procedure is being activated and that the crisis team will take over.
- Communication protocols and contact and dispatch lists.
- Draft texts for the most common communications during the crisis.
- A summary of current laws and regulations.
- Measures to ensure that everyone is well prepared if a crisis occurs and who is responsible for it.
- The annual budget necessary to keep the risk plan up to date and people trained.
- Reporting structure indicating the end of the crisis.
- How the crisis and the crisis plan will be evaluated after a crisis.
- How the crisis plan will be updated.

Ensure that individuals who play a role in combating a crisis are trained. Conduct regular drills. Ensure there is a central command centre and that communication systems are always operational.

Worst-case scenarios

A worst-case scenario is the most severe possible outcome that can reasonably occur in a given situation. The crisis plan should include such scenarios and not just the obvious ones.

Planning worst-case scenarios not only shapes your crisis plan but also directly affects the design and approach to the work itself. So, not just what to do if the building collapses but perhaps outsource the work to a design firm with better quality control, and so on.

Well-develop crisis plans ensure that preventive measures are taken and necessary changes are initiated.

PERSPECTIVE COMPETENCES

9. IMPLEMENTING CHANGES

Projects are initiated to implement change. How do the organisation's vision and mission affect project implementation? How do programmes and a portfolio affect project governance? How do the development frameworks to be adopted affect project delivery? To better understand this, we take a closer look at these aspects in this chapter.

Chapter 9.01 Strategy – The project is placed within the organisation's change strategy. What are the organisation's mission, vision and strategy? How is performance management designed within an organisation? How are investment analyses carried out on which investment decisions are based?

Chapter 9.02 Programme Management – What is a programme? How is a programme organised? What is the lifecycle, and what are the core documents of a programme? What are the implications of a programme on a project?

Chapter 9.03 Portfolio Management – What is a portfolio, and what is the difference between portfolio management and management by projects? How is a portfolio organised, and what is the heartbeat of a portfolio? How are projects prioritised within a portfolio?

Chapter 9.04 Supporting Functions and Implementing Project, Programme, and Portfolio Management – What are the characteristics of a permanent PMO, and what are the implications of a permanent PMO for managing projects? How can the organisation successfully implement project, programme, and portfolio management?

Chapter 9.05 Development Frameworks – How are development frameworks applied within organisations? What are the characteristics of Agile, Scrum, Kanban and Lean Six Sigma frameworks, and how do you use these frameworks in projects?

Together, these chapters describe how projects can be positioned in the changing environment of organisations.

9.01 STRATEGY

PURPOSE

The purpose of this chapter is to enable the individual to understand the strategy and strategic processes to manage projects within the context of the organisation's strategy.

LEARNING OBJECTIVES

- Corporate mission, vision, and core values;
- Strategic objectives;
- Benchmarking;
- SWOT analysis;
- Aligning with the organisation's mission, vision and strategic objectives;
- Ten Schools of Thought (advanced);
- Business model Canvas (advanced);
- McKinsey 7S model (advanced);
- Strategic performance management (advanced);
- Balanced Scorecard and strategy map (advanced);
- Performance dashboards (advanced);
- EFQM model (advanced);
- Net Present Value calculation (advanced);
- Payback period and break-even point (advanced).

DEFINITIONS

Mission: The purpose of an organisation.
Vision: A compelling idea or future state for an organisation, product or service.
Core value: A fundamental belief that underpins our actions.
Strategy: How an individual, group or organisation wants to achieve its goals.

INTRODUCTION

Projects establish their raison d'être in their contribution to the organisation's strategy to achieve the objectives arising from its vision and mission within its core values. It is, therefore, of utmost importance to know the mission, vision, and core values of the sponsoring organisation and its stakeholders. This also provides an opportunity to better justify the project's delivery and identify opportunities to contribute to these objectives. Projects can also be initiated to contribute to defining or developing the organisation's mission, vision, core values, and strategies.

POSITIONING

It is important to assess, right from the start, how the proposed project fits in with the goals and values of the sponsoring organisation and the stakeholders. This largely determines the justification for the project, how the project should be delivered, and how the project results should be shaped.

During the project definition stage, this should be further elaborated. During project delivery, this should be monitored and explicitly evaluated at stage transitions. It won't be the first time these objectives and values get lost in the daily hectic of realising the project on time. At project closure, the alignment with the goals and values should be confirmed and recorded in the end-of-project report.

ALIGN WITH ORGANISATIONAL MISSION, VISION AND STRATEGIC OBJECTIVES

Project values, such as the project deliverables, objectives, outcomes and benefits, should all align with the organisation's mission, vision and strategic objectives. These project values can be derived directly from them or the derived objectives at the business or functional level. Based on these, key performance indicators, targets, and the project's critical success factors can be determined. During project delivery, both the deployment of the project success factors and the achievement of the key performance targets should be monitored.

ORGANISATIONAL MISSION, VISION, AND CORE VALUES

The organisation's mission and vision enable people to connect with the organisation and direct their actions. Not surprisingly, management often pays a lot of attention to these. Besides the mission and vision, the organisation's core values are also important. Core values are the fundamental convictions that form the basis for our actions. Core values serve as the moral and ethical compass of the organisation.

Mission and mission statement

The mission is the purpose of why an organisation exists. Through their mission, they indicate who they are and what they do. A mission statement should be brief and easy to remember. A mission statement helps staff and management to stay focused on the reason for its existence and makes it clear to others what the organisation stands for. The mission statement should be reviewed every five to ten years or as needed.

Vision and vision statement

A vision describes a compelling idea or future state for an organisation, product or service and is, therefore, a guideline for the changes that need to be implemented. A good vision statement:

- Is short and concise, easy to remember and simple to understand;
- Is appropriate to the degree of change that needs to be made;
- Appeals to reason and emotion;
- Is relevant to all stakeholders;
- Is sufficiently robust to remain valid throughout the period of change;
- Does not contain deadlines and performance targets;
- Contains sufficient information to legitimise the investments.

A good vision statement is *Motivating, Ambitious, Generic, Inspiring and Communicative* (MAGIC).

> *Martin Luther King, during his speech on 28 August 1963: 'I have a dream that one day, on the red hills of Georgia, the sons of former slaves and the sons of former slave owners will be able to sit down together at a table of brotherhood.'*

Timelines and performance targets are usually not included in the vision. That will come later when an organisation translates the vision into a strategy. In the vision, the organisation describes how they want to be seen, not how they want to achieve it. This does not always go according to plan. That's why they don't describe the solution in the vision. Several roads lead to Rome (the desired future).

Core values

Core values are the fundamental beliefs that underpin our actions. Core values are important for the organisation's identity. They guide their people; they determine the attitudes and behaviour of staff and management.

Normally, three to six core values usually give a good picture of an organisation. Fewer core values often don't cover what is essential. More core values provide too little direction and make what the organisation stands for unclear. Core values need to be specific: core values such as 'customer-orientated' and 'service-orientated' are not specific enough because every company is expected to be customer- and service-orientated.

> *According to Disney Careers, their corporate values are optimism, innovation, decency, quality, community, and storytelling (2020).*

Communicating one's own mission and core values is becoming increasingly important. This is how an organisation attracts the right people and the right customers. By acting consistently based on their core values, they also become more reliable in their network with other parties. Changing an organisation's core values costs much time and energy.

STRATEGY AND STRATEGIC OBJECTIVES

A strategy outlines how an individual, group or organisation intends to achieve its goals. An organisation's strategy is based on its vision and the underlying mission and core values. There are many ways for an organisation to develop, refine, or renew an organisational strategy. This is often done based on a benchmark and SWOT analysis. Within an organisation, multiple strategies are usually focused on simultaneously.

For each of these strategies, strategic objectives are defined. These are goals that the organisation aims to achieve, usually within three to five years. From these objectives, business and functional-level objectives are derived, which have a shorter time span, usually one to three years. It is essential to determine the strategy to which the project should contribute and to agree on this with all parties involved. Are we supporting business continuity or preparing the organisation for the future? A lack of clarity on this subject can do great harm.

Difference between tactic and strategy

For an organisation, a strategy is the main plan that it guides towards its vision. Tactics are the specific actions or manoeuvres to implement a chosen strategy. A strategy is more significant than tactics. However, the two should go together, or the strategy will fail.

> *You want to go on holiday to Spain. Since you have little money, you decide to hitchhike (strategy). You can stand next to a major motorway ramp or post an application on the website, but you choose to approach truck drivers who regularly drive to Spain and ask them if you can travel with them (tactics). Fortunately, this turned out well.*

BENCHMARKING

A benchmark is defined as a reference by which things are compared but is also defined as the evaluation against such a reference value. Organisations benchmark their own performance with that of the best competitors in the market (external benchmarking). We distinguish between performance, process and strategic benchmarking. In addition, benchmarking can also be applied between departments and business units within the same organisation (internal benchmarking).

A *performance benchmark* compares the performance of the company's processes and products with the best performance of its competitors. A *process benchmark* compares the processes, skills and competences contributing to the organisation's success. A *strategic benchmark* compares the strategies of how organisations achieve competitive advantage.

First, determine which processes and performances you want to benchmark and which organisations you want to compare them with. Then, carry out the benchmark, develop improvement proposals, and implement these improvements. Check the results. Finally, perform a new benchmark to check how your organisation has developed compared to other organisations. Realise that it is often not easy to gather (reliable) information from competitors.

SWOT ANALYSIS

In a SWOT analysis, the organisation's strengths, weaknesses, opportunities, and threats are identified and analysed. Based on this, an organisation can develop, refine, or renew its strategy. Strengths and weaknesses relate to the own organisation and the products and services provided. Opportunities and threats relate to the external circumstances and developments to which the organisation and its products and services are exposed (see Figure 9.01.01).

In the confrontation matrix that subsequently arises, the internal and external elements oppose each other, and strategies can be determined. When setting up the confrontation matrix, it is advisable not to include too many elements. The risk may arise that the overview will be lost and connections will not be recognised. An ideal SWOT analysis contains three to five strategies per combination after the first selection.

The SWOT team can then select the most promising strategy per combination. This ultimately leads to four possible strategies (see Figure 9.01.02):

» *Grow strategy* – How do we use our strength to exploit the opportunities?
» *Defend strategy* – How do we use our strength to avert the threats?
» *Improve strategy* – How do we strengthen our weaknesses to exploit the opportunities?
» *Crisis strategy* – How do we strengthen our weaknesses to avert threats or withdraw?

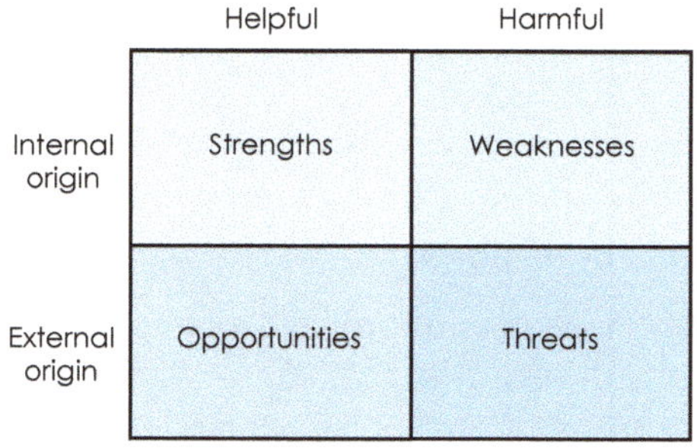

Figure 9.01.01 SWOT analysis

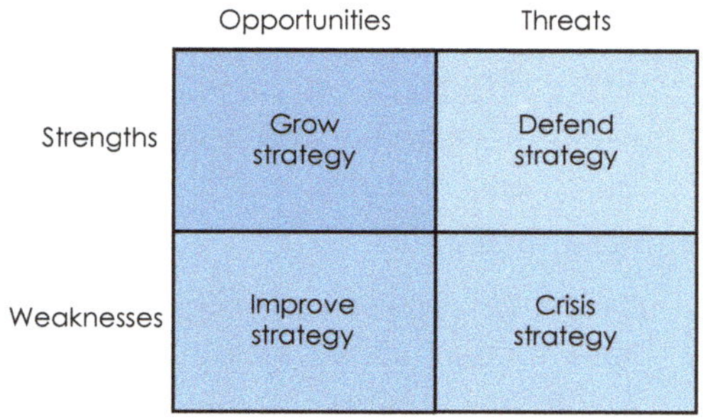

Figure 9.01.02 Confrontation matrix

Based on these four possible strategies, you can finally determine one or two strategies to implement. Make sure the SWOT team is a good reflection of the organisation. Ensure a careful external analysis and be specific. Assure that the intended policy does not distort the analysis. And finally, have the SWOT team guided by an expert facilitator the first time.

RESPONSIBILITIES

The project sponsor is accountable for the strategic goals and the underlying mission, vision and core values being properly translated into the project assignment. The project manager is responsible for their application and monitors them for the project's duration.

ADVANCED

TEN SCHOOLS OF THOUGHT (ADVANCED)

Organisation strategies can be developed in many different ways. In the *Ten Schools of Thought*, Henry Mintzberg (2013) presented a framework that describes ten approaches to define strategies.

1. *Design school* – This approach focuses on achieving a match between internal strengths and weaknesses and external opportunities and threats. This works well in a stable market where you have sufficient knowledge about yourself and the market.
2. *Planning school* – The changed situation is designed and implemented based on a well-thought-out step-by-step plan. This assumes the ability to predict the circumstances and the actions of others to a high degree. The issue arises when things don't go according to plan.
3. *Positioning school* – Here, first, the position of the own products on the market is determined. Then the market is analysed, and finally, based on this, the strategy determines how to improve the position of its own products in the market. This school also assumes that the market is what it is.
4. *Entrepreneurial school* – This approach puts the focus on the CEO. It is mostly observed in small businesses. With this approach, the company follows whatever the CEO says.
5. *Cognitive school* – With this approach, people's perceptions and information are studied. It is rooted entirely in understanding the customers. Based on this understanding, you can improve or communicate more effectively to obtain strategic advantages.
6. *Learning school* – This approach focuses on learning from the past: what worked well and what didn't. This is effective when the company and the circumstances are stable.
7. *Power school* – Here, the firm follows the people in power. This can refer to people within their own organisation, customers and other stakeholders. Problems arise when they stop listening to feedback.
8. *Cultural school* – This approach is based on the belief that the company has immense human and cultural capital that can give a proper direction to the firm. Problems arise when you cannot unify the people behind a joint idea of change.
9. *Environmental school* – Here, the focus on the environment predominates. What will happen to the environment? How will we become sustainable? This is mainly applied when there is a total dependency on environmental factors.
10. *Configuration school* – This approach is based on the belief that the strategy cannot be derived from a simple set of values. The organisation is repeatedly configured until it reaches the desired result.

For the characteristics of these ten schools of thought, see Table 9.01.01. Depending on the circumstances, different approaches can be followed and can also be combined.

	School of thoughts	Strategy	Main Focus
1	Design school	Conceptual	Strategy based on SWOT analyses
2	Planning school	Formal	Formal process with clear steps and techniques
3	Positioning school	Analytical	Strategy based on the competitive position
4	Entrepreneurial school	Visionary	Strategy based on vision of the entrepreneur
5	Cognitive school	Mental	Strategy based on mental perspectives customers
6	Learning school	Emergent	Strategy development as a learning process
7	Power school	Power-based	Strategy based on following powered positions
8	Cultural school	Ideological	A social process that builds on corporate culture
9	Environmental school	Passive	The environment is central actor
10	Configurational school	Episodic	Organisations can be seen as configurations

Table 9.01.01 The Ten Schools of Thought, according to Mintzberg (2013)

BUSINESS MODEL CANVAS (ADVANCED)

A business model provides a blueprint for an organisation. It is the rationale for how an organisation creates, delivers and retains value and can be used to examine desired business options. The new versus the current situation is a source for initiating many projects and aligns projects with the organisation's vision and strategic objectives. A commonly used model is the *Business Model Canvas* (Osterwalder, et al, 2010). This business model consists of four main areas, divided into nine building blocks (see Figure 9.01.03).

Sales:

- *Customer segments* – Which target groups and specific customers can we distinguish? What are the wishes and needs of those target groups and specific customers?
- *Channels* – What is our marketing strategy? How do we keep our customers informed about our offer? How can the customers purchase the products and services?
- *Customer relationships* – How do we interact with the different customer segments? Which segments provide us with the most revenue?

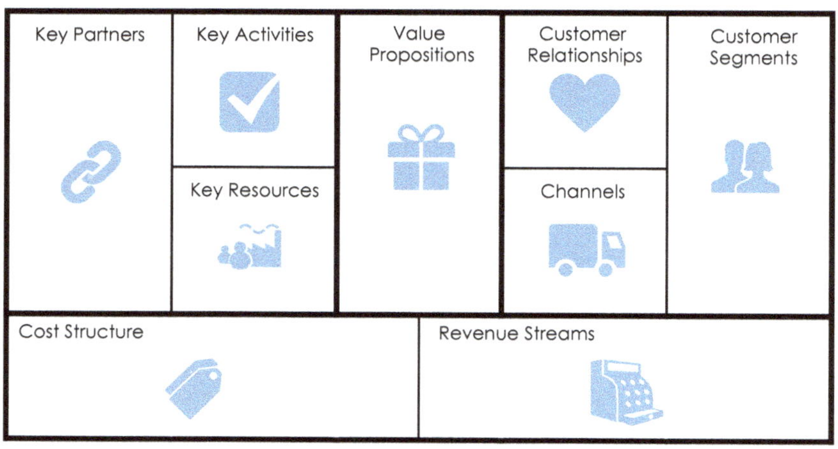

Figure 9.01.03 Business model Canvas (Osterwalder, et al, 2010)

Value:

- *Value proposition* – What added value do you offer our customers? How do we differ from your competitors in this regard?

Production:

- *Key activities* – What are your core activities to deliver your value proposition, distribute our products and services, and maintain and enhance customer relations?
- *Key resources* – What are the most important company assets? This concerns people, materials, equipment, and the necessary permits and financing.
- *Key partners* – Who are your main partners and suppliers? Which key resources do they provide you with? Which key activities do they perform?

Cost and revenues:

- *Revenue streams* – How are revenues generated? What is the contribution of each stream? How many customers and how much turnover is needed to be profitable?
- *Cost structure* – What are the costs of sales and internal operating costs? Which resources and activities are the most expensive?

With the Business Model Canvas, a coherent business model can be developed for an entire organisation, a work unit or an individual product or service. Applying this business model often demonstrates that changes in one business aspect also trigger changes in others. Collaborating with a new partner can lead to offering new services and a change in the relationship with the customers. Initiating a new sales channel may result in new value propositions, new customers, new resources, et cetera. In other words, a project result usually brings about more changes than initially expected. This insight is important for both the decision to initiate the project and the project design but is, of course, also crucial for implementing the project output in the organisation.

7S-MODEL VAN MCKINSEY (ADVANCED)

McKinsey's 7S model (50Minutes.com, 2015) is a more internally orientated business model. The concrete elements are strategy, structure and systems. The soft elements are style, staff, skills and shared values (see Figure 9.01.04).

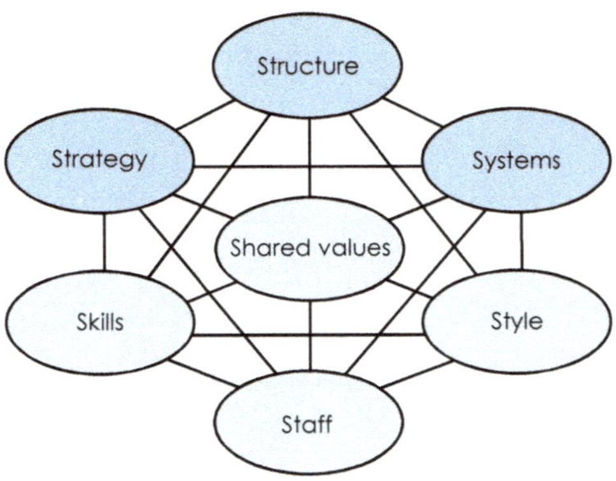

Figure 9.01.04 7S-model Mc Kinsey (50Minutes.com, 2015)

- *Strategy* – What are the strategic goals and how should these be realised?
- *Structure* – How is the organisation set up? What are the organisational structure and division of tasks? Who is accountable for what?
- *Systems* – What methods and procedures are applied? What is the infrastructure? How does communication take place, and what is the level of bureaucracy?
- *Style* – How is the company managed, how do they interact, and what is the leadership style?
- *Staff* – What is the size of the organisation and the profile of its staff and management? This also included the quality and quality of the workforce and their motivation.
- *Skills* – What are the competences of the workforce? What differentiates them from others?
- *Shared values* – What are the core beliefs and shared values guiding behaviour and actions?

All factors are interrelated. If you change one factor, other factors will change too. In an optimally functioning organisation, all factors are effectively interrelated.

STRATEGIC PERFORMANCE MANAGEMENT (ADVANCED)

Strategic performance management is the process in which the organisation's mission, vision, strategy and objectives are translated to all organisational levels and made measurable through critical success criteria and performance indicators to direct the organisation.

A common step-by-step plan for setting up performance management is as follows:

- Confirm the mission, core values and vision of the organisation;
- Formulate a strategy map and a blueprint for the new organisation;
- Appoint an owner for each strategic goal;
- Define one or more *key performance indicators* (KPIs) with the owner for each strategic goal;
- Determine for each KPI the current value and the objectives to be achieved over time;
- Formulate the actions that need to be taken to achieve those objectives;
- Configure a performance dashboard;
- Periodically monitor the progress of the actions and the realisation of the targets;
- Take corrective actions where necessary;
- Regularly update the strategy map and the targets to be achieved;
- Evaluate the effectiveness of performance management (at least twice a year).

Performance should be determined as a derivative of the organisation's strategy. Ensure that all important aspects are included and that there is not too much emphasis on one or just a few aspects. Also, ensure that both the organisation's efforts and results are measured. Ensure that the individual performance of employees is in line with the overriding organisation goals. Make sure that the correct behaviour initiated by the performance management system is actually rewarded.

Balanced Scorecard

The *Balanced Scorecard* (Kaplan & Norton, 1996) defines four perspectives on which organisational goals, performance indicators and associated objectives can be determined in conjunction. The model's strength is that it encompasses both financial and non-financial goals.

The four perspectives of the Balanced Score Card are (see Figure 9.01.05):

- *Innovation and learning perspective* – What are our learning and innovation goals?
- *Internal business perspective* – What are the necessary performances of the internal processes?
- *Customer perspective* – What are our customer-related goals?
- *Financial perspective* – What are our financial goals?

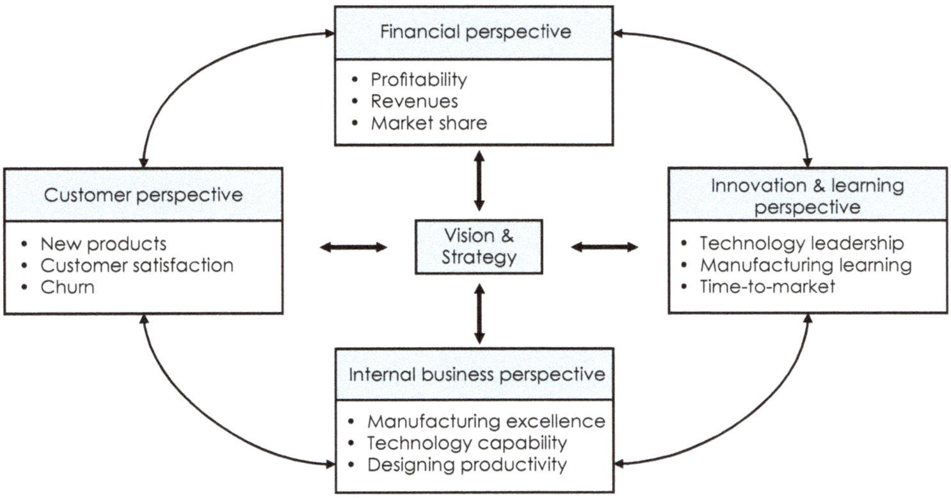

Figure 9.01.05 Balanced scorecard

The logical structure of the BSC is formed not only by the relationship between the four perspectives but also BY the causal relationships between the individual (sub)goals within these perspectives.

Strategy map

A strategy map visualises the key performance goals within the various business perspectives of the organisation and the interdependencies with which a business strategy can be realised. This makes a strategy map an important tool to translate strategy into action. A strategy map is, in principle, free of form. However, the Kaplan and Norton strategy map based on the Balanced Scorecard is most commonly used (see Figure 9.01.06).

Start working based on the organisation's long-term strategy; that gives focus. Show goals, not performance indicators or actions, that will come later. Avoid too many dependencies.

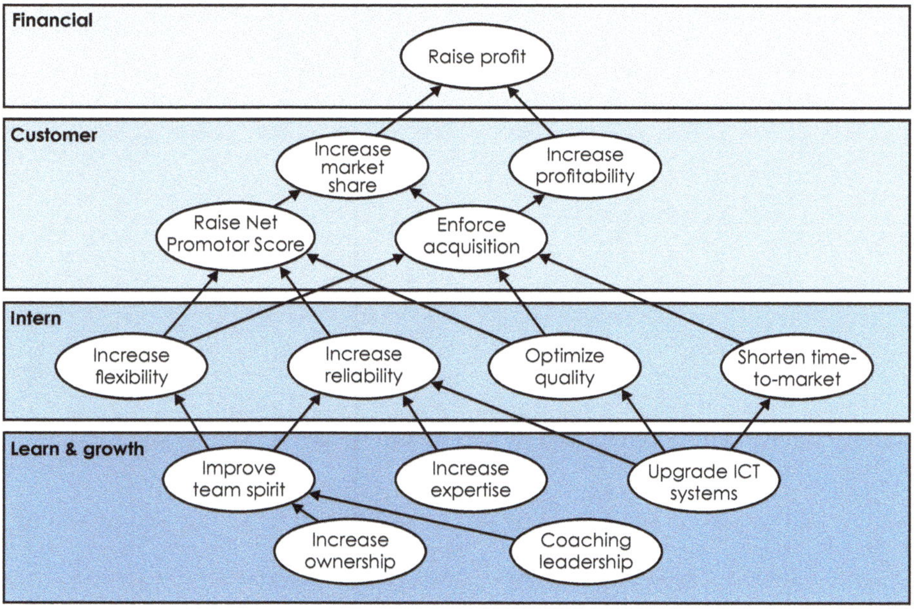

Figure 9.01.06 Example strategy map

Key Performance Indicators

After drawing up the strategy map, you can define the *key performance indicators* (KPIs). A KPI is an important performance measure used to determine the degree of progress towards a specific goal.

It is important to choose good KPIs. The performance indicator should be relevant and valid. Does the KPI reflect what you want to measure? Can the KPI also be influenced by other factors? An incorrectly chosen KPI can lead to undesired behaviour. Once the KPIs have been determined, the objectives to be realised can be set SMART for each KPI.

> *If the goal is to strengthen the position in the mortgage market, you can take the total amount of mortgages granted as a KPI or the total return on mortgages. The former is easier to measure; the latter is more accurate. The former also often leads to providing risky mortgages, which only puts your own organisation at risk.*

Performance dashboards

Finally, corresponding performance dashboards can be set up. A performance dashboard is a user interface that provides values related to a particular goal or business process. We distinguish strategic, operational and analytical dashboards.

- *Strategic dashboard* – This dashboard provides an overview of the most important KPIs of the organisation. Don't include details, and ensure the dashboard is visible on one screen. Limit the overview to a dozen KPIs (preferably less) and limit the number of filter options (see Figure 9.01.07).

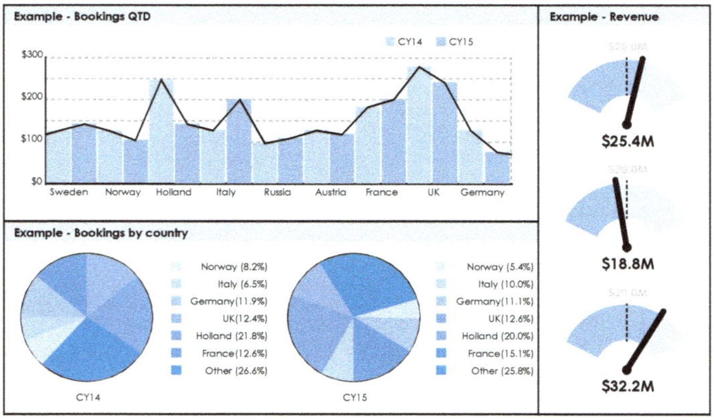

Figure 9.01.07 Example strategic dashboard

- *Operational dashboard* – This dashboard only contains operational KPIs, such as the number of outstanding calls and the longest waiting time for a helpdesk. An operational dashboard usually contains real-time data.
- *Analytical dashboard* – This dashboard contains a large amount of operational data that can be filtered according to various insights. It is often inevitable that users have to scroll through this dashboard.

EFQM MODEL (ADVANCED)

A widely used model for organisational excellence and continuous improvement is the EFQM model (EFQM, 2021). EFQM is the European Foundation for Quality Management. The EFQM model is based on three questions and seven criteria:

Why does the organisation exist, for what purpose, and why this particular strategy? (Direction)

1. *Purpose, vision, and strategy* – Focus on defining a purpose that inspires, an ambitious vision, and a strategy that delivers results.
2. *Organisational Culture and Leadership* – Focuses on guiding the organisation's culture and values, creating the conditions to realise change.
3. *Engaging stakeholders* – Focuses on engaging customers, people, business and governance stakeholders, society, partners and suppliers.

How does it plan to execute its purpose and implement its strategy? (Execution)

4. *Creating sustainable value* – Focuses on generating value and how it is created, communicated, sold and delivered.
5. *Driving performance and transformation* – Focuses on preparing for the future while performing today. Key elements include innovation and technology and using data, information, knowledge, critical assets, and resources.

What has been accomplished so far? What are the aspirations for the future? (Results)

6. *Stakeholder perception* – Focuses on results derived from feedback from key stakeholders about their experiences with the organisation.
7. *Strategic and operational performance* – Focuses on the results related to the organisation's performance to fulfil its purpose and fitness for the future.

Furthermore, EFQM offers a diagnostic tool, RADAR. This tool can be used in conjunction with the EFQM model to help identify where an organisation's current strengths and opportunities for improvement lie and to describe the organisation's future in terms of its desired outcomes and the necessary actions to be taken to achieve them.

INVESTMENT CALCULATIONS (ADVANCED)

Based on the goals to be achieved, operational plans can be prepared and the necessary projects initiated. However, separate business cases should first be prepared for individual projects. Do the planned benefits outweigh the investments? Various techniques can be used for such an investment analysis. Well-known techniques are the return on investment, various rates on return, the net present value, the payback period and the break-even point analyses.

Return on Investment (ROI)

Return on investment (ROI) measures the return on investment compared to the total investment. ROI is typically expressed as a percentage. There are various ways to calculate the ROI. Therefore, clarifying the equation (to be) used first is important. The most common equation is:

» ROI = (Net gains on investment during a period of time / Total cost of investment) x 100.

Generally, ROI is easy to calculate. However, it does not consider items such as time frame, opportunity cost, and the effect of inflation. ROI can be calculated annually to solve the first problem. Furthermore, ROI can be used to refer to all kinds of benefits, not just financial ones, such as the number of new customers, revenue growth, or CO2 reduction relative to the investment, et cetera.

Rates of Return

There are various rates of return on capital. The *Rate of Return* (RoR) is the total gain on an investment over a period, expressed as a percentage of the initial investment. The *Annualised Rate of Return* (ARR) is the average annual return to get from the initial investment to the current value.

> *If you receive 10% return per year, your initial investment of €100 will be after 1 year: 1.1 x €100 = €110; after 2 years: 1.1 x €110= €121; and after 3 years: 1.1 x €121 = €133.10.*
>
> - *The (total) Rate of Return is: RoR = 133,10 /100 = 0.331 or 33.10%.*
> - *The Annualised Rate of Return is: ARR = 10%.*

The *Internal Rate of Return* (IRR) is the discount rate at which the net present value of an investment is zero. See the next section on Net Present Value.

NET PRESENT VALUE ANALYSIS (ADVANCED)

The *Net Present Value* (NPV) of an investment is the sum of the present values of the cash flows generated by that investment over a period of time. The NPV analysis is usually applied when the period of use covers a large number of years. This is because cash flows in the (distant) future have (much) less value than cash flows at present. If you want to compare cash flows over such a period, future cash flows should first be converted to their present value. Converting future cash flows to their present value is done based on a discount rate set by the organisation.

Cash is King

For investment analyses, the principle 'cash is king' applies. This means that investment calculations are based on cash flows and not on revenues and expenditures.

WACC

The cost of capital is expressed in the WACC. The WACC is the *Weighted Average Cost of Capital*. It is the current weighted average costs of financing a company's operations based on their debts (interest) and equity (dividend).

Discount rate

The discount rate covers future cash flows into current cash flows. The discount rate is higher than the WACC due to the risk involved in implementing projects. Typically, discount rates range from 10% and 20%, depending on the type of organisation and the market in which it operates. Discount rates in an organisation tend to remain the same over a period of time.

Cash flow

Cash Flow (CF) is the net balance of a company's incoming and outgoing cash over a given period, usually one year. Outgoing cash flows are valued negatively, and incoming cash flows are positively valued.

NPV calculation

To convert future cash flows to their present value, we use the same technique when calculating what a current amount will be worth in the future, but now vice versa. Instead of multiplying the amount each year by an interest rate, we now divide the future cash flow each year by the discount rate to convert that amount back to the present.

If you know the expected cash flows associated with the investment and you know the applicable discount rate (i), you can calculate the NPV of the investment (see Table 9.01.02). Here, the current year is referred to as year 1, the following year as year 2, the successive year as year 3, and so on.

If the discount rate (i) is 10%, then the *Discounted Cash Flow* (DCF) is (see Table 9.01.02):

- Year 1: – € 50 remains – € 50.
- Year 2: – € 100 is now worth: – € 100 / 1.10 = – € 91 (recalculate backwards once).
- Year 3: – € 100 is now worth: – € 100 / 1.102 = – € 83 (recalculate backwards twice).
- Year 4: + € 100 is now worth: + € 100 / 1.103 = + € 75 (recalculate backwards three times).

Et cetera.

Years	1	2	3	4	5	6	7
Cash flow	-50	-100	-100	100	150	150	50
Discounted cash flow (based on i=10%)	-50	-91	-83	75	102	93	28
Cumulated discounted cash flow	-50	-141	-224	-148	-46	47	75
Discount factor (based on 10%)	1	0.909	0.826	0.751	0.683	0.621	0.564

Table 9.01.02 Example calculation NPV

In the example, the *Cumulated Discounted Cash Flow* (CDCF) over seven years is: -€50 – €91 – €83 + €75 + €102 + €93 + €28 = + € 75.

This investment has thus a positive NPV and is, therefore, interesting from a financial point of view.

NPV formulas

Taking the present as year 1, you can calculate the Discounted Cash Flow (DCF) of year 'n' at a discount rate 'i' using the formula: $DCF = CF / (1 + i)^{n-1}$.

When calculating the DCF of year n, you should always calculate that cash flow back to the present (n – 1) times: the 2nd year, you should calculate it back once; the 3rd year, you should calculate it back twice; the 4th year you should calculate it back three times, et cetera (see example above).

The NPV of the investment is the *Cumulated Discounted Cash Flow* (CDCF) over the period of time is the addition of all the individual DCFs of the various years. The NPV can then be calculated using the formula: $NPV = CDCF = \sum CF / (1 + i)^{n-1}$. The symbol $\sum$ stands for 'the sum of'.

> *Cash Flow in year n:* $CF_n = Inflow_n - Outflow_n$
> *Discounted Cash Flow of year n:* $DCF_n = CF_n / (1 + i)^{n-1}$
> *Cumulated Discounted Cash Flow over the years 1-n:* $CDCF_n = \sum DCF_n / (1 + i)^{n-1}$

Discount factor

To avoid calculating the different values for $1/(1 + i)^{n-1}$, you can also use a table with the different discount factors. These indicate the $1/(1 + i)^{n-1}$ values over the various years at the different discount rates (see Table 9.01.03).

In Table 09.01.03, the discount factors for the different years at the discount rate of 10% are: 0.909 (2), 0.826 (3), 0.751 (4), 0.683 (5), 0.621 (6), 0.564 (7), and 0.513 for the year 8.

Year	6%	7%	8%	9%	10%	11%	12%
2	0.943	0.935	0.926	0.917	0.909	0.901	0.893
3	0.890	0.873	0.857	0.843	0.826	0.812	0.797
4	0.840	0.816	0.794	0.772	0.751	0.731	0.712
5	0.792	0.763	0.735	0.708	0.683	0.659	0.636
6	0.747	0.713	0.681	0.650	0.621	0.593	0.567
7	0.705	0.666	0.630	0.596	0.564	0.535	0.507
8	0.665	0.623	0.583	0/547	0.513	0.482	0.452

Table 9.01.03 Discount rates

Internal Rate of Return (IRR)

If the total of all planned investments with a positive NPV exceeds the available budget, you should rank the investments in order of profitability. This can be done by calculating the *Internal Rate of Return* (IRR) of each investment. The IRR is the discount rate at which the net present value is zero. The higher the IRR, the more attractive the investment is from a financial point of view.

Opportunity costs

Opportunity costs are the missed returns of the best alternative. When calculating the NPV of an investment, these missed returns should be included as opportunity costs in the calculation.

> *An organisation owns a piece of land and wants to build a new office on it. The costs for the construction of that office are estimated at € 1.2 million. Buying an office elsewhere costs € 1.3 million. This makes the first option seem cheaper. However, the sale of the piece of land is expected to yield € 0.2 million. If you include these opportunity costs in the calculation, the new building actually 'costs' € 1.4 million and buying an office elsewhere is the best option financially.*

Sunk costs

Sunk costs are costs that have already been incurred and cannot be undone, no matter what decision is made. Sunk costs should not be included in the investment analyses because these costs remain regardless of the outcome of the decision.

PAYBACK PERIOD (ADVANCED)

The payback period is the period of time required to recover the investment costs. This period is calculated based on the nominal values of the cash flows. The payback period is only used as a criterion when investments need to be recovered within a short period, usually within three years and sometimes even within one year. In those situations, the discount rate does not have much effect.

BREAK-EVEN POINT (ADVANCED)

The break-even point is the number of products that should be sold to recover the investment's costs (see Figure 9.01.08). This criterion is mainly applied to investments in commercial products. This criterion is also calculated from the nominal values and is usually used in an initial analysis to justify the investment.

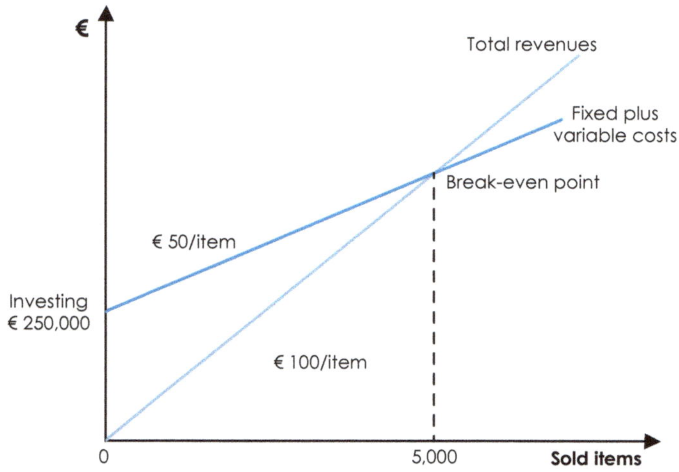

Figure 9.01.08 Example break-even point

Suppose that, based on an investment of € 250,000, products can be manufactured for € 50 and sold for € 100 each. The break-even point is then: € 250,000/(€ 100 – € 50) = 5,000 products.

9.02 PROGRAMME MANAGEMENT

PURPOSE
The purpose of this chapter is to enable the individual to effectively participate in and manage the impact of programmes on projects.

LEARNING OBJECTIVES
- What is a programme, and what are the characteristics of a programme;
- Differences between projects and programmes;
- When do you choose a programme (advanced);
- Programme organisation roles and responsibilities (advanced);
- Integration between projects and programmes (advanced);
- Multi-organisation programmes (advanced);
- Benefit management (advanced);
- Programme lifecycle (advanced);
- Core documents of a programme (advanced).

DEFINITIONS
Programme: A temporary organisation of interrelated projects and business activities managed in a coordinated way to enable the implementation of change and the realisation of benefits to achieving a strategic goal.
Programme management: The coordinated management of projects and business activities in order to enable the implementation of change and the realisation of benefits to achieve a strategic goal.

INTRODUCTION
Projects are rarely isolated – especially not when strategic objectives should be realised. That is when the results of several projects are needed to develop the capabilities that will enable the organisation to implement the necessary changes and realise the associated benefits. It gets even more complicated when multiple organisational units are needed to implement those changes and realise those benefits. This does not just happen; it has to be organised. Welcome to Programme Management!

Knowing how such programmes are initiated and managed is vital as it directly affects the initiation and management of the underlying projects.

POSITIONING
More and more, programmes are initiated to implement strategic changes in the organisation. In those situations, the programme will initiate the underlying projects (vision-driven programmes). However, programmes may also materialise bottom-up if it transpires that the various projects and changes cannot be managed effectively in isolation (emergent programmes). Finally, programmes can emerge from changes in legislation and regulations (compliance programmes).

PROGRAMME AND PROGRAMME MANAGEMENT
A programme is a temporary organisation to coordinate the management of interrelated projects and business activities to enable the implementation of change and the realisation of benefits to achieving a strategic goal. Each component retains

its own management. Programme management is the coordinated management of these components.

If an organisation decides to enter a new market, each manager may do so independently. They may also decide to set up a task force with participants from the business units involved to align those units' activities and to initiate and coordinate the necessary projects. The programme is then the task force. This task force is only considered successful if the new marker is successfully entered and the expected benefits are realised. A programme is, therefore, much more than just initiating and coordinating several projects.

Such a task force is chaired by one of the board members (the programme sponsor) and assisted by someone responsible for the daily coordination of the work (programme manager). The participants from the relevant business units participating in the task force are called business change managers. The programme manager is usually supported by a programme office.

DIFFERENCES BETWEEN PROJECTS AND PROGRAMMES

Programmes differ from projects in several ways. Deliverables drive a project; a programme is driven by its vision of the end state. A project coordinates work packages; a programme coordinates projects and business activities. A project delivers products and services; a programme implements change and realises benefits. A project ends after handing over the output; a programme should be closed deliberately (see Figure 9.02.01).

Also, programmes often exhibit more complexity than projects in terms of the interrelatedness and interdependence of elements. A collaborative approach, becomes more important. Effective programmes also provide a greater likelihood of achieving the overarching strategic goals and efficient use of resources, satisfying the needs of the stakeholders.

Project	Programme
• Driven by deliverables	• Driven by vision of 'end state'
• Coordinates work packages	• Coordinates projects and business activities
• Delivers products and services	• Implements change and realises benefits
• More straight forward	• More interrelatedness and interdependencies
• More team driven	• A collaborative approach is more important
• Ends by handing over the output	• Should be deliberately closed

Figure 9.02.01 Differences between projects and programmes

Implementing changes and realising benefits is an ongoing effort. If a programme is successful, there is a tendency to continue it. Nothing wrong with that; however, it then becomes part of the ongoing operations and is no longer a programme, as it is no longer a temporary organisation.

RESPONSIBILITIES

Within the programme, the programme sponsor is accountable for the programme's success. The programme manager is responsible for the daily management of the programme and for initiating and coordinating the projects within the programme. Business change managers are operationally responsible for implementing the changes in their individual business units.

Within the programme, as the project manager, you should coordinate with the programme manager, your fellow project managers, and the business change managers. You should also coordinate with the programme office on the project's progress and the application of methods, tools, techniques and competences. The programme office can act as project assurance on behalf of the project sponsor.

ADVANCED
PROGRAMME ORGANISATION (ADVANCED)

In a programme, it is important that the programme sponsor comes from the top of the organisation, and all concerned business units are represented in the task force. And finally, there should be a separate coordinator who initiates and coordinates the various projects.

If we translate that into management terms, then there is a programme sponsor (chairman), there is a programme board (task force), there are business change managers (the representatives of the various business units), and there is a programme manager (the coordinator). The involved senior managers are called sponsors; collectively, they are called the sponsor group (see Figure 9.02.02).

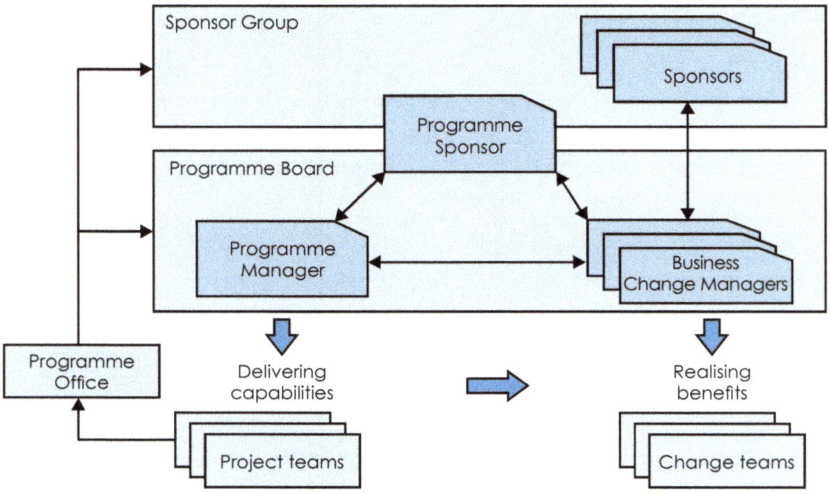

Figure 9.02.02 Programme organisation structure

Programme sponsor – A programme should realise strategic goals. Therefore, it is inevitable that the programme sponsor is a senior member of the permanent organisation. The programme sponsor is the ultimate owner of the programme and is accountable for its success.

Programme manager – The programme manager is in charge of the daily management of the programme and initiating and coordinating the necessary projects.

Sponsors – The responsibility of the programme sponsor does not alter the fact that every business manager remains accountable for implementing the changes and realising the benefits within their own business unit. The programme sponsor cannot and should not take over this responsibility. Within the programme, the top managers of the involved business units are called the sponsors.

Sponsor group – All the directly involved top managers form the programme sponsor group. The programme sponsor is also a member of this sponsor group. The sponsor group is (a subset of) the highest decision-making body in the organisation that decides on the programme's initiation, direction and conclusion. The sponsor group also makes the necessary funding available. The programme sponsor reports on the programme to this sponsor group. The sponsor group can also be the parent portfolio board (see Chapter 9.03 Portfolio Management).

Business change managers – The *Business Change Managers* (BCMs) are in charge of daily implementing the changes and realising benefits in the business units. The BCMs are the link between the programme and the respective business units. The BCMs are usually senior staff members of these business units.

Programme board – The programme sponsor, the programme manager and the business change managers form the programme board. Sponsors of the most important projects, key figures from the business organisation such as the financial director, and representatives of important suppliers can be added to the programme board if necessary.

Programme office – A separate office is usually set up to support the programme manager in their daily management of the programme. The programme office also defines and ensures the application of the desired methods, tools, and techniques within the programme on its behalf. Finally, it can assume the assurance role toward the respective programme components.

Integration projects and programmes

Projects in programmes have their own organisation. However, it may be desirable to partially integrate project and programme roles (see Figure 9.02.03).

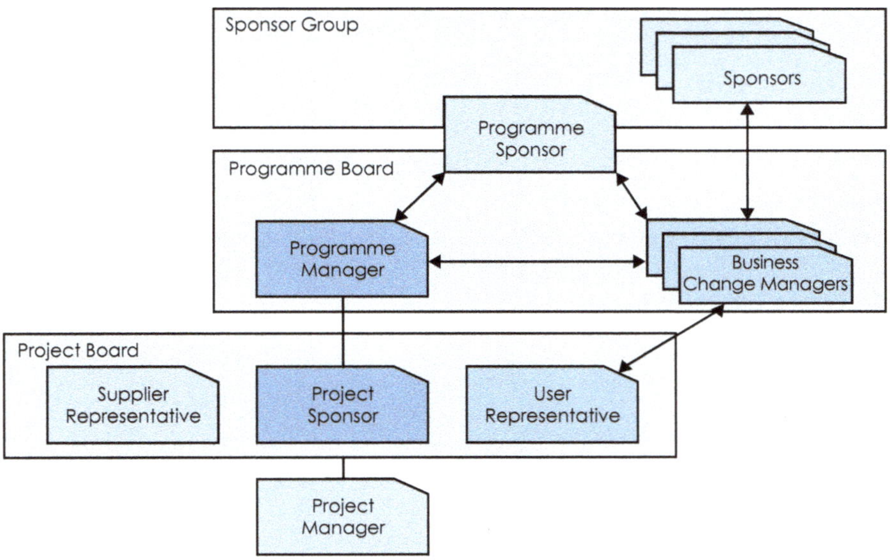

Figure 9.02.03 Integration project and programme roles

The programme manager can fill the role of the project sponsor. This may be desirable for a strategic project within the programme. For more regular projects, it is advisable to appoint one of the sponsors as the project sponsor to ensure the involvement and ownership of the respective business unit.

The business change manager role in a programme ties in with the role of the user representative in a project. The user representative in the project board should ensure that the project delivers what is necessary to achieve the agreed goals within the organisation. Furthermore, they should also ensure that, with the project output, the envisaged changes will be implemented and benefits will be realised. That is in line with the responsibility of the business change manager in a programme.

Such integration of project and programme roles better aligns the projects and the programme. The disadvantage is that responsibilities are stacked, and the circle of people involved in the programme is limited, which can lead to problems concerning support and commitment. The rest of the organisation will then see the programme as a responsibility of a limited group of people only. That is a real risk.

In large programmes, the many project boards in the programme can cause the programme to become unmanageable. It is then advisable to set up boards for specific themes and or work streams only or delegate the project board function to the programme manager and only set up a programme board. A theme is a logical grouping of projects and activities focused on a particular sub-goal within the programme. A workstream is a logical grouping of projects and activities around certain type of work such as IT, facilities, HRM and so on.

MULTI-ORGANISATION PROGRAMMES (ADVANCED)

Programmes are also regularly initiated and implemented jointly by collaborating organisations or a network of organisations. Together, they aim to achieve goals they cannot achieve on their own (see Figure 9.02.04). A well-known example is a public-private partnership between a public body and private parties. This might involve, for example, a neighbourhood development in which housing associations, property developers with a clear land position, and the municipality work together to achieve common goals.

The sponsor group will then consist of the administrative representatives of the organisations involved who have agreed to realise certain objectives together. The business change managers in the programme board are the operational representatives of the organisations involved. The programme sponsor is preferably the administrative representative of the most influential sponsor in this partnership, but it can also be an independent external professional in this case.

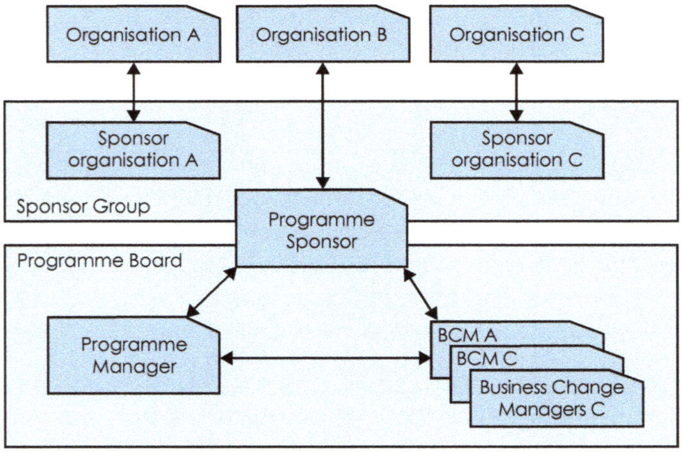

Figure 9.02.04 Multi-organisation programmes

BENEFITS MANAGEMENT (ADVANCED)

Benefits management is the whole of management activities to optimise the potential benefits and minimise the negative impacts of an initiative. A benefit is an advantage resulting from the outcome. A negative consequence or dis-benefit is something disadvantageous resulting from an outcome. Benefits management is not about realising the change itself but about maximising the benefits and minimising the dis-benefits resulting from a change.

A programme is initiated to achieve a strategic goal and its associated benefits. Therefore, benefit management is a fundamental part of managing a programme. It starts even before the actual start of the programme and continues after the completion of the programme. Benefits management includes identifying, defining, monitoring and measuring the benefits to be realised.

What is the added value we want to realise? How are we going to realise it? Who is responsible for this? Will the planned change actually deliver the intended benefits? And if not, what should we do to realise these benefits still? What other benefits can we realise with the changes? What are the possible negative effects that the programme may have? And who is responsible for minimising these negative consequences? This is certainly not easy.

Nevertheless, benefits management is crucial and should be at the heart of any change. Benefits management steers the implementation of changes. It also maintains the link between the changes to be implemented and the strategic goals to be achieved. And it also helps to increase involvement and create ownership among management and other stakeholders.

Benefits map

A goal tree or benefits map is usually drawn up to identify the benefits. A benefits map visualises the goals and sub-goals to be achieved and their interrelationships. Identifying the benefits first top-down and then completing the benefits map bottom-up is common. A benefits map corresponds to a strategy map within the business organisation. A goal-effort network can be created by linking the individual benefits to the required projects and activities. The concepts of goal and benefit are interchangeable here (see Figure 9.02.05).

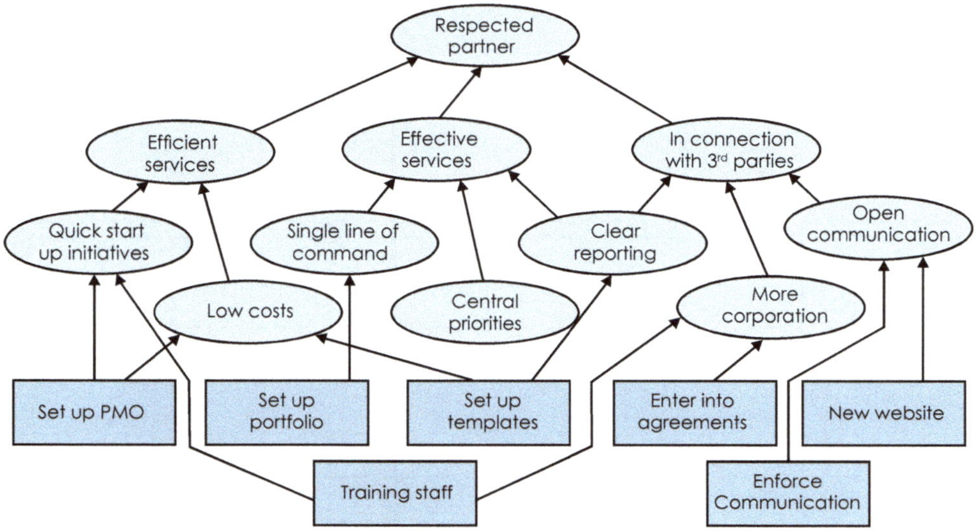

Figure 9.02.05 Goal-effort network

Benefits realisation plan

A benefits realisation plan is a plan that outlines the development of the benefits to be achieved over time, with the most critical project outputs required to achieve them and with the planned benefits reviews. (see Figure 9.02.06). Finally, the plan includes the necessary resources to measure and evaluate the benefits periodically.

Key Performance Indicators (KPIs) with associated targets should be established for all benefits. All benefits should be broken down to such a level that individual performance agreements can be made with the respective business units. These performance agreements are usually laid down in a covenant.

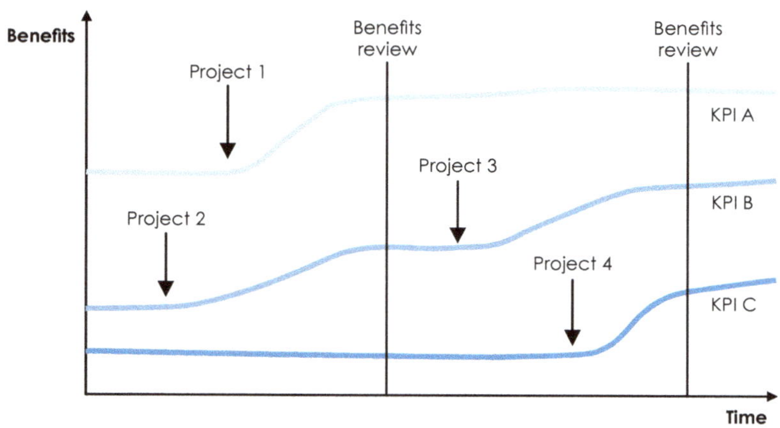

Figure 9.02.06 Example of benefits development, projects delivery and benefits review over time

PROGRAMME LIFECYCLE (ADVANCED)

A programme consists of several stages (see Figure 9.02.07):

Initiating a programme

This stage is triggered by a mandate from the sponsor group (top-down) or the need for projects or business units to create a coordinating management level (bottom-up). A programme sponsor is assigned, and a programme outline and a programme definition plan are prepared. Based on both, the sponsor group authorises the programme sponsor to install the programme board, assign the programme manager, and start the definition stage.

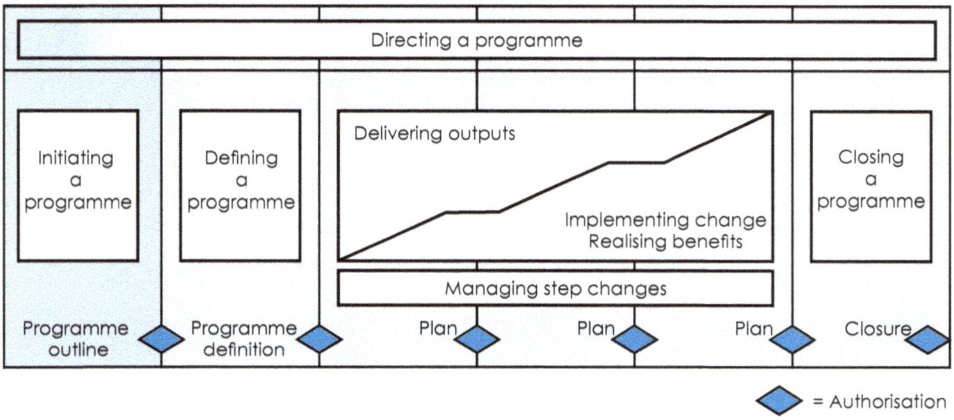

Figure 9.02.07 Programme lifecycle

Defining a programme

The definition stage lays the foundation for the programme's implementation. The programme vision is sharpened, and the benefits map is prepared. Next, the target operating model and the programme plan are developed, the programme's business case is completed, and the plan for the 1st step change is drawn up. Based on all these elements, the sponsor group authorises the programme and implementation of the 1st step change.

Managing step changes

Implementing the envisaged changes and realising benefits usually takes place in several step changes. Projects are grouped around such distinct step changes.

Between step changes, the programme manager initiates the required projects and ensures that the necessary capabilities are delivered. This enables business change managers to implement the required changes and realise the envisaged benefits. In doing so, step changes need to be sustainably embedded in the organisation. At the end of each step change, the sponsor group decides whether to continue the programme or not (go/no-go decision).

Close a programme

Programmes tend to go on forever. It then becomes part of the business organisation. To enable new programmes to start, a programme that has primarily achieved its strategic goals and predicted benefits or has nothing left to contribute should be closed, and the delegated tasks, responsibilities and powers transferred back to the business organisation.

CORE DOCUMENTS (ADVANCED)

The core documents of a programme comprise the documents that define the scope and direction of the programme. Core documents are developed in the definition stage and updated at least at each stage transition:

- *Vision document* – A description of how the organisation wants to be seen by others in relation to the strategic goal to be achieved. The vision document describes a compelling future that appeals to hearts and minds with implied added value for all stakeholders. The vision is the dot on the horizon to which we strive (see Chapter 9.01 Strategy).
- *Benefits map* – The visualisation of goals and sub-goals to be achieved in a programme and their interrelationships. It provides the criteria against which the various alternatives of the target operating model are assessed.
- *Target operating model* – An outline description of the future state and capabilities of the envisaged changed situation (see, for example, *Business Canvas model*, Chapter 9.01 Strategy). This model is the guide for all project outputs to be delivered and changes to be implemented.
- *Benefits realisation plan* – A plan outlining the development of the benefits to be realised over time with the planned delivery of the enabling project outputs and the planned benefit reviews.
- *Programme plan* – A high-level plan for realising the envisaged capabilities, changes, and benefits to achieve the programme's strategic goal.
- *Programme business case* –The business justification for the programme. The business cases of the individual projects are derived from this business case.

9.03 PORTFOLIO MANAGEMENT

PURPOSE

The purpose of this chapter is to enable the individual to effectively participate in and manage the impact of portfolio management on projects.

LEARNING OBJECTIVES

- The characteristics of portfolio management and management by projects;
- The differences between programme, portfolio management and management by projects;
- Prioritise programmes and projects (advanced);
- Portfolio organisation (advanced);
- Portfolio processes (advanced).

DEFINITIONS

Portfolio: A set of projects and programmes, which are not necessarily related, brought together to provide optimum use of the organisation's resources to achieve the organisation's strategic goals while minimising portfolio risk.
Portfolio management: The coordinated management of a set of projects and programmes, which are not necessary related, brought together to provide optimum use of the organisation's resources to achieve the organisation's strategic goals while minimising portfolio risk.
Management by projects: The coordinated management of a set of projects brought together to provide optimum use of the available resources to achieve the objectives of these projects in an efficient and effective way while minimising the risks.

INTRODUCTION

As the living environment expands, changes are occurring at an increasingly rapid pace. The implementation of changes has become a constant factor. For companies, the ability to implement changes is a necessity to survive. For governments and institutions, it has become essential in meeting the ever-changing public and political demands.

Many organisations are adapting to this or are planning to do so. In addition to their 'production' environment, they also set up a permanent 'change' environment. Portfolio management is such an environment that enables an organisation to initiate and coordinate projects and programmes in a structured manner. Management by projects is the application of processes, methods, skills, knowledge and experience to achieve project objectives more efficiently and effectively. It is vital to understand how these frameworks function as they directly affect the initiation and management of the underlying projects.

POSITIONING

Projects are authorised through portfolio management and management by projects; project decisions are made, resources allocated, and necessary frameworks established. Furthermore, project progress and results are monitored. Projects should periodically report to these managements.

PORTFOLIO MANAGEMENT

Portfolio management is the coordinated management of a set of projects and programmes, which are not necessarily related, brought together to provide optimum use of the organisation's resources to achieve the organisation's strategic goals while minimising portfolio risk. To do so, portfolio management should be able to answer the following questions:

- Are we doing the right things?
- Are we doing things correctly?
- Are we carrying out the work according to schedule?
- Are we achieving the benefits and goals as anticipated?

The primary responsibility of portfolio management is to ensure that the correct projects and programmes are initiated, whereby special attention is paid to deploying critical resources. It should also ensure that projects and programmes are implemented effectively. This is often done by setting up a knowledge centre that develops and ensures the application of best practices within the portfolio (see Chapter 9.04 Supporting Functions and Implementing Project, Programme, and Portfolio Management).

Furthermore, portfolio management should ensure that projects and programmes are implemented according to plan and monitor their overall progress. Finally, it should ensure that the expected benefits and strategic objectives are realised. This is achieved by setting criteria for determining benefits and linking projects and programmes to performance management. All in all, quite a task. Portfolio management should, therefore, not be taken lightly and should have its own support unit, the portfolio office.

Not all projects are authorised and monitored by the portfolio. Small, non-critical projects within individual business units often remain their responsibility. Projects within programmes are initiated and monitored by those programmes. However, deploying resources for these projects fall under portfolio management as it has to reserve capacity for them.

Projects within the portfolio are authorised by the portfolio. Furthermore, the portfolio allocates the necessary resources and makes go/no-go decisions in those projects. Most communication with the portfolio goes through the support office. They also often fulfil the role of project assurance. Since the portfolio is responsible for the optimal use of resources, it can order a project to speed up or slow down and sometimes even close prematurely to make way for other initiatives.

The latter says nothing about the project's performance. What matters is the added value to the organisation and the optimal use of the available resources. In this context, project marketing may be important; do this in consultation with the project sponsor. The continuation of the project is primarily in their interest.

MANAGEMENT BY PROJECTS

Management by projects is the coordinated management of a set of projects to provide optimum use of the available resources to achieve the objectives of these projects efficiently and effectively way while minimising the risk. It is usually done by:

- Establishing an efficient and effective governance structure;

- Developing and implementing best practices to carry out projects;
- Setting up a joint project office to better support projects;
- Training and coaching of project managers and project staff;
- Making use of 'pools' to enable better deployment of people and resources;
- Central purchasing of products and services and hiring of staff.

Management by projects is not about managing the individual projects themselves or implementing change and realising benefits; it is about establishing a project environment where projects can achieve their objectives efficiently and effectively. Management by projects is a permanent endeavour for those who deliver projects. That can be a supplier, contractor, or separate entity within a customer organisation. Within management by projects, projects are not necessarily related.

Management by projects is usually performed as an ongoing activity. Within management by projects, projects are often carried out for a wide range of customers. Occasionally, management by projects is set up for a specific assignment.

DIFFERENCES BETWEEN PROGRAMME, PORTFOLIO MANAGEMENT AND MANAGEMENT BY PROJECTS

In practice, the terms programme, portfolio and management by projects are often used interchangeably. Yet they clearly have different meanings. Programme management is a temporary endeavour. Portfolio management and management by projects are basically an ongoing responsibility. In programmes, projects and activities are interrelated; in portfolios and management by projects not necessarily. Programmes aim to realise benefits and achieve a strategic goal. Portfolio management and management by projects aim to optimise the use of available resources; in portfolio management to achieve the overall organisation's strategic goals; in management by projects to achieve projects objectives efficiently and effectively. Portfolio management is applied in a customer organisation. Management by projects can be applied wherever projects are carried out. Portfolio management encompasses projects and programmes; management by projects just projects (see Figure 9.03.01).

Features	Programme management	Portfolio management	Management by projects
Responsibility	To implement change and realise benefits to achieve a strategic goal	Optimal use of available resources to achieve the organisation's strategic goals	Optimum use of available resources to achieve the project's objectives in an efficient and effective way
Scope	Interrelated projects and business activities	Projects and programmes, not necessarily related	Projects, not necessarily related
Lifecycle	Temporary	Permanent	Permanent (usually)
Organisation	Own organisation	Customer organisation	By those who deliver projects

Figure 9.03.01 Differences between programme, portfolio management and management by projects

RESPONSIBILITIES

Portfolio management authorises the projects within the portfolio and usually takes go/no-go decisions. It also establishes the governance structure projects should comply with. Management by projects defines the best practices based on which projects should be carried out.

ADVANCED

PRIORITISE PROJECTS AND PROGRAMMES (ADVANCED)

Prioritising initiatives within a portfolio is essential to portfolio management. This is not easy because initiatives are often difficult to compare in terms of purpose and direction. Should we invest in our operational reliability or improve our customer relations? You can only spend your money once. The most effective way to set priorities is top-down rather than immediately weighing individual initiatives against each other.

Divide – Divide all strategic objectives first into several coherent categories. These categories are often called 'buckets'. Sometimes this classification is similar to the Balanced Scorecard. In most cases, however, a separate classification is used. Limit the number of categories (see Figure 9.03.02). Maintain this classification for several years.

Figure 9.03.02 Example classification into buckets

Allocate – Allocate the available investment budget across these categories based on the assessment of the current situation. How much has been spent on the various categories in recent years? What did we achieve with it? What are the competitors doing? What are our targets next year? And finally, based on all this, how can we best allocate our investment budget across the categories to gain the most benefit for the organisation as a whole?

Identify – Identify the current and new initiatives. Which projects and programmes will continue? Which initiatives do we want to initiate next year? What are the expected cost and duration of these initiatives? It is important that the planned initiatives have already been worked out and approved by the responsible business unit manager and are not just a wish list.

Categorise – Assign the current and new initiatives to one of the categories. Initiatives will often contribute to more than one category. However, to keep the process manageable, each initiative should only be assigned one category.

Prioritise – Prioritise the initiatives within each category within the available budget of that category. This is best achieved by a small team from the business units involved, chaired by one of the portfolio board members. This ultimately results in a complete list of projects and programmes for the entire portfolio. The projects and programmes which are not selected are parked. A multicriteria analysis is often used to prioritise these initiatives (see Chapter 8.04, Resourcefulness).

Specific aspects can be used for the different categories. The Enhance Market Position category could include turnover, market share, and customer satisfaction. The Business

Continuity category could include risk, and quality costs. However, a multi-criteria analysis cannot be used to prioritise initiatives within the portfolio as a whole, as a portfolio comprises several strategic categories.

Balance – Balance the timing of the projects and programmes during the year based on the available resources, the interdependencies, and the impact on the various organisational units, while minimising the overall portfolio risks. You should avoid all new initiatives starting at the beginning of the year. Then you will have too few architects at the start and a surplus at the end of the year. You should also avoid having different projects simultaneously working on the same critical assets.

> *In order to enhance operational efficiency, the decision was made to integrate the various call centres. Unfortunate, when the new call centre went live, Sales had just launched a major campaign. As a result, many complaints arose during the introduction, which was exactly what they wanted to avoid.*

Plan – Plan the portfolio for next year. When should the ongoing projects be completed? When should the new projects and programmes be started, and when should the various results be implemented? What is the expected use of resources and budget during the year? Who is working on critical assets and when? The portfolio plan is regularly referred to as the portfolio roadmap.

PORTFOLIO ORGANISATION (ADVANCED)

Portfolio management is usually assigned to a portfolio board mandated by the organisation's highest governing body (see Figure 9.03.03). The chairman of the portfolio board is, preferably, one of the senior members of the board of directors and, thus, the link between the portfolio board and the board of directors.

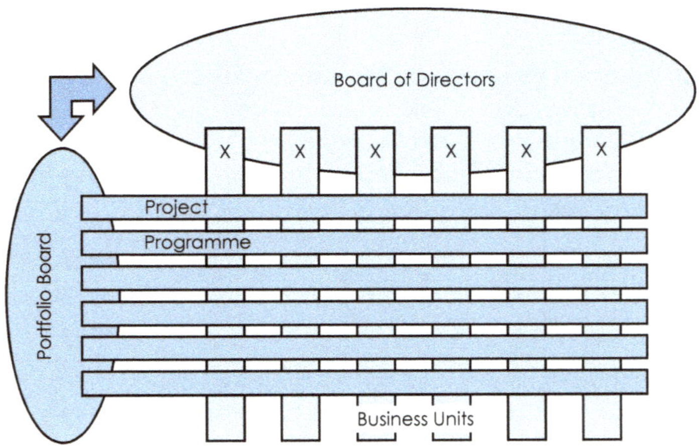

Figure 9.03.03 Position of the portfolio board in the permanent organisation

The portfolio manager is responsible for supporting the portfolio board and the daily management of the portfolio. The portfolio manager is supported by a portfolio office. This office usually supports the portfolio manager in all four responsibility areas.

Separate portfolios can be set up for different operating companies or categories of projects and programmes. In this case, an enterprise portfolio is set up to coordinate the sub-portfolios and the overarching projects and programmes.

PORTFOLIO LIFECYCLE (ADVANCED)

Portfolio management is inextricably linked to the annual budget round. First, based on the organisation's five-year plan, the targets and available budget for next year are set. Then the portfolio and portfolio roadmap is determined in several budget rounds.

During the year, the status of ongoing projects and programmes is reviewed periodically (usually monthly). Planned initiatives are checked against approved targets and authorised if applicable. Typically, the portfolio and the portfolio roadmap are updated quarterly at key points and thoroughly mid-year (see Figure 9.03.04).

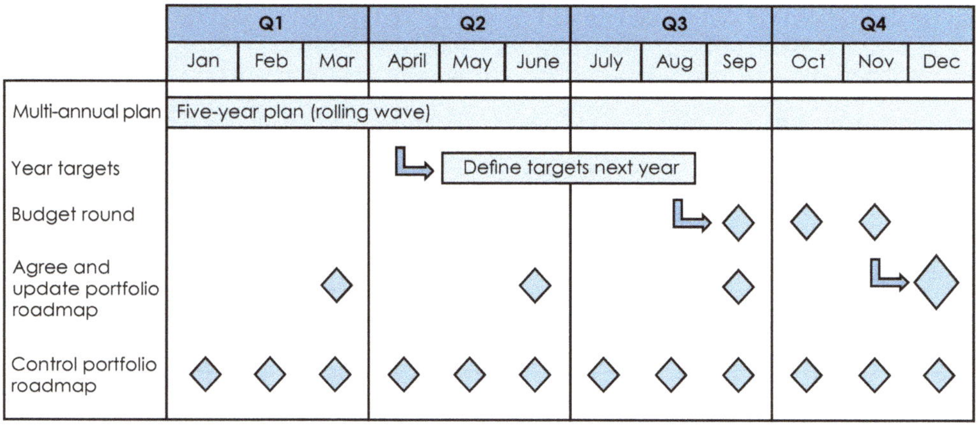

Figure 9.03.04 Example portfolio lifecycle

Operational decisions can be made by the portfolio manager. The more important decisions should be submitted to the portfolio board for approval. These decisions take extra time as they have to be fitted into the portfolio board's meeting schedule.

9.04 SUPPORTING FUNCTIONS AND IMPLEMENTING PPP MANAGEMENT

PURPOSE

The purpose of this chapter is to enable the individual to effectively make use of the supporting functions and contribute to the implementation of project, programme, and portfolio (PPP) management in the organisation.

LEARNING OBJECTIVES

- Characteristics of a permanent PMO;
- A possible service portfolio of a permanent PMO;
- The added value of a permanent PMO;
- ISO 21502:2020 Guidance on Project Management (advanced);
- Implementing a project, programme and portfolio organisation (advanced);
- IPMA Organisational Competence Baseline (advanced);
- Identifying the maturity level of a PPP organisation (advanced).

DEFINITIONS

Project, Programme and Portfolio organisation (PPP organisation): A permanent management domain within an organisation to manage projects, programmes, and portfolios.
Project Management Office (PMO): An organisational unit that facilitates the decision-making process within a project, programme and portfolio organisation.
Knowledge centre: An organisational function providing and maintaining standards to improve service delivery and organisational learning.

INTRODUCTION

Within the permanent organisation, often various functions have been set up, on the one hand, to support the project, and on the other hand, to ensure that the project operates within the governance of the permanent organisation. Knowing these supporting functions' processes and services is paramount to manage projects efficiently and effectively.

Nowadays, more and more supporting functions are provided or channelled via a permanent Project Management Office (PMO). However, many organisations are not yet equipped that way. Implementing a permanent *Project, Programme and Portfolio* (PPP) organisation is no sinecure and, despite its advantages, often meets with a lot of resistance.

POSITIONING

At the project definition stage, you should agree with the supporting functions/PMO on what services they will provide and whether they will be provided by their office or on-site. During delivery, you should periodically inform them about the project's progress according to the reporting standards. At stage transitions, you should provide them with the necessary information so that they can prepare project decisions to be taken at programme, portfolio, or corporate level. Where appropriate, you should notify them of relevant lessons learned.

PURPOSE AND CHARACTERISTICS OF A PERMANENT PMO

The main purpose of a permanent PMO is to ensure consistency, efficiency, and effectiveness in project, programme, and portfolio management activities throughout the organisation. A permanent PMO:

- Facilitates the decision-making process in a portfolio;
- Defines and maintains guidelines for project and programme management;
- Supports the implementation of projects and programmes;
- Assures the proper implementation of the projects and programmes within the portfolio.

Towards projects, it acts as a support and oversight function to project managers and project teams, providing them with the necessary tools, methodologies, and resources to deliver projects successfully.

Structure

In its simplest form, a permanent PMO consists of a single individual or a single office. In a more complex form, a PMO consists of a central office with various local offices (hub and spoke). Some PMOs have established a separate knowledge centre to define and maintain project and programme management guidelines. In most cases, however, this function is performed integrally within the PMO, with each PMO member being responsible for maintaining one or more guidelines.

Knowledge Centre

To maintain guidelines within the portfolio, it is recommended that for each guideline a responsible officer is appointed, assisted by a team of subject matter experts. This is to ensure that these guidelines remain practical and are also accepted and supported by the relevant managers and support officers. Furthermore, it is best to agree on an exchange procedure. The guidelines are valid and should be followed until an improved version replaces them. Ensure that the stakeholders agree on this in advance and that respected subject matter experts are part of the review teams. Finally, the agreed guidelines should be formally approved by the manager in charge.

Variety of PMOs

If the PMO consists of only one individual, it usually does no more than provide an overview of ongoing projects and programmes and define and maintain agreed guidelines. In its most comprehensive form, the PMO also maintains a pool of project and programme managers and support officers who can be assigned to individual projects and programmes. Usually, a PMO is a physical department, but it can also be a virtual unit. In the latter case, the support is provided by individual employees within different business units.

Deployment of support officers

Support officers can be assigned part-time or full-time to individual projects and programmes. This can be for the full range of support or just for a specific task or service. In all cases, it is advisable to agree in advance on which services are to be provided and whether this will be done centrally or on-site. It is best to do this based on a service portfolio with norm values, costs, and time estimates for each service.

Service portfolio

The service portfolio of a PMO should consist of all services that the support officers can provide. This portfolio can vary widely (see Chapter 5.01 Project Definition Stage). The most common services are:

- Set up and close the project administration at project start and end;
- Set up and maintain the document management system and project files;
- Assist in preparing and updating plans and budgets;
- Set up and maintain management procedures and registers;
- Assist with procurement and contract management;
- Collect data and forecasts and prepare reports;
- Assist in planning and requesting resources;
- Administer new resources and support the introduction of new project members;
- Assist in the project team and project board meetings and take minutes;
- Assist with quality activities, maintain the quality register and archive quality records;
- Assist with risk activities, maintain the risk register and archive risk records;
- Assist with change control activities, maintain issue registers and archive issue reports;
- Maintain configuration items records and provide configuration status accounts;
- Provide expertise in the use of supporting tools and techniques.

In addition, secretarial work may be included, such as booking meeting rooms and making travel and accommodation arrangements.

Organisation

Usually, a separate head of PMO leads the PMO. This person reports to the director of projects or the portfolio manager. Sometimes, the portfolio manager themself is the head of the PMO. If PMO officers are assigned to individual projects, they report operationally to the respective project managers but functionally to the head of the PMO.

ADDED VALUE OF A PERMANENT PMO

Depending on the size and responsibilities of the permanent PMO, the added value for the various stakeholders varies.

Management – The PMO can provide an overview of initiatives, assist in selecting the right initiatives and creating the portfolio roadmap, establish and maintain guidelines, provide timely and consistent information to make strategic decisions and ensure that expected benefits are realised in coordination with the regular staff departments.

Project and programme managers – The PMO can provide them with accelerated start-up and closure, a consistent approach, qualified support, practical and proven guidelines, and up-to-date knowledge of the latest tools and techniques. Moreover, the PMO contributes significantly to timely and consistent management decision-making and resource allocation as it supports portfolio management processes.

Support officers – The PMO can provide them structural training and coaching on-the-job, career opportunities, support through proven guidelines, the availability of adequate tools and techniques, and structured updates on the latest developments.

Moreover, the PMO can provide additional support when needed. Finally, support officers become full members of a respected organisational unit.

Users/business units – The PMO can ensure timely and consistent involvement, fit-for-use and fit-for- purpose changes, minimal disruption, and maximum contribution to business operations based on established guidelines. Moreover, the PMO ensures timely information about imminent changes and that those changes match the change capacity of the relevant business units.

Internal and external suppliers – The PMO can help them to ensure an even deployment of resources and a central point of contact for resource allocation for the projects and programmes.

A mature permanent PMO contributes in this way to:

- *Governance* – Critically examining and questioning the principles;
- *Working method* – Ensuring the introduction of guidelines;
- *Lessons learned* – Recording and implementing lessons learned;
- *Implementation* – Training and coaching staff and management;
- *Transparency* – Providing timely, accurate and relevant information;
- *Project assurance* – Checking whether agreements are met;
- *Document control* – Maintaining management documents and records;
- *Benefit realisation* – Reporting on realised benefits to management.

RESPONSIBILITIES

The project manager should apply the tools, techniques and best practices as the permanent PMO prescribes and tailor those to the project's requirements. You should also report progress to the permanent PMO so that they can keep the management informed and pass on lessons learned to improve applicable guidelines. The permanent PMO, in turn, should ensure that proper guidelines, tools and techniques are available, that you have adequate support, and that the established guidelines are applied.

ADVANCED

IMPLEMENTING A PPP ORGANISATION (ADVANCED)

Introducing a PPP organisation is a major change and is best implemented as a programme. It is necessary to involve stakeholders directly in the change and to appoint change managers in the customer organisation concerned. This can be best done by 'early adopters': people who are enthusiastic about the change and will start using the new guidelines as soon they become available. These are the people with whom the introduction of the new way of working can take shape.

A prerequisite for effective implementation is that the need for change is made explicit and is also perceived as such by top management. Mere dissatisfaction with the current situation is not enough. Once the sense of urgency has been established, a vision of the new situation needs to be developed and associated benefits defined. An outline of the PPP organisation should be set up and how the PPP will be implemented.

It is best to develop a project management handbook and implement the most important systems first. At this stage, it is essential to train the early adaptors in project management so that they can contribute to the further development of the handbook. A permanent PMO can be set up, and pilot projects can be started. The project management teams involved, including the project board members, should be trained and coached.

Assess the results and, if successful, only then set up a company-wide implementation. Finally, secure the PPP organisation in the organisation's quality system. By implementing lessons learned, improvements can be made, and project-based work in the organisation can be further developed.

The implementation should be clearly communicated to all parties involved. Many people need to be involved. Potential quick wins should be identified, implemented and celebrated, and possible obstacles should be quickly removed. Provide an environment wherein mistakes are allowed. You can get help, but you have to participate!

Pros and cons

Organisations have different reasons for introducing a PPP organisation. Customer organisations can respond quickly and effectively to changes. Supplier organisations can implement projects more quickly, efficiently, and effectively.

By setting up a separate change organisation, the necessary resources can more easily be made available and the permanent organisation is relieved of the burden. When implementing changes through the permanent organisation, there is a risk of suboptimisation. All changes-related decisions have to be made through the permanent reporting lines. This overloads the line organisation, leaving line management with less time for its actual work or with a risk that the necessary changes do not take place, with all its consequences. The final responsibility and coordination of changes lie only at the highest level of the organisation, and there is a considerable distance towards the (external) customer.

A disadvantage is the creation of a matrix structure (two bosses). The organisation becomes more complex. Conflicts of interest become more visible. Some responsibilities and powers are transferred. On the other hand, in a pure line organisation, the conflicts about the changes to be made often remain more implicit, which can ultimately be even more damaging.

Resistance

Resistance to introducing a PPP organisation stems directly from the organisational changes involved. People often derive their status from their current position and powers, do not see the need for change, and are uncertain about what the change means for them. In this way, introducing project management is just a 'normal' organisational change, with all its characteristics, problems and resistances and one that impacts straight the organisation's core.

ISO 21502: 2020, GUIDANCE ON PROJECT MANAGEMENT (ADVANCED)

The ISO 21502:2020 provides guidance on project management concepts and practices.

ISO 21502:2020 defines a project as a temporary endeavour to achieve one or more defined objectives. These project objectives should contribute to outcomes and the realisation of benefits for stakeholders, including the sponsoring organisation, other internal and external organisation stakeholders, customers and their stakeholders.

An outcome is defined as the change resulting using the output from a project. A benefit is defined as a created advantage, value or another positive effect. Outcomes and benefits result from using the project output. Projects can be responsible for ensuring that those outcomes and those benefits are realised.

The ISO 21502;2020 describes:

- Project management concepts;
- Prerequisites for formalising project management in organisations;
- Integrated project management practices (activities);
- Management practices.

Project management concepts

The project management concepts describe the project context, the project governance, the project lifecycle, the project organisation and the project management competences.

Project context – Selected opportunities and threats are the reasons for initiating projects and the basis for the project's business case. The outputs from projects enable outcomes which should realise benefits for the sponsoring organisations, as well as for internal or external stakeholders.

Project governance – The principles, policies, and framework by which the project organisation is directed and controlled. The responsibility for maintaining project governance is usually assigned by the sponsoring organisation to the project sponsor/ project board.

Project lifecycle – The number and names of a project's stages depend upon the type of project being undertaken, desired governance, and the anticipated risk. The stages can reflect the delivery approach.

Project organisation – The project organisation is a temporary structure that defines the project's roles, responsibilities and authorities in the project. Individuals are assigned by titles to specific roles in the project organisation.

Competences of project management – According to ISO 21502:2020, these can be categorised into technical, behavioural and business competences, which is comparable to the ICB4.

Prerequisites for formalising project management in organisations

There are various prerequisites that an organisation should consider before establishing an environment for implementing, maintaining and improving project management. ISO 21502: 2020 describes considerations for implementing project management, how to facilitate continuous improvement of project management and how to ensure an alignment with the organisational processes and systems.

Integrated PM practices

Integrated project management practices cover the practices to be used when undertaking a project, from pre-project to post-project activities. The purposes of the individual practices are:

- *Pre-project activities* – To verify the project is worth starting;
- *Overseeing a project* – To oversee the project by the sponsoring organisation;
- *Directing a project* – To enable the project to remain relevant in the organisational context;
- *Initiating a project* – To establish the foundation for project delivery and verify that the project is justified;
- *Controlling a project* – To perform the daily management including stages and work packages;
- *Managing delivery* – To plan, execute, and deliver the individual work packages;
- *Closing a project* – To confirm project completion and manage project closure;
- *Post-project activities* – To verify that outcomes and the expected benefits are being realised.

IPMA ORGANISATIONAL COMPETENCE BASELINE (ADVANCED)

The IPMA Organisational Competence Baseline (OCB, 2019) describes the concept of organisational competence in project management and explains what an organisation should do to improve itself continuously. Organisational competence in this respect is the ability of organisations to integrate people, resources, processes, structures and cultures into projects, programmes and portfolios within a supporting control and management system.

The IPMA OCB describes five groups of organisational competences: governance, management, organisational alignment, resources and people competences. These five groups are, in turn, subdivided into 18 competence elements (see Figure 9.04.01).

However, the OCB is neither a textbook nor a cookbook. Instead, it indicates WHAT should be done and not HOW.

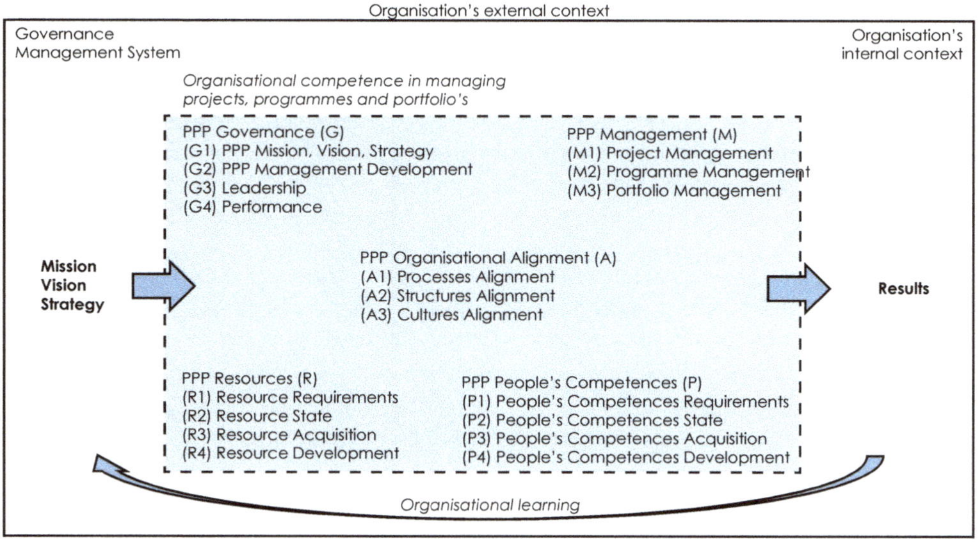

Figure 9.04.01 OCB competence elements (IPMA, 2019)

IDENTIFYING THE MATURITY LEVEL (ADVANCED)

IPMA Delta is an assessment model to determine the competence of an organisation to manage projects based on the IPMA-OCB. The IPMA Delta assesses this competence based on five competence classes, whereby a competence class is defined as a state in which an organisation can manage a particular aspect systematically and effectively. This assessment provides a baseline on which improvements can be made. These five competence classes are (see Figure 9.04.02):

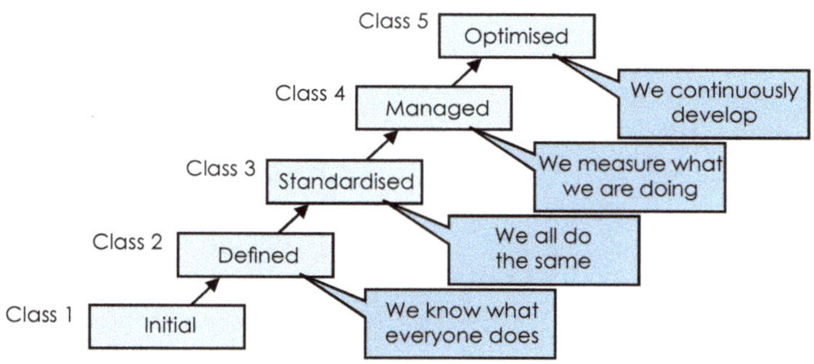

Figure 9.04.02 IPMA Delta competence classes

Initial – Project results are mainly achieved based on personal qualities. Projects often exceed time and budget and deliver only part of the agreed output. PPP processes and structures are virtually non-existent. Successes are not repeatable.

Defined – PPP standards are only partially implemented. Project management is still primarily the responsibility of the individual business units. No PPP improvement process is in place. Line managers have only limited knowledge of their role in projects. Projects still score poorly in terms of time, cost and deliverables. The status of projects is already visible to management at milestones.

Standardised – Almost all PPP standards are in place and are applied. A centralised PMO has also been established, PPP competences are tracked and developed, and line management can fulfil their role within projects. Resources are managed, and project deliverables are usually delivered on time and within budget. Senior management is actively involved in project management and is visibly committed.

Controlled – All PPP standards are in place and are applied across the organisation. The central PMO acts as a knowledge centre and is part of the training programme for aspiring professionals. Project management is regularly evaluated based on which improvements are implemented. Line managers are evaluated on their performance in projects. Projects are often delivered on time, within budget, and to the full satisfaction of stakeholders.

Optimising – All PPP standards are fully implemented and applied across the organisation. The entire PPP organisation is constantly developing. Standards are tailored to individual projects and programmes. Top management is actively involved in the projects and programmes and often acts as a project or programme sponsor. The quality of project delivery is assessed and improved based on key performance indicators. Projects are almost always delivered on time, within budget, and to the full satisfaction of stakeholders.

IPMA Delta uses questionnaires like other maturity models to determine the current maturity level. Based on the ambition level, the difference between the current and desired situation can be determined, and an improvement plan can be developed. With a higher maturity level, projects and programmes can run more smoothly and are implemented more efficiently and effectively (see Figure 9.04.03).

Progressing to the next competence class is quite a job and requires decisive management and a lot of effort. A single step takes at least one year. However, significant benefits can be achieved with each step. Literature shows that a 15% performance improvement in change capacity can be realised per step. Most organisations are still at a competence classes 1, 2 or 3 regarding project management. When it comes to programme and portfolio management, organisational competences are generally even lower.

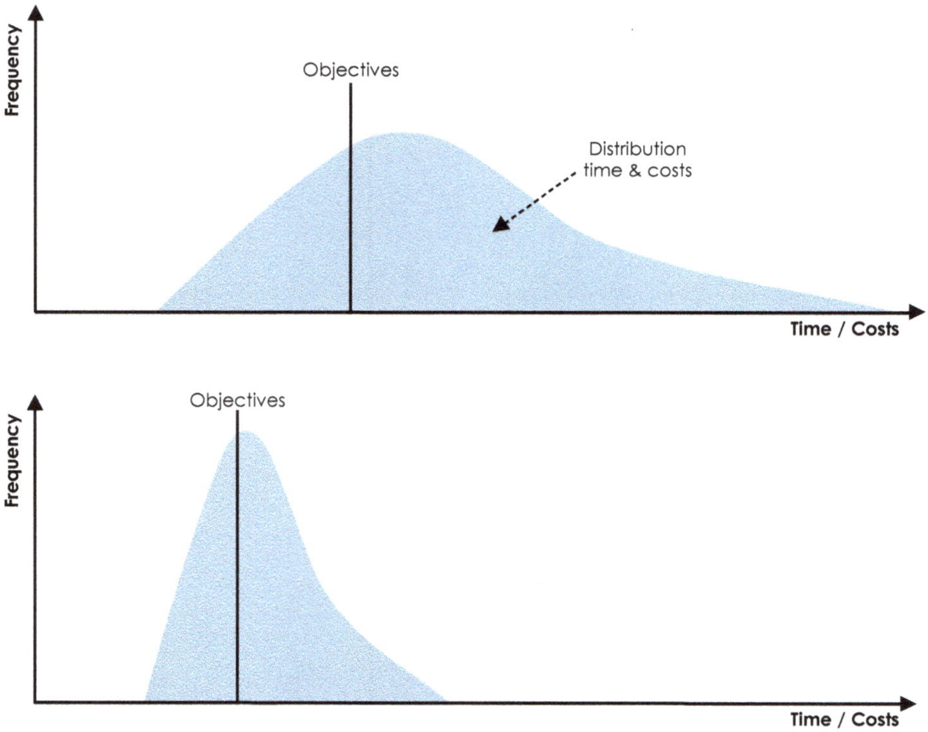

Figure 9.04.03 Expected improvement due to higher maturity class

9.05 DEVELOPMENT FRAMEWORKS

PURPOSE

The purpose of this chapter is to enable the individual to understand various development frameworks and to manage the project in conjunction with these frameworks.

LEARNING OBJECTIVES

- What is Agile and the principles and values of Agile as laid down in the Agile Manifesto;
- The characteristics of the Scrum framework;
- Applying Scrum within a project context versus continuous development;
- The characteristics of Lean Six Sigma and the seven forms of waste (advanced);
- The characteristics of Kanban (advanced).

DEFINITIONS

Development framework: A framework to develop delivering products in a structured way.
Agile: A conceptual approach to implement changes iteratively and incrementally.
Scrum: A lightweight framework to adaptively develop or improve products.
Kanban: A framework to optimise the workflow by visualising and limiting the work in progress.
Lean Six Sigma: A framework to improve performance by systematically removing waste and reducing variation, based on a team effort.

INTRODUCTION

A project management approach should be tailored to the work to be carried out and how it will be done. It makes quite a difference whether a project is developed Waterfall or iteratively and whether it is delivered all at once or incrementally. This also affects the role and position of the project manager. This chapter looks closely at the Agile way of working and its impact on project management.

POSITIONING

The project mandate often already indicates how the project output is to be developed. This approach is confirmed or determined in the project outline and further elaborated in the project definition stage. It is essential that the chosen approach fits the project deliverables, project conditions and organisational culture. In the project definition stage, the intended releases are also scheduled.

Even in an Agile approach, the project manager should facilitate the work and report on the progress to management and other stakeholders. You also need to ensure that the chosen approach remains effective, the work is performed within the agreed tolerances, and the agreed quality activities are carried out and documented Further ensure that the deliverables are implemented as agreed and important lessons are forwarded to the appropriate bodies. At the conclusion of the project, you should ensure that the project is dismantled and the team is discharged as in any other project. Avoid that the project drifts unnoticed into operational use.

AGILE

Agile means flexible. It is a conceptual approach to implementing changes iteratively and incrementally. Iterative in this context means that products are developed cyclically. Incremental in this context means that the output is delivered in a series of small steps.

Manifesto for Agile Software Development

Towards the end of the last century, software projects were performed formally with detailed specifications at the start and extensive documentation at the end. As a result, many projects failed because this approach did not meet the rapidly changing technical developments and user needs within software development.

This created a strong desire to make software development more agile. In 2001, this was formalised in the *Manifesto for Agile Software Development*. This manifesto states Agile values as follows:

- Individuals and interactions over processes and tools;
- Working software over comprehensive documentation;
- Customer collaboration over contract negotiation;
- Responding to change over following a plan.

This manifesto is based on the following twelve principles:

1. Our highest priority is to satisfy our customers;
2. Welcome changing requirements, even late in development;
3. Deliver working software frequently;
4. Business people and developers should work together daily throughout the project;
5. Build projects around motivated individuals;
6. The most effective way of conveying information is through face-to-face conversation;
7. Working software is the primary measure of progress;
8. Agile processes promote sustainable development;
9. Continuous attention to technical excellence and good design enhances agility;
10. Simplicity – the art of maximising the amount of work not done – is essential;
11. The best results emerge from self-organising teams;
12. Regular reflections on how to become more effective.

This movement is very successful. This is also because the principles are essentially good best practices. Many projects are now carried out in an Agile way of working. At present, there are already more than 100 Agile frameworks. Existing frameworks are also included under this umbrella. In addition, Agile is increasingly being applied outside the field of software development. In principle, an Agile approach can be applied in all disciplines. The Agile approach is also being increasingly integrated into traditional project management approaches, and all kinds of hybrid forms of work emerge. Please note: applying Agile in a project is not a matter of 'yes or no'. The question is 'how much'. Scrum, Kanban and Lean Six Sigma (LSS) are well-known Agile frameworks.

Agile working in business as usual and in projects

Agile working can be applied within business as usual and in projects. Within business as usual, permanent Agile teams are responsible for continuously developing existing products. Only if the development of new products cannot be accommodated within this framework, separate Agile projects are initiated. Upon completion, these temporary teams are being disbanded again. Further development of the new product is then assigned to one of the existing development teams. If necessary, these teams are expanded for this purpose (see Figure 9.05.01).

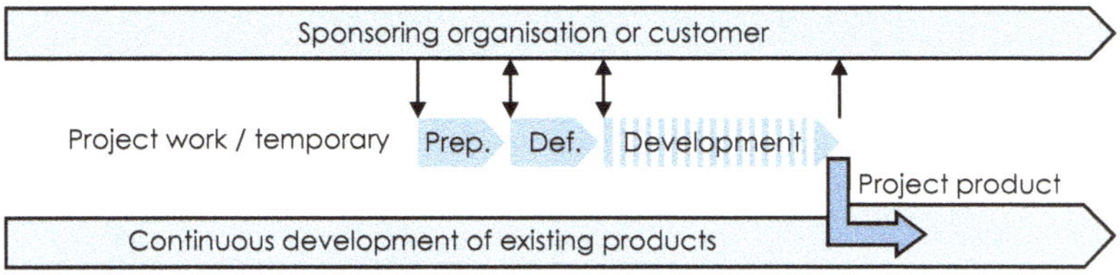

Figure 9.05.01 Agile in project versus Agile in continuous development

In continuous development, work that cannot be completed within a timebox is almost automatically moved to the next timebox. Within projects, minor items that cannot be developed within a timebox are dropped to meet the time constraints set.

Agile basics

Agile is characterised by self-managing teams, timeboxes, an iterative approach, techniques such as backlogs and stand-ups, and incremental delivery of dispatchable products at the end of each timebox (see Figure 9.05.02). The term backlog refers to a list of outstanding items. A stand-up is a short meeting to discuss progress on key issues, held standing.

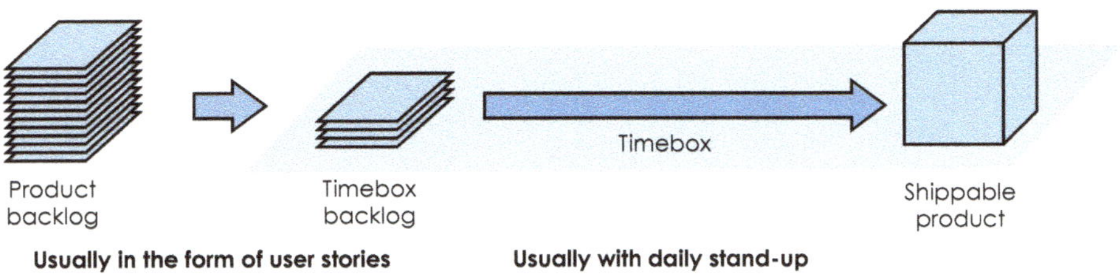

Figure 9.05.02 Agile basics

This basic structure falls within an overall approach consisting of a product vision, a product roadmap and a series of releases. A release is a set of functions put into use simultaneously. This can be at the end of each timebox and after several timeboxes have been completed.

In Agile projects, self-managing teams form the basis of the project. They are fully responsible for realising the products to be delivered via short iterations in fixed timeboxes. The requirements are determined by the user representative (product owner) in consultation with the delivery team.

Whereas in traditional projects, scope and quality are set, and efforts are made to control time and costs, Agile projects are driven by the number of features delivered within a predetermined period (see Figure 9.05.03). Accept that the customer doesn't need everything. Many features are rarely used or not used at all. By prioritising the functions/features and developing them in that order, the customer gets what they really want sooner and the project can be delivered on time. Less important features are dropped or moved to continuous development.

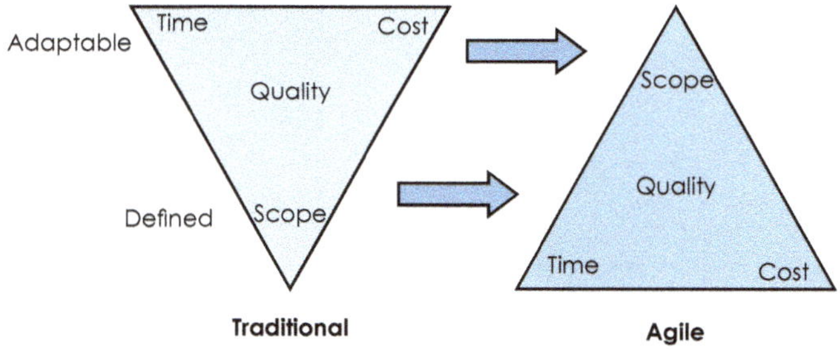

Figure 9.05.03 What to flex and what to fix

The features with the highest priority are usually also the best defined. Conversely, one could even say: 'If we cannot adequately specify a feature, the urgency might not be as high as claimed.'

Another principle of Agile is that nothing is perfect all at once. Repeated feedback is needed to achieve a good result. Customers and users often don't know what they really want until they see the first results. Furthermore, like the delivery team, customers and users gradually discover newer and better solutions. It would be a waste not to make use of them. It does mean that previously delivered results sometimes have to be adjusted. That is unfortunate, but there is no point in continuing on the wrong path. Since individual iterations are usually short, adjusting previous results is usually not a big problem.

A common statement is that Agile is only suitable for software development projects. This is incorrect. Agile can be applied in any project where strong collaboration with users is required and incremental delivery is an option. The advantage of Agile projects is that developers and users work together from the start. Wherever this is important, an Agile approach delivers benefits.

SCRUM

In Scrum, the work is carried out in multidisciplinary self-managing teams that, in short sprints, deliver dispatchable products. In their latest *Scrum Guide* (2020), Ken Schwaber and Jeff Sutherland define Scrum as a lightweight framework that helps people, teams, and organisations generate value through adaptive solutions for complex problems.

Scrum is based on empiricism and lean thinking. Empiricism is the approach that holds that knowledge comes from experience, and decisions are made based on observations. Lean thinking is the approach that focuses on value-adding processes and activities.

Empiricism is based on transparency, inspection and adaptation. The processes and work should be visible to those performing the work and receiving the results. The artefacts and progress should be inspected frequently and thoroughly to detect potential variances and problems. If any aspects of the process and the resulting products are unacceptable, the applied process or products should be adjusted.

Scrum values

The successful use of Scrum depends on people being committed, focused, open, respectful and courageous. The Scrum team is committed to achieving its goals and supporting each other. Their primary focus is on making the most progress toward achieving these goals. The team and its stakeholders speak openly about the work and its challenges. Scrum team members respect each other as capable, independent people. They also dare to do the right thing and solve challenging problems.

Scrum team

The Scrum team consists of a product owner, a Scrum master and developers. Scrum teams are cross-functional, meaning they have all the skills needed to create value in each sprint. They are also self-managing, which means together, they decide who does what, when and how.

A typical Scrum team comprises ten or fewer individuals to prevent sub-teams from emerging. The Scrum team is collectively responsible for creating a useful and valuable increment. The product owner and the Scrum master can actively participate as developers within the team.

Product owner – Accountable for maximising the value delivered by the Scrum team. They are also accountable for developing and communicating the product goal, creating and ordering the product backlog, and ensuring it is clear, visible and understandable.

A good product owner has the confidence of management, has authority, is business-orientated, is persuasive, knows the market and the product, understands the development process and is available to the developers, users and other stakeholders. The product owner acts as change authority within the Scrum framework. The product owner is an individual, not a committee.

Developers – Accountable for developing the backlog items into increments. They are responsible for creating the sprint plan, delivering quality by meeting the Definition of Done and holding each other accountable for their responsibilities. The developed increments are the collective responsibility of all developers. Make sure all required disciplines are covered. Prevent work differentiation.

Scrum master – The individual responsible for setting up Scrum successfully within a team or organisation. The Scrum master coaches the team members, overcomes barriers (impediments) and ensures that all Scrum events take place effectively. The Scrum master may also coach product owners in their responsibilities.

Scrum artefacts

Scrum's artefacts are the product backlog, sprint backlogs and increments.

Product backlog – An evolving and ordered list of what is still needed to develop or improve a product. It is the single source of work for the Scrum team. It also includes the project goal. The product goal describes the future state of the product to be developed.

The initial product backlog is prepared in the project definition stage. The product backlog is constantly changing, on the one hand, because work is completed, and on the other, because wishes and requirements change. Only the product owner can modify the product backlog.

Sprint backlog – Contains the sprint goal (why), the backlog items selected for the sprint (what) and the sequence of work to deliver the increment (how). The sprint plan is the ordered list of backlog items to be developed and the current status of the work. The sprint backlog items should be detailed enough for developers to track their progress during the sprint. Only the Scrum team can modify the product backlog.

The sprint goal is the only objective for the sprint. The sprint goal is a short description (1 or 2 lines) of the overall improvement that should be achieved with the increment to be delivered. Sometimes, release backlogs (no Scrum term) are distinguished between the product and the sprint backlogs.

Increment – A concrete addition to the finished product towards the product goal that meets the Definition of Done. Multiple increments can be delivered within one sprint. All increments realised in a sprint should be presented in the sprint review. If required, an increment may already be released during a sprint. Make sure each increment works well with all previous increments.

Definition of Done (DoD) – List of criteria (checklist) that every backlog item should meet to be considered complete (Done). The DoD is prepared in the project definition stage and confirmed during the start of each sprint. The DoD should be distinguished from acceptance criteria. Acceptance criteria are the criteria the individual backlog items should meet.

Scrum events

Scrum has four formal events within an umbrella event, the sprint. (see Figure 9.05.04).

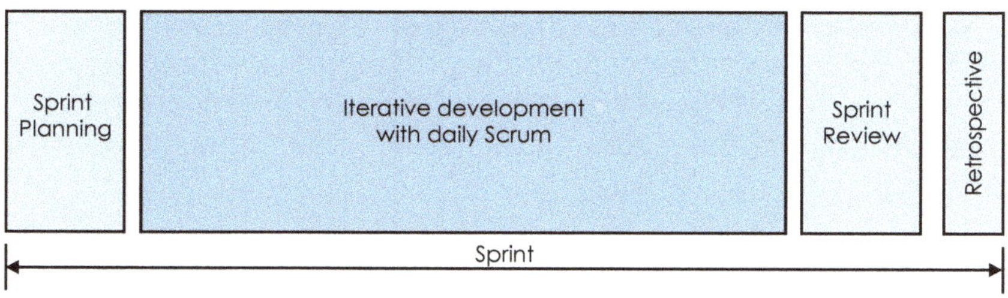

Figure 9.05.04 Scrum events

Sprint – Timebox with a fixed duration of up to one month, in which a ready product is created. The sprint starts with a sprint planning and ends with a sprint review and a retrospective. During the sprint delivery, the work is coordinated during daily Scrums. A task board is used to monitor progress. A sprint starts immediately after the end of the previous one.

Each sprint has a goal and a flexible plan that guides the work to be realised. The backlog items are developed in order of priority. Typically, the MoSCoW technique prioritises (see Chapter 4.04 Requirements and Objectives). If not all the work can be completed in the sprint, the team will drop the could-haves first and, if this is not enough, then the should-haves.

If the work turns out to be different than expected, the Scrum team may adjust the scope of the sprint backlog to ensure that the sprint goal can still be realised. Only the product owner can cancel a sprint (in consultation with the project manager) and only if the sprint goal is no longer achievable or obsolete. During the sprint, the product backlog is refined for future sprints.

Sprint planning – Sprint event in which the work to be performed in that sprint is determined and agreed upon by the Scrum team. The sprint backlog is developed and planned. Usually, backlog items are split into items of one day or less. This makes dividing an prioritising the work and tracking progress easier. By estimating the backlog items to be developed, they often make use of velocity techniques such as T-Shirt planning or Planning Poker and story points (see Chapter 5.06 Resources).

Daily Scrum – Daily stand-up by the developers to review progress. The daily Scrum typically takes no more than 15 minutes. Each developer gets 2 minutes to indicate what they are working on by answering the questions: (1) what have I done since the last time, (2) what will I do until the following daily Scrum, and (3) what issues do I have and what help do I need? Issues are called impediments. Impediments should be resolved before the next stand-up. If necessary, the Scrum master takes charge or escalates it to the project manager for further action.

Sprint review – Review of the outcome of the sprint by the entire Scrum team and invitees at the end of the sprint. The developers explain what is 'done' and not yet 'done' and indicate which problems they have faced and how they solved them. They demonstrate the completed work to the attendees, enable them to try the increments themselves, answer questions about it, and collect possible points of interest. Based on that, the product owner accepts or rejects the delivered increments on behalf of the customer and adjusts the product backlog. Changes in the market are also taken into account. The product owner then discusses the current product backlog and the likely completion date of the entire work. Finally, they all work together to determine what to do next.

Retrospective – Evaluation by the Scrum team at the end of the sprint to see how they can increase the quality of the increments and the effectiveness of the work: what went well, what can be improved and what needs to be improved? A check should also be done to see whether the agreed improvement from last time have been implemented and led to improvements. It makes no sense to define new ones if the previous improvements have not been followed up. It is recommended to limit the number of improvements per retrospective.

Other concepts

Other concepts often used within the Scrum framework are user stories, epics and the *Definition of Ready* (DoR), but these are not official Scrum concepts.

User story – Format to describe a backlog item from the perspective of the user, including why the user needs that functionality:

As [type of user], I [want/should] [action] so that [some reason].

> *As a buyer, I want to be able to choose from different payment options so that I can select a payment method that suits me best.*

Epic – A significant backlog item that has yet to be broken down into a set of smaller ones. Product backlog items are often defined in epics. An epic is often a backlog item that needs one or more sprints to be developed. Breaking down an epic into smaller backlog items is called backlog refinement.

Definition of Ready (DoR) – List of criteria that each backlog item should meet to start the work. These criteria are often represented by the acronym INVEST:
- *Independent* – Can be developed independently of other backlog items;
- *Negotiable* – Contains no specific solution; multiple solutions are possible;
- *Valuable* – The described backlog item provides added value;
- *Estimable* – It is easy to estimate the work that needs to be done;
- *Small* – The backlog item can be developed by one individual in (approximately) one day;
- *Testable* – The backlog item can be tested to determine whether it meets the requirements.

Monitoring progress

Several techniques can be used to monitor progress and communicate the work, such as a task board, information radiator, velocity, and a burn down and burn up chart.

Task board – Visualises the work planned (To Do), the work in progress (WIP) and the work done (Done) in three consecutive columns. The work is usually described in user stories on post-its and arranged in the column To Do in order of priority from top to bottom (see Figure 9.05.05). A task board is often referred to as a Scrum board.

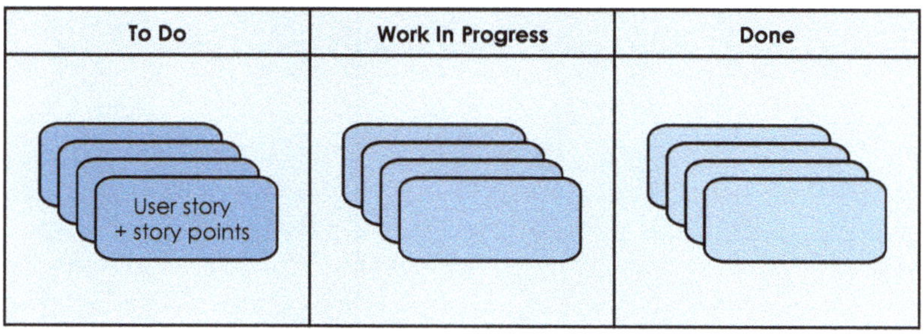

Figure 9.05.05 Task board

Information radiator – A wall or a large board, clearly visible to everyone, with all relevant information for an assignment, usually a sprint, release or project. Preferably, the information radiator is located in the developers' workspace. In addition to the task board, items such as the product and sprint goal, DoR and DoD, impediments, lessons learned, and the burn down and burn up charts may also be displayed.

Velocity – A measure of the amount of work a Scrum team performs during a sprint. Velocity is the most important measure of productivity in Scrum. Usually, an estimate is made in relation to a reference activity. Within Agile, the work required to perform that reference activity is called a story point. Known estimating techniques are Planning Poker and T-Shirt planning (see Chapter 5.05 People and Resources).

The velocity is calculated at the end of the sprint by adding up all the story points of the backlog items completed during the sprint. This velocity is the basis for the next sprint planning. The number of story points a team can achieve per sprint varies depending on the type of work, the team, and the team's experience.

Burn down chart – A specific version of the traditional slip chart (see Chapter 6.04 Control and Reporting) that shows the work still to be done. In a sprint, the outstanding work is expressed in the total story points of all backlog items still to be completed (see Figure 9.05.06). A burn down chart is usually used to track progress during a sprint.

Burn up chart – Displays the development of the total work 'done' and the outstanding work defined in the product backlog at the end of the successive sprints. The development of these two lines indicates when the total work to realise the product goal will be completed (see Figure 9.05.07).

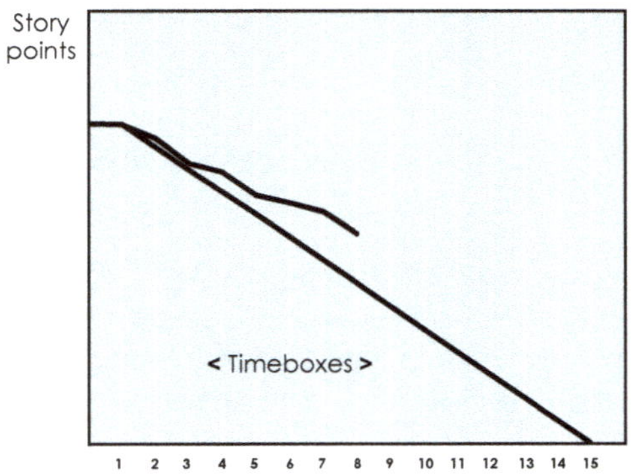

Figure 9.05.06 Burn down chart

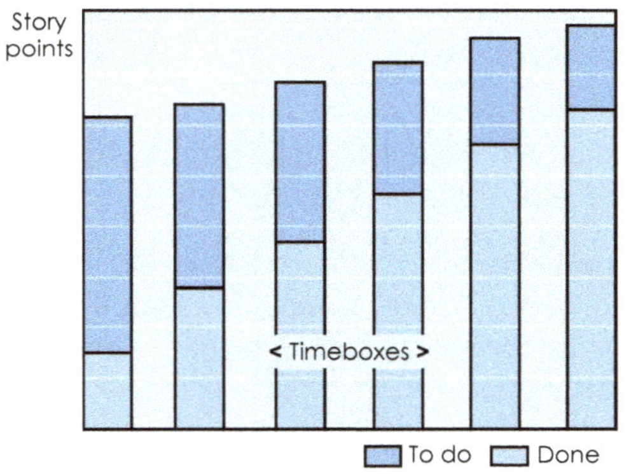

Figure 9.05.07 Burn up chart

Coordination between Scrum teams

If a Scrum team becomes too big, it should be split into multiple teams. Within a project, different Scrum teams can work on the same product with the same product backlog and the same product owner and Scrum master. On the other hand, different Scrum teams can work on different products with different product backlogs, product owners and Scrum masters. In both cases, Scrum teams need to coordinate with each other. This is done in a Scrum-of-Scrum, in which one or more team members participate.

Scrum in projects

Scrum can be used effectively in a project context but is unsuitable for managing a project in isolation. Scrum does not describe how projects are initiated and investment decisions are taken, nor how management can take responsibility for the investments and how projects will be closed upon completion.

Scrum also does not know project roles such as project sponsor, project manager and work package manager. When a Scrum team works within a project and is responsible for a work package, the product owner usually also fulfils the role of a work package manager. If multiple Scrum teams operate within one work package, there is often a separate work package manager to whom the individual product owners report. If the entire project is carried out by one Scrum team, then the product owner may also fulfil the role of project manager within the project.

Agile in a project lifecycle

A project may consist of merely a series of delivery timeboxes, with increments being put into use at the end of each timebox. On the other hand, the products may be developed in one or more stages, consisting of one or more releases, each consisting of multiple delivery timeboxes. Which combination of timeboxes, releases and stages fits best depends on the project and its context. Moreover, some work packages may be developed Waterfall and others Agile.

In the project preparation stage, determine which part of the project will be delivered in Agile. Create a product vision, define a customer journey and validate key hypotheses. The product vision is the customer's overarching goal with the product or system. The customer journey is how the customer is expected to use a particular product or system. When setting up the project management team, ensure proper integration with the Agile roles. Ensure that potential product owners are involved in the project definition stage. Within Agile, the project preparation stage is also known as *project chartering* or *project visioning*.

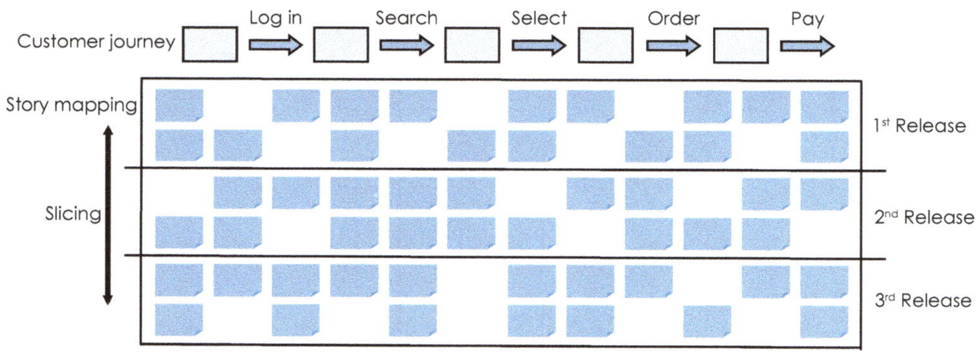

Figure 9.05.08 Slicing backlog items into releases

In the project definition stage, develop a story map based on the customer journey and have the product owners prepare the initial product backlogs. Group the backlogs into successive releases by 'slicing' the backlog items into progressive combinations (see Figure 09.05.08). The first release should consist of the *Minimum Marketable Product* (MMP). A Minimal Marketable Product is the smallest possible set of backlog items that creates a desired user experience and, therefore, can be used or marketed successfully.

Prepare the project plan/product roadmap with the successive stages and releases. Prepare the business case based on the best, worst and expected outcome. Define the work standards to be applied and the procedures and regulations to be followed. Agree on the Definition of Ready and the Definition of Done and have the release backlog prepared for the first release. Within Agile, the project definition stage is sometimes also called *Sprint zero*.

At stage transitions, organise a formal workshop with the teams to evaluate the work delivered, the Agile performance, the benefits realised, and the project's overall status. Define any lessons learned, and update expectations. Then update the project plan and business case, and prepare the plan for the next stage/release and the end-of-stage report for approval by the project sponsor/ project board (go/no-go decision).

At project closure, organise a formal workshop with the teams to evaluate the project's success, lessons learned, and any follow-up action recommendations. Prepare an end-of-project report and ensure that acceptance of the project output is confirmed and the discharge and formal closure of the project by the project sponsor.

The relevant management information can be captured in individual documents but also in e-mails, on a shared portal or in a PowerPoint presentation, as Agile aims to reduce documentation.

RESPONSIBILITIES

Even in an Agile approach, the project manager is responsible for initiating the project, preparing and monitoring the project plan/road map, and communicating between the delivery team and management. The role of the project manager can best be described as 'structuring and facilitating'.

ADVANCED

LEAN SIX SIGMA (ADVANCED)

Lean is a way of working that relies on a joint team effort to improve value for money for the customer by systematically removing waste (Muda), overburden (Muri) and unevenness of work (Mura). This creates maximum added value for the customer with minimal effort.

Six Sigma is a disciplined, data-driven approach to eliminating defects. Sigma is a measure of deviation from the standard. Realising six sigma entails that the process should not result in more than 3.4 defects per million opportunities. This approach requires detailed measurement of the performance.

The two methods can easily be applied together. Lean (the lean organisation) focuses on pace and reducing waste. Six Sigma (the perfect organisation) focuses on reducing the variation in production and business processes. Lean Six Sigma (LSS) offers a framework for continuously improving an organisation.

LSS philosophy

The philosophy of LSS is that:

- We can only control processes once we know how these processes progress and we have measured the actual performance of these processes.
- By minimising waste, we increase customer satisfaction and improve financial results.

LSS principles

The principles of LSS can be summarised as follows:

- *Value* – Specify the added value of the end product for the customer;
- *Value stream* – Define all activities of the process;
- *Flow* – Remove all unnecessary activities and avoid overload and irregularities;
- *Pull* – Put the customer in the lead; use the 'just in time' principle;
- *PDCA* – Implement a continuous improvement process and strive for perfection.

LSS focuses on what really matters to the customer. This approach leads to simultaneous cost reduction, increased customer satisfaction, and shorter turnaround times. With LSS, you invest in your people and use their knowledge and skills.

LSS process models

LSS has two process models: a process model for continuous (incremental) improvement of processes (DMAIC) and a process model for a process (re)design (DMADV).

The five main processes for incremental process improvement (DMAIC) are:

- *Define* – Defines the quality goals that match the customer demand and the organisational strategy;
- *Measure* – Measures the core aspects of the current process and collects relevant data;
- *Analyse* – Examines the collected data and looks for cause-effect relationships;
- *Improve* – Improves existing processes and conducts pilots to determine process capacity;
- *Control* – Sets up control systems, monitors the improvements and takes corrective actions if necessary.

The five main processes for the process (re)design (DMADV are:

- *Define* – Defines the quality goals that match the customer demand and the organisational strategy;
- *Measure* – Measures the core aspects of the current process and collects the relevant data;
- *Analyse* – Examines the characteristics to develop alternatives;
- *Design* – Designs the (improved) processes;
- *Verify* – Sets up pilots, tests the design, implements the processes in the production environment and delivers the result to the process owners.

Seven classic forms of waste

Within Lean, seven forms of waste are defined. As the origin of LSS lies in the manufacturing industry, the classic forms of waste are based on the manufacturing industry:

- *Production* – Over-or under-production of finished and semi-finished products;
- *Transport* – Unnecessary movement and handling of products;
- *Storage* – Unnecessary or incorrect storage of products;
- *Process* – Defective process design, use of faulty or incorrect tools;
- *Defects* – Error detection, rejection, waste and recovery;
- *Waiting* – Delay or wait for previous or next process steps;
- *Motion* – Ergonomics of the working environment, unnecessary movements of people.

LSS roles and responsibilities

LSS usually recognises two roles within the team: the Black Belt and the team members. In addition, LSS recognises a sponsor and a Master Black Belt who supports, coaches and monitors the Black Belt. For minor process improvements, Green Belts can be used. They can implement minor improvements within their own business processes under the supervision of a Black Belt.

KANBAN (ADVANCED)

Kanban is a framework to optimise the workflow. This is realised by visualising the workflow using a Kanban board and limiting the amount of work in progress by applying a limited number of 'signal cards' (see Figure 09.05.09).

The number of signal cards corresponds to the available capacity of the team. New work has to wait in a queue until a signal card becomes available. Kanban was initially invented to manage *Just In Time* (JIT) manufacturing processes.

Unlike Scrum, within Kanban, employees can continue with their regular work. Initially, the original work processes remain the same. Finally, Kanban does not work with timeboxes. New tasks are picked up as soon as the work in progress is completed.

Kanban philosophy

The philosophy is that:

- By visualising the workflow, the problem areas become more visible;
- By limiting the work in progress, the throughput increases.

Kanban principles

The Kanban principles can be summarised as follows:

- Continue with what you are doing now;
- Initially respect the current roles and responsibilities;
- Pursue evolutionary changes;
- Encourage leadership actions at all levels.

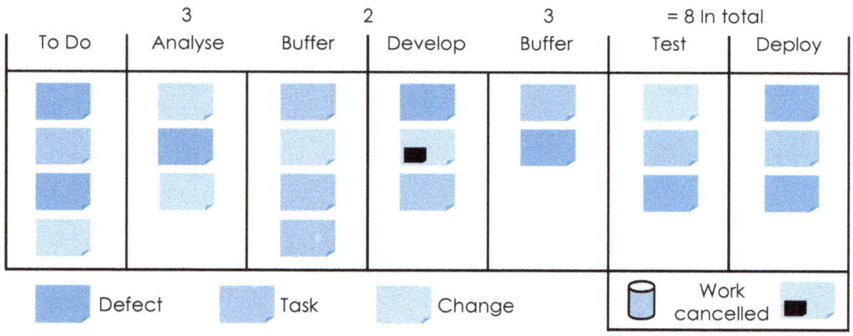

Figure 09.05.09 Example Kanban board

Implement a Kanban approach

Introducing Kanban is an evolutionary process. Start by focusing on quality. Then reduce work in progress. Deliver as often as possible and optimise supply versus demand. Prioritise your input queue and increase predictability by controlling the causes of variability in the system (e.g. available key people). If necessary, introduce buffers prior to bottlenecks in the process to ensure throughput.

To implement Kanban:

- Visualise the work process on a control board (Kanban board).
- Define the different types of work (change, incident, problem, maintenance, et cetera).
- Align supply and demand. Add buffers to control the throughput per process step.
- Make working agreements on, for example, expected lead time.
- For each process step, determine the maximum number of work units in progress (see the number at the top of each column in Figure 9.05.09).
- Record how and when prioritisation of the input buffers takes place and how products are transferred to the receiving party.
- Include a buffer at the beginning and end for coordinating work with the inputting and receiving parties.
- Define what information will be recorded on the design cards (ID number, title, description, and input and completion date).
- Agree on colours for the different types of work. Bottlenecks can be recorded on a red Post-it and linked to a signal card.
- Annotate if work items are cancelled during the process. This provides insight to the requesters and increases the quality of the input process ('Work cancelled' in Figure 9.05.09).
- Record all service agreements and policy guidelines.
- Implement feedback loops such as stand-ups and reviews;
- Measure the lead time per service type and optimise the process.

Kanban can be combined with other methods or frameworks, such as Scrum.

10. INTERNAL CONTEXT

A project does not stand alone, it takes place in an environment that is often complex and constantly changing. In doing so, the project organisation should take into account the governance of the customer and supplier organisations because they co-determine the design and delivery of the project.

Chapter 10.01 – Organisation Theories – Explains aspects such as staff and line functions, tasks and responsibilities, the span of control, and the differences between hierarchical and flat organisations. Furthermore, the relationship between the project and the permanent organisation, organisational elements according to Mintzberg, and Total Quality Management are discussed.

Chapter 10.02 – Personnel Management – Discusses what personnel management comprises and the role of the project manager, functional manager and personnel manager. It further explains the concept of competence management and single-, double-, and triple-loop learning.

Chapter 10.03 – Financial Administration – Covers various aspects related to financial accounting. The permanent organisation imposes a financial regime which project accounting needs to comply with. Project costs and forecasts should be included in the financial records and, ultimately, in the organisation's financial reporting.

Together, these chapters form the contextual competences of the project manager in relation to the internal context of the permanent organisation.

10.01 ORGANISATION THEORIES

PURPOSE

The purpose of this chapter is to enable the individual to align the project with the organisation's decision-making and reporting structures and quality requirements.

LEARNING OBJECTIVES

- The primary processes in permanent organisations;
- Line and staff departments;
- Span and depth of control;
- The pros and cons of a flat and a hierarchical organisation;
- Segregation of functions;
- Interfaces between the project and permanent organisation;
- Operational, functional and hierarchical lines of command;
- Characteristics of project matrix, autonomous, and project coordination structures;
- Systems and system approach and the use in projects (advanced);
- Organisational structures, according to Mintzberg (advanced);
- Total Quality Management (advanced).

DEFINITIONS

Permanent organisation: An organisation structured to accomplish its raison d'être permanently.

Governance: Principles, policies and framework by which an organisation is directed and controlled.

Primary process: The object-orientated system of activities by which an organisation legitimises and realises its raison d'être.

Line department: A department responsible for a part of the primary process of an organisation.

Staff department: A department which supports the management in her tasks with specialised advisory and support functions.

Matrix organisation: An organisational structure in which the project manager shares responsibilities with functional managers for determining the priorities of those assigned to the project.

Autonomous project structure: An organisational structure where the project is set up independently of the permanent organisation, with team members being transferred to their new position and giving up their current position.

Functional project structure: An organisational structure in which the project is organised and carried out via the functional departments of the permanent organisation.

INTRODUCTION

Projects are carried out within the context of the permanent organisation. Therefore, it is of the utmost importance to understand the structures and processes of the permanent organisation to manage the interface with the organisation efficiently and effectively.

What are the primary processes in a permanent organisation? What are the authorities of the respective line and support departments? What is the distinction between flat and hierarchical organisations, and how do the span and depth of control affect the project? What does the separation of functions imply? Furthermore, what are the interfaces between the project and sponsoring organisation? What are the different lines of command, and what are the most common structures to align projects and the permanent organisation?

POSITIONING

These organisations' governance, structures, and processes are vital throughout the project lifecycle. The sponsoring organisation or customer provides the project's mandate and goal, deliverables, requirements and constraints, as well as the principles and policies by which the project is directed and controlled throughout the project lifecycle. The supplier organisation often establishes additional frameworks and principles to realise the deliverables.

PERMANENT ORGANISATION

A permanent organisation is an organisation structured to accomplish its raison d'être permanently. This can be companies, NGOs, government agencies and anything in between. The term 'permanent organisation' is used to distinguish it from the temporary nature of the project organisation. A permanent organisation is also called a line or corporate organisation but can also be referred to as a parent organisation in relation to a project.

Primary process

The primary process is the object-orientated system of activities by which an organisation legitimises and realises its raison d'être. The primary process involves transformation and transaction processes. Transformation processes are those processes that change and relocate products, such as production and transport. Transaction processes trigger an exchange, such as purchases and sales. Transactional processes anchor the primary process to the environment and, in particular, to the market.

Based on this definition, departments such as Marketing, Communications, Research and Development and Administration are not part of the primary process. Also, Management Control and Technical Support and Maintenance are not part of the primary process. Management control comprises the control processes needed to control the primary process. Technical support and maintenance include the processes aimed at maintaining the primary process. When drawing processes, it is common to depict the control processes above and technical support and maintenance processes below the primary processes (see Figure 10.01.01).

Line and staff departments

Based on the above, we distinguish line and staff departments. Line departments are responsible for the primary process of an organisation and have their own authority. Staff departments support the line management in their tasks with specialised advisory and support functions. In principle, they can only issue directives and instructions on behalf of the management. Well-known examples of staff departments are Finance, Human Resources, and Legal.

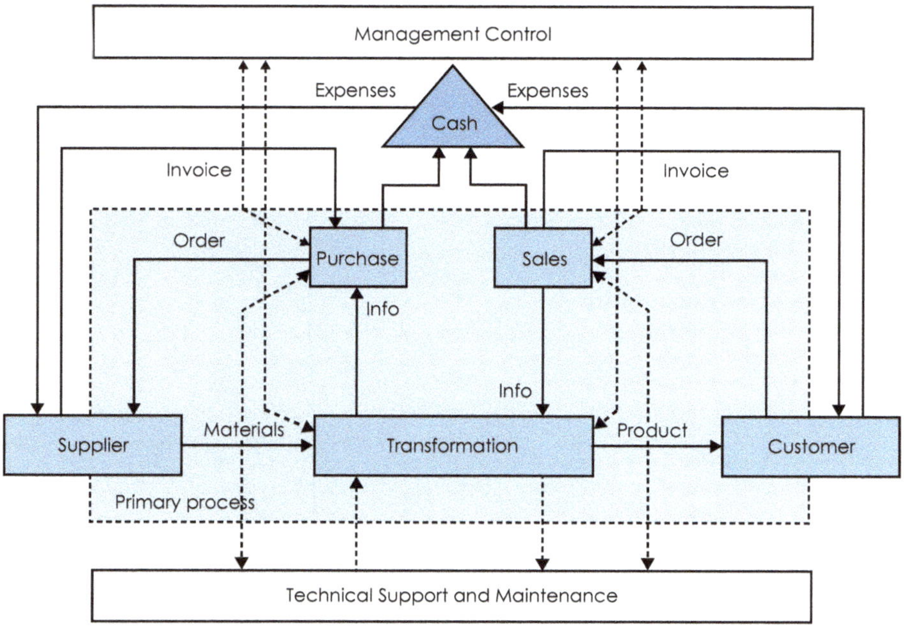

Figure 10.01.01 Example of a primary process

Line departments are drawn vertically below the parent function. Staff departments are drawn in a sidebar of the vertical structure (see Figure 10.01.02).

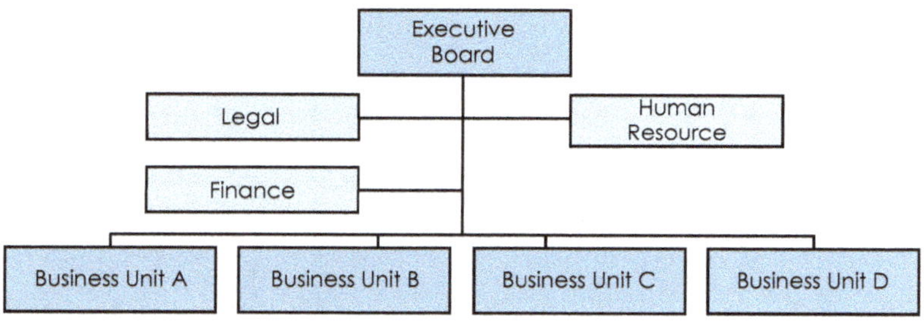

Figure 10.01.02 Annotation line and staff departments

Span and depth of control

The span of control is the number of employees that effectively can be managed directly. That has its limits. If they try to manage too many people directly, the quality of control decreases, and with it, the organisation's effectiveness. The average span of control is about 1 in 10 but can reach 1 in 25 or more. This depends on the organisational structure, the type of work, and aspects such as the organisational culture and the competence and availability of the manager and those who report to them. With the current shift towards self-managing teams, the span of control is increasing.

With a more significant number of employees, more decisions need to be delegated. The manager will only participate in the more strategic decisions, which usually leads to more job satisfaction among employees. If the manager wants to maintain complete control in such situations, communication and decision-making will be hampered, hindering the effective delivery of the work. A large span of control creates a flat organisation; a small span of control creates a hierarchical organisation.

The depth of control is the number of management layers between the top of the organisation and the workers at the workplace. It is determined by the available information technology and the degree of directive or goal-orientated control. It is essential to find an effective balance between these two elements.

Flat versus hierarchical organisation

A hierarchical organisation is an organisation with relatively numerous management layers. A flat organisation has relatively few management layers (see Figure 10.01.03).

Hierarchical organisations rely on a vertical chain of command. They tend to have more specialised departments than flat organisations. This gives employees more opportunities to move up the ladder gradually. Reporting lines are clear. However, there is a risk of bureaucracy and the creation of silos. Large organisations tend to have a hierarchical structure to facilitate their size.

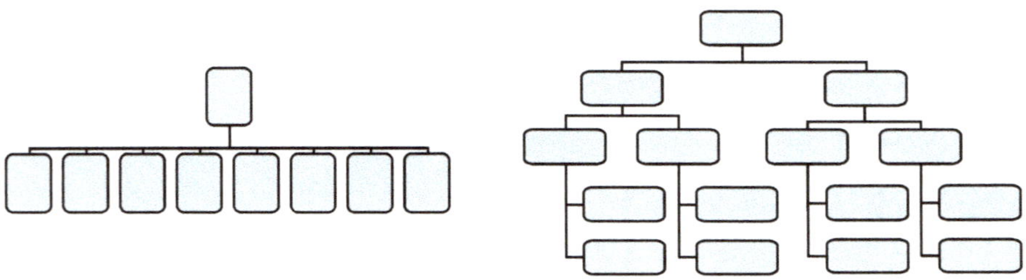

Figure 10.01.03 Flat versus hierarchical organisation

Flat organisations have little or no middle management. They are often more transparent, which enhances internal communication and enables quick decision-making. Employees often have more responsibility. However, flat organisations can lead to a lack of supervision and direction. Small organisations and start-ups tend to have a flat organisation as they have less need for structure.

For projects, a hierarchical organisation means that management decisions usually have to be reconfirmed by the next management level and are more subject to administrative procedures. In such situations, management decisions typically take longer and are more often subject to conflicting views. This should be duly taken into account in the management of projects.

Separation of functions

This principle states that distinct procurement and contract management functions should not be performed by one person or within one area. This is to prevent fraud and other security issues. Five functions are distinguished here:

- Authorisation – Approval to carry a task (e.g. project sponsor);
- implementation – Performing the work, e.g., purchase of goods (e.g. project manager);

- Custody – Storing the goods received (e.g. warehouse manager);
- Registration – Recording the events (e.g. administrator);
- Reconciliation – Controlling that the records are consistent, accurate, and complete (e.g. controller).

Depending on the critical values and risks, functions should be separated more strictly. From the point of view of the reliability of the internal processes, the controlling function should always be kept separate from the other functions. The separation of functions directly impacts the permanent organisation's governance over the project and the distribution of tasks, responsibilities and authority within the project.

INTERFACES BETWEEN PROJECT AND PERMANENT ORGANISATION

Interfaces between the project and the permanent organisation occur at different levels. This also almost automatically implies that alignment at these interfaces should also be made at different levels within the permanent organisation. Here, we usually distinguish operational, tactical and strategic interfaces:

- *Strategic level* – This level determines the governance, structures, and processes within which projects are implemented. Is it via a matrix structure, an autonomous project structure or a project-coordination structure? Are projects organised via programmes or a portfolio? How are costs and resources assigned, and how is the senior management informed?
- *Tactical level* – Here, the business case establishes the link between the project and the sponsoring organisation. Is it clear what the project needs from the sponsoring organisation and what the sponsoring organisation can expect from the project at completion?
- *Operational level* – At this level, the sponsoring organisation defines the project requirements, provides the resources, and accepts the project output. The sponsoring organisation also applies the project output to realise the anticipated benefits.

Lines of command

In addition, when managing the project, we need to take into account the control that managers within the permanent organisation continue to have over the people deployed in the project. Here, we can distinguish an operational, functional and hierarchical command line. In fact, each employee has three bosses (see Figure 10.01.04).

The operational boss tells you what to do, which activities you should carry out and when the work should be completed. The functional boss tells how you should carry out the work. The hierarchical boss determines your salary and your development path. These three command lines can be combined in one individual but can also be assigned to different persons. In the latter case, there needs to be coordination between the various bosses.

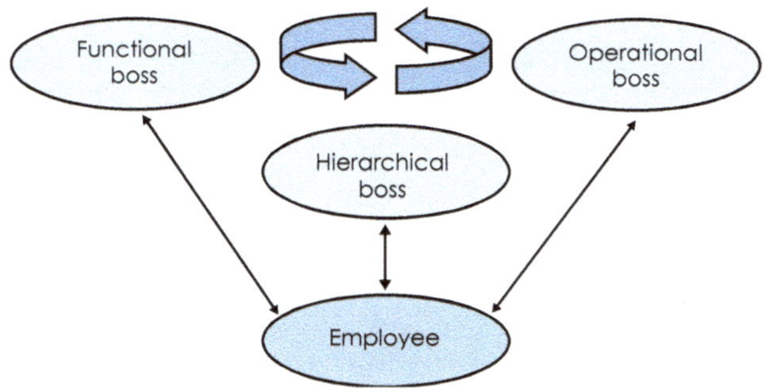

Figure 10.01.04 The three different lines of command for every employee

ORGANISATIONAL MODELS

Based on allocation these three lines of command, the relationship between the project and the permanent organisation can be shaped differently. The most common forms are the project matrix structure, the autonomous project structure and the functional project structure. In the examples below, the position of the project sponsor is equivalent to that of the business unit manager. This may vary per project.

Matrix organisation

The matrix project structure is the most common form of positioning projects in relation to the permanent organisation. In this structure, the roles of the operational, functional and hierarchical boss are split. The role of the operational boss within the project is delegated to the project manager. The other roles remain inside the permanent organisation. Therefore each team member has two bosses: the project manager inside the project and the supervisor or business unit manager within the permanent organisation (see Figure 10.01.05).

This can work very effectively but can also cause a lot of tension, especially if the employee has to work both within the project and operations. Also, the decision-making by the management is sometimes complicated and delayed because the project sponsor is involved in directing their own business units and the project. But the project can also make effective use of the expertise of the various employees within the permanent organisation. Also, projects within a matrix organisation can be launched quickly. Finally, deploying employees from the permanent organisation can increase acceptance of the project output within their organisation.

Autonomous project structure

In an autonomous project structure, the project organisation is set up independently of the permanent organisation. In such structure, team members are being transferred to their new position and giving up their current position. In the case of an autonomous project structure, the project organisation is usually a separate legal entity at a separate location. All the lines of command are within the project organisation. The project manager is then the operational, functional and hierarchical boss of the team members. Such a structure is usually set up by a contractor when it has to carry out a large and risky project for one of its customers (see Figure 10.01.06).

An advantage of this structure is the clear lines of command. All team members are 100% dedicated to the project. Also, the decision-making process is simpler. A disadvantage is that initiating and dismantling such a project takes extra time and effort. The use of specialists from the permanent organisation is also not self-evident. Finally, there is a chance that much expertise will go to waste at the end of the project as employees cannot return to their previous positions and apply elsewhere because their old positions have been filled.

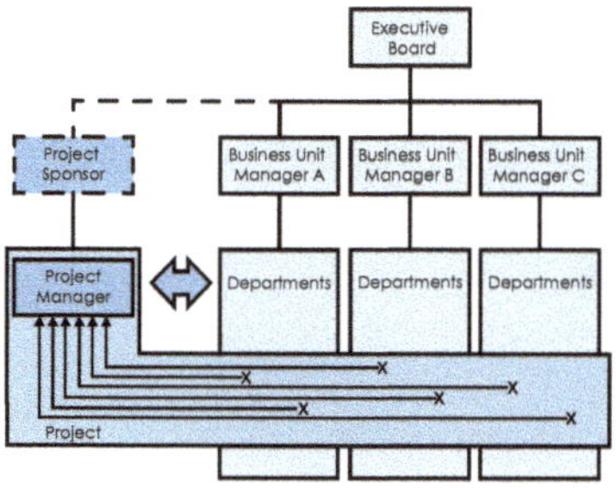

Figure 10.01.05 Matrix

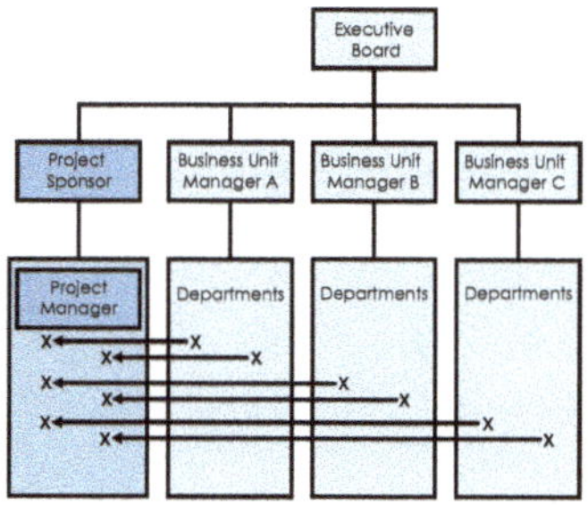

Figure 10.01.06 Autonomous

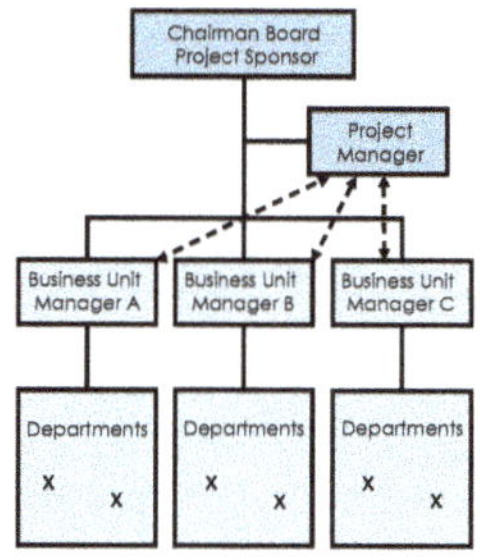

Figure10.01.07 Functional

Functional project structure

In a functional project structure, the project is organised and carried out via the functional departments of the permanent organisation. The project sponsor is the director, the work package leaders are the heads of the department, and the project board meeting is just an item on the agenda of the Executive Board meeting. The project manager only facilitates this process (see Figure 10.01.07).

An advantage of this structure is the clear reporting lines. Every department manager allocates their own people to the project based on their expertise. Furthermore, the teams within a department are homogeneous.

A disadvantage is that, except at the highest level, ultimately, no one is responsible for the project. There is a lot of vertical communication, and the lines of communication are lengthy. Moreover, everything goes through the existing communication channels, putting a heavy burden on those channels. Furthermore, there is a risk of suboptimisation per department. The project will also likely become/remain subordinate to other (departmental) priorities. Finally, there is often limited horizontal collaboration between departments/teams, which results in limited engagement and a poor customer-orientated result. The project manager has only a reporting function.

RESPONSIBILITIES

The project manager should establish interfaces with the permanent organisations on strategic, tactical and operational levels, and ensure that the project is carried out accordingly. The strategic level determines the governance for the project, the tactical level the need and purpose but also the business justification, and the operational level of the requirements and the output to be delivered. The project sponsor is accountable to the sponsoring organisation or customer for this.

ADVANCED

SYSTEMS APPROACH (ADVANCED)

A systems approach is an effective means of analysing organisations and designing the interfaces between a project and the permanent organisation. It can also be applied to design the interfaces of the project outputs with the systems they are meant to operate with. Finally, a systems approach can be used to design the internal processes in the project itself.

A system is a set of interrelated or interacting elements. Systems are always part of larger systems and contain subsystems themselves. Each system strives for equilibrium with its environment (homeostasis). A systems approach is a method of studying phenomena as a whole with interdependencies and interactions with the environment.

Systems theory is the interdisciplinary study of natural and man-made systems. This theory aims to understand the complexity and interdependencies between and within systems. In systems theory, discussing whether something is a system, subsystem, or element is of secondary significance. What is important is the awareness that everything is interconnected with everything else.

System description

Systems can be subdivided into subsystems and elements up to the level that sufficient insight is obtained to answer the questions asked. The rest can remain in a black box. Systems can be described by defining their boundaries, interfaces, and interconnections with other systems and the environment.

A black box is an element of which its interaction with other systems or elements is known, but not how it functions itself. A system boundary is an element that marks the limit of a system. An interface is an intermediary where two systems interact. The interconnection is what interacts between two systems (see Figure 10.01.08). Integration is the merging of two or more systems into a larger system.

It is nice to know that a status report is submitted to the portfolio board (interface) every month. Not less important is which information these reports should contain (interconnections). You can't define the one if you don't know what comprises the other.

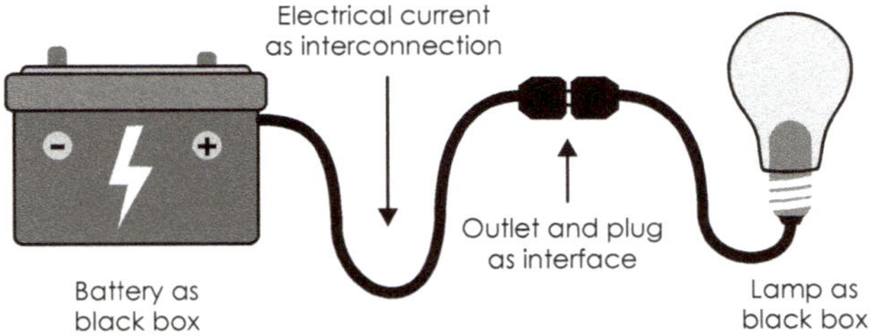

Figure 10.01.08 Example of black boxes, interfaces and interconnections

System control

In systems, we distinguish feedforward and feedback control. Feedforward control takes place at the input. Feedback control takes place at the output (see Figure 10.01.09).

When approaching a slope with a car, you accelerate in advance to ensure that you maintain the car's speed (feedforward). With cruise control, the system registers that the car's speed is decreasing and then accelerates (feedback). When tolerances are in danger of being exceeded, we should escalate this to the next level of management (feedforward). We should not wait until tolerances are exceeded (feedback).

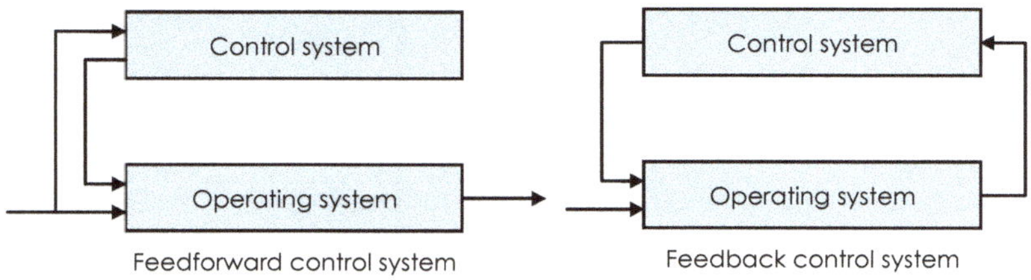

Figure 10.01.09 Feedforward and feedback control

A project as a system

The output of the project can be described as a system. This system should function properly within the business systems. However, a project also consists of interconnected and interacting elements and can therefore also be seen as a system. This can refer to different aspects of a project. For example, a project can be viewed as a social, a production, or an information system. In the latter approach, we can systematically check whether all relationships and communication lines between the various entities within a project, as well as between the project and the environmental entities, are adequately fulfilled, but also whether feedback is arranged.

Managing interfaces

The interfaces between different (sub)systems are a source of disruption and errors in the mutual collaboration between (sub)systems. For example, managing interfaces comes into play when various teams have to work simultaneously in the same location. When is one team ready so that the next team can start? The project manager is responsible for managing those interfaces. But if you are wise, you put the operational responsibility for managing those interfaces on the parties responsible for realising the (sub-)systems involved. An intermediate solution is to make one of the teams/ contractors responsible for coordinating the interfaces.

Managing integration

Integration is the process of merging different systems into one. Integration comes into play the moment designs and deliverables are realised based on the various component and product specifications (see Verification and validation, Chapter 5.03 Quality). Integration is an integral part of a project and, therefore, an important focus area for the project manager. The project manager should ensure that the individual work packages are integrated, resulting in the delivery of the desired end result. The project manager should also ensure that the integrated parts are tested as one working system, in addition to testing the individual subsystems, and that they are tested in conjunction with the existing business systems.

ORGANISATIONAL CONFIGURATIONS FRAMEWORK (ADVANCED)

When you want to align the project with the permanent organisation, it is important to realise that these can vary widely. According to Mintzberg (2009), organisations can be distinguished based on the core elements of the organisation, the primary coordination mechanism and the type of decentralisation, resulting in six configurations.

Core elements

Mintzberg (1992) distinguishes six organisational core elements, five visible and one invisible (ideology). Those core elements are (see Figure 10.01.10):

- *Strategic apex* – Top management and supporting staff, directing the entire organisation;
- *Middle line* – The middle management between the operating core and the strategic top;
- *Operating core* – The people who carry out the primary activities;
- *Technostructure* – The analysts, outside the middle line, who formally plan and direct the work;
- *Support staff* – The people outside the operating core that support it;
- *Ideology* – The halo of beliefs and traditions, norms, values and culture.

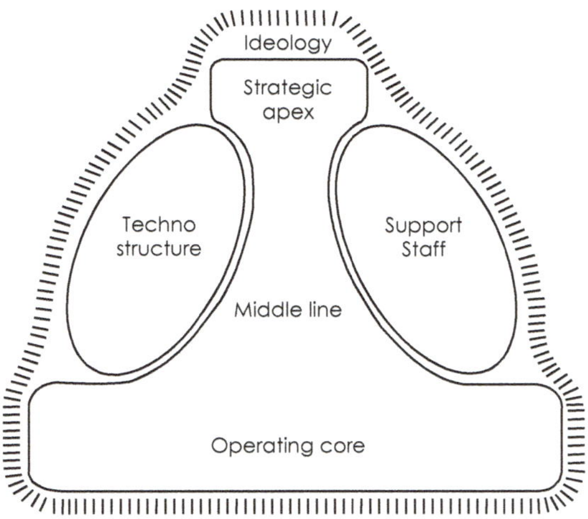

Figure 10.01.10 Core elements, according to Mintzberg (1992)

Coordinating mechanism

Organisations can coordinate their work in several fundamental ways:

- Direct supervision – Through orders and control from the immediate supervisor;
- Standardisation of outputs – Through the specification of products and services;
- Standardisation of skills – Through education and training;
- Standardisation of work – Through procedures and work instructions;
- Standardisation of norms – Through the perception of common beliefs;
- Mutual adjustment – Through coordination at the workplace.

As work becomes more complex, coordination shifts from mutual adjustment through direct supervision to standardisation, and eventually back to mutual adjustment.

Decentralisation

Organisations can decentralise their authority in three fundamental ways:

- *Vertical decentralisation* – The extent to which power is delegated downwards;
- *Horizontal decentralisation* – The extent to which power is delegated to staff;
- *Selective decentralisation* – The extent to which power is delegated to different units.

Configurations

Based on the above, Mintzberg first defined five configurations. Later, he added missionary and political organisations (see Table 10.01.01).

Configuration	Core elements	Coordinating mechanism	Decentralisation	Forces
Entrepreneurial organisation	Strategic apex	Direct supervision	Vertical and horizontal centralisation	Centralise
Diversional organisation	Middle line	Standardisation of output	Limited vertical decentralisation	Balkanise
Professional bureaucracy	Operating core	Standardisation of skills	Vertical and horizontal decentralisation	Professionalise
Machine bureaucracy	Technostructure	Standardisation of work	Limited horizontal decentralisation	Rationalise
Adhocracy	Support staff	Mutual adjustment	Selective decentralistation	Collaborate
Missionary	Ideology	Standardisation of norms	Pure decentralistation	Visionary
Political	None	None	Vary	None

Table 10.01.01 Configurations, according to Mintzberg

Entrepreneurial organisation – The strategic apex is the core element. It uses direct supervision as the main coordinating mechanism and applies vertical and horizontal centralisation. The emphasis is on entrepreneurship to seize opportunities. This type of configuration is generally located in start-ups and dot-com companies. The strategic apex exerts a centralising pull, enabling them to control decision-making.

Diversional organisation – The middle line is the core element. It uses standardisation of output as the main coordination mechanism and applies limited vertical decentralisation down to a divisional level. The technostructure is at corporate level to provide services to all departments with support staff at each department. Business activities are typically categorised into products or services, customer groups or geographical locations. This type of configuration is generally located at large enterprises. The middle line exerts a balkanising pull to concentrate power toward its own unit.

Professional bureaucracy – The operating core is the core element. It uses the standardisation of skills as the main coordinating mechanism and applies vertical and horizontal decentralisation. The support staff is typically vast and provides clerical and maintenance support for the operational core. This type of configuration is generally located at universities and hospitals. The operational core exerts a professionalising pull to minimise the influence of others on their work.

Machine bureaucracy – The technostructure is the core element. It uses the standardisation of work as the main coordinating mechanism and applies limited horizontal decentralisation. The environment for a machine bureaucracy is stable, and it seeks internal efficiency. This type of configuration is generally located at manufacturers and large government bodies. The technostructure exerts a rationalising pull to control the operating core.

Adhocracy – The support staff is the core element. It uses the mutual adjustment as the main coordinating mechanism and applies selective patterns of decentralisation. Business activities are often non-routine and use advanced technology. They seek innovation to adapt to changing conditions. This type of configuration is generally located at research and development firms. The support staff exerts a collaborative pull to get involved in the organisation's core activities.

Missionary – The ideology is the core element. It uses the standardisation of norms as the main coordinating mechanism and applies pure decentralisation. All organisation members more or less equally share the power. This type of configuration is generally located at special interest groups. Ideology exerts a normative pull on the people in the organisation.

Political – Here, members are torn apart by their conflicting forces. If no outward force prevails, the organisation acquires a political configuration without a stable form of centralisation or decentralisation.

When the balance between the different pulling forces shifts, it creates a lot of friction. Mintzberg's model helps us to explain much of what we encounter in organisations.

TOTAL QUALITY MANAGEMENT (ADVANCED)

Total Quality Management (TQM) comprises several frameworks focused on continuously improving product and process integrity. The philosophy behind TQM is that quality is the responsibility of all parties involved. TQM not only significantly affects the permanent organisation but also strongly determines the alignment between the project and the permanent organisation and how the work will be delivered and managed within the project itself.

Most TQM includes seven principles:

1. *Customer focus* –Meet customer requirements and strive to exceed their expectations;
2. *Leadership* – Create conditions in which people strive to achieve quality objectives;
3. *Engagement of people* – Empower competent people to increase their capacity to deliver value;
4. *Process approach* – Apply process thinking and acting to achieve quality objectives;
5. *Continuous improvement* – Focus on continuously improving product and process quality;
6. *Evidence-based decision-making* – Make use of data to support the decision-making process;
7. *Relationship management* – Develop strong relationships with suppliers and partners.

TQM requires accurate performance measurements and makes use of quality cycles like Deming's (see Chapter 5.04 Quality). Ensure all parties involved are trained and committed to its success. To deliver total quality management, various quality management frameworks can be applied, such as Lean Six Sigma (see Advanced in Chapter 9.05, Development Frameworks).

THEORY OF CONSTRAINT (ADVANCED)

Theory Of Constraints (TOC), developed in 1985 by E.M. Goldratt, is a method used to identify and resolve the most limiting factor (the constraint) in production. A constraint (bottleneck) is anything that prevents the organisation from achieving its goal.

Five Focusing Steps – A cyclic process for identifying and eliminating constraints:

- *Identify* – Identify the current constraint, e.g., a large inventory often builds up just before a constraint.
- *Exploit* – Maximise throughput using available resources (quick wins).
- *Subordinate* – Focus on the remaining process flow. Ensure it never obstructs the constraint.
- *Elevate* – If needed, implement more substantive changes to 'break' the constraint
- *Repeat* – Once the constraint is broken, move to the next one.

Thinking Processes – Focus on answering the questions: what needs to be changed?; what should be the result?; and what is needed to achieve it?

Besides equipment, constraints can be policies, paradigms and the market itself. Policies are the required or recommended way of working. Paradigms are deeply engrained beliefs or habits. They are often the underlying foundation of the policies. The market becomes the constraint when the production capacity exceeds sales. The current way of working is by far the most common constraint.

Implementing new organisational policies requires careful planning, effective communication, and thoughtful enactment. Involve key stakeholders, subject matter experts and relevant departments. Further, obtain management support, assign responsibilities, communicate to all involved, address resistance and concerns, generate quick wins, provide training, apply a pilot or proof of concept, monitor and evaluate, and finally reinforce and recognise. However, it all starts by creating a sense of urgency by establishing the constraint that prevents the organisation from achieving its goal (see Chapter 6.05 Change and Transformation).

10.02 PERSONNEL MANAGEMENT

PURPOSE

The purpose of this chapter is to enable the individual to align the project with human resource processes and functions.

LEARNING OBJECTIVES

- Characteristics of personnel policy and personnel management;
- Knowledge management (advanced);
- Competence management in projects (advanced);
- Single-loop, double-loop, and triple-loop learning (advanced).

DEFINITIONS

Personnel policy: The guidelines that govern the relationships with employees to attain organisational objectives.
Personnel management: That aspect of management aimed at implementing the personnel policy within the organisation.
Competence management: That aspect of management aimed at identifying and developing the necessary employees competences to attain organisational objectives.
Knowledge management: That aspect of management aimed at identifying, organising, storing and sharing knowledge and information within the organisation to attain organisational objectives.

INTRODUCTION

Many employees work on projects almost continuously. Project-based working and managing projects are often essential competences for an organisation. Also, a large part of employee development often occurs in a project environment. Therefore, personnel management cannot be a responsibility of the permanent organisation alone. Project managers often have a derived responsibility with regard to the personnel management of their team members.

In addition, the human resources function provides multifaceted support to the project regarding staff deployment, temporary employment, training, salaries, incentives, stress reduction, welfare, and ethics. A well-developed relationship with personnel management can significantly increase the utilisation and quality of available staff.

POSITIONING

Personnel management plays an important role throughout the project lifecycle. You should ensure compliance with the permanent organisation's personnel policy, both in the selection and deployment of the team members. Pay special attention to their working conditions and competence development, regularly discuss their performance with them, and support their managers in their performance and appraisal interviews. At completion, it is necessary to conduct a final performance review and provide feedback on their development to their manager. Finally, support them when returning to their department or to a new workplace.

PERSONNEL POLICY AND PERSONNEL MANAGEMENT

Personnel policy includes the guidelines that govern the relationships with employees to achieve the organisational goals and objectives. Personnel policy expresses top management's view on their staff and includes specific objectives and guidelines regarding staffing, training, salaries, motivation, et cetera. Personnel policy has a direct link to organisational change and development.

Personnel management is that aspect of management aimed at the implementation of the personnel policy within the organisation. Aspects of personnel management are:

- Job description and job assessment;
- Personnel planning and administration;
- Selection and recruitment;
- Compensation policy and employment conditions;
- Working conditions and absenteeism policy;
- Career development, education and training;
- Performance and appraisal interviews;
- Termination and outplacement of personnel.

The *Human Resource* (HR) manager develops the personnel policy and advises management accordingly. Top management is accountable for personnel management. The line managers are responsible for the personnel management in their department. The HR manager should ensure this is done according to the current policy and support them with its implementation.

PERSONNEL MANAGEMENT IN PROJECTS

In a matrix organisation structure, the project manager has a derived responsibility for personnel management within the project. You should follow the company's personnel policy and support the absenteeism policy. Support your team member's career development. Inform their managers about their performance and support them in their performance appraisals. Even though salary, promotion, and incentives are the responsibility of their line manager, you have an advisory and supporting role in this.

People often acquire the most knowledge while working. Ensure junior team members get instructions on doing the work and understand the underlying principles. Pair a junior with a senior team member. Encourage knowledge sharing. Introduce peer reviews.

Although interconnected, personnel management should not be confused with resource management. In resource management, you should ensure the necessary resources are available and properly allocated to the project. In personnel management, you need to make sure that the company's personnel policy is followed within the project.

RESPONSIBILITIES

The organisation's top management is accountable for the personnel policy. The line manager, supported by the personnel manager, is responsible for implementing this policy. The project manager has a derived responsibility for personnel management within their project. In doing so, the project manager needs to coordinate with the line and HR management. The HR manager can support the project manager with their personnel management responsibilities.

ADVANCED

KNOWLEDGE MANAGEMENT (ADVANCED)

Knowledge management is that aspect of management aimed at identifying, organising, storing and sharing knowledge and information within the organisation to attain organisational objectives. This can cover all types of information but is mainly linked to knowledge about primary processes, such as logistics and production figures, prices of materials and services, costs of hiring staff, and market and customer information. Nowadays, such knowledge is often stored in databases with extensive search functions.

Such databases are also progressively developed for projects. These may include checklists of risks, applicable norms and standards, RASCIs, and information flow diagrams that have been proven effective in previous projects.

Usually, the departments directly involved are entrusted with managing and developing such databases, as they have the most to gain from it. This is strongly preferable to individuals keeping their own private files unless knowledge is only relevant at the individual level.

These databases are also beneficial for collecting time estimates. In doing so, it is essential that the estimates also include the conditions under which the work was carried out and that they are corrected for the losses incurred to avoid those losses being built into the standards by default (see Chapter 5.05 Resources).

COMPETENCE MANAGEMENT (ADVANCED)

Competence management is that aspect of management aimed at identifying and developing the necessary employees' competences to attain organisational objectives. It provides a basis for companies to achieve and maintain a competitive advantage.

Determine the core competences that are important to the organisation. Develop competence profiles for the various job descriptions and link them to the result areas and performance indicators. In doing so, use or develop a competence framework. Finally, develop a competence development strategy. Education, training, and coaching, but also recruitment and guiding towards other work are instruments to give substance to such a strategy.

Projects and project managers can contribute to competence management for projects by helping to develop competence profiles and performance indicators for the various result areas within projects, as well as by providing team members opportunities for training and coaching.

SINGLE-, DOUBLE-, AND TRIPLE-LOOP LEARNING (ADVANCED)

When behavioural change is needed, we distinguish single-, double-, and triple-loop learning (Argyris, 1999). In projects, we should pay attention to all three levels of learning (see Figure 10.02.01).

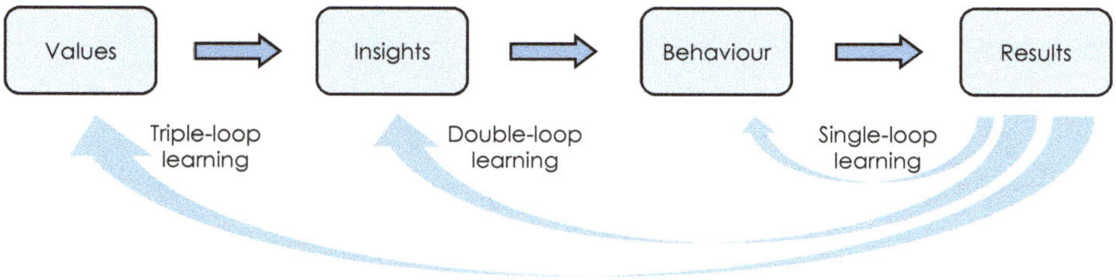

Figure 10.02.01 Single-, double-, and triple-loop learning (Argyris, 1999)

Single-loop learning – Learning how to improve things to get a better result. It focuses on doing things right. Causality might be observed but is usually not addressed. Single-loop learning is acquiring knowledge by trial and error.

Double-loop learning – Identifying and understanding the cause of the problems and the underlying assumptions. It is about adjusting the approach to get a better result; e.g., what is happening, and why is it happening? Double-loop learning is about doing the right things.

Triple-loop learning – Examining our values and beliefs to ensure we do what matters. It is about understanding how we make decisions that shape our work and developing new behaviours that align with our values and motivations.

Competence development can be much more effective by distinguishing what kind of learning is involved.

10.03 FINANCIAL ADMINISTRATION

PURPOSE

The purpose of this chapter is to enable the individual to align the project with finance and control processes and functions.

LEARNING OBJECTIVES

- Fixed and variable costs and direct and indirect costs;
- Principles of financial administration (advanced);
- Accounting (advanced);
- Annual accounts (advanced);
- Investments and depreciations (advanced);
- OPEX and CAPEX (advanced);
- Financial models for funding (advanced);
- Cash flow calculation for investment analysis (advanced);
- Valuation of projects in financial accounting (advanced);
- Allocation of indirect costs (advanced).

DEFINITIONS

Variable costs: Costs that change due to a change in production.
Fixed costs: Costs that do not change due to a change in production as long as productivity remains within certain limits.
Direct costs: Costs that are allocated directly to an object.
Indirect costs: Costs that are not allocated directly to an object.

INTRODUCTION

The financial situation of the sponsoring organisation determines the requirements and preconditions within which projects should be carried out. The finance and control function of the sponsoring organisation often sets mandatory rules, procedures and guidelines. Conversely, projects directly affect the organisation's financial situation, both in terms of expenditure and the potential (financial) benefits that can be realised. It is, therefore, important to know the outline of financial accounting in permanent organisations and how financial decisions are made.

POSITIONING

Knowledge of financial and control processes within the sponsor organisation is important at the start of a project and at gate reviews when the business case needs to be prepared and updated. Furthermore, it is essential when cost estimates have to be prepared, financial decisions have to be made, and financial reporting has to be prepared. Therefore, knowledge of financial and control processes within the sponsoring organisation is important throughout the project lifecycle.

COST CLASSIFICATION

Costs can be classified into fixed and variable costs but can also be classified based on how costs are allocated to products or services. Based on the latter, costs can be classified into direct and indirect costs (see Figure 10.03.01).

Cost classification	Direct costs	Indirect costs
Fixed costs	Purchase drilling machine	Office and general expenses
Variable costs	Manhours	Use meeting rooms

Figure 10.03.01 Examples of costs categories

Fixed and variable costs

Variable costs change due to a change in production. Fixed costs don't as long as production remains within certain limits. The extent to which variable costs respond to a change in operating pressure can vary from one cost item to another.

Variable costs can be divided into:

- *Linear (proportional) variable costs* – Costs increase or decrease proportionally to the change in production;
- *Progressive variable costs* – Costs increase more than proportionally to the increase in production;
- *Degressive variable costs* – Costs increase less than proportionally to the increase in production.

Most variable costs are linear at average production capacity. Progressive variable costs often occur when the organisation approaches its maximum capacity. The additional costs are then caused by overtime, extra wear and tear on equipment or expensive hiring. Variable costs can decrease as production increased during low workloads. Lower unit costs can then be realised by purchasing larger quantities. Unit costs can also fall when staff become more routine in their work. An example of fixed costs would be the rental costs of the business premises.

Direct and indirect costs

Direct costs are costs that are allocated directly to an object. Indirect costs are costs that are not allocated directly to an object. This differs per organisation and situation.

Indirect costs are usually allocated to the project through a surcharge on direct costs. Sometimes indirect costs are allocated to the project via a surcharge on the project's total cost estimate or a combination of both. The calculation of the indirect costs is always based on a predetermined production. If, in reality, more or less is produced in a financial year than budgeted, then there is over-or under-absorption.

Preparing cost estimate

When preparing a cost estimate, it is important to distinguish between variable and fixed costs and direct and indirect costs. Indirect costs should be allocated to the project via a specific surcharge percentage. The project manager should ensure that indirect costs are not forgotten or charged twice, direct and indirect. It will not be the first time that travel and telephone expenses are charged directly to the project, even though these costs were already included as a surcharge to the hourly rates.

RESPONSIBILITIES

The project manager needs to have basic financial knowledge to be a discussion partner for line managers in general and controllers in particular. They should be able to place their project in the context of the organisation's financial status.

ADVANCED

PRINCIPLES OF FINANCIAL ACCOUNTING (ADVANCED)

Financial accounting records all economic facts within the permanent organisation. It calculates allocations and cost values for different tasks while overseeing spending. Financial accounting is based on a several principles. First, all calculations are made in money and valued at cost. Other principles are:

- *Allocation principle* – Consequences of transactions and other events are processed when they occur and not when the payments are made or received.
- *Continuity principle* – The valuation of the assets and liabilities is based on ongoing concern. This principle is abandoned only when it is clear that the organisation will no longer be continued.
- *Matching principle* – Expenses are allocated to the period in which the revenues for which they are incurred are realised.
- *Realisation principle* – Revenues and profits are not recognised until the related goods or services have been delivered or performed.
- *Precautionary principle* – Losses and risks should be included as soon as they are known.
- *Consistency principle* – The accounting policies should allow for inter-comparability across years and between organisations.

ACCOUNTING (ADVANCED)

Bookkeeping is the heart of financial accounting. All financial transactions are recorded in the bookkeeping. Accounting is based on double-entry bookkeeping. Each transaction is booked to one or more accounts on the credit side and of equal value on the debit side. Usually, accounting uses daybooks, journals, and ledgers (see Figure 10.03.02).

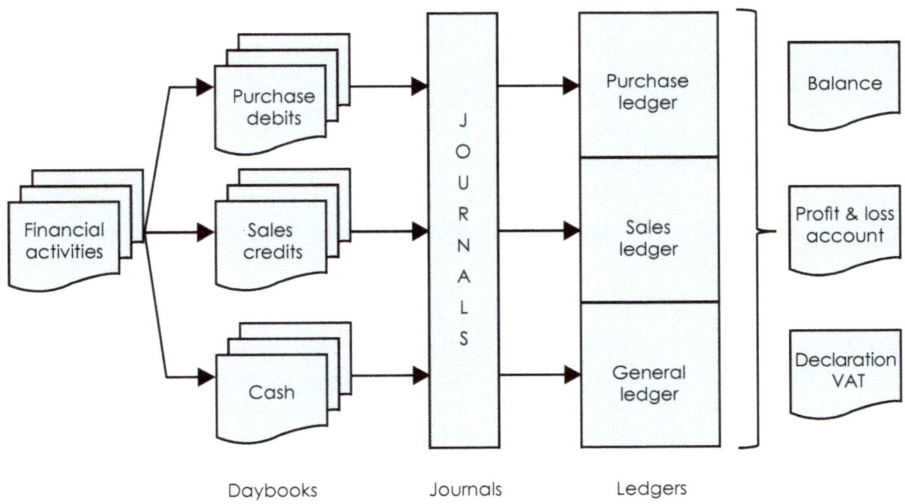

Figure 10.03.02 Structure bookkeeping

In a daybook, the original entries are recorded by date as they occur. The information in the daybooks is then transferred into one or more journals. They are also in chronological order, but they record credits and debits in balanced pairs. Each and every credit journal entry is matched by a debit journal entry. For example, a client's payment of € 1,500 of a sales invoice is booked on: debit Bank + € 1,500, and credit debtors – € 1,500 (see Figure 10.03.03).

Finally, all journal records are then booked into the correct ledger accounts. In contrast to journals, ledgers also show the balance of accounts before and after each transaction. Therefore, ledgers can be used to generate balance sheets and income statements. The main types are purchasing, sales, and general ledger.

Date	No.	Post	Debit	Credit
Received € 1,500 by bank from a debtor				
01-01	1	Bank	€ 1,500	
		To Debtors		€ 1,500
Goods purchased on account of € 10,000 net with 21% sales tax				
01-02	2	Stock	€ 10,000	
		VAT to be deducted	€ 2,100	
		To Creditors		€ 12,100
Goods sold on account of € 5,000 net with 21% sales tax. Purchase value € 4,000, realised gross sales result € 1,000.				
01-05	3	Debtors	€ 6,050	
		To revenue Sales		€ 5,000
		To Payable VAT		€ 1,050
		Cost of Sales	€ 4,000	
		To Stock		€ 4,000

Figure 10.03.03 Example journal entries

ANNUAL ACCOUNTS (ADVANCED)

For investment calculations, some knowledge about annual accounting is also desirable. An organisation is free to choose how its internal financial reporting is prepared. However, for external reporting, an organisation is bound by legal regulations. One of the most important documents for external reporting is the annual accounts. Annual accounts consist of a balance sheet, a profit and loss account, a cash flow statement, an explanation of these items, and a statement of the accounting policies used.

Balance sheet

A balance sheet is a statement of the assets and liabilities of an organisation at a specific moment in time. A balance sheet is prepared at the end of the financial year, usually on the 31st of December. A balance sheet usually contains the following items (see Figure 10.03.04):

Balance per 31-12						
Assets				**Liabilities**		
	2021	2020			2021	2020
Tangible fixed assets	€ 4,090	€ 3,600		Shareholder equity	€ 1,500	€ 1,500
Intangible fixed assets	€ 1,000	€ 1,000		Retained earnings	€ 1,850	€ 1,050
Financial fixed assets	€ 1,000	€ 1,000		Added retained earnings	€ 340	€ 800
Fixed assets	**€ 6,090**	**€ 5,600**		**Total equity**	**€ 3,690**	**€ 3,350**
				Provisions	€ 1,000	€ 1,000
Stock	€ 600	€ 550		Long-term liabilities	€ 2,000	€ 2,000
Receivables	€ 350	€ 400		Bank credit	€ 500	€ 250
Cash & cash equivalents	€ 400	€ 350		Current liabilities	€ 250	€ 300
Current assets	**€ 1,350**	**€ 1,300**		**Total liabilities**	**€ 3,750**	**€ 3,550**
Total assets	**€ 7,440**	**€ 6,900**		**total equity & liabilities**	**€ 7,440**	**€ 6,900**

Figure 10.03.04 Example balance sheet

- *Tangible fixed assets* – The tangible durable production assets such as property, plant and equipment owned by the company.
- *Intangible fixed assets* – The company's ownership of concessions, licences, intellectual rights, and payments for goodwill.
- *Financial fixed assets* – Participation in, for example, a subsidiary and securities held by the company.
- *Fixed assets* – Long-lived assets with more than one year of useful life. Fixed assets include tangible and intangible financial fixed assets.
- *Stock* – Include raw materials, components, semi-finished products and unsold products. Non-durable inventories, such as office supplies, are not valued. Stock is valued at cost.
- *Receivables* – Total debtors less the provision for uncollectible debtors. Debtors are the invoices that customers have yet to pay to the company. All receivables are valued net of VAT.
- *Cash and cash equivalents* – Includes coins, bank balances, and checks received but not yet deposited. Cash equivalents are any short-term securities with 90 days or fewer maturity periods.
- *Current assets* – Cash and assets usually converted to cash within the year. Current assets include inventories, receivables, cash and cash equivalents.
- *Total assets* – The total of fixed and current assets of the company.
- *Shareholders equity* – The nominal value of subscribed capital deposited by the shareholders. Changes in the value of shares of listed companies do not affect this.
- *Retained earnings* – The total profit not paid to the shareholders.
- *Added retained earnings* – The unpaid profit to the shareholders in this book year.
- *Total equity* – The total shareholder equity and retained earnings.
- *Provisions* – Reservation for future obligations. Provisions may only be recognized for concretely foreseen risks and liabilities such as major reorganisation, damage claims, and pensions.

- *Long-term liabilities* – Debts due over one year, such as mortgage loans.
- *Bank credit* – Temporary credit that is due within one year.
- *Current liabilities* – Other debts due within one year, such as accounts payable, taxes and premiums.
- *Total liabilities* – The total of the provisions, bank credit, and long-term and current liabilities.
- *Total equity and liabilities* – Always equals total assets.

Profit and loss account

The profit and loss (P&L) account is an overview of all costs and revenues of a company between two balance sheet moments. It almost always includes a period of one year (the financial year). A profit and loss account usually contains the following items (see Figure 10.03.05):

Profit & Loss account	2021
Net sales	**€ 3,800**
• Cost of sales	€ -1,000
Gross sales result	**€ 2,800**
• Operating costs	€ -1,583
EBITDA	**€ 1,217**
• Depreciation	€ -550
EBIT	**€ 667**
• Financial income and expenses	€ -100
Earnings before taxes	**€ 567**
• Tax 20%	€ -113
Result after taxes	**€ 454**
• Dividend	€ -114
Retained earnings	**€ 340**

Figure 10.03.05 Example profit and loss account

- *Net sales* – Invoiced turnover excl. VAT;
- *Cost of sales* – Costs directly attributable to sales, such as materials and outsourced work;
- *Gross sales result (gross margin, gross profit)* – Net sales minus the cost of sales;
- *Operational costs* – Costs of general business operations, such as rental costs;
- *Operational result (EBITDA)* – Gross sales result minus operational costs;
- *Depreciation* – Accounting decrease in value of tangible fixed assets;
- *Operational income (EBIT)* – The total operating income and expenses;
- *Financial income and expenses* – Net interest and expenditures of financing;
- *Earnings (net profit) before taxes* – Operating result minus financial income and expenses;
- *Corporation tax* – Tax payable over the net profit of the company;
- *Result (net profit) after tax* – Result before tax minus corporation tax;
- *Dividend* – The amount paid to the shareholders;
- *Retained earnings* – Earnings added to the reserves.

IFRS

The *International Financial Reporting Standards* (IFRS) are accounting standards for annual reports. All companies listed in Europe and many other countries should follow these guidelines. Under the IFRS, assets, receivables and liabilities should be valued at the fair value at which they can be traded or settled at that time between knowledgeable and willing parties.

This means that the value of the assets has to be revalued annually, with the possibility that these values will change significantly as a result of changes in the market. This should also be considered when calculating the business case in projects.

EBIT and EBITDA

An increasing number of international companies are working with the terms EBITDA and EBIT. These terms are prescribed in the USA accounting standards for annual reports.

EBITDA is the acronym for *Earnings Before Interest, Tax, Depreciation and Amortisation*. EBITDA is equal to the operational result. Depreciation is the decrease in the value of tangible fixed assets. Amortisation is the decrease in the value of intangible fixed assets. A distinction is made because depreciation should be taken into account when determining the corporate income tax, and amortisation not.

EBIT is the acronym for *Earnings Before Interest and Tax*. EBIT is equal to the operational income. EBIT defines the profitability of a company without considering the financial and tax-legal situation of the company.

OPEX and CAPEX

Expenditure can be divided into operational and capital costs. Operational costs, also called *Operational Expenditures* (OPEX), are all recurring expenses of the company used within the year. Capital costs, also called *Capital Expenditures* (CAPEX), are all costs incurred to develop sustainable means of production for more than one year.

OPEX is charged directly to the profit and loss account for the same year. CAPEX should be depreciated over the economic life of the relevant means of production and is therefore not charged directly to the current profit and loss account. Thus, by investing during the year, the cash flow position deteriorates, but the profit and loss account does not.

Costs needed to investigate the feasibility of investment and later implement the output are usually considered OPEX. Despite this being OPEX, these costs should also be included in the business case calculation.

Investments and depreciation

An investment in the context of financial accounting is the (financial) effort to acquire a fixed asset. Depreciation is the reduction in value during the economic life of a fixed asset. The annual depreciation in the P&L account of a fixed asset is the initial investment minus the expected residual value at the end of that asset's economic life, divided by the expected economic life of that asset.

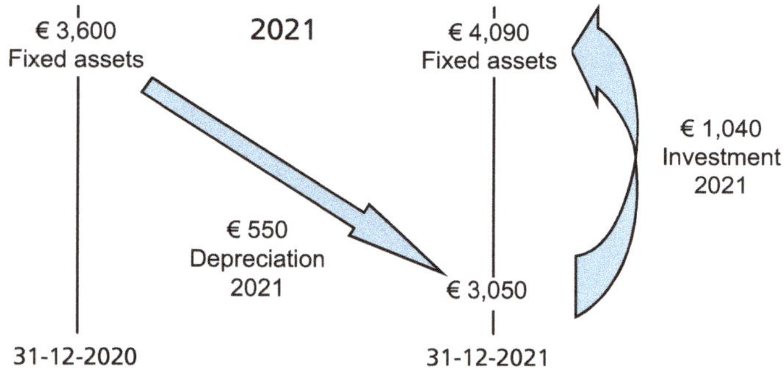

Figure 10.03.06 Relation value fixed assets and depreciation

The value of all investments is included in the balance sheet. Depreciation in a financial year is charged to the P&L account. But both values are, of course, connected. Based on the value of the fixed assets at the start of the financial year and the investments and depreciation in that year, the value of the fixed assets at the end of the financial year can be determined (see Figure 10.03.06).

Financial ratios

When assessing the financial health of an organisation, different ratios are used. The most common ratios are the debt-to-equity ratio and debt-to-asset ratio.

Debt-to-equity ratio – This ratio shows how much labilities a company has relative to its equity. It is calculated by dividing the company's total liabilities by its total equity. The debt-to-equity ratio is used to assess a company's solvency. This is the company's ability to meet its long-term financial obligations. In the example in Figure 10.03.04, the ratio in 2021 is 3750/3690 = 1.02.

Debt-to-asset ratio – This ratio measures how much debt a company has relative to its assets. It is calculated by dividing a company's total liabilities by its total assets. The debt-to-asset ratio is used to assess a company's liquidity. This is the company's ability to meet its short-term financial obligations. In the example in Figure 10.03.04, the ratio in 2021 is 3750/7440 = 0.50.

There are no universally good or bad values for these ratios. These vary by sector. It is essential to compare the company's ratios to its industry peers.

CALCULATION OF NET CASH FLOW (ADVANCED)

For investment analyses, expected net cash flows over the years due to that investment are applied. The net cash flow in a book year can best be derived from the earnings before taxes:

- Plus depreciation – This is included in the P&L account but is not a cash flow.
- Minus investments – These are actual expenses not included in the P&L account.
- Minus increase in the stock and current receivables and liabilities.

An increase in the stock and current receivables and liabilities is capital that cannot be directly withdrawn from the company (see Figure 10.03.04):

31-12-2021: € 600 (stock) + € 350 (receivables) – € 250 (current liabilities) =	€ 700
31-12-2020: € 550 (stock) + € 400 (receivables) – € 300 (current liabilities) =	– € 650
Increase in capital not directly withdrawable from the company	+ € 50

Based on the example balance sheet and P&L account, the cash flow over 2020 is:

• Earnings before tax 2021	+ € 567
• Plus depreciation	+ € 550
• Minus investments	- € 1,04
• Minus increase in capital not directly withdrawable from the company	- € 50
• Net cash flow in 2021	+ €2

VALUATION OF PROJECTS (ADVANCED)

The implementation of projects often takes longer than one financial year. Since they represent value, the work in progress of these projects should be capitalised on the balance sheet. Within this, a distinction is made between profit-taking on delivery ('Completed Contract' method) and profit-taking in proportion to the performance made ('Percentage of Completion' method). The choice depends on whether the profit on the already completed part of the project can be reasonably estimated or not.

In the completed contract method, all costs and revenues of the project are only taken at its completion. Until then, all costs incurred are recorded as work in progress. Work in progress is work commissioned by third parties that have not yet been invoiced. Project costs are, therefore, not recognised in the balance sheet and P&L account until completion.

In the percentage of completion method, the profits and losses are already taken during the project:

- % completed to date = actual costs to date / total expected costs at completion.
- Total turnover to date = % completed to date x total sales value.
- Turnover this year = total turnover to date – total turnover up to and including last year.
- Earnings this year = turnover minus costs this year.

ALLOCATION OF INDIRECT COSTS (ADVANCED)

We distinguish direct and absorption costing methods for accounting for production-related costs. The direct costing method (variable costing or marginal costing) focuses only on direct variable costs. Production costs are considered variable costs. Periodic costs are considered fixed costs. A direct costing method is a practical tool that uses cost accounting to make short-term production and sales planning decisions.

Absorption Costing (AC) or integral cost accounting includes all costs related to producing goods or services. Commonly used Absorption Costing techniques include the *Traditional Costing method*, the *Cost Centre method*, and the *Activity Based*

Costing method, which involves an increasingly finer-grained allocation of indirect costs to the different cost objects.

Traditional costing method

Under the traditional costing method, indirect costs are allocated to cost objects based on a predetermined overall overhead rate. The overall overhead rate is the estimated overhead/estimated total direct costs of all cost objects in that financial year.

Cost centre method

This method allocates indirect costs to the project via cost centres. A cost centre is a real or fictional business unit delivering a homogeneous performance.

- *Main cost centre* – A business unit where finished goods are manufactured (e.g. assembly area);
- *Independent cost centre* – A business unit where a product or service is provided to a main cost centre (e.g. drawing office);
- *Service cost centre* – A cost centre where general services are provided to other cost centres (e.g. canteen costs).

Indirect costs are allocated to the individual cost centres via allocation keys. Based on predetermined production quantities, a cost price per product or service is calculated (see Figure 10.03.07). If, in reality, more or less is produced in a financial year than budgeted, then there is over-or under-absorption.

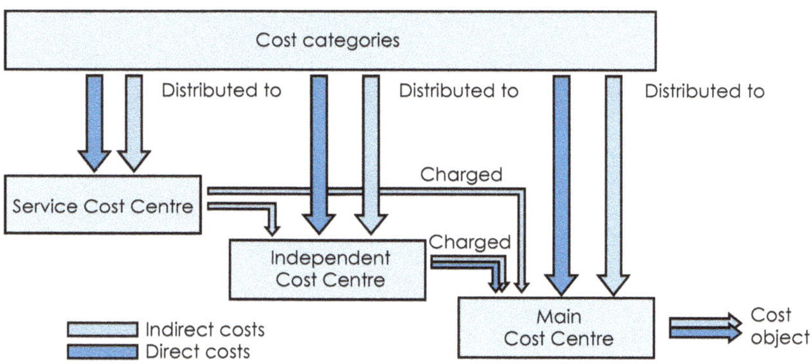

Figure 10.03.07 Cost allocation with the cost centre method

Activity Based Costing method

Activity-Based Costing (ABC) is based on activities (cost drivers). They are the fundamental tasks and processes an organisation undertakes to produce products or deliver services. Under this method, indirect costs are allocated to the individual cost drivers, with the cost driver rate then being the total allocated costs divided by the predetermined quantities of that cost driver. Based on these cost driver rates, the cost per product or service can then be calculated.

11. EXTERNAL CONTEXT

In addition to the internal environment, the project manager should also take into account the external environment in which the permanent organisation operates and, thus, also in which the project operates.

Chapter 11.01 – Health, Safety, Security, and Environment (HSSE) – Deals with the laws underlying these competence areas. Environmental and health and safety laws and regulations exert a tight regime on many projects. The project manager needs to know which HSSE regulations are relevant to the project and how to act accordingly.

Chapter 11.02 – Sustainability – This chapter discusses sustainability in projects and the concept of corporate social responsibility and how it affects the implementation of the project and project deliverables.

Chapter 11.03 – Laws and Legislation – Contract law and the fulfilment of obligations under those contracts form the core of this chapter. Attention is also paid to unlawful acts and copyright, patent and trademark law, and different law theories.

Chapter 11.04 – Influence and Interests – The environment strongly influences organisations. To deal with this properly, you should dare to take responsibility for doing what needs to be done.

Chapter 11.05 – Culture and Values – In most projects, you have to deal with cultural differences. Careful alignment with cultural values creates alignment at the level of 'this is how we do it here'.

Together, these chapters form the key contextual competences for the project manager from the external environment.

11.01 HEALTH, SAFETY, SECURITY AND ENVIRONMENT

PURPOSE

The purpose of this chapter is to enable the individual to identify and ensure that the project complies with all relevant health, safety, security, and environmental issues in a project.

LEARNING OBJECTIVES

- The basics of the health and safety legislation;
- The components of the health and safety plan for a project;
- The consequences resulting from the duty of care;
- The legal responsibility of the project manager;
- Security precautions for a project;
- The General Data Protection Regulation;
- The application of environmental legislation.

DEFINITIONS

Health: The state of well-being from a mental, physical and social point of view.
Security: Protection of a person or object against violence, threat, danger or damage.
Safety: A condition in which one is protected from danger, hazards or injury.
Environment: Conditions in which individuals, animals, and plants live or work.
Duty of care: A moral or legal obligation to care for the safety or well-being of others.

INTRODUCTION

Society is becoming increasingly aware of the importance of *Health, Safety, Security, and Environment* (HSSE). The consequences of violating HSSE regulations are becoming increasingly serious. The project manager should know which HSSE regulations are relevant to the project. This is no easy feat. Moreover, the regulations and their potential impact relate not only to the implementation of the project itself but also to the project deliverables. Although regulations vary per country, some general rules should be considered.

Most organisations have converted these standards and regulations into an internal code applicable across the organisation, including the project, programme and portfolio domain.

POSITIONING

Even before a project starts, you should look for relevant standards and regulations that may directly or indirectly affect the project. A clear assessment of the HSSE aspects should be carried out in the project definition stage, both with respect to the project and the project output throughout the product lifecycle. Since much only becomes clear during the course of the project, the potential HSSE impact on the project and the project output and of the project and project output on HSSE should be continuously monitored and reassessed, at least at each stage transition.

HEALTH AND SAFETY LEGISLATION

Health and safety are mostly linked to construction projects. However, this can also be an issue within an office environment. Back problems, RSI, and stress are common reasons people get sick. They may be bullied, working conditions may be unhealthy, and people may feel unsafe.

Risk assessment

The first step should always be to perform a risk assessment of the planned activities concerning health and safety. Familiarise yourself with the applicable legislation and the company policies, engage subject matter experts, involve your team, the project sponsor, and other stakeholders, and inquire about the lessons learned from the past.

Health and safety plan

Next, prepare a health and safety (H&S) plan. For construction sites, this may be mandatory. Implementing a well-thought-out H&S plan is essential to keep workers and the community safe while a construction project is in progress. An H&S plan should include a risk assessment. An H&S plan should document the following:

- H&S policy statement – Formal organisational statement about health and safety;
- List of responsible personnel – Who is responsible at which project stage?
- How and when people will be trained – This may be mandatory and should be repeated;
- How often are inspections carried out – Are rules followed, and is the plan properly implemented?;
- Mandatory certifications –Which and for whom;
- Personal protective equipment – Such as safety helmets and safety shoes;
- Local rules and regulations – Such as the ban on smoking in restricted areas;
- Safety procedures and measures – Such as installing guardrails and placing warning signs;
- Extreme weather measures – What to do in the event of hurricanes and the like;
- Safety and emergency contact details – Phone numbers and email addresses;
- Reporting instructions and procedures in case of safety incidents and accidents;
- Data collection and reporting – How to keep records and keep management informed;
- How often the safety plan should be updated – Periodically and linked to the start of new activities;
- How safety measures should be enforced – What to do in case of repeated violations;
- How complaints should be filed and followed up.

Other projects do not require such a comprehensive H&S plan. Usually, you can refer to the H&S plan of the permanent organisation. However, this should not be assumed automatically. Within the project, the project manager remains responsible.

For construction sites, it is recommended that there is a separate safety officer. In other situations, it may be advisable to appoint a confidential officer. In the latter case, ensuring the confidential officer's independence and protecting the whistle-blower's position is essential. Ensure that the safety or confidential officer is well-trained and has visible support from management. Understand that the most important thing about an H&S plan is its implementation and follow-up.

Duty of care

The employer is liable for damages employees suffer while performing their work unless the employer proves that it has fulfilled its duty of care. 'Duty of care' means that the employer should take any necessary measures, within reason, to protect and prevent the employee from suffering damage in the performance of the assigned work. An employee is only liable for the damage if they caused the accident intentionally or through deliberate recklessness.

> *The carpenter took the safety cap off the sawing machine. It was easier to work that way. As a result, he seriously injured his hand when he tried to cut a board to size. He now holds the employer liable for the medical costs. The court granted the claim because the carpenter could remove the safety cap, contrary to the safety instructions.*

This responsibility goes beyond the legal requirements insofar as it is reasonable and fair, and is not limited to the construction site. The duty of care applies in many industries and also applies to the responsible project manager.

> *During demolition work, a splinter penetrated the employee's safety glove despite the class 2 safety gloves, which the employer had provided him as required by law. The infected wound caused dystrophy that finally affected the entire body. The employee became severely disabled as a result.*
>
> *The court held the employer liable for the employee's injuries because it was foreseeable that splinters could fly around during demolition work, and class 3 safety gloves had not been made available, although these are only slightly more expensive and probably could have prevented the injury.*

Legal responsibility of the project manager

The project manager is the highest safety officer within the project. You are responsible for ensuring a risk assessment is carried out and an H&S plan is drawn up and implemented. If an accident occurs and you are negligent in performing your duties, you can be held personally responsible for this based on an unlawful act (tort). If the Public Prosecution Service suspects gross negligence, they may even prosecute you under criminal law.

SECURITY

Security protects a person or object against violence, threat, danger or damage. This can come from outside the organisation and from within, such as through fraud and theft. When analysing risks to cope with danger, internal causes should never be ignored.

Surveillance is often one of the measures resulting from a security risk analysis. Security is increasingly outsourced. Almost every company today is connected to a *Private Alarm Centre* (PAC).

Nowadays, data security is an increasingly important issue that virtually every project manager has to deal with. This includes preventing data theft, breach of files, disruption of the systems used, ransomware, and disclosure of information. You cannot hide behind the security measures of the permanent organisation. You have your own responsibility in this.

GENERAL DATA PROTECTION REGULATION

Many countries have data protection regulations. Since 2018, the *General Data Protection Regulation* (GDPR) has been applied across the *European Union* (EU). Globally, many companies enact this regulation as they do business with companies within the EU.

The GDPR regulates how organisations should handle personal data. Organisations should register all personal data recorded and processed, adequately protect these data, have their own data protection policy, act accordingly, and make it public.

Organisations may only process personal data on one of the legal grounds specified in the GDPR:

- Contractual necessity – To perform an agreement, e.g., to prepare an invoice;
- Consent – When the individual concerned has given consent;
- Legal obligations – To give effect to the law, such as registration in the municipal register;
- Vital interests – To protect a person's life, health or safety;
- Perform a task in the public interest or by public authority;
- Legitimate interests – To pursue a legitimate business interest, e.g., to prevent fraud.

Under the GDPR, organisations should state in advance how and why they will use personal data. This is usually done through a privacy statement. Organisations may use personal data for other purposes only if these are consistent with the original purposes and only under strict conditions.

Under the GDPR, everyone has the right to access, correct, and transfer their data, and in some situations, the right to be forgotten. Organisations should also inform them how they use their data.

Only those who need to process these data should have access to it. Hired staff should sign a privacy statement in advance. Wherever possible, personal data should be anonymised. Additional rules apply to specific categories of personal data, such as religion, race, health and criminal record. The project manager is responsible for ensuring GDPR compliance in their project.

ENVIRONMENTAL LEGISLATION

Environmental laws and regulation are the laws and regulations that protect air and water quality, wildlife, and environmental health. Environmental legislation varies substantially in different countries. Where some countries lead the way, others lag far behind. There can also be a vast difference between stated intentions and actual legislation.

Environmental laws and regulations regulate the interaction between humans and nature to reduce environmental threats and improve public health. This is not without debate. Insights on environmental issues and related legislation may change during the project's course. Therefore, the project manager should pay attention to environmental issues and legislation throughout the project.

Environmental legislation is relevant not only for infrastructure and construction projects, but also for many other projects. What chemicals are used in developing and producing the new products and in its use and eventual disposal?

It is also important to know how long certain permits are valid and when they should be reapplied. Changes to the existing situation may require notification or even a new permit. This is not always clear, but it can be decisive for initiating a project. Environmental permits may also be linked to other permits. This reduces bureaucracy but complicates the conditions under which a permit is issued.

Before implementing the project, it should be realised that no single law regulates everything. There is often a patchwork of complementary, overlapping and sometimes contradictory legislation. Permits should be applied for from different authorities, have different procedures and deadlines, and might have different participation and objection procedures. Seek proper advice on this from subject-matter experts.

RESPONSIBILITIES

The project manager is the highest safety officer within the project and is responsible for the HSSE aspects in the project and of the project deliverables. Team members should report unsafe and unhealthy work situations.

11.02 SUSTAINABILITY

PURPOSE

The purpose of this chapter is to enable the individual to ensure that the project complies with relevant sustainability principles and objectives.

LEARNING OBJECTIVES

- Sustainable development;
- The principle of People, Planet, Profit (3Ps);
- Sustainable development in projects;
- Corporate Social Responsibility (CSR);
- Triple Bottom Line (TBL);
- The 10 principles of the UN Global Compact (advanced);
- ISO standard 26000 Corporate social responsibility (advanced).

DEFINITIONS

Sustainable development: The development to meet the present needs without compromising the ability of future generations to meet their needs;
People, Planet, Profit: The principle that companies focus equally on social, environmental and economic impacts;
Triple Bottom Line (TBL): An accounting framework in which People, Planet, and Profit have equal importance;
Corporate Social Responsibility (CSR): The obligation that a company should play a positive role in the community and consider the environmental and social impact of business decisions that goes beyond what the law requires or what is socially appropriate.

INTRODUCTION

Organisations are becoming increasingly aware of the need for and benefits of sustainable business. Nowadays, sustainability is no longer an option but an essential condition for everything we do. Projects should be designed in such a way that both the implementation of the project and the project result we deliver are sustainable.

The project manager should follow (or even exceed) guidelines and rules on sustainable development from within the organisation and from the wider society and realise a workable balance between the demands of society and the impacts on the eco-environment and economy.

POSITIONING

Sustainable development is not something you do only once in the project. Sustainable development should be a guiding principle throughout the project regarding the approach and deliverables. Focus on sustainable development during the project assessment before the project starts, when preparing the project management plan in the project definition stage, and throughout the project delivery.

SUSTAINABLE DEVELOPMENT

The *UN World Commission on Development and Environment* defines sustainable development as *the development that meets the needs of the present without compromising the ability of future generations to meet their own needs*. This implies that the extraction of renewable resources should not exceed the rate of their renewal and that the absorption capacity of the environment to assimilate waste should not be exceeded, not only when producing goods and services but throughout the lifecycle and value chain of that product or service.

Sustainable development can be achieved by reducing consumption levels, recycling residual waste (circular economy), and or applying cleaner technologies. To achieve sustainability, we probably need all three.

PEOPLE, PLANET, PROFIT (3PS MODEL)

People, Planet, Profit is the principle that companies focus equally on social, environmental and economic impacts:

- *People* – The social interests and well-being of the people;
- *Planet* – The sustainability of our natural environment and resources;
- *Profit* – The raison d'être and the continuity of an organisation in the longer term.

A sustainable enterprise has committed itself to this principle. Sustainable entrepreneurship aims to discover, create, and exploit business opportunities that contribute to social and environmental benefits for others in society. Sustainable entrepreneurship does not just happen; it requires a long-term vision that should be embedded in the organisation's core processes.

Subscribing to the 3Ps principles is more than just complying with labour and environmental laws. It includes a commitment to pay as much attention to social and environmental issues as to profit. In pursuing better organisational performance, a conscious effort should also be made to improve social and environmental aspects.

SUSTAINABLE DEVELOPMENT IN PROJECTS

At a minimum, projects should be implemented per the sustainability vision of the organisations involved. This applies to the products to be delivered and how the project is carried out. The project may even have to contribute directly to the organisation's ambitions to realise its sustainability vision.

According to Schippers and Silvius (2014), sustainability criteria should be explicitly included in project design and project management to be effective. This starts with assessing the project in a broader context. Time and spatial boundaries need to be defined more broadly when sustainability is included.

Scope and deliverables – The scope should be redefined if social and environmental considerations are taken, recognising the broader context and impact of the project approach and the project deliverables. How do you ensure deliverables can be easily maintained, repaired, upgraded, decommissioned and disposed of? How can we enable materials to be easily reused upon disposal?

Stakeholder analysis and communication – Sustainability will likely lead to identifying more different stakeholders and a more proactive and open communication with them, including environmental pressure groups and human rights groups.

Risks and opportunities – From a sustainable perspective, the project's long-term social and environmental impacts over the entire product lifecycle should be taken into account. This requires a broader-than-normal risk analysis. Furthermore, a more precautionary approach should be considered, as environmental and social impacts are much more difficult to predict, and corrective measures usually require much more effort to be effective.

Project design – Consider how the project output will be developed. Think beyond how things are typically done. Consider offsite and modular construction. Ensure users and other stakeholders participate in the project. Ensure flexible delivery to accommodate changes during project implementation.

Quality – Focus more on fit for use and purpose than is standard in traditional projects. Quality expectations and acceptance criteria should be outcome rather than output orientated. Quality requirements should also reflect the product lifecycle and include economic, social and environmental aspects of the outputs and outcomes to be realised.

Business case – The business justification should include financial and non-financial social and environmental costs, risks and benefits. Financial analysis alone is insufficient in this context. A multicriteria analysis should include all these aspects.

Resources – Consider appropriate wages, workload, working conditions, and work-life balance, as well as cultural differences, equal treatment, inclusiveness, equal opportunities, and personal development.

Procurement – Value social and environmental performance when selecting suppliers. The responsibility for sustainability does not stop at the edge of the project but includes the entire supply chain. Avoid bribery and non-ethical behaviour in procurement processes. For materials, consider the total lifecycle of the products.

Control and reporting – Proactive and open communication on the project also includes social and environmental performances, issues and risks.

If the sustainable approach is not yet self-evident, preparing a separate sustainability management plan is recommended next to the regular project management plan. Like the project management plan, this SMP should be managed throughout the project lifecycle and updated at stage transitions and project closure. Involve the corporate sustainability or CSR officer, if there is one. As sustainability in projects and project management is still evolving, evaluating and sharing lessons learned with others regularly is imperative.

CORPORATE SOCIAL RESPONSIBILITIES

Corporate Social Responsibility is defined by the *International Organization for Standardisation* (ISO) as: *'the responsibility of an organisation for the impacts of its decisions and activities on society and the environment through transparent and ethical behaviour that contributes to sustainable development, including health and the welfare of society; takes into account the expectations of stakeholders; is in compliance with applicable law and consistent with international norms of behaviour; is integrated throughout the organisation and practiced in its relationships.'*

Corporate Social Responsibilities (CSR) is the active, voluntary but not optional, social role an organisation undertakes that goes beyond complying with legal requirements. CSR aims at sustainable business, balancing Profit, People and Planet. The essence of social responsibility is the willingness of an organisation to integrate social and environmental considerations into its decision-making and to account for the impact of its decisions and activities on society and the environment. CSR also emphasises the responsibility and accountability an organisation has for the transparency and ethics of its behaviour, also towards its stakeholders. These dimensions are also inextricably linked to CSR.

A commitment to CSR includes the obligation to publicly report on the company's impact concerning social and environmental issues. The triple bottom line is a framework for reporting on these impacts. Other standards, such as the UN *Sustainable Development Goals* (SDGs) and the *European Sustainable Reporting Standard* (ESRS), can be linked to this classification.

THE TRIPLE BOTTOM LINE (TBL)

In 1994, John Elkington introduced the *Triple Bottom Line* (TBL) concept to transform the financial accounting-focused into a comprehensive approach that also measures the organisation's impact on social welfare and environmental health (Savitz, 2013). The bottom line refers to profit or loss, which appears at the bottom of a profit and loss statement in the annual accounts. The triple bottom line adds a social and environmental bottom line to the traditional financial bottom line.

The aim is not to add up the three bottom lines but to consider each bottom line on its own merits. This is difficult enough, as within each bottom line, multiple aspects are to be considered, and per initiative, the criteria vary. Economic criteria for companies might be turnover and profitability; for governments, job growth and personal income may be the key performance indicators. The same applies to both other bottom lines. Possible aspects might be:

- Social welfare – Unemployment rate, female employment rate, percentage of the population with education, travel times but also life expectancy, et cetera;
- Environmental impact – Concentration of toxic substances in the atmosphere, excessive nutrients, fossil fuel consumption, solid waste management, change in land use, amount of plastic in the oceans, biodiversity, et cetera.

The strength of the TBL is that it can be adapted on a case-by-case basis. In doing so, the key is not defining the TBL but developing support for the aspects chosen and the KPIs set and measuring them all the way through. This should be taken up early, and users should be involved from the beginning to avoid heated and deconstructive discussions later on. In this context, users are all those who have to deal with the consequences of the decisions taken. Doing nothing or delaying is also a decision.

The main value of the TBL lies in the awareness of the broader implications of each initiative, including in the long term, the more comprehensive consultation upfront, and then the consistent measurement of the KPIs agreed upon throughout the process.

Fortunately, with awareness of the importance of sustainability swiftly expanding, more and more tools are being developed to assess the sustainable impact of initiatives. These range from rudimentary checklists to sustainable impact certification programmes. In addition, more and more software tools are becoming available to assess and manage various aspects of CSR strategies in projects.

RESPONSIBILITIES

At a minimum, the project manager should ensure that the project is carried out in line with the sustainability vision of the organisations involved and that social and environmental aspects are taken into account as much as possible within the project assignment.

ADVANCED

THE 10 PRINCIPLES OF THE UN GLOBAL COMPACT (ADVANCED)

The *United Nations Global Compact* provides a framework for companies to align their business with universally accepted principles on human and labour rights, environment and anti-corruption and asks them to promote them within their sphere of influence. These principles are derived from their Universal Declaration of Human Rights and internationally recognised declarations, such as from the International Labour Organisation and United Nations conventions. These principles are:

Human rights

1. Companies should support and respect the human rights proclaimed by the United Nations;
2. Ensure that they are not accomplices in human rights violations.

Labour rights

3. Companies should uphold freedom of association and recognition of the right to collective bargaining;
4. Eliminate all forms of forced and compulsory labour;
5. Eliminate all forms of child labour;
6. Eliminate discrimination in employment and occupation.

Environment

7. Companies should support a prudent approach to environmental challenges;
8. Take actions to promote greater environmental responsibility;
9. Encourage the development and diffusion of environmentally friendly technologies.

Anti-corruption

10. Companies should counter all forms of corruption, including extortion and bribery.

By incorporating these into their business, companies fulfil their primary responsibilities towards people and the planet and lay the foundation for long-term success. Some labels already prescribe these principles as a condition for obtaining their brand. Flagrant violations of these principles result in no longer being financed for its activities.

ISO 26000 CORPORATE SOCIAL RESPONSIBILITY (ADVANCED)

The *ISO 26000: 2010* is the guideline for organisations to conduct corporate social responsibilities. This international standard offers principles, fundamental practices, core subjects and policies on integrating socially responsible behaviour into the organisation.

Principles

The ISO 26000 contains seven principles for corporate social responsibility. According to ISO 26000, an organisation should:

- Be accountable for its impact on society, the economy and the environment;
- Be transparent in its decisions and activities that impact society and the environment;
- Act ethically based on honesty, equity and integrity;
- Respect, consider and respond to the interests of its stakeholders;
- Respect the rule of law (mandatory);

- Respect international norms of behaviour while respecting the rule of law;
- Respect human rights and recognise their importance and universality.

Fundamental practices

In addition to these principles, ISO 26000 recognises two fundamental practices: (1) the recognition by an organisation of its social responsibility and (2) the identification of and engagement with its stakeholders. An organisation is responsible for the consequences of its decisions and activities over which it has formal and or actual control.

Core subjects

An organisation complying with CSR should address the following core subjects (see Figure 11.02.01):

- *Organisational governance* –This concerns integrating the principles of social responsibility into the decision-making and activities of the organisation.
- *Human rights* – This concerns the recognition and respect for human rights, not only within its own organisation but also within its sphere of influence.
- *Labour practices* – This concerns people's right to earn money through freely chosen work and the right to fair and reasonable working conditions. It also includes recognition of workers' organisations in collective bargaining on social issues related to employment.

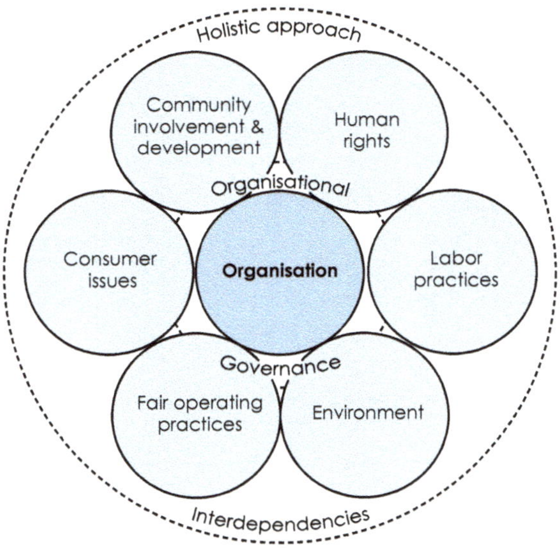

Figure 11.02.01 The seven core subjects ISO standard 26000

- *The environment* – This concerns protecting the environment, taking precautions to prevent environmental risks and applying the 'polluter pays' principle.
- *Fair operating practices* – This concerns ethical business practices such as preventing corruption, pursuing fair competition and respecting the property rights of others.
- *Consumer issues* – This concerns providing fair marketing information, promoting sustainable consumption and, where appropriate, supporting the vulnerable and disadvantaged.

- *Community involvement and development* – This concerns engaging stakeholders, including supporting civil institutions and building community relationships.

These topics affect almost all project management processes.

Human rights

Human rights are the fundamental rights of all human beings. The first category concerns civil and political rights, such as the right to life and liberty, equality before the law, and freedom of expression. The second category concerns economic, social and cultural rights, such as the right to work, food, and the highest attainable standard of health (see Chapter 7.02 Personal Integrity and Personality).

Human rights are inherent, inalienable, universal, indivisible and interdependent and transcend laws and cultural traditions:

- *Inherent* – They belong to every individual by the simple fact that they are human beings;
- *Inalienable* – People cannot give them up, neither can they be taken away;
- *Universal* – They apply to everyone, regardless of status;
- *Indivisible* – Human rights cannot be selectively denied;
- *Interdependent* – Rights contribute to the realisation of other rights.

11.03 LAWS AND LEGISLATION

PURPOSE
The purpose of this chapter is to enable the individual to ensure that the project complies with all relevant laws and legislations.

LEARNING OBJECTIVES
- Form-free and formal agreements;
- Conditions an agreement should meet;
- Shortcomings in the fulfilment of an agreement;
- Legal offence/tort;
- Regulatory agencies;
- Responsibility of the project manager in law enforcement;
- Different law theories (advanced);
- Areas of law (advanced);
- Principles of intellectual property (advanced).

DEFINITIONS
Agreement: A negotiated and typically legally binding arrangement on a course of action.
Default: A failure to fulfil an obligation.
Unlawful act/tort: An act or omission of an act that is illegal and causes harm to another.
Breach of contract: A shortcoming attributable to one of the contract parties.
Force majeure: An (unforeseeable) circumstance that prevents someone from fulfilling a contract and for which one cannot be held responsible.

INTRODUCTION
As a project manager, you have to deal with many legal aspects, such as permits, agreements, copyrights and patents, as well as possible shortcomings in fulfilling agreements and legal offences. Knowing the legal aspects at key points, mitigating legal risks, and knowing when to seek legal advice is essential.

POSITIONING
Throughout the project, agreements are made, and contracts are concluded and performed. Each stage of contract formation, conclusion, performance and settlement may give rise to conflicts. Throughout the project, actions may be taken or, on the contrary, omitted that could be considered unlawful or even give rise to prosecution. Legal issues may even directly affect the project approach and design itself. At least at stage transitions and project closure, legal issues should be evaluated, and lessons learned passed on to the appropriate bodies.

AGREEMENTS
An agreement is a negotiated and typically legally binding arrangement on a course of action. There are form-free and formal agreements. A formal agreement is an agreement that is only legally valid if certain formal requirements are met. For

example, an agreement to transfer copyright should be in writing to be legally valid. However, most agreements are form-free. Such an agreement takes effect as soon as parties have reached a consensus. Form-free agreements are also called verbal agreements. The fact that such an agreement is legally binding does not mean it is of good quality. Also, the burden of proof of such an agreement is difficult. Unless the law states otherwise, agreements are form-free.

Conditions an agreement should meet

Agreements never arise spontaneously; people should act in one way or another. For a legally enforceable agreement, it is necessary that:

- Parties have the authority to act.
- There is mutual consent.
- The agreement is not contrary to law, public order or morality.

Authority to act

In agreements between organisations, both parties should check whether the individual acting on behalf of the other is authorised to represent them. The powers of representation within an organisation are recorded in the *Chamber of Commerce* trade register. This register is public and can even be consulted on the internet. Precisely because of the public nature of this register, a contracting party cannot, in principle, invoke the other party's lack of authority after concluding a contract: one could have checked this beforehand.

Of course, an individual can also be authorised within the company to enter into a particular agreement. Furthermore, based on their position, the other party may assume that people have some power of representation. For example, consumers may presume that salespersons are authorised to sell items to customers at a set price. Whether the youngest clerk is also authorised to provide large one-off discounts is disputable.

A similar issue arises within projects. It is often taken for granted that the people in charge are authorised to carry out the work within the framework of the agreement. But is that really the case? Who is authorised to agree on additional work or can approve the purchase of materials and services? Who is authorised to agree on time, quality and money, even if this is within the framework of the agreement? It is, therefore, advisable from the outset to establish unambiguously what the authorities are of those in charge and which decisions should be escalated to the next level.

Mutual consent

For an agreement to be legally enforceable, there should be mutual consent, i.e., an offer should be made and accepted. An offer can be made verbally, in writing, by displaying goods in a shop window or by placing an advertisement. However, it should always include the subject it relates to, the quantity offered and the price asked. If any of these aspects are missing, it is not an offer but an invitation to make an offer.

> *The text in an advertisement reads: 'For sale, cabinet, for any reasonable price.' This is not an offer but an invitation to make an offer.*

As long as the offer is not (yet) accepted, the individual or organisation who made the offer can still withdraw it. The offer can also expire. This happens when:

- The offer is rejected.
- When a verbal offer is not immediately accepted.
- When a written offer is not accepted within a reasonable period of time.

To avoid confusion, it is best to explicitly state how long the offer remains valid and whether it has or will expire.

Intent and declaration of intent

For an agreement to be legally valid, the intention and the declaration of intent should correspond. Even if they don't correspond, the agreement is still valid unless the individual who accepted the offer could have known that a mistake was involved.

> *A customer buys a car for € 10,000. A week later, the salesperson tells him they made a mistake and that the price should have been € 500 higher. In this case, the price remains € 10,000.*
>
> *A customer sees an advertisement for a new bed for € 1.80. He immediately orders the bed. However, the shop informs him of a mistake and that the price should be € 180. There is no agreement. The buyer could have known that a mistake had been made.*

Defect on consent

There may be situations where the intention and the consent correspond but where the consent is defective. This is called a defect of consent. A mistake, threat, fraud, and abuse of circumstances can cause a defect of consent. In that case, the agreement is voidable.

A mistake is made if the contract is concluded based on the wrong information. A mistake can only be invoked if the other party knew this and did nothing about it. However, each party should take its owns measures within reasonable limits to avoid mistakes. There may be an abuse of circumstances in the case of a strong economic closeness, a high degree of inexperience or levity or an abnormal state of mind.

Not contrary to law, public order or morality

The freedom of parties to conclude an agreement is not 100%. The law may dictate that certain agreements cannot be made. This applies, in particular, to labour and tenancy law. Labour law, for example, can prescribe a minimum wage, maximum working hours and certain dismissal rules.

Non-compliance with public order or morality can arise from written and unwritten law, e.g., concerning disturbing the night's rest, immoral conduct on the public highway, and intent or gross negligence.

SHORTCOMINGS IN THE FULFILMENT OF AN AGREEMENT

Regarding the shortcoming in fulfilling an agreement, we distinguish between best-effort and performance agreements (see Chapter 6.01 Procurement).

Best-effort agreement – An agreement to perform specific tasks to the best of their ability without guaranteeing a particular result. That result is expected or hoped for but not part of the agreement itself. The supplier is only *in default* when they have not (correctly) delivered their effort on time. The proof of the default lies with the customer.

Performance agreement – An agreement to deliver a result within predefined terms and conditions. Not delivering, or not delivering properly and or on time, always results in a shortcoming. If a shortcoming is due to one of the parties, it is a *breach of contract*. If the shortcoming is not due to one of the parties, then it is called *force majeure*. A force majeure is an (unforeseeable) circumstance that prevents someone from fulfilling a contract and for which one cannot be held responsible (an act of God).

Compensation for damages can only be claimed if the debtor is *in default*. A debtor is in default only after it is given a notice of default, in which it is given a reasonable period to perform and fails to perform within that period. Only in case of a *fatal deadline* (e.g., forgetting to deliver the wedding dress on the wedding day) will the debtor be in default without formal notice. A fatal deadline is a non-extendable period within which performance should be delivered.

If an employee or subcontractor causes a breach of contract, this does not release the supplier from its liability. In this context, we speak of the *risk liability* of the contractor. In case of breach of contract, compensation for tangible and also intangible damages can be claimed. If one of the parties fails to fulfil its obligation in an agreement, the other party is entitled to suspend its own obligation. In general, you can only terminate the agreement if the other party is *in default*.

UNLAWFUL ACT/TORT

A tort or unlawful act is an act or omission of an act that is illegal and causes harm to another.

The law gives three reasons why an act can be regarded as unlawful:

- An infringement of a right, such as an infringement of copyright;
- An act or omission in violation of a legal obligation, such as committing a criminal offence;
- An act or omission contrary to morality.

Acting contrary to morality is the most important form of an unlawful act. The court examines whether a standard of care has been violated, such as endangerment, nuisance, professional errors, unlawful publications, or unfair competition.

It is essential to understand that a tort does not always mean liability and the right to compensation. If you want to claim damages, you should also prove that the tort is attributable to the perpetrator; there is damage, a causal link between the tort and the damage, and the violated norm should protect against the damage caused (relativity).

In the event of compensation, not only the actual damage can be recovered, but also the costs incurred to limit the damage and the expenses incurred to determine and claim the damage.

REGULATORY AGENCIES

Regulatory agencies are independent public bodies established by law to set and enforce standards for a particular industry or sector to protect the public interest. They also often set permitted tariff adjustments, facilitate dispute resolution, and advise and counsel the government on policy issues.

Regulatory authorities conduct periodic audits and cost and performance analyses. However, it is up to the project itself to demonstrate compliance with applicable regulations. Identifying these regulations in advance and providing the necessary documentation to demonstrate compliance is essential. Recognise and manage regulators as stakeholders, align processes and procedures with them and consult experts. Non-compliance can have severe consequences for the project, both materially and in terms of reputation. Regulators can impose fines, as well as prohibit the commissioning of project deliverables.

RESPONSIBILITY OF THE PROJECT MANAGER IN LAW ENFORCEMENT

In criminal law, not only those who break the rules are at fault, but also anyone who creates, facilitates, or maintains a prohibited situation. They are vicariously liable. Project managers may also be vicariously liable if they had the position to intervene, did not do so, and knowingly accepted the risk that the prohibited act took place. The guiding principle is that a supervisor is vicariously liable unless they can prove they are not to blame.

> *The organisation provides employees with a tablet with specific software for their work. However, some of your team members use this tablet to commit fraud. You may then be held vicariously liable for any damage caused and for the criminal acts of those team members unless you can prove that you took reasonable measures to prevent this.*

RESPONSIBILITIES

The project manager is responsible for the daily management of the project, including the legal aspects. They should ensure that all agreements and contracts in the project are clearly and unambiguously recorded and carried out, that the project is conducted per the relevant regulations and legislation, and that legal risks are mitigated. They should know when to seek legal advice. Further, they are responsible for law enforcement in their project. The project sponsor is accountable for the project and, therefore, also for the final decisions taken regarding the legal aspects of the project.

ADVANCED

AREAS OF LAW (ADVANCED)

In jurisdiction, we distinguish between private and public law. Private law is the law that regulates the relationship between citizens, such as personal and family, commercial, property, and contract law. Public law regulates the relationship between citizens and the state and between different branches of the state, such as state, administrative, criminal, and fiscal law (see Figure 11.03.01).

Private or Civil Law	Public Law
• Personal and Family Law	• State Law
• Commercial Law	• Administrative Law
• Property Law	• Criminal Law
• Contract Law	• Tax or Fiscal Law

Figure 11.03.01 Jurisdictions

State or constitutional law concerns the political governance of a state or country. Administrative law concerns the governance of public bodies that administer public policies. Criminal law concerns criminal offences and the consequences of these actions. Fiscal or tax law governs the assessment and collection of taxes in a legal context. The fields and types of law can vary per country.

In projects, you will have to deal mainly with contract law. Realise that parties can be sued under multiple jurisdictions. Failure to comply with HESSE regulations can be administratively fined, criminally prosecuted, and lead to civil damages. The burden of proof varies by jurisdiction.

INTELLECTUAL PROPERTY LAW (ADVANCED)

Intellectual property (IP) laws mainly include:

- *Copyright* – The exclusive right of an author to publish or reproduce their works of literature, science or art. Copyright also includes portrait and image rights.
- *Patent right* – The right of the patent holder to prohibit others from commercially exploiting their invention in exchange for disclosure of that invention.
- *Trademark right* – The exclusive right to use a particular trademark, such as a logo or product name.

The intellectual property right gives the owner the right of use. This right is divided into the right of enjoyment and disposition. The right of enjoyment entitles the owner to the actual use of its property. The right of disposition authorises the owner to perform all conceivable legal acts relating to its property. The owner may transfer all or part of its IP rights to another individual (IP assignment).

Staff and service providers

It is important to establish who owns which IP rights. The same rules do not apply to all IPs and may vary from country to country. In an employment relationship, IP rights generally belong to the employer. In case external consultants are involved, the IP rights of the work developed usually belong to them unless the contract clearly stipulates otherwise. It is essential to explicitly include the desired allocation of rights in advance in the various contracts.

Licences

Objects of IP rights can be transferred to third parties. It goes without saying that, that this should be clearly set out in writing. Such a licence may also be registered in one of the applicable registers, so the licensee can also invoke rights against third parties. However, it should not unduly restrict the free movement of goods or services or violate the applicable antitrust laws.

11.04 POWER AND INTERESTS

PURPOSE

The purpose of this chapter is to enable the individual to use power and interest techniques to achieve stakeholder satisfaction and deliver the agreed results within time, budget and quality constraints.

LEARNING OBJECTIVES

- Projects related to power and interests;
- Power and authority;
- Principles of persuasion;
- PESTLE analysis;
- Sources of interest (advanced).

DEFINITIONS

Power: The ability to exert their will over others.
Authority: The right/position to set frameworks, give orders, and take decisions.
Influence: The effect of exercised power.
Interest: Something that benefits an individual, group or organisation or, if infringed, puts them at a disadvantage.
PESTLE analysis: A strategic framework to analyse and evaluate external macro-environmental factors that may influence an organisation's interests.

INTRODUCTION

There where projects are implemented, situations are influenced, and interests are served or infringed. You should exert your influence and dare to use formal and informal sources of power to serve your interest for the greater good. By actively using these sources of power, you take responsibility for the implementation and purpose of the project. Also, consider the sustainability and corporate social responsibility of the sponsoring organisation, the stakeholders involved, and your own position in these. Understand the power and interests of others so that you can take them into account when preparing and implementing the project. After all, power and influence arise in relationship with others.

POSITIONING

Projects are carried out in the context of their environment. During the project preparation stage, the power and interest of the various stakeholders are reflected in all aspects of the project outline. In the project definition stage, this is elaborated into the project design and, ultimately, the project management plan. The power and interests of the various stakeholders are an essential part of the stakeholder analyses. During the delivery stage, internal and external parties need to be carefully involved so that the project is not adversely affected by environmental forces, and they can even be used for the benefit of the project. Involving stakeholders is an important part of the art of project management.

PROJECTS RELATED TO POWER AND INTERESTS

Before using power and influence for the greater good of the project, you need to assess and understand the power and interests of the stakeholders. Conduct a stakeholder analysis and engage with them. Assess their interests, ambitions, influence and power, and potential impact on the project.

Investigate the sources of interest and assess their formal and informal power and influences. In doing so, don't just look at the group and or organisations they represent but also at their personal ambitions and interests. These may differ. Since power and influence arise in relationships with others, preparing a stakeholder map may help. Also, assess their attitude towards the project (see Chapter 4.02 Stakeholders).

Furthermore, take their personal working style into account. A person's personality directly impacts their power and influence, but also how they exert it. Finally, culture and values also play an important role (see Chapter 11.05 Culture and Values).

A good way to understand their interests and ambitions is to explore together what the success criteria and success factors are for the project (see Chapter 5.02 Project Design). In doing so, you should also explore how to engage them to benefit the project (see Chapter 4.02 Stakeholders).

POWER AND AUTHORITY

Power is defined as the ability to exert their will over others. This links power to an individual, group or organisation. Power is also not static. Circumstances or the involvement of new people can change the balance of power. Abuse of power can lead to counterforces. Hersey, Blanchard and Johnson (2008) distinguish the following types of power:

Formal power or legitimate power – This type of power is determined by the formal or legitimised position held by an individual, group or organisation. Formal power is important for the project sponsor and the other project board members, as it directly determines their decision-making power and the ability to shield the project from adverse influences. Depending on your position, you also have more or less formal power.

Power to reward – This concerns the power you have to reward someone. The power of reward is usually linked to formal or legitimate power. A functional manager can give an employee a raise or a promotion. As a project manager, you can give a team member a more challenging role or task.

Coercive power – This is about having the power to punish someone. This power is typically linked to formal or legitimate power. A functional manager can revoke an employee's accrued rights or withhold expected rewards. As a project manager, you can give a team member a lesser role or may involve them less in decision-making. You need to consider carefully about whether this will be effective in the long run.

Connection power – One's influential connections determine this type of power. Project managers who have worked carefully to build relationships with influential people can fall back on them for support in difficult situations. Projects are not just about 'What can I do?' but often also about 'Who do I know?' Building a supportive and collaborative network is essential to exerting influence effectively.

Expertise power – Expertise power refers to power based on proven expertise. Within projects, people with expertise get others on board based on their in-depth understanding of the project approach within the context in which the project is defined and implemented.

Information power – The additional information at your disposal determines this type of power. You can better oversee and understand the game of mutual influence if you are more broadly informed. You can realise benefits for the project based on that extra information more easily.

Reference power – This type of power is embedded in someone's attitude, charisma and authenticity. The people being led and influenced have confidence in the leader's personality. This creates a willingness to follow. People with referential power derive their authority from being seen as role models by others.

Using power with integrity and competence strengthens your influence and increases the likelihood that stakeholders will follow you. Doing so increases the likelihood of project success: the extent to which the project results satisfy relevant stakeholders.

Be aware that power is based on the perception of yourself and others about the situation. Exerting power means influencing people's perception of the situation so that you can achieve the results you envisage.

Formal power lies in the position an individual holds. Connection, expertise, information, and reference power lie in the person. Reward and coercive power can be both.

Authority is the right/position to set frameworks, give orders, and take decisions. Within an organisation or institute, authority follows the hierarchy. Authority is then granted to senior officials to achieve the organisational objectives. Authority is then linked to formal power.

PRINCIPLES OF PERSUASION

In 1984 Cialdini formulated six persuasion principles to increase and strengthen your influence. The principle of Unity was formulated later (Cialdini, 2021). These principles particularly affect decision-making concerning purchasing and consumption but can also be very well applied in other circumstances, such as in projects.

Principle of reciprocity – In almost every culture, reciprocity is a fundamental norm. It is defined as the mutually felt obligation within a relationship to reciprocate a gift with a counter-gift. This could be by providing extra information, involving individuals in decision-making, giving individuals extra time if possible, et cetera. By consciously investing in this, you create a good breeding ground for reciprocity.

Principle of commitment and consistency – Simply sending an updated schedule is insufficient. To gain genuine commitment, people should express their participation face-to-face. Promise creates debt. People want to be consistent and are eager to fulfil their explicitly given commitments.

Principle of social proof – Long queues make an impression. A slogan such as 'X people have also ordered ...' entices others to buy it too. 'Click the video for customer reviews!' makes the benefits of predecessors explicit and increases the likelihood that others will follow.

Principle of sympathy or liking – People seen as sympathetic are more likelier to receive a 'yes' than others. Kindness pays off. A powerful way to elicit sympathy is by empathising with the other person's needs. If you have to give a presentation, adapt your language and dress to your target audience. Make yourself heard and show with examples that you understand and appreciate the other person's world. *See Building rapport* in Chapter 7.03, Personal Communication.

Principle of authority – People usually trust authorities. 'Rated number 1 by the Consumers' Association' reinforces the message. Invite recognised subject-matter experts to underline the desired approach. This could be from the relevant field but also from unexpected quarters, such as having a sports coach come and tell how they led the team to the championship. A reference to a proven authority can also be made in constructing arguments. See *Building arguments* in Chapter 7.03, Personal Communication.

Principle of scarcity – People don't want to miss an opportunity. 'Only X rooms left' is an often-used slogan to encourage people to book the room now. With scarcity, you tap into people's underlying fears. Imagine not being able to acquire what someone else already has!

Principle of unity – People identify more easily with people who are 'cut from the same cloth'. Think of your family, the country you were born in, your school, and so on. Influencing from such a common reference is much easier because of the basic trust you feel. So if you know what you have in common with the other person, using that point to connect and exert your influence is effective.

Conformity theory

The conformity theory implies that people change their beliefs, actions or perceptions to conform to the groups they belong or want to belong to or those whose approval they seek. The conformity theory underwrites the principle of unity as defined by Cialdini.

PESTLE ANALYSIS

The PESTLE analysis provides insight into environmental factors you need to consider when exercising power and influence (see Figure 11.04.01). Knowing these environmental factors well and taking them into account can significantly increase your project's chances of success.

Political factors – A reliable and conscientious political environment provides stability and confidence to organisations. You can trust the rules and laws in place and how they are applied. Clear rules enable healthy development. Where politics is more centralised and autocratic, you have to be more alert to underlying currents. Room for growth is then mainly tied to those in power. To effectively run your project, it is necessary to be thoroughly acquainted with the laws, rules and political customs and adjust your actions accordingly.

Figure 11.04.01 PESTLE analysis

Economic factors – With an economic analysis, you look at various economic factors that may affect the project's success. Think of inflation, tax climate, funding possibilities, but also logistical connections with other businesses and customer organisations, labour market environment, et cetera. You can look at the comparative advantages of the country or region. What other companies are located in the region, and what contribution they can make to strengthen the power and influence of the company?

Social factors – With social analysis, you look at factors such as basic ethical attitudes; work attitudes; level of education; the collaboration between government, educational institutions and businesses; demographics; lifestyle and openness to other cultures. Healthy social relationships are desirable to leverage your power and influence. Are people willing and able to move with the mission and vision to which you want to give form and substance to? Also, numerical and historical social factors count in the analysis: what is the average age composition? What is the distribution of income? What are the cultural roots and related views on responsibility and work?

Technological factors – With technical analysis, you look at factors such as productivity; the degree of automation; innovation capacity; intellectual property protection; logistics and network capacity; supplier strength and flexibility, and the technological knowledge base. Where do you find the best technical breeding ground to build power and influence? How do you ensure you choose an environment equipped to develop and maintain the intended technological edge?

Legal factors – With a legal analysis, you look at the applicable laws and their impact on the ability to exercise power and influence. How is compliance with laws and regulations monitored? What are the rules for import/export? How do you comply with labour market laws? How should you deal with health and safety issues? What advertising and privacy codes do you comply with? Which social and environmental laws are you bound by?

Environmental factors – Much attention should be paid to the impact of business operations on the environment and vice versa. Environmental requirements for business operations are becoming increasingly stringent and thus need to be correctly analysed as a determining factor. The availability of energy resources, minerals and raw materials, climatic conditions, and existing infrastructures also play an important role in decision-making and resulting projects.

The attitude towards sustainability and corporate social responsibility of the sponsoring organisation or customer, and other stakeholders also play an essential role in this analysis. The PESTLE analysis provides insight into the environment within which power and influence are exercised and the opportunities and frameworks provided by the environment. Projects can be tailored accordingly.

RESPONSIBILITIES

When implementing a project, everyone is responsible for properly using their power and influence appropriate to their task or role to enable project success. This applies not only to the project result but also to its delivery. Project managers have their own responsibility in this. They will have to use their power and influence effectively, but also reliably and consciously, to achieve the desired result while giving attention and space to the power and influence of others.

ADVANCED

SOURCES OF INTEREST (ADVANCED)

Interests are matters that are beneficial to an individual, group or organisation or, if harmed, disadvantage them. Safeguarding these interests is essential for developing a future-proof business. Sources of interest are factors that serve the organisation's interest. If these sources are compromised, the benefits provided by these sources fall away. This can jeopardise the survival of the organisation. Many projects contribute to safeguarding the sources of interest of an organisation. Important sources of interest are:

Customers/Markets – Loyal customers serve your company's interests the most. They observe what the company does, buy their products and enjoy their service. By responding well to the needs of those target groups, they will remain loyal to the company. You can best maintain this source of interest by providing products and services that truly meet customers' needs. You can also apply new products and services to acquire new customers and markets. The bottom line is always: 'I serve my organisation optimally by serving their customers/clients to their full satisfaction.'

Land and raw materials – Utilising land can serve various interests. It can be cultivated and built on. The agricultural sector thrives primarily on the exploitation of the land. As such, it makes a substantial contribution to the economy. Not just for providing food but also for providing raw materials for products such as clothing and energy.

Minerals are also very important. Now, you see a switch from traditional mining, such as oil and gas, to mining special metals that enable us to build and use batteries, electric cars and wind turbines. Securing these raw materials is essential for sustaining today's economy. Countries that can supply such materials are critical strategic partners. Numerous projects are being set up to use renewable resources effectively. Today, more and more attention is being paid to the exploitation of land, and the use of raw and auxiliary materials is being subjected to new regulations and laws.

Production sources – High-quality machines convert raw materials into products essential to customers. New installations convert water flows, geothermal heat, solar and wind into energy. New production systems increase the efficiency and effectiveness of business processes. New information systems are becoming increasingly crucial for producing goods and services and becoming an indispensable part of new products themselves. Suppliers who create these systems and innovative components are a source of interest for many parties. For exploiting unique technology, patents should protect this 'source of interest'.

Infrastructures – For transporting products, energy, and information, well-functioning infrastructures are essential. Look at the problems we currently face when it comes to transporting energy, whether it is electricity, gas, hydrogen or any other form. Also, look at the entire logistics chain of parcel delivery companies such as Bol.com and

Amazon.com. And don't forget the storage and distribution of information through well-known platforms like Google and Instagram and the valuable information they acquire around the users of these platforms. Having a well-functioning digital infrastructure is very important these days.

Human talent – Setting up, operating and maintaining production assets and infrastructure requires human talent. Knowledge of infrastructure, where lifelong learning is possible, is in the interests of almost every organisation. Collaboration between vocational schools and companies is essential for the continuous development of talent. Also, we see the increasing importance of online learning. Although automation, robotisation and artificial intelligence are gaining ground, human talent often remains essential to achieving a winning edge. The availability of human talent should be protected by providing excellent and inspiring working conditions and challenging job prospects. This source of interest can be temporarily covered by, for example, non-compete agreements, but this is not a long-term solution.

Capital – Investing in means of production and infrastructure costs money. However, capital is scarce, and organisations or individuals that provide the necessary funds want to receive profitable interest on the loans or dividends on the equity provided; otherwise, they will not provide the funds. As a result, the focus remains on shareholder value. This may erode other sources of interest.

Projects are increasingly being co-funded through crowdfunding. In this way, supporting economic activity becomes more visible to the community. Even banks require certain investments to be financed in this way. This is not only a form of risk management; it also shows the community's support, which is increasingly important these days.

Laws and treaties – Laws and treaties are made to serve and align common interests. They have a strong influence on individuals and companies. Therefore, companies and action groups exert a strong influence on political parties through the use of lobbyists. After all, the government has a wide range of power because of its legislative role. When safeguarding interests, certain laws should be maintained or replaced by new ones, preferably from companies' and interest groups' perspectives. This is the main centre of focus for most lobbyists.

Culture – In this context, culture does not mean cultural heritage but how people interact with each other and, in particular, how people act in companies and organisations. This determines how leadership should be provided, how people work together, and how to best market products. Organisations and companies may be interested in perpetuating or changing a particular cultural perspective. This can affect whether or not directive management is accepted or social unrest arises (see Chapter 11.05 Culture and Values).

11.05 CULTURE AND VALUES

PURPOSE

The purpose of this chapter is to enable the individual to recognise and integrate the influence of internal and external cultural aspects on the project design, objectives, processes, sustainability of the outcomes and agreed outcomes.

LEARNING OBJECTIVES

- Projects related to culture and values;
- Dimensions of national cultures;
- Organisational culture model;
- Organisational culture and decision-making (advanced).

DEFINITIONS

National culture: The total of core beliefs, values and expectations shared by most country's residents.
Organisational culture: The way members of an organisation interact with each other, their work and the outside world, to achieve the organisation's goals and objectives.
Values: A set of internalised concepts or moral guiding principles on which individuals base their actions.
Culture change: The change in core beliefs, values and expectations within an organisation or country.
Culture-conscious action: An action that is consciously and effectively aligned with the applicable culture of the organisation and or society to achieve goals and objectives.

INTRODUCTION

Culture exerts a strong influence on people's actions. They are ingrained behavioural patterns embedded in a set of solid inner beliefs. To successfully launch a project, it is necessary to fit in with the existing culture. Assess the culture and values of the society and the organisation and their implications for the project. If a transition is needed to achieve the intended benefits, remember that changing ingrained habits takes time. When people don't really feel a need to change, they quickly fall back into their old habits (see Chapter 6.05 Organisational Change and Transformation).

POSITIONING

In a project, people from different cultures and with different values have to work together, and they also have to deal with different cultures and values of users and other stakeholders. This affects the project from the very beginning of the project to its closure and beyond.

From the very beginning, the project assignment should take into account the ingrained behavioural patterns and the underlying values and beliefs of all parties involved. In the project definition stage, it is important to discuss the fundamental value of collaboration, the cultural patterns of the users and other stakeholders involved, and how to pay attention to these. During delivery, in addition to content, there should be constant attention to the cultures and values of people and any problem that may arise from these differences. Attention to the values and beliefs embedded in concrete behaviour is a form of respect for everyone's culture. This respect is a crucial factor for project success.

PROJECTS RELATED TO CULTURE AND VALUES

In projects, you have to assess the culture and values of the society and the formal and informal culture and values within the organisation and their implications for the project.

Regarding the culture and values of the society, you should consider not only the location of the project but also the culture of origin of the key stakeholders and members of the project team. This is even more important when dealing with virtual project teams (see Chapter 8.03 Teamwork). To understand the differences between the various national cultures, you can use Hofstede's study. For organisational culture, you can refer to Schein's organisational culture model and the various organisational cultures and their characteristics as defined by Quinn and Cameron. The model of Schein shows that visual artefacts and symbols and the espoused values and beliefs do not always match the underlying basis assumptions in the organisation. Especially as an organisation consists of multiple groups and entities they can fundamentally differ (for all, see below).

Engage with stakeholders, and reflect on their cultures and values. People may have different beliefs and values affecting the project's collaboration (see 'Spiral Dynamics', Chapter 8.01 Relationships and Engagement). It is important to have an open mind. Engage with stakeholders and realise it isn't always what it looks like. Within the project team, it is of great importance to spend time and energy to build an effective team culture you can rely on (see *Developing a project culture in*, Chapter 8.03, Teamwork).

DIMENSIONS OF NATIONAL CULTURES

How people value and respect each other and how they interact depends largely on their cultural background. It is, therefore, important to have knowledge of people's cultural backgrounds and their dominant characteristics. To investigate this, Hofstede (2011) conducted an extensive survey of 11,600 IBM employees working in 50 countries. Based on this survey, he first distinguished four dimensions of national cultures. Two dimensions were added at a later stage based on subsequent surveys. These dimensions are:

Power distance index (PDI)

Power distance is the extent to which people expect and accept that power is unevenly distributed. In societies with high power distance, such as Arab and Latin American countries, Russia or China, people are more likely to conform to decisions made from the hierarchy. In countries within northern Europe, the United States and Australia, where the power distance is minior, people expect to be involved when making decisions. The power space for the hierarchy to make and implement decisions is smaller, and decentralisation is more popular than centralisation.

Individualism vs collectivism (IDV index)

An individual society manifests itself through weak ties between individuals. This leads to an appreciation of independence. Countries that score high on this are, for example, the United States and the Scandinavian countries. A society is collectivist if individuals, from birth, form part of strong, close-knit groups that offer protection in exchange for loyalty. Countries that score high in this respect include Latin American and Asian countries such as Japan, South Korea, Taiwan and Indonesia.

In collectivist cultures, family members often hold important positions in the organisation. You will be given assignments only when you are truly part of the group and have shown respect, gained trust, and been accepted. As a leader, you are subservient to the group. When decisions are made at the expense of group members, such as a dismissal, apologies are in order, unlike in America, where you are valued as an individual if you have fulfilled your dreams and become successful on your own merit without the help of your family.

Masculinity vs femininity (MAS index)

In masculine societies, gender roles are distinctly separated. Men are expected to be assertive, ambitious and tough, while women should be modest, tender and caring. A clear division of roles between men and women is common. Countries with a strong masculine culture include Japan, English-speaking countries, Germany, Austria, Italy, and Latin American countries. In feminine societies, gender roles overlap more, and men and women are mutually responsible for caring for relationships, quality of life and livelihood. Scandinavian countries, Thailand, South Korea, and Suriname, are good examples of this.

In masculine cultures, conflicts are more likely to be resolved by 'assertively standing up for yourself' than by 'negotiating the best compromise'. To distinguish oneself from others, deepening and broadening the task content is valued. In feminine cultures, discussing necessary procedures and strengthening social relationships within the team are highly valued.

Uncertainty avoidance (UA Index)

People may avoid uncertain situations because they feel threatened by unknown or uncertain circumstances. In a society where people harbour feelings of uncertainty, laws, procedures, rules and control mechanisms are important. Abnormal behaviour is not tolerated. Examples of countries with high uncertainty avoidance are Latin America, southern Europe, and Japan. In cultures with low uncertainty avoidance, people are more likely to accept what happens. Life is full of risks, so when something happens, you still have the opportunity to respond effectively. Doing so makes you open to conflict, whereas in cultures with high uncertainty avoidance, these are preferably avoided. Singapore, China, Sweden, Britain and the United States are good examples of this.

In cultures with high uncertainty avoidance, people express their emotions more easily. Rules, clear, straightforward answers, and precise job descriptions are perceived as pleasant and safe. People also prefer specialists who have earned their spurs with specific solutions rather than generalists who help you to find your own solution. You are also expected to pay attention to operational issues and the decision content so that team members feel confident that implementation is feasible and can be controlled.

In cultures with low uncertainty avoidance, showing emotions is often perceived as excessive. In these cultures, uncertainty is okay. Time will provide the answers. Disagreements are allowed, and people readily engage in conflict. Both are viewed as a way to solve problems. Rules are optional. With some flexibility, you can always work things out together.

Long-term vs short-term orientation (LTO Index)

Additional research by Michael Bond, known as the *Chinese Value Survey*, reveals a fifth dimension of national culture. It is about long-term versus short-term orientation. Long-term orientation is defined as the pursuit of future rewards, especially through encouraging thriftiness and persistence. Depending on what time and context demand, these cultures follow a pragmatic course towards the future. They can change and weigh up opportunities that come their way. Practicality, if necessary for the future, transcends traditions. Countries like Russia, China and Japan score high with this.

Short-term orientated cultures represent virtues focused on the past and the present, respect for tradition, concern for stability and the social need for reciprocation in giving favours and gifts. Social change is viewed with suspicion because it can harm traditions and the associated values. Saudi Arabia, Iran, Canada, the United States, and the United Kingdom are good examples of countries that score low on long-term orientation.

In long-term cultures, the moment and the context determine which steps should be taken towards the future. The adage is: 'If you view your present situation and circumstances, you will know how to act' The ability to adapt is not anchored in universal rules for what is right and wrong but depends on situational circumstances to which you adapt yourself flexibly. In short-term cultures, the traditional past tells you what to do now. The adage is: 'Hold on to the traditions and values in which your actions are anchored'. Personal fortitude and loyalty to the country's culture are perceived as important traits.

Indulgence versus restraint (IVR index)

Further research by Michael Minkov on the World Value Survey revealed a sixth dimension. The dimension of indulgence versus restraint emerged from the questions on happiness, control over one's life, and the importance of leisure. Indulgence represents relatively unfettered satisfaction of basic, natural human desires like enjoying life and having fun. Countries such as Venezuela, Mexico, Sweden, and Nigeria score high here. Restraint reflects the belief that the need for satisfaction should be contained. Social norms should regulate it. Countries that score high on this are Pakistan, Estonia, Latvia, Lithuania and Eastern European countries.

In restrained cultures, moral discipline is high, and there is more pessimism than optimism. On average, more people are introverted, and a lower percentage feel healthy. The adage is: 'Hold back'. In an indulgent culture, freely expressing your opinion is normal, and optimism, enjoying life and having fun are valued. Relatively more people are extroverts and feel happy and healthy. The adage is: 'Live your life!'

Dealing with cultural differences

When dealing with other groups or societies, it is wise to suspend judgement. Chapter 7.03 describes building rapport as a powerful quality for connecting with others. One learns to understand the other better by viewing things from their perspective. Also, through carefully observing displayed behaviour and showing interest in the backgrounds of this behaviour, you gain insight into other cultures. Project managers who excel in this show respect and appreciation for the culture they engage in. In the longer term, this also gives them room to integrate some of their own cultural insights into the culture they have entered.

ORGANISATIONAL CULTURE MODEL

People behave differently in different organisations because the organisation's culture is different. That is what makes understanding an organisation's culture so important. The organisational culture is defined as how members of an organisation interact with each other, with their work and with the outside world to achieve the organisation's results and objectives. These jointly achievable results and goals are also the unifying element within an organisational culture.

According to Schein (2008), organisational culture comprises shared assumptions developed through external adaptation and internal integration. External adaptation (upstream) is the organisation's adaptation to the environment, as well as to its own organisation's mission and strategy and the availability of people and resources. We behave this way because the environment demands it from us. Internal integration (undercurrent) is about internalising what is labelled normal behaviour in the organisation. This is how we do it here. According to Schein, organisational culture is best understood by looking at the artefacts and symbols, the espoused values and beliefs, and the fundamental underlying assumptions of an organisation (see Figure 11.05.01).

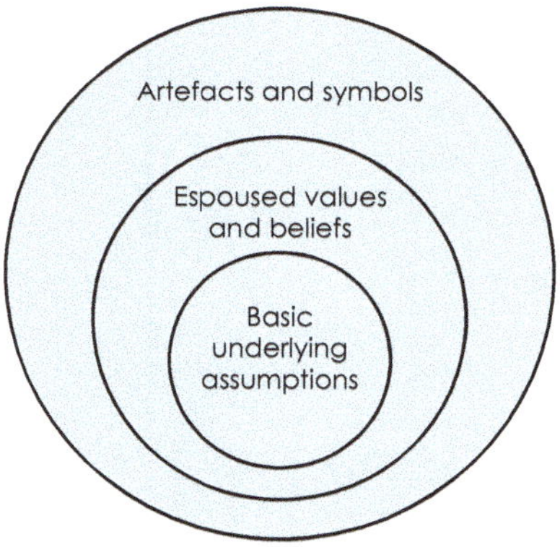

Figure 11.05.01 Schein's model of an organisation culture (Schein, 2008)

Artefacts

These are the visible and tangible elements of the organisation's culture, such as office layout, dress code, logos, and architecture. It is what you see when you enter a building. It immediately accords a positive, neutral or negative feeling.

> *'Why is the sales department upstairs when sales are closely related to project development downstairs?'*

By asking yourself such questions, you are trying to understand the organisation's values, beliefs and underlying assumptions. It is essential that you explore this further to understand the organisation's culture.

Espoused values

You can find out the espoused values by talking to people. How they work, and why they handle things as they do. Telling stories they are proud of and anecdotes about how things were done. But beware! Sometimes, they only tell you the stories that reflect the organisation's official mission and policies. If so, the fundamental beliefs and values remain tacitly hidden when in fact, they determine daily behaviour.

> *'Give them leeway to sell because they can open doors that will otherwise remain closed. In our department, we solve technical problems. Besides: we usually know how to get hold of the customer's contacts ourselves for the necessary answers!'*
>
> *Sales and project development are separated in many organisations. After all, winning contracts is something completely different from developing project deliverables. In some cases, separating these departments is justifiable and acceptable. However, sometimes the existing culture exerts a negative or limiting influence on the organisation's survival. For example, as projects become more complex, inadequate pre-consultation between sales and project development may lead to loss-making projects. The belief 'We solve the technical problems' then deserves at least a deepening in the form of 'We determine customer needs together with sales.'*

Underlying basic assumptions

This level of organisational culture is virtually obscure, yet, at the same time, it is the most stable and also the most ingrained. It encompasses people's underlying values, beliefs and assumptions when doing their jobs. Values, beliefs and assumptions they feel comfortable with and in which they have always excelled. Changing this is no easy feat. However, if a change is necessary, these underlying values, beliefs and assumptions should be made visible first. Then, you can introduce new values and beliefs through training and reflection,.

> *Pre-consultation of the project organisation was set up to arrive at a more accurate quote for the customer, but underlying basic assumptions hampered real collaboration between sales and the project managers.*
>
> *'A project is just a set of components, which we always offer from our catalogue,' and 'We receive a commission, but not a consultation fee.'*
>
> *The old world of component sales had always been successful. Therefore, the transition to project sales is quite challenging.*
>
> *A professional checklist has been created based on new customer enquiries. Sales now use it to assess customer needs. As a result, they better understand the needs, can calculate more accurately, and realise more margin. Internally, working together to develop this checklist and changing the commission structure positively impacted the embedding of the new values in daily behaviour.*

Culture-conscious action

Culture-aware actions are those that are consciously and effectively aligned with the prevailing culture of the organisation and or society to achieve goals and objectives. To create sustainable change, it is necessary to understand the underlying culture. Since most projects involve change, cultural awareness is an important competence for every project professional.

RESPONSIBILITIES

It is the responsibility of all parties within the project to observe the organisation's culture. Without this, the project will not get off to a good start. Attention to culture means attention to the underlying values, beliefs and assumptions from which people perform their work. The resulting beliefs are embedded in behaviour. Respect and feeling for the underlying assumptions, values, beliefs and associated behaviour create space for effortless delivery of the work and implementation of the necessary changes.

ADVANCED

ORGANISATIONAL CULTURE AND DECISION-MAKING (ADVANCED)

Organisational culture is an important aspect of how decisions are made in organisations. Decisions affect people and, therefore, their interests. Decisions are thus constantly surrounded by a certain political charge. Quinn & Cameron (2011) distinguish four cultural models in their research (see Figure 11.05.02). The horizontal axis distinguishes *internal versus external focus*. The vertical axis distinguishes *flexibility and freedom* of action versus manageability and stability of action.

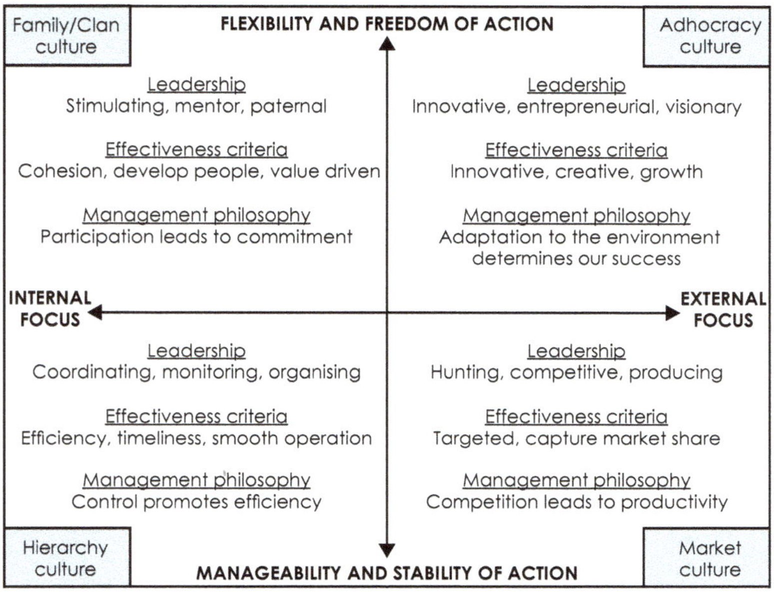

Figure 11.05.02 Culture models based on competitive values (Quin & Cameron, 2011)

In a hierarchical culture, management aspects and internal control should be considered more than in an adhocratic culture. If you ignore this, your behaviour will soon be perceived as unrestrained and uncontrolled. Conversely, if you want to implement tight control measures in an adhocracy culture, you immediately face a wall of social and political resistance. From their perception, these measures will be at the expense of innovative capacity and freedom of creative thinking. The underlying assumptions about what is valuable lead to resistance to tighter control mechanisms.

In a family culture, participation and attention to personal development are core values. A tightly managed, goal- and market-orientated attitude will be perceived as limiting the relative freedom of action and personal awareness. If this move is necessary, examining why this is necessary is needed. Conversely, people who are used to and love the market culture will not immediately be able to appreciate the relative freedom and conversations about maintaining connection and commitment to each other that characterise the family culture. They will perceive this as slow and unfocused.

Quinn (2015) has also elaborated on the management roles appropriate to the distinct cultures (see Figure 11.05.03).

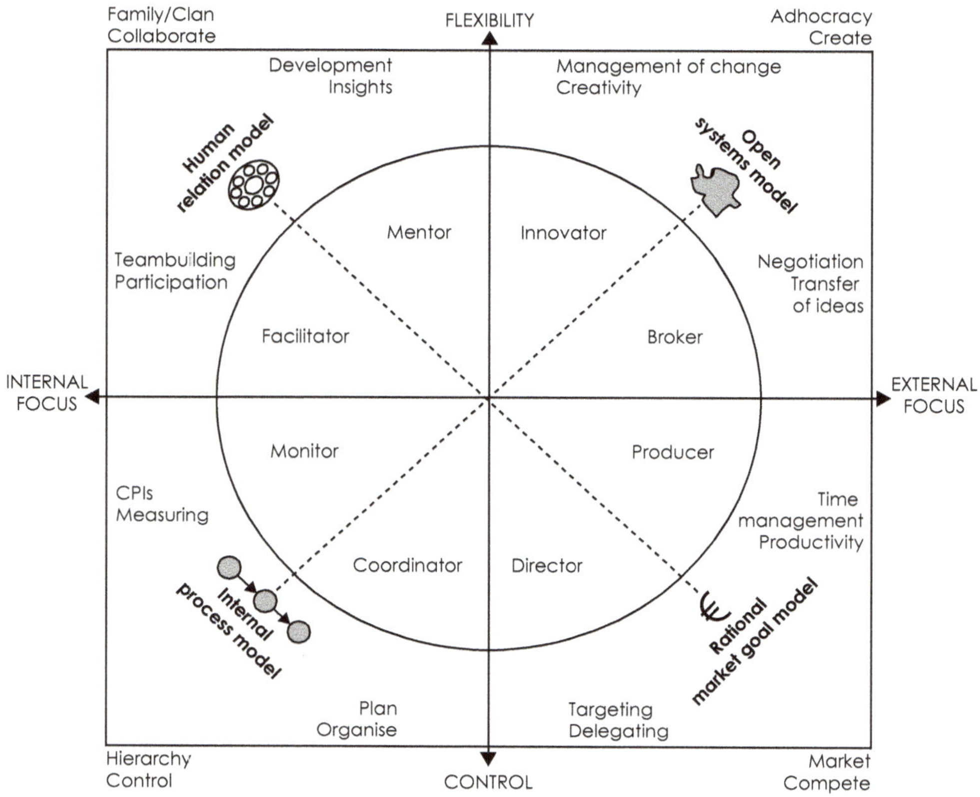

Figure 11.05.03 Manager's value perspective and roles (Quin, 2015)

Management roles in a hierarchy culture: internal focus and control

The (project) manager fulfils the role of coordinator. You ensure the realisation of the project output by designing and organising work processes and planning and coordinating the work between functions. Within this culture, the project manager also fulfils the role of monitor. Based on a tight internal organisation with clear procedures and guiding indicators, you ensure that the project develops according to the standards and remains under the client's supervision through measurements. Decision-making is strongly focused on controlling internal processes. In case of deviations, a reasoned justification is provided. Through go-no-go decisions, the hierarchy determines whether projects continue.

Management roles in a family culture: internal focus and flexibility of action

The (project) manager fulfils the role of facilitator. You ensure that conflicts do not escalate and pay close attention to team development, strengthening team spirit, and participative decision-making. You also fulfil the role of mentor, focused on developing individual team members and strengthening interpersonal communication. Organising workshops where searching for answers together fits well into this culture.

Management roles in an adhocracy culture: external focus and flexibility of action

The (project) manager fulfils the role of innovator. Together with their team, they ensure that change is dealt with effectively and creatively. You also perform the broker role, using all your negotiating talents to match innovative ideas with client needs. Central to decision-making is the desire to exploit opportunities and chances through flexible working methods.

Management roles in a market culture: external focus and controlled action

The (project) manager fulfils the role of producer. You make every effort to deliver the requested products on time, within budget, and according to the specifications, and you motivate your team to achieve this. You also perform the role of director. You create clear images of the work to be delivered and set goals and tight schedules for delegating the work effectively. In this culture, you see the project as a genuine endeavour to realise project deliverables the customer accepts.

Align the project approach with the culture.

According to this management model, a project should be firmly embedded in an organisation's existing culture. By doing this, you demonstrate your ability to clearly and distinctly align your role perception with the prevailing role perception of the culture in which the project is carried out. Assertively fulfilling your role is thus not simply doing what your own preferences are but requires a good antenna for the social and political preferences of the context you are part of. These preferences are usually not explicitly expressed but have developed over time. Being attentive to people, their interests and how they are used to doing things is thus a crucial success factor in projects.

> *Angela worked for a while as a project manager at a dynamic company, where she could be honest and forthright with employees about how the work could best be realised. All involved were quite pleased with her performance.*
>
> *Next, she got an assignment at a company with a strict hierarchy. After approaching several employees spontaneously, a line manager told her that this is not the way things were done here and that deploying staff was part of his job. After familiarising herself with this, she effortlessly switched to this mode of operation. Once the required capacity was assigned officially, she still conducted the necessary conversations to reach a controlled, mutually accepted approach with the assigned project staff.*

If, as a project manager, you want to change the status quo, realise that you will first have to co-exist within the existing culture. This conveys that you value the way people work and interact. At some point, this allows you to submit your own perspectives on improving work performance. Often, a change of culture is not necessary. The key is to appreciate and accept the underlying values and beliefs. From that appreciation, you can match the desired project approach to the culture you have arrived at.

ANNEX

GLOSSARY

5xWhy	A more intuitive root cause analysis, based on repeatedly asking the why-question.
Acceptance criterion	The value on a defined scale that the project output should meet to be acceptable.
Active listening	A listening technique in which the listener adopts an activating and encouraging attitude.
Agile	A conceptual approach to implement changes iteratively and incrementally.
Agreement	A negotiated deal on actions to be taken.
Analogy technique	A technique for developing ideas by association using an analogy as inspiration.
Analytic problem solving	A structured and methodical approach to solve a particular problem or issue.
As-built documents	Specialist documents that show how the final product was actually built.
Assertiveness	Standing up for one's own opinion, needs or interests in a non-abusive, tactful way.
Audit	A systematic, independent and documented process to determine whether the implementation processes comply with the quality guidelines, standards and procedures, and are efficient and effective.
Authority	The right/position to set frameworks, give orders, and make decisions.
Autonomous project structure	An organisational structure where the project is set up separately from the permanent structure of the organisation.
Award criteria	Criteria based on which a proposal or quotation is awarded.
Bank guarantee	A security issued by a bank to pay a debt, when or if the debtor fails to settle it.
Baseline measurement	The description of the actual status quo.
Baseline scenario	The anticipated development in case of no investment.
Baseline	An established status or situation that serves as a reference for further work.
BATNA	The best alternative to a negotiated agreement.
Benchmark	A reference value against which things are compared.
Benefit management	All managerial tasks that focus on identifying and optimising potential benefits and minimising negative impacts of initiatives.
Benefits review	An assessment of whether the envisaged benefits are or have been realised.
Best effort agreement	An agreement to perform specific tasks to the best of their ability.
Black box	An element whose interaction with other elements is known, but not how it functions.
Brainstorming	A technique with the intent to develop as many ideas as possible about a particular topic by free association.
Breach of contract	A contractual shortcoming attributable to one of the contract parties.
Break-even point	The number of products that should be sold to recover the investment's costs.
Brown paper session	An interactive session where a brown paper screen or wall is used to collect ideas or solutions from the participants.
Budgeting	Allocating financial resources for a particular purpose.
Building rapport	The process of establishing a positive and harmonious relationship, characterised by mutual trust, understanding, and respect.

Burnout A mental condition in which an individual is emotionally and physically exhausted and unable to perform optimally.

Business case The business justification to invest.

Care ethics The ethical approach where the interest and care of others determine the best action.

Cash flow Cash and cash equivalents being transferred in a given period.

Change authority An individual or entity authorised to approve change requests and off-specifications.

Change budget A budget allocated to the change authority to finance change requests.

Change control A process used to ensure that changes to a product or service are controlled and coordinated.

Change management That aspect of management aimed at helping people, organisations and societies to change or transform, achieving intended benefits and goals.

Change request A request for approval to change a product or service.

Change An alteration of a product, service, a condition or a situation.

Communication channel How to convey information.

Communication plan A plan describing how, when, by whom, with which stakeholders, and for what purpose communication will take place, with the necessary costs and resources to do so.

Communication Exchange of information.

Competence management That aspect of management aimed at identifying and developing the necessary employees competences to attain organisational objectives.

Configuration Item (CI) An entity within a configuration that satisfies an end-use function and of which configuration information should be controlled.

Configuration item record The registered configuration information of a configuration item.

Configuration management database The database that contains all configuration item records.

Configuration management The aspect of management that focuses on technical and administrative direction over the lifecycle of a configuration item, its configuration status, and related configuration information.

Conflict de-escalation Interventions in order to resolve a conflict.

Conflict management style A characteristic behaviour for resolving conflicts.

Conflict phase A distinctive gradation of severity and depth of a conflict.

Conflict A disagreement between parties over opposing interests, values, goals or actions.

Contingency reserve A reserve for foreseen issues and risks (known-unknowns).

Contract A legally binding agreement setting out mutual obligations and rights.

Control point A usually predetermined moment in time when the progress of the work is assessed and reported on.

Conversation A verbal exchange of information between two or more people.

Core value A fundamental belief that underpins your actions.

Corporate Social Responsibility (CSR) The obligation that a company should play a positive role in the community and consider the environmental and social impact of business decisions that goes beyond what the law requires or what is socially appropriate.

Cost breakdown structure A hierarchical cost breakdown into cost objects, cost items, and cost categories.

Cost category A type of resource used to realise cost objects.

Cost control The process of controlling expenditures and outstanding financial obligations against the available budget.

Cost estimating The process of forecasting financial resources needed for a particular purpose.

Cost item An expenditure to realise a cost object.

Cost object An object for which costs are separately allocated and controlled.

Crashing The use of extra resources on the critical path to reduce overall duration.

Creative problem-solving A problem-solving approach using creative techniques in order to come up with new and original solutions to a particular problem or issue.

Crisis A situation of intense difficulty requiring a quick response.

Critical path The longest chain of activities to be carried out in a plan.

Culture change The change in core beliefs, values and expectations within an organisation or country.

Culture of openness A culture where people are encouraged to interact and discuss complex issues openly, helping to become more innovative, creative and responsive to change.

Culture-conscious action An action which is consciously and effectively aligned with the applicable culture of the organisation and or society to achieve goals and objectives.

Customer An individual, group or organisation receiving the deliverables.

Daily Scrum A 15-minute event for the developers of the Scrum team to inspect the progress toward the sprint goal and adapt the sprint.

Dashboard A user interface that indicates values related to a particular goal or business process.

Data The bare text, figures, numbers or graphs.

Decision point A control point where the project is reviewed to decide whether or not it can proceed and whereby, if so, the budget for the next stage is released (gate).

Decision to fund The decision to authorise the delivery of the project (2nd project decision).

Decision to justify The decision to authorise the project definition stage (1st project decision).

Decision tree A graphical calculation technique to evaluate the implications of several courses of action in the presence of uncertainty.

De-commissioning The systematic and controlled close-down of the project, including dismantling the facilities, and closure of the project records and contracts.

Default A failure to fulfil an obligation.

Definition of Done (DoD) The list of criteria (checklist) that every backlog item should meet to be considered complete (Done).

Delphi method A structured and iterative technique used to gather and distil insights and opinions of a group of experts on a particular topic, whereby they do not know who is providing what input.

Delta measurement The difference in development between the baseline scenario and investing.

Deontology The ethical approach that focuses on the normative ethical position based on rules.

Depreciation The allowable accounting depreciation of an investment over a period of time.

Depth of control The number of management layers between the top of the organisation and the workers at the workplace.

Development framework A framework to develop delivering products in a structured way.

Devil's triangle The model used to visualise the triple constraint theory.

Direct costs Costs that are allocated directly to an object.

Discharge Official release of the duty to perform work.

Distress Tension caused by a prolonged or sudden severe imbalance between load and load capacity and that negatively influences behaviour.

Document management system A mostly computerised system used to store and manage documents.

Document management The aspect of management that focuses on the effective identification, collection, storage, and sharing of documents.

Document tracking matrix A matrix in which responsibilities for the various documents are plotted against individuals or roles.

Document Written, printed, or electronic matter containing information or that serves as an official record.

Duty of care The moral or legal obligation to care for the safety and well-being of others.

Earned Value Analysis A technique to assess the work's progress based on the planned and earned value and the actual costs.

Effectiveness The extent to which the desired outcome is achieved.

Efficiency The proportion of output to the utilization of resources.

Emotional intelligence The ability to recognise one's own emotions and those of others, and to handle these emotions well in social relationships.

End-of-project report The report at the end of the project detailing the project results and performance to obtain release of duty to perform.

End-of-stage report A report at stage transition detailing the project status, stage performance, and updated project management plan to obtain authorisation for the next stage.

Environment Conditions in which individuals, animals, and plants live or work.

Ethics Moral principles governing a person's behaviour.

Eustress Tension that provides creativity, energy and motivation and positively influences behaviour.

Evaluation An assessment of activities carried out and their results to identify areas of process improvement.

Exception plan A plan that replaces the plan of which tolerances are (or threaten to be) exceeded.

Exception report A report detailing the cause and consequences of an exception, and options to continue.

Extrinsic motivated Doing things because you experience them as external impulses to be followed.

Fast track The partial overlapping of critical activities to accelerate progress.

Feasibility study A research into whether a desired outcome is realistic and feasible.

Feedback A reaction given to someone about their performance or behaviour, and desired performance or future behaviour.

Fishbone diagram A root cause diagram to determine the basic underlying reasons that cause a variation, defect or risk, also known as Ishikawa diagram and cause and effect diagram.

Fit for purpose A term used to indicate that a product or service is suitable for the intended purpose.

Fit for use A term used to indicate that a product or service is readily available for use.

Fixed costs Costs that do not change as a result of a change in production, as long as productivity remains within certain limits.

Float (Total Float) The period by which an activity can be delayed from its earliest start without delaying the plan's completion, assuming that all other activities are performed according to plan.

Flowchart A visualisation of a process. A flowchart often uses separate symbols for activities, decision points, documents, storage, input and output.

Force majeure A circumstance that prevents someone from fulfilling a contract and for which they cannot be held responsible.

Formal power Power based on the legitimised formal position.

Function separation The uncoupling of operational and controlling tasks.

Functional conflict A conflict that eventually contributes to improving decisions or cooperation.

Functional project structure An organisational structure in which the project is organised and carried out via the functional departments of the permanent organisation.

Functional requirement A specific function a product should fulfil.

Gantt chart A graphical depiction showing the duration of activities along a time bar.

General terms and conditions A set of recurring supporting conditions that can be referred to so that they do not have to be included in the contracts themselves.

Governance Principles, policies, and framework by which an organisation is directed and controlled.

Group thinking A behavioural symptom which portrays a team that is too focused on its own functionality and, therefore, is blind to surrounding signals.

Handover The legal and physical transfer of the project output to the customer organisation.

Health The state of well-being from a mental, physical and social point of view.

Histogram A bar chart showing the frequency of outcomes, giving different input value, in corresponding bar lengths.

Impediment Anything that prevents, hinders or slows down progress.

In default Failure to fulfil a contractual obligation on time after notice of default.

Increment A concrete addition to an existing product towards the product goal that meets the definition of done.

Incremental approach An approach in which the output is delivered in a series of small steps.

Indirect costs Costs that are not allocated directly to an object.

Influence The effect of exercised power.

Informal power The power based on personal characteristics or advantages.

Information management The aspect of management that focuses on the effective identification, collection, storage, and exchange of information.

Information The assumed meaning given to data received or provided.

Initial project decision (decision to justify) The decision to authorise the project definition stage.

Inspection A systematic assessment of a product or process by one or more specialists to determine whether it meets the specifications.

Interest Something that benefits an individual, group or organisation or, if infringed, puts them at a disadvantage.

Interface A point where systems interact.

Intrinsic motivated Doing things because you experience them from within yourself as meaningful, fun and engaging.

Investment appraisal The analysis of whether an investment is profitable, affordable and aligned with an organisation's strategy.

Investment The (financial) effort to acquire an asset that can be used for an extended period of time (more than one year).

Ishikawa diagram See fishbone diagram.

Issue register A log used for recording and maintaining information on issues that need to be formally addressed.

Issue An event or condition that has or almost certainly will occur, was not foreseen, and needs management attention to be resolved or dealt with.

Iterative approach An approach in which the products are developed cyclic.

Kaizen A philosophy which encourages continuous improvement in all aspects of result-orientated collaboration.

Kanban A framework to optimise the workflow by visualising and limiting the work in progress.

Key Performance Indicator (KPI) An important performance measure used to determine the degree of progress towards achieving targets.

Kick-off The first meeting at the start of a project or stage to initiate an effective and efficient delivery of that project or stage.

Knowledge centre An organisational function providing and maintaining standards to improve service delivery and organisational learning.

Knowledge management The aspect of management aimed at identifying, organising, storing and sharing knowledge and information within the organisation to attain organisational objectives.

Leadership style How a leader accomplishes their team's objective by motivating them to work towards a common goal and focusing on their well-being.

Leadership Directing and motivating others in their role and tasks to realise goals.

Lean Six Sigma A framework to improve business processes and team performance by systematically removing waste and reducing variation.

Lessons learned The knowledge gained during the work, that benefits the work and ensures that it is carried out more efficiently in the future.

Letter of Credit (LOC) A document in which a bank guarantees that a payment for a purchase will be received on time and for the correct amount.

Letter of Intent (LOI) A document describing the process agreements and plans to reach a legal agreement.

Line department A department responsible for a part of the primary process of an organisation.

Longlist A list of potential qualified external parties that can submit a proposal or quotation.

Management By Exception (MBE) A management philosophy that only requires escalation to the next management level if it is predicted that the agreed tolerances are to be exceeded.

Management By Objectives (MBO) A management philosophy that focuses on the joint setting of goals and monitoring progress.

Management by projects The coordinated management of a set of projects brought together to provide optimum use of the available resources to achieve the objectives of these projects in an efficient and effective way while minimising the risks.

Management reserve A reserve for unforeseen issues and risks (unknown-unknowns).

Management The whole of all managerial tasks necessary to realise a planned result. This includes planning, organising, controlling and directing an individual, group, or organisation.

Margin A provision to cover inaccuracies in the estimates.

Matrix organisation An organisational structure in which the project manager shares responsibilities with functional managers to determine the priorities of those assigned to the project.

Maturity model A model to measure the ability of an organisation to manage a particular discipline.

Meeting A gathering within a specific timeframe to discuss subjects to reach a judgement or decision.

Milestone slip chart A graphical representation of when the various milestones are expected to be achieved at successive control points.

Milestone An important event that provides visible evidence of progress.

Mind mapping A visual method used to organise ideas or solutions in a coherent manner around a central problem or issue.

Miscommunication The situation where the receiver interprets the message differently than intended.

Mission The purpose of an organisation.

Model A representation of a concept, idea, or reality.

Motivation The inner desire and determination to work in a disciplined way towards concrete results.

Multi criteria analysis A technique that provides a systematic approach to support complex decision-making according to predetermined criteria and objectives.

National culture The total of core beliefs, values and expectations shared by a vast majority of a country's residents.

Negotiation strategy The approach you take when negotiating.

Negotiation A consultation aimed at reaching an agreement.

Net present value analysis An analysis of the profitability of a planned investment by comparing the present value of that investment's envisaged incoming and outgoing cash flows over its lifetime.

Noise in communication Any source that distracts us from receiving the intended message correctly.

Norm A set of rules that parties voluntarily agree on about the quality of their products, services or processes.

Off-specification A product or service that should be delivered but currently is not or is forecasted not to be.

Openness An attitude that is open to new ideas, opinions or arguments and actively encourages exchanging ideas, opinions and arguments.

Opportunity costs The missed returns of the best alternative.

Opportunity A possible event or situation that, if it occurs, might have a positive impact on the achievement of the objectives.

Organisational change The change in an organisation's characteristics and or configurations, whereby the organisation's behaviour also changes sustainably.

Organisational culture The way members of an organisation interact with each other, their work and the outside world, to achieve the organisation's goals and objectives.

Outsourcing Transferring business functions to an external party.

Payback period The period required to recover the investment's costs.

People, Planet, Profit The principle that companies focus equally on social, environmental and economic impacts.

Performance agreement An agreement to deliver an output within predefined terms and conditions.

Performance readiness The combination of the employee's ability to perform their tasks and the level of confidence and/or willingness to actually do so.

Permanent organisation An organisation structured to accomplish its raison d'être permanently.

Personal integrity Acting per their own moral and ethical values and principles.

Personal time management The ability to create focus by making conscious decisions and organising your personal schedule accordingly.

Personnel management That aspect of management aimed at implementing the personnel policy within the organisation.

Personnel policy The guidelines that govern the relationships with employees to attain organisational objectives.

PESTLE analysis A strategic framework to analyse and evaluate external macro-environmental factors that may influence an organisation's interests.

Phasing model A widely used phasing that serves as a reference for the phasing of future projects.

Pilot A small scale implementation used to demonstrate the viability of an idea.

Portfolio management The coordinated management of a set of projects and programmes, which are not necessary related, brought together to provide optimum use of the organisation's resources to achieve its strategic goals while minimising portfolio risk.

Portfolio A set of projects and programmes, which are not necessarily related, brought together to provide optimum use of the organisation's resources to achieve it strategic goals while minimising portfolio risk.

Positional negotiation A negotiating style which focuses on taking positions to achieve goals.

Post-investment review The post-project assessment of the initial investment decision.

Power of attorney The authority to enter into financial commitments.

Power The ability to exert your will over others.

Precedence chart An activity network with a schematic representation of dependencies over time, based on activities on node.

Presentation An oral transmission of information to a group, typically visually supported.

Primary process The object-orientated system of activities by which an organisation legitimises and realises its raison d'être.

Principled negotiation A negotiating style which focuses on achieving a win/win agreement.

Priority The importance of a fact, an outcome or condition relative to others items.

Probability tree A graphical representation to evaluate several options with uncertain outcomes.

Process quality The quality of the process undertaken.

Procurement The process of buying or obtaining goods and or services from external parties.

Product backlog An evolving ordered list of what is needed to develop or improve a product.

Product breakdown structure (PBS) A breakdown of the products to be delivered.

Product description The description of a product, including the purpose, composition, quality criteria and by whom and how the product will be reviewed and approved.

Product flow diagram A diagram showing the development sequence and interdependencies of the products to be delivered.

Product lifecycle The sequence of stages of a product from the first idea through construction and use until decommissioning and demolition.

Product owner The person who is accountable for maximising the product's value resulting from the Scrum team's work.

Product quality The quality of the product delivered.

Productivity The amount of work done per period.

Professional ethics The ethical approach to making conscious choices to comply with standards and values in implementing your profession.

Programme management The coordinated management of projects and business activities in order to enable the implementation of change, and the realisation of benefits to achieve a strategic goal.

Programme A temporary organisation of interrelated projects and business activities managed in a coordinated way to enable the implementation of change, and the realisation of benefits to achieving a strategic goal.

Project (management) approach A high-level description of how the project will be realised and managed, including the main principles and essential choices for success.

Project accounting The extra compatible accounts to be kept by the project in addition to the business accounting.

Project assignment The assignment of the project manager to realise the project.

Project assurance The planned and systematic actions on behalf of the individual members of the project board to provide confidence that a project will be successful.

Project benefit An advantage resulting from a project outcome.

Project board The highest governance board in the project responsible for the overall direction and management of the project within the constraints and directions set by the sponsoring organisation or customer.

Project constraint A limitation or restriction within which a project should be carried out.

Project controls The set of activities to ensure the implementation of the project in a controlled way.

Project criterion A condition a project should meet to be acceptable.

Project decision A decision by the sponsoring organisation or customer to go ahead with the project (go/no-go decision).

Project definition stage The first stage of the project in which a sound basis is laid for delivering the project output.

Project deliverable A tangible or intangible element to be realised by the project.

Project delivery stage The stage of the project in which the actual design and development of the project output takes place.

Project design A charcoal sketch, blueprint or high-level project architecture.

Project dis-benefit A disadvantage resulting from a project outcome.

Project discharge The official release of the project manager's duty to perform.

Project evaluation The assessment of the activities undertaken and the associated results to identify areas of improvement for future projects.

Project filing structure The structure of folders in which project documents are stored.

Project goal What the sponsoring organisation or customer wants to achieve with the project output.

Project governance The principles, policies, and framework by which the project organisation is directed and controlled.

Project lifecycle The sequence of stages and phases from project definition until project closure.

Project Management Office (PMO) An organisational unit that facilitates the decision-making process within a project, programme and portfolio organisation.

Project management plan The plan that describes how the project is being carried out and controlled.

Project management product A product specifically designed to control an aspect of the project.

Project management success The extent to which the project manager's performance satisfies the relevant stakeholders.

Project management team The project manager and core team members leading the project.

Project management All managerial tasks necessary to deliver the project deliverables successfully. This involves planning, organising, monitoring, and controlling all aspects of the project, leading the team, and motivating all people involved.

Project manager The individual responsible for the daily management of the project to achieve the project deliverables and enable project success.

Project mandate The authorisation of the sponsoring organisation or customer to initiate the project.

Project objective A target within which the project should be realised.

Project organisation The temporary organisation in which the project output is realised.

Project outcome The result of a change enabled by the project output.

Project outline The description of the project assignment, which serves as the basis for the project definition stage.

Project output The total of the project deliverables that forms the project result.

Project phase A period within a project with its own characteristics and with a predetermined output. Project phases can overlap.

Project plan A high-level plan to realise the project output.

Project preparation stage The period prior to the start of the project in which the project outline is formulated and agreed upon.

Project sign off The formal acceptance of the project results by the sponsoring organisation or customer, acknowledging that everything has been delivered according to the contract and other specified documents. This completes the project in full.

Project sponsor The individual accountable for the project's success to the sponsoring organisation or customer, and owner of the project's business case.

Project stage A period within a project, separated from other periods, with a predetermined output, and concluded with a go/no-go decision. Project stages cannot overlap.

Project start-up A workshop with the project (management) team and other key stakeholders to develop a sound basis for the project or next stage.

Project success criteria The aspects on which mainly the success or failure of a project is defined by the various stakeholders.

Project success factors The aspects that strongly influence the success or failure of a project.

Project success The extent to which the completed project satisfies the relevant stakeholders.

Project support A role within the project management team that supports the project manager in daily management by providing certain administrative services and specific tasks.

Project team A team that realises specialist products within a project.

Project, Programme and Portfolio organisation (PPP organisation) A permanent management domain within an organisation to manage projects, programmes, and portfolios.

Project A unique, temporary, multidisciplinary, and organised endeavour to realise agreed deliverables within predefined requirements and constraints.

Proof of concept A small-scale demonstration to determine whether a solution is viable.

Protocol of delivery The protocol signed by the supplier and customer organisation to confirm the legal transfer of the project output to the customer organisation.

Prototype A simplified version of the result to explore workability.

Purchase The act of buying goods and or services from external parties.

Quality criteria The set of features and characteristics that can be tested and measured to confirm that the quality objectives have been met.

Quality expectations A wish or statement about the quality expected from the project output.

Quality management The aspect of management aimed at directing and controlling an organisation regarding quality.

Quality register A log used for recording planned and conducted quality activities.

Quality requirement A condition or capability a product or service should meet to be acceptable.

Quality review An assessment by a team of relevant stakeholders to determine whether a deliverable meets the established quality criteria.

Quality The extent to which a set of features and characteristics of a product, service or process satisfy stated or implied needs.

RAG-code An acronym for Red, Amber, and Green which function as traffic lights to indicate the status of a particular aspect and whether action is needed.

Regulation A mandatory provision with a legal basis issued by an administrative authority.

Reliability Operating consistently, in accordance with anticipated behavior and agreed-upon standards.

Requirement specification The documented total set of requirements the project output should meet.

Requirement A condition or capability needed to solve a problem or achieve an objective.

Residual items The defects, damages or imperfections that have been noticed and recorded at the closeout assessment, and need to be rectified.

Resistance A hesitation or refusal to accept, comply or agree with something.

Resource levelling The optimisation of allocating resources which may affect the critical path.

Resource management The aspect of management that focuses on the identification, analysis, acquisition, planning, deployment, monitoring and adjustment of resources required.

Resource plan A plan for allocating resources (except money).

Resource smoothing The optimisation of allocating resources, without affecting the overall duration of the plan.

Resource-time variance graph A graph showing planned resources in successive periods.

Risk action-holder An individual responsible for taking a risk response delegated by the risk owner.

Risk appetite The risks an individual, group or organisation is willing to take in achieving its objectives.

Risk aversion The tendency to prefer outcomes with low uncertainty.

Risk capacity The amount of risk an organisation can bear in achieving its objectives.

Risk exposure The extent to which an initiative or organisation is exposed to risks.

Risk impact An outcome of a risk, if it occurs, affecting objectives.

Risk liability The organisation's liability of the actions of its employees and contractors in relation to its clients.

Risk management The aspect of management that aims at the effective identification, analysis and evaluation of risks and the planning and implementation of risk responses.

Risk matrix A probability-impact grid to categorise risks by probability and impact.

Risk owner An individual or entity responsible for managing a specific risk.

Risk probability The likelihood that a risk may actually occur.

Risk profile The nature and exposure of risks faced by an initiative or organisation.

Risk proximity The period in which a risk may occur.

Risk register A log used for recording identified risks and associated risk measures.

Risk source An element that poses a risk.

Risk tolerance The limit value above which risks should be escalated to the next management level.

Risk A possible event or situation that, if it occurs, might have a negative impact on the achievement of the objectives.

Root cause analysis A systematic process used to identify the underlying causes of a particular problem or issue.

Safety A condition in which one is protected from danger, hazards or injury.

Scope configuration An arrangement of the scope in a particular composition.

Scope creep A slow and almost unmarked scope change without formally capturing the new scope.

Scope demarcation A description of what does not belong to the scope to determine it more precisely.

Scope The work and deliverables to accomplish.

Scrum master The individual responsible for setting up and running Scrum successfully within a team or organisation.

Scrum team A small, self-managing, and cross-functional team that is accountable for creating a valuable, useful increment at every sprint.

Scrum A lightweight framework to adaptively develop or improve products.

Security Protection of an individual or object against violence, threat, danger or damage.

Selection criteria Criteria based on which organisations are selected to submit a proposal or quotation.

Self-motivation Propelling yourself into action and actively pursuing set goals.

Shortlist A list of external organisations to be invited to submit a proposal or quotation.

Situational leadership A leadership style whereby you adapt to circumstances as they arise.

Slip chart A visual representation illustrating a value in comparison to the initial plan at consecutive control points.

Span of control The number of people that a supervisor or manager can effectively oversee directly.

Specification A precise description of the characteristics of an item.

Sponsoring organisation The organisation that commissioned and funds the work and makes the final go/no-go decisions. This can be corporate, programme management or an external client.

Sprint backlog A plan by and for the developers to realise the sprint goal.

Sprint planning The sprint event in which the work to be performed in that sprint is determined and agreed upon.

Sprint retrospective A sprint event to find ways to increase the quality and effectiveness of the work of the sprint team.

Sprint review A sprint event to inspect the output of the sprint and determine the necessary remaining time.

Sprint A timebox of a fixed length of one month or less to create one or more increments.

Staff department A department which supports the management in her tasks with specialised advisory and support functions.

Stage plan A plan to manage and control the work within a stage.

Stakeholder engagement The coordinated actions to effectively involve stakeholders to complete an initiative successfully.

ACRONYMS

3Ps	People, Planet, Profit
ABC	Activity-Based Costing
AC	Actual Costs
ARR	Annualised Rate of Return
AT	Actual Time
BAC	Budget At Completion
BAFO	Best And Final Offer
BATNA	Best Alternative to a Negotiated Agreement
BCM	Business Change Manager
CAD	Computer Added Design
CAPEX	Capital Expenditures
CBS	Cost Breakdown Structure
CDCF	Cumulated Discounted Cash Flow
CE	Competence Element
CF	Cash Flow
CI	Configuration Item
CIR	Configuration-Item Record
CMDB	Configuration Management Database
CPI	Cost Performance Index
CSR	Corporate Social Responsibility
CTA	Cost Trend Analysis
CV	Cost Variance
D	Duration
DCF	Discounted Cash Flow
DMADV	Define, Measure, Analyse, Design, Verify
DMAIC	Define, Measure, Analyse, Improve, Control
DoD	Definition of Done
DoR	Definition of Ready
EAC	Estimate At Completion
EBIT	Earnings Before Interest and Tax
EBITDA	Earnings Before Interest, Tax, Depreciation and Amortisation
EF	Earliest Finish
EFQM	European Foundation for Quality Management
ES	Earliest Start
ESRS	European Sustainable Reporting Standard
ETC	Estimate To Complete
EU	European Union
EV	Earned Value
EVA	Earned Value Analysis
FAT	Factory Acceptance Test
GDPR	General Data Protection Regulation
GP	General Partnership
GROW	Goals, Reality, Opportunities and Way Forward
GTD	Getting Things Done
H&S	Health and Safety
HR	Human Resource
HSSE	Health, Safety, Security and Environment
ICB	Individual Competence Baseline
IFRS	International Financial Reporting Standards
IP	Intellectual Property
IPMA	International Project Management Association
IRR	Internal Rate of Return
ISO	International Organization for Standardization
JIT	Just In Time
KPI	Key Performance Indicator
LF	Latest Finish
LOI	Letter Of Intend
LS	Latest Start
LSS	Lean Six Sigma
MAGIC	Motivating, Ambitious, Generic, Inspiring, Communicative
MBE	Management By Exception
MBO	Management By Objectives
MMP	Minimal Marketable Product
MOSCOW	Must-have, Should-have, Could-have and Won't-have
MOU	Memorandum Of Understanding
MTA	Milestone Trend Analysis
MVP	Minimal Viable Product
NPV	Net Present Value
OBS	Organisation Breakdown Structure
OCB	Organisational Competence Baseline
OPEX	Operational Expenditure
PBS	Product Breakdown Structure

PC	Percentage Complete
PD	Planned Duration
PDCA	Plan-Do-Check-Act
PEB	Project Excellence Baseline
PEM	Project Excellence Model
PESTLE	Political, Economic, Social, Technological, Legal, Environmental
PMO	Project Management Office
PMP	Project Management Plan
POC	Proof Of Concept
PPP	Project, Programme, Portfolio
PS	Project Support
PSU	Project Start-Up
PV	Planned Value
RAM	Responsibility Assignment Matrix
RASCI	Responsible, Accountable, Support, Consulted, Informed
REBT	Rational Emotive Behaviour Therapy
RFC	Request For Change
RFI	Request For Information
RFP	Request For Proposal
RFQ	Request For Quotation
RFS	Request For Solution
ROI	Return On Investment

RoR	Rate of Return
SAT	Site Acceptance Test
SCM	Supply Chain Management
SDG	Sustainable Development Goals
SIG	Special Interest Group
SLA	Service Level Agreement
SMART	Specific, Measurable, Achievable, Relevant, Time-related
SMP	Sustainable Management Plan
SOP	Standard Operating Procedure
SPI	Schedule Performance Index
SV	Schedule Variance
TBL	Triple Bottom Line
TCO	Total Cost of Ownership
TOC	Theory Of Constraints
TQM	Total Quality Management
TTA	Time Trend Analysis
UN	United Nations
VAC	Variance At Completion
VAR	Variation
WACC	Weighted Average Cost of Capital
WBS	Work Breakdown Structure
WIP	Work In Progress
ZOPA	Zone Of Possible Agreement

LITERATURE

50Minutes.com (2015). *McKinsey 7S Framework.* 50Minutes.com. ISBN 978280626

Aken, T. van. (2014). *De weg naar projectsucces.* Dutch 4th revised edition. Van Haren Publishing. ISBN 9789087533113.

Allen, D. (2002). *Getting things done. The art of stress-free productivity.* Penguin Books. ISBN 9780142000281.

Apke, L. (2015). *Understanding The Agile Manifesto. A Brief & Bold Guide to Agile.* Lulu.com. ISBN 9781312863910.

Argyris, C. (1985). *Action science. Concepts, Methods, and Skills for research and intervention.* Jossey Bass. ISBN 9780875896656.

Argyris, C. (1999). *On Organizational Learning.* 2nd edition. Wiley-Blackwell. ISBN 9780631213093.

Beck, D.E., Larsen, T.H., Solonin, S., Viljoen, R. & Johns, T.Q. (2018). *Spiral Dynamics in Action Humanity's Master Code.* John Wiley & Sons. ISBN 9781119387183.

Belbin, R.M. (2022). *Team Roles at Work.* Routledge. ISBN 9780367756000.

Bennis, W. (2009). *On becoming a leader. The leadership classic.* Basic Books. ISBN 9780465014088.

Blackburn, S.G. (2022). *The JOHARI Window Model. The definitive guide.* Coach LLC Publishing. ASIN B09T3NWLKB.

Blanchard, K. & Peal, N.V. (1988). *The Power of Ethical Management.* William Morrow. ISBN 9780688070625.

Bono, de, E. (1973). *Lateral thinking. Creativity step by step.* Harper Colophon. ISBN 9789013136401.

Bono, de, E. (1999). *Six thinking hats.* Back Bay books. ISBN 9780316178310.

Bos, R. ten. (2005). *For Business Ethics.* 1st Edition. Routledge. ISBN 9780415311359.

Broder, J.F. & Tucker, E. (2012). *Risk Analysis and the Security Survey.* 4th Edition. Butterworth-Heinemann. ISBN 9780123822338.

Byttebier, I. & Vullings, R. (2015). *Creativity in business. The basic guide for generating and selecting ideas.* BIS Publishers. ISBN 9789063693800.

Cialdini, R.B. (2021). *Influence, new and expanded. The psychology of persuasion.* Harper Business. ISBN 9780062937650.

Clarke, J. (1999). *Office politics. A survival guide.* Spiro press. ISBN 9781858355320.

Covey, Stephen R. (2004). *The seven habits of highly effective people. Powerful lessons in personal change.* Free press. ISBN 9780743269513.

Deci, E.L. & Ryan, R.M. (2013). *Handbook of Self Determination research.* University of Rochester press. ISBN 9781580461566.

Dryden, W. (2012). *Getting started with REBT. A concise guide for clients.* Routledge. ISBN 9781135479091.

Dugdale, D. & Lyne, S. (2010). *Budgeting Practice and Organisational Structure.* 1st Edition. CIMA Publishing. ISBN 97800809655901.

EFQM (2021). *The EFQM Model.* Revised 2nd Edition. EFQM. ISBN 9789052368702.

Fernandes, G. (2021). *Improving and Embedding Project Management Practice in Organisations A mixed methodology research.* Lambert Academic Publishing. ISBN 9786023307009.

Fink, S. (2021). *Crisis management.* iUniverse Inc. ISBN 9780595090792.

Fisher, R., Ury, W.L. & Patton, B. (2011). *Getting to Yes. Negotiating agreement without giving in. The international bestseller of the Harvard negotiation project.* Penguin Publishing group. ISBN 9780143118756.

Fleming. Q.W. & Koppelman, J.M. (2010). *Earned Value Project Management.* 4th Edition. Project Management Institute. ISBN 9781935589082.

Friedlob, G.T. & Welton R.E. (2008). *Keys to Reading an Annual Report (Barron's Business Keys).* 4th Edition. Barron's Educational Series. ISBN 9780764139154.

Goldratt E.M. & Cox, J. (1984). *The Goal.* North River Press. ISBN 9780884271956.

Goldratt E.M. (1997). *Critical Chain.* North River Press. ISBN 139780884271536.

Goleman, D. (2005). *Emotional Intelligence: Why it can matter more than IQ.* Random House Publishing Group. ISBN 9780553383713.

Goleman, D. (2017). *Leadership That Gets Results.* Harvard Business Review Press. ISBN 9781633692626

Granovetter, M.S. (1973). *The strength of weak ties.* In American Journal of Sociology, Volume 78.

Graves, C.W. (1970). *Levels of existence an open system of values.* In Journal of Humanistic Psychology, Page 131–155.

Groote, G., Hugenholtz-Sasse, C. & Klaassen, D. (2011). *Projecten leiden: methoden en technieken voor projectmatig werken.* Dutch edition. Spectrum. ISBN 9789049107628.

Hedeman, B.H., Fredriksz, H. & Vis van Heemst, G. (2012). *Project Management Based on PRINCE2.* 6th Edition. Van Haren Publishing. ISBN 9789087534967.

Hedeman, B.H. & Riepma, R. (2018). *Projectmanagement op basis van ICB Versie 4.* Dutch Edition. 4th Edition. Van Haren Publishing. ISBN 9789401803816.

Hedeman, B.H. (2012). *Programmamanagement op basis van MSP® 2011 Edition.* Dutch 3rd edition. Van Haren Publishing. ISBN 9789087536916.

Hersey, P., Blanchard, K.H. & Johnson, D.E. (2008). *Management of organizational behavior. Leading Human resources.* 9th Edition. Pearson College Div. ISBN 9780131441392.

Herzberg, F., Mausner B. & Snyderman Bloch, B. (1993). *The motivation to work.* Routledge. ISBN 9781560006343.

Herzberg, F. (2003), *One More Time How Do You Motivate Employees?*, in Harvard Business Review, January pp. 87–96.

Hisrich, R., Peters, M., & Shepherd, D. (2013). *Entrepreneurship.* 10th Edition. McGraw Hill. ISBN 9780078112843.

Hofstede, G., Hofstede, G.J. & Minkov, M. (2010). *Cultures and organizations. Software of the mind. Intercultural cooperation and its importance for survival.* The McGraw Hill companies. ISBN 9780071664189.

Imai, M. (1986). *KAIZEN. The key to Japan's competitive success.* McGraw-Hill Education. ISBN 9780075543329.

IPMA (2015). *Code of Ethics and professional conduct®. Moving the profession forward by acting ethically.* © IPMA

IPMA Delta® (2015). *Moving organisations forward translating strategy into results.* © IPMA Brochure

IPMA (2019). *Organisational Competence Baseline® for Developing Competence in Managing by Projects.* Version 1.1. ISBN 9789492338068 (pdf) or ISBN 9789492338075 (print).

IPMA (2015). *Individual Competence Baseline® for Project, Programme & Portfolio Management.* Version 4.0. IPMA Publications. ISBN 9789492338013 (PDF) or ISBN 9789492338006 (print).

IPMA (2016). *Project Excellence Baseline® for Achieving Excellence in Projects and Programmes.* Version 1.0. ISBN 9789492338051 (PDF) or ISBN 9789492338044 (print).

International Organization for Standardization (2020). *ISO 21502:2020 –, Project, programme and portfolio management – Guidance on project management.* ISBN 9789267112039.

Ishikawa, K. (1996). *Guide to Quality Control.* Asian Productivity Organisation. ISBN 99789283310365.

ISO/TC 258 (2022). *ISO 21503:2022 – Project, programme and portfolio management – Guidance on programme management.* Edition 2. ISO.org.

ISO/TC 46/SC 11 (2019). *ISO 30301:2019 – Information and Documentation – Management systems for records – Requirements.* Edition 2. ISO.org.

ISO/TC 258 (2022). *ISO 21504:2022 – Project, programme and portfolio management – Guidance on portfolio management.* ISO.org.

ISO/TC 262 (2018). *ISO 31000:2018 – Risk management, A practical guide.* ISO.org.

ISO/TMBC (2010). *ISO 26000:2010 – Guidance on social responsibility.* ISO.org.

ISO/TC 176/SC 1. ISO 9000:2015 – *Quality management systems – Fundamentals and vocabulary.* Edition 4. ISO.org.

ISO/TC 176/SC 2 (2017). *ISO 10007:2017 – Quality management – Guidelines for configuration management.* ISO.org.

Johnson, J. (2020). *Chaos 2020 Beyond Infinity.* The Standish Group.

Juran, J. (1988). *Quality Control Handbook.* 4th Edition. McGraw Hill, ISBN 9780070331761.

Kaplan, R.S. & Norton D.P. (1996). *The Balanced Score Card: Translating Strategy into Action.* Harvard Business Review Press. ISBN 9780875846514.

Kaptein, M. (2017). *The living code. Embedding ethics into the corporate DNA.* Routledge. ISBN 9781906093143.

Karasek, R.A. (1992). *Healthy work Stress, Productivity and the Reconstruction of Working Life.* Basic books. ISBN 9780465028962.

Katie, B. (2021). *Loving what is. Four questions that can change your life.* Harmony Books. ISBN 9781846046971.

Kiran, D.R. (2016). *Total Quality Management Key Concepts and Case Studies.* 1st Edition. Butterworth-Heinemann. ISBN 9780128110355.

Laufer, A. (2016). *Breaking the code of project management.* Palgrave MacMillan. ISBN 9780230608030.

Leary, T. (2004). *Interpersonal diagnosis of personality A functional theory and methodology for personality evaluation.* Wipf & Stock Pub. ISBN 9781592447763.

Likert, R. (1987). *New Patterns of Management.* Garland Science. ISBN 9780070378506.

Locke, E.A. & Latham G.P. (2017). *New developments in Goal Setting and Task Performance.* Routledge. ISBN 9780815390879.

Loomans, P. (2017). *Time surfing. The Zen approach to keeping time on your side.* Watkins Publishing. ISBN 9781786780911.

Luecke, R. (2004). *Crisis Management: Mastering the Skills to Prevent Disasters.* Harvard Business Review Press. ISBN 9781591394372.

Mastenbroek, W.F.G. (1994). *Conflict management and organizational development.* Wiley. ISBN 9780471941415.

McGregor, D. & Cutcher-Gerschenfeld, J. (2006). *The Human Side of Enterprise, Annotated Edition.* McGraw Hill. ISBN 9780071462228.

Meadows, D.H. (2008). *Thinking in Systems.* Chelsea Green Publishing. ISBN 9781603580557.

Mintzberg, H. (2013). *Rise and Fall of Strategic Planning.* Free Press. ISBN 9781476754765.

Mintzberg, H. (1992). *Structure in Fives, Designing Effective Organizations.* Pearson. ISBN 9780138554798.

Muller, E., Rosenthal, U., Helsloot I. & E.R.G. Dijkman, van (2013) *Crisis. Studies over crisis en crisisbeheersing.* Dutch Edition. Kluwer. ISBN 9789013121186.

Nusbaumer Knaflic, C. (2023). *Storytelling with you. Plan, create, and deliver a stellar presentation.* John Wiley & sons. ISBN 9781394160303.

Ofman, D. (2004). *Core qualities A gateway to Human resources.* Cyan communications. ISBN 9789055942404.

Ofman, D. (2019). *Core quadrant game a unique and inspiring way to know yourself and others better. Core quadrants, cards.* Core Quality International. ISBN 9789077987025.

Osterwalder, A. & Pigneur, Y. (2010). *Business Model Generation.* John Wiley and Sons. ISBN 9780470876411.

Pink, D.H. (2011). *Drive The surprising truth about what motivates us.* Riverhead books. ISBN9781594484803.

Pondy, L.R. (1967). *Organizational conflict. Concepts and models.* In Administrative science Quarterly, September, Page 296320.

Pondy, L.R. (1992). *Reflections on organizational conflict.* In Journal of organizational behavior, volume 13.

Pyzdek, T., Keller, P. (2013). *The Handbook for Quality Management, 2nd Edition. A Complete Guide to Operational Excellence.* McGraw Hill. ISBN 9780071799249.

Quinn, R.E., St'Claire, L.S., Faerman, S.R., Thompson, M.P. & McGrath, M.R. (2020). *Becoming a Master Manager A Competing Values Approach.* Wiley. ISBN 9781119710967.

Quinn, R.E. & Cameron K.S. (2011). *Diagnosing and Changing Organizational Culture Based on the Competing Values Framework.* 3rd Edition. Jossey Bass. ISBN 9780470650264.

Raison, M. (2022). *The power of impossible thinking. How to turn your impossible ideas into reality.* Yellow Ideas Publishing. ISBN 9798370358708.

Rampersad, H.K. (2001). *Total Quality Management. An Executive Guide to Continuous Improvement.* Springer. ISBN 9783540679677.

Renkema, J. (2020). *Schrijfwijzer. Met taaltips en oefeningen op schrijfwijzer.nl.* Dutch Edition. Boom. ISBN 9789024409686.

Ries, E. (2011). *The Lean Startup: How Today's Entrepreneurs Use Continuous Innovation to Create Radically Successful Business.* Independently published. ISBN 9798391079088.

Rogers, E.M. (2010). *Diffusion of Innovations.* 4th Edition. Free Press. ASIN B003YUC6G4.

Savitz, A.W. & Weber, K. (2013). *The Triple Bottom Line.* Jossey-Bass. ISBN 9781118226223.

Schein, E,H. & Schein, P.A. (2016). *Organizational Culture and Leadership.* 5th Edition. Wiley and Sons. ISBN 9781119212041.

Schein, E.H. (1998). *Process Consultation Revisited Building the Helping Relationship.* Addison Wesley Longman. ISBN 9780201345964.

School Press (2004). *Crisis Management Mastering the Skills to Prevent Disasters (Harvard Business Essentials).* Harvard Business Review Press. ISBN 9781591394372.

Schuyler, J.R. (2018). *Risk and Decision Analysis in Projects 3.1st Edition.* CreateSpace Independent Publishing Platform. ISBN 9781719014236.

Schulz von Thun Friedemann (2008). *Miteinander reden 1 Störungen und Klärungen Allgemeine Psychologie der Kommunikatizion.* Rowohlt Taschenbuch. ISBN 9783499624070.

Scouller, J. (2011). *The three levels of leadership.* Management books. ISBN 9781852526818.

Selye, H. (1978). *The Stress of Life.* McGraw Hill companies. ISBN 9780070562127.

Senge, P. (2006). *The fifth discipline The art and practice of the learning organization.* Revised & updated Edition. Doubleday. ISBN 9780385517256.

Sheen, R. & Gallo, A. (2015). *HBR Guide to Building Your Business Case (HBR Guide Series).* Harvard Business Review Press. ISBN 9781633690028.

Shenhar, A.J. & Dvir, D. (2007). *Reinventing Project Management The Diamond Approach to Successful Growth & Innovation.* Harvard Business review Press. ISBN 9781591398004.

Shiba, S. & Walden, D. (2006). *Breakthrough management.* Confederation of Indian industry. ASIN BOOE2RMJZG.

Shiba, S. & Walden, D. (2007). *Four practical revolutions in management.* Taylor & Francis. ISBN 9781563273889.

Shim, J. (2009). *Schaum's Outline of Financial Management.* 3th Edition. McGraw Hill education. ISBN 9780071635318.

Silvius, G., Schipper, R., Planko, J. & Brink, J. van den (2012). *Sustainability in Project Management.* 1st Edition. Gower. ISBN 9781409431695.

Taylor, P. (2011). *Leading Successful PMOs How to Build the Best Project Management Office for Your Business.* 1st Edition. Routledge. ISBN 9781409418375.

The Art of Service (2020). *EBITDA. A complete guide.* EBITDA Publishing. ISBN 9781867421337.

The KPI Institute, smartKPI.com, et al. (2015). *The Health, Safety, Security and Environment KPI Dictionary 160+ Key Performance Indicator Definitions.* The KPI Institute. ISBN 9781515307181.

Thomas, K.W. (2002). *Thomas Kilmann conflict mode instrument.* CPP, Inc. ASIN B0006SA34O.

Toulmin, S.E. (2013). *The uses of argument,* Updated Edition. Cambridge University press. ISBN 9780521534833.

Tronto, J. (2013). *Caring democracy markets, equality and justice.* New York University Press. ISBN 9780814782781.

Tronto, J. (1993). *Moral boundaries. A political argument for an ethic of care.* Routledge. ISBN 9780415906425.

Tuckman, B. (1965). *Developmental Sequence in Small Groups.* In Psychological Bulletin, Volume 63, Number 6, pp 383399.

Vroom, V.H. & Yetton, P.W. (2010). *Leadership and decision making.* University of Pittsburgh Press. ISBN 9780822952657.

INDEX

Symbols

A

B

C

D

E

F

G

H

I

J

K

L

M

N

O

P

Q

R

S

T

U

V

W

Z

www.ingramcontent.com/pod-product-compliance
Lightning Source LLC
Chambersburg PA
CBHW041747220926
51847CB00013B/129
* 9 7 8 9 4 0 1 8 1 0 9 2 0 *